ALMANAC *of*
ARCHITECTURE
& DESIGN
2001

ALMANAC *of* ARCHITECTURE & DESIGN 2001

Edited by
James P. Cramer

Foreword by
Blair Kamin

Greenway Group, Inc.
Greenway Consulting
Greenway Communications, LLC
Counsel House Research
Washington D.C., Chicago, Atlanta

CMD Group, Inc.
Atlanta, Mexico City, Stockholm, Sydney, Toronto

Editor: James P. Cramer
Managing Editor: Jennifer Evans
Greenway Group Editorial and Research Staff: Jan
    Akers, Corinne Cramer, Lee Cuthbert, Kerry
    Harding, Elisabeth Houston, Mary Pereboom,
    Beth Seitz
Consulting Architectural Historian: Jane Wolford
Index: Kay Wosewick, Pathways Indexing

Printed in the
United States of America

Published by: Greenway Communications, LLC
30 Technology Parkway South
Suite 200
Norcross, GA 30092
(800) 726-8603
www.greenwayconsulting.com

ISBN: 0-9675477-1-7
ISSN: 1526-4017

Distributed in the U.S. by:
R.S Means Company, Inc.
PO Box 800, 63 Smiths Lane
Kingston, MA 02364-0800
(800) 334-3509
www.rsmeans.com

CONTENTS

CONTENTS (CON'T)

CONTENTS (CON'T)

CONTENTS (CON'T)

CONTENTS (CON'T)

FOREWORD

Blair Kamin

This book reminds me of the old time capsules that were tucked away in the bowels of skyscrapers, filled with things like autographed baseballs, ice hockey pucks, and high-toned letters written to future generations by various VIPs. It's a cultural artifact that tells the story of architecture at the dawn of millennium, yet in contrast to those bygone time capsules, it doesn't make us wait 50 or 100 years to unlock its secrets. They're all here, right now, right in these pages, and what they present—along with the kind of useful, delightful and thought-provoking nuggets of information you expect to find in an almanac—is the tale of a profession experiencing equal measures of prosperity and anxiety.

On the surface, everything looks great. All the arrows architects want to go up, like the annual value of construction, are going up. And all the arrows architects want to go down, like office building vacancy rates, are going down. Design firm principals are making very good money—certainly more, I can say from looking at my own relatively meager paycheck, than the journalists who critique their work. But beneath the surface, there's tension roiling, and its chief source, as Rem Koolhaas cleverly observes in his acceptance speech for the 2000 Pritzker Architecture Prize, is the shift from "brick and mortar" to "click and mortar."

Ricardo Legorreta, the 2000 AIA Gold Medallist, also notes the computer's rising influence in his acceptance speech and broadens the reasons for concern, saying poignantly: "For the first time we question how long our buildings should last. We wonder where globalization, technology and fashion are leading us. And often we consider that architecture has lost its leadership and wonder if we are only at the service of commercial, technological, political and superficial interests."

The damage, unfortunately, does not stop there. "Our personal lives are also affected by this turmoil," Legorreta adds. "We often live sur-

rounded by ugly environments, inhuman spaces, packed with a continuous stress and futile activities. More and more we lose interest
and devote less time to thinking, meditating and appreciating family
life, friendship and love."

Anyone who knows anything about architecture today—anyone who
has seen the mean-spirited buildings that deaden our cityscapes with
their banality and brutality—knows that there is an awful truth in
these remarks. Yet it is to the great credit of the *Almanac's* editor,
James P. Cramer, and its managing editor, Jennifer Evans, that they
have included the speeches of the Pritzker, AIA Gold Medal, and
AIA Firm Award winners for the first time in this, the second edition of the book. It's fitting that these addresses come near the
beginning of the *Almanac*. For they form a kind of framework that
puts all the information that follows into perspective and elevates its
importance to what really matters-not what architecture does for the
bottom line, but how it affects the human spirit.

What I also like about this book is that it is a book, and not one of
those World Wide Web list of lists, or a Web site where you type in
some key words and the search engine mechanically spits the information back at you. Bor-ing! Flipping through a collection of facts
like this one is all about serendipity and a sense of discovery. It's like
being in a good city, where you can bump into something or someone you never expected. So as an ambitious young architect pages
through the book's long list of awards (architects, it seems, have
found as many ways to congratulate themselves as journalists), he or
she may stumble over a fascinating fact (the amount of steel in Sears
Tower, for example, is enough to build 50,000 cars). Or perhaps he
or she will stop to read an epigram like Ralph Erskine's: "The job of
buildings is to improve human relations: architecture must ease
them, not make them worse." Wisdom like that belongs on a screen
saver.

A strong sense of order is just as essential to a good book as it to
good architecture, and the logical progression of information in the
Almanac certainly is welcome given the rush of unfiltered information that is coming at us in the Computer Age. To be sure, this book

is more about words and numbers than images; if you are looking for a synthesis of the latest aesthetic trends, better go to the bookstore at MoMA. But the *Almanac* nevertheless tells a significant story, one that is as much about our ever-evolving architecture culture as it is about architecture itself.

An anthropologist seeking to paint a picture of today's design world might read the table of contents of this book in the following way: There is, first, the matter of how architecture culture marks time (the calendar). Then we come across some big ideas that are percolating today (the award winners' speeches and student essays). After that, we see what architecture culture deems worthy of recognition (awards and honors). We grasp how it divides itself into groups and sub-groups (organizations), where it stores treasured objects (museums), who are its chieftains (noted individuals), and so on, through the obituaries of key figures.

Along the way are chapters like "Records, Rankings & Achievements" — a sort of "Guinness Book of Records of Architecture and Design" that names, among other things, the longest covered bridges in the world. In addition, plenty of useful things get covered, like the birthdays of famous architects (now I have no excuse for not sending Stanley Tigerman and Helmut Jahn a card) and a list of National Trust for Historic Preservation-approved historic hotels (beats the Holiday Inn, I'll bet). But the chapter I find most intriguing is one of the shortest—a three-page list of architectural bookstores. It hints at what may be truly useful about this book—its ability to build communities.

A caution: I don't mean the *Almanac* is the publishing equivalent of one of those romantically-conceived New Urbanism towns where everybody supposedly sits on the front porch in a rocking chair, just like Grandma and Grandpa did, and talks endlessly with their neighbors out there on the sidewalk. Instead, this book recognizes the reality that in today's world, communities of interest are just as important as traditional communities based on a shared sense of place. And so, it wisely lists the Web address for just about everything in its pages. In addition, the chapter on museums comes complete with a list of upcoming exhibitions that tells us where we can go for intellectual nourishment whether we're in San Francisco or Stockholm. The aforementioned list of architecture bookstores serves the same function, promoting common interests rather than individual achievement. That's all to the good. If there is one thing we have learned so far in this time of exploding computer usage, it is that information can help to build communities, both real and virtual.

In many other ways, however, we seem to be at sea, awash in a normless world where there no longer seems to be a governing set of architectural ideas. We have rules for protecting the great buildings of the past, which appear in the chapter on design and historic preservation—the Secretary of the Interior's Standards for Rehabilitation, a Ten Commandments-like series of prohibitions (Thou shalt not use chemical or physical treatments, such as sand-blasting, that cause damage to historic materials, and so forth). But we do not have rules for creating the landmarks of the future, even if we do have triumphs like Frank Gehry's Guggenheim Museum in Bilbao, Spain. This is, as Koolhaas unflinchingly says, "a post-ideological era," one that is utterly different from the shared values and the broad-based movement of mid-century modernism. "We respect each other, but we do not form a community," he says in his Pritzker speech. "We have no project together" and have no discourse, either, about such profoundly important issues as settlement or human co-existence.

That sounds pretty bleak, but architecture is, by nature, an optimistic profession, and the *Almanac* reflects that optimism. You can see it in the many, relatively new awards given for environmentally-conscious, or green, architecture. And you can feel it in several of the epigrams, like Charles Correa's notion that the architect is a visionary agent of change. Indeed, there is a sense of visionary optimism—mixed with controlled rage—in the words of both Legorreta, who urges architects to create not just better living standards, but a better quality of life, and Koolhaas, who sees in the virtual utopias made possible by the computer a new standard, one that demands that architects come to grips with issues like the plundering of the environment and global poverty.

These are bracing wake-up calls and they raise the entire *Almanac* to a higher level. For in the end, this is a book that doesn't simply tell you what is or what was. Rather, it explores what could be, even what should be. In other words, the *Almanac* is more than a mere compilation of numbers and words, and charts and graphs. It is about ideas as well as information. And those ideas address the future of architecture, its very soul. The contents of those old-fashioned time capsules were never as rich—or as provocative—as that.

INTRODUCTION

The purpose of the *Almanac of Architecture & Design 2001* is multi-fold: to provide a single, comprehensive source for facts, records, and rankings for the architecture and design professions; to provide information about design leaders, both past and present; to provide economics and metrics that are useful to architects and designers in improving, expanding, and understanding their profession and their work; and finally, to provide a more complete understanding of the key forces that are reshaping the design professions and the buildings and products that designers create for our world.

We have built upon last year's highly successful inaugural edition of the *Almanac of Architecture & Design 2000* in numerous significant ways. In addition to updating all the entries, we have expanded coverage in each of our sections from museum exhibitions and award programs to the rankings of degree programs. You will also notice that we augmented the index to include subjects and places as well as people. The most exciting change, however, is the inclusion of notable speeches and essays, including the acceptance speeches from the Pritzker Prize laureate, Rem Koolhaas; the AIA Gold Medal recipient, Ricardo Legorreta; and the Architecture Firm Award winner, Gensler by Arthur Gensler; as well as essays from recent graduates, Tiffany Lin and Robyn Wissel, on their experience at America's best design schools.

The associations, museums, and design firms around the world have made important contributions to this *Almanac*. The top designers and architects themselves have also been key sources for us. It has been a joy to work with so many quality people around the world who gladly schedule us into their priorities. This much I can say for sure: in design and architecture there are many admirable people who are dedicated to learning and improving and contributing to the design professions and, ultimately, the quality of services they provide their to clients and the public.

In his book *The Right Stuff,* Tom Wolfe describes what it took the best pilots to succeed. He used an architecture metaphor that can also serve us here with the *Almanac*. I share his words with you:

> *A career in flying was like climbing one of those ancient Babylonian pyramids made of a dizzy progression of steps and ledges, a ziggurat, a pyramid extraordinarily high and steep; and the idea was to prove at every foot of the way up that pyramid that you were one of the elected and anointed ones who had the right stuff and could move higher and higher and even – ultimately, God willing, one day – that you might be able to join that special few at the very top, that elite who had the capacity to bring tears to men's eyes, the very Brotherhood of the Right Stuff itself.*

The *Almanac of Architecture and Design 2001* recognizes those who have achieved the top, which includes the selfless contributions of designers as well as the achievements of star architects. The *Almanac* not only displays facts on top level accomplishments but includes coverage of significant contributions to the enhancement of the quality of life through design. I'm reminded of the words of Sir Norman Foster when he accepted the AIA Gold Medal:

> *I have always believed passionately that architecture and design is a social art – and not a luxury – that it is concerned with the quality of life – the creation of benefits – about caring and sharing. Social concern is one of the most powerful driving forces of architecture.*

Foster's words underlie our daily work on the *Almanac* year around and motivate us to seek out the best. Why recognize success? Because quality is important! New achievements, benchmarks, and records reshape and improve the quality of life. It is in this regard that this *Almanac* is essentially about places and people and is borne out of the needs of people.

Hundreds of people helped us to compile the information in the *Almanac of Architecture & Design 2001*. I would like to extend a special thanks to the organizations and their leaders who share with us daily the changes, updates, and new information. To our many friends at

CMD Group, we thank you for co-sponsoring our research and offering your own databases for inclusion. Even as you read this, the Greenway Consulting staff is diligently working on the next edition, under the leadership of our architectural historian, Jennifer Evans, the very effective managing editor of the *Almanac*. Lastly, much thanks goes to Blair Kamin, the architecture critic of the *Chicago Tribune*, for his thoughtful and spirited foreword.

To each of you who support our mission, we extend our special thanks and offer our wishes to you for a prosperous and meaningful year – by design.

James P. Cramer

CALENDAR

JANUARY EVENTS AND DEADLINES

Residential Architect Design Awards
Submissions due January 10
(202) 736-3407

Heimtextil Frankfurt
Frankfurt, Germany
January 10-13
www.heimtextil.de

Maison & Objet
Paris, France
January 12-16
(703) 522-5000

Domotex 2001
Hanover, Germany
January 13-16
www.domotex.de

Engineering Excellence Awards
Submissions due Janury 15
www.acec.org

Abbott Lowell Cummings Award
Submissions due January 15
www.vernaculararchitecture.org

Restoration and Renovation
Washington, D.C.
January 15-17
www.egiexhib.com

ACEC Engineering Excellence Awards
Submissions due January 16
www.acec.org

Interior Design Show
Toronto, Canada
January 18-21
www.interiordesignshow.com

International Design Competition, Osaka
Submissions due January 19
www.jidpo.or.jp/japandesign/jdf/html/en_ind
ex.html

RENOVEHOTEL: Conference and Exhibition
for Hotel, Restaurant and Public Building
Renovation
Paris, France
January 20-24
www.reedexpo.com

Society for Environmental Graphic Design
Design Awards
Submissions due January 29
www.segd.org

International Air Conditioning, Heating,
Refrigerating Exposition
Atlanta, GA
January 29-31
www.ahrexpo.com

BraunPrize
Submissions due January 31
www.braunprize.com

Hospitality Design Leadership Summit 2001
Vail, Colorado
January 31- Februray 2
(888) 383-6829

TEXBO: International Trade Fair for Interior
Decoration, Creative Home Design, Object
and Planning
Salzburg, Austria
January 31 - February 3
www.reedexpo.com

JANUARY 2001

SUN	MON	TUES	WED	THURS	FRI	SAT
	1 *New Year's Day*	2	3	4 Helmut Jahn	5	6
7	8	9	10 John Wellborn Root	11	12	13
14	15 *Martin Luther King Jr. Day*	16	17	18	19	20
21	22	23 Gottfried Böhm	24	25	26	27 Felix Candela
28	29	30	31			

Notes for Events & Anniversaries

FEBRUARY EVENTS AND DEADLINES

International Design Resource Awards
Submissions due February 1
www.designresource.org

Urban Land Institute Annual Conference
Paris, France
February 1
www.uli.org

Pacific Home Fashion Fair
Las Vegas, NV
February 1-2
www.heimtextil.de

New York Home Textiles Market
New York City, NY
February 4-8
(800) 235-3512

***Metropolis* West Conference**
San Francisco, CA
February 7-8
www.metropolismag.com

**National Association of Home Builders
International Builder's Show**
Atlanta, GA
February 9-12
www.nahbexpos.com

**The Emergent Building Technologies
Conference: Integrating People, Technology &
Design**
Las Vegas, NV
February 12-13
www.energentbuildingtech.com

**American Institute of Architects Grassroots
Convention**
Washington, D.C.
February 14-17
www.e-architect.com

**ASTROBAU: International Trade Fair for
Building Products and Related Services**
Salzburg, Austria
February 15-18
www.reedexpo.com

National Engineers Week
February 18-24
www.eweek.org

**TED: Technology Entertainment and Design
Conference**
Monterey, CA
February 21-24
www.ted.com

**6th World Congress of Tall Buildings and
Urban Habitats**
Melbourne, Australia
February 26-March 2
www.icms.com.au/tbuh

World of Concrete 2001
Las Vegas, NV
February 27-March 2
www.worldofconcrete.com

**EXPOTERM: International Exhibition for
Energy, Heating, Refrigeration, Air-
Conditioning Control Systems**
Lyon, France
February 28 - March 3
www.reedexpo.com

**Eurotips: Furniture and Interior Design
Components Exhibition**
Lyon, France
February 28-March3
www.reedexpo.com

FEBRUARY 2001

SUN	MON	TUES	WED	THURS	FRI	SAT
				1	2	3 Alvar Aalto
4	5	6	7 Ernest Flagg	8	9 J.J.P. Oud	10
11	12 Etienne-Louis Boulée	13	14	15	16	17
18	19 *President's Day*	20	21 Hendrik Petrus Berlage	22	23	24 Charles LeBrun
25	26	27	28 Frank Gehry			

Notes for Events & Anniversaries

MARCH EVENTS AND DEADLINES

AIA Continental Europe International Design Awards
Submissions due March 1
www.aiaeurope.org

Coram Design Award
Submissions due March 1
www.coram.nl

Design-Build for Hospitality and Healthcare Conference
Las Vegas, NV
March 1-2
www.dbia.org

Inter Con
Tampa, FL
March 1-2
www.cisca.org

South Florida Furniture & Accessory Market
Ft. Lauderdale, FL
March 2-4
www.kemexpo.com

American Planning Association National Planning Conference
New Orleans
March 10-14
www.planning.org

Sustainable Development Conference & Trade Show
Atlanta, GA
March 14-16
www.southface.org

***Business Week/Architectural Record* Awards**
Registration due March 16
www.e-architect.com

Association of Collegiate Schools of Architecture Annual Meeting
Baltimore, MD
March 16-20
www.acsa-arch.org

5th European International Conference on Design Management
Amsterdam, The Netherlands
March 18-20
www.dmi.org

National Green Building Conference
Seattle, WA
March 18-20
www.nahbrc.org

GlobalShop
Chicago, Illinois
March 22-24
www.globalshop98.com

Hospitality Design 2001: Expo and Conference
Las Vegas, NV
March 29-31
www.hdexpo.com

Interior Design Competition
Submissions due March 31
www.iida.org

MARCH 2001

SUN	MON	TUES	WED	THURS	FRI	SAT
				1	2	3
4	5	6 Michaelangelo	7 Samuel Sloan	8	9	10 Leopold Eidlitz
11	12 André LeNôtre	13	14 James Bogardus	15	16	17
18	19	20	21	22	23	24 Jane Beverly Drew
25	26	27 William Lescaze	28	29 Raymond Hood	30 Hans Hollein	31

Notes for Events & Anniversaries

APRIL EVENTS AND DEADLINES

National Town Meeting on Main Street
Indianapolis, IN
April 1-4
www.mainstreet.org

International Council for Innovation and Research in Building and Construction Congress
Wellington, New Zealand
April 2-6
www.branz.org.nz/cib/

Triennial CIB World Building Congress: Performance in Product and Process
Wellington, New Zealand
April 2-6
www.cibworld.nl

NeoCon South
Atlanta, GA
April 4-5
(800) 677-6278

Multipolar Patterns of Urban Development
Lodz, Poland
April 4-7
Email: zerm@krysia.uni.lodz.pl

International Sustainable Development Research Conference
Manchester, UK
April 5-6
www.erpenvironment.org

4th International Symposium on Asia Pacific Architecture
Honolulu, HI
April 5-7
http://web1.arch.hawaii.edu/events/symposium4/

Society of Architectural Historians Annual Meeting
Toronto, Ontario, Canada
April 18-22
www.sah.org

International Home Furnishings Market
High Point, NC
April 19-27
www.merchandisemart.com

American Solar Energy Society Annual Conference
Washington, D.C.
April 21-25
www.ases.org

***Business Week/Architectural Record* Awards**
Submissions due April 23
www.e-architect.com

Facility Forum
Dallas, TX
April 23-25
www.facilityforum.com

EnvironDesign5
Atlanta, GA
April 25-27
www.environdesign.com

Vernacular Architecture Forum Annual Meeting
Newport, RI
April 25-29
www.vernaculararchitecture.org

6th Annual Conference on Design Management in the Digital Environment
Pasadena, CA
April 30-May 1
www.dmi.org

The Newport Symposium
Newport, RI
April 30-May 2
www.newportmansions.org

APRIL 2001

SUN	MON	TUES	WED	THURS	FRI	SAT
1 Mario Botta	2	3	4	5	6	7 Leon Krier
8 Kisho Kurokawa	9 Jørn Utzon	10	11	12	13	14 Peter Behrens
15 *Easter*	16 Ove Arup	17	18	19	20	21
22 Edward Larrabee Barnes	23	24 John Russell Pope	25	26 I.M. Pei	27 C.R. Cockerell	28
29	30					

Notes for Events & Anniversaries

MAY EVENTS AND DEADLINES

American Institute of Architects Architecture Firm Award
Submissions due in May
www.e-architect.com

Space Syntax 2001 @Georgia Institute of Technology
Atlanta, GA
May 7-11
http://murmur.arch.gatech.edu/~3sss/

Sustain 2001 - The World Sustainable Energy Exhibition & Conference
Amsterdam, The Netherlands
May 8-10
www.sustain2001.com

Society for Industrial Archeology Annual Conf.
Washington, D.C.
May 10-13
www.ss.mtu.edu/IA/sia.html

American Consulting Engineers Council Annual Convention
San Antonio, TX
May 13-16
www.acec.org

National Preservation Week
May 13-19
www.nthp.org

Heimtextil Americas
Miami, FL
May 16-18
www.heimtextil.de

American Institute of Architects National Convention
Denver, CO
May 17-20
www.e-architect.com

Decorex USA
New York, NY
May 19-22
www.glmshows.com/decorex

International Contemporary Furniture Fair
New York City, NY
May 19-22
www.icff.com

Surtex
New York City, NY
May 20-22
www.surtex.com

2001 International Conference on Project Cost Management
Beijing, China
May 24-27
www.srb.org.hk/2001_conf/

Seventh International Conference on Structural Studies, Repairs and Maintenance of Historical Buildings
Bologna, Italy
May 28-30
www.wessex.ac.uk/conferences/2001/stremaho1/

LightFair International
Las Vegas, NV
May 29 - June 1
www.lightfair.com

SOIS: Southwestern Ontario Industrial Show
Kitchener, Canada
May 29-30
www.reedexpo.com

Society for Environmental Graphic Design Annual Conference
Miami, FL
May 30- June 2
www.segd.org

Royal Architecture Institute of Canada Festival of Architecture
Halifax, Canada
May 30-June 2
www.raic.org

UN	MON	TUES	WED	THURS	FRI	SAT
		1	2	3 Aldo Rossi	4 Bruno Taut	5
	7	8 Charles Atwood	9 Rafael Moneo	10	11	12 Daniel Libeskind
3	14 Helena Syrkus	15	16	17	18 Walter Gropius	19
0	21	22 Marcel Breuer	23 Robert A.M. Stern	24	25	26
7 William Robert Ware	28 Charles F.A. Voysey *Memorial Day*	29	30	31		

Notes for Events & Anniversaries

JUNE EVENTS AND DEADLINES

IBEX: International Building Exposition
Hong Kong
June
www.reedexpo.com

Canadian Council on Rehabilitation and Work World Congress
Montreal, Canada
June 1-5
www.ccrw.org

Environmental Design Research Association Annual Conference
Edinburgh, Scotland
June 3-6
www.edra.org

Fourth European Project Management Conference
London, U.K.
June 3-7
www.pmi.org

International Conference on Innovation Systems in Construction
Ottawa, Canada
June 6-7
www.cibworld.nl

International Design Conference in Aspen
Aspen, CO
June 6-9
www.idca.org

Third International Conference on Ecosystems and Sustainable Development
Alicante, Spain
June 6-8
www.wessex.ac.uk/conferences/2001/ecosud01/

Ecospheres: Land, Water, and Populations Conference
Lincoln, Nebraska
June 11-14
www.unl.edu/ecospheres

Association of Collegiate Schools of Architecture International Conference
Istanbul, Turkey
June 15-19
www.acsa-arch.org

Building Owners & Managers Association (BOMA) Annual Convention/Office Building Show
San Diego, CA
June 17-19
www.boma.org

International Conference on Facilities Management
Innsbruck, Austria
June 17-19
www.cibworld.nl

International Interior Design Association (IIDA) Annual Meeting
June 17-19
www.iida.org

A/E/C Systems Show
Chicago, Illinois
June 18-21
www.aecsystems.com

NeoCon
Chicago, IL
June 18-20
www.merchandisemart.com

Buildings - New York
New York, NY
June 19-20
www.reedexpo.com

International Conference on Construction
Hong Kong, China
June 19-21
www.cibworld.nl

Continued on pg. 14

JUNE 2001

SUN	MON	TUES	WED	THURS	FRI	SAT
					1 Norman Foster	**2** Carlo Scarpa
3	**4**	**5** Asher Benjamin	**6**	**7**	**8** Bruce Goff	**9**
10	**11**	**12** John Roebling	**13**	**14** Kevin Roche	**15**	**16**
17 George Howe	**18**	**19** Charles Gwathney	**20**	**21** Paolo Soleri	**22**	**23**
24 Gerrit Rietveld	**25** Suzana Antonakakis	**26** Matthew Nowicki	**27**	**28**	**29**	**30**

Notes for Events & Anniversaries

JUNE EVENTS AND DEADLINES (CON'T)

Interior Lifestyle
Tokyo, Japan
June 20-22
www.heimtextil.de

Construction Specifications Institute Annual Convention & Exhibition
Dallas, TX
June 21-24
www.csinet.org/confer/conhome.htm

ASHRAE Annual Meeting
Cincinnati, OH
June 23-27
www.ashrae.org

International Conference on Building Envelope Systems and Technologies
Ottawa, Canada
June 27-29
www.nrc.ca/icbest

JULY EVENTS AND DEADLINES

Renewable Energy
Brighton, U.K.
July
www.reedexpo.com

URBAN 21 - Global Conference on the Urban Future
Berlin, Germany
July 4-6
www.urban21.de

CAAD Futures 2001
Eindhoven, The Netherlands
July 8-11
www.caadfutures.arch.tue.nl/2001

World Planning Conference
Shanghai, China
July 11-15
www.hku.hk/cupem/worldcongress/

Hanssem International Interior Design Competition
Submissions due July 16-19
www.hanssemcompe.com

League of Historic American Theaters Annual Conference
New York City, NY
July 17-21
www.lhat.org

1st International Conference on Innovation in Architecture, Engineering and Construction
Loughborough, UK
July 18-20
www.lboro.ac.uk/cice/aec/

2001: A Planning Odyssey (SCUP's 36th Annual Conference)
Boston, MA
July 21-25
www.scup.org/36

APPA 2001 Educational Conference & 88th Annual Meeting
Montreal, Canada
July 22-24
www.appa.org

JULY 2001

SUN	MON	TUES	WED	THURS	FRI	SAT
1	2	3	4 *Independence Day*	5	6 Herman Hertzberger	7
8 Philip Johnson	9 Michael Graves	10	11	12 Buckminster Fuller	13	14 Moshe Safdie
15	16	17	18	19	20	21
22	23 Richard Rogers	24	25	26	27	28 Santiago Calatrava
29	30	31				

Notes for Events & Anniversaries

AUGUST EVENTS AND DEADLINES

**American Institute of Architects Honor
Awards for Architecture**
Submissions due in August
www.e-architect.com

**American Institute of Architects Honor
Awards for Interior Architecture**
Submissions due in August
www.e-architect.com

**Illuminating Engineers Society of North
America Annual Conference**
Ottowa, Canada
August 5-7
www.iesna.org

**American Institute of Building Design
Convention**
Montreal, Canada
August 8-12
www.aibd.org

**"Design for Architecture" 9th International
Alvar Aalto Symposium**
Jyväskylä, Finland
August 10-12
www.alvaraalto.fi

**Industrial Designers Society of America
National Conference**
Boston, MA
August 15-18
www.idsa.org

**U.S. Green Building Council's Annual
Members Summit**
Tucson, AZ
August 19-22
www.usgbc.org

**The Transformation to Sustainable Planning:
Decision-Making, Models and Tools**
Newcastle upon Tyne, U.K.
August 29-September 1
www.sustainable-cities.org.uk

SUN	MON	TUES	WED	THURS	FRI	SAT
			1 Martin Roche	**2**	**3**	**4**
5	**6** Jacques-Denis Antoine	**7**	**8**	**9** Eileen Gray	**10**	**11** Peter Eisenman
12	**13**	**14** Sverre Fehn	**15**	**16**	**17**	**18** Pietro Belluschi
19	**20** Eero & Eliel Saarinen	**21**	**22**	**23**	**24**	**25**
26	**27**	**28**	**29**	**30**	**31**	

Notes for Events & Anniversaries

SEPTEMBER EVENTS AND DEADLINES

Interiors Magazine Awards
Submissions due in September
(646) 654-5786

American Institute of Architects Honor Awards for Regional & Urban Planning
Submissions due in September
www.e-architect.com

American Institute of Architects 25 Year Award
Submissions due in September
www.e-architect.com

American Society of Architectural Perspectivists Annual Convention
Yellowstone National Park, Wyoming
September 6-9
www.appa.org

Society of Architectural Historians of Great Britain Annual Conference
Stirling, England
September 6-9
www.sahgb.org.uk

International Casual Furniture & Accessories Market
Chicago, Illinois
Septemebr 12-16
www.merchandisemart.com

IIDEX/NeoCon Canada
Toronto, Canada
September 13-14
www.merchandisemart.com

Alice Davis Hitchcock Book Award
Submissions due September 15
www.sah.org

Antoinette Forrester Downing Award
Submissions due September 15
www.sah.org

Philip Johnson Award
Submissions due September 15
www.sah.org

Spiro Kostof Book Award
Submissions due September 15
www.sah.org

APPA's Institute for Facilities Management
Scottsdale, AZ
September 16-20
www.appa.org/education

Design on the Edge
Lexington, KY
September 20
(859) 257-3106

American Consulting Engineers Council Fall Conference
Orlando, FL
September 20-22
www.acec.org

American Society of Landscape Architects Annual Meeting
Montreal, Canada
September 22-24
www.asla.org

London Open House
London, England
September 23-23
www.londonopenhouse.org

World Workplace 2001
Kansas City, MO
September 23-25
www.worldworkplace.org

Decorex International
London, U.K.
September 23-26
www.decorex.com

The National Association of Women in Construction 2001 Conference
Anchorage, AK
September 26-29
www.nawic.org

SEPTEMBER 2001

SUN	MON	TUES	WED	THURS	FRI	SAT
						1
2 Renaldo Giurgola	3 Louis Sullivan *Labor Day*	4 Kenzo Tange	5 Rudolf M. Schindler	6	7 Andres M. Duany	8
9	10	11 Peter Eisenman	12	13	14 Renzo Piano	15
16 Fumihiko Maki	17	18 Peter Smithson	19	20 Stanley Tigerman	21	22
23	24	25 Francesco Borromini	26	27	28	29
30						

Notes for Events & Anniversaries

OCTOBER EVENTS AND DEADLINES

Association for Computer Aided Design in Architecture Conference
October
www.acadia.org

International Workshop on Architectural Management
Reading, UK
October

American Institute of Architects Edward G. Kemper Award
Submissions due in October
www.e-architect.com

American Institute of Architects Institute Honors for Collaborative Achievement
Submissions due in October
www.e-architect.com

American Institute of Architects Thomas Jefferson Awards for Public Architecture
Submissions due in October
www.e-architect.com

American Institute of Architects Whitney Young, Jr. Award
Submissions due in October
www.e-architect.com

American Institute of Architects Young Architects Award
Submissions due in October
www.e-architect.com

American Institute of Architects/ACSA TOPAZ Medallion
Submissions due in October
www.e-architect.com

CERSAIE: International Exhibition of Ceramics for the Building Industry and Bathroom Furnishings
Bologna, Italy
October 2-7
www.cersaie.it

Urban Land Institute Fall Meeting
Boston, MA
October 3-7
www.uli.org

Chicago Design Show
Chicago, Illinois
October 4-7
www.chicagodesign.com

International Council of Societies of Industrial Design Congress & XXII General Assembly
Seoul, Korea
October 7-11
www.icsid.org

Design Management Institute International Design Management Conference
Chatham, MA
October 14-18
www.dmi.org

National Trust for Historic Preservation National Preservation Conference
Providence, RI
October 16-21
www.nthp.org

International Home Furnishings Market
High Point, NC
October 18-26
www.merchandisemart.com

FEDCON
Washington, D.C.
October 23
www.nacf.com/fedcon

North American Construction Forecast
Washington, D.C.
October 23-24
www.nacf.com

Design-Build Institute Annual Conference
Boston, MA
October 24-26
www.dbia.org

Continued on pg. 22

SUN	MON	TUES	WED	THURS	FRI	SAT
	1	2	3 Denise Scott Brown	4	5	6 Le Corbusier
7	8 *Columbus Day*	9	10	11	12 Richard Meier	13
14	15	16	17	18	19	20
21	22	23 Paul Rudolph	24 Charlotte Perriand	25	26	27 *Yom Kippur*
28	29	30	31 Charles Moore			

Notes for Events & Anniversaries

OCTOBER EVENTS AND DEADLINES (CON'T)

DesigNation4
Miami, FL
October 25-29
www.DesigNation.net

**International Conference on Urban
Waterfront Planning, Development & Culture**
New York City, NY
October 26-28
www.waterfrontcenter.org

**RAIA Governor General's Medals for
Architecture**
Submissions due October 31
www.raic.org

Great American Main Street Award
Submissions due October 31
www.mainst.org

NeoCon New York
New York City, NY
October 31-November 1
www.merchandisemart.com

NOVEMBER EVENTS AND DEADLINES

**Project Management Insitute 2001 - First to
the Future**
Nashville, TN
November 1-10
www.pmi.org

Architectural Digest Home Design Show
New York City, NY
November 1-3
www.merchandisemart.com

**Frank Lloyd Wright Building Conservancy
Annual Conference**
Lakeland, FL
November 1-4
www.swcp.com/flw

**Society for American City and Regional
Planning History Ninth Biennial Conference
of Planning History**
Philadelphia, PA
November 1-4
www.urban.uiuc.edu/sacrph/index.html

BATIMAT: International Building Exhibition
Paris, France
November 5-10
www.reedexpo.com

**Association of Collegiate Schools of Planning
Annual Conference**
Cleveland, OH
November 8-11
www.uwm.edu/Org/acsp/index.htm

Build Boston
Boston, MA
November 13-15
www.buildboston.com

**International Project Management Congress
2001**
Tokyo, Japan
November 19-21
www.enaa.or.jp/JPMF/

ISES Solar World Congress
Adelaide, Australia
November 25 - December 2
www.ises.org/ises.nsf

NeoCon West
Los Angeles, CA
November 29-30
www.merchandisemart.com

NOVEMBER 2001

SUN	MON	TUES	WED	THURS	FRI	SAT
				1	2 Susana Torre	3
4	5	6	7	8	9 John Mervin Carrère	10
11 James Renwick	12	13	14	15	16	17 Rem Koolhaas
18	19	20	21	22 *Thanksgiving*	23	24
25	26	27	28	29 Gottfried Semper	30 Andrea Palladio	

Notes for Events & Anniversaries

DECEMBER EVENTS AND DEADLINES

Hugh Ferriss Memorial Prize
Submissions due in December
www.asap.org

P/A Awards
Submissions due in December
www.architecturemag.com

Symposium on Healthcare Design
Nashville, TN
December 5-8
(508) 647-8637

**American Institute of Architecture Students
Annual Forum**
Washington, D.C.
December 27, 2001 - January 1, 2002
www.aiasnatl.org

DECEMBER 2001

SUN	MON	TUES	WED	THURS	FRI	SAT
						1 Joan Edelman Goody
2	**3**	**4** Gae Aulenti	**5** Ricardo Bofill	**6**	**7**	**8**
9	**10**	**11**	**12**	**13**	**14**	**15** Oscar Niemeyer
	Hanukkah					
16 Ralph Adams Cram	**17**	**18**	**19**	**20** Elizabeth Plater-Zyberk	**21**	**22**
23	**24**	**25** *Christmas Day*	**26**	**27**	**28**	**29**
30	**31**					

Notes for Events & Anniversaries

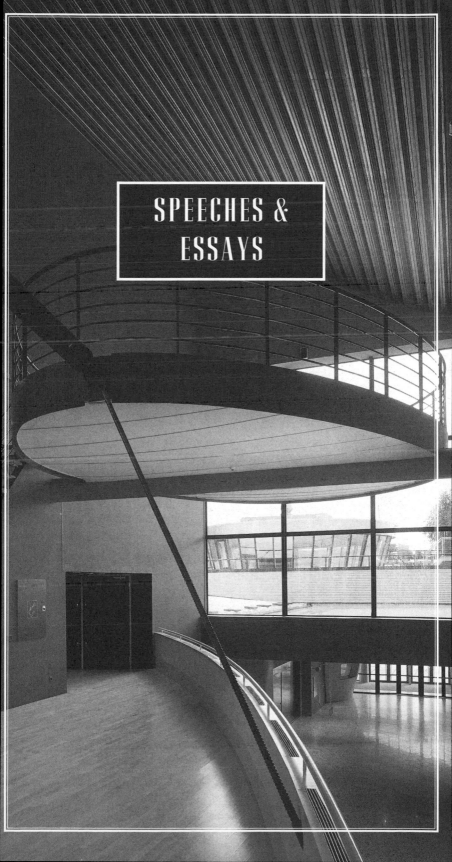

SPEECHES &
ESSAYS

AIA Gold Medal 2000 — Ricardo Legorreta

The 2000 AIA Gold Medallist, Ricardo Legorreta, delivered the following acceptance speech at the Accent on Architecture Gala at the National Building Museum in Washington, D.C. on January 28, 2000.

Jesús Reyes-Heroles, Mexican Ambassador to the USA:
Ronald Skaggs, President of the AIA:
My brilliant sponsor, David Messersmith:
Dear AIA Colleagues:
Dear Friends:

I am deeply moved and extremely happy. Instead of a long speech I briefly want to share with you my thoughts and emotions. I don't remember a specific day or moment in which I decided to be an architect. It came out so naturally! There is no art or architecture background in my family: I only remember that when I notified my father, a professional banker, (sometimes I say that I am an architect by reaction) of my decision to enter the school of Architecture at the Universidad Nacional Autónoma de México, the next day he said to me: "try to be the best" and gave me a subscription to *L'Architecture d'aujourd'hui* magazine.

Since that moment I devoted all my enthusiasm and passion, the main reason for living, to the most beautiful profession in the world: Architecture.

In addition to being my father, best friend and tennis partner, "Don Luis," that was the way I used to call him, was in love with his country. He drove the family all around Mexico developing inside of me a deep love and admiration for my country and countrymen. Little by little I realized that the U.S. had a faulted image of Mexico. We only showed you charros, tequila, and siesta. So I made it an object of mine to devote time to teach others about the architectural values of Mexico.

AIA Gold Medal 2000 Acceptance Speech (Con't)

Thanks to our beloved Charles Moore, I started to teach in the USA and awake and promote among students an exchange between our two countries; together with Buz Yudell, another dear friend, we still maintain and foster that exchange. Then one day my wonderful fellow countryman, the actor Ricardo Montalban, asked me to design his L.A. home – that was the beginning of my professional practice in this country.

Throughout all these years, I have only received from you support, understanding, friendship and love. For this I can't thank you enough. To be recognized and honored by my American colleagues goes beyond any of my greatest wishes or dreams.

I was far from home in Israel when Michael Stanton woke me up at 6 a.m. to give me the great news that I had won the AIA Gold Medal. I thought I was dreaming. It took me hours to realize it was true. I woke up Victor, who was profoundly asleep, and called everybody in Mexico. Michael, I must tell you, that despite your apologies, I will never forget that phone call. The best of all.

Tonight I am here with most of my family; Mr. Reyes Heroles, official representative of my country; my long life partner Noe Castro; my son Victor, "actual partner and boss"; some of my best American and Mexican clients that have become some of my best friends: Cindy Pritzker, Carlos and Laura Lavinda, Pedro Cerisola, Ed and Camille Penhoet, Sandy and Jeanne Robertson and Bill Rutter. I thank them and all my clients that couldn't be here for believing in me. Thanks to David Messersmith, the most brilliant sponsor you can imagine and finally to all of those that are here to celebrate your decision to award me the AIA Gold Medal.

I still feel it is a dream – the happiest dream in my professional life, one that I share and celebrate with you. The recognition is not only to me because I don't believe in geniuses. It also belongs to all the people that work in my office, associate architects and consultants, without whom this couldn't have been possible.

AIA Gold Medal 2000 Acceptance Speech (Con't)

It is also a recognition to my country. Mexico is a country of architects. Architecture is one of the pillars of our culture and part of our daily life: every Mexican is an architect by heart. If it wasn't for Mexico, for the valuable inspiration I have received since my childhood from visiting the Mexican landscape, cities, villages, churches, convents and haciendas, if it wasn't for my teachers, friends and the Mexican people I couldn't be here. In the name of my country and countrymen. I thank you very much.

In this particular moment of architecture, your decision confirms, once more, that the AIA recognitions are beyond cultural, economical and political interests – you are a truly professional institution. I am proud to join the much admired and distinguished Gold Medallists group, and to share this year celebration with Rick Lowe, Gensler Associates, and my dear friend Richard Meier.

Being the 2000 Gold Medallist invites me to share with you a special meditation.

After a controversial 20th century with two world wars, deep social, economical and educational differences, impressive medical and technological progress, we are entering a globalized 21st century full of expectations and unlimited possibilities of success but also of failures. The speed of technological progress continues and the latitude of generations is getting shorter and shorter, at this moment we talk about having a new generation every seven years. God knows what will be the gap in the future.

More and more humanity has the feeling of being dominated by the machine. Human beings are loosing credibility. Young people start to believe that computers and virtual intelligence are superior to human imagination and creativity and that soon they will be able to tell us better than ourselves what decision we should make and which way we should go. For the first time in history man seems to be one step behind machines.

AIA Gold Medal 2000 Acceptance Speech (Con't)

Obviously architecture is not exempt from this situation. For the first time we question how long our buildings should last, we wonder where globalization, technology and fashion are leading us, and often we consider that architecture has lost its leadership and wonder if we are only at the service of commercial, technological, political and superficial interests.

Our personal lives are also affected by this turmoil. We often live surrounded by ugly environments, inhuman spaces, packed with a continuous stress and futile activities. More and more we loose interest and devote less time to thinking, meditating and appreciating family life, friendship and love.

By nature I am a passionate optimist, and the AIA Gold Medal makes me more passionate and optimistic. My dear colleagues, I invite you to work together and take advantage of this brilliant future, full of opportunities – I invite you to bring architecture to the level it deserves. To devote all our talent, passion and knowledge to create better living conditions for humanity – not only better living standards but better quality of life.

Let's stop building monuments to ourselves and with humility, use technology, information and knowledge as tools to serve humanity and create better environments, better cities, better places to learn, work, rest and meditate by recuperating the true values of life: such as peace, spirituality and love. Mankind transcends by the beauty of its thinking and achievements - beauty is the best way for us to transcend.

The measure of human being's success is in direct proportion to his commitment to excellence. Let us help countries, perhaps planets, governments and all kinds of people to be happier and enjoy life. Remember, giving is a fundamental element of happiness.

Let us design buildings and spaces that not only comply with cost, codes, safety, and physical space but above all give the users aesthetic

AIA Gold Medal 2000 Acceptance Speech (Con't)

and spiritual emotions, happiness and encourage better understanding between different races, nationalities, belief, economical levels, ages and interests. By working together to achieve this, architecture will recover the recognition it deserves.

On my behalf I leave with you my love, friendship, gratitude and with respect and admiration for I.M. Pei. I make the same promise he did when, in 1979, he was awarded the Gold Medal:

"I will do the best I can to be a better man because only that way I can be a better architect."

God bless you.

Courtesy of the American Architectural Foundation

Architecture Firm Award 2000 – Gensler

Arthur Gensler, co-founder of Gensler, the 2000 AIA Architecture Firm Award winner, delviered the following acceptance speech at the Accent on Architecture Gala at the National Building Museum in Washington, D.C. on January 28, 2000.

First, all of us at Gensler want to thank The American Institute of Architects for this wonderful award. It is an honor for us to be recognized. I don't think it really hit home until last night, when I saw our name carved on the wall of the Institute's headquarters along with the other outstanding firms from the past. But the biggest thrill is for me to be here this evening to receive this honor and to share the stage with Ricardo Legorreta, who is really the architect of the hour and one of the truly great architects of our time.

People often ask me how you control a large firm. You don't. I learned a long time ago that to build a great organization, you hire people smarter than you are and then get out of their way. I'm honored to have such a collaborative, entrepreneurial, talented, creative, and energetic team to share this award with. Gensler is an employee-owned team of 1,900 people with 106 partners, who continually stretch and share their talents across our one-firm firm. Not all of them could make it here tonight, but let me introduce the leadership team of our firm: Margo Grant Walsh, our Vice Chairman; Ed Friedrichs, our President and fellow FAIA member; Tony Harbour, a Board member with responsibility for our Design Steering Committee and our London office; Joe Brancato, Robin Klehr, and Walter Hunt, all Managing Principals of our New York office; my son David Gensler, who co-manages our London office; Jim Furr, also FAIA and Managing Principal of our Houston office: Diane Hoskins, Managing Principal of our Washington DC office; Dan Winey, Managing Principal of our San Francisco office; Andy Cohen, Managing Principal of our Los Angeles office, my son Douglas Gensler, who manages our Boston office; Darrel Fitzgerald, another FAIA, who manages our Atlanta office; and of course Jim Follett, also FAIA, who started the firm with me in San Francisco and now

Opposite: Arthur Gensler
Photographer: ©Kit Morris 1999

Architecture Firm Award 2000 Acceptance Speech (Con't)

manages our Chicago office.

Last but not least, my wife Drue, a member of our Board, who helped me launch the firm and set its direction. When Jim, Drue and I started our firm 35 years ago with $200 in the bank and very few contacts, I can assure you we never anticipated our being here tonight. It has been an incredible trip and we still have a long way to go.

People sometimes ask me if I anticipated the amazing growth of our firm. The answer is, of course, "No," but I always find myself adding that growth is not the issue. Providing our clients with responsive design solutions is the issue, and the real trick is to do this across a closely linked network of offices. Everything we are today is attributable to our clients – not just because they give us the opportunities, but because they encourage us to learn from them, grow with them, go with them across the country and then across the globe. Because of this, we've always been quite fearless in pushing the envelope of architectural services. We were fortunate to start our firm with a focus on work that fell below the radar screen for many architects – space planning and interiors. Hopefully, we had some effect on these services being a significant part of most firms' work today.

We currently have about 1,200 active clients, many for over 20 years, and, luckily for us, they are a roster of the world's leading companies. Most of these organizations are changing dramatically. As their world changes, ours is changing, too, constantly expanding the horizons of our work and our services. Our clients look to us now to develop design solutions, based on an understanding of their business. They look to us to design projects that align with their business strategies. They understand, more than they did 90 years ago, that the quality and performance of their facilities are as critical to their success as their people, process and their technology.

Architecture knits these strategic elements together. And this is why today our profession has a unique opportunity to recapture our leadership role. Whether we're talking about a large or a small firm, this is the profession's time- and we must seize it. If we fail to do so, others will come forward. If we take the lead, they will follow. Together,

Architecture Firm Award 2000 Acceptance Speech (Con't)

we can make a better world, a world in which we will all prosper.

I've been in this profession for over 40 years and I can honestly say that I've never seen as many opportunities and such a shortage of skilled people to do them. I'm sure others here have a similar problem. We learned early on to exclude no one in our search for smart and talented people. Architecture is a big tent – there's room for men and women of every background and every possible specialty. I'm proud of our firm's record in that area.

Our host tonight is the American Architectural Foundation. Let me take this opportunity to mention their excellent Buildings Connection Program, which teaches an appreciation for design among young people, in grades K-8, so they will grow up to value architecture and design and, hopefully, consider it as a career.

We need the best and the brightest in our profession to take on the responsibilities and opportunities that we are being offered. I hope that each of you will support this program in your community. When you talk to these young people, I hope you can feel their excitement about design and their desire to help the environment. Our profession has a particular responsibility to take the lead on these issues. We need to be courageous in pressing for livable cities, for sustainability, for decent and affordable housing, for a world, in other words, that we can feel proud to leave to our children and grandchildren.

Let me end by thanking you again for selecting Gensler as the Architectural Firm of the Year. Particular thanks are due to Michael Stanton, the Past President of the Institute, who so ably sponsored our nomination. The mission of our firm is to make great places not just for our clients, but for the people and communities who experience our work and whose lives are enhanced by our solutions. You honor all of them, but especially our clients, in giving us this wonderful award.

Thank you very much.

Courtesy of the American Architectural Foundation

Pritzker Architecture Prize 2000 – Rem Koolhaas

Rem Koolhaas, the 2000 Pritzker Prize Laureate, delivered the following acceptance speech at the Jerusalem Archaeological Park, Israel on May 29, 2000.

I have prepared a short speech – and maybe I should start with an anecdote. It may be a strange anecdote, but coming from the Netherlands, and being born in 1944, meant paradoxically that I was ignorant of the issue of Jewishness until the age of 21. In my youth, in my country, it was completely unusual to indicate anyone's religious or racial background, and it was an issue that we never spoke about. That changed drastically when I first came to New York and was welcomed on the Institute for Architecture and Urban Studies led by the architect Peter Eisenman, who deserves, in my view, the Pritzker Prize even more than me. The first time I was there, Peter took me by my coat like this, in a very aggressive way, and said, "Do you know why you're here, Koolhaas?" And I said, "No." "You are here to represent the Gothic element." So that put me in my place, and probably explains some of the feelings of my situation here.

Anyway, I want to begin by performing my thank yous. I thank Cindy Pritzker and the Pritzker Family and its foundation for their exceptional identification with architecture. I thank the jury who made such an inspired decision this year. I thank my partners at my office O.M.A. Each and every 550 of them have made the contribution that now turns out to be critical. I thank the Harvard Design School for supporting my double life as a futurist. And I thank my clients who triggered our work by burdening us with their needs.

After my thank yous I have written three little anecdotes, or three little episodes, that for me indicate both the recent past of architecture, the current situation of architecture and the, perhaps, imminent future of architecture. And, I want to discuss some of the potential evolutions that I – if I'm not careful – will blow away the evolution that may happen in the imminent future. I want to start in 1950 – fifty years ago.

Pritzker Architecture Prize 2000 Acceptance Speech (Con't)

Fifty years ago, the architectural scene was not about a unique individual, the genius, but about the group – the movement. There was no scene. There was an architectural world. Architecture was not about the largest possible difference, but about the subtleties that could be developed within a narrow range of similarities within the generic. Architecture was a continuum that ended with urbanism. A house was seen as a small city. The city was seen as a huge house. This kind of architecture saw itself as ideological. Its politics stretched all the way from socialism to communism and all the points in between. Great themes were adopted from beyond architecture, not from the imagination of the individual architect's brain.

Architects were secure in their alignment with what was then called society, something that was imagined and could be fabricated. It is now 2000, 50 years after the idyllic caricature that I just described for you. We have Pritzkers. There are a fair amount here sitting on the first row. Therefore, we have unique and singular identities, signatures even. We respect each other, but we do not form a community. We have no project together. Our client is no longer the state or its derivations but the private individuals that often embark on daring ambitions and expensive trajectories, which we architects support whole heartily.

The system is final. The market economy. We work in a post--ideological era and, for lack of support, we have abandoned the city or any more general issues. The themes we invent and sustain are our private mythologies, our specializations. We have no discourse about territorial organization, no discourse about settlement or human co-existence. At best our work brilliantly explores and exploits a series of unique conditions. The fact that this site's archeological aspect is emphasized above its political charge shows that political innocence is an important part of the contemporary architect's equipment.

I am grateful that the jury's text for the 2000 prize casts me as defining new kinds of relationships, both theoretical and practical, between architecture and the cultural situation. That is indeed a sense of what I'm trying to do. Although I am very bad at predicting

Pritzker Architecture Prize 2000 Acceptance Speech (Con't)

the future, too preoccupied by the present, let us speculate for a moment about the next fifty year interval - architecture as it will be practiced in two thousand fifty, or if we are lucky, a little bit sooner.

One development is certain. In the past three years, brick and mortar have evolved to click and mortar. Retail has become e-tail and we cannot exaggerate the importance of those things enough. Compared to the occasional brilliance of architecture now, the domain of the virtual has asserted itself with a wild and messy abandon and is proliferating at a speed that we can only dream of. For the first time in decades, and maybe in millennia, we architects have a very strong and fundamental competition. The communities we cannot imagine in the real world will flourish in virtual space. The territories and demarcations that we maintain on the ground are merged and morphed beyond recognition in a much more immediate, glamorous, and flexible domain – that of the electronic.

After four thousand years of failure, PhotoShop and the computer create utopias instantly. At this ceremony, in this location, architecture is still fundamentally committed to mortar, as if only the proximity to one of the largest piles assembled in the history of mankind reassures us about another two thousand years of lease on our particular niche and our future credibility. But the rest of the world has already liberated architecture for us. Architecture has become a dominant metaphor, a controlling agent for everything that needs concept, structure, organization, entity, form. Only we architects don't benefit from this redefinition, marooned in our own Dead Sea of mortar.

Unless we break our dependency on the real and recognized [when using] architecture as a way of thinking about all issues, from the most political to the most practical, and liberate ourselves from eternity to speculate about compelling and immediate new issues, such as poverty, the disappearance of nature, architecture will maybe not make the year two thousand fifty.

Thank you.

Courtesy of the Hyatt Foundation

Architecture Student Essay
Tiffany Lin

The editors of the Almanac of Architecture & Design *asked a recent architecture graduate from Cornell University, last year's Top School for Architecture (see page 367), to contribute an essay on a student's unique perspective about design education and the future of the profession. Tiffany Lin studied architecture at Cornell where she graduated in May 2000 with a Bachelor of Architecture degree. She currently works at Michael Graves & Associates in Princeton, New Jersey.*

It is an engaging task for a recent graduate to reflect upon the college experience relative to only a few months in the professional world. Although the disparity between education and practice in architecture is readily discussed and debated, a true understanding of this disconnect can only be found in the day to day experience in the workplace. The strength of an architecture education is its focus on teaching one to see, question, and think conceptually and analytically. In school, the relationship between the intellectual issues of our discipline and the practical aspects of building-making is often left uncultivated. Tension between the theory of architecture and the reality of practice significantly contributes to a recent graduate's challenge of negotiating the transition from school to profession.

Architecture school is all-encompassing. No other discipline allows for the exploration of virtually every subject through a single creative medium. "Architecture" is taught as a vehicle for discovery and discussion. It is an invaluable education in developing a critical eye for our surroundings and questioning the conventions of history, culture, social interaction and their relationship to the making of space. In school we learn the to live, see, think, and breathe as architects – architects of ideas. Passionate faculty members, each with their own ideological positions and endeavors, are role models for our fanatical lifestyles. We thrive on criticism, competition, and discussion. Motivated by a spirit of camaraderie, we often have desk-crits with fellow students to discuss ideas and share in the search for answers and discoveries. We have pin-ups with faculty to further develop these ideas. Guest critics from around the world convene in remote

Architecture Student Essay (Con't)

locations to participate in our design reviews and indoctrinate us with inspiration and excitement for the field. We are obsessive. We live the work. It is an intense atmosphere of energy, creativity and devotion that consumes our lives. Architecture students are often stereotyped as exclusive and enigmatic. In part this is true, not because we are antisocial or elitist but because we do not know anything else. Studio is our passion, our social life, our connection to each other and the university.

But what happens when we are jettisoned from our beloved studios after graduation and this lifestyle can no longer be sustained? Working in a firm has made it particularly clear that architects are, even if it is in the most romantic form, in a service industry. We rely on funding from clients to make a living and, *more importantly,* to make architecture. It seems for most offices the ideal, the question, and the provocation of Architecture must yield to the economic necessity of running a business. And to run a business efficiently so everyone can go home with a salary (of sorts) means that people must be tasked. The exhausting door-schedules, wall sections, millwork details, plumbing plans, and innumerable design alternatives must be done. Although these are indeed the tedious aspects of architecture that one must learn to eventually 'practice,' it is easy to lose perspective of the bigger picture when our immediate task often seems trivial and uninteresting. Given this scenario, it is critical that we are inspired by the more grand vision of our employers. Considering the amount of effort relative to the reward, the possibility of discontentment and reevaluation of one's path is common in the architectural field, especially for the recent graduate. The question everyone seems to be asking in their first humbling, sometimes frustrating trimester of work is: Do I really want all that defines a career in architecture?

In an architecture firm large or small, corporate or conceptual, financially stable or struggling, our job as the 'intern' is usually to learn our task, do it well, and pull the long hours without complaint. The entire profession seems to survive on a kind of built-in rights-of-pas-

Architecture Student Essay (Con't)

sage cycle. From the extensive interview process we go through, it is evident that our employers are somewhat interested in our individual talents and ideas. But it is also understood that this is not our time and there are tasks to be done. As the rookie, our job is to do the grunt work just as they did when they first graduated. It is an uneasy transition from being the sole author of a project in school, responsible for the design, creation and presentation of our work, to being on a team of architects where we are only responsible for a diminutive task in the grand scope of a project. The complex processes of architectural production are overwhelming and are foreign to the subjects offered in academia. In school, the design process culminated with the final review. Exploratory collages, models, drawings, and texts conveyed our ideas brilliantly and were unscathed by budget, code, politics and other realities of practice. The notion of 'client' was of our own invention to stimulate a project's development and unbridle new discoveries. Now, when process continues into the seemingly contradictory business aspects of architecture, where with the AV consultants, lawyers, and misinformed clients unwittingly dismember the intellectual objectives of 'Architecture,' we are initially bewildered and a little discouraged.

Today, for most it takes extraordinary vision and optimism to work in a firm and continue to be devoted to the idea of becoming an architect. Historically, architects have been 'trained' with particular skills to work in offices. Contemporary architectural education teaches us to think, analyze, critique and essentially *be* offices. This shift in ideology has set up an internal friction in the professional world that is difficult for a recent graduate to mediate. It is important at this transitional time in our careers that we as interns must carefully observe the complex entirety of the architectural practice in order to make well-informed decisions that best serve our long-term goals. It is additionally important that architects conduct their practices with integrity for the discipline such that the internship period offers motivation for discovery and dedication. We must not lose focus on our connection to the fundamental basis of architecture that has to do with vision, tactility, and creation. The possibility of constructing

Architecture Student Essay (Con't)

alternate models for practice can offer new and exciting career potentials. Architecture's allied fields also create the opportunity for formulating offices that may not need to be at the mercy of the singularity of the profession. The enthusiasm and idealism that we take from our educational experiences must be synthesized with the constituent realities of architectural practice in order for young architects to ultimately find a path to artistic and intellectual satisfaction.

Interior Design Student Essay

Robyn Wissel

The editors of the Almanac of Architecture & Design *asked a recent interior design graduate from the University of Cincinnati, last year's Top School for Interior Design (see page 366), to contribute an essay on a student's unique perspective about design education and the future of the profession. Robyn Wissel studied interior design at the University of Cincinnati where she graduated in June 2000 with a Bachelor of Design degree. She currently works at FRCH Design in their specialty retail design studio.*

My Reward

What does it mean to design? By definition, design is to develop something in a skillful or artistic way. Sounds simple, yet after five years of college courses and "co-op" experiences, difficult to rationalize. I define design as an evolution: the development of something into a more involved or useful form. This is not limited to just the design of objects or spaces, but also includes personal fulfillment.

Naivete

On my first day of college, the class was asked to name an interior designer or any designer for that matter. The class sat quietly, as everyone looked around at one another. The only designer named was Frank Lloyd Wright. Considering this, it is apparent how cultivated I have become. Society's, often misinformed, idea of the knowledge a designer must possess is unrealistic. I was unaware of the breath of knowledge that lie ahead. Entering college five years ago, with only a notion of what the design profession was about, I fancied the idea that I had figured it all out: "design something to look good and people will love it." This was ignorant to the process, the history, the theory, the principles, and the emotional implications. There was so much to learn, so much to see. Who was I? Who did I want to become?

Knowledge Gained

Design is indeed a rewarding vocation. It embraces an understand-

Interior Design Student Essay (Con't)

ing of the past and an awareness of the present, resulting in a pre-sumption of the future. My education began as a metamorphosis with a foundation built on design principles. Through the combina-tion of architectural history (precedent), design charettes (innova-tion), knowledge (realism), and intuition (emotion), I became a pro-fessional concerned with poetics and passion. I learned that design is an inclusive process. It involves reaching into the past, searching for prior experience, wisdom, creativity, and knowledge and interpreting it into present day application, while challenging current perception. I recognized design as a love/hate relationship, elusive to the author and often misinterpreted by the audience. Complex and sometimes under appreciated, to the victor goes the spoils. One of the principles that stands out most clearly in my mind is a conversation with one of my professors. During a desk critique, he instructed me that when designing, always reach for the "senses," remembering that design embraces sight, sound, smell, touch, and taste and that these senses are triggered by memory recall. My eyes opened to the power and fulfillment of design. He challenged me to approach design as the power to effect someone's environment, at work and at play. Rewarding in its ability to recall an experience from memory, design can challenge or qualify current perception. Design was beginning to challenge my perception.

Personal Evolution

The University of Cincinnati provided an integral part of my evolu-tion from student to professional. I clearly never expected it to be so gratifying. Having the opportunity to participate in a co-operative education experience, alternating quarters of scholastic and profes-sional curriculum, the knowledge I gained has been immeasurable. Experiencing various design typologies, employers, and consumers proved to be eye opening and key to my personal and professional growth. My understanding of design flourished, becoming more complex and less contrived. I learned the "business" of design, while embracing the diversities of both new employers and geographic relocations across the nation. Co-op fostered personal confidence to design for the real world. Just as school had provided the first steps

Interior Design Student Essay (Con't)

of design: factual information, theoretical principles, and knowledge, co-op embraced this knowledge and put it to the test on a daily basis. Early in my professional career I decided to "explore," choosing a market segment I had not worked in previously. Specialty retail became my next challenge. A continual learning cycle, with new projects, mentors, trends, and ideas, my career always challenges. This is the reward.

Personal Reward

Often left unnoticed or unrecognized; reward is a catalyst for the design profession. Educational reward lies in the history and theory I have learned: the people, the places, and the objects. The co-op experience is rewarding as the first step in a series of many towards my career: the chances, the applications, the failures, and the praises. And now as a career I find the opportunity for design to be rewarding in the ability to grow in experience, recognition, and perspective.

My job is to design, to create, to innovate, to reinvent, and to question the interrogative. Everyday I get to try new things, explore new avenues and do something I love with a fervent passion. Some people only dream of this. I live this. It is the opportunity to grow personally as a leader, as a team member, and as a professional within the design community. The reward is to continually evolve.

AWARDS & HONORS

ACSP Distinguished Educator Award

The ACSP Distinguished Educator Award is presented annually by the Association of Collegiate Schools of Planning (ACSP) in appreciation of distinguished service to planning education and practice. Nominations are welcomed from chairs and faculty members of ACSP member schools and are reviewed by the award committee. Recipients are chosen for their scholarly contributions, teaching excellence, service to the profession, and significant contributions to planning education and/or practice.

For additional information about the Distinguished Educator Award, visit ACSP's Web site at *www.uwm.edu/Org/acsp/*.

1983	Harvey Perloff, University of California, Los Angeles
1984	John Reps, Cornell University
1986	F. Stuart Chapin, University of North Carolina at Chapel Hill
1987	John Friedmann, University of California, Los Angeles
1989	John Dyckman, Johns Hopkins University
1990	Barclay Gibbs Jones, Cornell University
1991	Britton Harris, University of Pennsylvania
1992	Melville Branch, University of Southern California
1993	Ann Strong, University of Pennsylvania
1994	John A. Parker, University of North Carolina at Chapel Hill
1995	Alan Feldt, University of Michigan
1996	Martin Meyerson, University of Pennsylvania
1997	Lloyd Rodwin, Massachusetts Institute of Technology
1998	Michael Teitz, University of California, Berkeley
1999	Lisa Redfield Peattie, Massachusetts Institute of Technology
2000	Melvin M. Webber University of Calfornia, Berkeley

Source: Association of Collegiate Schools of Planning

Aga Khan Award for Architecture

Granted once every three years, the Aga Khan Trust for Culture's Aga Khan Award for Architecture recognizes outstanding contributions to the built environment in the Muslim world. The diversity of winning projects includes individual buildings, restoration and re-use schemes, large-scale community developments, and environmental projects. In addition to the physical, economic, and social needs of a region, this award seeks to emphasize the importance of cultural and spiritual aspects of a project. The Steering Committee, comprised of internationally distinguished architects and scholars, governs this complex three-year process of nominations and technical review in addition to the selection of the Master Jury, which selects the final winning entries. Eligible projects must have been completed within the past 25 years and in use for a minimum of two years. An award of US $500,000 is apportioned between each cycle's winners.

For more information about this award and photographs, drawings and descriptions of the 1998 award recipients, visit the Aga Khan Award for Architecture's Web site at *www.akdn.org*.

1980

Agricultural Training Centre
Nianing, Senegal
UNESCO/BREDA (Senegal)

Medical Centre
Mopti, Mali
André Ravereau (France)

Courtyard Houses
Agadir, Morocco
Jean-François Zevaco (Morocco)

Sidi Bou Saïd
Tunis, Tunisia
Technical Bureau of the Municipality,
    Planners (Tunisia)

Halawa House
Agamy, Egypt
Abdelwahed El-Wakil (England)

Rüstem Pasa Caravanserai
Edirne, Turkey
Ertan Çakirlar (Turkey)

Ertegün House
Bodrum, Turkey
Turgut Cansever

Turkish Historical Society
Ankara, Turkey
Turgut Cansever and Ertur Yener (Turkey)

Inter-Continental Hotel and Conference
    Centre
Mecca, Saudi Arabia
Rolf Gutbrod and Frei Otto (Germany)

National Museum, Doha, Qatar
Michael Rice and Co. (England) and
    Design and Construction Group
    (Greece)

Aga Khan Award for Architecture (Con't)

Water Towers
Kuwait City, Kuwait
VBB, Sune Lindström and Joe Lindström,
    Björn and Björn Design, Stig Egnell
    (Sweden)

Ali Qapu, Chehel Sutun and Hasht
    Behesht
Isfahan, Iran
ISMEO – Istituto Italiano per il Medio ed
    Estremo Oriente (Italy)

Mughal Sheraton Hotel
Agra, India
ARCOP Design Group (Canada)

Kampung Improvement Program
Jakarta, Indonesia
KIP Technical Unit (Indonesia)

Pondok Pesantren Pabelan
Central Java, Indonesia
Amin Arraihana and Fanani (Indonesia)

1983
Hafsia Quarter
Tunis, Tunisia
Association de Sauvegarde de la Médina
    de Tunis (Tunisia)

Darb Qirmiz Quarter
Cairo, Egypt
Egyptian Antiquities Organization and
    German Archaeological Institute
    (Egypt)

Sherefudin's White Mosque
Visoko, Bosnia-Herzegovina
Zlatko Ugljen with D. Malkin, Engineer
    (Bosnia-Herzegovina)

Residence Andalous
Sousse, Tunisia
Serge Santelli (France) and Cabinet
    GERAU (Tunisia)

Hajj Terminal, King Abdul Aziz
    International Airport
Jeddah, Saudi Arabia
Skidmore, Owings and Merrill (USA)

Ramses Wissa Wassef Arts Centre
Giza, Egypt
Ramses Wissa Wassef (Egypt)

Tanjong Jara Beach Hotel and Rantau
    Abang Visitors' Centre
Kuala Trengganu, Malaysia
Wimberly, Wisenand, Allison, Tong and
    Goo (USA) with Arkitek Bersikutu
    (Malaysia)

Great Mosque of Niono
Niono, Mali
Lassina Minta (Mali)

Nail Çakirhan Residence
Akyaka Village, Turkey
Nail Çakirhan (Turkey)

Azem Palace
Damascus, Syria
Michel Ecochard (France) and Shafiq al-
    Imam (Syria)

Tomb of Shah Rukn-i-'Alam
Multan, Pakistan
Awqaf Department (Pakistan)

1986
Social Security Complex
Istanbul, Turkey
Sedad Hakki Eldem (Turkey)

Dar Lamane Housing Community
Casablanca, Morocco
Abderrahim Charai and Abdelaziz Lazrak
    (Morocco)

Aga Khan Award for Architecture (Con't)

Mostar Old Town
Bosnia-Herzegovina
Stari-Grad Mostar (Bosnia-Herzegovina)

Al-Aqsa Mosque
al-Haram al-Sharif, Jerusalem
Isam Awwad (Jerusalem) and ICCROM
  (Italy)

Yaama Mosque, Yaama
Tahoua, Niger
Falké Barmou (Niger)

Bhong Mosque, Bhong
Rahim-Yar Khan, Pakistan
Rais Ghazi Mohammad, Patron (Pakistan)

1986 Honorable Mentions
Shushtar New Town
Shushtar, Iran
DAZ Architects (Iran)

Kampung Kebalen Improvement
Surabaya, Indonesia
Surabaya Kampung Improvement
  Program, with the Surabaya Institute of
  Technology, and the Kampung Kebalen
  Community (Indonesia)

Ismaïliyya Development Projects
Ismaïliyya, Egypt
Culpin Planning (England)

Saïd Naum Mosque
Jakarta, Indonesia
Atelier Enam Architects and Planners
  (Indonesia)

Historic Sites Development
Istanbul, Turkey
Touring and Automobile Association of
  Turkey (Turkey)

1989
Great Omari Mosque
Sidon, Lebanon
Saleh Lamei-Mostafa (Egypt)

Rehabilitation of Asilah
Morocco
Al-Mouhit Cultural Association, Patron
  (Morocco)

Grameen Bank Housing Program
Bangladesh
Grameen Bank (Bangladesh)

Citra Niaga Urban Development
Samarinda, Indonesia
Antonio Ismael Risianto, PT Triaco, and
  PT Griyantara Architects (Indonesia)

Gürel Family Summer Residence
Çanakkale, Turkey
Sedat Gürel (Turkey)

Hayy Assafarat Landscaping and Al-Kindi
  Plaza
Riyadh, Saudi Arabia
Bödeker, Boyer, Wagenfeld and Partners,
  Landscape Architects (Germany)
Beeah Group Consultants, Architects
  (Saudi Arabia)

Sidi el-Aloui Primary School
Tunis, Tunisia
Association de la Sauvegarde de la Médina
  de Tunis (Tunisia)

Corniche Mosque
Jeddah, Saudi Arabia
Architect: Abdelwahed El-Wakil (England)

Ministry of Foreign Affairs
Riyadh, Saudi Arabia
Henning Larsen (Denmark)

Aga Khan Award for Architecture (Con't)

National Assembly Building, Sher-e-
Bangla Nagar
Dhaka, Bangladesh
Louis I. Kahn with David Wisdom and
Associates (USA)

Institut du Monde Arabe
Paris, France
Jean Nouvel, Pierre Soria and Gilbert
Lezénés, with the Architecture Studio
(France)

1992
Kairouan Conservation Program
Kairouan, Tunisia
Association de Sauvegarde de la Médina
de Kairouan (Tunisia)

Palace Parks Program
Istanbul, Turkey
Regional Offices of the National Palaces
Trust (Turkey)

Cultural Park for Children
Cairo, Egypt
Abdelhalim Ibrahim Abdelhalim (Egypt)

East Wahdat Upgrading Program
Amman, Jordan
Urban Development Department,
Planners (Jordan)
Halcrow Fox Associates and Jouzy and
Partners, Feasibility Studies (Jordan)

Kampung Kali Cho-de
Yogyakarta, Indonesia
Yousef B. Mangunwijaya (Indonesia)

Stone Building System
Dar'a Province, Syria
Raif Muhanna, Ziad Muhanna, and Rafi
Muhanna (Civil Engineer), (Syria)

Demir Holiday Village
Bodrum, Turkey
Turgut Cansever, Emine Ögün, Mehmet
Ögün, and Feyza Cansever (Turkey)

Panafrican Institute for Development
Ouagadougou, Burkina Faso
ADAUA Burkina Faso (Burkina Faso)

Entrepreneurship Development Institute
of India
Ahmedabad, India
Bimal Hasmukh Patel (India)

1995
Restoration of Bukhara Old City
Uzbekistan
Restoration Institute of Uzbekistan,
Tashkent, and the Restoration Office of
the Municipality of Bukhara,
Uzbekistan

Conservation of Old Sana'a
Yemen
General Organization for the Protection of
the Historic Cities of Yemen (Yemen)

Reconstruction of Hafsia Quarter II
Tunis, Tunisia
Association de Sauvegarde de la Médina
(Tunisia)

Khuda-ki-Basti Incremental Development
Scheme
Hyderabad, Pakistan
Hyderabad Development Authority and
Tasneem Ahmed Siddiqui (Pakistan)

Aranya Low-Cost Housing
Indore, India
Vastu-Shilpa Foundation, Balkrishna V.
Doshi (India)

Aga Khan Award for Architecture (Con't)

Great Mosque and Redevelopment of the
Old City Centre
Riyadh, Saudi Arabia
Rasem Badran (Jordan)

Menara Mesiniaga
Kuala Lumpur, Malaysia
T.R. Hamzah & Yeang Sdn. Bhd.
(Malaysia)

Kaedi Regional Hospital
Kaedi, Mauritania
Association pour le Développement
naturel d'une Architecture et d'un
Urbanisme Africains (Mauritania)

Mosque of the Grand National Assembly
Ankara, Turkey
Behruz Cinici and Can Cinici (Turkey)

Alliance Franco-Sénégalaise
Kaolack, Senegal
Patrick Dujarric (Senegal)

Re-Forestation Program of the Middle East
Technical University
Ankara, Turkey
Middle East Technical University,
Landscaping and Planners

Landscaping Integration of the Soekarno-
Hatta Airport
Cengkareng, Indonesia
Aéroports de Paris, Paul Andreu (France)

1998

Rehabilitation of Hebron Old Town
Hebron, Palestine
Engineering Office of the Hebron
Rehabilitation Committee (Palestine)

Slum Networking of Indore City
Indore, India
Himanshu Parikh, Civil Engineer (India)

Lepers Hospital
Chopda Taluka, India
Per Christian Brynildsen and Jan Olav
Jensen (Norway)

Salinger Residence
Bamgi, Selangor, Malaysia
Jimmy C.S. Lim (Malaysia)

Tuwaiq Palace
Riyadh, Saudi Arabia
OHO Joint Venture (Atelier Frei Otto,
Buro Happold, Omrania)

Alhamra Arts Council
Lahore, Pakistan
Nayyar Ali Dada (Pakistan)

Vidhan Bhavan
Bhopal, India
Charles Correa (India)

Chairman's Awards
*On two occasions the Chairman's Award has
been granted. It was established to honor the
achievements of individuals who have made considerable lifetime achievements to Muslim architecture but whose work was not within the scope
of the Master Jury's mandate.*

1980   Hassan Fathy (Egypt)
1986   Rifat Chadirji (Iraq)

Source: The Aga Khan Trust for Culture

**As designers, we have the
opportunity and obligation to
explore moral issues in the
course of our work. Often, the
questions are just as important as the answers, for in the
end we are only what we do.**

Scott Simpson

AIA Continental Europe International Design Awards

The AIA Continental Europe chapter's International Design Awards, sponsored by Herman Miller, recognize excellent architecture in Europe. Members of the chapter, European licensed architects, and U.S. AIA chapter members with a project located within the AIA Continental Europe chapter's territory are eligible. Projects completed within the previous six years may be submitted in one of the following categories: new construction; historic preservation, adaptive re-use and remodeling; interiors; or urban design and planning. A panel of U.S. and European professionals with expertise in all categories evaluate the entries, choosing as many awards as they deem worthy of merit.

For additional information about the AIA Continental Europe chapter and their design awards, visit their Web site at *www.aiaeurope.org*.

2000 Winners

1st Prize:
Buchholz Sports Center
Uster, Switzerland
Camenzind Gafensteiner Architects
(Switzerland)

2nd Prize:
Urbanitzacio Riera Canyado
Barcelona, Spain
M.M.A.M.B. (Spain)

3rd Prize:
Zahrebska 23-25
Prague, Czech Republic
Petr Franta Architects & Assoc. (Czech
Republic)

Award of Excellence:
Elevator and Renewal of Space in the Old
Town Hall Tower
Prague, Czech Republic
ATREA Co. (Czech Republic)

Karlova 21 Corporate Offices
Prague, Czech Republic
Prague Investments and Vladimir
Dankovsky (Czech Republic)

Parc de la Solidaritat
Barcelona, Spain
M.M.A.M.B. (Spain)

2000 Jury:
Petre Bilek (Czech Republic)
Kristin Feireiss (Netherlands)
Josep Maria Montaner (Spain)

Source: AIA Continental Europe

Opposite: Zahrebska 23-25, Prague, Czech Republic, Petr Franta Architects & Associates

AIA Gold Medal

The Gold Medal is The American Institute of Architects' highest award. Eligibility is open to architects or non-architects, living or dead, whose contribution to the field of architecture has made a lasting impact. The AIA's Board of Directors grants no more than one Gold Medal each year, occasionally granting none.

For more information, contact the AIA's Honor and Awards Dept. at (202) 626-7586 or visit their Web site at *www.e-architect.com*.

1907	Sir Aston Webb	1967	Wallace K. Harrison
1909	Charles Follen McKim	1968	Marcel Breuer
1911	George Browne Post	1969	William Wilson Wurster
1914	Jean Louis Pascal	1970	Richard Buckminster Fuller
1922	Victor Laloux	1971	Louis I. Kahn
1923	Henry Bacon	1972	Pietro Belluschi
1925	Sir Edwin Landseer Lutyens	1977	Richard Joseph Neutra*
1925	Bertram Grosvenor Goodhue	1978	Philip Cortelyou Johnson
1927	Howard Van Doren Shaw	1979	Ieoh Ming Pei
1929	Milton Bennett Medary	1981	Joseph Luis Sert
1933	Ragnar Östberg	1982	Romaldo Giurgola
1938	Paul Philippe Cret	1983	Nathaniel A. Owings
1944	Louis Henri Sullivan	1985	William Wayne Caudill*
1947	Eliel Saarinen	1986	Arthur Erickson
1948	Charles Donagh Maginnis	1989	Joseph Esherick
1949	Frank Lloyd Wright	1990	E. Fay Jones
1950	Sir Patrick Abercrombie	1991	Charles W. Moore
1951	Bernard Ralph Maybeck	1992	Benjamin Thompson
1952	Auguste Perret	1993	Thomas Jefferson*
1953	William Adams Delano	1993	Kevin Roche
1955	William Marinus Dudok Hilversum	1994	Sir Norman Foster
1956	Clarence S. Stein	1995	Cesar Pelli
1957	Ralph Walker (Centennial Medal of Honor)	1997	Richard Meier
1957	Louis Skidmore	1999	Frank Gehry
1958	John Wellborn Root	2000	Ricardo Legorreta
1959	Walter Gropius	2001	*Finalists:*
1960	Ludwig Mies van der Rohe		Michael Graves
1961	Le Corbusier (Charles Edouard Jeanneret-Gris)		Kisho Kurokawa
1962	Eero Saarinen*		James Stewart Polshek
1963	Alvar Aalto		
1964	Pier Luigi Nervi		
1966	Kenzo Tange		

* honored posthumously
Source: The American Institute of Architects

Opposite: El Camino Real Hotel, Cancun, Mexico, Ricardo Legorreta
Photographer: Lourdes Legorreta

AIA Honor Awards

The American Institute of Architecture's (AIA) Honor Awards celebrate outstanding design in three areas: Architecture, Interior Architecture, and Regional & Urban Design. Juries of designers and executives present separate awards in each category.

Additional information and entry forms may be obtained by contacting the AIA Honors and Awards Department at (202) 626-7586 or by visiting their Web site at *www.e-architect.com*.

2000 AIA Honor Awards for Architecture Recipients:

The AIA Honor Awards for Architecture have been presented annually since 1949 to projects which have best met their own requirements. Projects are judged individually and not against each other in one of two categories: design resolution and design advancement.

Center Street Park and Ride
Des Moines, Iowa
Herbert Lewis Kruse Blunck

Desert Housing for Low-income Seniors
Indian Wells, California
Studio E Architects

The Getty Center
Los Angeles, California
Richard Meier & Partners

Grand Central Terminal
New York, New York
Beyer Blinder Belle Architects & Planners

The Hill County Jacal
Pipe Creek, Texas
Lake/Flato Architects

Kaufmann House Restoration
Palm Springs, California
Marmol and Radziner Architects

Kuala Lumpur City Centre, Phase 1
Kuala Lumpur, Malaysia
Cesar Pelli & Associates, with associate
architect Adamson Associates

Le Fresnoy National Studio for
Contemporary Arts
Tourcoing, France
Bernard Tschumi Architects

Mashantucket Pequot Museum and
Research Center
Mashantucket, Connecticut
The Polshek Partnership

Massachusetts Museum of Contemporary
Art
North Adams, Massachusetts
Bruner/Cott & Associates

Methow Valley Cabin
Winthrop, Washington
James Cutler Architects

Neugebauer House
Naples, Florida
Richard Meier & Partners with general
contractor Newbury North Associates

Opposite: Methow Valley Cabin, Winthrop, WA,
James Cutler Architects
Photographer: Art Grice

AIA Honor Awards (Con't)

Olympia Fields Park and Community
 Center
Olympia Fields, Illinois
Weiss/Manfredi Architects

U.S. Port of Entry
Point Roberts, Washington
The Miller/Hull Partnership

Women's Memorial and Education Center
Arlington, Virginia
Weiss/Manfredi Architects

Jury:
 Robert Kliment, Chair
 Thomas Bosworth
 Andrea Clark Brown
 Daniel Gregory
 Gerald Horn
 Tracey Hunte
 M. David Lee
 Elizabeth Corbin Murphy

2000 AIA Honor Awards for Interior Architecture Recipients:

The AIA Honor Awards for Interior Architecture honor excellence in interior design projects of all types and sizes, worldwide. The award's intent is to highlight the diversity of interior architecture projects. All architects licensed in the U.S. are eligible to submit entries.

Ackerman McQueen Advertising
 Executive Offices
Tulsa, Oklahoma
Elliott + Associates Architects

City Hall Improvement Project
San Francisco, California
Heller • Manus Architects (supervising
 architects), with Komorous-Towey
 Architects/Finger & Moy Architects

Colleen B. Rosenblat Jewelry Showroom
 and Office
Hamburg, Germany
Gabellini Associates

Farnsworth House
Plano, Illinois
Lohan Associates Inc.

Fifth Avenue Duplex
New York, New York
Shelton, Mindel & Associates

Helmut Lang Flagship Retail Boutique
New York, New York
Gluckman Mayner Architects

Iwataya Passage
Fukuokashi, Japan
WalkerGroup/CNI

Long Meadow Ranch Winery
St. Helena, California
Turnbull Griffin Haesloop

Ocean Liner Dining Room and Lounge
Miami, Florida
Shelton, Mindel & Associates Architects

The Offices of Greenwell Goetz Architects
 Design Studio
Washington, D.C.
Greenwell Goetz Architects

Seiji Ozawa Hall at Tanglewood
Lenox, Massachsetts
William Rawn Associates Architects Inc.

SHR Perceptual Management Workspace
Scottsdale, Arizona
Morphosis Architects

Opposite: Dining Room and Lounge aboard the Mercury cruise ship, Miami, FL, Shelton, Mindel & Associates Architects
Photographer: Michael Moran Photography

AIA Honor Awards (Con't)

St. Jean Vianney Catholic Church
Sanctuary
Baton Rouge, Louisiana
Trahan Architects

Jury:
Neil Frankel, Chair
Richard Pollack
Ronnette Riley
Susan Szenasy
Jane Weinzapfel

2000 AIA Honor Awards for Regional and Urban Design Recipients:

The AIA Honor Awards for Regional and Urban Design seek to recognize the expanding role of architects in planning our communities. Owners, agencies, organizations, architects and others involved in regional or urban design projects may submit them to the competition. A U.S. licensed architect must be involved in the project.

Bahcesehir, Istanbul
Torti Gallas and Partners-CHK Inc. with
associate architect Akin Oktay, Insas
Insaat Taahut Ve Ticaret A.S.

Central Waterfront Development Plan
Hong Kong, China
Skidmore, Owings & Merrill International

Eastward Ho: A Regional Vision for
Southeast Florida
Southeast Florida
Daniel Williams

Mid-Embarcadero Open Space/Ferry
Terminal
San Francisco, California
The ROMA Design Group

Park/Madison Avenue Development
Project
Detroit, Michigan
Schervish Vogel Consulting Architects

Pennsylvania Convention Center
Philadelphia, Pennsylvania
Thompson, Ventulett, Stainback &
Associates Inc. (design architect), with
associate architect/architect of record
Vitetta and consulting architect
Kelly/Maiello Inc.

Pennsylvania Station Redevelopment
New York, New York
Skidmore, Owings & Merrill

Did you know...

Since 1995, the following firms have won the most AIA Honor Awards:

Skidmore, Owings and Merrill – 11
Gabellini Associates – 5
Hardy Holzman Pfeiffer
Associates – 5
Shelton, Mindel & Associates – 5
Herbert Lewis Kruse Blunk
Architecture– 4
Polshek Partnership Architects– 4
Bohlin Cywinski Jackson– 3
Kallman, McKinnell & Wood
Architects– 3
Richard Meier & Partners– 3

Source: Design Intelligence

AIA Honor Awards (Con't)

Shanghai Waterfront Redevelopment
   Master Plan
Shanghai, China
Skidmore, Owings & Merrill with associ-
   ate architect Shanghai Urban Planning
   and Design Research Institute

The Village of Park DuValle
Louisville, Kentucky
Urban Design Associates, with LaQuatra
   Bonci & Associates Landscape
   Architecture; Stull & Lee; William
   Rawn Associates Architects Inc.;
   Tucker & Booker Inc.; Sabak, Wilson &
   Lingo Inc.

Windsor Town Center
Vero Beach, Florida
Scott Merrill, AIA

Jury:
   Douglas S. Kelbaugh, Chair
   Lance Brown
   Elizabeth Plater-Zyberk
   Mayor M. Susan Savage
   Daniel Solomon

Source: The American Institute of Architects

AIA Honors for Collaborative Achievement

The American Institute of Architects (AIA) annually presents their Honors for Collaborative Achievement award to recognize achievements in influencing or advancing the architectural profession. Recipients may be individuals or groups. Nominees must be living and may have been active in any number of areas, including administration, art, collaborative achievement, construction, industrial design, information science, professions allied with architecture, public policy, research, education, recording, illustration, and writing and scholarship.

For more information, refer to the AIA's Web site at *www.e-architect.com* or contact the AIA's Honors and Awards Department at (202) 626-7586.

1976
- Edmund N. Bacon
- Charles A. Blessing
- Wendell J. Campbell
- Gordon Cullen
- James Marston Fitch
- The Institute for Architecture and Urban Studies
- New York City Planning Commission and New York City Landmarks Preservation Committee
- Saul Steinberg
- Vincent J. Scully Jr.
- Robert Le Ricolais

1977
- Claes Oldenburg
- Louise Nevelson
- Historic American Buildings Survey
- Arthur Drexler
- G. Holmes Perkins
- The Baroness Jackson of Lodsworth DBE (Barbara Ward)
- Walker Art Center
- City of Boston
- Pittsburgh History & Landmarks Foundation
- Montreal Metro System

1978
- Frederick Gutheim
- Richard Haas
- Dr. August Komendant
- David A. Macaulay
- National Trust for Historic Preservation
- Stanislawa Nowicki
- John C. Portman Jr.
- Robert Royston
- Nicholas N. Solovioff
- Robert Venturi

1979
- Douglas Haskell
- Barry Commoner
- John D. Entenza
- Bernard Rudofsky
- Steen Eiler Rasmussen
- National Endowment for the Arts
- Christo
- Bedford-Stuyvesant Restoration
- Charles E. Peters
- Arthur S. Siegel (posthumous)

1980
- Cyril M. Harris
- Sol LeWitt
- Robert Campbell

AIA Honors for Collaborative Achievement (Con't)

Committee for the Preservation of
  Architectural Records
Progressive Architecture Awards Program
The Rouse Company for Faneuil Hall
  Marketplace
John Benson
M. Paul Friedberg
Jack E. Boucher
Mrs. Lyndon B. Johnson

1981

Kenneth Snelson
Paul Goldberger
Sir Nikolaus Pevsner
Herman Miller, Inc.
Edison Price
Colin Rowe
Reynolds Metals Company
Smithsonian Associates

1982

"Oppositions" (Institute for Architecture
  & Urban Studies)
Historic New Harmony, Inc.
The MIT Press
Jean Dubuffet
Sir John Summerson
The Plan of St. Gall
The Washington Metropolitan Area
  Transit Authority
William H. Whyte

1983

The Honorable Christopher S. Bond,
  Governor of Missouri
Donald Canty
Fazlur Khan (posthumous)
Knoll International
Christian Norberg-Schulz
Paul Stevenson Oles

1984

Reyner Banham
Bolt, Beranek & Newman
Cooper-Hewitt Museum
Inner Harbor Development of the City of
  Baltimore

His Highness the Aga Khan
T.Y. Lin
Steve Rosenthal
San Antonio River Walk
Bruno Zevi

1985

Ward Bennett
Kenneth Frampton
Esther McCoy
Norman McGrath
The Hon. John F. Seiberling
Weidlinger Associates
Nick Wheeler
Games of the XXIII Olympiad
Cranbrook Academy of Art
Central Park

1986

Cathedral Church of St. John the Divine
Antoinette Forrester Downing
David H. Geiger
Gladding, McBean & Company
William H. Jordy
Master Plan for the United States Capitol
Adolf Kurt Placzek
Cervin Robinson
Rudolf Wittkower (posthumous)

1987

James S. Ackerman
Jennifer Bartlett
Steven Brooke
The Chicago Architecture Foundation
Jules Fisher & Paul Marantz, Inc.
Charles Guggenheim
John B. Jackson
Mesa Verde National Park
Rizzoli International Publications, Inc.
Carter Wiseman

1988

Spiro Kostof
Loeb Fellowship in Advanced
  Environmental Studies, Harvard
  University
Robert Smithson (posthumous)

AIA Honors for Collaborative Achievement (Con't)

Society for the Preservation of New
England Antiquities
Sussman/Prejza & Company, Inc.
Robert Wilson

1989

Battery Park City Authority
American Academy in Rome
Eduard Sekler
Leslie E. Robertson
Niels Diffrient
David S. Haviland
V'Soske

1990

The Association for the Preservation of
Virginia Antiquities
Corning Incorporated
Jackie Ferrara
Timothy Hursley
Marvin Mass
Mary Miss
Peter G. Rolland
Joseph Santeramo
Taos Pueblo
Emmet L. Wemple

1991

James Fraser Carpenter
Danish Design Centre
Foundation for Architecture, Philadelphia
The J.M. Kaplan Fund
Maguire Thomas Partners
Native American Architecture (Robert
Easton and Peter Nabokov)
Princeton Architectural Press
Seaside, Florida
Allan Temko
Lebbeus Woods

1992

Siah Armajani
Canadian Centre for Architecture
Stephen Coyle
Milton Glaser
The Mayors' Institute on City Design
The Municipal Art Society of New York

John Julius Norwich
Ove Arup & Partners Consulting
Engineers PC
Peter Vanderwarker
Peter Walker

1993

ADPSR (Architects/Designers/Planners
for Social Responsibility)
Michael Blackwood
The Conservation Trust of Puerto Rico
Benjamin Forgey
The Gamble House
Philadelphia Zoological Society
The Princeton University Board of
Trustees, Officers and the Office of
Physical Planning
Jane Thompson
Sally B. Woodbridge
World Monuments Fund

1994

Joseph H. Baum
Beth Dunlop
Mildred Friedman
Historic Savannah Foundation
Rhode Island Historical Preservation
Commission
Salvadori Educational Center on the Built
Environment
Gordon H. Smith
The Stuart Collection
Sunset Magazine
Judith Turner

1995

The Art Institute of Chicago, Dept. of Arch
ASAP (The American Society of
Architectural Perspectivists)
Friends of Post Office Square
The University of Virginia, Curator and
Architect for the Academical Village/
The Rotunda
Albert Paley
UrbanArts, Inc.
Dr. Yoichi Ando

AIA Honors for Collaborative Achievement (Con't)

1996

Boston by Foot, Inc.
William S. Donnell
Haley & Aldrich, Inc.
Toshio Nakamura
Joseph Passonneau
Preservation Society of Charleston
Earl Walls Associates
Paul Warchol Photography, Inc.

1997

Architecture Resource Center

1998

Lian Hurst Mann
SOM Foundation
William Morgan

1999

Howard Brandston
Jeff Goldberg
Ann E. Gray
Blair Kamin
Ronald McKay
Miami-Dade Art in Public Places
Monacelli Press
New York Landmarks Conservancy

2000

The Aga Khan Award for Architecture
Douglas Cooper
Dr. Christopher Jaffe
Donald Kaufman and Taffy Dahl
William Lam
San Antonio Conservation Society
F. Michael Wong

Source: The American Institute of Architects

Architects, sculptors and painters, we must all return to the crafts. For art is not a profession. There is no essential difference between the artist and the craftsman.

Walter Gropius

Alice Davis Hitchcock Book Award

The Alice Davis Hitchcock book award has been granted annually by the Society of Architectural Historians (SAH) since 1949. It is given to a publication by a North American scholar, published within the preceding two years, that demonstrates a high level of scholarly distinction in the field of the history of architecture.

For more information contact the SAH at (312) 573-1365 or visit their Web site at *www.sah.org*.

1949
Colonial Architecture and Sculpture in Peru by Harold Wethey (Harvard University Press)

1950
Architecture of the Old Northwest Territory by Rexford Newcomb (University of Chicago Press)

1951
Architecture and Town Planning in Colonial Connecticut by Anthony Garvan (Yale University Press)

1952
The Architectural History of Newport by Antoinette Downing and Vincent Scully (Harvard University Press)

1953
Charles Rennie Macintosh and the Modern Movement by Thomas Howarth (Routledge and K. Paul)

1954
Early Victorian Architecture in Britain by Henry Russell Hitchcock (Da Capo Press, Inc.)

1955
Benjamin H. Latrobe by Talbot Hamlin (Oxford University Press)

1956
The Railroad Station: An Architectural History by Carroll L. V. Meeks (Yale University Press)

1957
The Early Architecture of Georgia by Frederick D. Nichols (University of N.C. Press)

1958
The Public Buildings of Williamsburg by Marcus Whiffen (Colonial Williamsburg)

1959
Carolingian and Romanesque Architecture, 800 to 1200 by Kenneth J. Conant (Yale University Press)

1960
The Villa d'Este at Tivoli by David Coffin (Princeton University Press)

1961
The Architecture of Michelangelo by James Ackerman (University of Chicago Press)

1962
The Art and Architecture of Ancient America by George Kubler (Yale University Press)

1963
La Cathédrale de Bourges et sa Place dans L'archtietture Gothique by Robert Branner (Tardy)

1964
Images of American Living, Four Centuries of Architecture and Furniture as Cultural Expression by Alan Gowans (Lippincott)

1965
The Open-Air Churches of Sixteenth Century Mexico by John McAndrew (Harvard University Press)

Alice Davis Hitchcock Book Award (Con't)

1966
  Early Christian and Byzantine Architecture by Richard Krautheimer (Penguin Books)

1967
  Eighteenth-Century Architecture in Piedmont: the open structures of Juvarra, Alfieri & Vittone by Richard Pommer (New York University Press)

1968
  Architecture and Politics in Germany, 1918-1945 by Barbara Miller Lane (Harvard University Press)

1969
  Samothrace, Volume III: The Hieron by Phyllis Williams Lehmann

1970
  The Church of Notre Dame in Montreal by Franklin Toker (McGill-Queen's University Press)

1971
  no award granted

1972
  The Prairie School; Frank Lloyd Wright and his Midwest Contemporaries by H. Allen Brooks (University of Toronto Press)

  The Early Churches of Constantinople: Architecture and Liturgy by Thomas F. Mathews (Pennsylvania State University Press)

1973
  The Campanile of Florence Cathedral: "Giotto's Tower" by Marvin Trachtenberg (New York University Press)

1974
  FLO, A Biography of Frederick Law Olmstead by Laura Wood Roper (Johns Hopkins University Press)

1975
  Gothic vs. Classic, Architectural Projects in Seventeenth-Century Italy by Rudolf Wittkower (G. Braziller)

1976
  no award granted

1977
  The Esplanade Ridge (Vol.V in The New Orleans Architecture Series) by Mary Louise Christovich, Sally Kitredge Evans, Betsy Swanson, and Roulhac Toledano (Pelican Publishing Company)

1978
  Sebastiano Serlio on Domestic Architecture by Myra Nan Rosenfeld (Architectural History Foundation)

1979
  The Framed Houses of Massachusetts Bay, 1625-1725 by Abbott Lowell Cummings (Belknap Press)

  Paris: A Century of Change, 1878-1978 by Norma Evenson (Yale University Press)

1980
  Rome: Profile of a City, 312-1308 by Richard Krautheimer (Princton University Press)

1981
  Gardens of Illusion: The Genius of Andre LeNotre by Franklin Hamilton Hazelhurst (Vanderbilt University Press)

1982
  Indian Summer: Luytens, Baker and Imperial Delhi by Robert Grant Irving (Yale Univ. Press)

1983
  Architecture and the Crisis of Modern Science by Alberto Pérez-Goméz (MIT Press)

1984
  Campus: An American Planning Tradition by Paul Venable Turner (MIT Press)

1985
  The Law Courts: The Architecture of George Edmund Street by David Brownlee (MIT Press)

Alice Davis Hitchcock Book Award (Con't)

1986

The Architecture of the Roman Empire: An Urban Appraisal by William L. MacDonald (Yale University Press)

1987

Holy Things and Profane: Anglican Parish Churches in Colonial Virginia by Dell Upton (MIT Press)

1988

Designing Paris: The Architecture of Duban, Labrouste, Duc and Vaudoyer by David Van Zanten (MIT Press)

1989

Florentine New Towns: Urban Design in the Late Middle Ages by David Friedman (MIT Press)

1990

Claude-Nicolas Ledoux: Architecture and Social Reform at the End of the Ancient Régime by Anthony Vidler (MIT Press)

1991

The Paris of Henri IV: Architecture and Urbanism by Hilary Ballon (MIT Press)
Seventeenth-Century Roman Palaces: Use and the Art of the Plan by Patricia Waddy (MIT Press)

1992

Modernism in Italian Architecture, 1890-1940 by Richard Etlin (MIT Press)

1994*

Baths and Bathing in Classical Antiquity by Fikret Yegul (MIT Press)

1995

The Politics of the German Gothic Revival: August Reichensperger by Michael J. Lewis (MIT Press)

1996

Hadrian's Villa and Its Legacy by William J. MacDonald and John Pinto (Yale University Press)

1997

Gottfried Semper: Architect of the Nineteenth Century by Harry Francis Mallgrave (Yale University Press)

1998

The Dancing Column: On Order in Architecture by Joseph Rykwert (MIT Press)

1999

Dominion of the Eye: Urbanism, Art & Power in Early Modern Florence by Marvin Trachtenberg (Cambridge University Press)

2000

The Architectural Treatise in the Renaissance by Alina A. Payne (Cambridge University Press)

---

* *At this time the SAH altered their award schedule to coincide with their annual meeting, and no award for 1993 was granted.*

Source: Society of Architectural Historians

American Academy of Arts and Letters Academy Awards

The American Academy of Arts and Letters grants their annual Academy Award to an architect(s) as an honor of their work and an encouragement to their ongoing creativity. The prize consists of a $7500 cash award. Recipients must be citizens of the United States. Members of the Academy are not eligible.

For more information, contact the American Academy of Arts and Letters at (212) 368-5900.

1991   Rodolfo Machado and Jorge Silvetti
1992   Thom Mayne and Michael Rotondi, Morphosis
1993   Franklin D. Israel
1994   Craig Hodgetts and Hsin-Ming Fung
1995   Mack Scogin and Merrill Elam
1996   Maya Lin
1997   Daniel Libeskind
1998   Laurie Olin
1999   Eric Owen Moss
2000   Will Bruder
       Jesse Reiser and Nanako Umemoto

Source: American Academy of Arts and Letters

If we are to build a beautiful world, and I can't imagine a more necessary and finer ambition, we must become fully aware of the importance of facts and feelings of the quality of life.

Alden B. Dow

American Academy of Arts and Letters Gold Medal for Architecture

The American Academy of Arts and Letters grants a gold medal in the arts in rotation among painting, music, sculpture, poetry, architecture, and many other categories. The entire work of the architect is weighed when being considered for the award. Only citizens of the United States are eligible.

For more information contact the American Academy of Arts and Letters at (212) 368-5900.

1912   William Rutherford Mead
1921   Cass Gilbert
1930   Charles Adams Platt
1940   William Adams Delano
1949   Frederick Law Olmsted
1953   Frank Lloyd Wright
1958   Henry R. Shepley
1963   Ludwig Mies van der Rohe
1968   R. Buckminster Fuller
1973   Louis I. Kahn
1979   I. M. Pei
1984   Gordon Bunshaft
1990   Kevin Roche
1996   Philip Johnson

Source: American Academy of Arts and Letters

Architecture is that great living creative spirit which from generation to generation, from age to age, persists, creates, according to the nature of man, and his circumstances as they change.

Frank Lloyd Wright

Apgar Award for Excellence

The Apgar Award for Excellence recognizes individuals whose interpretation and evaluation of America's built environment has heightened public awareness toward the importance of excellence in building and urban design, community revitalization, and city and regional planning. Established in 1998 by former National Building Museum Trustee Mahlon Apgar IV and his wife, Anne N. Apgar, the objective of the award is to encourage the communication of knowledge, experience, and ideas about the built environment among policymakers, professionals, and the general public through any form of print or electronic media. Nominations are reviewed by a panel of architecture professionals including journalists, academics, and practitioners. Recipients are awarded a $1500 honorarium and are invited to participate in public programs at the Museum.

For more information about the Apgar Award, contact the National Building Museum at (202) 272-2448 or visit them on the Internet at *www.nbm.org*.

1999   Samuel Mockbee
2000   Earl Blumenauer

Source: National Building Museum

> If I could build one building in my life, I want to build a building that people feel in the stomach — you can call it comfort, beauty, excitement, guts, tears... There are many ways to describe the reaction to architecture, but tears are as good as any.
>
> *Philip Johnson*

Architecture Firm Award

The American Institute of Architects (AIA) awards its Architecture Firm Award annually to an architecture firm for "consistently producing distinguished architecture." The highest honor that the AIA can bestow on a firm, the Board of Directors confers the award. Eligible firms must claim collaboration within the practice as a hallmark of their methodology and must have been producing work as an entity for at least 10 years.

For more information, visit the AIA on the Internet at *www.e-architect.org* or contact the AIA Honors and Awards Department at (202) 626-7586.

1962	Skidmore, Owings & Merrill	1985	Venturi, Rauch and Scott Brown
1964	The Architects Collaborative	1986	Esherick Homsey Dodge & Davis
1965	Wurster, Bernardi & Emmons	1987	Benjamin Thompson & Associates
1967	Hugh Stubbins & Associates	1988	Hartman-Cox Architects
1968	I.M. Pei & Partners	1989	Cesar Pelli & Associates
1969	Jones & Emmons	1990	Kohn Pedersen Fox Associates
1970	Ernest J. Kump Associates	1991	Zimmer Gunsul Frasca Partnership
1971	Albert Kahn Associates, Inc.	1992	James Stewart Polshek and Partners
1972	Caudill Rowlett Scott	1993	Cambridge Seven Associates Inc.
1973	Shepley Bulfinch Richardson Abbott	1994	Bohlin Cywinski Jackson
1974	Kevin Roche John Dinkeloo & Associates	1995	Beyer Blinder Belle
1975	Davis, Brody & Associates	1996	Skidmore, Owings & Merrill
1976	Mitchell/Giurgola Architects	1997	R. M. Kliment & Frances Halsband Architects
1977	Sert, Jackson and Associates	1998	Centerbrook Architects and Planners
1978	Harry Weese & Associates	1999	Perkins & Will
1979	Geddes Brecher Qualls Cunningham	2000	Gensler
1980	Edward Larrabee Barnes Associates	2001	*Finalists:*
1981	Hardy Holzman Pfeiffer Associates		Arquitectonica
1982	Gwathmey Siegel & Associates, Architects		Herbert Lewis Kruse Blunck
1983	Holabird & Root, Architects, Engineers & Planners		Tigerman McCurry Architects
1984	Kallmann, McKinnell & Wood, Architects		

Source: The American Institute of Architects

Opposite: Austin-Bergstrom International Airport, Austin, TX, Gensler
Photographer: John Edward Linden

Arnold W. Brunner Memorial Prize

The American Academy of Arts and Letters annually recognizes an architect who has contributed to architecture as an art with the Arnold W. Brunner Memorial Prize. A prize of $5000 is granted to each recipient. Eligibility is open to architects of any nationality.

For more information, contact the American Academy of Arts and Letters at (212) 368-5900.

1955	Gordon Bunshaft
	Minoru Yamasaki, Honorable Mention
1956	John Yeon
1957	John Carl Warnecke
1958	Paul Rudolph
1959	Edward Larrabee Barnes
1960	Louis I. Kahn
1961	I. M. Pei
1962	Ulrich Franzen
1963	Edward Charles Basset
1964	Harry Weese
1965	Kevin Roche
1966	Romaldo Giurgola
1968	John M. Johansen
1969	Noel Michael McKinnell
1970	Charles Gwathmey and Richard Henderson
1971	John Andrews
1972	Richard Meier
1973	Robert Venturi
1974	Hugh Hardy with Norman Pfeiffer and Malcolm Holzman
1975	Lewis Davis and Samuel Brody
1976	James Stirling
1977	Henry N. Cobb
1978	Caesar Pelli
1979	Charles W. Moore
1980	Michael Graves
1981	Gunnar Birkerts
1982	Helmut Jahn
1983	Frank O. Gehry
1984	Peter K. Eisenman
1985	William Pederson and Arthur May
1986	John Hejduk
1987	James Ingo Freed
1988	Arata Isozaki
1989	Richard Rogers
1990	Steven Holl
1991	Tadao Ando
1992	Sir Norman Foster
1993	Jose Rafael Moneo
1994	Renzo Piano
1995	Daniel Urban Kiley
1996	Tod Williams and Billie Tsien
1997	Henri Ciriani
1998	Alvaro Siza
1999	Fumihiko Maki
2000	Toyo Ito

Source: American Academy of Arts and Letters

Architects deal with the oldest forms of man's concern: his shelter, and, even more, his need for beauty and personal expression.

Nathaniel Owings

ASLA Medal

Every year the American Society of Landscape Architects (ASLA) awards its highest honor, the ASLA Medal, to an individual who has made a significant contribution to the field of landscape architecture. The following individuals were chosen for their unique and lasting impact through their work in landscape design, planning, writing and/or public service. Eligibility is open to non-members of the ASLA of any nationality.

For more information, contact the ASLA at (202) 898-2444 or visit their Web site at *www.asla.org*.

1971	Hideo Sasaki	1990	Ray Freeman
1972	Conrad L. Wirth	1991	Meade Palmer
1973	John C. Simonds	1992	Robert S. "Doc" Reich
1974	Campbell E. Miller	1993	A. E. "Ed" Bye Jr.
1975	Garrett Eckbo	1994	Edward D. Stone Jr.
1976	Thomas Church	1995	Dr. Ervin Zube
1977	Hubert Owens	1996	John Lyle
1978	Lawrence Halprin	1997	Julius Fabos
1979	Norman T. Newton	1998	Carol R. Johnson
1980	William G. Swain	1999	Stuart C. Dawson
1981	Sir Geoffrey Jellicoe	2000	Carl D. Johnson
1982	Charles W. Eliot II		
1983	Theodore O. Osmundson		
1984	Ian McHarg		
1985	Roberto Burle Marx		
1986	William J. Johnson		
1987	Phillip H. Lewis Jr.		
1988	Dame Sylvia Crowe		
1989	Robert N. Royston		

Source: American Society of Landscape Architects

I have all my life been considering distant effects and always sacrificing immediate success and applause to that of the future.

Frederick Law Olmsted

ASLA Professional Awards

The American Society of Landscape Architects' (ASLA) annual Professional Awards program is intended to encourage the profession of landscape architecture by rewarding works of distinction and to generate increased visibility for the winners and the profession in general. Entries are accepted for placement in one of four areas: design, analysis & planning, research, and communication. Eligibility is open to any landscape architect or, in the case of research and communication, any individual or group. Awards are granted on three levels: Presidents Award of Excellence, the highest distinction with only one granted in each category; Honor Awards, given to no more than five percent of the total number of entries in each category; and Merit Awards, determined by the discretion of the jury. Juries for each category are comprised of landscape professionals and appointed by the ASLA's Professional Awards Committee.

For additional information, visit the ASLA's Web site at *www.asla.org* or contact them at (202) 898-2444.

2000 Design Awards Recipients:
Honor Awards:
Reid Residence, Houston, TX
The Office of James Burnett

Hoboken South Waterfront, Hoboken, NJ
Arnold Associates / Wilday Joint Venture

The New Riverfront, Hartford and East
   Hartford, CT
Carol R. Johnson Associates, Inc.

Beth Israel Memorial Garden,
   Houston, TX
GLS Landscape Architecture

Merit Awards:
Advantica Plaza, Spartanburg, SC
Peter Lindsay Schaudt while employed by:
   Clark Tribble Harris & Li Architects
   (currently LS3P Architects)

8 Bedons Alley, Charleston, SC
Nelson-Byrd Landscape Architects

Northeastern University, Boston, MA
Pressley Associates, Inc.

Desert Lives at the Phoenix Zoo: Bighorn
   Sheep and Arabian Oryx, Phoenix, AZ
Floor & Associates, Inc.

Sydney Olympics 2000, Sydney, Australia
Hargreaves Associates

Trampoline and Willow Garden,
   Chaumont-sur-Loire, France
Landworks Studio, Inc.

Richmond Canals, Ricmond, VA
Wallace Roberts and Todd, LLC

Dallas Area Rapid Transit Mall, Dallas, TX
Sasaki Associates, Inc.

ASLA Professional Awards (Con't)

Gateway Science School, St. Louis, MO
Joe McGrane of EDAW, Inc

H.U.D. Plaza Improvements, Wash. DC
Martha Schwartz, Inc.

Jury:
Everett Fly, Robert Murase, Laurin B.
Askew Jr.

2000 Analysis & Planning Award Recipients:
President's Award of Excellence:
Sonoran Preserve, Phoenix, AZ
City of Phoenix Landscape Architects: Gail
Brinkman, Joe Cascio, Jim Coffman,
Joseph Ewan, Walt Kinsler, Terry
Newman, Janet Waibel

Honor Awards:
St. Louis Downtown Development Action
Plan, St. Louis, MO
EDAW, Inc.

Massachusetts Historic Cemetery
Preservation Initiative, Massachusetts
Walker-Kluesing Design Group

Merit Awards:
Mountain View Cemetary, Vancouver,
B.C., Canada
Philips Wuori Long Inc. - Margot Long,
Principal

Georgia Tech Wayfinding Master Plan,
Georgia Tech, Atlanta, GA
Moore Iacofano Goltsman, Inc.

Southwood, Tallahassee, FL
Sasaki Associates, Inc.

Alexandria Urban Master Plan,
Alexandria, LA
Patrick C. Moore, ASLA Landscape
Architects/Site Planners

California State University Monterey Bay
Master Plan, Seaside and Mariana, CA
Sasaki Associates, Inc.

Canyon Forest Village II Corp., Tusayan, AZ
Design Workshop, Inc.

Pikes Peak Multi-Use Plan, Pikes Peak, CO
Design Workshop, Inc.

Jury:
John Parsons, Tom Papandrew, Meg
Maguire

2000 Research Award Recipients:
Honor Awards:
Visualizing and Testing Views of a
Changing National Forest Policy
Landscape, Mount Hood National
Forest, Oregon
Robert Ribe and Edward Armstrong,
University of Oregon; Paul Gobster and
Pat Greene, USDA Forest Service

Merit Awards:
Conserving Dutch Landscape Spatial
Diversity, The Netherlands
Harry Dijkstra, Ranneke Roos, Lon
Schone, Jetty van Lith-Kranendonk,
James F. Palmer

Jury:
Perry Howard, Joan Nassauer, Jim Urban

Communications Award Recipients:
President's Award of Excellence:
Land Marks Series
Peter Walker, Owner/Publisher,
Spacemaker Press; James Truelove,
Associate Publisher

Merit Awards:
Lakescaping for Wildlife and Water
Quality

ASLA Professional Awards (Con't)

Fred J. Rozumalski, Barr Engineering; Carrol L. Henderson - Minnesota Department of Natural Resources; Carolyn J. Dindorf - Hennepin Conservation District

A Guide to the Landscape Architecture of Boston
Jack Ahern; Hubbard Educational Trust Advisory Committee; John F. Furlong; Carol R. Johnson; Marion Pressley; Lynn Wolff; Karen Good, Project Manager

Youth Power Guide
Urban Places Project, Umass; YouthPower/El Arco Iris Holyoke, MA

TimePlaces Heritage Signs, Mountains to Sound Greenway, WA
Jones & Jones Architects and Landscape Archtiects, PSC - Nancy Rottle, Grant Jones, Curt Warber; Other team members: Tom Atkins, Steve Durrant

Cultural Landscape Currents
National Park Service, Historic Landscape Initiative, The Cultural Landscape Foundation

ReLeaf Nashville, Nashville, TN
Hawkins Partners, Inc.

The Once and Future Forest
Andropogon Associates, LTD.

Las Vegas Springs Preserve, Las Vegas, NV
University of Nevada at Las Vegas

Guide to Developing a Preservation Maintenance Plan for Historic Landscape
Margaret Coffin, Regina Bellavia, Charles Pepper

Jury:
Perry Howard, Joan Nassauer, Jim Urban

Source: American Society of Landscape Architects

Auguste Perret Prize

The International Union of Architects (UIA) grants the triennial Auguste Perret Prize to an internationally renowned architect or architects for their work in applied technology in architecture.

For more information, visit the UIA's Web site at *www.uia-architectes.org.*

1961
  F. Candela (Mexico)
  Honorary Mention:
  The Architects of the British Ministry for Education Office and the Architects of the Office for the Study of Industrial and Agricultural Buildings of Hungary
1963
  K. Mayekawa (Japan)
  J. Prouvé (France)
1965
  H. Sharoun (GFR)
  Honorary Mention: \
  H. and K. Siren (Finland)
1967
  F. Otto and R. Gutbrod (GFR)
1969
  Karel Hubacek (Czechoslovakia)
1972
  E. Pinez Pinero (Spain)
1975
  A.C. Erickson and team (Canada)
  Honorary Mention:
  J. Cardoso (Brazil)

1978
  Kiyonori Kitutake (Japan)
  Piano & Rogers (Italy/United Kingdom)
1981
  G. Benisch (GFR)
  Honorary Mention:
  J. Rougerie (France)
1984
  Joao Baptista Vilanova Artigas (Brazil)
1987
  Santiago Calatrava (Spain)
  Honorary Mention:
  C. Testa (Argentina)
1990
  Adien Fainsilber (France)
1993
  KHR AS Arkitekten (Denmark)
1996
  Thomas Herzog (Germany)
1999
  Ken Yeang (Malaysia)

Source: International Union of Architects

By definition, a building is a sculpture because it is a three-dimensional object.

Frank Gehry

Business Week/Architectural Record Awards

The *Business Week/Architecture Record* Awards recognize creative design solutions with an emphasis on the achievement of business goals through architecture. Co-sponsored by The American Institute of Architects, the awards are judged by a jury of business leaders, public officials, and designers. Eligible projects must have been completed within the past three years and must be submitted jointly by the architect and the client. Projects may be located anywhere in the world.

For additional information, call (202) 682-3205 or visit the AIA on the Internet at *www.e-architect.org*.

2000 Award Winners:

Sticks Inc.
Des Moines, IA
Herbert Lewis Kruse Blunck Architecture

Hanjin Container Terminal
Los Angeles, CA
Robert Stewart Architect & Caldwell
　　Architects

Fukuoka Prefectural and International
　　Hall
Fukuoka, Japan
Emilio Ambasz & Associates

Valeo Technical Center
Auburn Hills, MI
Davis Brody Bond

Saint-Hyacinthe School of Trades and
　　Technologies
Quebec, Canada
ABCP Architecture

Rose Center for Earth and Space,
　　American Museum of Natural History
New York, NY
Polshek Partnership Architects

Mahindra United World College of India
Pune, India
Christopher Charles Benninger & Assoc.

The Children's Place Corp. Headquarters
Secaucus, NJ
Davis Brody Bond

Ground Zero
Marina del Rey, CA
Shubin + Donaldson Architects

Jury:

Carol Ross Barney, Chair
William Agnello
Julie Anixter
Edward Ciffone
Henry N. Cobb
Julie Eizenberg
Robin M. Ellerthorpe
James O. Jonassen
Wilson Pollack
Eric Richert
Yvonne Szeto
Jane Weinzapfel

Source: Architectural Record/Business Week

Opposite: Saint-Hyacinthe School of Trades and Technologies, Quebec, Canada, ABCP Architecture. Photo: Denis Farley, Montreal, Quebec, Canada

Carlsberg Architectural Prize

The Carlsberg Architectural Prize is awarded every four years to a living architect or group of architects who has produced works of enduring architectural and social value. As part of Carlsberg's long-standing patronage of the arts, Carlsberg A/S established this prize in 1991 to promote the benefits of quality architecture. Nominations are culled from the international architectural press, and the jury is comprised of architects, scholars, and members of the press. Winners of this international award receive a prize amount equal to $220,000 US.

For more information visit the Carlsberg Web site at *www.carlsberg.com/info/*.

1992 Tadao Ando, Japan
1995 Juha Leiviskä, Finland
1998 Peter Zumthor, Switzerland

Source: Carlsberg A/S

Opposite: Peter Zumthor
Photographer: Arno Balzarini

Design for Humanity Award

Every year the American Society of Interior Designers (ASID) grants the Design for Humanity Award to an individual or institution that has made a significant contribution toward improving the quality of the human environment through design related activities that have had a universal and far-reaching effect. A committee appointed by the ASID Board reviews the nominations. The award is presented at ASID's annual national convention.

For additional information about the Design for Humanity Award, contact the ASID at (202) 546-3480 or on the Internet at *www.asid.org.*

1990	The Scavenger Hotline	1996	Wayne Ruga and the Center for Health Design
1991	E.I. Du Pont de Nemours & Company	1997	Barbara J. Campbell, *Accessibility Guidebook For Washington, D.C.*
1992	The Preservation Resource Center	1998	William L. Wilkoff, District Design
1993	Neighborhood Design Center	1999	AlliedSignal, Inc.-Polymers Division
1994	Elizabeth Paepcke & The International Design Conference in Aspen	2000	Victoria Schomer
1995	Cranbrook Academy of Art		

Source: American Society of Interior Designers

I am convinced that we can attain an acceptable degree of comfort by following the rules of nature.

Stefan Behnisch

Design for Transportation National Awards

Co-presented by the Department of Transportation (DOT) and the National Endowment for the Arts (NEA), the Design for Transportation National Awards are presented every five years for functional, innovative transportation system projects which solve problems by uniting form and function. Both agencies established criteria for judging, which is carried out by a multi-disciplinary jury of professionals. Entries must achieve one or more of the following DOT goals: tie America together through intermodal and multi-modal connections; enhance the environment through compatibility with community life and the physical surroundings; demonstrate sensitivity to the concerns of the traveling public; and provide a secure and safe traveling environment. Innovation, aesthetic sensibility, technical and functional performance, and cost efficiency must all be demonstrated. Awards are presented at two levels, the highest being Honor Awards, followed by Merit Awards. The following projects won an Honor Award in 2000.

Photographs and jury comments for both the Honor and Merit Award recipients can be found on the Internet at *http://ostpxweb. dot.gov.*

2000 Honor Awards:

Admiral Clarey Bridge
Pearl Harbor, Oahu, Hawaii

Grand Central Terminal
New York, New York

Dallas Area Rapid Transit
Dallas, Texas

Historic Columbia River Highway State
Trail
Columbia River Gorge, Oregon

Terminal B/C, Ronald Reagan
Washington National Airport
Washington, D.C.

River Relocation Project
Providence, Rhode Island

Westside Light Rail
Portland, Oregon

United States Port of Entry
Calexico, California

Memorial Tunnel Fire Ventilation Test
Program
Charleston, West Virginia

The Bat Dome Culvert
Laredo, Texas

Vessel Traffic Services Project
Lower Mississippi River

Design for Transportation National Awards (Con't)

2000 Jury:
Alex Krieger, Chair

Architecture, Interior Design, and Historic Preservation:
Alex Krieger, Chair
Kate Diamond
Hanan A. Kivett
Mary Means
Donald Stull

Engineering:
James Poirot, Chair
Jonathan Esslinger

Patricia Galloway
John M. Kulicki
M. John Vickerman

Landscape Architecture, Urban Design, Planning, Art and Graphic Design:
Elizabeth Moule, Chair
Wendy Feuer
Roger K. Lewis
Weiming Lu
Lynda Schneekloth

Source: U.S. Department of Transportation and National Endowment for the Arts

Did you know...

At the height of the Roman Empire, the Romans succeeded in constructing over 50,000 miles of roads throughout Europe, North Africa, and the Middle East.

Designer of Distinction Award

The Designer of Distinction Award is granted by the American Society of Interior Designers (ASID) to an ASID interior designer whose professional achievements have demonstrated design excellence. Eligibility is open to members in good standing who have practiced within the preceding ten years. Nominations are accepted by ASID's general membership body and reviewed by jury selected by the National President. This is a merit based award and, thus, is not always granted annually.

For more information, visit the ASID on the Internet at *www.asid.org* or contact them at (202) 546-3480.

1979   William Pahlman
1980   Everett Brown
1981   Barbara D'Arcy
1982   Edward J. Wormley
1983   Edward J. Perrault
1984   Michael Taylor
1985   Norman Dehaan
1986   Rita St. Clair
1987   James Merricksmith
1988   Louis Tregre
1994   Charles D. Gandy
1995   Andre Staffelbach
1996   Joseph Minton
1997   Phyllis Martin-Vegue
1998   Janet Schirn
1999   Gary E. Wheeler
2000   Paul Vincent Wiseman

Source: American Society of Interior Designers

Did you know...

David Rowland's 40 in 4 wire-rod chair, designed in 1963, utilized such exacting engineering tolerances that, as its name implies, forty could be stacked in a four foot high space, a characteristic which has continued to make it popular among commercial and institutional organizations.

Designs of the Decade: Best in Business 1990 – 1999 Awards Competition

The Industrial Designers Society of America (IDSA) and *Business Week* magazine co-sponsored the Designs of the Decade: Best in Business 1990 – 1999 Awards Competition to recognize the most compelling design/business success stories of the 1990s. Entries were open to anyone who designed a product introduced for sale anywhere in the world between January 1, 1990 and July 1, 1999 in one of seven categories. A jury of business executives and designers reviewed each submission and considered the role of design in the product idea, the breadth of design involvement in product strategy, the impact of the design on corporate performance in financial and marketing terms, and overall design quality.

For photographs and the success stories of all the Gold, Silver, and Bronze level winners, visit IDSA's Web site at *www.idsa.org*.

Gold Winners:

Business & Industrial Products
  iMac
  Apple Design Staff

  Palm Pilot
  Palo Alto Products International and Palm
    Computing design staff

  PowerShot Forward Action Staple Gun
   IDI/Innovations & Development Inc. and
    WorkTools Inc.

Consumer Products
  Gillette Sensor for Women Razor
  Gillette design staff

  Motorola TalkAbout SLK Two-Way Radio
  Motorola design staff

  Nike Triax sport watches
  Nike design staff and Astro Products Inc.

  OXO Good Grips Kitchen Tools
  Smart Design

  Sony PlayStation
  Sony design staff

Environmental Designs
  no Gold level winners chosen

Furniture
  Aeron Chair
  Stumpf, Weber + Associates and
    Chadwick & Associates

Medical & Scientific Equipment
  no Gold level winners chosen

Packaging, Graphics & User Interface
  Hush Puppies Branding
  Fitch Inc.

Opposite: Aeron Work Chair, Herman Miller
Photographer: Nick Merrick © Hedrich Blessing

Designs of the Decade: Best in Business 1990 – 1999 Awards Competition (Con't)

Transportation

BMW 3 Series
BMW design staff

VW New Beetle
Volkswagen design staffs in the U.S. and
Germany

Jury:

Charles Jones, Chair
Robert Hayman
Marco Iansiti
Dr. Lorraine Justice
Dr. Stephano Marzano
Luis Pedraza
Noel Zeller

Source: Business Week *and Industrial Designers Society of America*

Did you know...

In 1931, when Normal Bel Geddes redesigned the Oriole stove, an all-white enameled gas range, it not only caused an immediate doubling of its sales and was copied by other stove manfactures but it made corporations aware of the benefits of good design.

Distinguished Professor Award

The Association of Collegiate Schools of Architecture's (ACSA) Distinguished Professor Award is presented annually for "sustained creative achievement" in the field of architectural education, whether through teaching, design, scholarship, research, or service. Eligible candidates must be living faculty of an ACSA member school for a minimum of 10 years or be otherwise allied with architectural education at an ACSA member school. Students or faculty of an ACSA member school may make nominations. Each year, an Honors and Awards Committee recommends a maximum of five candidates to the ACSA Board. Winners are entitled to use the title 'ACSA Distinguished Professor' for life.

For additional information about the ACSA Distinguished Professor Award, contact the Association at (202) 785-2324, or visit their Web site at *www.acsa-arch.org*.

1984-85
 Alfred Caldwell, Illinois Institute of
  Technology
 Robert S. Harris, Univ. of Southern Calif.
 Fay Jones, Univ. of Arkansas
 Charles Moore, Univ. of Texas at Austin
 Ralph Rapson, Univ. of Minnesota

1985-86
 James Marston Fitch, Columbia Univ.
 Leslie J. Laskey, Washington Univ.
 Harlan McClure, Clemson Univ.
 Edward Romieniec, Texas A & M Univ.
 Richard Williams, U. of Illinois,
  Champaign-Urbana

1986-87
 Christopher Alexander, Univ. of
  California, Berkeley
 Harwell Hamilton Harris, North Carolina
  State Univ.
 Stanislawa Nowicki, Univ. of Pennsylvania
 Douglas Shadbolt, Univ. of British
  Columbia
 Jerzy Soltan, Harvard Univ.

1987-88
 Harold Cooledge, Jr., Clemson Univ.
 Bernd Foerster, Kansas State Univ.
 Romaldo Giurgola, Columbia Univ.
 Joseph Passonneau, Washington Univ.
 John G. Willams, Univ. of Arkansas

1988-89
 Peter R. Lee, Jr., Clemson Univ.
 E. Keith McPheeters, Auburn Univ.
 Stanley Salzman, Pratt Institute
 Calvin C. Straub, Arizona State Univ.
 Blanche Lemco van Ginkel, Univ. of
  Toronto

1989-90
 Gunnar Birkerts, Univ. of Michigan
 Olivio C. Ferrari, Virginia Polytechnic
  Institute
 George C. Means, Jr., Clemson Univ.
 Malcolm Quantrill, Texas A & M Univ.

1990-91
 Denise Scott Brown, Univ. of
  Pennsylvania
 Panos Koulermos, Univ. of Southern Calif.

Distinguished Professor Award (Con't)

William McMinn, Cornell Univ.
Forrest Wilson, The Catholic Univ. of
America
David Woodcock, Texas A & M Univ.

1991-92
M. David Egan, Clemson Univ.
Robert D. Dripps, Univ. of Virginia
Richard C. Peters, Univ. of California,
Berkeley
David L. Niland, Univ. of Cincinnati

1992-93
Stanley W. Crawley, Univ. of Utah
Don P. Schlegel, Univ. of New Mexico
Thomas L. Schumacher, Univ. of
Maryland

1993-94
George Anselevicius, Univ. of New Mexico
Hal Box, Univ. of Texas at Austin
Peter McCleary, Univ. of Pennsylvania
Douglas Rhyn, Univ. of Wisconsin-
Milwaukee
Alan Stacell, Texas A & M Univ.

1994-95
Blake Alexander, Univ. of Texas at Austin
Robert Burns, North Carolina State Univ.
Robert Heck, Louisiana State Univ.
Ralph Knowles, Univ. of Southern
California

1995-96
James Barker, Clemson Univ.
Mui Ho, Univ. of California, Berkley
Patricia O'Leary, Univ. of Colorado
Sharon Sutton, Univ. of Minnesota
Peter Waldman, Univ. of Virginia

1996-97
Colin H. Davidson, Universite de
Montreal
Michael Fazio, Mississippi State Univ.
Ben J. Refuerzo, Univ. of Calif., Los
Angeles
Max Underwood, Arizona State Univ.
J. Stroud Watson, Univ. of Tennessee

1997-98
Roger H. Clark, North Carolina State
Univ.
Bob E. Heatly, Oklahoma State Univ.
John S. Reynolds, Univ. of Oregon
Marvin E. Rosenman, Ball State Univ.
Anne Taylor, Univ. of New Mexico

1998-99
Ralph Bennett, Univ. of Maryland
Diane Ghirardo, Univ. of Southern
California
Robert Greenstreet, Univ. of Wisconsin-
Milwaukee
Thomas Kass, Univ. of Utah
Norbert Schoenauer, McGill Univ.
Jan Wampler, Massachusetts Inst. of Tech.

2000
Maelee Thomson Foster, Univ. of Florida
Louis Inserra, Pennsylvania State Univ.
Henry Sanoff, North Carolina State Univ.

Source: Association of Collegiate Schools of Architecture

Dubai International Award for Best Practices in Improving the Living Environment

The United Nations' Center for Human Settlements (HABITAT), in conjunction with the Municipality of Dubai, United Arab Emirates, biennially awards the Dubai International Award for Best Practices in Improving the Living Environment to initiatives that have made outstanding contributions to improving the quality of life in cities and communities worldwide. The first Best Practices award was presented in 1996 following an international conference on best practices held in Dubai. In 2000, over 700 submissions were received from more than 120 countries. Each project is reviewed for its compliance with the three criteria for a Best Practice: impact, partnership, and sustainability. The award is open to all organizations, including governments and public and private groups. Winners receive a $30,000 prize, trophy and certificate. In addition, all entries are listed in a Best Practices database at *www.bestpractices.org* that contains over 1100 solutions to the common social, economic and environmental problems of an urbanizing world.

For additional information, contact HABITAT at (212) 963-4200, or on the Internet at *www.bestpractices.org*.

2000 Winners:

Luanda Sul Self-financed Urban Infrastructure, Angola

Public Security, Human Rights and Citizenship, Brazil

Creating a Sustainable Community, Hamilton-Wentworth Vision 2020/Air Quality, Canada

Comprehensive Re-vitalisation of Urban Settlements, Chengdu, China

Democratisation of Municipal Management, Cotacachi Canton, Ecuador

Cost Effective and Appropriate Sanitation Systems, India

Women's Empowerment Programme, Nepal

Spanish Greenways Programme, Spain

Shambob Brick Producers Co-operative, Sudan

Tourism and Coastal Zone Management, Cirali, Turkey

2000 Jury:

Prof. W. Cecil Steward, USA (Chair)

Hon. Dato Dr. Siti Zaharah Bt Sulaiman, Malaysia

Claudia Ximena Balcazar, Colombia

Hussain Nasser Ahmed Lootah, Dubai Municipality, UAE

Mayor Josiah K. Magut, Kenya

Source: United Nationals Center for Human Settlements

Edward C. Kemper Award

Edward C. Kemper served as Executive Director of The American Institute of Architects (AIA) for nearly 35 years, from 1914 to 1948. The Edward C. Kemper Award honors an architect member of the AIA who has similarly served as an outstanding member of the Institute.

For more information, visit the AIA on the Internet at *www.e-architect.org* or contact the AIA Honors and Awards Department at (202) 626-7586.

1950 William Perkins	1981 Robert L. Durham
1951 Marshall Shaffer	1982 Leslie N. Boney Jr.
1952 William Stanley Parker	1983 Jules Gregory
1953 Gerrit J. De Gelleke	1984 Dean F. Hilfinger
1954 Henry H. Saylor	1985 Charles Redmon
1955 Turpin C. Bannister	1986 Harry Harmon
1956 Theodore Irving Coe	1987 Joseph Monticciolo
1957 David C. Baer	1988 David Lewis
1958 Edmund R. Purves	1989 Jean P. Carlhian
1959 Bradley P. Kidder	1990 Henry W. Schirmer
1960 Philip D. Creer	1991 John F. Hartray Jr.
1961 Earl H. Reed	1992 Betty Lou Custer*
1962 Harry D. Payne	1993 Theodore F. Mariani
1963 Samuel E. Lunden	1994 Harry C. Hallenbeck
1964 Daniel Schwartzman	1995 Paul R. Neel
1965 Joseph Watterson	1996 Sylvester Damianos
1966 William W. Eshbach	1997 Harold L. Adams
1967 Robert H. Levison	1998 Norman L. Koonce
1968 E. James Gambaro	1999 James R. Franklin
1969 Philip J. Meathe	2000 James A. Scheeler
1970 Ulysses Floyd Rible	
1971 Gerald McCue	** Honored posthumously*
1972 David N. Yerkes	*Source: The American Institute of Architects*
1973 Bernard B. Rothschild	
1974 Jack D. Train	
1975 F. Carter Williams	
1976 Leo A. Daly	
1977 Ronald A. Straka	**Design has become the public art of our time.**
1978 Carl L. Bradley	
1979 Herbert E. Duncan Jr.	*Steven Holt*
1980 Herbert Epstein	

Engineering Excellence Awards

The American Consulting Engineers Council's (ACEC) Engineering Excellence Awards are an annual competition that begins at the state level, with finalists moving to the national competition. Each year one project receives the "Grand Conceptor" Award, and up to 23 other projects receive either Grand or Honor Awards. Projects are judged by a panel of 20 – 25 engineers and infrastructure experts on the basis of uniqueness and originality; technical value to the engineering profession; social and economic considerations; complexity; and how successfully the project met the needs of the client. Projects must be entered in one of nine categories: studies, research and consulting engineering services, building support systems; structural systems; surveying and mapping; environmental; water and wastewater; water resources; transportation; and special projects. Any firm engaged in the private practice, consulting engineering, or surveying is eligible to participate. Entries must be submitted to an ACEC Member Organization.

For photographs and descriptions of the winning projects, visit *www.acec.org/programs/2000eeaawards.htm* on the Internet.

2000 Grand Conceptor Award Winner:
Structural System
  AEOS 3.67 Meter Telescope Facility
  Kihei, Hawaii
  SATO & ASSOCIATES, INC.

2000 Grand Award Winners:
Studies, Research and Consulting Engineering Services
  Village Creek WWTP Wet Weather
    Treatment Improvement
  Arlington, Texas
  Camp Dresser & McKee, Inc.

Structural Systems
  Excavation Support For Tunnel
    Construction
  Boston, Massachusetts
  GEI Consultants Inc./Hatch Mott
    MacDonald/Weidlinger Associates Inc.

Structural
  SAFECO Field
  Seattle, Washington
  Skilling Ward Magnusson Barkshire, Inc.

Water And Wastewater
  Penn Forest Dam Replacement
  Trachsville, Pennsylvania
  Gannett Fleming

Transportation
  US 75 North Central Expwy. Reconstruction
  Dallas, Texas
  HDR Engineering, Inc.; Bridgefarmer &
    Associates, Inc.; Carter & Burgess,
    Inc./Lochwood Andrews & Newnam
    Joint Venture; Brown & Root Services;
    HNTB Corporation; Halff Associates,
    Inc.

Engineering Excellence Awards (Con't)

Riverfront Plaza and Founders Bridge
Hartford, Connecticut
Berger, Lehman Associates

Special Projects
Cape Hatteras Light Station Relocation
Buxton, North Carolina
Law Engineering and Environmental
Services, Inc.

2000 Honor Awards
*Studies, Research, And Consulting Engineering
Services*
Florida Keys Owners Demo Project
Big Pine Key, Florida
Ayres Associates

Building/Technology Services
New York Presbyterian Hospital
Modernization
New York City, New York
Syska & Hennessy, Inc.

Structural Services
Oregon State Library Renovation
Salem, Oregon
KPFF Consulting Engineers

Surveying And Mapping Technology
Statewide DOQQ Conversion/Web-Based
GIS
Frankfort, Kentucky
GRW Aerial Surveys, Inc.

Environmental
Edwards Dam Removal and Site
Restoration
Augusta, Maine
Woodard & Curran and E-Pro Engineering

Rocket Fuel Facilities Neutralization
Tobe ICBM Bases, Kazakhstan
Harding Lawson Associates

A New Approach To Groundwater
Remediation
Sun Prairie, Wisconsin
RMT, Inc.

Water And Wastewater
Water System Flood Response and
Restoration
Grand Forks, North Dakota
Advanced Engineering and Environmental
Services, Inc.

Sweetwater River Groundwater Facilities
Chula Vista, California
Boyle Engineering Corporation

Town of Lakeview Wastewater Treatment
Project
Lakeview, Oregon
Anderson Engineering & Surveying, Inc.

Water Resources
Tongue River Revival
Decker, Montana
ESA Consultants Inc.

Transportation
TRAX Light Rail Project
Salt Lake City, Utah
Carter & Burgess, Inc.

Golf Cart Bridges at Bridges of Rancho
Santa Fe
Rancho Santa Fe, New Mexico
T.Y. Lin International

Mid-City E Route Park Road Tunnels
Washington, D.C.
Parsons Transportation Group Inc. and
Corddry, Carpenter, Dietz & Zack

Opposite: SAFECO Field, Seattle, WA, NBBJ (architect), Skilling Ward Magnusson Barkshire Inc.
(engineer)
Photographer: Tim Hursley

Engineering Excellence Awards (Con't)

First Avenue South Bridge
Seattle, Washington
Parsons Brinckerhoff and Kaiser
  Engineers

Special Projects
91st Avenue WWTP Pipeline
  Rehabilitation
Tolleson, Arizona
Brown and Caldwell

Source: American Consulting Engineers Council

Did you know...

Phoenix's Bank One Ballpark(1998, Ellerbe Becket) contains a 5,940 ton retractable roof which opens in only 5 minutes.

GSA Design Awards

The U.S. General Services Administration (GSA) presents biennial Design Awards as part of its Design Excellence Program, which seeks the best in design, construction, and restoration for all Federal building projects. The Design Awards were developed to encourage and recognize innovative design in Federal buildings and to honor noteworthy achievements in the preservation and renovation of historic structures.

For additional information about the GSA Design Awards or to view photographs and descriptions of the 1998 winners, visit GSA's Web site at *http://designawards.gsa.gov.*

1998 Honor Award Recipients:

Architecture

Ronald Reagan Building and International Trade Center
Washington, D.C.
Pei Cobb Freed & Partners Architects, LLP and Ellerbe Becket

National Data Processing Center, Bureau of the Census, U.S. Department of Commerce
Bowie, Maryland
Tobey + Davis/ Davis, Brody, Bond

Mark O. Hatfield U.S. Courthouse
Portland, Oregon
Kohn Pedersen Fox Associates, P.C. and BOORA Architects

U.S. Port of Entry
Point Roberts, Washington
The Miller/Hull Partnership

Graphic Design

Booklet, "United States Court of Appeals Building for the Ninth Circuit,"
San Francisco, California
Rightside Imaging

Signage, Mark O. Hatfield U.S. Courthouse
Portland, Oregon
Mayer/Reed

1998 Citation Recipients:

Architecture

Robert C. Byrd U.S. Courthouse
Charleston, West Virginia
Skidmore Owings and Merrill LLP

On the Boards

U.S. Courthouse and Federal Building
Central Islip, New York
Richard Meier & Partners and The Spectorgroup

U.S. Post Office and Courthouse
Brooklyn, New York
R.M. Kliment & Frances Halsband Architects

William J. Nealon Federal Building and U.S. Courthouse
Scranton, Pennsylvania
Bohlin Cywinski Jackson, Architects

Historic Preservation/Conservation

Edward Gignoux U.S. Courthouse
Portland, Maine
Leers Weinzapfel Associates Architects

GSA Design Awards (Con't)

Restoration of Alexander Calder's Flamingo
Chicago, Illinois
McKay Lodge Fine Arts and Conservation
Laboratory, Inc.

Engineering
"Engineering and Environmental Study"
for U.S. Courthouse and Federal
Building
Phoenix, Arizona
Ove Arup & Partners

Landscape Architecture
Jacob Javitz Plaza
New York, New York
Martha Schwartz, Inc.

Urban Planning
Urban Design Guidelines for Physical
Perimeter and Entrance Security: An
Overlay to the Master Plan for the
Federal Triangle
Washington, D.C.
Sorg and Associates, P.C.

"Governors Island Land Use Study," New
York Harbor
New York, New York
Beyer Blinder Belle Consortium

Art
Federal Triangle Flowers, Ronald Reagan
Building and International Trade
Center
Washington, D.C.
Stephen Robin

Boundary Markers, National Building
Museum
Washington, D.C.
Raymond Kaskey

Justice Warren B. Rudman U.S.
Courthouse
Concord, New Hampshire
Diana K. Moore

Africa Rising
290 Broadway, New York, New York
Barbara Chase-Riboud

Architectural Glass, Robert C. Byrd U.S.
Courthouse
Charleston, West Virginia
David Wilson

Lens Ceiling, Federal Building and U.S.
Courthouse
Phoenix, Arizona
James Carpenter

Graphic Design
"Renewing the Commitment," 30th
Anniversary of the Architectural
Barriers Act
Tullier Marketing Communications

Jury:
Robert A.M. Stern (Chair)
Charles Durrett
Leslie Gallery-Dilworth
Arthur Gensler
Paul Hawkes
Pamela Hellmuth
Fred Kelley
Tom Moran
Garth Rockcastle
Allison Williams

Source: U.S. General Services Administration

Hugh Ferriss Memorial Prize

The Hugh Ferriss Memorial Prize is awarded annually by the American Society of Architectural Perspectivists (ASAP) to recognize excellence in architectural illustration. This international awards program is open to all current members of the Society. A traveling exhibition, Architecture in Perspective, co-sponsored by the Otis Elevator Company, highlights the winners and selected entries and raises awareness of the field.

To see the winning drawings, visit the ASAP's Web site at *www.asap.org/aip.html.*

1986
   Lee Dunnette, AIA and James Record
1987
   Richard Lovelace, *One Montvale Avenue*
1988
   Thomas Wells Schaller, AIA, *Proposed Arts and Cultural Center*
1989
   Daniel Willis, AIA, *Edgar Allen Poe Memorial (detail)*
1990
   Gilbert Gorski, AIA, *The Interior of the Basilica Ulpia*
1991
   Luis Blanc, *Affordable Housing Now!*
1992
   Douglas E. Jamieson, *BMC Real Properties Buildings*
1993
   David Sylvester, *Additions and Renovations to Tuckerton Marine Research Field Station*

1994
   Rael D. Slutsky, AIA, *3rd Government Center Competition*
1995
   Lee Dunnette, AIA, *The Pyramid at Le Grand Louvre*
1996
   Paul Stevenson Oles, FAIA, *Hines France Office Tower*
1997
   Advanced Media Design, *World War II Memorial*
1998
   Wei Li, *Baker Library Addition, Dartmouth College*
1999
   Serge Zaleski, *Five Star Deluxe Beach Hotel*
2000
   Thomas W. Schaller, *1000 Wilshire Blvd.*

Source: American Society of Architectural Perspectivists

I.D. Annual Design Review

I.D. magazine's Annual Design Review began in 1954 and today is considered America's largest and most prestigious industrial design competition. Entries are placed in one of seven separate categories (consumer products, graphics, packaging, environments, furniture, equipment, concepts and student work) and reviewed by juries of leading practitioners. Within each category, projects are awarded on three levels: Best of Category, Design Distinction, and Honorable Mention. Winning entries are published in a special July/August issue of *I.D.* magazine. The following products received the Best of Category award.

For additional information about the Annual Design Review, contact *I.D.* magazine at (212) 447-1400.

2000 Best of Category Winners:

Consumer Products:
  Yamaha Silent Cello
  Yamaha Corporation

  Pico Walnut Opener
  Ralph Krämer

  Jurors:
  Nasir Kassamali, Bonnie Mackay, Freeman
    Thomas

Graphics:
  Your Private Sky: R. Buckminster Fuller
  Lars Müller

  Jurors:
  Seam Adams, Janet Froelich, J. Abbott
    Miller, Paul Sahre

Packaging
  Blu Dot 2D/3D Packaging
  Werner Design Werks

  Jurors:
  Lisa Naftolin, Scott Stonwell, Allison
    Muench Williams

Environments
  Vitra Showroom at Neocon 1999
  Boym Partners

  Vista Point
  Bruce Tomb, Kris Force, Jayne Roderick

  Jurors:
  Walter Chatham, Emanuela Frattini
    Magnusson, Elizabeth Ranieri

Furniture:
  Sagesse
  Annick Magac

  Jurors:
  Neil Frankel, Troy Halterman, Grace
    Jeffers

Equipment
  PRS Photochemical Recycling Center
  IDEO Products Development

  T-Bird Tea-Brewing Machine
  Design Stream

  Jurors:
  Cathy Bailey, Ben Fether, Roger Minkow

I.D. Magazine Annual Design Review (Con't)

Concepts:

Kitchen Sink, Dishwasher and Essential
  Range Washing Machine
Electrolux

Personal Satellite Assistant
NASA, Ames Research Center

Student Work:

Eco Wall Garden
Cynthia Nicole Gordon, University of
  Washington

Curlybot
Phil Frei, MIT Media Lab

Jurors:
Janet Abrams, Judy Ellis, Peter Hall,
  Chuck Hoberman

Source: I.D. Magazine

**Every article of furniture
should, at first glance, pro-
claim its real purpose.**

Charles Eastlake

IDSA Education Award

The Industrial Designers Society of America (IDSA) grants the Education Award to recognize excellence in industrial design education. Educators are presented this award in honor of their significant and distinguished contributions.

For additional information, visit IDSA on the Internet at *www.idsa.org.*

1988	Arthur J. Pulos Syracuse University	1994	Hin Bredendieck Georgia Institute of Technology
1989	Robert Lepper Carnegie Mellon University		Joseph Koncelik Ohio State University
1990	Edward Zagorski University of Illinois, Champaign-Urbana	1996	Toby Thompson Rochester Institute of Technology
1991	James Alexander Art Center College of Design	1997	Marc Harrison Rhode Island School of Design
1992	Strother MacMinn Art Center College of Design	1998	Bruce Hannah Pratt Institute
	Robert Redmann University of Bridgeport	1999	Michael Nielsen Arizona State University
1993	Vincent Foote North Carolina State University	2000	Katherine McCoy Illinois Institute of Technology
	Herbert Tyrnauer California State University at Long Beach		Michael McCoy Illinois Institute of Technology

Source: Industrial Designers Society of America

Industrial Design Excellence Awards (IDEA)

The Industrial Design Excellence Awards (IDEA), co-sponsored by *Business Week* magazine and the Industrial Designers Society of America (IDSA), are presented annually to honor industrial design worldwide. Any U.S. designer or non-U.S. designer whose produce is distributed in North America may enter their designs in one of nine categories. Each year a jury of business executives and design professionals issue as many awards as they deem necessary, evaluating over 1,000 entries on the following criteria: design innovation, benefit to the user, benefit to the client/business, ecological responsibility, and appropriate aesthetics and appeal. Gold, silver, and bronze level citations are granted. The following designs received the Gold award in 2000.

For detailed descriptions, photographs, and contact information for all Gold, Silver, and Bronze winners, visit the IDSA on the Internet at *www.idsa.org*.

IDEA2000 Gold Award Winners:

Business & Industrial Products

Apple Cinema Display
Apple Computer

"Eclipse" Gasoline Dispenser
Herbst LaZar Bell

SC4000 Sit-Down Counterbalanced Lift Truck
Crown Equipment, Design Central, and Ergonomic Systems Design

Virtual Ink Mimio™
Fitch and Virtual Ink

WP2000 Series Pallet Truck
Crown Equipment and Design Central

Consumer Products

ASF Paper Shredder
Staubitz Design Associates and Michilin Manufacturing

Bandit
Speck Product Design

Infinity Prelude MTS Loudspeaker System
Ashcraft Design

iSub
Apple Computer

Mouse Sander
Black & Decker

NEC Z1 Personal Computer
Hauser

New Vision 1 Television
Philips Design

OrangeX OJex Manual Juicer
Smart Design

Sportscope Flex-Fit Bicycle Helmets
Design Workshop and Biokinetics

TR5 Fitness Bicycle
Strategix I.D.

View-Master Virtual Viewer
Fisher-Price and Priestman Goode

Industrial Design Excellence Awards (IDEA) (Con't)

Design Exploration
Culinary Art
Philips

Johnson & Johnson Independence 3000
Personal Transporter
Roche Harkins Design

JBREWS Sentry Unit & Transport Case
Carlson Technology, Dept. of Defense
Joint Program Office, and Betac

MainFrame (Vadem Allegro) Research
ZIBA Design

Rug Power and Communications Grid
3rd Uncle Design and Teknion Furniture
Systems

Thumbscript & Prototype Communicator
Smart Design/Thumbscript Development

Water Bug/Power Bug
Great Stuff

"Without Thought" Concept
IDEO

Digital Media & Interfaces
MPEG 4-Net Application
Samsung Electronics

Volume Analysis
GE Medical Systems

Environmental Designs
Accord 15
APCO Graphics

Ackerman McQueen Advertising
Executive Offices
Elliott + Associates Architects

Crayola Cafe & Store
Burdick Group

Levi's Mothership Exhibit
Mauk Design

Furniture
Resolve System™
Olive 1:1

SATURNO Lighting Poles
Emilio Ambasz & Associates

Medical & Scientific Products
Intima II
BD Medical Systems

Mixing Station & Syringe Components
Coleman Product Design

Neurometrix NC-stat™
Product Genesis

Packaging & Graphics
Michael Graves Design Packaging
Design Guys

Student Design
bebo
Michael Stefan Leoniak, Art Center
College of Design

Bigelow Tea Series Boxes
Kee-sook Jeon, Art Center College of
Design

Wayfinding for Seniors
Rick Hoobler, Hillary Carey, Ignacio
Filippini, Jacey Stroback, and
Lisa Glass, Carnegie Mellon University

Transportation
BMW K1200 LT Motorcycle
BMW

IDEA2000 Jury:
Patricia Moore, Chair
Michelle Berryman
Leslie Gallery Dilworth
Ricardo Gomes
Gray Holland

Opposite: The "Eclipse" Gasoline Dispenser, Herbst
LaZar Bell

Industrial Design Excellence Awards (IDEA) (Con't)

IDEA2000 Jury (Con't)

Henry Kim

Dan Klitsner

Jane Langmuir

Noel Mayo

Devin Moore

Ruth Soenius

Leslie Speer

Molly Follette Story

Bronwen Walters

Cooper Woodring

Edward Zagorski

Source: Industrial Designers Society of America

Did you know...

Since 1996 the following design firms have won the most IDEA awards:

IDEO – 43
Ziba Design – 26
Fitch – 18
frogdesign – 17
Pentagram – 14
Altitute – 13
Lunar Design – 12
Hauser – 11
Herbst LaZar Bell – 11
Smart Design – 9

Source: Business Week

Interior Design Competition

The Interior Design Competition is presented jointly each year by the International Interior Design Association (IIDA) and *Interior Design* magazine. The Competition was established in 1973 to recognize outstanding interior design and to foster new interior design ideas and techniques. Winning projects appear in Interior Design magazine, and the "Best of Competition" winner receives a $5,000 cash prize.

For more information, contact IIDA at (888) 799-IIDA or visit their Web site at *www.iida.org*.

2000 Best of Competition:
Eleven Madison Park
New York, NY
Bentel & Bentel Architects/Planners
  (Locust Valley, NY)

2000 Award Winners:
America Online Creative Centers
Dulles, VA
Ai (Washington, DC)

Klasky Csupo, Inc.
Hollywood, CA
Area (Los Angeles, CA)

Quiksilver Corporate Headquarters
Huntington Beach, CA
BAUER AND WILEY Architects (Newport Beach, CA)

Apple Computer, Inc./CompUSA
San Francisco, CA
Eight Inc. (San Francisco, CA)

Nokia IPRG
Mountain View, CA
Gensler (San Francisco, CA)

Eleven Inc.
San Francisco, CA
Eight Inc. (San Francisco, CA)

Santa Fe Residence
Santa Fe, NM
Brukoff Design Associates, Inc.
  (Sausalito, CA)

The Brown Residence
Cambridge, MA
Diane McCasstery and David Stern
  (Boston, MA)

2000 Jury:
Laura Barnett
Alan Lauck
Gary Lee
Judy Niedermaier
Lauren Rottet
John Robert Wiltgen

Source: International Interior Design Association and Interior Design *magazine*

Interiors' Annual Design Awards

Since 1980, *Interiors* magazine has hosted its Annual Design Awards competition to honor and recognize outstanding interior design projects. Entries are judged in one of twelve building types. A jury of design professionals selects winners based on aesthetics, design creativity, function, and achievement of client objectives. Winners are honored at an Annual Awards Breakfast in New York.

For more information, contact *Interiors* at (212) 536-5141.

2000 Award Winners:

Best Large Office
TBWA/Chiat/Day West Coast Headquarters
Los Angeles, California
Clive Wilkinson Architects

Best Small Office
Urban Innovations
Chicago, Illinois
Eva Maddox Associates

Best Restaurant
Ideya Restaurant
New York, New York
PNB Design

Best Healthcare Facility
Charles B. Rangel Comm. Health Center
New York, New York
HLW International

Best Retail Project
Gucci
London, UK
Studio Sofield

Best Educational Facility
New York University dormitory
New York, New York
Davis Brody Bond

Best Public Space
Iwataya Passage
Fukuoka, Japan
Walker Group/CNI

Best Showroom
"Modern Living Space"
Toronto, Canada
Cecconi Simone

Best Residence
Spear Loft
New York, New York
Form Follows Function

Best Hotel
W New York
New York, New York
Rockwell Group

Best Entertainment Venue
American Cinematheque at the Egyptian
 Theater
Hollywood, California
Hodgetts + Fung Design Associates

Best Sports Fitness Facility
No winner

2000 Jury:
Paola Antonelli
Rand Elliott, FAIA
William McDonough
Nestor Santa-Cruz
Laurinda Spear

Source: Interiors

International Design Award, Osaka

Through its biennial International Design Award, Osaka, the Japan Design Foundation honors organizations and individuals who have made a significant contribution to the promotion of industry culture and the betterment of society through their design work. The award embraces all fields of the design profession. Nominations are solicited from leading figures in design from around the world. Winners are selected by a jury of five Japanese members.

For more information, visit the Japan Design Foundation on the Internet at *www.jidpo.or.jp/japandesign/jdf/html/en_index.html* or email them at *jdf@silver.ocn.ne.jp*.

1983
- Chermayeff & Geismar Associates (USA)
- Maria Benktzon & Sven-Eric Juhlin (Sweden)
- Paola Navone (Italy)
- Pentagram (United Kingdom)
- *Honorary Award for the Encouragement of Design Activities:* Prime Minister, Margaret Thatcher (United Kingdom)

1985
- Bang & Olufsen A/S (Denmark)
- Philip Johnson (USA)
- Bruno Munari (Italy)
- Douglas Scott (United Kingdom)
- *Honorary Award:* Tadashi Tsukasa (Japan)

1987
- Kenji Ekuan (Japan)
- Norman Foster (United Kingdom)
- The Netherlands PTT (Netherlands)

1989
- Otl Aicher (Federal Republic of Germany)
- Jens Nielsen (Denmark)
- Frei Otto (Federal Republic of Germany)
- Yuri Borisovitch Soloviev (U.S.S.R)

1991
- Fritz Hansens Eft. A/S (Denmark)
- Fumihiko Maki (Japan)
- Antti Nurmesniemi and Vuokko Eskolin-Nurmesniemi (Finland)

1993
- Department of Architecture and Design of the Museum of Modern Art, New York (USA)
- Yusaku Kamekura (Japan)

1995
- Tadao Ando (Japan)
- Lawrence Halprin (USA)
- Arthur J. Pulos (USA)

1997
- Hans J. Wegner (Denmark)

1999
- Pasqual Maragall (Spain)
- Ryohin Keikaku Co., Ltd. (Japan)

Source: Japan Design Foundation

J.C. Nichols Prize for Visionary Urban Development

The Urban Land Institute (ULI) created the J.C. Nichols Prize for Visionary Urban Development to honor an individual or an institution who has made a commitment to responsible urban community development. As a founding member of the Urban Land Institute and whose work as a visionary developer includes the Country Club Plaza in Kansas City, the award's namesake, J.C. Nichols, embodies the ULI's commitment to fostering responsible land use and reputable development. Nominees can be drawn from a wide range of disciplines, including but not limited to architects, researchers, developers, journalists, public officials, and academics, and must be U.S. or Canadian citizens. A jury of urban experts, each representing diverse backgrounds and experiences, reviews the nominations. Recipients receive a $100,000 honorarium.

For additional information, visit the ULI on the Web at *www.uli.org* or contact them at (202) 624-7000.

2000   Mayor Joseph P. Riley Jr.

Source: Urban Land Institute

A place where a small boy, as he walks through it, may see something that will tell him what he wants to do with his whole life.

Louis Kahn's definition of a city

Jean Tschumi Prize

The Jean Tschumi Prize is awarded by the International Union of Architects (UIA) to individuals for their significant contribution to architectural criticism or architectural education.

For more information, visit the UIA's web site at *www.uia-architectes.org*.

1967 J.P. Vouga (Switzerland)
1969 I. Nikolaev (USSR)
      P. Ramirez Vazquez (Mexico)
1972 J.B. Vilanova Artigas (Brazil)
1975 R. Banham (U.K.)
1978 Rectory and Faculty of
      Architecture of the University
      of Lima (Peru)
1981 Neville Quarry (Australia)
      Honorary Mention:
      Jorge Glusberg
      (Argentina) and Tadeusz
      Barucki (Poland)
1984 Julius Posener (GDR)
1987 C. Norberg-Schulz (Norway)
      A. L. Huxtable (USA)

1990 Eduard Franz Sekler (Austria);
      Honorary Mention:
      Dennis Sharp (U.K.) and
      Claude Parent (France)
1993 Eric Kumchew Lye (Malaysia)
1996 Peter Cook (U.K.); Liangyong Wu
      (P.R. of China)
      Honorary Mention:
      Toshio Nakamura and the
      Mexican editor COMEX
1999 Juhani Pallasmaa (Finland)
      Honorary Mention:
      Jennifer Taylor (Australia)

Source: International Union of Architects

Design is not so much about the end product as it is about the process.

Clement Mok

Kenneth F. Brown Asia Pacific Culture & Architecture Design Award

Every two years the School of Architecture at the University of Hawai'i at Manoa and the Architects Regional Council of Asia (ARCASIA) sponsor the Kenneth F. Brown Asia Pacific Culture & Architecture Design Award program to recognize outstanding examples of contemporary architecture in Asia and the Pacific Rim that successfully balance spiritual and material aspects and demonstrate a harmony with the natural and cultural settings. Through this award program the sponsors hope to promote the development of humane environments within the multicultural Asia Pacific region as well as inspire a more culturally, socially, and environmentally appropriate approach to architecture. In order to be eligible, projects must have been completed within the previous 10 years and be located in Asia or countries that touch the Pacific Ocean. Winners receive a $US 25,000 cash prize and are invited to speak at the International Symposium on Asia Pacific Architecture.

For additional information or to view photographs and descriptions of winning projects, visit *www2.hawaii.edu/~kbda/* on the Internet.

2000 Award Winner:
    Arthur and Yvonne Boyd Education
        Center "Riverside"
    Nowra, New South Wales, Australia
    Glenn Murcutt, Wendy Lewin, Reginald
        Lark, Architects Equally in Association
        (Australia)

2000 Honorable Mentions:
    Kim Ok-gill Memorial Hall
    Seoul, Korea
    Kim In-Cheurl (Korea)

    Shanti, A Weekend House
    Alibaug, Maharashtra, India
    Rahul Mehrotra (India)

    LMW Corporate Office
    Coimbatore, India
    Rahul Mehrotra (India)

    26 Everton Road
    Singapore
    Richard K.F. Ho (Singapore)

2000 Jury:
    Kenneth F. Brown, chair (U.S.)
    A. I. Abdelhalim (Egypt)
    C. Anjalendran (Sri Lanka)
    Ricardo Legorreta (Mexico)
    Thomas M. Payette (U.S.)

Source: University of Hawai'i at Manoa, School of Architecture

Opposite: The Arthur and Yvonne Boyd Education Center; Nowra, New South Wales, Australia; Glenn Murcutt, Wendy Lewin, Reginald Lark, Architects Equally in Association

Keystone Award

Created by the American Architectural Foundation (AAF) in 1999, the Keystone Award honors individuals who have furthered the Foundation's vision "of a society that participates in shaping its environment through an understanding of the power of architecture to elevate and enrich the human experience." The award's objective is to recognize and encourage leadership that results in citizen participation in the design process, and advances communication with key decision-makers about how design issues affect a community's quality of life. Nominees may include, but are not limited to, patrons, advocates, critics, activists, clients, government representatives, and educational leaders. The award selection committee is comprised of experts in the fields of community development, communication, design, preservation, and government. Presentation of the award is made at the annual Accent on Architecture Gala in Washington, D.C. in January.

For additional information, contact the AAF at (202) 626-7500 or on the Web at *www.aafpages.org*.

1999   The Honorable Richard M. Daley
2000   Rick Lowe

Source: American Architectural Foundation

Design is one of the most forceful influences on behavior and is a part of everything we human beings experience... It's this connection between design, emotion, and behavior that gives design its power.

Penny Bonda

Lewis Mumford Prize

Every two years the Society for American City and Regional Planning History (SACRPH) grants the Lewis Mumford Prize to the best book in American city and regional history. Winners are chosen based on originality, depth of research, quality of writing, and the degree to which the book contributes to a greater understanding of the rich history of American city or regional planning. The presentation of a plaque and $500 cash prize is made at the Society's biennial conference.

For additional information, visit the Society on the Internet at *www.urban.uiuc.edu/sacrph/index.html.*

1991-93
> *The New York Approach: Robert Moses, Urban Liberals, and Redevelopment of the Inner City* by Joel Schwartz (Ohio State University Press)

1993-95
> *The City of Collective Memory: Its Historical Imagery and Architectural Entertainments* by M. Christine Boyer (MIT Press)

1995-97
> *City Center to Regional Mall: Architecture, the Automobile, and Retailing in Los Angeles, 1920-1950* by Richard Longstreth (MIT Press)

1997-99
> *Boston's Changeful Times: Origins of Preservation and Planning in America* by Michael Holleran (Johns Hopkins)

Honorable Mention:
> *Remaking Chicago: The Political Origins of Urban Industrial Change* by Joel Rast (Northern Illinois University Press)

Source: Society for American City and Regional Planning History

Town planning is not industrial design, the city is not a functional object, aesthetically sound or otherwise; the city is an artificial landscape built by human beings in which the adventure of our life unfolds.

Constant Nieuwenhuys

Michael Tatum Excellence in Education Award

The Michael Tatum Excellence in Education Award was created by the International Interior Design Association (IIDA) and sponsored by Tecknion to honor outstanding interior design educators. The Award also celebrates the life and career of Michael Tatum, an outstanding educator and IIDA member who passed away in 1998. When reviewing the nominations, the awards committee considers excellence in teaching, innovative teaching techniques, student mentoring, contributions to the profession, creative scholarship, including the publication of scholarly research, and leadership in interior design education within the community. Nominees must be full-time faculty at FIDER-accredited schools. Recipients are awarded a $5,500 cash prize and are invited to present a scholarly paper to the IIDA membership.

For more information about the Tatum Award, contact IIDA at (312) 467-1950 or visit them on the Internet at *www.iida.org*.

1999 Joy Dohr
      University of Wisconsin at Madison

2000 Henry P. Hildebrandt
      University of Cincinnati

Source: International Interior Design Association

Mies van der Rohe Award for European Architecture

Established in 1987 by the European Commission, the European Parliament, and the Mies van der Rohe Foundation, the Mies van der Rohe Award for European Architecture seeks to highlight notable projects within the context of contemporary European architecture. Works by European architects which are constructed in the member states of the European Union and associated European states within the two years following the granting of the previous award are eligible for the program. Winning projects are chosen for their innovative character and excellence in design and execution by an international panel of experts in the field of architecture and architectural criticism. The Award consists of a 50,000 Euro cash prize and a sculpture by Xavier Corberó, a design inspired by the Mies van der Rohe Pavilion.

For more information, visit the Mies van der Rohe Foundation's Web site at *www.miesbcn.com*.

1988
    Borges e Irmão Bank
    Vila do Conde, Portugal
    Alvaro Siza Vieira

1990
    New Terminal Development
    Stansted Airport, London, England
    Norman Foster & Partners

1992
    Municipal Sports Stadium
    Badalona, Barcelona, Spain
    Esteve Bonell and Francesc Rius

1994
    Waterloo International Station
    London, England
    Nicholas Grimshaw & Partners

1996
    Bibliotèque Nationale de France
    Paris, France
    Dominique Perrault

1999
    Art Museum in Bregenz,
    Bregenz, Austria
    Peter Zumthor

Source: Mies van der Rohe Foundation

Did you know...

Alvar Aalto's Finnish Pavilion at the 1939 New York World's Fair popularized Scandinavian organic design in the United States.

Mies van der Rohe Award for Latin American Architecture

A sister award to the Mies van der Rohe Award for European Architecture, this biennial award recognizes projects in Mexico, Central America, South America, Cuba, and the Dominican Republic. The Foundation created the award in 1987 to bring greater attention to contemporary Latin American architecture by honoring works of considerable conceptual, aesthetic, technical, and construction solutions. In order to be eligible, projects must have been completed within the previous two years prior to the granting of the Award and be located in a member country. The Award itself is identical to that of the European award, a cash prize of 50,000 Euros and a sculpture by Xavier Corberó inspired by the pillars of the Mies van der Rohe Pavilion in Barcelona.

For more information, visit the Mies van der Rohe Foundation's Web site at *www.miesbcn.com.*

1998
   Televisa Headquarters
   Mexico City
   TEN Arquitectos

2000
   São Paulo State Picture Library Building,
      restoration and adaptation
   São Paulo, Brazil
   Paulo A. Mendes da Rocha Arquitetos
      Associados

Source: Mies van der Rohe Foundation

National Building Museum Honor Award

Since 1986 the National Building Museum has honored individuals and organizations that have made an exceptional contribution to America's built history. The award is presented each year at an elegant gala held in the Museum's Great Hall, which has often been the site of the Presidential Inaugural Ball since 1885.

For more information, contact the National Building Museum at (202) 272-2448 or visit their Web site at *www.nbm.org*.

1986 J. Irwin Miller
1988 James W. Rouse
1989 Senator Daniel Patrick Moynihan
1990 IBM
1991 The Rockefeller Family
1992 The Civic Leadership of Greater Pittsburgh
1993 J. Carter Brown
1994 James A. Johnson and Fannie Mae
1995 Lady Bird Johnson
1996 Cindy and Jay Pritzker

1997 Morris Cafritz, Charles E. Smith, Charles A. Horsky and Oliver T. Carr Jr.
1998 Riley P. Bechtel and Stephen D. Bechtel Jr. of the Bechtel Group
1999 Harold and Terry McGraw and The McGraw-Hill Companies
2000 Gerald D. Hines

Source: National Building Museum

National Design-Build Awards

Every year the Design-Build Institute of America (DBIA) honors exemplary design-build projects through its National Design-Build Awards. Through this award program, the DBIA's goal is to promote the design-build process as an effective project delivery method and recognize outstanding design-build projects. Submitted entries in each category are evaluated on their overall success in fulfilling the owner/user's project goals. The projects' achievement within the design-build approach of efficiency, performance, architecture, risk management, and problem solving and the design team's use of innovation to add value are also considerations. Projects completed within the last five years that met the criteria of a qualified design-build contract are eligible. When merited, the jury may choose to grant the Design-Build Excellence Award to those projects which were outstanding but fell short of the National Design-Build Award.

For additional, visit DBIA's Web site at *www.dbia.org* or contact them at (202)682-0110.

2000 Recipients:

Best Private Project Over $15 million

Old Navy Pacific Distribution Center, Fresno, CA
James N. Gray Company (design-builder/designer/eng./const.)

Honor Award:

Radisson Hotel, Brisbane, CA
Webcor Builders (design-builder/const.)
Pahl, Pahl, Pahl Architects (designer)
Culp & Tanner (eng.)

Best Private Project Under $15 million

Sauer-Danfoss Manufacturing Facility, Lawrence, KS
Story Design Ltd. (design-builder/designer/const.)
Rietz Consultants Ltd. (structural eng.)
KJWW Engineering Consultants, PC (mechanical/electrical eng.)

Raytheon Missile Systems Conference Center, Tucson, AZ
Sundt Construction, Inc. (design-builder/const.)
SmithGroup (designer)

Honor Award:

Indiana Automotive Fasteners Manufacturing Plant/Office Headquarters, Greenfield, IN
Kajima Construction Services, Inc. (design-builder/designer/const.)
Heapy Engineering (eng.)

Northwest Airlines DC10 Maintenance Hanger, Detroit Metropolitan Wayne County Airport, Romulus, MI
Walbridge Aldinger Company (design-builder/const.)
Farrand & Associates Inc. Architects (designer)
Ruby & Associates PC (eng.)

National Design-Build Awards (Con't)

Best Public Project Over $15 million

St. Charles County Family Arena, St. Charles, MO

J.S. Alberici Construction Company, Inc. (design-builder/const.)

Hastings & Chivetta Architects, Inc. (architect)

Acoustical Design Group (acoustical eng.)

Bay Engineering (civil eng.)

Alper Ladd, Inc. (structural eng.)

McGrath, Inc. (mechanical eng.)

Shannon & Wilson (geotechnical eng.)

Wiegmann & Associates (HVAC D/B eng.)

Murphy Company (plumbing eng.)

Sachs Electric (electrical eng.)

San Francisco Civic Center Complex, San Francisco, CA

HSH Design/Build Inc. (design-builder)

Skidmore, Owings & Merrill (designer)

Clark Construction Group, Inc. (const.)

Hines (development manager)

Honor Award:

Linwood and Howard Avenue Ozonation Facilities, Milwaukee, WI

Black & Veatch Construction Inc./J.S. Alberici Construction Company Joint Venture (design-builder)

HNTB Corporation (designer)

Black & Veatch LLP (eng.)

J.S. Alberici Construction Co. Inc. (const.)

Special Recognition for Sustainable Design-Build:

BEQ-MCPON Plackett Manor and Naval Hospital-Great Lakes Naval Station, Great Lakes, IL

James McHugh Construction Co. (design-builder/const.)

Wight & Co. (designer)

SmithGroup, Inc. (eng.)

Best Public Project Under $15 million

McCoy Baseball Stadium Renovation/Expansion, Pawtucket, RI

O. Ahlborg & Sons/Heery International Joint Venture (design-builder/const.)

Heery International (designer/structural eng.)

Robinson Green Beretta (civil eng.)

Maguire Group (mechanical/electrical/ plumbing eng.)

C.A. Pretzer Associates (structural forensics/berm structures)

New Heights Elementary School, East Grand Forks, MN

M.A. Mortenson Company (design-builder/const.)

DLR Group (designer/eng.)

Honor Award:

Aircraft Paint Facility - Tinker Air Force Base, Oklahoma City, OK

The Austin Company (design-builder/designer/eng./const.)

Alameda County Recorder's Building, Oakland, CA

Hensel Phelps Construction Company (design-builder/const.)

Kaplan McLaughlin Diaz (designer)

Gayle Manufacturing Co. (structural eng.)

Critchfield Mechanical (mechanical eng.)

Sasco Electrical (electrical eng.)

Rehabilitation/Renovation/Restoration:

Jackson Hall Remodel - University of Minnesota, Minneapolis, MN

M.A. Mortenson Company (design-builder/const.)

Architectural Alliance (designer)

Ericksen Roed & Associates (structural eng.)

Metropolitan Mechanical Contractors, Inc./Dunham & Associates (mech. eng.)

Elliott Contracting Corporation/Dunham & Associates (electrical eng.)

National Design-Build Awards (Con't)

Excellence Award:

Outrigger Waikoloa Beach Resort
Renovation, Waikoloa, HI
Charles Pankow Builders Ltd. (design-
builder/const.)
Architects Hawaii, Ltd. (designer)
Robert Englekirk Consulting Structural
Engineers (structural eng.)
Lincolne Scott & Kohloss (mechanical eng.)
Moss Engineering (electrical eng.)

Honor Award:

Tolson Youth Activities Ctr., Fort Bragg, NC
Beers/Davidson and Jones Group (design-
builder/const.)
Williams-Russell & Johnson Inc. (arch./eng.)

Best Civil Project Over $15 million

Route 133, Section 1A-Highstown Bypass,
East Windsor Township, NJ
Schiavone Construction Company, Inc.
(design-builder/const.)
Goodkind & O'Dea Inc. (designer/eng.)

B&O Capacity Improvement Project, East
Gary, IN to Greenwich, OH
Sverdrup Civil, Inc. (design-builder/
designer/eng./const.)

Best Civil Project Under $15 million

Aqueduct Improvement Proj., Cranston, RI
CDM Engineers and Constructors, Inc.
(design-builder)
Camp Dresser & McKee Inc. (design/eng.)
RD Installations Inc./Fyfe Inc./Structural
Preservations Systems, Inc. (const.)

Best Industrial/Process Project Over $25 million

Amtrak Acela Maintenance Facilities, Ivy
City Yard, Washington, DC;
Southhampton Yard, Boston, MA;
Sunnyside Yard, Queens, NY
STV Construction Services (design-
builder/designer/eng.)
Slattery Skanska (const.)

Honor Award:

Oxford Automotriz de Mexico
Stamping/Assembly Facility, Ramos
Arizpe, Coahuila, Mexico
Kitchell S.A. de C.V./Kitchell Constructors
Inc. of Arizona (design-builder)
SmithGroup, Inc. (designer/eng.)
Kitchell S.A. de C.V. (const.)

Best Industrial/Process Project Under $25 million

Power and Desalinization Plant,
Ascension Island, UK
Caddell Construction Company, Inc.
(design-builder/const.)
Southern Division, Naval Facilities
Engineering Command, U.S. Navy
(designer)
Robert and Company (eng.)

Excellence Award:

Knapheide Mfg. Facility, Quincy, IL
The Korte Company (design-builder/ const.)
Korte Design/Christner, Inc. (designer)
Ibrahim Engineering (eng.)

Best Project Under $5 million

Peoria Production Shop
Manufacturing/Assembly Facility,
Peoria, IL
River City Construction, LLC (design-
builder/const.)
River City Design Group, LLC (designer)
Brown Engineers, Inc. (structural eng.)
Austin Engineering (civil eng.)

Honor Award:

Superior Consultant's Microsoft Solutions
Center, Alpharetta, GA
Heery International, Inc. (design-
builder/designer/eng./const.)
The Lauck Group (design consultant)

Source: Design-Build Institute of America

National Historic Planning Landmarks

Every year the American Institute of Certified Planners (AICP), the American Planning Association's (APA) professional and educational arm, grants National Historic Planning Landmark status to up to three historically significant projects to the planning profession that are at least 25 years old. In addition, projects must have initiated a new direction in planning, made a significant contribution to the community, and be available for public use and viewing.

For additional information about National Historic Planning Landmarks, contact the AICP at (202) 872-0611 or visit them on the Web at *www.planning.org*.

Arizona
   The Salt River Project (1911)

California
   Bay Conservation and Development Commission and Creation of the San Francisco Bay Plan (1965-69)
   East Bay Regional Park District, San Francisco (1934)
   Los Angeles Co. "Master Plan of Highways" (1940) and "Freeways for the Region" (1943)
   Napa County Agricultural Preserve (1968)
   Petaluma Plan (1971-72)
   San Francisco Zoning Ordinance (1867)

Colorado
   Speer Boulevard, Denver

District of Columbia
   Euclid v. Ambler, US Supreme Court (1926)
   First National Conference on City Planning (1909)
   National Resources Planning Board (1933-43)
   Plan of Washington, DC (1791)

Georgia
   Plan of Savannah (1733)

Hawaii
   Hawaii's State Land Use Law (1961)

Illinois
   "Local Planning Administration" (1941)
   Merriam Center, Chicago (1930+)
   Plan of Chicago (1909)
   Plan of Park Forest (1948)
   Plan of Riverside (1869)

Indiana
   New Harmony (1814-27)

Kentucky
   Lexington Urban Service Area (1958)

Louisiana
   Plan of the Vieux Carre, New Orleans (1721)

Maryland
   Columbia (1967+)
   Greenbelt (A Greenbelt Town, 1935+)
   Plan of Annapolis (1695)

Massachusetts
   "Emerald Necklace" Parks, Boston (1875+)
   Founding of the Harvard University Graduate Planning Program (1929)

National Historic Planning Landmarks (Con't)

Michigan

Kalamazoo Mall (1956)

Missouri

Country Club Plaza, Kansas City (1922)

Founding of the American City Planning Institute (ACPI, 1917)

Kansas City Parks Plan (1893)

Montana

Yellowstone National Park (1872)

New Jersey

"Radburn" at Fair Lawn (1928-29)

Society for the Establishment of Useful Manufactures Plan for Paterson (1791-92)

Southern Burlington County (NJ) NAACP v Township of Mount Laurel (1975)

Yorkship Village, Camden (1918)

New York

Bronx River Parkway and the Westchester County Parkway System (1907+)

Central Park, New York City (1857)

First Houses, New York City (1935-36)

Forest Hills Gardens (1911+)

Founding of the American City Planning Institute (ACPI, 1917)

Grand Central Terminal, New York City (1903-13)

Long Island Parkways (1885) and Parks (1920s)

New York City Zoning Code (1916)

New York State Adirondack Preserve & Park

New York State Commission of Housing and Regional Planning (1923-26)

Regional Plan of New York & Environs (1929)

Second Regional Plan of the Regional Plan Association of New York (1968)

Sunnyside Gardens (1924+)

University Settlement House and the Settlement House Movement (1886)

North Carolina

Blue Ridge Parkway (1935+)

Ohio

Cincinnati Plan of 1925

Cleveland Group Plan (1903)

Founding of Ohio Planning Conference (1919)

Greenhills (A Greenbelt Town, 1935+)

Oregon

Oregon's Statewide Program for Land Use (1973)

Pennsylvania

Plan of Philadelphia (1683)

Rhode Island

College Hill Demonstration of Historic Renewal, Providence (1959)

South Carolina

First American Historic District, Charleston (1931)

Tennessee

Plan of Metro Government, Nashville/Davidson County (1956)

Tennessee Valley Authority (1933+)

Town of Norris (1933)

Texas

"A Greater Fort Worth Tomorrow" (1956)

Paseo del Rio, San Antonio (1939-41)

Utah

Plat of the City of Zion (1833)

Virginia

Blue Ridge Parkway (1935+)

Jeffersonian Precinct, University of Virginia (1817)

Monument Avenue Historic District, Richmond (1888)

Roanoke Plans (1907; 1928)

National Historic Planning Landmarks (Con't)

West Virginia
   Appalachian Trail (1921+)

Wisconsin
   Greendale (A Greenbelt Town, 1935+)
   Wisconsin Planning Enabling Act (1909)

Wyoming
   Yellowstone National Park (1872)

Source: American Institute of Certified Planners

Did you know...

The Country Club Plaza in Kansas City, MO (1922) was the first automobile-oriented suburban shopping center.

National Historic Planning Pioneers

Every year the American Institute of Certified Planners (AICP), the American Planning Association's (APA) professional and educational arm, designates up to three National Historic Planning Pioneers for their significant contributions and innovations to American planning. Recipients have impacted planning practice, education, and/or theory on a national scale with long-term beneficial results. Their contributions must have occurred no less than 25 years ago.

For additional information about National Planning Pioneers, contact the American Institute of Certified Planners at (202) 872-0611 or visit them on the Web at *www.planning.org*.

Charles Abrams	Harlean James
Frederick J. Adams	T.J. Kent Jr.
Thomas Adams	George Edward Kessler
Edmund N. Bacon	Pierre Charles L'Enfant
Harland Bartholomew	Kevin Lynch
Edward M. Bassett	Benton MacKaye
Edward H. Bennett	Ian Lennox McHarg
Alfred Bettman	Albert Mayer
Walter H. Blucher	Harold V. Miller
Ernest John Bohn	Corwin R. Mocine
Daniel Hudson Burnham	Arthur Ernest Morgan
Charles H. Cheney	Robert Moses
F. Stuart Chapin Jr.	Lewis Mumford
Paul Davidoff	Jesse Clyde Nichols
Frederic Adrian Delano	John Nolen Sr.
Earle S. Draper	Charles Dyer Norton
Simon Eisner	Charles McKim Norton
Carl Feiss	Frederick Law Olmsted Sr.
George Burdett Ford	Frederick Law Olmsted Jr.
Paul Goodman	"Outdoor Circle, The"
Percival Goodman	Harvey S. Perloff
Aelred Joseph Gray	Clarence Arthur Perry
Frederick Gutheim	John Reps
S. Herbert Hare	Jacob August Riis
Sid J. Hare	Charles Mulford Robinson
Elisabeth Herlihy	James W. Rouse
John Tasker Howard	Charlotte Rumbold
Henry Vincent Hubbard	Mel Scott
Theodora Kimball Hubbard	Ladislas Segoe

National Historic Planning Pioneers (Con't)

Flavel Shurtleff
Mary K. Simkhovitch
William E. Spangle
Clarence S. Stein
Rexford Guy Tugwell
Lawrence T. Veiller
Francis Violich
Charles Henry Wacker
Lillian Wald
Gordon Whitnall
Donald Wolbrink
Edith Elmer Wood
Henry Wright
Catherine Bauer Wurster

Source: American Institute of Certified Planners

National Medal of Arts

The National Medal of Arts was established by Congress in 1984 to honor individuals and organizations "who in the President's judgement are deserving of special recognition by reason of their outstanding contributions to the excellence, growth, support and availability of the arts in the United States." All categories of the arts are represented; although awards are not always granted in each category every year. No more than 12 medals may be awarded per year. Individuals and organizations nationwide may make nominations to the National Endowment for the Arts (NEA). The National Council on the Arts reviews these nominations and makes recommendations to the President of the United States for final selection of the annual medal. The following individuals received this honor for their work in the design profession.

Visit the NEA's Web site at *www.arts.endow.gov* for additional information or nomination forms.

1988 I.M. Pei - Architect
1989 Leopold Adler - Preservationist
1990 Ian McHarg - Landscape Architect
1991 Pietro Belluschi - Architect
1992 Robert Venturi and Denise Scott
         Brown - Architects
1995 James Ingo Freed - Architect
1997 Daniel Urban Kiley - Landscape
         Architect
1998 Frank Gehry - Architect
1999 Michael Graves - Architect

Source: National Endowment for the Arts

When the process of building is so carefully thought out that the product is thereby raised above the utilitarian, we call the product architecture.

Dora P. Crouch

P/A Awards

The P/A Awards were first handed out in 1954 by *Progressive Architecture* magazine and are now presented annually by *Architecture* magazine. The awards are designed to "recognize design excellence in unbuilt projects." A jury of designers and architects selects the winners.

For more information, visit the magazine on the Internet at *www.architecturemag.com* or call (212) 536-6221.

2000 P/A Award Winners:

The Blur Building
Yverdon-les-Bains, Switzerland
Diller + Scofidio

M.I.T. Residence 2001
Cambridge, Massachusetts
Steven Holl Architects

Torus House and Studio for Eric Wolf
Columbia Country, New York
Preston Scott Cohen

A Shroud for Bathing
New Orleans, Louisiana
Eskew+

Nelson-Atkins Museum of Art Expansion
Kansas City, Missouri
Steven Holl Architects

2000 P/A Award Citations:

Inner City Arts Addition and Renovation
Los Angeles, California
Michael Maltzan Architecture

Big Belt House
Meagher County, Montana
William E. Massie

MTA 101 Pedestrian Bridge
Los Angeles, California
Morphosis

Tulane University Center Addition and
  Remodel
New Orleans, Louisiana
Vincent James Associates

SPA
Culver City , California
Eric Owen Moss Architects

JVC Convention and Exhibition Center
Zapopan, Mexico
TEN Arquitectos

InSideOutSide House
Houston, Texas
Studio Works

Dundas Square
Toronto, Canada
Brown & Storey Architects

Pennsylvania Station Redevelopment
  Project
New York, New York
Skidmore, Owings & Merrill

2000 P/A Award Jury:

Richard Koshalek
Michael Rotondi
Brigitte Shim
Ben Van Berkel
Marion Weiss

Source: Architecture *magazine*

Philip Johnson Award

With its Philip Johnson Award, the Society of Architectural Historians (SAH) annually recognizes an outstanding architectural exhibition catalogue. In order to be eligible for this annual recognition, the catalogue must have been published within the preceding two years.

For more information contact the SAH at (312) 573-1365 or visit their Web site at *www.sah.org.*

1990
> *Los Angeles Blueprints for Modern Living: History and Legacy of the Case Study Houses* by Elizabeth A.T. Smith (The Museum of Contemporary Art and MIT Press)

1991
> *Architecture and Its Image: Four Centuries of Architectural Representation, Works from the Collection of the Canadian Centre for Architecture* by Eve Blau and Edward Kaufman, eds. (The Canadian Centre for Architecture and MIT Press)

1992
> no award granted

1993
> *The Making of Virginia Architecture* by Charles Brownell (Virginia Museum of Fine Arts and the University Press of Virginia)

> Louis Kahn: In the Realm of Architecture by David Brownlee (The Museum of Contemporary Art and Rizzoli International)

1994
> *Chicago Architecture and Design 1923-1993: Reconfiguration of an American Metropolis* by John Zukowsky (Prestel and Art Institute of Chicago)

1995
> *The Palladian Revival: Lord Burlington, His Villa and Garden in Chiswick* by John Harris (Yale University Press)

1996
> *The Perspective of Anglo-American Architecture* by James F. O'Gorman (The Athenaeum of Philadelphia)

> *An Everyday Modernism: The Houses of William Wurster* by Marc Treib (San Francisco Museum of Modern Art and the University of California Press)

1997
> *Sacred Realm: The Emergence of the Synagogue in the Ancient World* by Steven Fine (Yeshiva University Museum and Oxford University Press)

1998
> *Building for Air Travel: Architecture and Design for Commercial Aviation* by John Zukowsky (Art Institute of Chicago and Prestel)

1999
> *The Work of Charles and Ray Eames: a Legacy of Invention* by Donald Albrecht (The Library of Congress, Vitra Design Museum, and Abrams Publishing)

2000
> *E.W. Godwin: Aesthetic Movement Architect and Designer* by Susan Weber Soros (Yale University Press)

Source: Society of Architectural Historians

Praemium Imperiale

The Praemium Imperiale is awarded by the Japan Art Association, Japan's premier cultural institution, for lifetime achievement in the fields of painting, sculpture, music, architecture, and theater/film. The following individuals received this honor for architecture which includes a commemorative medal and a 15,000,000 yen ($125,000 approx.) honorarium.

For more information visit the Japan Art Association's Web site at *www.japanart.or.jp/en/.*

1989 I. M. Pei (United States)
1990 James Stirling (U.K.)
1991 Gae Aulenti (Italy)
1992 Frank Gehry (United States)
1993 Kenzo Tange (Japan)
1994 Charles Correa (India)
1995 Renzo Piano (Italy)
1996 Tadao Ando (Japan)
1997 Richard Meier (United States)
1998 Alvaro Siza (Portugal)
1999 Fumihiko Maki (Japan)
2000 Richard Rogers (U.K.)

Source: Japan Art Association

Make no small plans; they have no magic to stir men's blood. Make big plans; aim high in hope and in work, remembering that a noble and logical diagram once recorded will never die, but long after we are gone will be a living thing.

Daniel Burnham

Presidential Design Awards

Established by President Ronald Reagan in 1983, the Presidential Design Awards recognize outstanding contributions to federal design by government agencies and employees and private designers in the categories of architecture, engineering, graphic design, historic preservation, interior design, landscape architecture, industrial & product design, and urban design & planning. The Presidential Design Awards are administered by the National Endowment for the Arts (NEA) and are presented every four years. The program includes two levels of awards: Federal Design Achievement Awards are merit awards given by the National Endowment for the Arts as its highest recognition of quality design; and Presidential Awards for Design Excellence are presented by the President of the United States for design of the highest quality in accordance with international standards. Works that have been sponsored, authorized, commissioned, produced or supported by the Government of the United States of America and completed in the 10 years prior to the date of the award are eligible. Projects are judged based on their purpose, leadership, cost, aesthetics and performance. For Round Four of the Presidential Design Awards in 1995, the jury selected 75 projects to receive Federal Design Achievement Awards. Of these, nine were recommended to receive Presidential Awards for Design Excellence, which are listed below.

For a detailed description of the winners from both award programs and photographs of the projects listed below, visit the NEA's Web site at *www.arts.endow.gov*.

1995 Presidential Awards for Design Excellence Recipients:

Focus: HOPE Center for Advanced
  Technologies
Detroit, Michigan
Smith Hinchman & Grylls Assoc., Inc.

The Byron White United States
  Courthouse
Denver, Colorado
Michael Barber Architecture

United States Holocaust Memorial Museum
Washington, DC
Pei Cobb Freed & Partners

United States Holocaust Memorial
  Museum Permanent Exhibition
Washington, DC
Ralph Appelbaum Associates Incorporated

The Double Arch Bridge of the Natchez
  Trace Parkway
Franklin, Tennessee
Figg Engineering Group

Presidential Design Awards (Con't)

Interstate 90 Completion Project
Seattle, Washington
Washington State Department of
   Transportation

River Relocation Project
Providence, Rhode Island
William D. Warner, Architects & Planners
   and Maguire Group, Inc.

The Cooper-Hewitt, National Museum of
   Design, Smithsonian Institution
New York, New York
Smithsonian Institution, Cooper-Hewitt,
   National Design Museum

FDA Food Label Design
Greenfield/Belser Ltd.

Juries:

Donlyn Lyndon (chair)

*Architecture/Preservation and Interior Design
Jury:*
   Graham Gund (chair), Beverly Russell,
   Adèle Naudé Santos, Dr. Sharon E. Sutton,
   Jane Thompson, Cynthia Weese, Amy
   Weinstein

*Graphic Design and Product/Industrial Design
Jury:*
   Richard Saul Wurman (chair), Bryce
   Ambo, Robert Brunner, Matthew Carter,
   Nancye Green, Richard Poulin, Patrick
   Whitney, Lorraine Wild

*Landscape Architecture, Urban Design and
Planning Jury:*
   Everett L. Fly (chair), Michael Barker,
   Catherine Brown

Engineering Jury:
   Guy Nordenson (chair), Joseph P. Colaco,
   Virginia Fairweather, Joe Passonneau

Source: U.S. General Services Administration and the
National Endowment for the Arts

Pritzker Architecture Prize

In 1979 Jay and Cindy Pritzker, through the Hyatt Foundation, established the Pritzker Architecture Prize to inspire greater creativity among the architectural profession and to generate a heightened public awareness about architecture. Today it is revered as one of the highest honors in the field of architecture. The Prize is awarded each year to a living architect whose body of work represents a longstanding, significant contribution to the built environment. Nominations are accepted every January from any interested party. Architects from all nations are eligible. Laureates of the Pritzker Prize receive a $100,000 grant, citation certificate, and a bronze medallion.

For additional information, visit their Web site at *www.pritzker prize.com.*

1979	Philip Johnson (United States)	1991	Robert Venturi (United States)
1980	Luis Barragan (Mexico)	1992	Alvaro Siza (Portugal)
1981	James Stirling (U.K.)	1993	Fumihiko Maki (Japan)
1982	Kevin Roche (United States)	1994	Christian de Portzamparc
1983	Ieoh Ming Pei (United States)		(France)
1984	Richard Meier (United States)	1995	Tadao Ando (Japan)
1985	Hans Hollein (Austria)	1996	Rafael Moneo (Spain)
1986	Gottfried Boehm (Germany)	1997	Sverre Fehn (Norway)
1987	Kenzo Tange (Japan)	1998	Renzo Piano (Italy)
1988	Gordon Bunshaft (United States)	1999	Sir Norman Foster (U.K.)
	Oscar Niemeyer (Brazil)	2000	Rem Koolhaas (Netherlands)
1989	Frank O. Gehry (United States)		
1990	Aldo Rossi (Italy)		

Source: The Pritzker Architecture Prize

Opposite: Nexus Housing, Fukuoka, Japan, Rem Koolhaas
Photographer: Kawano

Pulitzer Prize for Architectural Criticism

As one of the many lasting contributions he made to the field of journalism, Joseph Pulitzer established the Pulitzer Prize as an incentive to excellence in journalism, music, and letters. Over the years the scope of the awards has been expanded from its original 1917 configuration. Since 1970, the Pulitzer Prize Board has awarded a prize for distinguished journalistic criticism. In the past this category has included winners in the arts, culture, and literary fields. The following individuals received this honor for their work in architectural criticism.

Visit the Pulitzer Prize's Web site at *www.pulitzer.org* for a detailed history, chronology, and archive of past winners.

1970	Ada Louise Huxtable	1990	Allan Temko
	The New York Times		*San Francisco Chronicle*
1979	Paul Gapp	1996	Robert Campbell
	Chicago Tribune		*The Boston Globe*
1984	Paul Goldberger	1999	Blair Kamin
	The New York Times		*Chicago Tribune*

Since 1980 the Pulitzer Prize Board has also acknowledged the two finalists in each category. The following individuals were finalists for their work in architectural criticism.

1981	Allan Temko	1988	Allan Temko
	San Francisco Chronicle		*San Francisco Chronicle*
1983	Beth Dunlop	1997	Herbert Muschamp
	The Miami Herald		*The New York Times*

Source: The Pulitzer Prize Board

RAIA Gold Medal

The Gold Medal is the highest honor bestowed by the Royal Australian Institute of Architects (RAIA). It is presented annually to an architect to recognize a career of distinguished service achieved through a body of designs of high merit, advancement of the architecture profession, or an endowment of the profession in a distinguished manner. Gold medallists are nominated by their peers in confidence, and a jury comprised of past medallists and the national president make the final selection. Since 1970, the Gold Medallist traditionally delivers the AS Hook Address, named in memory of the early RAIA promoter Alfred Samuel Hook, that provides insight into the life, work, and principles of the Gold Medallist and the state of the profession at the time.

For additional information about the Gold Medal or to read past AS Hook Addresses, visit the RAIA on the Internet at *www.raia.com.au.*

1960	Emeritus Prof. Leslie Wilkinson	1983	Gilbert Ridgway Nicol and Ross Kingsley Chisholm
1961	Louis Layborne-Smith		
1962	Joseph Charles Fowell	1984	Philip Sutton Cox
1963	Sir Arthur Stephenson	1985	Prof. Richard Norman Johnson
1964	Cobden Parkes	1986	Richard Butterworth
1965	Sir Osborn McCutcheon	1987	Daryl Sanders Jackson
1966	William Rae Laurie	1988	Romaldo Giurgola
1967	William Purves Race Godfrey	1989	Robin Findlay Gibson
1968	Sir Roy Grounds	1990	Prof. Peter McIntyre
1969	Robin Boyd	1991	Donald Campbell Rupert Bailey
1970	Jack Hobbs McConnell	1992	Glenn Marcus Murcutt
1971	Frederick Bruce Lucas	1993	Kenneth Frank Woolley
1972	Edward Herbert Farmer	1994	Neville Quarry
1973	Jørn Utzon	1995	no award granted
1974	Raymond Berg	1996	Denton Corker Marshall
1975	Sydney Edward Ancher	1997	Roy Simpson
1976	Harry Seidler	1998	Gabriel Poole
1977	Ronald Andrew Gilling	1999	Richard Leplastrier
1978	Mervyn Henry Parry	2000	John Morphett
1979	Harold Bryce Mortlock		
1980	John Hamilton Andrews		
1981	Colin Frederick Madigan		*Source: Royal Australian Institute of Architects*
1982	Sir John Wallace Overall		

RAIC Gold Medal

The Royal Architectural Institute of Canada (RAIC) began its Gold Medal program in 1967 to recognize the achievements of architects or individuals related to the field and their contributions to Canada's built environment. As the RAIC Gold Medal is merit based, awards are not always granted yearly.

For more information, contact the RAIC at (613) 241-3600 or visit their Web site at *www.raic.org*.

1967	Mayor Jean Drapeau	1985	John Bland
1968	The Right Honorable Vincent Massey	1986	Ed Zeidler
1970	Dr. Eric R. Arthur	1989	Raymond T. Affleck
1970	The Late John A. Russell	1991	Phyllis Lambert
1973	Professor Serge Chermayeff	1992	Doug Shadbolt
1976	Dr. Constantinos Doxiadis	1994	Barton Myers
1979	John C. Parkin	1995	Moshe Safdie
1981	Jane Jacobs	1997	Raymond Moriyama
1982	Ralph Erskine	1998	Frank O. Gehry
1984	Arthur Erickson	1999	Douglas Cardinal

Source: The Royal Architectural Institute of Canada

RIBA Royal Gold Medal

Presented annually for distinction in architecture, the Royal Gold Medal is presented by Her Majesty the Queen on the advice of the Royal Institute of British Architects (RIBA). Since it was first granted by Queen Victoria in 1848, the RIBA confers the Royal Gold Medal annually.

For additional information, visit the RIBA on the Internet at *www.architecture.com.*

1848	Charles Robert Cockerell	1882	Baron von Ferstel
1849	Luigi Canine	1883	Fras. Cranmer Penrose
1850	Sir Charles Barry	1884	William Butterfield
1851	Thomas L. Donaldson	1885	H. Schliemann
1852	Leo von Klenze	1886	Charles Garnier
1853	Sir Robert Smirke	1887	Ewan Christian
1854	Philip Hardwick	1888	Baron von Hansen
1855	J. I. Hittorff	1889	Sir Charles T. Newton
1856	Sir William Tite	1890	John Gibson
1857	Owen Jones	1891	Sir Arthur Blomfield
1858	August Stuler	1892	Cesar Daly
1859	Sir George Gilbert Scott	1893	Richard Morris Hunt
1860	Sydney Smirke	1894	Lord Leighton
1861	J. B. Lesueur	1895	James Brooks
1862	Rev. Robert Willis	1896	Sir Ernest George
1863	Anthony Salvin	1897	Dr. P.J.H.Cuypers
1864	E. Violett-le-Duc	1898	George Aitchison
1865	Sir James Pennethorne	1899	George Frederick Badley
1866	Sir M. Digby Wyatt	1900	Rodolfo Amadeo Lancani
1867	Charles Texier	1901	*(Not awarded due to the death of Queen Victoria)*
1868	Sir Henery Layard		
1869	C.R. Lepsius	1902	Thomas Edward Collcutt
1870	Benjamin Ferrey	1903	Charles F. McKim
1871	James Fergusson	1904	Auguste Choisy
1872	Baron von Schmidt	1905	Sir Aston Webb
1873	Thomas Henry Wyatt	1906	Sir L. Alma-Taderna
1874	George Edmund Street	1907	John Belcher
1875	Edmund Sharpe	1908	Honore Daumet
1876	Joseph Louis Duc	1909	Sir Arthur John Evans
1877	Charles Barry	1910	Sir Thomas Graham Jackson Bart
1878	Alfred Waterhouse	1911	Wilhelm Dorpfeld
1879	Marquis de Vogue	1912	Basil Champneys
1880	John L. Peerson	1913	Sir Reginald Blomfield RA
1881	George Godwin	1914	Jean Louis Pascal

RIBA Royal Gold Medal (Con't)

1915	Frank Darling	1960	Pier Luigi Nervi
1916	Sir Robert Rowand Anderson	1961	Lewis Mumford
1917	Henri Paul Nenot	1962	Sven Gottfrid Markeluis
1918	Ernest Newton RA	1963	The Lord Holford
1919	Leonard Stokes	1964	E. Maxwell Fry
1920	Charles Louis Girault	1965	Kenzo Tange
1921	Sir Edwin Landseer Lutyens	1966	Ove Arup
1922	Thomas Hastings	1967	Sir Nikolaus Pevsner
1923	Sir John James Burnet	1968	Dr. Richard Buckminster Fuller
1924	(Not awarded)	1969	Jack Antonio Coia
1925	Sir Giles Gilbert Scott	1970	Sir Robert Mathew
1926	Ragnar Ostberg	1971	Hubert de Cronin Hastings
1927	Sir Herbert Baker	1972	Louis I. Kahn
1928	Sir Guy Dawber	1973	Sir Leslie Martin
1929	Victor Alexandre Frederic Laloux	1974	Powell & Moya
1930	Sir Percy Scott Worthington	1975	Michael Scott
1931	Sir Edwin Cooper	1976	Sir John Summerson
1932	Dr. Hendrik Petrus Berlage	1977	Sir Denys Lasdun
1933	Sir Charles Reed Peers	1978	Jorn Utzon
1934	Henry Vaughan Lanchester	1979	The Office of Charles and Ray Eames
1935	Willem Marinus Dudok	1980	James Stirling
1936	Charles Henry Holden	1981	Sir Philip Dowson
1937	Sir Raymond Unwin	1982	Berthold Lubetkin
1938	Ivar Tengborn	1983	Sir Norman Foster
1939	Sir Percy Thomas	1984	Charles Correa
1940	Charles Francis Annesley Voysey	1985	Sir Richard Rogers
1941	Frank Lloyd Wright	1986	Arata Isozaki
1942	William Curtis Green	1987	Ralph Erskine
1943	Sir Charles Herbert Reilly	1988	Richard Meier
1944	Sir Edward Maufe	1989	Renzo Piano
1945	Victor Vesnin	1990	Aldo van Eyck
1946	Sir Patrick Abercrombie	1991	Coin Stansfield Smith
1947	Sir Albert Edward Richardson	1992	Peter Rice
1948	Auguste Perret	1993	Giancarlo de Carlo
1949	Sir Howard Robertson	1994	Michael and Patty Hopkins
1950	Eliel Saarinen	1995	Colin Rowe
1951	Emanuel Vincent Harris	1996	Harry Seidler
1952	George Grey Wornum	1997	Tadao Ando
1953	Le Corbusier (C.E. Jeanneret)	1998	Oscar Niemeyer
1954	Sir Arthur George Staphenson	1999	Barcelona, Spain
1955	John Murray Easton	2000	Frank Gehry
1956	Dr. Walter Adolf Georg Gropius		
1957	Hugo Alvar Henrik Aalto		
1958	Robert Schofield Morris		
1959	Ludwig Mies van der Rohe		

Source: Royal Institute of British Architects

Opposite: Frank Gehry
Photographer: Thomas Mayer

Rudy Bruner Award for Urban Excellence

The biennial Rudy Bruner Award for Urban Excellence is awarded to projects which approach urban problems with creative inclusion of often competing political, community, environmental, and formal considerations. Established in 1987, the Award recognizes one Gold Medal Winner and four Silver Medal winners. Any project which fosters urban excellence is eligible to apply. A multi-disciplinary Selection Committee performs an on-site evaluation of each finalist before final selections are made.

For photographs and project descriptions, visit the Bruner Foundation on the Internet at *www.brunerfoundation.org* or contact them at (617) 876-8404.

1999 Gold Medal Winner:
Yerba Buena Gardens
San Francisco, CA

1999 Silver Winners:
ARTScorpsLA, Inc.
Los Angeles, California

National Aids Memorial Grove, Golden Gate Park
San Francisco, California

Parkside Preservation
Philadelphia, Pennsylvania

The Portland Public Market
Portland, Maine

1999 Selection Committee:
Curtis Davis, AIA
Lawrence P. Goldman
Min Kantrowitz, AICP, M. Arch
Rick Lowe, Founding Director
Frieda Molina
Hon. Tom Murphy

Source: The Bruner Foundation

Good cities and good neighborhoods are made with a certain amount of building harmony and an understanding that buildings are a background for human activity in the public realm.

Elizabeth Plater-Zyberk

Russel Wright Award

Established by Manitoga, The Russel Wright Center in Garrison, New York, the Russel Wright Award honors individuals who are working in the tradition of the mid-twentieth century design pioneer Russel Wright (1904-1976) to provide outstanding design to the general public. Russel Wright was a well-known home furnishings designer in the 1930s through the 1950s who throughout his career maintained the importance of making well-designed objects accessible to the public. The 75-acre wooded landscape he sculpted, Manitoga, is on the National Register of Historic Places and includes Dragon Rock, the home he designed that exemplifies his philosophy that architecture should enhance rather than dominate its surroundings.

For additional information about the Russel Wright Award, contact the Russel Wright Center, Manitoga, at (914) 424-3812 or *www.manitoga.org.*

2000   Michael Graves

Source: Manitoga, The Russel Wright Center

My goal is to bring to American culture an intimacy with nature.

Russel Wright

SEGD Design Awards

The Society for Environmental Graphic Design's (SEGD) Design Awards recognize the best in environmental design – the planning, design, and specifying of graphic elements in the built and natural environment. Eligible projects include signage, wayfinding systems, mapping, exhibit design, themed environments, retail spaces, sports facilities and campus design. A jury of professionals reviews the entries to determine which projects best help to identify, direct, inform, interpret, and visually enhance our surroundings. Three levels of awards are granted – Honor Awards, Merit Awards, and the Juror Award. Winners are announced at SEGD's annual conference each spring and are honored in an annual exhibition and bi-annual publication.

For photographs and project description of all the winning entries, visit SEGD's Web site at *www.segd.org*.

2000 Honor Awards:

The Endurance: Shackleton's Legendary Antarctic Expedition
American Museum of Natural History, New York
AMNH Exhibition Department

Hancock Park
Los Angeles, California
Sussman/Prejza & Company

Levi's Mothership Exhibit, Magic Show
Las Vegas, Nevada
Mauk Design

Tiles of the Ocean
Lisbon, Portugal
Chermayeff & Geismar

CompUSA (Apple Computer)
San Francisco, California
marchFIRST (formerly US Web/CKS) and Eight, Inc.

2000 Merit Awards:

Board of Trade Sculpture
Kansas City, Missouri
Gastinger Walker Harden Architects

The Block at Orange
Orange, California
CommArts

Specialty Graphics for Paris Las Vegas Casino Resort
Las Vegas, Nevada
Studio Arts & Letters

Wildhorse Saloon
Walt Disney World Pleasure Island, Lake Buena Vista, Florida
Daroff Design/DDI Architects/DDI Graphics

Chicago Streetscape Signage Standards Manual
Chicago, Illinois
Two Twelve Harakawa

SEGD Design Awards (Con't)

Aveda Retail Prototype
Southdale, Minnesota
Gensler (New York)

Ducati Showroom Prototype
New York, New York
Gensler (New York)

Epidemic! The World of Infectious Disease
American Museum of Natural History,
    New York
AMNH Exhibition Department

Geneva Telecom'99
Geneva, Switzerland
Nth Degree

Pasadena Unified School District
Pasadena, California
Hunt Design Associates

Grand Central Terminal Retail Directory
    Map and Metro North Map
New York, New York
Two Twelve Harakawa

Birmingham Flight Sequence
Birmingham, Alabama
Lorenc/Yoo Design

Salem State College
Salem, Massachusetts
Solbert Perkins Design Collaborative

Frank G. Wells Building
Burbank, California
Venturi, Scott Brown & Associates with
    HKS Architects

Downtown Indianapolis Signage Program
Indianapolis, Indiana
Corbin Design

Paradise Valley Mall Children's Playcourt
Paradise Valley, Arizona
Thinking Caps

Concord Mills
Concord, North Carolina
Kiku Obata & Company

Concerns of the Day (student entry)
Market House Gallery, Providence, Rhode
    Island
Cheryl Hanba and Molly Schoenhoff

Levi's Original Spin Store Design
New York, Chicago, Boston
Morla Design

Camper Gallery: Whittlin' History
Delaware Agricultural Museum & Village,
    Dover, Delaware
Ueland Junker McCauley Nicholson

Michael Graves Press Event
The Whitney Museum of American Art,
    New York
Design Guys

Federal Reserve Interpretive Plaques
Federal Reserve Bank 9th District HQ
HOK

USAID, Reagan Building
Washington, DC
Chermayeff & Geismar

Michael Jordan's The Steakhouse
New York, New York
Rockwell Group

The Home Depot – The Legend
Atlanta, GA
Caribiner International

Corning Museum of Glass
Glass Innovation Center, Corning, New
    York
Ralph Appelbaum Associates

SEGD Design Awards (Con't)

Flight of the Creative Spirit: Robert
  Crawford
Fairbanks North Star Borough School
  District, Eiclson AFB, Alaska
Koryn Rolstad Studios

Monsanto Childcare Center
St. Louis, Missouri
Hellmuth, Obata & Kassabaum (HOK)
  with Tempus Fugit

Village Works: Photographs by Women in
  China's Yunnan Province
Wellesley, Massachusetts
Pentagram Design

Nike World Campus North Expansion
Beaverton, Oregon
Ambrosini Design

Nike World Campus: "The Park"
Beaverton, Oregon
Ambrosini Design

Stay Cool! Air Conditioning America
National Building Museum, Wash. DC
Pentagram Design

Teledesic Headquarters
Bellevue, Washington
NBBJ Graphic Design

2000 Juror Award:
  Muvico Paradise 24 Theater
  Davie, Florida
  Development Design Group

2000 Jury:
  Anne Tryba, Chair
  Alexander Isley
  David Manfredi
  Karal Ann Marling
  Michael Stanton

Source: Society for Environmental Graphic Design

Sir Patrick Abercrombie Prize

The International Union of Architects (UIA) grants this triennial award to an internationally renowned architect or architects for significant work in town planning and territorial development.

For more information, visit the UIA's Web site at *www.uia-architectes.org*.

1961 Town Planning Service of the City of Stockholm (S. Markelius and G. Onblahd, Sweden)

1963 G. Dioxiadis (Greece)

1965 C. Buchanan and team (United Kingdom)
T. Farkas and team (Hungary)

1967 G. De Carlo (Italy)

1969 H. Bennet and team (United Kingdom)
Honrary Mention:
Belaunde Terry (Peru)

1972 Centre for Experimentation, Research and Training (Morocco)

1975 Iosif Bronislavovitch Orlov and Nilolai Ivanovitch Simonov (USSR)

1978 The City of Louvain la Neuve (Belgium)

1981 Warsaw architects (Poland) for the reconstruction of their capital
Honorary Mention:
M. Balderiotte and team (Argentina)

1984 Hans Blumenfeld (Canada)
Lucio Costa (Brazil)

1987 AIA Regional/Urban Design Assistance Team (R/UDAT) (USA)
Honorary Mention:
Eduardo Leira (Spain)
L. Bortenreuter, K. Griebel and H.G. Tiedt for the remodeling of the city center of Gera (Germany)

1990 Edmund N. Bacon (USA)

1993 Jan Gehl (Denmark)

1996 Juan Gil Elizondo (Mexico)

1999 Karl Ganser (Germany)
Honorary Mention:
Master plan of the city of Shenzhen (People's Republic of China)

Source: International Union of Architects

Design is dream-building. It is the process by which we are remaking the world in our own image.

Alan Robbins

Sir Robert Matthew Prize

The International Union of Architects (UIA) awards the Sir Robert Matthew Prize triennially to an internationally renowned architect or architects whose work has improved the quality of human settlements.

For more information, visit the UIA's web site at *www.uia-architectes.org.*

1978 John F.C. Turner (U.K.)
1981 Hassan Fathy (Egypt);
      Honorary Mention:
      Rod Hackney (U.K.) and
      Hardt Walther Hamer (GFR)
1984 Charles Correa (India)
1987 Housing Reconstruction
      Programme for the City of
      Mexico (Mexico)
1990 Department of Architecture of
      the Singapore Housing &
      Development Board
      (Singapore)

1993 Laurie Baker (U.K.)
1996 Professor Giancarlo De Carlo (Italy)
      Jury citation:
      Oberste Baubehörde (the
      German team under the guid-
      ance of architect Benno
      Brugger and led by Hans Jörg
      Nussberger)
1999 Martin Treberspurg (Austria)
      Honorary Mention:
      Development & Construction
      Branch of the Hong Kong
      Housing Department

Source: International Union of Architects (UIA)

Did you know...

Since the establishment of Singapore's public housing authority in 1960, they have built over 800,000 apartments in which 86% of their population live.

Spiro Kostof Book Award

The Society of Architectural Historians (SAH) grants the annual Spiro Kostof Award to a work that has made the greatest contribution to understanding the historical development of the change in urbanism and architecture.

For more information, contact the SAH at (312) 573-1365 or visit their Web site at *www.sah.org.*

1994
Architecture Power and National Identity by Lawrence J. Vale (Yale University Press)

1995
In the Theatre of Criminal Justice: The Palais de Justice in Second Empire Paris by Katherine Fischer Taylor (Princeton University Press)

1996
The Topkapi Scroll: Geometry and Ornament in Islamic Architecture by Gülru Necipoglu (Getty Center for the History of Art and Humanities)

1997
The Projective Cast: Architecture and Its Three Geometries by Robin Evans (MIT Press)

Auschwitz: 1270 to the Present by Debórah Dwork and Robert Jan van Pelt (Norton)

1998
The Architects and the City by Robert Bruegmann (University of Chicago Press)

Magnetic Los Angeles by Gregory Hise (Johns Hopkins Press)

1999
City Center to Regional Mall: Architecture, the Automobile and Retailing in Los Angeles, 1920-1950 by Richard Longstreth (MIT Press)

Housing Design and Society in Amsterdam: Reconfiguring Urban Order and Identity, 1900-1920 by Nancy Stieber (University of Chicago Press)

2000
The Architecture of Red Vienna 1919-1934 by Eve Blau (MIT Press)

Source: Society of Architectural Historians

Star Award

Through its Star Award the International Interior Design Association (IIDA) recognizes individuals who have made an outstanding contribution to the interior design profession. No more than one award is granted each year. However, as this is merit based, awards are not always given each year. Although non-members are eligible for the Star Award, the IIDA Board of Directors, the selection body, only accepts nominations from IIDA Fellows, chapter presidents, and directors.

For more information about the Star Award, visit IIDA's Web site at *www.iida.org* or contact them at (888) 799-4432.

1985	Lester Dundes	1994	Michael Kroelinger
1986	William Sullivan	1995	Douglas R. Parker
1987	Orlando Diaz-Azcuy	1997	Michael Wirtz
1988	Paul Brayton	1998	Charles and Ray Eames
1989	Florence Knoll Bassett	1999	Michael Brill
1990	Beverly Russell	2000	Eva L. Maddox
1991	Stanley Abercrombie		
1992	M. Arthur Gensler Jr.		
1993	Sivon C. Reznikoff		

Source: International Interior Designers Association

Opposite: Eva Maddox

Thomas Jefferson Award for Public Architecture

The Thomas Jefferson Award for Public Architecture is presented annually by The American Institute of Architects (AIA) to recognize and foster the importance of design excellence in government and infrastructure projects. Awards are presented in three categories:

- Category One – Private sector architects who have amassed a portfolio of accomplished and distinguished public facilities (C1)
- Category Two – Public sector architects who produce quality projects within their agencies (C2)
- Category Three – Public officials or others who have been strong advocates for design excellence (C3)

For more information, visit the AIA on the Internet at *www.e-architect.org* or contact the AIA Honors and Awards Department at (202) 626-7586.

1992 James Ingo Freed (C1)
George M. White (C2)
The Honorable Patrick J. Moynihan (C3)

1993 The Honorable Jack Brooks (C3)

1994 Richard Dattner (C1)
M.J. "Jay" Brodie (C2)
The Honorable Joseph P. Riley Jr. (C3)

1995 Herbert S. Newman (C1)
Edward A. Feiner (C2)
Henry G. Cisneros (C3)

1996 Thomas R. Aidala (C2)
The Honorable Douglas P. Woodlock (C3)

1997 John Tarantino (C2)
Richard A. Kahan (C3)
Hunter Morrison (C3)

1998 Arthur Rosenblatt (C2)

1999 Lewis Davis (C1)
Robert Kroin (C2)

2000 Charles Emil Peterson (C2)
Jay Chatterjee (C3)

Source: The American Institute of Architects

TOPAZ Medallion

The TOPAZ Medallion is jointly awarded by The American Institute of Architects (AIA) and the American Collegiate Schools of Architecture (ACSA) to honor individuals who have made an outstanding contribution to the field of architectural education. Candidates are nominated by colleagues, students and former students. Recipients have made a significant impact on the field of architecture, expanded into fields beyond their specialty, and affected a lasting impact on their students.

For additional information about this award program, visit the AIA's Web site at *www.e-architect.com.*

1976	Jean Labatut Princeton University
1977	Henry Kamphoefner North Carolina State University
1978	Lawrence Anderson MIT
1979	G. Holmes Perkins University of Pennsylvania
1980	Serge Chermayeff Yale University
1981	Marcel Breuer Harvard University
1982	Joseph Esherick University of California, Berkeley
1983	Charles E. Burchard Virginia Polytechnic University
1984	Robert Geddes Princeton
1985	Colin Rowe Cornell University
1986	Vincent Scully Jr. Yale University
1987	Ralph Rapson University of Minnesota
1988	John Hejduk Cooper Union
1989	Charles Moore, University of California, Berkeley
1990	Raymond L. Kappe Southern California Institute of Architecture
1991	Kenneth B. Frampton Columbia University
1992	Spiro Kostof University of California, Berkeley*
1993	Mario Salvadori Columbia University
1994	Harlan E. McClure Clemson University
1995	Henry N. Cobb Harvard University
1996	Denise Scott Brown University of Pennsylvania
1997	Donlyn Lyndon University of California, Berkeley
1998	Werner Seligmann Syracuse University
1999	W. Cecil Steward University of Nebraska
2000	Alan H. Balfour Rensselaer Polytechnic Institute

* honored posthumously

Source: The American Institute of Architects

Twenty-Five Year Award

Awarded annually by The American Institute of Architects (AIA), the Twenty-Five Year Award is presented to projects which excel under the test of time. Projects must have been completed 25 to 35 years ago by an architect licensed in the United States, though the nominated facility may be located anywhere in the world. To be eligible submissions must still be carrying out their original program and demonstrate a continued viability in their function and form.

For more information, visit the AIA on the Internet at *www.e-architect.org* or contact the AIA Honors and Awards Department at (202) 626-7586.

1969
Rockefeller Center
New York City, NY
Reinhard & Hofmeister; Corbett, Harrison & MacMurray

1971
The Crow Island School
Winnetka, IL
Perkins, Wheeler & Will; Eliel & Eero Saarinen

1972
Baldwin Hills Village
Los Angeles, CA
Reginald D. Johnson; Wilson, Merrill & Alexander; Clarence S. Stein

1973
Taliesin West
Paradise Valley, AZ
Frank Lloyd Wright

1974
S.C. Johnson & Son Administration Building
Racine, WI
Frank Lloyd Wright

1975
Philip Johnson's Residence ("The Glass House")
New Caanan, CT
Philip Johnson

1976
860-880 North Lakeshore Drive Apartments
Chicago, IL
Ludwig Mies van der Rohe

1977
Christ Lutheran Church
Minneapolis, MN
Saarinen, Saarinen & Associates; Hills, Gilbertson & Hays

1978
The Eames House
Pacific Palisades, CA
Charles and Ray Eames

1979
Yale University Art Gallery
New Haven, CT
Louis I. Kahn, FAIA

1980
Lever House
New York City, NY
Skidmore, Owings & Merrill

1981
Farnsworth House
Plano, IL
Ludwig Mies van der Rohe

Opposite: Smith House, Darien, CT, Richard Meier & Partners
Photograph © Scott Frances/Esto

Twenty-Five Year Award (Con't)

1982
Equitable Savings and Loan Building
Portland, OR
Pietro Belluschi, FAIA

1983
Price Tower
Bartlesville, OK
Frank Lloyd Wright

1984
Seagram Building
New York City, NY
Ludwig Mies van der Rohe

1985
General Motors Technical Center
Warren, MI
Eero Saarinen and Associates with Smith,
Hinchman & Grylls

1986
Solomon R. Guggenheim Museum
New York City, NY
Frank Lloyd Wright

1987
Bavinger House
Norman, OK
Bruce Goff

1988
Dulles International Airport Terminal
Building
Chantilly, VA
Eero Saarinen and Associates

1989
Vanna Venturi House
Chestnut Hill, PA
Robert Venturi, FAIA

1990
The Gateway Arch
St. Louis, MO
Eero Saarinen and Associates

1991
Sea Ranch Condominium I
The Sea Ranch, CA
Moore Lyndon Turnbull Whitaker

1992
The Salk Institute for Biological Studies
La Jolla, CA
Louis I. Kahn, FAIA

1993
Deere & Company Administrative Center
Moline, IL
Eero Saarinen and Associates

1994
The Haystack Mountain School of Crafts
Deer Isle, ME
Edward Larrabee Barnes

1995
The Ford Foundation Headquarters
New York City, NY
Kevin Roche John Dinkeloo and
Associates

1996
The Air Force Academy Cadet Chapel
Colorado Springs, CO
Skidmore, Owings & Merrill

1997
Phillips Exeter Academy Library
Exeter, NH
Louis I. Kahn, FAIA

1998
Kimbell Art Museum
Fort Worth, TX
Louis I. Kahn, FAIA

1999
The John Hancock Center
Chicago, IL
Skidmore, Owings & Merrill

2000
The Smith House
Darien, CT
Richard Meier & Partners

Source: The American Institute of Architects

UIA Gold Medal

Every three years at the World Congress of the International Union of Architects (UIA), the UIA awards its Gold Medal to a living architect who has made an outstanding achievement to the field of architecture. This honor recognizes the recipient's lifetime of distinguished practice, contribution to the enrichment of mankind, and the promotion of the art of architecture.

For more information, visit the UIA's Web site at *www.uia-architectes.org*.

1984   Hassan Fathy (Egypt)
1987   Reima Pietila (Finland)
1990   Charles Correa (India)
1993   Fumihiko Maki (Japan)
1996   Rafael Moneo (Spain)
1999   Ricardo Legorreta (Mexico)

Source: International Union of Architects

Did you know...

A recent survey of the American Institute of Architecture Students revealed that the following firms are the most admired by students today:

1. Frank Gehry
2. Richard Meier
3. Morphosis
4. Tadao Ando
5. SOM

Source: Counsel House Research

Urban Land Institute Awards for Excellence

The Urban Land Institute Awards for Excellence follow the organization's mission "to provide responsible leadership in the use of land in order to enhance the environment." Considered by many the most prestigious award within the development community, the Urban Land Institute has recognized outstanding land development projects throughout the world since 1979. Submissions are accepted from developers in the United States and Canada (except for the International Award which is worldwide in scope) and judged by a panel of experts. Winning entries represent superior design, improve the quality of the built environment, exhibit a sensitivity to the community, display financial viability, and demonstrate relevance to contemporary issues.

For more information about the awards, contact the Urban Land Institute at (800) 321-5011 or visit their Web site at *www.uli.org.*

1999 Awards for Excellence recipients:

Bayou Place, *Houston, Texas* (Rehabilitation Small-Scale)
The Cordish Company, (owner/developer)
Gensler (architect)
Tribble & Stephens (contractor)

Bonita Bay, *Bonita Springs, Florida* (Residential Large-Scale)
Bonita Bay Properties Inc. (owner/developer)
Wilson Miller (planning & engineering)
Tom Fazio (golf course architect)
Arthur Hill (golf course architect)
Diedrich NBA (clubhouse architect)

Chicago Public Schools' Capital Improvement Program, *Chicago, Illinois* (Special Award)
Chicago Public Schools (owner/developer)
DeStefano and Partners (managing architect)
Educational Design Group Enterprise
Bovis Management Group (construction management)

The Commons at Calabasas, *Calabasas, California* (Commercial/Hotel Small-Scale)
Caruso Affiliated Holdings (owner/developer)
Caruso Affiliated Holdings/David W. Williams, AIA (architect)
Richard Sawyer (specialty design consultant)
Sasaki Associates (landscape architect)

Coors Field, *Denver, Colorado* (Special Award)
Denver Metropolitan Major League Baseball Stadium District (owner/developer)
HOK Sports Facilities Group Inc. (key consultant)

East Pointe, *Milwaukee, Wisconsin* (Mixed-Use Small-Scale)
Milwaukee Redevelopment Corporation & Mandel Group Inc. (owner/developer)
Nagle, Hartray, Danker, Kagan & McKay Architects (architects)
Eppstein-Uhen Architects Inc. (architects)

Urban Land Institute Awards for Excellence (Con't)

Hualalai at Historic Ka'upulehu, *Ka'upulehu-Kona, Hawaii* (Recreational Large-Scale)
Ka'upulehu Makai Venture/Haulalai Development Company (owner/developer)
Hill Glazier Architects (hotel architect)
Riecke, Sunnland, Kono Architects Ltd. (residential architect)
Belt Collins Hawaii (land planner)
Golden Bear International (Nicklaus Design) (golf course architect)

John Hancock Center, *Chicago, Illinois* (Rehabilitation Large-Scale)
U.S. Equities Realty Inc. (owner/developer)
Cook Hiltscher Associates (architect)
Turner Construction Co. (contractor)

Normandie Village, *Los Angeles, California* (Residential Small-Scale)
1747 Normandie Partners L.P. (owner/developer)
ONE Company Architecture + ONE (architect)
Katherine Spitz & Associates (landscape architect)

7th & Collins Public Parking/Retail Facility, *Miami Beach, Florida* (Commercial/Hotel Small-Scale)
City of Miami Beach (public owner/developer)
Goldman Properties (private owner/developer)
Arquitectonica (ARQ) (architect)
McCarthy Building Company (contractor)
Desman Associates (engineer)
Rosenberg Design Associates (landscape architect)

Vinohradsky Pavilion, *Prague, Czech Republic* (International)
Prague Investments, a.s. (owner/developer)
Ing. Arch. Milan Vesely Ing. Linor Fabián, Karel Dudych Loxia, a.s (key consultants)

1999 Jury:
Eugene Kohn, Chair
Toni Alexander
Karen B. Alschuler
Daniel A. Biederman
Joseph E. Brown
A. Larry Chapman
James H. Callard
Lewis M. Goodkin
Robert Nilsson
H. Pike Oliver
Diana B. Permar
Robert N. Ruth
Edward D. Stone Jr.

Source: Urban Land Institute

The public worth of architecture resides partly in what buildings do...and partly in what buildings say.

Paul Spencer Byard

Veronica Rudge Green Prize in Urban Design

Established by Harvard University in 1986, the Veronica Rudge Green Prize in Urban Design awards excellence in urban design with an emphasis on projects that contribute to the public spaces in cities and improve the quality of urban life. The Prize is awarded biennially by a jury of experts in the field of architecture and urban design. Nominations are made to the Harvard Design School by a panel of critics, academics, and practitioners in the field of architecture, landscape architecture, and urban design. Eligible projects must be larger in scope than a single building and must have been constructed within the last 10 years. Winners receive a monetary award and certificate.

Additional information about the award can be found on the Internet at *www.gsd.harvard.edu/prizes/grn.html*.

1988
Ralph Erskine, Byker Redevelopment in Newcastle upon Tyne, U.K.

Alvaro Siza Vieira, Malagueira Quarter Housing Project in Evora, Portugal

1990
The City of Barcelona, Urban Public Spaces of Barcelona

1993
Fumihiko Maki, Hillside Terrace Complex, Tokyo, Japan

Luigi Snozzi, Master Plan and Public Buildings of Monte Carasso, Switzerland

1996
Mexico City, Restoration of the Historic Center of Mexico City and Ecological Restoration of the District of Xochimilco

1998
Sir Norman Foster and Foster and Partners, subway system in Bilbao, Spain and the development of Carré d'Art Plaza in Nîmes, France.

Source: *Harvard Graduate School of Design/School of Architecture*

We in the architecture profession should be making more generous surroundings and smaller spaces that open onto real places of interaction where people can meet and activities can take place.

Herman Herzberger

Vincent J. Scully Prize

The National Building Museum founded the Vincent J. Scully Prize to recognize practice, scholarship, and criticism in the design professions – architecture, landscape architecture, historic preservation, city planning, and urban design. By naming the prize after Vincent J. Scully, America's renowed architectural scholar, mentor, and critic whose lifetime of work made a tremendous impact on the profession, the Museum hopes to celebrate others who have yielded a significant contribution to the betterment of our world. The award carries a $25,000 honorarium, and the recipient is invited to present a lecture at the Museum.

For more information about the Vincent J. Scully Prize, contact the National Building Museum at (202) 272-2448 or visit them on the Internet at *www.nbm.org*.

1999 Vincent J. Scully
2000 Jane Jacobs

Source: National Building Museum

Whitney M. Young, Jr. Award

The American Institute of Architects (AIA) bestows the Whitney M. Young Jr. Award annually upon an architect or architecturally oriented organization that makes a significant contribution toward meeting the challenge set forth by Mr. Young to architects: to assume a professional responsibility toward current social issues. These issues are ever present and flexible and include such things as housing the homeless, affordable housing, minority and women participation in the profession, disability issues, and literacy.

For more information, visit the AIA on the Internet at *www.e-architect.org* or contact the AIA Honors and Awards Department at (202) 626-7586.

1972	Robert J. Nash	1988	Habitat for Humanity
1973	Architects Workshop of Philadelphia	1989	John H. Spencer
1974	Stephen Cram*	1990	Harry G. Robinson III
1975	Van B. Bruner Jr.	1991	Robert Kennard
1976	Wendell J. Campbell	1992	Curtis J. Moody
1980	Leroy M. Campbell*	1993	David Castro-Blanco
1981	Robert T. Coles	1994	Ki Suh Park
1982	John S. Chase	1995	William J. Stanley III
1983	Howard Hamilton Mackey Sr.	1996	John L. Wilson
1984	John Louis Wilson	1997	Alan Y. Taniguchi
1985	Milton V. Bergstedt	1998	Leon Bridges
1986	The Rev. Richard McClure Prosse*	1999	Charles McAfee
1987	J. Max Bond Jr.	2000	Louis L. Weller

* Honored posthumously

Source: The American Institute of Architects

Wolf Prize for Architecture

Dr. Ricardo Wolf established the Wolf Foundation in 1976 in order to "promote science and arts for the benefit of mankind." In this vein, the Wolf prize is awarded annually to outstanding living scientists and artists in the fields of agriculture, chemistry, mathematics, medicine, physics, and the arts. The awards, an honorarium of US$100,000 and a diploma, are presented each year in Jerusalem's Chagall Hall. In the arts category, the Wolf Prize rotates annually between architecture, music, painting, and sculpture. The following individuals received this honor for their contribution to the field of architecture.

For more information about the Wolf Prize, contact the Wolf Foundation at +972 (9) 955 7120 or visit their Web site at *www.aquanet.co.il/wolf.*

1983   Ralph Erskine (Sweden)

1988   Fumihiko Maki (Japan)
        Giancarlo de Carlo (Italy)

1992   Frank O. Gehry (US)
        Jorn Utzon (Denmark)
        Sir Denys Lasdun (U.K.)

1996   Frei Otto (Germany)
        Aldo van Eyck (Holland)

Source: Wolf Foundation

> **Beautiful buildings are more than scientific. They are true organisms...using the best technology by inspiration rather than the idiosyncrasies of mere taste or averaging by the committee mind.**
>
> *Frank Lloyd Wright*

Young Architects Award

The Young Architects Award is presented annually by The American Institute of Architects (AIA) to an architect in the early stages of his or her career who has made "significant contributions" to the profession. The competition is open to AIA members who have been licensed to practice for less than 10 years; the term "young architect" has no reference to the age of nominees.

For additional information about the Young Architects Award visit the AIA online at *www.e-architect.org* or contact the AIA Honors and Awards Department at (202) 626-7586.

1993
Joan M. Soranno
Vicki L. Hooper
Thomas Somerville Howorth
Brett Keith Laurila

1995
William A. Blanski
Anne Tate

1996
Christopher W. Coe
George Thrush
Keith Moskow

1997
Robert S. Rothman
William J. Carpenter
Michael A. Fischer
Brad Simmons

1998
J. Windom Kimsey
Jose Luis Palacious
Karin M. Pitman
Charles Rose
Karl W. Stumpf
David Louis Swartz
Maryann Thompson
Randall C. Vaughn

1999
Father Terrence Curry
Victoria Tatna Jacobson
Michael Thomas Maltzan
David T. Nagahiro
Peter Steinbrueck

2000
Mary Katherine Lanzillotta
Andrew Travis Smith

Source: The American Institute of Architects

ORGANIZATIONS

American Architectural Foundation (AAF)

Headquartered in America's oldest museum devoted to architecture, Washington D.C.'s Octagon, the American Architectural Foundation (AAF) is dedicated to furthering the public's understanding of architecture and the human experience. The nonprofit AAF sponsors education and outreach programs which foster public participation in the design process, encourages public stewardship of America's architectural heritage, and promotes alliances between architects and their communities. It is also a repository for a growing architectural archive of over 60,000 drawings, 30,000 photographs, and more.

Address:
1735 New York, Avenue NW
Washington, D.C. 20006
Telephone: (202) 626-7500
Internet: www.amerarchfoundation.com

American Consulting Engineers Council (ACEC)

The American Consulting Engineers Council (ACEC) represents private engineering firms in the U.S. by promoting their interests and providing educational opportunities to members. Specifically, the goals of the group are to help members achieve higher business standards, ensure ethical standards are maintained, act as an information clearinghouse, advise on legislation, and to support the advancement of engineering. The ACEC was formed by the union of the American Institute of Consulting Engineers and the Consulting Engineers Council in 1973. Today it is the largest national organization of consulting engineers. Fifty-two state and regional Member Organizations represent more than 5,700 engineering firms. These firms employ more than 250,000 engineers, architects, land surveyors, scientists, technicians and other professionals who design approximately $100 billion of private and public works annually.

Address:
1015 15th St, NW, #802
Washington, DC 20005
Telephone: (202) 347-7474
Internet: www.acec.org

Did you know...

The foundation and floor slabs of the Sears Tower contain 2 million cubic feet of concrete – enough to build an eight-lane highway five miles long.

American Institute of Architects (AIA)

Representing the professional interests of America's architects and seeking to increase national design literacy among the public, The American Institute of Architects (AIA) provides education, government advocacy, community redevelopment and public outreach activities with and for its 62,000 members. With 305 local and state AIA organizations, the Institute monitors closely legislative and regulatory actions at all levels of government. It provides professional development opportunities, industry standard contract documents, information services, and a comprehensive awards program.

Address:
1735 New York Ave., NW
Washington, DC 20006
Telephone: (202) 626-7300 or (800) AIA-3837
Internet: www.e-architect.com

All buildings have a public facade, acting positively or negatively on public space, enriching or impoverishing it.

Leon Krier

American Institute of Architecture Students (AIAS)

The American Institute of Architecture Students (AIAS) is a non-profit, independent, student-run organization that seeks to promote excellence in architecture education, training and practice, as well as to organize architecture students and promote the practice of architecture. The AIAS was formed in 1956 and today serves over 7,500 undergraduate and graduate architecture students. More than 150 chapters at U.S. and Canadian colleges and universities support members with professional development seminars, community projects, curriculum advisory committees, guest speakers and many other programs.

Address:
1735 New York Avenue, NW
Washington, DC 20006
Telephone: (202) 626-7472
Internet: www.aiasnatl.org

Did you know...

A recent survey of the AIAS revealed the students' top concerns about the future of the profession:

1. **Technology expansion and how to embrace and enhance design**
2. **Job security & economic stability**
3. **Lack of respect for the profession and the value and importance of quality design**
4. **Green architecture/sustainable design**
5. **Urban renewal issues and the preservation of quality places**

Source: Counsel House Research

American Planning Association (APA)

The American Planning Association (APA) represents 30,000 planners, officials and citizens involved with urban and rural planning issues. Sixty-five percent of APA's members are employed by state and local government agencies. The mission of the organization is to encourage planning that will contribute to public well-being by developing communities and environments that meet the needs of people and society more effectively. APA is headquartered in Washington, D.C. and has 46 regional chapters. The American Institute of Certified Planners (AICP) is APA's professional and educational arm, certifying planners who have met specific criteria and passed the certification. The group also has research, publications, conference, and education components.

Address:
1776 Massachusetts Ave., NW
Washington, D.C. 20036
Telephone: (202) 872-0611
Internet: www.planning.org

Did you know...

In 1929 Harvard became the first school in the United States to offer a graduate program in city planning.

American Society of Interior Designers (ASID)

The American Society of Interior Designers (ASID) was formed in 1975 with the consolidation of the American Institute of Designers (AID) and the National Society of Interior Designers (NSID). It serves over 30,000 members with continuing education, government affairs, conferences, publications, online services, and more. Members include residential and commercial designers, 3,500 manufacturers of design-related products and services, also know as Industry Partners, and 7,500 students of interior design. ASID has 49 chapters throughout the United States.

Address:
608 Massachusetts Avenue, NE
Washington, DC 20002-6006
Telephone: (202) 546-3480
Internet: www.asid.org

Did you know...

The Bureau of Labor projects that employment in the interior design industry will grow by 27% between 1996 and 2006.

American Society of Landscape Architects (ASLA)

Representing the landscape architecture profession in the United States since 1899, the American Society of Landscape Architects (ASLA) currently serves over 13,000 members through 47 chapters across the country. The ASLA's goal is to advance knowledge, education, and skill in the art and science of landscape architecture. The benefits of membership include a national annual meeting, *Landscape Architecture* magazine, continuing education credits, seminars and workshops, professional interest groups, government advocacy, and award programs. In addition, the U.S. Department of Education has authorized the Landscape Architectural Accreditation Board (LAAB) of the ASLA as the accrediting agency for landscape architecture programs at U.S. colleges and universities.

Address:
636 Eye Street, NW
Washington, DC 20001-3736
Telephone: (202) 898-2444
Internet: www.asla.org

Did you know...

Landscape architect Beatrix Farrand was the only female founding member of the American Society of Landscape Architects.

Architects' Council of Europe (ACE)

Membership of the Architects' Council of Europe (ACE) is comprised of most European representative bodies of the architecture profession. Their constitution states: "The Association of member organizations shall be a non-profit association...as the Liaison Committee of the Representative Bodies of the profession of Architecture, be dedicated to the better understanding of cultural values and the promotion of the highest standards of education and practice in architecture, and shall seek to ensure and shall promote the independence and integrity of the Architectural Profession within the European Community and shall, in these matters, act as its Liaison Committee in seeking, insofar as possible, consensus among the Member Organizations; and shall, without prejudice to the right of Derogation set out at Article 11.5 of this Constitution, promote and represent the common interests of the Profession of Architect in the European Community." Currently the ACE is focusing on deregulation, sustainability issues, and continued work on opening up avenues of communication throughout Europe among politicians, developers, and members of the construction industry.

Address:
Avenue Louise 207 b. 10 1050
Brussels, Belgium
Telephone: (32-2) 645-0905
Internet: www.ace-cae.org

Architectural Institute of Japan (AIJ)

The Architectural Institute of Japan (AIJ) is an academic association with nearly 40,000 members. The organization, dedicated to cultivating the talents of its members and promoting architectural quality in Japan, celebrated its 100th anniversary in 1986. AIJ activities include publications, research, prizes, lectures, exhibitions, and library services. The Board of Directors consists of the President, five Vice Presidents, 18 General Directors, and nine Directors representing the nine local chapters.

Address:
26-20, Shiba 5-chome, Minato-ku
Tokyo 108-8414 Japan
Telephone: +81-3-3456-2051
Internet: www.aij.or.jp

Construction Specifications Institute (CSI)

Headquartered in Alexandria, Virginia, the Construction Specifications Institute (CSI) represents nearly 18,000 members, including architects, engineers, specifiers, contractors, building owners, facility managers, and product manufacturers. As a professional association, CSI provides technical information, continuing education, conferences, and product shows for members. It strives to meet the industry's need for a common system of organizing and presenting construction documents, as demonstrated by its MasterFormat™ system and the new Uniform Drawing System™, which are quickly becoming an industry standard. CSI also publishes The *Construction Specifier*, a monthly magazine featuring articles on technologies, applications, legal issues, trends, and new products.

Address:
601 Madison Street
Alexandria, Virginia 22314-1791
Telephone: (800) 689-2900 or (703) 684-0300
Internet: www.csinet.org

Council on Tall Buildings and Urban Habitat (CTBUH)

The Council on Tall Buildings and Urban Habitat (CTBUH) was established to study and report on all aspects of the planning, design, construction, and operation of tall buildings. The group is sponsored by architecture, engineering, and planning professionals. One of the Council's major focuses is the publication of monographs on tall buildings, as well as studying not only the technological factors related to tall buildings, but the social and cultural aspects of the structures. They maintain an extensive database of tall buildings and produce the definitive list of the world's tallest buildings. The Council Headquarters is located at Lehigh University in Bethlehem, Pennsylvania.

Address:
CTBUH – Lehigh University
11 East Packer Avenue
Bethlehem, PA
Telephone: (610) 758-3515
Internet: www.ctbuh.org

Very tall buildings enter into a realm that many cultures consider sacred. In my native Spanish, 'sky' and 'heaven' are the same word.

Cesar Pelli

**Design-
Build
Institute of
America
(DBIA)**

The Design-Build Institute of America (DBIA) is a
voice supporting the integrated design-build project
delivery method. Founded in 1993, DBIA membership includes design-builders, contractors, design
professionals, subcontractors, representatives of government agencies, and other professionals. The
DBIA strives to improve the level of design-build
practice, to disseminate educational information,
and to furnish advice and support to facility owners
and users. Toward this end, the Institute's programs
include dissemination and development of standard
procedures and formats, promotion of design-build
in public forums and with private corporations and
government agencies, educational programs, and
providing information support and assistance to
members.

Address:
1010 Massachusetts Avenue, N.W.
Suite 350
Washington, D.C. 20001
Telephone: (202) 682-0110
Internet: www.dbia.org

Design Futures Council (DFC)

The Design Futures Council (DFC) is a Washington D.C. think-tank with the mission to explore trends, changes, and new opportunities in design, architecture, engineering, and building technology for the purpose of fostering innovation and improving the performance of member organizations. Participants represent a full spectrum of design, manufacturing, and service professionals. Council activities include proprietary surveys, industry focus groups, futures invention workshops, and conference facilitation. Members receive a host of benefits, including the semi-monthly newsletter *DesignIntelligence*.

Address:
11921 Freedom Drive, Suite 550
Reston, VA 20190
Telephone: (800) 726-8603

The future calls for highly integrative design which is inclusive rather than exclusive.

Peter Schneider

Design Management Institute (DMI)

The Design Management Institute (DMI) is a professional organization that primarily serves senior design executives and other executives involved in the development of products, communications, and environments, as well as educators. Through its conferences, publications, and research, DMI strives to be the international authority and advocate on design management. Their quarterly *Design Management Journal*, the industry's only scholarly journal, emphasizes contemporary design management thinking with features from the world's leading experts in design management.

Address:
29 Temple Place
Boston, MA 02111-1350
Telephone: (617) 338-6380
Internet: www.dmi.org

Industrial Designers Society of America (IDSA)

Since 1965, the Industrial Designers Society of America (IDSA) has been dedicated to communicating the value of industrial design to society, business, government, and the general public. IDSA serves its constituency through its professional journal *Innovations*, award programs, annual conference, research, networking opportunities, and promotion of the practice at all levels of government.

Address:
1142 Walker Rd
Great Falls, VA 22066
Telephone: (703) 759-0100
Internet: www.idsa.org

I am not a designer. I try to be a happiness producer.

Philippe Starck

Initiative for Architectural Research (IAR)

The Initiative for Architectural Research (IAR) was formed by the Association of Collegiate Schools of Architecture (ACSA), American Institute of Architects (AIA) and Architectural Research Centers Consortium (ARCC) primarily to serve as an advocate for architectural research, to serve as a clearinghouse for information about architectural research, and to facilitate research efforts that address specific needs of the architectural profession. The IAR produces *A/R: Architecture/Research*, the directory of architectural research abstracts from universities, architecture firms, national laboratories, and research centers throughout the US and Canada, as well as co-producing the annual Research Awards with *Architecture* magazine.

Address:
IAR c/o ACSA
1735 New York Avenue, NW
Washington, DC 20006
Telephone: (202) 785-2324
Internet: www.architectureresearch.org

International Council of Societies of Industrial Design (ICSID)

The International Council of Societies of Industrial Design (ICSID) strives to advance the discipline of industrial design worldwide. This non-profit, non-governmental organization was formed in 1957 and is supported by 152 organizations and societies in 53 countries. Through these groups, ICSID represents approximately 150,000 professionals. Member groups work with an Advisory Senate and Executive Board in the areas of practice, education, promotion, and development to enhance the profession.

Address:
Yrjönkatu 11 E
00120 Helsinki
Finland
Telephone: +358 9 696 22 90
Internet: www.icsid.org

Did you know...

Jens Risom's 1941-2 angled and canted chair with webbing, which was patented in 1945, was the first chair created for Hans Knoll and his new contemporary furniture company.

International Federation of Interior Architects/Designers (IFI)

The goals of the International Federation of Interior Architects/Designers (IFI) are to promote the interior architecture and design profession, to represent its practitioners, to act as a clearinghouse for professional and cultural information, to encourage international cooperation, and to assist and serve the industry. The IFI engages in a number of activities to further these ends, such as maintaining a public relations program, lobbying for policies benefiting the practice, organizing conferences and supporting minimum standards of education and a Code of Ethics and Practice. Its membership is composed of professional interior design organizations in countries throughout the world.

Address:
P.O. Box 91640
Auckland Park
Johannesburg, 2006
South Africa
Telephone: +27 11 4772279
Internet: www.ifi.co.za

International Federation of Landscape Architects (IFLA)

The International Federation of Landscape Architects (IFLA) represents various national associations of landscape architects. The non-profit, non-governmental organization was formed in 1948 to promote the practice of landscape architecture and to establish standards of professional practice throughout the world. The IFLA is governed by a World Council with jurisdiction over regional councils. Members join IFLA through their national membership associations; although, individuals from countries which do not have a national representative group may also join. The IFLA publishes a newsletter twice a year and sponsors a biennial World Conference. Other regional meetings are held on a regular basis.

Address:
4 rue Hardy, RP no 914
78009 Versailles
Cedex, France
Internet: www.ifla.net

International Interior Design Association (IIDA)

With a mission of promoting excellence in interior design and advancing the practice through knowledge, the International Interior Design Association (IIDA) provides a variety of services and benefits for its 11,000 members. It advocates for design excellence, nurtures the interior design community worldwide, maintains educational standards, responds to trends in business and design, and provides a wealth of information about interior design and related issues. The organization maintains 9 international regions with more than 30 chapters and 64 U.S. city centers.

Address:
341 Merchandise Mart
Chicago, IL 60654
Telephone: (312) 467-1950
Internet: www.iida.org

Design shapes the way we live. So it ought to serve everyone.

Eva Maddox

International Union of Architects (UIA)

Founded in 1948, the International Union of Architects (UIA) is an international, non-governmental organization dedicated to uniting the architects of the world. Through its 92 UIA Member Sections, the group represents over a million architects. The UIA's mission is to represent architects and promote the practice with other professional organizations worldwide, other non-governmental organizations, and intergovernmental institutions. The UIA General Secretariat is the Union's executive body and the administrative center for the coordination of relations between the UIA Member Sections and their activities. A personal information service is available from the General Secretariat, allowing architects to keep up with UIA activities, its partners, and Member Sections.

Address:
51, rue Raynouard
75 016 Paris, France
Telephone: 33 (1) 45 24 36 88
Internet: www.uia-architectes.org

The architect represents neither a Dionysian nor an Apollinian condition: here it is the mighty act of will, the will which moves mountains, the intoxication of the strong will, which demands artistic expression. The most powerful men have always inspired the architects; the architect has always been influenced by power.

Friedrich Nietzsche

Japan Institute of Architects (JIA)

The Japan Institute of Architects (JIA) serves to define and promote the social and legal status of professional architects in Japan and to promote their interests abroad. Currently, JIA represents over 6,300 members through 10 chapters. A member of the Architects Regional Council Asia (ARCASIA) as well as the International Union of Architects (IUA), the Japan Institute of Architects was formed in 1987 when the Japan Architects Association (JAA) and the Japan Federation of Professional Architects Association (JFPAA) united.

Address:
2-3-18, Jingumae
Shibuya-ku, Tokyo
150-0001 Japan
Telephone: +81-3-3408-7125
Internet: http://web.jia.or.jp/jia/intro/about_e/main.htm

Joslyn Castle Institute for Sustainable Communities

Housed in Omaha, Nebraska's historic 1902 Joslyn Castle, the Joslyn Castle Institute for Sustainable Communities is a partnership among Nebraska state government, the Joslyn Art Museum, the University of Nebraska College of Architecture, and other public and private organizations. The Institute focuses on promoting sustainable development through outreach and education programs, as well as research. Its goal is to encourage communities to develop by balancing economic, social and environmental needs. The institute is one of 18 centers worldwide partnering with the United Nations Center for Human Settlement (UNCHS) in its Best Practices in Local Leadership Program (BLP).

Address:
3902 Davenport Street
Omaha, Nebraska 68131
Telephone: (402) 595-1902
Internet: www.libfind.unl.edu/JCI/

Did you know...

The Roy Lee Walker Elementary School, designed by SHW Group and completed in July 2000, is Texas' first sustainable school project in both its design and curriculum.

National Institute of Building Sciences (NIBS)

The National Institute of Building Sciences (NIBS) serves the public interest by promoting a rational regulatory environment for the building community, facilitating the introduction of new technology, and disseminating technical information. NIBS was established by Congress as an authoritative national source on building science and technology issues. It is a non-governmental, non-profit organization. Of its 21-member Board of Directors, 15 are elected and six are appointed by the President of the United States with the approval of the U.S. Senate. NIBS committees are integral in establishing industry-wide standards for the construction industry. They also publish many books on specific building technologies and techniques.

Address:
1090 Vermont Avenue, NW, Suite 700
Washington, DC 20005-4905
Telephone: (202) 289-7800
Internet: www.nibs.org

National Organization of Minority Architects (NOMA)

The National Organization of Minority Architects (NOMA) was formed in 1971 for the purpose of enhancing diversity in architecture. Today there are 12 NOMA chapters and 19 student chapters across the country, increasing recognition on university campuses and providing access to government policy makers. The organization works to advance minority architects, from job placement for college students to aiding member firms in securing contracts. NOMA annually holds a conference, organizes a design award program, and produces a newsletter.

Address:
Internet: www.noma.net

Royal Architectural Institute of Canada (RAIC)

The Royal Architectural Institute of Canada (RAIC) "works towards a future in which Canadians will view our total environment, both natural and built, as our most important asset and the Institute's members as essential to its creation and maintenance." Established in 1907, the Institute represents more than 3,000 architects, educators, and graduates of accredited Canadian schools of architecture. The organization focuses its activities in five areas: publications, symposia and exhibitions, research, awards, and practice committees.

Address:
55 Murray Street, Suite 330
Ottawa, Ontario, K1N 5M3
Canada
Telephone: (613) 241-3600
Internet: www.raic.org

Royal Australian Institute of Architects (RAIA)

The Royal Australian Institute of Architects (RAIA) represents over 8,000 members in Australia and overseas, largely through eight state chapters. Established in 1929, the RAIA seeks to raise awareness among the public about the value of architecture and the importance of good design and to promote creativity and continuous training among its members. Their mission is to "unite architects to advance architecture." Each year the RAIA sponsors the Architecture Awards in the states and territories, culminating in a national prize. The group also publishes Australia's premier architecture magazine, *Architecture Australia*, and the highly regarded and regularly updated *Environment Design Guide*.

Address:
2a Mugga Way
Red Hill ACT 2603
Australia
Telephone: (02) 6273 1548
Internet: www.raia.com.au

Royal Institute of British Architects (RIBA)

Founded in 1834, the Royal Institute of British Architects (RIBA) was one of the world's first architectural associations. Representing more than 32,000 members in over 100 countries, the RIBA is a worldwide organization committed to the improvement and enjoyment of the physical environment. Its mission is "the advancement of architecture and the promotion of the acquirement of the knowledge of the arts and sciences connected therewith." The organization sponsors several prestigious award programs including the Stirling Prize and the Royal Gold Medal. Their RIBA Architecture Gallery features many exhibits on architecture and design each year. Members also have access to Ribanet Conference, a global communication system connecting architects through their computers, allowing them to use electronic conferencing to exchange ideas, share files, participate in one-to-one online chats, and send and receive emails. RIBA membership is open to anyone, whether an architect or a patron of the practice. Established in 1934, RIBA's British Architectural Library is the largest and most comprehensive resource in the United Kingdom for research and information on all aspects of architecture.

Address:
66 Portland Place
London W1N 4AD UK
Telephone: 44 171 580 5533
Internet: www.architecture.com

Society of Architectural Historians (SAH)

Since its founding in 1940, the Society of Architectural Historians (SAH) has sought to promote the history of architecture. The membership of SAH ranges from professionals such as architects, planners, preservationists, and academics to those simply interested in architecture. The Society produces a quarterly journal and monthly newsletter and organizes study tours and an annual conference There are also a number of associated, although independent, local chapters. The SAH's national headquarters is located in the architecturally significant Charnley-Persky House which was designed in 1891 by the firm of Dankmar Adler and Louis Sullivan. Guided tours of the house are offered.

Address:
1365 North Astor Street
Chicago, Illinois 60610-2144
Telephone: (312) 573-1365
Internet: www.sah.org

We may live without her, and worship without her, but we cannot remember without her How cold is all history, how lifeless all imagery, compared to that which the living nation writes, and the uncorrupted marble bears!

John Ruskin

Society for Environmental Graphic Design (SEGD)

The Society for Environmental Graphic Design (SEGD) is a non-profit organization formed in 1973 to promote public awareness of and professional development in environmental graphic design. This interdisciplinary field encompasses the talents of many design professionals, including graphic designers, architects, landscape architects, product designers, planners, interior designers, and exhibition designers, in the planning and design of graphic elements that shape our built and natural environments. Practitioners in this field design graphic elements to help identify, direct, inform, interpret, and visually enhance our surroundings. From wayfinding systems and mapping to exhibit design and themed environments, environmental graphic design impacts our experiences everywhere. SEGD offers its members an interdisciplinary network to support and enhance their efforts in this growing discipline, a bi-monthly newsletter, annual conference, design award program, technical bulletins, job bank listings, and many other formal and informal resources.

Address:
401 F Street NW, Suite 333
Washington, DC 20001
Telephone: (202) 638-5555
Internet: www. segd.org

United Nations Centre for Human Settlements (Habitat)

The United Nations Centre for Human Settlements (Habitat) was established in 1978 as the lead agency for coordinating human settlements and development activities within the United Nations family, focusing on the following priority areas: shelter and social services; urban management; environment and infrastructure; and assessment, monitoring, and information. Habitat supports and works in partnership with governments, local authorities, non-governmental organizations, and the private sector. Currently, Habitat has over 200 operational programs and projects underway in 80 countries, focusing on urban management, housing, basic services, and infrastructure development. Habitat promotes sustainable human settlement development through policy formulation, capacity-building, knowledge creation, and the strengthening of partnerships between governments and civil society. In 1996, the United Nations General Assembly designated Habitat as a focal point for the implementation of the Habitat Agenda, the global plan of action adopted at the second United Nations Conference on Human Settlements.

Address:
P. O. Box 30030
Nairobi, Kenya
Tel: (254-2) 623153
Internet: www.unchs.org

Urban Land Institute (ULI)

Formed in 1936 as a research arm of the National Association of Real Estate Boards (now the National Association of Realtors), the Urban Land Institute (ULI) is an independent institution dedicated to promoting the responsible use of land to enhance the total environment. The group represents 15,000 professionals in 50 states and 52 countries. ULI activities include research, forums and task forces, awards, education, and publishing.

Address:
1025 Thomas Jefferson Street, NW
Suite 500 West
Washington, DC 20007
Telephone: (202) 624-7000
Internet: www.uli.org

The only thing worse than vulgar urbanism is tasteful urbanism.

Robert Venturi

U.S. Green Building Council

The U.S. Green Building Council was formed in 1993 to integrate, educate, and provide leadership for building industry leaders, environmental groups, designers, retailers, and building owners as they strive to develop and market products and services which are environmentally progressive and responsible. The Council includes more than 250 organizations worldwide with a common interest in green building practices, technologies, policies, and standards. Member groups have access to a clearinghouse of resources, plus many networking opportunities.

Address:
110 Sutter Street, Suite 140
San Francisco, CA 94104
Telephone: (415) 445-9500
Internet: www.usgbc.org

Did you know...

The new wood-framed visitor's center at Zion National Park in Utah was designed to use 70% less energy than a conventional building.

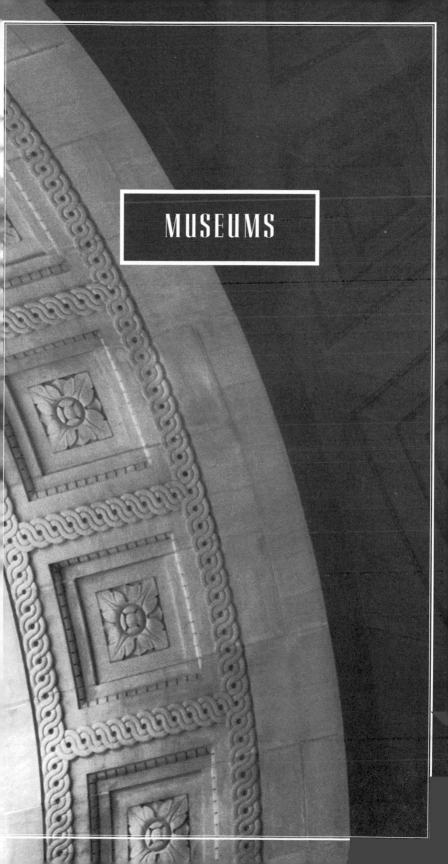

MUSEUMS

Alvar Aalto Museum

Founded in 1966, Finland's Alvar Aalto Museum houses a permanent collection of the designer/architect's work, produces publications related to his career, and oversees conservation of his buildings. Additionally, the Museum arranges Aalto exhibits worldwide. Its architectural collection contains 1,200 original models and artifacts designed by Aino and Alvar Aalto, as well as a photo archive and reproductions of Aalto's original drawings. A library featuring architecture and literature centered around Alvar Aalto is open to researchers and students by appointment.

Address:
Alvar Aallon katu 7
40600 Jyvaskyla, Finland
Telephone: +358 (0) 14 624 809
Internet: www.alvaraalto.fi

Exhibition Schedule:
Alvar Aalto. Architect
Permanent Exhibit

Lighting with Atmosphere: Finnish Candleholders
November 30, 2000 – February 25, 2001

The World in Miniature: Architecture and Environmental Design by Schoolchildren
March 3 – April 1, 2001

Young Designers from Finland
April-May

Rax Rinnekangas – Photographs
June – July

Design for Architecture
August 8 – October 25, 2001

Light Fittings / Alvar Aalto
Beginning November 1, 2001

Architektur Zentrum Wien

The Architektur Zentrum Wien was founded in 1993 by the Austrian Federal Government and the City of Vienna as a forum to promote Austrian architecture. Through their national and international exhibitions, publications, workshops, and panel discussions, the museum is Austria's premier venue for contemporary architecture and urban design. In addition, they host the annual Viennese Seminar on Architecture and the Vienna Architecture Congress. A database on contemporary Austrian architecture is maintained by the museum and available on a limited basis on the Internet. The library, which will be open to the public once the planned library expansion is complete, contains 700 international architecture and art periodicals and a growing collection of books and exhibition catalogues.

Address:
Museumsplatz 1
1070 Vienna
Austria
Telephone: +43 522 31 15 23
Internet: www.azw.at

Exhibition Schedule:
(contact the museum for an updated schedule)

Art Institute of Chicago, Department of Architecture

The Art Institute of Chicago encompasses The School of the Art Institute of Chicago and a museum with ten curatorial departments. Collections at the Art Institute include: African and Amerindian Art, American Art, Architecture, Asian Art, Ancient Art, European Painting, Photography, European Decorative Arts and Sculpture, Prints and Drawings, Textiles, Arms and Armor and Twentieth-Century Painting and Sculpture. The Department of Architecture at the Art Institute was established in 1981 from the architectural drawings collection within the Burnham Library of Architecture (founded in 1912) and the architectural fragments collection of the Department of American Arts. The Ernest R. Graham Study Center for Architectural Drawings houses a collection of more than 130,000 architectural sketches and drawings, largely of designs by Chicago architects, including Walter Burley Griffin, Louis Sullivan, Ludwig Mies van der Rohe and Frank Lloyd Wright. The collection also features architectural models and fragments, including a reconstruction of the Adler and Sullivan trading room from the Chicago Stock Exchange (1893-94). The Burnham Library of Architecture, one of the first organizations in the United States to collect architectural drawings, architects' papers, and primary documentary materials, is open to researchers and scholars.

Address:
111 South Michigan Avenue
Chicago, Illinois 60603
Telephone: (312) 443-3949
Internet: www.artic.edu/aic

Art Institute of Chicago Department of Architecture (Con't)

Exhibition Schedule:

Skyscrapers. The New Millennium
August 19, 2000 - January 15, 2001

Chicago Architects
June 3, 2000 - March 2001

2001. Building for Space Travel
March 24 - October 2, 2001

All Aboard! Architecture, Design, and Rail Travel for the Twenty-first Century
December 8, 2001 - July 28, 2002

Did you know...

The Tribune Tower international design competition in 1922 paid a total of $100,000, equivalent to more than $1 million today, in prize money.

Athenaeum of Philadelphia

The Athenaeum of Philadelphia was founded in 1814 to collect and disseminate information related to American history and the "useable arts." The not-for-profit, member-supported library contains a vast architecture and interior design collection with an emphasis on the period 1800 to 1945. The library is open to qualified readers without charge. The Athenaeum's National Historic Landmark building, designed by John Nott in 1845 near Independence Hall, is also open to the public as a museum furnished with American fine and decorative arts from the first half of the nineteenth century. They offer public programs, lectures and changing exhibitions, as well as administering trusts that provide awards and grants.

Address:
219 S. Sixth Street
Philadelphia, PA 19106-3794
Telephone: (215) 925-2688
Internet: www.PhilaAthenaeum.org

Exhibition Schedule:
(check with the museum for an updated schedule)

Canadian Centre for Architecture (CCA)

Montréal's Canadian Centre for Architecture (CCA) is a museum and study center devoted to local, national and international architecture, landscape design, and urban planning disciplines that contribute to the built environment of the past and present. Their exhibits are intended to reveal the richness of architectural culture and to heighten the public's awareness of contemporary issues in architecture. The CCA occupies an award-winning building designed by Peter Rose in 1989 and the adjacent 1874 Shaughnessy House. Its garden, designed by Melvin Charney, serves as both an urban garden and outdoor museum of architecture.

Address:
1920 Baile Street
Montréal, Québec
Canada H3H 2S6
Telephone: (514) 939-7026
Internet: www.cca.qc.ca

Exhibition Schedule:
Cities in movement
November 15, 2000 - April 1, 2001

Beginning in early 2001 and extending through 2003, the CCA launches a series of 5 exhibitions under the umbrella title Modern Architecture in the Making. *These are the first two installations:*

Soane
May 9, 2001 - September 9, 2001

Mies in America
October 17, 2001 – January 20, 2002

Cooper-Hewitt, National Design Museum, Smithsonian Institution

The Cooper-Hewitt, National Design Museum, Smithsonian Institution is the only museum in the U.S. devoted exclusively to the study of historical and contemporary design. Reflecting the belief that design links individuals, societies and the natural environment, the museum's program addresses five key issues: function, innovation & creativity, communication, history & criticism, and context. Four curatorial departments care for and evaluate the Museum's collections: applied arts and industrial design, drawings and prints, textiles, and wallcoverings. The Museum's interests also encompass graphic design, architecture, urban planning, and environmental design.

Address:
2 East 91st Street
New York, New York 10128
Telephone: (212) 849-8400
Internet: www.si.edu/ndm/

Exhibition Schedule:
The OPulent Eye of Alexander Girard
September 12, 2000 – March 18, 2001

Masterpieces from the Vitra Design Museum: Furnishings of the Modern Era
October 10, 2000 - February 4, 2001

Aluminum by Design: Jewelry to Jets
March 20 – July 15, 2001

A Room with a View: Landscape and Wallpapers
April 24 – October 14, 2001

Glass of the Avant-Garde: From the Vienna Secession to the Bauhaus
September 4, 2001 – January 6, 2002

Easier Living: Russel Wright and the Modern Domestic Environment
November 20, 2001 - March 10, 2002

Danish Center for Architecture, Gammel Dok

The Danish Center for Architecture, located in the historic 1882 harbor-front warehouse Gammel Dok, is devoted to the advancement of architecture and urban design and to raising awareness of the importance of quality design among professionals, institutions, government, and the public. It serves as a platform for debate and a forum for the display of projects and ideas that strive to improve the physical environment. In addition, they host exhibits on Danish and international architecture, maintain a database of contemporary Danish architecture, define architecture policies, and promote knowledge of architecture in the Danish public schools.

Address:
Strandgade 27B
1401 Copenhagen K
Denmark
Telephone: +45 32 57 19 30
Internet: www.gammeldok.dk

Exhibition Schedule:
CITY within CITY
October 13, 2000 – February 2001

ArkitekturGalleriet 2001
January 2001 – December 2001

Exceptional Places
Permanent Changing Exhibit, beginning April 2001

Danish Design Center

The Danish Design Center was founded in 1977 to promote Danish design within Denmark and abroad. Through its exhibits, lectures, design competitions, publications, library, and design management consultation services, the Danish Design Center stands at the forefront of the promotion of good design within the industrial design profession and for the benefit of society as a whole. In January 2000 they opened their new building, which was designed by one of Denmark's premier architects, Henning Larsen, across from Tivoli Gardens.

Address:
H C Andersens Boulevard 27
1553 Copenhagen V, Denmark
Telephone: +45 33 69 33 69
Internet: www.ddc.dk

Exhibition Schedule:
Kurage
December 1, 2000 – January 1, 2001

Re(f)use
January 10 – March 11, 2001

Fantasy Design
January 20 – March 18, 2001

Design Icons
March 21 – June 10, 2001

Fiskars' Design
March 27 – May 27, 2001

Danish Design Prize
June – July 2001

Bysted Design
August 4 – September 23, 2001

The Fifth Quarter
September 29 – December 2, 2001

Travel Light
October 4 – January 6, 2002

Design Museum

Located in London's South Bank area in a converted 1950s warehouse, the Design Museum is the only museum devoted exclusively to 20th century industrial design. Since its founding in 1989 by the Conran Foundation, the Museum's many changing exhibits and educational programs have offered an insight into the role of design and mass production in our everyday lives. Its exhibits include the Collection gallery, which highlights historical trends and design of the past 100 years; the Review gallery, featuring new, innovative designs and prototypes; and many special exhibitions. The Museum's reach is further extended through its extensive educational program of contract teaching, outreach activities, teacher training courses, and resources for classroom use.

Address:
Shad Thames
London
SE1 2YD
United Kingdom
Telephone: 0171 378 6055
Internet: www.designmuseum.org

Exhibition Schedule:
Review Gallery
Permanent Exhibit

Collection Gallery
Permanent Exhibit

Isambard Kingdom Brunel: Recent Works
October 27, 2000 – February 25, 2001

Design Sense: Rewarding Sustainable Design
November 17, 2000 – January 21, 2001

Luis Barragan
March – July 2001

Heinz Architectural Center, Carnegie Museum of Art

Opened by the Carnegie Museum of Art in 1993, the Heinz Architectural Center is dedicated to the collection, study, and exhibition of architectural drawings and models. Though its scope is international, it does foster a principle interest in the architecture of western Pennsylvania. The museum also maintains one of only three architectural cast collections in the world, and the only one in North America.

Address:
4400 Forbes Avenue
Pittsburgh, PA 15213-4080
Telephone: (412) 622-3131
Internet: www.cmoa.org

Exhibition Schedule:
Inside Out: New Perspectives on the Heinz Architectural Center's Collection
October 28, 2000 – January 21, 2001

Aluminum by Design
October 28, 2000 – February 11, 2001

Forum: Aluminum in Contemporary Architecture
November 18, 2000 – February 4, 2001

Folds, Blobs, and Boxes: Architecture in the Digital Era
February 3 – May 27, 2001

Light! The Industrial Age, 1750-1900, Art & Science, Technology & Society
April 7 – July 29, 2001

Landscapes of Retrospection: The Magoon Collection of British Drawings and Prints, 1739 – 1860
June 9 – September 23, 2001

Dream Street: Photographs by W. Eugene Smith
November 10, 2001 – February 10, 2002

The Lighthouse: Scotland's Centre for Architecture, Design & the City

The Lighthouse is one of Europe's largest temporary exhibition venues devoted to promoting access, involvement and participation in architecture and design. The themes of their exhibits range from architecture and design to the city, including monograph shows of architectural and design practices, object led exhibitions of the best products, and experimental explorations of issues related to urban living. The Lighthouse is located in the former 1895 Glasgow Herald building designed by Charles Rennie Mackintosh, Glasgow's celebrated architect, designer and artist. It also houses the Mackintosh Interpretation Centre, a facility for the study of the work and legacy of Charles Rennie Mackintosh.

Address:
11 Mitchell Lane
Glasgow, G1 3NU
U.K.
Telephone: +44 (0) 141 221 6362
Internet: www.thelighthouse.co.uk

Exhibition Schedule:
Waves
November 9, 2000 – January 7, 2001

Electric City
November 26 , 2000 – February 25, 2001

Channel 4
March 10 – July 22, 2001

Second City First
dates to be determined

Produced In Scotland
dates to be determined

Richard Murphy Architects
dates to be determined

Museum of Finnish Architecture

The Museum of Finnish Architecture maintains a large collection of drawings and photographs related to Finnish architecture as well as an extensive architectural library. The Museum organizes exhibits about Finnish architecture and 20th century design issues, which they host in Helsinki, as well as throughout Finland and abroad. In addition, they publish books and host lectures to generate support and promote interest in Finnish design.

Address:
Kasarmikatu 24, 00130
Helsinki, Finland
Telephone: +35 8-9-85675100
Internet: www.mfa.fi

Exhibition Schedule:
Helsinki Forum
October 31, 2000 – February 24, 2001

Architectural Competitions
March 2001

West is East is West: Mies van der Rohe
March-April 2001

"Poor boy" wooden statues
April-June 2001

Concrete Spaces, Aarno Ruusuvuori's Concrete Architecture from the 1960s
June-September 2001

The World of Scale Models
Fall 2001

Traveling Exhibitions:
20th Century Architecture: Finland
Architektur im Ringturm, Vienna, Austria: through Feb. 2001
Sevilla, Spain: Autumn 2001

Museum of Modern Art (MoMA)

New York City's Museum of Modern Art (MoMA) encompasses six curatorial areas, including the world's first department devoted to architecture and design. Established in 1932, the Department of Architecture and Design's collection contains architectural documents, drawings, and photographs, including the Ludwig Mies van der Rohe Archive and collections from other leading architects. They also maintain over 3,000 design objects, from furniture to tools, automobiles, and textiles and a 4,000 piece graphic design collection. The Lily Auchincloss Study Center for Architecture and Design is open by appointment to researchers who are interested in accessing reference materials related to the Museum's collection of design objects, posters, architectural drawings, models and periodicals.

Address:
11 West 53 Street
New York, NY 10019
Telephone: (212) 708-9400
Internet: www.moma.org

Exhibition Schedule:
Workspheres: Designing the Workplace of Tomorrow
February 8 – May 8, 2001

Mies in Berlin
June 21 – September 11, 2001

Traveling Exhibitions:
The Un-Private House
Armand Hammer Museum of Art, UCLA
October 4, 2000 – January 7, 2001

The Un-Private House
The Museum of Contemporary Art (MACBA), Barcelona, Spain
January – April 2001

National Building Museum

Established by an act of Congress in 1980, the National Building Museum, a private, nonprofit institution, is dedicated to exploring all facets and disciplines of the built environment. From architecture, urban planning, and construction to engineering and design, the Museum reveals the connections between the way we build and the way we live. The Museum is located in Washington D.C.'s historic 1887 Pension Bureau Building designed by U.S. Army General Montgomery C. Meigs. The Museum's impressive Great Hall with its colossal Corinthian columns is often the site of the President's Inaugural Ball among many other gala events. Through its exhibitions and education programs, the Museum serves as a forum for exchanging information about topical issues such as managing suburban growth, preserving landmarks, and revitalizing urban centers.

Address:
401 F Street NW
Washington, DC 20001
Telephone: (202) 272-2448
Internet: www.nbm.org

Exhibition Schedule:
WOOD: An American Tradition
September 9, 2000 – April 22, 2001

Metropolitan Perspectives: Smart Growth and Choices for Change
October 11, 2000 – March 4, 2001

Drawing the Future: Design Drawings for the 1939 New York World's Fair
October 13, 2000 – January 14, 2001

Monuments, Mills, and Missile Sites: Thirty Years of the Historic American Engineering Record (HAER)
October 26, 2000 – April 29, 2001

National
Building
Museum
(Con't)

Exhibition Schedule (Con't)

On the Job: Design and the American Office
November 18, 2000 – June 24, 2001

William Price: From Arts and Crafts to Modern Design
December 1, 2000 – April 29, 2001

General Services Administration's 2000 Award Winners
March 29 – July 8, 2001

The Architecture of R.M. Schindler
June 29 – October 7, 2001

Tools As Art VI: Instruments of Change
Permanent Exhibit

Washington: Symbol and City
Permanent Exhibit

Building a Landmark: The National Building Museum's Historic
Home
Permanent Exhibit

Netherlands Architecture Institute

Located at the edge of Museumpark in the center of Rotterdam and housed in a building designed by Jo Coenen in 1993, the Netherlands Architecture Institute (NAI) is a museum and cultural institution concerned with architecture, urban design and space planning. Through its exhibitions and other programs, the NAI strives to inform, inspire and stimulate architects and laymen alike about the value of design. The NAI possesses one of the largest architectural collections in the world with over 15 kilometers of shelving containing drawings, sketches, models, photographs, books and periodicals, including work by virtually every important Dutch architect since 1800. This collection, as well as its 40,000 volume library, is open to researchers. Lectures, study tours, and a variety of publications are also offered by the NAI.

Address:
Mueumpark 25
3015 CB Rotterdam
Netherlands
Telephone: 31 (0) 10-4401200
Internet: www.nai.nl/nai_eng.html

Exhibition schedule:
Two Centuries of Architecture in the Netherlands
Permanent Exhibition

Towards Totalscape: Contemporary Japanese Architecture, Urban Design and Landscape Architecture
October 21, 2000 – January 14, 2001

The Appearance of the Netherlands: The Residential Area of the Future
November 18, 2000 – January 7, 2001

Kazuyo Sejima
December 2, 2000 – January 14, 2001

Netherlands Architecture Institute (Con't)

Exhibition schedule (Con't)

Francine Houben
January 20 – February 25, 2001

Richard Meier
February 1 – April 15, 2001

Villa Sonneveld
Beginning March 2001

Jo Coenen
March 9 – April 29, 2001

Young German Architects
March 17 – May 6, 2001

Material World
Beginning April 8, 2001

J.J.P. Oud
May 12 – August 26 , 2001

Happiness City Space
Autumn 2001 – Spring 2002

Norwegian Museum of Architecture

Founded by the National Association of Norwegian Architects in 1975, the Norwegian Museum of Architecture (NAM) collects, processes, and disseminates information and material concerned with architecture, with a focus towards the 20th century. The Museum is housed in one of Oslo's oldest buildings, Kongrens gate 4, part of which dates to 1640. The Museum boasts an archive of over 200,000 drawings and photographs and is available to researchers by appointment. In the past, the Museum's exhibits have been concerned with various aspects of Norwegian architecture, from the work of individuals to overviews of contemporary architecture. The Museum also hosts traveling exhibitions which are typically in English.

Address:
Kongens gate 4, N-0153
Oslo, Norway
Telephone: +47-22 42 40 80
http://www.mnal.no/nam/NAM-eng.html

Exhibition Schedule:
History of Buildings: 1000 Years of Norwegian Architecture
Permanent Exhibit

Young and Prosperous
February 22 – March 26, 2001

Contemporary Norwegian Architecture: 1995–2000
April 4 – June 3, 2001

Drawings from the Collection
June 7 – July 9, 2001

Architect Chr. H. Grosch: 1801–1865
September 14, 2001

**Norwegian
Museum of
Architecture
(Con't)**

Traveling Exhibitions in Norway:
Architect Alexis de Chateauneuf—Hamburg—Oslo—London
Oslo City Hall

Architect Chr. H. Grosch: 1801–1865
May 20 – September 1, 2001, Old Theater, Halden

Traveling Exhibitions abroad:
Contemporary Norwegian Architecture: 1995–2000
Bibliotheca Alexandrina, Egypt (tentative)

Sverre Fehn –architect
Spring 2001, Munich, Germany
May 2001, Vienna, Austria

The Octagon

Located one block west of the White House, The Octagon was one of Washington, D.C.'s first residences. It was designed by Dr. William Thornton, the first architect of the U.S. Capitol and was completed in 1801. John Tayloe III and his descendants owned the home until it was purchased by The American Institute of Architects (AIA) in 1902 to serve as its headquarters. The American Architectural Foundation (AAF), the foundation established by the AIA in 1942, purchased the building in 1968 and opened it to the public as a museum in 1970. A National Historic Landmark, the Octagon is the oldest architecture and design museum in the United States.

Address:
1799 New York Ave. NW
Washington, D.C., 20006
Telephone: (202) 638-3105
Internet: www.aafpages.org/aafmodel/TheOctagon.htm

Exhibition Schedule:
If These Walls Could Talk: The Octagon's 200th Birthday
Late January - October 2001

Sculpture by John Mors (outdoors)
May – June 2001

Architecture: The Essence of the Image, Photos by Carolyn Johnson
June – July 2001

AIA Honor Awards
August 2001

Colors with Lucas Blok and Jeff Becom
September – October 2001

Timothy Makepeace: Sculpture and Drawings
November – December 2001

Skyscrapers: The New Millennium
November 16, 2001 – April 30, 2002

RIBA Architecture Gallery

The Royal Institute of British Architects' (RIBA) RIBA Architecture Gallery (formerly known as the RIBA Architecture Centre) features both historical and contemporary architecture and design exhibitions. Through exhibitions, talks, publications, events for children and the family, the Internet and collaborations, it provides a cultural focus for the communication and presentation of architecture and a forum for debate and the exchange of ideas.

Address:
66 Portland Square
London W1H 4AD UK
Telephone: +44 (0)171 580 5533
Internet: www.architecture.com

Exhibition Schedule:
Hugo Haering and The Secret of Form
January – March 2001

2001 An Architectural Odyssey
February – August 2001

San Francisco Museum of Modern Art

Originally named the San Francisco Museum of Art when it opened in 1935, the "modern" in San Francisco Museum of Modern Art (SFMOMA) was added in 1975 to more accurately describe its mission. SFMOMA's international permanent collection consists of over 18,000 works, including 5,600 paintings, sculptures and works on paper; approximately 9,800 photographs; 3,200 architectural drawings, models and design objects, and a growing collection of works related to the media arts. In 1983, the Museum established its Department of Architecture and Design, the first museum on the West Coast to do so. The department focuses on architecture and design projects pertaining to the Bay Area, California, the American West, and Pacific Rim. Its growing collection focuses on architecture, furniture design, product design, and graphic design from both historic and contemporary periods. The department's Architecture and Design Forum also organizes lectures, symposia, and competitions.

Address:
151 Third Street
San Francisco, CA 94103-3159
Telephone: (415) 357-4000
Internet: www.sfmoma.org

Exhibition Schedule:
Hiroshi Sugimoto: The Architecture Series
November 10, 2000 – March 4, 2001

Selections from the Permanent Collection of Architecture and Design
November 10, 2000 – March 4, 2001

*010101: Art in Technological Times
January 1, 2001(online)/March 3, 2001 (galleries) – July 8, 2001

Allan Wexler: Custom Built
March 30– June 24, 2001

San Francisco
Museum of
Modern Art
(SFMOMA)
(Con't)

Exhibition Schedule (Con't)

Revelatory Landscapes
May – September 2001 (at locations throughout the Bay Area)

California Pottery: From Missions to Modernism
July 20 – October 14, 2001

**If New York keeps on per-
mitting the building of
skyscrapers, each one having as many people every
day as we used to have in a
small city, disaster must
overtake us.**

Thomas Alva Edison, 1926

Sir John Soane's Museum

Sir John Soane's Museum in London has been open to the public since the mid-19th century. Originally the home of Sir John Soane, R.A., architect (1753 – 1837), in 1833, Soane negotiated an Act of Parliament to settle and preserve the house and his collections of art and antiques for the benefit of amateurs and students in architecture, painting, and sculpture. As a Professor of Architecture at the Royal Academy, Soane arranged his books, casts, and models so that the students might have easy access to them. He opened his house for the use of the Royal Academy students the day before and the day after each of his lectures. Today, as Soane requested, the house has, as much as possible, been left as it was over 150 years ago. The Museum's extensive research library is open to researchers by appointment. Staff is available to help with queries relating to many fields including: the restoration of authentic historic interiors, architectural history from the 17th century to the early 19th century, the conservation of drawings and works of art and methods of display, archives, and architectural models.

Address:
13 Lincoln's Inn Fields
London, WC2A 3BP
United Kingdom
Telephone: +44 (0) 171-405 2107
Internet: www.soane.org

Exhibition Schedule:
Ongoing exhibition of Sir John Soane's Home

Skyscraper Museum

The Skyscraper Museum is devoted to the study of historical, contemporary and future high-rise buildings. Located in Lower Manhattan, the birthplace of the skyscraper, the Museum was founded in 1996 as a private, not-for-profit, educational corporation and has presented many exhibits in temporary spaces throughout Manhattan. Its mission expands the traditional view of skyscrapers as objects of design and products of technology, viewing them also as investments in real estate, sites of construction, and places of work and residence. In late 2001, the Museum will open in its permanent home in New York's Battery Park City with expanded facilities for permanent and temporary exhibits, as well as a bookstore and study area.

Address (beginning late 2001):
25 Battery Place
New York, NY, 10281
Telephone: (212) 968-1961
Internet: www.skyscraper.org

Exhibition Schedule:
Skyscraper/City
Debuts 2002

Please visit the museum's Web site for information about their current location, gallery hours, and program schedule.

A machine that makes the land pay.

Cass Gilbert's definition of a skyscraper.

Swedish Museum of Architecture

Stockholm's Swedish Museum of Architecture serves as a repository of information about Swedish architecture, maintains a collection of architectural artifacts, and, through its exhibitions, educates people about the architectural heritage of Sweden. Its archives contain over 2,000,000 architectural drawings and nearly 600,000 photographs. The Museum's permanent exhibition, the History of Swedish Building, covers a period of 1,000 years of Swedish design.

Address:
Skeppsholmen, SE-111 49
Stockholm, Sweden
Telephone: 08-587 270 00
Internet: www.arkitekturmuseet.se

Exhibition Schedule:
The History of Swedish Building
permanent exhibit

Niemeyer – A Modernistic Cultural Heritage
October 7, 2000 – January 14, 2001

Utopia and Reality – Swedish Modernism 1900 –1960
At Moderna Museet, in co-operation with the Arkitekturmuseet
October 7, 2000 – January 14, 2001

Mies van der Rohe Architecture and Design in Stuttgart, Barcelona, Brno
January 27 – April 16, 2001

Projects from The National Association of Swedish Architects
May 2001

Guide to Swedish Architecture
June – August 2001

Housing of Tomorrow
September – October 2001

Architecture and Other Art Forms
November 2001 – January 2002

Vitra Design Museum

Germany's Vitra Design Museum is dedicated to documenting the history and current trends in industrial furniture design. Changing exhibitions are housed in a building Frank O. Gehry designed for the Vitra Design Museum in 1989. Items from the Vitra's permanent collection are housed in the Vitra Fire Station, designed by Zaha Hadid in 1993, and may be viewed by the public on special guided tours only. In addition to its changing exhibits and expansive permanent collection, the Vitra sponsors international travelling exhibitions around the world. The Museum also conducts student workshops, publishes books on design, and manufactures special editions of objects.

Address:
Charles-Eames-Str. 1
D-79576 Weil am Rhein
Germany
Telephone: + 49 7621 702 35 78
Internet: www.design-museum.com

Exhibition Schedule:
Obsession! (from the Vitra Design Museum collection)
November 11, 2000 – April 22, 2001

Blow Up – Shaped Air in Design, Architecture, Fashion and Art
May 4, 2001 – September 9, 2001

Isamu Noguchi
September 22, 2001 – May 3, 2002

Traveling Exhibitions:
Verner Panton
Grassimuseum, Leipzig, Germany:
November 4, 2000 – January 7, 2001

Verner Panton
Schloß Schönbruna, Vienna, Austria:
April 6 – July 1, 2001 (tentative)

Vitra Design Museum, Berlin

On July 1, 2000 the Vitra Design Museum opened a branch in Berlin, the first of many planned branches throughout Europe and the U.S. This location will continue the tradition of the museum's patronage of architecture; it will occupy a 1924-26 former transformer plant, "Humboldt," originally designed by Hans Heinrich Müller, an impressive monument of industrial architecture in the Prenzlauer Berg district of Berlin. The large converted transformer halls will house exhibits intended to raise popular awareness of design and architecture.

Address:
Kopenhagener Straße 58
D-10437 Berlin
Germany
Telephone: +49 30 473 777 0
Internet: www.design-museum.com/berlin.asp

Exhibition Schedule:
Blow Up – Shaped Air in Design, Architecture, Fashion and Art
October 28, 2000 – February 4, 2001

Ron Arad
January 19, 2001 - May 20, 2001

Frank Lloyd Wright – The Living City
March 4, 2001 - October 14, 2001

Ludwig Mies van der Rohe - Furniture and Buildings in Stuttgart, Barcelona, Brno
October 27, 2001 - January 20, 2002

Opposite: The Vitra Design Museum, Berlin in the former transformer station, Humboldt
Photo courtesy of the Vitra Design Museum Berlin

NOTED
INDIVIDUALS

Chancellors of The American Institute of Architects' College of Fellows

Since the founding of The American Institute of Architects' College of Fellows in 1952, the Chancellor is elected, now annually, by the Fellows to preside over the College's investiture ceremonies and business affairs.

1952-53	Ralph Thomas Walker	1983	William C. Muchow
1954-55	Alexander C. Robinson III	1984	Bernard B. Rothschild
1956	Edgar I. Williams	1985	Donald L. Hardison
1957-60	Roy F. Larson	1986	Vladimir Ossipoff
1961-62	Morris Ketchum	1987	S. Scott Ferebee Jr.
1963-64	Paul Thiry	1988	C. William Brubaker
1965-66	George Holmes Perkins	1989	Preston Morgan Bolton
1967-68	Norman J. Schlossman	1990	William A. Rose Jr.
1969-70	John Noble Richards	1991	Robert B. Marquis
1971-72	Jefferson Roy Carroll Jr.	1992	L. Jane Hastings
1973	Ulysses Floyd Rible	1993	John A. Busby Jr.
1974	Albert S. Golemon	1994	Thomas H. Teasdale
1975	Robert S. Hutchins	1995	Robert T. Coles
1976	William Bachman	1996	Ellis W. Bullock Jr.
1977	Phillip J. Meathe	1997	Jack DeBartolo Jr.
1978	George Edward Kassabaum	1998	Harold L. Adams
1979	David Arthur Pugh	1999	Jimmy D. Tittle
1980	Robert L. Durham	2000	Robert A. Odermatt
1981	Leslie N. Boney Jr.	2001	Harold Roth
1982	William Robert Jarratt		

Source: The American Institute of Architects

Good design is not important, it is imperative. Good design costs little more. It is an attitude of the mind. It is not about cost.

Stuart Lipton

Fellows of the American Academy in Rome

Every year the American Academy in Rome grants fellowships to study and work in Rome at the Academy's center for independent study, advanced research, and creative work. Also known as the Rome Prize, the fellowships are granted in a broad range of fields including design, music, literature, and archaeology. The following individuals have been the recipients of the Rome Prize for design related disciplines.

Architecture:

Stanley Abercrombie, FAAR'83
Kimberly A. Ackert, FAAR'97
Anthony Ames, FAAR'84
Joseph Amisano, FAAR'52
Amy Anderson, FAAR'81
Ross S. Anderson, FAAR'90
Richard W. Ayers, FAAR'38
Clarence Dale Badgeley, FAAR'29
Gregory S. Baldwin, FAAR'71
Marc Balet, FAAR'75
Richard Bartholomew, FAAR'72
Frederick Blehle, FAAR'87
James L. Bodnar, FAAR'80
Thomas L. Bosworth, FAAR'81
Charles G. Brickbauer, FAAR'57
Cecil C. Briggs, FAAR'31
Turner Brooks, FAAR'84
Andrea Clark Brown, FAAR'80, AIA
Theodore L. Brown, FAAR'88
William Bruder, FAAR'87
Marvin Buchanan, FAAR'76
Walker O. Cain, FAAR'48
Peter Carl, FAAR'76
Daniel Castor, FAAR'98
Judith Chafee, FAAR'77
Coleman Coker, FAAR'96
Caroline B. Constant, FAAR'79
Frederic S. Coolidge, FAAR'48
Roger Crowley, FAAR'85
Teddy Edwin Cruz, FAAR'92
Thomas V. Czarnowski, FAAR'68
Royston T. Daley, FAAR'62

Spero Daltas, FAAR'51
Douglas Darden, FAAR'89
Thomas L. Dawson, FAAR'52
Joseph De Pace, FAAR'85
Andrea O. Dean, FAAR'80
Kathryn Dean, FAAR'87
Judith Di Maio, FAAR'78
Ronald L. Dirsmith, FAAR'60
Robert Ward Evans, FAAR'73
James Favaro, FAAR'86
Ronald C. Filson, FAAR'70, FAIA
Garrett S. Finney, FAAR'95
Mark M. Foster, FAAR'84
Robert M. Golder, FAAR'63
Alexander C. Gorlin, FAAR'84
Michael Graves, FAAR'62, RAAR'78
James A. Gresham, FAAR'56
Brand Norman Griffin, FAAR'74
Olindo Grossi, FAAR'36
Michael Gruber, FAAR'96
Michael Guran, FAAR'71
Steven Harby, FAAR'00
George E. Hartman, FAAR'78, RAAR'96
John D. Heimbaugh, Jr., FAAR'70
George A. Hinds, FAAR'84
Peter Hopprier, FAAR'77
Elizabeth Humstone, FAAR'86
Sanda D. Iliescu, FAAR'95
Franklin D. Israel, FAAR'75
Erling F. Iversen
David J. Jacob, FAAR'58, RAAR'71
Allan B. Jacobs, FAAR'86, RAAR'96
James R. Jarrett, FAAR'59

Fellows of the American Academy in Rome (Con't)

E. Fay Jones, FAAR'81

Wesley Jones, FAAR'86

Wendy Evans Joseph, FAAR'84

Henri V. Jova, FAAR'51

Robert Kahn, FAAR'82

Spence Kass, FAAR'81

Stephen J. Kieran, FAAR'S 1

Grace R. Kobayaski, FAAR'90

Johannes M.P. Knoops, FAAR'00

Peter Kommers, FAAR'76

Eugene Kupper, FAAR'83

James R. Lamantia, FAAR'49

James L. Lambeth, FAAR'79

Gary Larson, FAAR'83

Thomas N. Larson, FAAR'64

John Q. Lawson, FAAR'81

David L. Leavitt, FAAR'50

Celia Ledbetter, FAAR'83

Diane Lewis, FAAR'77

Paul Lewis, FAAR'99

Roy W. Lewis, FAAR'86

George T. Licht, FAAR'37

Theodore Liebman, FAAR'66

Robert S. Livesey, FAAR'75

John H. MacFadyen, FAAR'54

Robert Mangurian, FAAR'77

Tallie B. Maule, FAAR'52

Arthur May, FAAR'76

David Mayernik, FAAR'89

John J. McDonald, FAAR'83

William G. McMinn, FAAR'82

Cameron McNall, FAAR'92

D. Blake Middleton, FAAR'82

Henry D. Mirick, FAAR'33

Robert Mittelstadt, FAAR'66

Grover E. Mouton III, FAAR'73

Vincent Mulcahy, FAAR'77

Anne Munly, FAAR'96

Theodore J. Musho, FAAR'61

Robert Myers, FAAR'54

John Naughton, FAAR'85

Stanley H. Pansky, FAAR'53

William Pedersen, FAAR'66

Charles O. Perry, FAAR'66

Warren A. Peterson, FAAR'55

Thomas M. Phifer, FAAR'96

Warren Platner, FAAR'56

Antoine S. Predock, FAAR'85, FAIA

George L. Queral, FAAR'88

Patrick J. Quinn, FAAR'80

Jason H. Ramos, FAAR'91

William Reed, FAAR'68

Walter L. Reichardt, FAAR'33

Jesse Reiser, FAAR'85

Richard Rosa, FAAR'99

Peter Miller Schmitt, FAAR'72

Thomas L. Schumacher, FAAR'69, RAAR'91

J. Michael Schwarting, FAAR'70

Frederic D. Schwartz, FAAR'85

Daniel V. Scully, FAAR'70

Catherine Seavitt, FAAR'98

Werner Seligmann, FAAR'81

Thomas Silva, FAAR'89

Jorge Silvetti, FAAR'86

Thomas G. Smith, FAAR'80

Barbara Stauffacher Solomon, FAAR'83

Friedrich St. Florian, FAAR'85

Charles Stifter, FAAR'63

James S. Stokoe, FAAR'79

John J. Stonehill, FAAR'60

Wayne Taylor, FAAR'62

Milo H. Thompson, FAAR'65

Duane Thorbeck, FAAR'64, FAIA

James Timberlake, FAAR'83

Robert H. Timme, FAAR'86

Fred Travisano, FAAR'82

William Turnbull, Jr., FAAR'80

James Velleco, FAAR'77

Robert Venturi, FAAR'56

Austris J. Vitols, FAAR'67

Peter D. Waldman, FAAR'00

Craig H. Walton, FAAR'82

Robert A. Weppner, Jr., FAAR'36

Nichole Wiedemann, FAAR'97

Fellows of the American Academy in Rome (Con't)

Charles D. Wiley, FAAR'48
Tod Williams, FAAR'83
Christian Zapatka, FAAR'91
Astra Zarina, FAAR'63

Landscape Architecture

Eric Armstrong, FAAR'61
E. Bruce Baetjer, FAAR'54
Julie Bargmann, FAAR'90
Richard C. Bell, FAAR'53, RAAR'75
Stephen F. Bochkor, FAAR'57
Elise Brewster, FAAR'98
Robert T. Buchanan, FAAR'59
Richard Burck, FAAR'82
Vincent C. Cerasi, FAAR'50
Henri E. Chabanne, FAAR'34
Linda J. Cook, FAAR'89
Joanna Dougherty, FAAR'86
F. W. Edmondson, FAAR'48 (1)
Jon S. Emerson, FAAR'67
Eric Reid Fulford, FAAR'92
Ralph E. Griswold, FAAR'23
Edgar C. Haag, FAAR'79
Robert Mitchell Hanna, FAAR'76
Stephen C. Haus, FAAR'79
Dale H. Hawkins, FAAR'52
Elizabeth Dean Hermann, FAAR'87
Gary R. Hilderbrand, FAAR'95
Walter Hood, FAAR'97
Alden Hopkins, FAAR'35
Dr. Frank D. James, FAAR'68
Dean A. Johnson, FAAR'66
Mary Margaret Jones, FAAR'98
John F. Kirkpatrick, FAAR'39
Robert S. Kitchen, FAAR'38
Albert R. Lamb, III, FAAR'70
Edward Lawson, FAAR'21
Tom Leader, FAAR'99
James M. Lister, FAAR'37
Roger B. Martin, FAAR'64
Laurel McSherry, FAAR'00
Stuart M. Mertz, FAAR'40

Stacy T. Moriarty, FAAR'84
Richard C. Murdock, FAAR'33
Norman T. Newton, FAAR'26, RAAR 67
Peter O'Shea, FAAR'96
Laurie D. Olin, FAAR'74, RAAR'90
Don H. Olson, FAAR'62
Thomas R. Oslund, FAAR'92
Nell H. Park, FAAR'33
George E. Patton, FAAR'51
Paul R. V. Pawlowski, FAAR'69
Peter M. Pollack, FAAR'71
Thomas D. Price, FAAR'32
Charles A. Rapp, FAAR'72
Michael Rapuano, FAAR'30
Peter G. Rolland, FAAR'78, FASLA
Leslie A. Ryan, FAAR'95
Peter Lindsay Schaudt, FAAR'91, ASLA
Terry Schnadelbach, FAAR'66
Seth H. Seablom, FAAR'68
Stephen Sears, FAAR'00
Charles Sullivan, FAAR'85
Jack Sullivan, FAAR'83
Charles R. Sutton, FAAR'32
Erik A. Svenson, FAAR'58
L. Azeo Torre, FAAR'76
Morris E. Trotter, FAAR'35
James R. Turner, FAAR'76
Daniel Tuttle, FAAR'88
Michael R. Van Valkenburgh, FAAR'88
E. Michael Vergason, FAAR'80
Craig P. Verzone, FAAR'99
Richard K. Webel, FAAR'29, RAAR'63
Professor James L. Wescoat, FAAR'97
Brooks E. Wigginton, FAAR'50
Gall Wittwer, FAAR'96
John L. Wong, FAAR'81
Prof. Ervin H. Zube, FAAR'61

Historic Preservation and Conservation

Elmo Baca, FAAR'00
Prof. Margaret Holben Ellis, FAAR'94
Shelley Fletcher, FAAR'98

Fellows of the American Academy in Rome (Con't)

Eric Gordon, FAAR'97

Anne Frances Maheux, FAAR'96

Pablo Ojeda-O'Neill, FAAR'96

Alice Boccia Paterakis, FAAR'00

Leslie Rainer, FAAR'99

Bettina A. Raphael, FAAR'94

Thomas C. Roby, FAAR'95

Catherine Sease, FAAR'95

Prof. Frederick Steiner, FAAR'98

Jonathan Thorton, FAAR'99

Dr. George Wheeler, FAAR'97

Design Arts

William Adair, FAAR'92

Gerald D. Adams, FAAR'68

Thomas Angotti, FAAR'90

Donald Appleyard, FAAR'75

Joseph H. Aronson, FAAR'74

Morley Baer, FAAR'80

Gordon C. Baldwin, FAAR'78

Phillip R. Baldwin, FAAR'94

Karen Bausman, FAAR'95

Ellen Beasley, FAAR'89

Anna Campbell Bliss, FAAR'84

Robert W. Braunschweiger, FAAR'74

Paul M. Bray, FAAR'97

Steven Brooke, FAAR'91

Michael B. Cadwell, FAAR'99

Heather Carson, FAAR'99

John J. Casbarian, FAAR'86, FAIA

Adele Chatfield-Taylor, FAAR'84

Walter Chatham, FAAR'89

Morison S. Cousins, FAAR'85

Russell Rowe Culp, FAAR'80

Phoebe Cutler, FAAR'89

Joseph Paul D'Urso, FAAR'88

Paul Davis, FAAR'98

Robert S. Davis, FAAR'91

Robert De Fuccio, FAAR'76

Robert Regis Dvorak, FAAR'72

Hsin-ming Fung, FAAR'92

Jeanne Giordano, FAAR'87

Miller Horns, FAAR'90

Robert Jensen, FAAR'76

June Meyer Jordan, FAAR'71

Wendy Kaplan, FAAR'00

J. Michael Kirkland, FAAR'70

Robert Kramer, FAAR'72

George Krause, FAAR'77, RAAR'80

Norman Krumholz, FAAR'87

Michael Lax, FAAR'78

Debra McCall, FAAR'89

R. Alan Melting, FAAR'70

Donald Oenslager

Donald Peting, FAAR'78

William L. Plumb, FAAR'86

William Reed, FAAR'68

Julie Riefler, FAAR'87

Mark Robbins, FAAR'97

Michael Rock, FAAR'00

Danny M. Samuels, FAAR'86

Mark Schimmenti, FAAR'98

Paul D. Schwartzman, FAAR'77

William V. Shaw, FAAR'68

Alison Sky, FAAR'78

Paul L. Steinberg, FAAR'82

Joel Sternfeld, FAAR'91

Michelle Stone, FAAR'78

Edward Marc Treib, FAAR'85

Kevin Walz, FAAR'95

Emily M. Whiteside, FAAR'82

Janet Zweig, FAAR'92

FAAR = Fellow of the American Academy in Rome

RAAR = Resident of the American Academy in Rome

Source: American Academy in Rome

Fellows of the American Academy of Arts and Sciences

Since its founding in 1780, the American Academy of Arts and Sciences has pursued its goal "To cultivate every art and science which may tend to advance the interest, honor, dignity, and happiness of a free, independent, and virtuous people." Throughout its history, the Academy's diverse membership has included the best from the arts, science, business, scholarship, and public affairs. Nominations for new members are taken from existing fellows and evaluated by panels from each discipline and the membership at large.

Design Professionals, Academics, and Writers:

Christopher Alexander '96
U. of Calif., Berkeley

Edward Larrabee Barnes '78
Edward Larrabee Barnes/
John M. Y. Lee Architects,
New York

Herbert Lawrence Block '59
Washington, D.C.

Denise Scott Brown '93
Venturi Scott Brown &
Assoc., Inc., Philadelphia

Robert Campbell '93
Cambridge, Mass.

Henry Nichols Cobb '84
Pei, Cobb, Freed & Partners,
New York

Peter D. Eisenman '00
Eisenman Architects, New York, NY

Kenneth Frampton '93
Columbia University

James Ingo Freed '94
Pei, Cobb, Freed & Partners,
New York

Frank Owen Gehry '91
Frank O. Gehry and Associates, Santa
Monica, Calif.

Lawrence Halprin '78
San Francisco, Calif.

Robert S.F. Hughes '93
Time Magazine

Ada Louise Huxtable '74
New York, N.Y.

Philip Johnson '77
Philip Johnson Architects,
New York

Gerhard Michael Kallmann '85
Kallmann, McKinnell and Wood,
Architects, Inc., Boston

(Noel) Michael McKinnell '85
Kallmann, McKinnell and Wood,
Architects, Inc., Boston

Richard Alan Meier '95
New York, NY

Henry Armand Millon '75
National Gallery of Art,
Washington, D.C.

William Mitchell '97
Massachusetts Institute of Technology

Fellows of the American Academy of Arts and Sciences (Con't)

I(eoh) M(ing) Pei '67
Pei, Cobb, Freed & Partners,
New York

Kevin Roche '94
Hamden, Conn.

Robert Rosenblum '84
New York University

Moshe Safdie '96
Moshe Safdie & Assoc., Sommerville,
Mass.

Vincent J. Scully '86
Yale University

Hugh Asher-Stubbins '57
Ocean Ridge, Fla.

Robert Venturi '84
Venturi Scott Brown & Assoc., Inc.,
Philadelphia

Foreign Honorary Members:

Charles Correa '93
Bombay, India

Carl Theodor Dreyer '65
Copenhagen, Denmark

Norman Robert Foster '96
Foster and Associates, London

Phyllis Lambert '95
Center Canadien d'Architecture, Montreal,
Quebec

Ricardo Legorreta '94
Mexico City, Mexico

Fumihiko Maki '96
Maki and Associates, Tokyo, Japan

J. Rafael Moneo '93
Harvard University

Oscar Niemeyer '49
Rio de Janeiro, Brazil

Renzo Piano '93
London, England

Alvaro Siza '92
Porto, Portugal

Kenzo Tange '67
Tokyo, Japan

Source: American Academy of Arts and Sciences

Fellows of The American Institute of Architects

The College of Fellows of The American Institute of Architects (AIA) is composed of AIA members who have been elected to Fellowship by a jury of their peers. Fellowship is granted for significant contributions to architecture and society and for achieving a high standard of professional excellence. Architect members who have been in good standing for at least 10 years may be nominated for Fellowship. The following individuals are current active members of The American Institute of Architects' College of Fellows.

A

Carlton S. Abbott, Williamsburg, VA
J. C. Abbott Jr., Sarasota, FL
James Abell, Tempe, AZ
Jan M. Abell, Tampa, FL
Stephen N. Abend, Kansas City, MO
Bruce A. Abrahamson, Minneapolis, MN
Max Abramovitz, Pound Ridge, NY
Raymond C. Abst, Modesto, CA
Harold L. Adams, Baltimore, MD
William M. Adams, Venice, CA
William T. Adams, Dallas, TX
Michael Adlerstein, New York, NY
P. Aguirre Jr., Dallas, TX
Loren P. Ahles, Minneapolis, MN
Thomas R. Aidala, San Francisco, CA
Roula Alakiotou, Chicago, IL
Charles A Albanese, Tucson, AZ
Richard K. Albyn, Pisgah Forest, NC
N. Sue Alden, Seattle, WA
Iris S. Alex, New York, NY
Cecil A. Alexander Jr., Atlanta, GA
Earle S. Alexander Jr., Houston, TX
Henry C. Alexander Jr., Coral Gables, FL
James G. Alexander, Boston, MA
A. Notley Alford, Englewood, FL
Stanley N. Allan, Chicago, IL

Maurice B. Allen Jr., Bloomfield Hills, MI
Ralph G. Allen, Chicago, IL
Rex W. Allen, Sonoma, CA
Robert E. Allen, San Francisco, CA
Robert E. Allen, Longview, TX
Gerald L. Allison, Newport Beach, CA
Killis P. Almond Jr., San Antonio, TX
Alfred S. Alschuler, Highland Park, IL
Ronald A. Altoon, Los Angeles, CA
Jesus E. Amaral, San Juan, Puerto Rico
Joseph Amisano, Atlanta, GA
Dorman D. Anderson, Seattle, WA
Harry F. Anderson, Oakbrook, IL
J. Timothy Anderson, Cambridge, MA
John D. Anderson, Denver, CO
Richard Anderson, Tucson, AZ
Samuel A. Anderson, Charlottesville, VA
William L. Anderson, Des Moines, IA
J. Philip Andrews, Pittsburgh, PA
Lavone D. Andrews, Houston, TX
Martha P. Andrews, Portland, OR
George Anselevicius, Albuquerque, NM
James H. Anstis, West Palm Beach, FL
Natalye Appel, Houston, TX
Richard M. Archer, San Antonio, TX
Peter F. Arfaa, Philadelphia, PA
Bruce P. Arneill, Glastonbury, CT
Chris Arnold, Palo Alto, CA

Fellows of The American Institute of Architects (Con't)

Christopher C. Arnold, Commerce Twp., MI

Robert V. Arrigoni, San Francisco, CA

Yvonne W. Asken, Portage, MI

Laurin B. Askew, Columbia, MD

Lee Hewlett Askew III, Memphis, TN

Neil L. Astle, Salt Lake City, UT

Louis D. Astorino, Pittsburgh, PA

Charles H. Atherton, Washington, DC

Tony Atkin, Philadelphia, PA

John L. Atkins, Research Triangle Park, NC

Eugene E. Aubry, Holmes Beach, FL

Seymour Auerbach, Chevy Chase, MD

Douglas H. Austin, San Diego, CA

Daniel Avchen, Minneapolis, MN

Donald C. Axon, Laguna Beach, CA

Alfred L. Aydelott, Carmel, CA

B

Howard J. Backen, Sausalito, CA

Edmund N. Bacon, Philadelphia, PA

David C. Baer, Houston, TX

Stuart Baesel, La Jolla, CA

Deon F. Bahr, Lincoln, NE

Ray B. Bailey, Houston, TX

William J. Bain Jr., Seattle, WA

Royden Stanley Bair, Houston, TX

Louis J. Bakanowsky, Cambridge, MA

David Baker, San Francisco, CA

Isham O. Baker, Washington, DC

Jack Sherman Baker, Champaign, IL

James Barnes Baker, London, England

Gregory S. Baldwin, Portland, OR

Samuel T. Balen, Waldport, OR

Rex M. Ball, Tulsa, OK

Richard S. Banwell, Walnut Creek, CA

Shalom S. Baranes, Washington, DC

Robert A. Barclay, Cleveland, OH

Paul H. Barkley, Falls Church, VA

John M. Barley, II, Jacksonville, FL

Charles C. Barlow, Jackson, MS

Edward L. Barnes, Cambridge, MA

Linda Barnes, Portland, OR

Jay William Barnes Jr., Austin, TX

Rebecca Barnes, Boston, MA

Jonathan Barnett, Washington, DC

Carol R. Barney, Chicago, IL

Howard R. Barr, Austin, TX

Raj Barr-Kumar, Washington, DC

Nolan E. Barrick, Lubbock, TX

Errol Barron, New Orleans, LA

Richard E. Barrow, Birmingham, AL

Richard W. Bartholomew, Philadelphia, PA

Armand Bartos, New York, NY

Edward C. Bassett, Mill Valley, CA

Fred Bassetti, Seattle, WA

Peter Batchelor, Raleigh, NC

Ronald J. Battaglia, Buffalo, NY

Jay S. Bauer, Newport Beach, CA

Edward Baum, Dallas, TX

Joseph D. Bavaro, Punta Gorda, FL

John Craig Beale, Dallas, TX

Burtch W. Beall Jr., Salt Lake City, UT

Leroy E. Bean, Petaluma, CA

Alan J. Beard, Portland, OR

Lee P. Bearsch, Binghamton, NY

William H. Beaty, Memphis, TN

William B. Bechhoefer, Bethesda, MD

Lee Becker, Washington, DC

Rex L. Becker, St. Louis, MO

Herbert Beckhard, New York, NY

Robert M. Beckley, Ann Arbor, MI

Michael Bednar, Charlottesville, VA

Carmi Bee, New York, NY

David W. Beer, New York, NY

Fellows of The American Institute of Architects (Con't)

Edgar C. Beery, Springfield, VA

Ann M. Beha, Boston, MA

Byron Bell, New York, NY

Frederic Bell, Long Island City, NY

M. Wayne Bell, Austin, TX

John Belle, New York, NY

Ralph C. Bender, San Antonio, TX

Barry Benepe, New York, NY

Daniel D. Bennett, Fayetteville, AR

David J. Bennett, Minneapolis, MN

Frederick R. Bentel, Locust Valley, NY

Maria A. Bentel, Locust Valley, NY

Kenneth E. Bentsen, Houston, TX

Frederick J. Bentz, Minneapolis, MN

Karl A. Berg, Denver, CO

Richard R. Bergmann, New Canaan, CT

Lloyd F. Bergquist, Bloomington, MN

Robert J. Berkebile, Kansas City, MO

Marlene J. Berkoff, San Rafael, CA

Anthony N. Bernheim, San Francisco, CA

Phillip Bernstein, New Haven, CT

K. Norman Berry, Louisville, KY

Richard J. Bertman, Boston, MA

Ronald P. Bertone, Middletown, NJ

Frederic A. Bertram, Clearwater, FL

Hobart Betts, Sag Harbor, NY

John H. Beyer, New York, NY

William Beyer, Minneapolis, MN

John H. Bickel, Louisville, KY

Frederick C. Biebesheimer, III, Old Lyme, CT

T. J. Biggs, Jackson, MS

Rebecca L. Binder, Playa Del Rey, CA

James Binkley, Arlington, VA

Lance L. Bird, Pasadena, CA

John R. Birge, Omaha, NE

Gunnar Birkerts, Bloomfield Hills, MI

James A. Bishop, Bellville, TX

George Bissell, Newport Beach, CA

J. Sinclair Black, Austin, TX

Walter S. Blackburn, Indianapolis, IN

Leonard D. Blackford, Sacramento, CA

Jan Gaede Blackmon, Dallas, TX

Boyd A. Blackner, Salt Lake City, UT

Peter Blake, Riverdale, NY

Frederick A. Bland, New York, NY

Wilfred E. Blessing, Oak Harbor, WA

Richard L. Blinder, New York, NY

Richard L. Bliss, Kirkwood, MO

Robert L. Bliss, Salt Lake City, UT

Ronald B. Blitch, New Orleans, LA

John D. Bloodgood, Des Moines, IA

Martin Bloomenthal, Princeton, NJ

Sigmund F. Blum, Naples, FL

Susan Blumentals, Brooklyn Center, MN

H. M. Blumer, Paradise Valley, AZ

Kirk V. Blunck, Des Moines, IA

William A. Blunden, Cleveland, OH

William E. Blurock, Newport Beach, CA

William Bobenhausen, Norwalk, CT

L. Kirkpatrick Bobo, Memphis, TN

Michael L. Bobrow, Los Angeles, CA

William N. Bodouva, New York, NY

Joe Boehning, Albuquerque, NM

Robert J. Boerema, Gainesville, FL

Joseph Boggs, Annapolis, MD

Walter F. Bogner, Larchmont, NY

Peter Bohlin, Wilkes Barre, PA

Friedrich K.M. Bohm, Columbus, OH

Mario H. Boiardi, Washington, DC

Stanley G. Boles, Portland, OR

Michael E. Bolinger, Baltimore, MD

Robert D. Bolling, Torrance, CA

Antonio R. Bologna, Memphis, TN

Preston M. Bolton, Houston, TX

James R. Bonar, Los Angeles, CA

J. Max Bond Jr., New York, NY

Fellows of The American Institute of Architects (Con't)

Charles Hussey Boney, Wilmington, NC

Leslie N. Boney Jr., Wilmington, NC

Paul D. Boney, Wilmington, NC

Dwight M. Bonham, Wichita, KS

Daniel Boone, Abilene, TX

David C. Boone, Santa Cruz, CA

Laurence O. Booth, Chicago, IL

Bill C. Booziotis, Dallas, TX

L. G. Borget, Houston, TX

Bernard Bortnick, Dallas, TX

Thomas L. Bosworth, Seattle, WA

Elmer E. Botsai, Honolulu, HI

Elmer Botsai, Honolulu, HI

Gary A. Bowden, Baltimore, MD

David M. Bowen, Fishers, IN

Gary Bowen, Omaha, NE

Ronald Gene Bowen, Middleton, WI

John A. Bower Jr., Philadelphia, PA

Paul D. Bowers Jr., Grand Rapids, MI

William A. Bowersox, Saint Louis, MO

Chester Bowles Jr., San Francisco, CA

J. Donald Bowman, Bellevue, WA

John Harold Box, Austin, TX

Robert A. Boynton, Richmond, VA

John Bozalis, Oklahoma City, OK

James H. Bradburn, Denver, CO

David R. Braden, Dallas, TX

Richard H. Bradfield, Clearwater, FL

Thomas G. Bradley, Decatur, IL

Clyde A. Brady, III, Orlando, FL

Scott W. Braley, Atlanta, GA

Ronald M. Brame, Dallas, TX

Joel Brand, Houston, TX

Robert Brannen, Boston, MA

Charles S. Braun, Longwood, FL

Richard M. Brayton, San Francisco, CA

William E. Brazley Jr., Matteson, IL

Melvin Brecher, Broomall, PA

William N. Breger, New York, NY

Simon Breines, Scarsdale, NY

John Michael Brendle, Denver, CO

Daniel R. Brents, Houston, TX

Adrienne G. Bresnan, New York, NY

Joseph Bresnan, New York, NY

Benjamin E. Brewer Jr., Houston, TX

Leon Bridges, Baltimore, MD

Stanford R. Britt, Washington, DC

Joseph M. Brocato Sr., Alexandria, LA

Myra M. Brocchini, Berkeley, CA

Ronald G. Brocchini, Berkeley, CA

Paul Broches, New York, NY

Raymond D. Brochstein, Houston, TX

William R. Brockway, Baton Rouge, LA

M. J. Brodie, Baltimore, MD

H. Gordon Brooks, II, Lafayette, LA

John W. Broome, Tualatin, OR

Robert C. Broshar, Clear Lake, IA

David J. Brotman, Los Angeles, CA

Charles E. Broudy, Philadelphia, PA

Jennie Sue Brown, Seattle, WA

Kenneth F. Brown, Honolulu, HI

Paul B. Brown, Traverse City, MI

Robert F. Brown Jr., Philadelphia, PA

Robert L. Brown Jr., Lithonia, GA

Terrance Brown, Albuquerque, NM

Woodlief Brown, Abilene, TX

George D. Brown Jr., Peekskill, NY

C. William Brubaker, Chicago, IL

Barry B. Bruce, Bellaire, TX

Van B. Bruner Jr., Haddonfield, NJ

Harry A. Bruno, Walnut Creek, CA

Larry S. Bruton, Portland, OR

Harvey Bryan, Belmont, MA

John H. Bryant, Stillwater, OK

Fellows of The American Institute of Architects (Con't)

Algimantas V. Bublys, Birmingham, MI

Marvin H. Buchanan, Berkeley, CA

James W. Buckley, Greensboro, GA

Michael P. Buckley, New Haven, CT

Huber H. Buehrer, Maumee, OH

John B. Buenz, Chicago, IL

Glenn A. Buff, Miami, FL

Henrik H. Bull, San Francisco, CA

Ellis W. Bullock Jr., Pensacola, FL

Thomas A. Bullock, Sr., Brenham, TX

W. Glenn Bullock, Knoxville, TN

Franklin S. Bunch, Sugar Land, TX

Richard S. Bundy, San Diego, CA

John H. Burgee, Montecito, CA

Charles E. Burgess, Houston, TX

J. Armand Burgun, Kitty Hawk, NC

Edward M. Burke, Austin, TX

James E. Burlage, Sausalito, CA

Robert Burley, Waitsfield, VT

Arthur L. Burns, Winter Haven, FL

John A. Burns, Alexandria, VA

Norma DeCamp Burns, Raleigh, NC

Robert P. Burns, Raleigh, NC

Rodger E. Burson, Wimberley, TX

John A. Busby Jr., Atlanta, GA

C. Joe Buskuhl, Dallas, TX

H. Kennard Bussard, Des Moines, IA

Jerome R. Butler, Chicago, IL

Theodore R. Butler, Minneapolis, MN

Fred W. Butner, Winston Salem, NC

Thomas K. Butt, Point Richmond, CA

Harold Buttrick, New York, NY

Paul S. Byard, New York, NY

Brent Byers, Austin, TX

Jeanne Byrne, Pacific Grove, CA

Arne Bystrom, Seattle, WA

C

Burns Cadwalader, Oakland, CA

Harold Calhoun, Houston, TX

Robert Campbell, Cambridge, MA

Wendell J. Campbell, Chicago, IL

H. F. Candela, Coral Gables, FL

Robert H. Canizaro, Jackson, MS

William T. Cannady, Houston, TX

Jamie Cannon, Town & Country, MO

Marvin J. Cantor, Fairfax, VA

Horace S. Cantrell Jr., Indianapolis, IN

Kenneth Harvey Cardwell, Berkeley, CA

Jean P. Carlhian, Boston, MA

William A. Carlisle, Columbia, SC

DeVon M. Carlson, Boulder, CO

Donald Edwin Carlson, Seattle, WA

Clyde R. Carpenter, Lexington, KY

Jack A. Carpenter, San Diego, CA

Edwin Winford Carroll, El Paso, TX

M. E. Carroll, Chevy Chase, MD

Marley Carroll, Charlotte, NC

W. T. Carry, Atlanta, GA

Chris Carson, San Antonio, TX

Donald K. Carter, Pittsburgh, PA

Virgil R. Carter, Newtown Square, PA

David R. Cartnal, San Jose, CA

Timothy A. Casai, Bloomfield Hills, MI

John Casbarian, Houston, TX

A. Cascieri, Lexington, MA

Donald W. Caskey, Irvine, CA

Heather W. Cass, Washington, DC

Joseph W. Casserly, Chicago, IL

John J. Castellana, Bloomfield Hills, MI

Stephan Castellanos, Stockton, CA

Samuel J. Caudill, Aspen, CO

Giorgio Cavaglieri, New York, NY

Fellows of The American Institute of Architects (Con't)

W. Brooks Cavin Jr., Shelburne, VT

Lawrence Chaffin Jr., Koloa, HI

Ann R. Chaintreuil, Rochester, NY

Alfred V. Chaix, South Pasadena, CA

Dean B. Chambliss, Denver, CO

Junius J. Champeaux, II, Lake Charles, LA

Lo-Yi Chan, Ashley Falls, MA

Wing T. Chao, Burbank, CA

L. William Chapin II, Alexandria, VA

Donald D. Chapman, Kula, HI

John S. Chase, Houston, TX

Walter F. Chatham, New York, NY

Peter Chermayeff, Boston, MA

Edith Cherry, Albuquerque, NM

Edward E. Cherry, Hamden, CT

Robert A. Chervenak, Mount Vernon, WA

Lugean L. Chilcote, Little Rock, AR

G. Cabell Childress, Castle Rock, CO

David M. Childs, New York, NY

Maurice F. Childs, Boston, MA

Susan Chin, New York, NY

Robert E. Chisholm, Miami, FL

Gordon H. Chong, San Francisco, CA

Frederick L. Christensen, Salinas, CA

George W. Christensen, Scottsdale, AZ

James W. Christopher, Salt Lake City, UT

Eric A. Chung, Radnor, PA

William C. Church, Portland, OR

Richard J. Chylinski, Los Angeles, CA

Mario J. Ciampi, Kentfield, CA

Robert L. Cioppa, New York, NY

Eugene D. Cizek, New Orleans, LA

George L. Claflen, Philadelphia, PA

John M. Clancy, Boston, MA

James F. Clapp Jr., Cambridge, MA

Gerald L. Clark, Havasu City, AZ

Roger H. Clark, Raleigh, NC

John P. Clarke, Trenton, NJ

Marshall F. Clarke, Greenville, SC

Fred W. Clarke III, New Haven, CT

Charles Clary, Destin, FL

Thomas R. Clause, Des Moines, IA

Jerry L. Clement, St. Louis, MO

Glen E. Cline, Boise, ID

Elizabeth Close, St. Paul, MN

Robert K. Clough, Chicago, IL

James A Clutts, Dallas, TX

Henry N. Cobb, New York, NY

R. F. Coffee, Austin, TX

Andrew S. Cohen, Middlebury, CT

Jack C. Cohen, Bethesda, MD

Martin H. Cohen, Armonk, NY

Stuart Cohen, Evanston, IL

Doris Cole, Concord, MA

Robert Traynham Coles, Buffalo, NY

David S. Collins, Cincinnati, OH

Donald Comstock, Sacramento, CA

William T. Conklin, Washington, DC

Richard T. Conrad, Sacramento, CA

W. M. Conrad, Kansas City, MO

John Conron, Santa Fe, NM

J. J. Conroy, Chicago, IL

Eugene E. Cook, Roselle, IL

Lawrence D. Cook, Falls Church, VA

Richard B. Cook, Chicago, IL

William H. Cook, Sonoita, AZ

Alexander Cooper, New York, NY

Jerome M. Cooper, Atlanta, GA

W. Kent Cooper, Washington, DC

Christopher Coover, Phoenix, AZ

Gerald M. Cope, Philadelphia, PA

Lee G. Copeland, Seattle, WA

C. Jack Corgan, Dallas, TX

Jack M. Corgan, Dallas, TX

William Corlett, Berkeley, CA

Araldo A. Cossutta, New York, NY

Fellows of The American Institute of Architects (Con't)

Walter H. Costa, Lafayette, CA

Leland Cott, Cambridge, MA

John O. Cotton, Marina Del Rey, CA

C. H. Cowell, Houston, TX

Dan C. Cowling, Little Rock, AR

David C. Cox, Washington, DC

Frederic H Cox, Richmond, VA

Warren J. Cox, Washington, DC

Whitson W. Cox, Carmichael, CA

Bruce I. Crabtree Jr., Nashville, TN

Kirk R. Craig, Greenville, SC

Steade Craigo, Sacramento, CA

George M. Crandall, Portland, OR

David A. Crane Tampa, FL

Ronald O. Crawford, Roanoke, VA

Martin W. Crennen, Helena, MT

Frank W. Crimp, Milton, MA

James H. Crissman, Watertown, MA

Edwin B. Crittenden, Anchorage, AK

K. C. Crocco, Chicago, IL

Charles B. Croft, Austin, TX

Edwin B. Cromwell, Little Rock, AR

Eason Cross Jr., Alexandria, VA

Samuel Crothers, III, Radnor, PA

R. L. Crowther, Denver, CO

Randolph R. Croxton, New York, NY

Metcalf Crump, Memphis, TN

Evan D. Cruthers, Honolulu, HI

John W. Cuningham, Minneapolis, MN

Ben Cunningham, St. Petersburg, FL

Gary M. Cunningham, Dallas, TX

Warren W. Cunningham, Philadelphia, PA

James L. Cutler, Bainbridge Is, WA

Bernard J. Cywinski, Havertown, PA

D

Charles E. Dagit Jr., Philadelphia, PA

Fernand W. Dahan, Rockville, MD

David A. Daileda, Springfield, VA

Curt Dale, Denver, CO

Todd Dalland, New York, NY

J. E. Dalton, Kent, OH

Leo A. Daly III, Washington, DC

Paul Damaz, East Hampton, NY

Sylvester Damianos, Pittsburgh, PA

Robert Damora, Bedford, NY

George E. Danforth, Chicago, IL

Arthur C. Danielian, Irvine, CA

George N. Daniels, Salt Lake City, UT

Stanley L. Daniels, Atlanta, GA

Doris Andrews Danna, St. Louis, MO

Robert F. Darby, Jacksonville, FL

Samuel N. Darby, Rockford, IL

Edwin S. Darden, Fresno, CA

Ben R. Darmer, Atlanta, GA

Richard Dattner, New York, NY

Theoharis L. David, New York, NY

D. G. Davidson, Washington, DC

Did you know...

The States with the most AIA Fellows are:
California — 383
Texas — 224
New York — 206
Illinois — 124
Massachusetts — 117
Florida — 94
Washington — 87
Pennsylvania — 76
Virginia — 68
Michigan — 63
District of Columbia — 60

Fellows of The American Institute of Architects (Con't)

David S. Davidson, Great Falls, MT

Robert I. Davidson, New York, NY

Albert J. Davis, Blacksburg, VA

Arthur Q. Davis, New Orleans, LA

Charles M. Davis, San Francisco, CA

Clark Davis, St. Louis, MO

Clark A. Davis, San Francisco, CA

Jerry A Davis, New York, NY

John M. Davis, Austin, TX

Lewis Davis, New York, NY

Nicholas Davis, Auburn, AL

Steven M. Davis, New York, NY

W. T. Davis, Greenville, SC

Clare Henry Day, Redlands, CA

Frederic L. Day Jr., Concord, MA

Natalie De Blois, San Antonio, TX

John Neff De Haas Jr., Bozeman, MT

Rey de la Reza, Houston, TX

Alfredo De Vido, New York, NY

Jack DeBartolo Jr., Phoenix, AZ

Rudolph V. DeChellis, Woodland Hills, CA

Vernon DeMars, Berkeley, CA

Kenneth DeMay, Watertown, MA

Louis DeMoll, Moylan, PA

J. R. DeStefano, Chicago, IL

Panayotis E. DeVaris, South Orange, NJ

E. L. Deam, Highland Park, IL

Robert C. Dean, Boston, MA

C. M. Deasy, San Luis Obispo, CA

Howard S. Decker, Chicago, IL

Ward W. Deems, Solana Beach, CA

Allan J. Dehar, New Haven, CT

Jorge Del Rio, San Juan, Puerto Rico

Homer T. Delawie, San Diego, CA

Eugene A. Delmar, Olney, MD

Sidney L. Delson, East Hampton, NY

Olvia Demetriou, Washington, DC

William Deno, Boulder, CO

Jos. Robert Deshayes, Caldwell, TX

Gary L. Desmond, Denver, CO

John J. Desmond, Baton Rouge, LA

Gita Dev, Woodside, CA

Suzanne Di Geronimo, Paramus, NJ

Antonio Di Mambro, Boston, MA

A P. DiBenedetto, Portland, OR

Eugene L. DiLaura, Milan, MI

Robert Diamant, Longboat Key, FL

J. J. J. Diamond, Jacksonville, FL

Katherine Diamond, Los Angeles, CA

Horacio Diaz, San Juan, Puerto Rico

James R. Diaz, San Francisco, CA

David R. Dibner, McLean, VA

Bruce Dicker, Portsmouth, NH

Gerald G. Diehl, Dearborn, MI

Paul E. Dietrich, Cambridge, MA

Robert H. Dietz, Apache Junction, AZ

William M. Dikis, Des Moines, IA

Frank Dimster, Los Angeles, CA

Philip Dinsmore, Tucson, AZ

David D. Dixon, Boston, MA

F. Dail Dixon Jr., Chapel Hill, NC

John M. Dixon, Old Greenwich, CT

Michael A. Dixon, St. Charles, IL

Lawrence S. Doane, San Francisco, CA

Jim C. Doche, Amarillo, TX

Peter H. Dodge, San Francisco, CA

George S. Dolim, San Francisco, CA

Peter Hoyt Dominick Jr., Denver, CO

Milford W. Donaldson, San Diego, CA

Janet Donelson, Seattle, WA

Richard C. Donkervoet, Baltimore, MD

Kermit P. Dorius, Newport Bch, CA

Albert A. Dorman, Los Angeles, CA

Richard L. Dorman, Santa Fe, NM

Robert W. Dorsey, Cincinnati, OH

Darwin V. Doss, Salem, OR

Fellows of The American Institute of Architects (Con't)

Betsey O. Dougherty, Costa Mesa, CA

Brian P. Dougherty, Costa Mesa, CA

Frank F. Douglas, Houston, TX

H. Robert Douglass, Missouri City, TX

C.R. George Dove, Washington, DC

Gerald A. Doyle, Phoenix, AZ

Peter G. Doyle, Houston, TX

Boris Dramov, San Francisco, CA

Helene Dreiling, Warrenton, VA

Roy M. Drew, San Diego, CA

Albert M. Dreyfuss, Sacramento, CA

Robert W. Drummond, Gainesville, FL

Andres Duany, Miami, FL

Martin David Dubin, Highland Park, IL

George A. Dudley, Rensselaerville, NY

J. Paul Duffendack, Leawood, KS

Herbert E. Duncan, Kansas City, MO

Foster W. Dunwiddie, Henderson, NV

Eugene C. Dunwody, Macon, GA

William L. Duquette, Los Gatos, CA

Almon J. Durkee, Traverse City, MI

William R. Dutcher, Berkeley, CA

Daniel L. Dworsky, Los Angeles, CA

E

Mary Jean Eastman, New York, NY

John P. Eberhard, Alexandria, VA

Jeremiah Eck, Boston, MA

Stanton Eckstut, New York, NY

Robert N. Eddy, Bakersfield, CA

Judith Edelman, New York, NY

Jared I. Edwards, Hartford, CT

David J. Edwards Jr., Columbia, SC

Albert Efron, Staten Island, NY

David L. Eggers, West Palm Beach, FL

Ezra D. Ehrenkrantz, New York, NY

John P. Ehrig, Merritt Island, FL

Joseph Ehrlich, Menlo Park, CA

Steven D. Ehrlich, Culver City, CA

Thomas N. Eichbaum, Washington, DC

John A. Eifler, Chicago, IL

Steven L. Einhorn, Albany, NY

Peter D. Eisenman, New York, NY

Sidney H. Eisenshtat, Los Angeles, CA

Richard Karl Eisner, Oakland, CA

Barry P. Elbasani, Berkeley, CA

Joseph L. Eldredge, Vineyard Hvn, MA

Charles N. Eley, San Francisco, CA

James H. Eley, Jackson, MS

Howard F. Elkus, Boston, MA

Harry Ellenzweig, Cambridge, MA

Robin M. Ellerthorpe, Chicago, IL

Dale R. Ellickson, Great Falls, VA

Benjamin P. Elliott, Rockville, MD

Rand L. Elliott, Oklahoma City, OK

John M. Ellis, New York, NY

James E. Ellison, Washington, DC

James W. Elmore, Phoenix, AZ

Frederick E. Emmons, Bel Tiburon, CA

Terrel M. Emmons, Springfield, VA

William Eng, Champaign, IL

Douglas K. Engebretson, West Springfield, MA

Mark C. Engelbrecht, Des Moines, IA

William L. Ensign, Annapolis, MD

Lawrence Enyart, Phoenix, AZ

Herbert Epstein, Delray Beach, FL

Elizabeth S. Ericson, Boston, MA

Jerome R. Ernst, Seattle, WA

Philip A. Esocoff, Washington, DC

Harold Lionel Esten, Silver Spring, MD

A. B. Etherington, Honolulu, HI

Deane M. Evans Jr., Arlington, VA

J. Handel Evans, Camarillo, CA

Ralph F. Evans, Salt Lake City, UT

Robert J. Evans, Marshall, CA

Fellows of The American Institute of Architects (Con't)

William S. Evans, Shreveport, LA

C. Richard Everett, Houston, TX

Gary Everton, Nashville, TN

Thomas J. Eyerman, Chicago, IL

F

Otto Reichert Facilides, Philadelphia, PA

William H. Fain Jr., Los Angeles, CA

James Falick, Houston, TX

Kristine K. Fallon, Chicago, IL

Jay David Farbstein, San Luis Obispo, CA

Michael Farewell, Princeton, NJ

Richard T. Faricy, Saint Paul, MN

Richard C. Farley, Denver, CO

Stephen J. Farneth, San Francisco, CA

Avery C. Faulkner, Delaplane, VA

Winthrop W. Faulkner, Chevy Chase, MD

James G. Fausett, Marietta, GA

Robert E. Fehlberg, Pleasanton, CA

Werner L. Feibes, Schenectady, NY

Daniel J. Feil, Washington, DC

Edward A. Feiner, Fairfax, VA

Jose Feito, Miami, FL

Curtis W. Fentress, Denver, CO

S. Scott Ferebee Jr., Charlotte, NC

Franklin T. Ferguson, Salt Lake City, UT

Richard E. Fernau, Berkeley, CA

Stephanie E. Ferrell, Tampa, FL

Miguel Ferrer, Santurce, Puerto Rico

Richard B. Ferrier, Arlington, TX

James D. Ferris, Michigan City, IN

Robert D. Ferris, San Diego, CA

M. L. Ferro, Weare, NH

Donald E. Ferry, Springfield, IL

Michael T. Fickel, Kansas City, MO

H. H. Field, Shirley, MA

John L. Field, San Francisco, CA

Robert A. Fielden, Las Vegas, NV

Michael M. Fieldman, New York, NY

Kenneth J. Filarski, Providence, RI

R. Jerome Filer, Miami, FL

Bob G. Fillpot, Norman, OK

Ronald C. Filson, New Orleans, LA

Curtis Finch, Lake Oswego, OR

James H. Finch, Alpharetta, GA

Robert A. Findlay, Ames, IA

Maurice N. Finegold, Boston, MA

Ira S. Fink, Berkeley, CA

Jerry V. Finrow, Seattle, WA

A. Robert Fisher, Belvedere, CA

James Herschel Fisher, Dallas, TX

John L. Fisher, Marysville, CA

Hollye C. Fisk, Dallas, TX

Michael A. Fitts, Nolensville, TN

Darrell A. Fitzgerald, Atlanta, GA

James T. Fitzgerald, Cincinnati, OH

Joseph F. Fitzgerald, Chicago, IL

Richard A. Fitzgerald, Houston, TX

Joseph H. Flad, Madison, WI

Earl Robert Flansburgh, Boston, MA

Ted Flato, San Antonio, TX

Joseph L. Fleischer, New York, NY

Richard J. Fleischman, Cleveland, OH

Norman C. Fletcher, Lexington, MA

David J. Flood, Santa Monica, CA

Colden R. Florance, Washington, DC

Luis Flores-Dumont, Santurce, Puerto Rico

J. Chadwick P. Floyd, Centerbrook, CT

Richard F. Floyd, Dallas, TX

W. Jeff Floyd Jr., Atlanta, GA

Ligon B. Flynn, Wilmington, NC

Michael Flynn, New York, NY

John W. Focke, Houston, TX

Bernd Foerster, Manhattan, KS

James Follett, Chicago, IL

Fellows of The American Institute of Architects (Con't)

Fred L. Foote, San Francisco, CA

Stephen M. Foote, Boston, MA

Peter Forbes, Boston, MA

Robert M. Ford, Starkville, MS

Russell Forester, La Jolla, CA

Bernardo Fort-Brescia, Miami, FL

James R. Foster, Fayetteville, AR

Richard Foster, Wilton, CT

Bruce S. Fowle, New York, NY

Bob J. Fowler, PE, CBO, Pasadena, CA

Marion L. Fowlkes, Nashville, TN

Sheldon Fox, Stamford, CT

Harrison Fraker, Berkeley, CA

Edward D. Francis, Detroit, MI

Jay E. Frank, Dallas, TX

Richard C. Frank, Gregory, MI

James R. Franklin, San Luis Obispo, CA

Gregory Franta, Boulder, CO

Ulrich J. Franzen, New York, NY

Robert J. Frasca, Portland, OR

James I. Freed, New York, NY

Beverly L. Freeman, Charlotte, NC

William W. Freeman, Burlington, VT

Jeffrey S. French, Philadelphia, PA

Thomas K. Fridstein, Chicago, IL

Stephen Friedlaender, Cambridge, MA

Hans A. Friedman, Evanston, IL

Rodney F. Friedman, Belvedere, CA

Edward Friedrichs, Santa Monica, CA

Louis E. Fry Jr., Washington, DC

Louis E. Fry, Washington, DC

Richard E. Fry, Ann Arbor, MI

Joseph Y. Fujikawa, Winnetka, IL

Albert B. Fuller Jr., St. Louis, MO

Frank L. Fuller, IV, Oakland, CA

Duncan T. Fulton, Dallas, TX

David F. Furman, Charlotte, NC

James E. Furr, Houston, TX

G

Robert C. Gaede, Cleveland, OH

Herbert K. Gallagher, Boston, MA

Leslie M. Gallery-Dilworth, Philadelphia, PA

Harvey B. Gantt, Charlotte, NC

Theodore Garduque, Honolulu, HI

Robert D. Garland Jr., El Paso, TX

Charles E. Garrison, Diamondhead, MS

Truitt B. Garrison, Granbury, TX

Alan G. Gass, Denver, CO

Fred C. Gast Jr., Portland, OR

Kirk A. Gastinger, Kansas City, MO

Martha M. Gates, Pittsford, NY

Robert F. Gatje, New York, NY

James B. Gatton, Houston, TX

F. E. Gaulden, Greenville, SC

John C. Gaunt, Lawrence, KS

Robert Geddes, Princeton, NJ

Barbara L. Geddis, Stamford, CT

William J. Geddis, Chestnut Hill, MA

Robert J. Geering, San Francisco, CA

Frank O. Gehry, Santa Monica, CA

Carolyn D. Geise, Seattle, WA

Martin B. Gelber, Los Angeles, CA

M. Arthur Gensler Jr., San Francisco, CA

David W. George, Southlake, TX

Frank Dan George, Stamford, CT

Reagan W. George, Willow City, TX

Robert S. George, San Bruno, CA

Stephen A. George, Pittsburgh, PA

Preston M. Geren, Fort Worth, TX

Phillip H. Gerou, Evergreen, CO

Joe P. Giattina Jr., Birmingham, AL

Dale L. Gibbs, Lincoln, NE

Donald H. Gibbs, Long Beach, CA

Randall C. Gideon, Fort Worth, TX

Sidney P. Gilbert, New York, NY

Fellows of The American Institute of Architects (Con't)

Victor C. Gilbertson, Minnetonka, MN

Wilmot G. Gilland, Eugene, OR

Norman M. Giller, Miami Beach, FL

W. Douglas Gilpin, Charlottesville, VA

James S. Gimpel, Chicago, IL

Raymond L. Gindroz, Pittsburgh, PA

David L. Ginsberg, New York, NY

Raymond Girvigian, South Pasadena, CA

Joseph Carl Giuliani, Washington, DC

Romaldo Giurgola, Australia

Richard E. Glaser, Cincinnati, OH

William R. Glass, Oakland, CA

David Evan Glasser, Fayetteville, AR

E. A. Glendening, Cincinnati, OH

Val Glitsch, Houston, TX

Richard J. Gluckman, New York, NY

Harold D. Glucksman, Union, NJ

James M. Glymph, Santa Monica, CA

Ronald V. Gobbell, Nashville, TN

James Goettsch, Chicago, IL

Alan E. Goldberg, New Canaan, CT

Steven M. Goldberg, New York, NY

M. H. Goldfinger, New York, NY

Ron Goldman, Malibu, CA

Nicholas Goldsmith, New York, NY

Roger Neal Goldstein, Boston, MA

Stanley J. Goldstein, West Orange, NJ

Harmon H. Goldstone, New York, NY

Harry A. Golemon, Houston, TX

Bennie M. Gonzales, Nogales, AZ

Donald W. Y. Goo, Honolulu, HI

R. L. Good, Dallas, TX

D. B. Goodhue, Monterey, CA

Cary C. Goodman, Kansas City, MO

John P. Goodman, Manlius, NY

Michael K. Goodwin, Phoenix, AZ

Joan E. Goody, Boston, MA

Ezra Gordon, Chicago, IL

Harry T. Gordon, Washington, DC

Robert E. Gould, Kansas City, MO

Ronald Gourley, Tucson, AZ

Brian Gracey, Knoxville, TN

Bernard J. Grad, Elberon, NJ

Bruce J. Graham, Hobe Sound, FL

Gary L. Graham, Boston, MA

Roy E. Graham, Washington, DC

Robert E. Gramann, Cincinnati, OH

Warren Wolf Gran, New York, NY

Charles P. Graves, Lexington, KY

Dean W. Graves, Kansas City, MO

Michael Graves, Princeton, NJ

David Lawrence Gray, Santa Monica, CA

Thomas A. Gray, Little Rock, AR

Lyn E. Graziani, Miami, FL

Robert E. Greager, Pleasant Ridge, MI

Dennis W. Grebner, St. Paul, MN

Aaron G. Green, San Francisco, CA

Curtis H. Green, Shorewood, MN

Richard J. Green, Cambridge, MA

Thomas G. Green, Boston, MA

Aubrey J. Greenberg, Chicago, IL

James A. Greene, Oviedo, FL

Sanford R. Greenfield, Westfield, NJ

Susan Greenwald, Chicago, IL

John O. Greer, Bryan, TX

Glenn H. Gregg, New Haven, CT

Nonya Grenader, Houston, TX

Raymond Grenald, Narberth, PA

James A. Gresham, Tucson, AZ

William C. Gridley, Washington, DC

L. Duane Grieve, Knoxville, TN

James R. Grieves, Baltimore, MD

Donald I. Grinberg, Boston, MA

Edward A. Grochowiak, San Diego, CA

Olindo Grossi, Manhasset, NY

William H. Grover, Centerbrook, CT

Fellows of The American Institute of Architects (Con't)

J. C. Grube, Portland, OR

Ernest A. Grunsfeld, Chicago, IL

Jordan L. Gruzen, New York, NY

John C. Guenther, St. Louis, MO

Francis A. Guffey II, Charleston, WV

Paul J. Gumbinger, San Mateo, CA

Graham Gund, Cambridge, MA

Brooks R. Gunsul, Portland, OR

Gerald Gurland, West Orange, NJ

William R. Gustafson, Philadelphia, PA

Dean L. Gustavson, Salt Lake City, UT

Cabell Gwathmey, Harwood, MD

Charles Gwathmey, New York, NY

Willard E. Gwilliam, Hayes, VA

H

E. Keith Haag, Cuyahoga Falls, OH

Lester C. Haas, Shreveport, LA

Wallace L. Haas Jr., Redding, CA

Donald J. Hackl, Chicago, IL

John B. Hackler, Charlotte, NC

L.R. Hahnfeld, Fort Worth, TX

Frank S. Haines, Honolulu, HI

William H. Haire, Stillwater, OK

Gaines B. Hall, Downers Grove, IL

Mark W. Hall, Toronto, ON

William A. Hall, New York, NY

Harry C. Hallenbeck, Sacramento, CA

Stanley I. Hallet, Washington, DC

Gerald Hallissy, Port Washington, NY

Anna M. Halpin, New York, NY

Frances Halsband, New York, NY

William Hamby, New York, NY

Robert L. Hamill Jr., Boise, ID

D.K. Hamilton, Bellaire, TX

E.G. Hamilton Jr., Dallas, TX

Theodore S. Hammer, New York, NY

Gerald S. Hammond, Cincinnati, OH

John Hyatt Hammond, Greensboro, NC

W. Easley Hamner, Cambridge, MA

Mark G. Hampton, Coconut Grove, FL

John Paul C. Hanbury, Norfolk, VA

Peter H. Hand, Atlanta, GA

J. Paul Hansen, Savannah, GA

Richard F. Hansen, Sanibel, FL

Robert E. Hansen, Hendersonville, NC

Ernest H. Hara, Honolulu, III

John M. Hara, Honolulu, HI

Dellas H. Harder, Columbus, OH

Donald L. Hardison, El Cerrito, CA

Hugh Hardy, New York, NY

John C. Harkness, Arlington, MA

Sarah P. Harkness, Lexington, MA

Frank Harmon, Raleigh, NC

Harry W. Harmon, Lake San Marcos, CA

John C. Haro, Scottsdale, AZ

Charles F. Harper, Wichita Falls, TX

David M. Harper, Coral Gables, FL

Robert L. Harper, Centerbrook, CT

James W. Harrell, Cincinnati, OH

David A. Harris, Washington, DC

Edwin F. Harris Jr., Raleigh, NC

James Martin Harris, Tacoma, WA

Robert S. Harris, Los Angeles, CA

Robert V.M. Harrison, Jackson, MS

Roy P. Harrover, Memphis, TN

Craig W. Hartman, San Francisco, CA

Douglas C. Hartman, Dallas, TX

Did you know...

Paul Williams (1884–1980) was the first African-American to be elected to The American Institute of Architects' College of Fellows.

Fellows of The American Institute of Architects (Con't)

George E. Hartman, Washington, DC

Morton Hartman, Highland Park, IL

William E. Hartmann, Castine, ME

John F. Hartray Jr., Chicago, IL

Timothy Hartung, New York, NY

Wilbert R. Hasbrouck, Chicago, IL

Dennis E. Haskell, Seattle, WA

Albert L. Haskins Jr., Raleigh North, NC

Peter M. Hasselman, Orinda, CA

Sami Hassid, Pleasant Hill, CA

Herman A. Hassinger, Moorestown, NJ

George J. Hasslein, San Luis Obispo, CA

L. J. Hastings, Seattle, WA

Marvin Hatami, Denver, CO

Harold D. Hauf, Sun City, AZ

Robert O. Hausner, Santa Fe, NM

Daniel J. Havekost, Denver, CO

Perry A. Haviland, Oakland, CA

Velpeau E. Hawes Jr., Dallas, TX

H. Ralph Hawkins, Dallas, TX

Jasper Stillwell Hawkins, Phoenix, AZ

William J. Hawkins III, Portland, OR

William R. Hawley, E Palo Alto, CA

Bruce A. Hawtin, Jackson, WY

Richard S. Hayden, New York, NY

J. F. Hayes, Cambridge, MA

John Freeman Hayes, Radnor, PA

Irving B. Haynes, Lincoln, RI

Edward H. Healey, Cedar Rapids, IA

Michael M. Hearn, San Francisco, CA

George T. Heery, Atlanta, GA

Clovis Heimsath, Austin, TX

Dan Heinfeld, Irvine, CA

John Hejduk, Bronx, NY

Margaret Helfand, New York, NY

Jeffrey Heller, San Francisco, CA

Maxwell Boone Hellmann, Cardiff by the Sea, CA

George F. Hellmuth, St. Louis, MO

A. C. Helman, Maitland, FL

David P. Helpern, New York, NY

James C. Hemphill Jr., Charlotte, NC

Arn Henderson, Norman, OK

John D. Henderson, San Diego, CA

Philip C. Henderson, Dallas, TX

James L. Hendricks, Rockwall, TX

William R. Henry, Jackson, MS

Donald C. Hensman, Pasadena, CA

Charles Herbert, Des Moines, IA

Robert G. Herman, San Francisco, CA

William W. Herrin, Huntsville, AL

Robert G. Hershberger, Tucson, AZ

Paul A. Hesson, San Antonio, TX

Charles R. Heuer, Charlottesville, VA

D. M. Hewitt, Seattle, WA

Warren Cummings Heylman, Spokane, WA

Mason S. Hicks, Fayetteville, NC

Charles C. Hight, Charlotte, NC

Dean F. Hilfinger, Bloomington, IL

Eric Hill, Detroit, MI

John W. Hill, Baltimore, MD

J. Robert Hillier, Princeton, NJ

Mark Hinshaw, Seattle, WA

Kem G. Hinton, Nashville, TN

Don M. Hisaka, Berkeley, CA

Gregory O. Hnedak, Memphis, TN

Paul S. Hoag, Bellevue, WA

Richard W. Hobbs, Washington, DC

Peter S. Hockaday, Seattle, WA

Murlin R. Hodgell, Norman, OK

Thomas H. Hodne, Minneapolis, MN

David C. Hoedemaker, Seattle, WA

August F. Hoenack, Bethesda, MD

David H. Hoffman, Evant, TX

David L. Hoffman, Wichita, KS

John J. Hoffmann, North Haven, CT

Fellows of The American Institute of Architects (Con't)

J. David Hoglund, Pittsburgh, PA
John A. Holabird, Chicago, IL
L. M. Holder, Austin, TX
Major L. Holland, Tuskegee, AL
Dwight E. Holmes, Tampa, FL
Jess Holmes, Henderson, NV
Nicholas H. Holmes Jr., Mobile, AL
Harry J. Holroyd, Columbus, OH
David A. Holtz, Potomac, MD
Malcolm Holzman, New York, NY
George W. Homsey, San Francisco, CA
Bobbie S. Hood, San Francisco, CA
Van D. Hooker, Albuquerque, NM
G. N. Hoover, Houston, TX
George Hoover, Denver, CO
Ray C. Hoover III, Atlanta, GA
Frank L. Hope Jr., San Diego, CA
Gene C. Hopkins, Detroit, MI
Edward M. Hord, Baltimore, MD
Howard N. Horii, Newark, NJ
Gerald Horn, Chicago, IL
Patrick Horsbrugh, South Bend, IN
T. Horty, Minneapolis, MN
Reginald D. Hough, Larchmont, NY
Marvin C. Housworth, Atlanta, GA
David C. Hovey, Winnetka, IL
J. Murray Howard, Charlottesville, VA
John Howey, Tampa, FL
Thomas S. Howorth, Oxford, MS
Charles K. Hoyt, Old Lyme, CT
Michael M. Hricak Jr., Venice, CA
Robert Y. Hsiung, Boston, MA
Charles A. Hubbard, Cortez, CO
Jeffrey A. Huberman, Charlotte, NC
Daniel Huberty, Seattle, WA
Richard W. Huffman, Philadelphia, PA
Stephan S. Huh, Minneapolis, MN
Robert E. Hull, Seattle, WA

Charles F. Hummel, Boise, ID
Fred E. Hummel, Sacramento, CA
Harry J. Hunderman, Northbrook, IL
Gregory Hunt, Washington, DC
Frances P. Huppert, New York, NY
Sam T. Hurst, Montecito, CA
Syed V. Husain, Kensington, CA
Mary Alice Hutchins, Portland, OR
Remmert W. Huygens, Wayland, MA
Bryden B. Hyde, Jarretsville, MD
Fred J. Hynek, Parker, CO

I

Dean Illingworth, Indianapolis, IN
Elizabeth W. Ingraham, Colorado Springs, CO
William A. Isley, Bainbridge Island, WA
H. Curtis Ittner, St. Louis, MO
Robert A. Ivy Jr., New York, NY

J

Huson Jackson, Lexington, MA
Mike Jackson, Springfield, IL
R. G. Jackson, Houston, TX
Ralph T. Jackson, Boston, MA
Bernard Jacob, Minneapolis, MN
Harry M. Jacobs, Oakland, CA
Stephen B. Jacobs, New York, NY
Hugh N. Jacobsen, Washington, DC
Phillip L. Jacobson, Seattle, WA
J. P. Jacoby, Menomonee Falls, WI
Helmut Jahn, Chicago, IL
Timm Jamieson, Roanoke, VA
Henry A. Jandl, Richmond, VA
William R. Jarratt, Ann Arbor, MI
Lloyd Jary, San Antonio, TX
Peter Jefferson, Highlands, NC
Jordan O. Jelks, Macon, GA

Fellows of The American Institute of Architects (Con't)

J. J. Jennewein, Tampa, FL

Richard W. Jennings, Austin, TX

Bruce H. Jensen, Salt Lake City, UT

David Jepson, Hartford, CT

Jon Adams Jerde, Venice, CA

John W. Jickling, Birmingham, MI

John M. Johansen, New York, NY

Anthony N. Johns Jr., Mt. Irvine, Trinidad & Tobaga

Arthur D. Johnson, Omaha, NE

Danie Johnson, Asheville, NC

Edwin J. Johnson, Dallas, TX

Floyd E. Johnson, Scottsville, VA

James H. Johnson, Denver, CO

Jed V. Johnson, Wappingers Falls, NY

Marvin R. Johnson, Raleigh, NC

Philip C. Johnson, New York, NY

Ralph E. Johnson, Chicago, IL

Scott Johnson, Los Angeles, CA

Walker C. Johnson, Chicago, IL

Yandell Johnson, Little Rock, AR

Norman J. Johnston, Seattle, WA

James O. Jonassen, Seattle, WA

Arthur E. Jones, Houston, TX

Bernard I. Jones, Carbondale, IL

E. Fay Jones, Fayetteville, AR

J. Delaine Jones, Troy, NY

Jack B. Jones, Tamuning, Guam

Johnpaul Jones, Seattle, WA

Paul Duane Jones, Kailua, HI

Renis Jones, Montgomery, AL

Robert Lawton Jones, Tulsa, OK

Rudard Artaban Jones, Urbana, IL

Bendrew G. Jong, Orinda, CA

Joe J. Jordan, Philadelphia, PA

David A. Jordani, Minneapolis, MN

Roberta W. Jorgensen, Irvine, CA

H. V. Jova, Atlanta, GA

Bruce D. Judd, San Francisco, CA

Yu Sing Jung, Boston, MA

Howard H. Juster, San Diego, CA

K

Carl F. Kaelber Jr., Pittsford, NY

Richard E. Kaeyer, Mt. Kisco, NY

Gerald Kagan, New Haven, CT

David T. Kahler, Milwaukee, WI

Charles H. Kahn, Chapel Hill, NC

Eino O. Kainlauri, Ames, IA

Harry Kale, Conshohocken, PA

Mark Kalin, Newton Center, MA

G. M. Kallmann, Boston, MA

Stephen H. Kanner, Los Angeles, CA

Gary Y. Kaplan, Red Bank, NJ

Richard H. Kaplan, Cleveland, OH

Raymond L. Kappe, Pacific Palisades, CA

Raymond John Kaskey, Washington, DC

Kirby M. Keahey, Houston, TX

Gustave R. Keane, Bradenton, FL

Jan Keane, New York, NY

Richard C. Keating, Marina Del Rey, CA

Douglas S. Kelbaugh, Ann Arbor, MI

Duane A. Kell, St. Paul, MN

John H. Kell, San Antonio, TX

Bernard Kellenyi, Red Bank, NJ

Larry J. Keller, Fairfax, VA

Frank S. Kelly, Houston, TX

F. L. Kelsey, Scottsdale, AZ

Diane Legge Kemp, Chicago, IL

William D. Kendall, Houston, TX

Robert N. Kennedy, Indianapolis, IN

Gertrude L. Kerbis, Chicago, IL

Thomas L. Kerns, Arlington, VA

William H. Kessler, Detroit, MI

Herbert A. Ketcham, Minneapolis, MN

Russell V. Keune, Arlington, VA

A.H. Keyes Jr., Washington, DC
Stephen J. Kieran, Philadelphia, PA
Lee F. Kilbourn, Portland, OR
James R. Killebrew, Grapevine, TX
Edward A. Killingsworth, Long Beach, CA
Tai Soo Kim, Hartford, CT
Tong S. Kimm, Apo
David R. H. King, Washington, DC
Dennis M. King, Huntington Woods, MI
Donald King, Seattle, WA
Gordon L. King, Sacramento, CA
. Bertram King, Asheville, NC
Leland King, Bodega Bay, CA
Sol King, Palm Beach, FL
M. Ray Kingston, Salt Lake City, UT
Paul Kinnison Jr., San Antonio, TX
Ballard H. Kirk, Columbus, OH
D. W. Kirk Jr., Fort Worth, TX
Stephen J. Kirk, Grosse Pointe Pk, MI
John M. Kirksey, Houston, TX
Peyton E. Kirven, Westlake Village, CA
Robert S. Kitchen, Ocean Hills, CA
Henry Klein, Mount Vernon, WA
. Arvid Klein, New York, NY
Robert M. Kliment, New York, NY
Stephen A. Kliment, New York, NY
Kenneth F. Klindtworth, Duck Key, FL
Lee B. Kline, Los Angeles, CA
Vincent G. Kling, Chester Springs, PA
James F. Knight, Gunnison, CO
Roy F. Knight, Tallahassee, FL
William H. Knight, Santa Rosa, CA
Stuart Knoop, Chevy Chase, MD
Charles M. Kober, Long Beach, CA
Carl Koch, Cambridge, MA
Steven Y. Kodama, San Francisco, CA
Edward J. Kodet Jr., Minneapolis, MN
Pierre F. Koenig, Los Angeles, CA

Alfred H. Koetter, Boston, MA
A. Eugene Kohn, New York, NY
Keith R. Kolb, Seattle, WA
Nathaniel K. Kolb Jr., Dallas, TX
Ronald Kolman, Savannah, GA
S. Richard Komatsu, El Cerrito, CA
Hendrik Koning, Santa Monica, CA
Norman L. Koonce, McLean, VA
James F. Kortan, Atlanta, GA
Panos G. Koulermos, La Crescenta, CA
Alexander Kouzmanoff, Rye Brook, NY
Gerhardt Kramer, Webster Groves, MO
Robert Kramer, Brookline, MA
M. Stanley Krause Jr., Newport News, VA
Eugene Kremer, Manhattan, KS
J. Richard Kremer, Louisville, KY
Jerrily R. Kress, Washington, DC
John L. Kriken, San Francisco, CA
Robert N. Kronewitter, Denver, CO
Kenneth C. Kruger, Santa Barbara, CA
James O. Kruhly, Philadelphia, PA
Rod Kruse, Des Moines, IA
Denis G. Kuhn, New York, NY
Julian E. Kulski, Orlean, VA
Ernest J. Kump, Zurich, Switzerland
Moritz Kundig, Spokane, WA
Theodore E. Kurz, Cleveland, OH
Peter Kuttner, Cambridge, MA
Sylvia P. Kwan, San Francisco, CA
Michael Kwartler, New York, NY

L

David N. LaBau, Bloomfield, CT
Ronald J. Labinski, Kansas City, MO
John W. Lackens Jr., Minneapolis, MN
Bill N. Lacy, Purchase, NY
Thomas Laging, Lincoln, NE

Fellows of The American Institute of Architects (Con't)

Henry J. Lagorio, Orinda, CA

Jerry Laiserin, Woodbury, NY

David C. Lake, San Antonio, TX

Charles E. Lamb, Annapolis, MD

James Lambeth, Fayetteville, AR

James I. Lammers, Chisago City, MN

Gregory W. Landahl, Chicago, IL

Peter H. Landon, Chicago, IL

D. E. Landry, Dallas, TX

Jane Landry, Dallas, TX

John M. Laping, West Amherst, NY

Arnold Les Larsen, Port Salerno, FL

Dayl A. Larson, Denver, CO

William N. Larson, Park Ridge, IL

William L. Larson, Omaha, NE

Carroll J. Lawler, West Hartford, CT

Charles E. Lawrence, Houston, TX

Jerry Lawrence, Tacoma, WA

Robert M. Lawrence, Oklahoma City, OK

David E. Lawson, Madison, WI

Elizabeth Lawson, Charlottesville, VA

William R. Lawson, Reston, VA

Franklin D. Lawyer, Houston, TX

John C. Le Bey, Savannah, GA

Robert LeMond, Fort Worth, TX

Glen S. LeRoy, Kansas City, MO

Benjamin B. Lee, Honolulu, HI

Donald R. Lee, Charlotte, NC

Elizabeth B. Lee, Lumberton, NC

John Lee, New York, NY

M. David Lee, Boston, MA

Gene Leedy, Winter Haven, FL

James M. Leefe, Sausalito, CA

Andrea P. Leers, Boston, MA

Gillet Lefferts, Darien, CT

Spencer A. Leineweber, Honolulu, HI

Lawrence J. Leis, Louisville, KY

Richard Leitch, South Laguna, CA

Herbert Lembcke, San Francisco, CA

James T. Lendrum, Phoenix, AZ

Peter A. Lendrum, Phoenix, AZ

Eason H. Leonard, Carmel, CA

Ralph Lerner, Princeton, NJ

Nicholas Lesko, Cleveland, OH

Francis D. Lethbridge, Nantucket, MA

Conrad Levenson, New York, NY

Brenda A. Levin, Los Angeles, CA

Richard D. Levin, Longboat Key, FL

Alan G. Levy, Philadelphia, PA

Eugene P. Levy, Little Rock, AR

Herbert W. Levy, Spring House, PA

Morton L. Levy, Houston, TX

Toby S. Levy, San Francisco, CA

Anne McCutcheon Lewis, Washington, DC

Calvin F. Lewis, Des Moines, IA

David Lewis, Homestead, PA

George B. Lewis, Oklahoma City, OK

Richard L. Lewis, Pebble Beach, CA

Roger K. Lewis, Washington, DC

Tom Lewis Jr., Kissimmee, FL

Walter H. Lewis, Champaign, IL

Alan C. Liddle, Lakewood, WA

Frederick Liebhardt, La Jolla, CA

Theodore Liebman, New York, NY

Bernard J. Liff, Pittsburgh, PA

John H. Lind, Iowa City, IA

David Lindsey, Seattle, WA

H. Mather Lippincott Jr., Moylan, PA

William H. Liskamm, San Rafael, CA

Robert A. Little, Cleveland, OH

Stanley C. Livingston, San Diego, CA

Thomas W. Livingston, Anchorage, AK

Walter R. Livingston Jr., Crum Lynne, PA

Peter Lizon, Knoxville, TN

W. Kirby Lockard, Tucson, AZ

James L. Loftis, Oklahoma City, OK

Fellows of The American Institute of Architects (Con't)

Donn Logan, Berkeley, CA

Dirk Lohan, Chicago, IL

Thomas E. Lollini, Berkeley, CA

Jerrold E. Lomax, Carmel Valley, CA

J. Carson Looney, Memphis, TN

R. Nicholas Loope, Phoenix, AZ

Gabor Lorant, Phoenix, AZ

Larry Lord, Atlanta, GA

George H. Loschky, Seattle, WA

John C. Loss, Whitehall, MI

Rex Lotery, Montecito, CA

William C. Louie, New York, NY

William Love, Los Angeles, CA

Wendell H. Lovett, Seattle, WA

Frank E. Lucas, Charleston, SC

Thomas J. Lucas, Southfield, MI

Lenore M. Lucey, Washington, DC

Carl F. Luckenbach, Ann Arbor, MI

Graham B. Luhn, Houston, TX

Anthony J. Lumsden, Los Angeles, CA

Frithjof Lunde, Center Valley, PA

Phillip Lundwall, Grand Rapids, MI

Victor A. Lundy, Bellaire, TX

Donald H. Lutes, Springfield, OR

Frederic P. Lyman, Sebeka, MN

Robert Dale Lynch, Pittsburgh, PA

Robert J. Lynch, Scottsdale, AZ

Donlyn Lyndon, Berkeley, CA

Maynard Lyndon, Kuessaberg, Germany

M

Michael Maas, W. Hampton Bch, NY

R. Doss Mabe, Los Angeles, CA

John E. MacAllister, San Francisco, CA

Donald MacDonald, San Francisco, CA

Virginia B. MacDonald, Kaneohe, HI

I. A. MacEwen, Tampa, FL

Ian MacKinlay, San Francisco, CA

Charles H. MacMahon, Deland, FL

Robert C. Mack, Minneapolis, MN

Eugene J. Mackey III, St. Louis, MO

John Macsai, Chicago, IL

Robert P. Madison, Cleveland, OH

Peter E. Madsen, Boston, MA

Theodore S. Maffitt Jr., Palestine, TX

Henry J. Magaziner, Philadelphia, PA

Gary Mahaffey, Minneapolis, MN

Victor C. Mahler, New York, NY

John E. Mahlum, Seattle, WA

C. R. Maiwald, Wilmington, NC

Marvin J. Malecha, Raleigh, NC

L. Vic Maloof, Atlanta, GA

Arthur E. Mann, Irvine, CA

Carter H. Manny Jr., Chicago, IL

Clark D. Manus, San Francisco, CA

Virginia S. March, Fairhope, AL

Roger W. Margerum, Detroit, MI

Phillip T. Markwood, Columbus, OH

Harvey V. Marmon Jr., San Antonio, TX

Jud R. Marquardt, Seattle, WA

Clinton Marr Jr., Riverside, CA

Mortimer M. Marshall Jr., Reston, VA

Richard C. Marshall, San Francisco, CA

Albert C. Martin, Los Angeles, CA

Christopher C. Martin, Los Angeles, CA

David C. Martin, Los Angeles, CA

Robert E. Martin, Toledo, OH

W. Mike Martin, Berkeley, CA

Walter B. Martinez, Miami, FL

Thomas S. Marvel, San Juan, Puerto Rico

Joseph V. Marzella, Wallingford, PA

Ronald L. Mason, Denver, CO

George Matsumoto, Oakland, CA

Edward H. Matthei, Chicago, IL

Robert F. Mattox, Boston, MA

Fellows of The American Institute of Architects (Con't)

Frank J. Matzke, St. Augustine, FL

John M. Maudlin-Jeronimo, Bethesda, MD

Laurie M. Maurer, Brooklyn, NY

Susan A. Maxman, Philadelphia, PA

Murvan M. Maxwell, Metairie, LA

Arthur May, New York, NY

Kenneth D. Maynard, Anchorage, AK

Charles F. McAfee, Wichita, KS

Charles McCafferty, Saint Clair Shores, MI

E. K. McCagg, II, Kirkland, WA

Joe M. McCall, Dallas, TX

Michael A. McCarthy, New York, NY

John McCartney, Washington, DC

Bruce McCarty, Knoxville, TN

Harlan E. McClure, Pendleton, SC

Wesley A. McClure, Raleigh, NC

Richard E. McCommons, Falls Church, VA

Robert E. McConnell, Tucson, AZ

Edward D. McCrary, Hillsborough, CA

M. Allen McCree, Austin, TX

Gerald M. McCue, Cambridge, MA

Grant G. McCullagh, Chicago, IL

James McCullar, New York, NY

Margaret McCurry, Chicago, IL

William A. McDonough, Charlottesville, VA

Connie S. McFarland, Tulsa, OK

A. S. McGaughan, Washington, DC

John M. McGinty, Houston, TX

Milton B. McGinty, Houston, TX

Richard A. McGinty, Hilton Hd Island, SC

John W. McGough, Spokane, WA

James R. McGranahan, Lacey, WA

Mark McInturff, Bethesda, MD

Herbert P. McKim, Wrightsville Beach, NC

David A. McKinley, Seattle, WA

Noel M. McKinnell, Boston, MA

Thomas L. McKittrick, College Station, TX

H. Roll McLaughlin, Carmel, IN

C. Andrew Andrew McLean, II, Atlanta, GA

James M. McManus, Glastonbury, CT

George A. McMath, Portland, OR

William G. McMinn, Coconut Grove, FL

E. Eean McNaughton Jr., New Orleans, LA

Carrell S. McNulty Jr., Cincinnati, OH

E. Keith McPheeters, Auburn, AL

John M. McRae, Starkville, MS

Charles B. McReynolds, Newport News, VA

Franklin Mead, Boston, MA

George C. Means Jr., Clemson, SC

Philip J. Meathe, Grosse Pte Farms, MI

David Meckel, San Francisco, CA

Henry G. Meier, Fishers, IN

Richard A. Meier, New York, NY

Carl R. Meinhardt, New York, NY

Lawrence P. Melillo, Louisville, KY

Roger C. Mellem, Port Republic, MD

R. A. Melting, New York, NY

John O. Merrill, Tiburon, CA

William Dickey Merrill, Carmel, CA

David R. Messersmith, Lubbock, TX

Robert C. Metcalf, Ann Arbor, MI

William H. Metcalf, McLean, VA

Andrew Metter, Evanston, IL

C. Richard Meyer, Seattle, WA

James H. Meyer, Richardson, TX

Kurt W. Meyer, Los Angeles, CA

Richard C. Meyer, Philadelphia, PA

Marshall D. Meyers, Pasadena, CA

Nancy A. Miao, New York, NY

Did you know...

Henry Hobson Richardson was the first member of the AIA to be advanced to a Fellow.

Fellows of The American Institute of Architects (Con't)

Linda H. Michael, Charlottesville, VA

Constantine E. Michaelides, St. Louis, MO

Valerius Leo Michelson, Minneapolis, MN

Robert Miklos, Boston, MA

Arnold Mikon, Detroit, MI

Juanita M. Mildenberg, Bethesda, MD

Don C. Miles, Seattle, WA

Daniel R. Millen Jr., Cherry Hill, NJ

David E. Miller, Seattle, WA

Ewing H. Miller, Port Republic, MD

George H. Miller, New York, NY

Henry F. Miller, Orange, CT

Hugh C. Miller, Richmond, VA

James W. Miller, Madison, WI

John F. Miller, Cambridge, MA

Joseph Miller, Washington, DC

L. Kirk Miller, San Francisco, CA

Leroy B. Miller, Santa Monica, CA

Richard Miller, Nashville, TN

Steven Miller, Prague, Czechoslovakia

William C. Miller, Salt Lake City, UT

Edward I. Mills, New York, NY

Michael Mills, Glen Ridge, NJ

Willis N. Mills Jr., Ponte Vedra Beach, FL

Lee Mindel, New York, NY

Adolfo E. Miralles, Altadena, CA

Henry D. Mirick, Fairless Hills, PA

Dan S. Mitchell, St. Louis, MO

Ehrman B. Mitchell Jr., Philadelphia, PA

Richard R. Moger, Port Washington, NY

Ronald L. Moline, Bourbonnais, IL

Robert B. Molseed, Annandale, VA

Lynn H. Molzan, Indianapolis, IN

Frank Montana, Dade City, FL

Joseph D. Monticciolo, Woodbury, NY

Curtis J. Moody, Columbus, OH

Thomas B. Moon, Rancho Santa Margarita, CA

Arthur C. Moore, Washington, DC

Barry M. Moore, Houston, TX

Gerald L. Moorhead, Houston, TX

Jesse O. Morgan Jr., Shreveport, LA

Robert Lee Morgan, Port Townsend, WA

W. N. Morgan, Jacksonville, FL

Howard H. Morgridge, Newport Beach, CA

Lamberto G. Moris, San Francisco, CA

Seth I. Morris, Houston, TX

Lionel Morrison, Dallas, TX

John Morse, Seattle, WA

James R. Morter, Vail, CO

Allen D. Moses, Kirkland, WA

Robert Mosher, La Jolla, CA

Samuel Z. Moskowitz, Naples, FL

Eric O. Moss, Culver City, CA

G. Michael Mostoller, Princeton, NJ

Kenneth L. Motley, Roanoke, VA

John K. Mott, Alexandria, VA

Edward A. Moulthrop, Atlanta, GA

Jennifer T. Moulton, Denver, CO

Frederic D. Moyer, Northbrook, IL

Frank R. Mudano, Clearwater, FL

Theodore Mularz, Ashland, OR

Paul Muldawer, Atlanta, GA

John W. Mullen III, Dallas, TX

Rosemary F. Muller, Oakland, CA

Harold C. Munger, Toledo, OH

Frank W. Munzer, Clinton Corners, NY

Charles F. Murphy, Mesa, AZ

Frank N. Murphy, Clayton, MO

David G. Murray, Tulsa, OK

Stephen A. Muse, Washington, DC

Robert C. Mutchler, Fargo, ND

John V. Mutlow, Los Angeles, CA

Donald B. Myer, Washington, DC

John R. Myer, Tamworth, NH

Barton Myers, Beverly Hills, CA

Ralph E. Myers, Prairie Village, KS

Fellows of The American Institute of Architects (Con't)

N

Daniel J. Nacht, Fair Oaks, CA

Barbara Nadel, Forest Hills, NY

Herbert N. Nadel, Los Angeles, CA

Chester Emil Nagel, Colorado Springs, CO

James L. Nagle, Chicago, IL

Louis Naidorf, Burbank, CA

Noboru Nakamura, Orinda, CA

C. S. Nakata, Colorado Springs, CO

Robert J. Nash, Oxon Hill, MD

Thomas M. Nathan, Memphis, TN

Kenneth H. Natkin, Esq., San Francisco, CA

James A. Neal, Greenville, SC

Paul R. Neel, San Luis Obispo, CA

Ibsen Nelsen, Vashon, WA

Edward H. Nelson, Tucson, AZ

James Richard Nelson, Wilmington, DE

John H. Nelson, Chicago, IL

T. C. Nelson, Kansas City, MO

Ede I. Nemeti, Houston, TX

Donald E. Neptune, Newport Beach, CA

John F. Nesholm, Seattle, WA

Barbara Neski, New York, NY

Julian J. Neski, New York, NY

Walter A. Netsch, Chicago, IL

Perry King Neubauer, Cambridge, MA

J. Victor Neuhaus, III, Hunt, TX

William O. Neuhaus, III, Houston, TX

David J. Neuman, Palo Alto, CA

Hans Neumann, Las Vegas, NV

S. Kenneth Neumann, Beverly Hills, MI

Peter Newlin, Chestertown, MD

Herbert S. Newman, New Haven, CT

Michael Newman, Winston-Salem, NC

Robert L. Newsom, Los Angeles, CA

Chartier C. Newton, Austin, TX

Doreve Nicholaeff, Osterville, MA

Robert Duncan Nicol, Oakland, CA

George Z. Nikolajevich, St. Louis, MO

Edward R. Niles, Malibu, CA

Ivey L. Nix, Atlanta, GA

Robert J. Nixon, Port Angeles, WA

George M. Notter Jr., Washington, DC

John M. Novack, Dallas, TX

Jimmie R. Nunn, Flagstaff, AZ

John Nyfeler, Austin, TX

O

W. L. O'Brien Jr., Research Triangle Park, NC

Thomas O'Connor, Detroit, MI

L. J. O'Donnell, Chicago, IL

Arthur F. O'Leary, County Louth, Ireland

Paul Murff O'Neal Jr., Shreveport, LA

Charles W. Oakley, Pacific Palisades, CA

Gyo Obata, Saint Louis, MO

Jeffrey K. Ochsner, Seattle, WA

Robert A. Odermatt, Berkeley, CA

Mary L. Oehrlein, Washington, DC

Rolf H. Ohlhausen, New York, NY

Richard M. Olcott, New York, NY

Edward A. Oldziey, Wyckoff, NJ

P. S. Oles, Newton, MA

H. B. Olin, Chicago, IL

Donald E. Olsen, Berkeley, CA

Carole J. Olshavsky, Columbus, OH

James W. Olson, Seattle, WA

Herbert B. Oppenheimer, New York, NY

Edward L. Oremen, San Diego, CA

Robert E. Oringdulph, Portland, OR

Gordon D. Orr Jr., Madison, WI

David William Osler, Ann Arbor, MI

G. F. Oudens, Chevy Chase, MD

Raymond C. Ovresat, Wilmette, IL

Kenneth Owens Jr., Birmingham, AL

Fellows of The American Institute of Architects (Con't)

P

C. J. Paderewski III, San Diego, CA

Elizabeth Seward Padjen, Marblehead, MA

Gregory Palermo, Des Moines, IA

Joshua J. Pan, Taipei, Taiwan

Solomon Pan, Tucson, AZ

Lester C. Pancoast, Miami, FL

John R. Pangrazio, Seattle, WA

Donald H. Panushka, Salt Lake City, UT

Dennis A. Paoletti, San Francisco, CA

Tician Papachristou, New York, NY

Laszlo Papp, New Canaan, CT

George C. Pappageorge, Chicago, IL

Nicholas A. Pappas, Richmond, VA

Ted P. Pappas, Jacksonville, FL

Charles J. Parise, Grosse Pointe Woods, MI

Ki Suh Park, Los Angeles, CA

Sharon C. Park, Arlington, VA

Alfred B. Parker, Gainesville, FL

Derek Parker, San Francisco, CA

Howard C. Parker, Dallas, TX

Leonard S. Parker, Minneapolis, MN

R. C. Parrott, Knoxville, TN

Steven A. Parshall, Houston, TX

Giovanni Pasanella, New York, NY

C. H. Paseur, Houston, TX

Joseph Passonneau, Washington, DC

Piero Patri, San Francisco, CA

Allen L. Patrick, Columbus, OH

R. Glen Paulsen, Ann Arbor, MI

Charles Harrison Pawley, Coral Gables, FL

Thomas M. Payette, Boston, MA

H. Morse Payne, Lincoln, MA

Richard W. Payne, Houston, TX

George Clayton Pearl, Albuquerque, NM

Bryce Pearsall, Phoenix, AZ

Charles Almond Pearson Jr., Arlington, VA

J. Norman Pease Jr., Charlotte, NC

John G. Pecsok, Indianapolis, IN

William Pedersen Jr., New York, NY

Gerard W. Peer, Charlotte, NC

William R. Peery, Clearwater, FL

I. M. Pei, New York, NY

Maris Peika, Toluca Lake, CA

John W. Peirce, Topsfield, MA

Cesar Pelli, New Haven, CT

William M. Pena, Houston, TX

Thompson E. Penney, Charleston, SC

David L. Perkins, Lafayette, LA

G. Holmes Perkins, Philadelphia, PA

L. Bradford Perkins, New York, NY

Norman K. Perttula, Aurora, OH

Stuart K. Pertz, New York, NY

Robert W. Peters, Albuquerque, NM

Carolyn S. Peterson, San Antonio, TX

Charles E. Peterson, Philadelphia, PA

Leonard A. Peterson, Chicago, IL

Edward G. Petrazio, Spanish Fort, AL

Eleanore Pettersen, Saddle River, NJ

Jay S. Pettitt Jr., Beulah, MI

Mark A. Pfaller, Elm Grove, WI

Norman Pfeiffer, Los Angeles, CA

J. D. Pfluger, Austin, TX

Barton Phelps, Los Angeles, CA

Frederick F. Phillips, Chicago, IL

W. Irving Phillips Jr., Houston, TX

J. Almont Pierce, Falls Church, VA

John Allen Pierce, Dallas, TX

Walter S. Pierce, Lexington, WA

Raymond A. Pigozzi, Evanston, IL

George J. Pillorge, Oxford, MD

Robert J. Piper, Winnetka, IL

Carl W. Pirscher, Windsor, Canada

John W. Pitman, Santa Barbara, CA

Peter A. Piven, Philadelphia, PA

Fellows of The American Institute of Architects (Con't)

Elizabeth Plater-Zyberk, Miami, FL

Charles A. Platt, New York, NY

Kalvin J. Platt, Sausalito, CA

G. Gray Plosser Jr., Birmingham, AL

Jan Hird Pokorny, New York, NY

Lee A. Polisano, London, England

William M. Polk, Seattle, WA

Wilson Pollock, Cambridge, MA

James Stewart Polshek, New York, NY

Ralph Pomerance, New York, NY

Leason F. Pomeroy, III, Santa Ana, CA

Lee H. Pomeroy, New York, NY

Lynn S. Pomeroy, Sacramento, CA

Gerrard S. Pook, Bronx, NY

Samuel D. Popkin, West Bloomfield, MI

William L. Porter, Cambridge, MA

John C. Portman Jr., Atlanta, GA

Penny H. Posedly, Phoenix, AZ

Raymond G. Post Jr., Baton Rouge, LA

Boone Powell, San Antonio, TX

James Pratt, Dallas, TX

Antoine Predock, Albuquerque, NM

William T. Priestley, Lake Forest, IL

Arnold J. Prima Jr., Washington, DC

Harold E. Prinz, Dallas, TX

Donald Prowler, Philadelphia, PA

Homer L. Puderbaugh, Lincoln, NE

David A. Pugh, Portland, OR

William L. Pulgram, Atlanta, GA

James G. Pulliam, Pasadena, CA

Joe T. Pursell, Jackson, MS

Michael Pyatok, Oakland, CA

Q

G. William Quatman, Kansas City, MO

Jerry L. Quebe, Chicago, IL

Robert W. Quigley, San Diego, CA

Marcel Quimby, Dallas, TX

Michael L. Quinn, Washington, DC

Richard W. Quinn, Avon, CT

R

Martin D. Raab, New York, NY

Bruce A. Race, Berkeley, CA

John A. Raeber, San Francisco, CA

Craig E. Rafferty, St. Paul, MN

George E. Rafferty, St. Paul, MN

Richard J. Rafferty, St. Paul, MN

Lemuel Ramos, Miami, FL

Peter A. Rand, Minneapolis, MN

Terry Rankine, Cambridge, MA

Raymond R. Rapp, Galveston, TX

Ralph Rapson, Minneapolis, MN

Howard Terry Rasco, Little Rock, AR

Peter T. Rasmussen, Tacoma, WA

John K. Rauch Jr., Philadelphia, PA

John G. Rauma, Minneapolis, MN

William L. Rawn, Boston, MA

James T. Ream, San Francisco, CA

Mark Reddington, Seattle, WA

Charles Redmon, Cambridge, MA

Louis G. Redstone, Southfield, MI

Ronald Reed, Cleveland, OH

Vernon Reed, Liberty, MO

William R. Reed, Tacoma, WA

Henry S. Reeder Jr., Cambridge, MA

Frank Blair Reeves, Gainesville, FL

I. S. K. Reeves, V, Winter Park, FL

Roscoe Reeves Jr., Chevy Chase, MD

Victor A. Regnier, Los Angeles, CA

Patrick C. Rehse, Phoenix, AZ

Pierce K. Reibsamen, Los Angeles, CA

Jerry Reich, Chicago, IL

Leonard H. Reinke, Oshkosh, WI

Ilmar Reinvald, Tacoma, WA

John Rex, Carpinteria, CA

M. Garland Reynolds Jr., Gainesville, GA

Fellows of The American Institute of Architects (Con't)

David A. Rhodes, Memphis, TN

James W. Rhodes, New York, NY

Kenneth Ricci, New York, NY

Paul J. Ricciuti, Youngstown, OH

David E. Rice, San Diego, CA

Richard L. Rice, Raleigh, NC

James W. Rich, Tulsa, OK

Lisle F. Richards, San Jose, CA

Heidi A. Richardson, Sausalito, CA

Walter J. Richardson, Newport Beach, CA

Charles H. Richter Jr., Baltimore, MD

David R. Richter, Corpus Christi, TX

Hans Riecke, Haiku, HI

James V. Righter, Boston, MA

Jorge Rigau, Rio Piedras, Puerto Rico

Jefferson B. Riley, Centerbrook, CT

Ronnette Riley, New York, NY

David N. Rinehart, La Jolla, CA

David Rinehart, Los Angeles, CA

M. Jack Rinehart Jr., Charlottesville, VA

Mark W. Rios, Los Angeles, CA

Darrel D. Rippeteau, Delray Beach, FL

Dahlen K. Ritchey, Bradfordwoods, PA

P. Richard Rittelmann, Butler, PA

James W. Ritter, Alexandria, VA

Richard E. Ritz, Portland, OR

I. L. Roark, Lawrence, KS

Jack Robbins, Berkeley, CA

Darryl Roberson, San Francisco, CA

Jaquelin T. Robertson, New York, NY

C. David Robinson, San Francisco, CA

Harry G. Robinson III, Washington, DC

J. W. Robinson, Atlanta, GA

Kevin Roche, Hamden, CT

Garth Rockcastle, Minneapolis, MN

George T. Rockrise, Glen Ellen, CA

Burton L. Rockwell, San Francisco, CA

Kenneth A. Rodrigues, San Jose, CA

Carl D. Roehling, Detroit, MI

Chester E. Roemer, St. Louis, MO

Ralph J. Roesling II, San Diego, CA

R. G. Roessner, Austin, TX

Archibald C. Rogers, Baltimore, MD

James G. Rogers III, New York, NY

John B. Rogers, Denver, CO

John D. Rogers, Asheville, NC

Craig W. Roland, Santa Rosa, CA

B. F. Romanowitz, Lexington, KY

James G. Rome, Corpus Christi, TX

Benjamin T. Rook, Charlotte, NC

Robert W. Root, Denver, CO

Richard M. Rosan, Washington, DC

William A. Rose Jr., White Plains, NY

Alan Rosen, Palm Desert, CA

Alan R. Rosen, Lake Forest, IL

Manuel M. Rosen, La Jolla, CA

Arthur Rosenblatt, New York, NY

Norman Rosenfeld, New York, NY

Edgar B. Ross, Tiburon, CA

James S. Rossant, New York, NY

Louis A. Rossetti, Birmingham, MI

Harold Roth, New Haven, CT

Richard Roth Jr., Freeport,

Edward N. Rothe, Edison, NJ

Martha L. Rothman, Boston, MA

Richard Rothman, Rising Fawn, GA

Bernard B. Rothschild, Atlanta, GA

Bernard Rothzeid, New York, NY

Maurice Rotival, Paris, France

Michael Rotondi, Los Angeles, CA

Lauren L. Rottet, Los Angeles, CA

Judith L. Rowe, Oakland, CA

Ralph T. Rowland, Cheshire, CT

Albert W. Rubeling Jr., Towson, MD

John Ruble, Santa Monica, CA

J. Ronald Rucker, Tyler, TX

J. W. Rudd, Knoxville, TN

Gordon E. Ruehl, Spokane, WA

Evett J. Ruffcorn, Seattle, WA

Fellows of The American Institute of Architects (Con't)

John A. Ruffo, San Francisco, CA

Herman O. Ruhnau, Riverside, CA

Peter L. Rumpel, Saint Augustine, FL

William W. Rupe, St. Louis, MO

T. T. Russell, Miami, FL

Walter A. Rutes, Scottsdale, AZ

H. Mark Ruth, Agana, Guam

Roger N. Ryan, N. Canton, OH

James E. Rydeen, Rio Verde, AZ

Donald P. Ryder, New Rochelle, NY

S

Werner Sabo, Chicago, IL

Harold G. Sadler, San Diego, CA

Moshe Safdie, Somerville, MA

Carol S. Sakata, Honolulu, HI

Raj Saksena, Bristol, RI

F. Cuthbert Salmon, Stillwater, OK

Nathaniel W. Sample, Madison, WI

Peter Samton, New York, NY

Danny Samuels, Houston, TX

Thomas Samuels, Chicago, IL

Gil A. Sanchez, Santa Cruz, CA

James J. Sanders, Seattle, WA

Linda Sanders, Walnut, CA

Donald Sandy Jr., San Francisco, CA

Adele N. Santos, San Francisco, CA

Carlos R. Sanz, Santurce, Puerto Rico

Charles M. Sappenfield, Sanibel, FL

Angel C. Saqui, Coral Gables, FL

Victor Saroki, Birmingham, MI

Louis Sauer, Pittsburgh, PA

Louis R. Saur, Clayton, MO

Robert W. Sawyer, Wilmington, NC

Peter M. Saylor, Philadelphia, PA

Sam Scaccia, Chicago, IL

Joseph J. Scalabrin, Columbus, OH

Mario L. Schack, Baltimore, MD

K. M. Schaefer, Kirkwood, MO

Robert J. Schaefer, Wichita, KS

Walter Schamu, Baltimore, MD

David Scheatzle, Tempe, AZ

James A. Scheeler, Reston, VA

Jeffrey Allen Scherer, Minneapolis, MN

G. G. Schierle, Los Angeles, CA

Arthur A. Schiller, Manhasset, NY

Don P. Schlegel, Albuquerque, NM

Frank Schlesinger, Washington, DC

Jon R. Schleuning, Portland, OR

John I. Schlossman, Hubbard Woods, IL

Roger Schluntz, Albuquerque, NM

Mildred F. Schmertz, New York, NY

Fred C. Schmidt, Oklahoma City, OK

Wayne S. Schmidt, Indianapolis, IN

R. Christian Schmitt, Charleston, SC

Herbert W. Schneider, Scottsdale, AZ

Walter Scholer Jr., Fort Myers, FL

John P. Schooley, Columbus, OH

Barnett P. Schorr, Seattle, WA

Charles F. Schrader, San Rafael, CA

Douglas F. Schroeder, Chicago, IL

Kenneth A. Schroeder, Chicago, IL

John H. Schruben, North Bethesda, MD

George A. D. Schuett, Glendale, WI

Kenneth E. Schwartz, San Luis Obispo, CA

Robert Schwartz, Washington, DC

Alan Schwartzman, Paris, France

Charles E. Schwing, Baton Rouge, LA

Alan D. Sclater, Seattle, WA

David M. Scott, Pullman, WA

William W. Scott, Taylors Falls, MN

Der Scutt, New York, NY

Jim W. Sealy, Dallas, TX

Linda Searl, Chicago, IL

Fellows of The American Institute of Architects (Con't)

Thomas J. Sedgewick, Clio, MI

Paul Segal, New York, NY

Lawrence P. Segrue, Visalia, CA

E. J. Seibert, Boca Grande, FL

Alexander Seidel, Belvedere, CA

Larry D. Self, St. Louis, MO

Theodore Seligson, Kansas City, MO

Bruce M. Sellery, Marina Del Rey, CA

Dale E. Selzer, Dallas, TX

John C. Senhauser, Cincinnati, OH

Ronald S. Senseman, Silver Spring, MD

Jerome M. Seracuse, Colorado Springs, CO

Diane Serber, Old Chatham, NY

Phillip K. Settecase, Salem, OR

Betty Lee Seydler-Hepworth, Franklin, MI

Richard S. Sharpe, Norwich, CT

John A. Sharratt, Boston, MA

James L. Shay, San Rafael, CA

Leo G. Shea, Leland, MI

John P. Sheehy, Mill Valley, CA

George C. Sheldon, Portland, OR

W. Overton Shelmire, Dallas, TX

Carol Shen, Berkeley, CA

John V. Sheoris, Grosse Pointe, MI

Herschel E. Shepard, Atlantic Beach, FL

Hugh Shepley, Manchester, MA

Patricia C. Sherman, Concord, NH

Takashi Shida, Santa Monica, CA

Roger D. Shiels, Portland, OR

Edward H. Shirley, Atlanta, GA

Philip A. Shive, Charlotte, NC

George Whiteside Shupee, Arlington, TX

Jack T. Sidener, Shatin, New Territories, PRC

Paul G. Sieben, Toledo, OH

Lloyd H. Siegel, Washington, DC

Robert H. Siegel, New York, NY

Charles M. Sieger, Miami, FL

Henry N. Silvestri, Corona Del Mar, CA

Brad Simmons, St. Louis, MO

Cathy J. Simon, San Francisco, CA

Mark Simon, Centerbrook, CT

Lawrence L. Simons, Santa Rosa, CA

Donal R. Simpson, Dallas, TX

Robert T. Simpson Jr., Berkeley, CA

Scott Simpson, Cambridge, MA

Howard F. Sims, Detroit, MI

Jerome J. Sincoff, St. Louis, MO

Donald I. Singer, Fort Lauderdale, FL

E. Crichton Singleton, Kansas City, MO

Charles S. Sink, Denver, CO

William H. Sippel Jr., Allison Park, PA

Michael M. Sizemore, Atlanta, GA

Ronald L. Skaggs, Dallas, TX

Norma M. Sklarek, Pacific Palisades, CA

Gary Skog, Southfield, MI

Murray A. Slama, Walnut Creek, CA

Clifton M. Smart Jr., Fayetteville, AR

Saul C. Smiley, Minnetonka, MN

Adrian D. Smith, Chicago, IL

Arthur Smith, Southfield, MI

Bill D. Smith, Dallas, TX

Bruce H. Smith, Pontiac, MI

Christopher J. Smith, Honolulu, HI

Cole Smith, Dallas, TX

Colin L. M. Smith, Cambridge, MA

Darrell L. Smith, Eugene, OR

Edward Smith, Salt Lake City, UT

Fleming W. Smith Jr., Nashville, TN

Frank Folsom Smith, Sarasota, FL

Hamilton P. Smith, Garden City, NY

Harwood K. Smith, Dallas, TX

Ivan H. Smith, Jacksonville, FL

John R. Smith, Ketchum, ID

Joseph N. Smith III, Atlanta, GA

Kenneth Smith, Jacksonville, FL

Macon S. Smith, Raleigh, NC

Fellows of The American Institute of Architects (Con't)

Stephen B. Smith, Salt Lake City, UT

T. Clayton Smith, Baton Rouge, LA

Tyler Smith, Hartford, CT

Whitney R. Smith, Sonoma, CA

David I. Smotrich, New York, NY

Neil H. Smull, Boise, ID

Richard Snibbe, New York, NY

Sheila Snider, Indianapolis, IN

Julie V. Snow, Minneapolis, MN

Walter H. Sobel, Chicago, IL

Daniel Solomon, San Francisco, CA

Richard J. Solomon, Chicago, IL

Stuart B. Solomon, Watertown, MA

James Hamilton Somes Jr., Portsmouth, NH

Hak Son, Santa Monica, CA

John R. Sorrenti, Mineola, NY

Charles B. Soule, Montgomery Village, MD

Michael Southworth, Berkeley, CA

Edward A. Sovik, Northfield, MN

George S. Sowden, Fort Worth, TX

Marvin Sparn, Boulder, CO

Laurinda H. Spear, Miami, FL

Lawrence W. Speck, Austin, TX

Michael H. Spector, New Hyde Park, NY

John H. Spencer, Hampton, VA

Tomas H. Spiers Jr., Camp Hill, PA

Pat Y. Spillman, Dallas, TX

Robert A. Spillman, Bethlehem, PA

Donald E. Sporleder, South Bend, IN

Joseph G. Sprague, Dallas, TX

Kent Spreckelmeyer, Lawrence, KS

Paul D. Spreiregen, Washington, DC

Bernard P. Spring, Brookline, MA

Everett G. Spurling Jr., Bethesda, MD

Dennis W. Stacy, Dallas, TX

Alfred M. Staehli, Portland, OR

Richard P. Stahl, Springfield, MO

Raymond F. Stainback Jr., Atlanta, GA

Duffy B. Stanley, El Paso, TX

William J. Stanley, III, Atlanta, GA

Jane M. Stansfeld, Austin, TX

Michael J. Stanton, San Francisco, CA

Earl M. Starnes, Cedar Key, FL

Frank A. Stasiowski, Newton, MA

Donald J. Stastny, Portland, OR

Russell L. Stecker, Montpelier, VT

John E. Stefany, Tampa, FL

Peter Steffian, Boston, MA

Charles W. Steger Jr., Blacksburg, VA

Douglas Steidl, Akron, OH

Carl Stein, New York, NY

Goodwin B. Steinberg, San Jose, CA

Robert T. Steinberg, San Jose, CA

Ralph Steinglass, New York, NY

Henry Steinhardt, Mercer Island, WA

Douglas E. Steinman Jr., Beaumont, TX

James A. Stenhouse, Charlotte, NC

Donald J. Stephens, Berlin, NY

Michael J. Stepner, San Diego, CA

Robert A. M. Stern, New York, NY

William F. Stern, Houston, TX

Preston Stevens Jr., Atlanta, GA

James M. Stevenson, Highland Park, IL

W. Cecil Steward, Lincoln, NE

William W. Stewart, Clayton, MO

Sherwood Stockwell, Wolcott, CO

Claude Stoller, Berkeley, CA

Neal P. Stowe Salt Lake City, UT

H. T. Stowell, Western Springs, IL

Ronald A. Straka, Denver, CO

Michael J. Stransky, Salt Lake City, UT

Frank Straub, Troy, MI

Carl A. Strauss, Cincinnati, OH

John R. Street Jr., Marietta, GA

Arthur V. Strock, Santa Ana, CA

Hugh Asher Stubbins Jr., Cambridge, MA

Fellows of The American Institute of Architects (Con't)

Sidney W. Stubbs Jr., Mount Pleasant, SC

Donald L. Stull, Boston, MA

Robert S. Sturgis, Weston, MA

Erik Sueberkrop, San Francisco, CA

Marvin D. Suer, Willow Grove, PA

John W. Sugden, Park City, UT

Douglas R. Suisman, Santa Monica, CA

Edward Sullam, Honolulu, HI

Patrick M. Sullivan, Claremont, CA

Gene R. Summers, Cloverdale, CA

Alan R. Sumner, Saint Louis, MO

Richard P. Sundberg, Seattle, WA

Donald R. Sunshine, Blacksburg, VA

Eugene L. Surber, Atlanta, GA

Charles R. Sutton, Honolulu, HI

Sharon E. Sutton, Seattle, WA

George Suyama, Seattle, WA

Eugene C. Swager, Peoria, IL

Robert M. Swatt, San Francisco, CA

Earl Swensson, Nashville, TN

Richard Swett, Copenhagen, Denmark

H. H. Swinburne, Philadelphia, PA

John M. Syvertsen, Chicago, IL

T

William B. Tabler, New York, NY

Edgar Tafel, Venice, FL

Marvin Taff, Beverly Hills, CA

Ray Takata, Sacramento, CA

Francis T. Taliaferro, Santa Monica, CA

R. H. Tan, Spokane, WA

Ted Tokio Tanaka, Marina Del Rey, CA

Virginia W. Tanzmann, Pasadena, CA

Charles R. Tapley, Houston, TX

A. Anthony Tappe, Boston, MA

H. Harold Tarleton, Greenville, SC

D. Coder Taylor, Glenview, IL

Marilyn J. Taylor, New York, NY

Richard L. Taylor Jr., Atlanta, GA

Walter Q. Taylor, Jacksonville, FL

Thomas H. Teasdale, Kirkwood, MO

Clinton C. Ternstrom, Los Angeles, CA

Roland Terry, Mt. Vernon, WA

Robert L. Tessier, Yarmouth Port, MA

B. C. Tharp, Montgomery, TX

Dorwin A. J. Thomas, Boston, MA

James B. Thomas, Houston, TX

James L. Thomas, Spartanburg, SC

Joseph F. Thomas, Pasadena, CA

Benjamin Thompson, Cambridge, MA

David C. Thompson, San Diego, CA

Milo H. Thompson, Minneapolis, MN

Robert L. Thompson, Portland, OR

Warren D. Thompson, Fresno, CA

Charles B. Thomsen, Houston, TX

Duane Thorbeck, Minneapolis, MN

Karl Thorne, Gainesville, FL

Oswald H. Thorson, Marco, FL

Stanley Tigerman, Chicago, IL

Patrick Tillett, Portland, OR

James H. Timberlake, Philadelphia, PA

Robert H. Timme, Los Angeles, CA

Leslie D. Tincknell, Saginaw, MI

James D. Tittle, Abilene, TX

Philip E. Tobey, Reston, VA

Calvin J. Tobin, Highland Park, IL

Logic Tobola II, El Campo, TX

Anderson Todd, Houston, TX

David F. M. Todd, New York, NY

Thomas A. Todd, Jamestown, RI

John Tomassi, Chicago, IL

James E. Tomblinson, Flint, MI

Frank Tomsick, San Francisco, CA

Coulson Tough, The Woodlands, TX

Fellows of The American Institute of Architects (Con't)

Dennis T. Toyomura, Honolulu, HI

Jack Train, Chicago, IL

Karl E. Treffinger Sr., West Linn, OR

Kenneth Treister, Coconut Grove, FL

Michael Tribble, Charlotte, NC

David M. Trigiani, Jackson, MS

William H. Trogdon, Olga, WA

Leroy Troyer, Mishawaka, IN

Charles N. Tseckares, Boston, MA

Edward T. M. Tsoi, Arlington, MA

Seab A. Tuck, III, Nashville, TN

Jack R. Tucker Jr., Memphis, TN

Thomas B. Tucker, San Diego, CA

Richard L. Tully, Columbus, OH

Emanuel N. Turano, Boca Raton, FL

John Gordon Turnbull, San Francisco, CA

Thomas P. Turner Jr., Charlotte, NC

Wilbur H. Tusler Jr., Kentfield, CA

James L. Tyler, Pacific Palisades, CA

Robert Tyler, Tarzana, CA

Anne G. Tyng, Philadelphia, PA

U

Edward K. Uhlir, Chicago, IL

Kenneth A. Underwood, Philadelphia, PA

Dean F. Unger, Sacramento, CA

Denorval Unthank Jr., Eugene, OR

Robert H. Uyeda, Los Angeles, CA

V

Joseph D. Vaccaro, Los Angeles, CA

Edward Vaivoda Jr., Portland, OR

William E. Valentine, San Francisco, CA

Joseph M. Valerio, Chicago, IL

William L. Van Alen, Wilmington, DE

Robert Van Deusen, Grand Junction, CO

George V. Van Fossen Schwab, Baltimore, MD

Thomas Van Housen, Minneapolis, MN

Peter van Dijk, Cleveland, OH

Harold F. VanDine Jr., Birmingham, MI

Johannes VanTilburg, Santa Monica, CA

Mitchell Vanbourg, Berkeley, CA

Harutun Vaporciyan, Huntington Woods, MI

Harold R. Varner, Berkley, MI

Leonard M. Veitzer, San Diego, CA

Thomas W. Ventulett, Atlanta, GA

Robert Venturi, Philadelphia, PA

Shirley J. Vernon, Philadelphia, PA

William R. Vick, Sacramento, CA

Robert L. Vickery, Charlottesville, VA

Wilmont Vickrey, Chicago, IL

Gregory D. Villanueva, Los Angeles, CA

John Vinci, Chicago, IL

Rafael Vinoly, New York, NY

Stephen Vogel, Detroit, MI

Leonard W. Volk II, Dallas, TX

A. R. Von Brock, Buchanan, VA

Robert J. Von Dohlen, W Hartford, CT

Richard L. Von Luhrte, Denver, CO

Bartholome Voorsanger, New York, NY

R. Randall Vosbeck, Vail, CO

William F. Vosbeck, Alexandria, VA

Thomas R. Vreeland, Century City, CA

R. E. Vrooman, College Station, TX

W

Hobart D. Wagener, Coronado, CA

William J. Wagner, Dallas Center, IA

Did you know...

In 1955, Elizabeth Coit became the first woman to be named a Fellow of the AIA.

Fellows of The American Institute of Architects (Con't)

John G. Waite, Albany, NY

Lawrence G. Waldron, Mercer Island, WA

Bruce M. Walker, Spokane, WA

Kenneth H. Walker, New York, NY

David A. Wallace, Philadelphia, PA

David D. Wallace, Westport, MA

Donald Q. Wallace, Lexington, KY

Les Wallach, Seattle, WA

Charles G. Walsh, Los Angeles, CA

Lloyd G. Walter Jr., Winston Salem, NC

W. G. Wandelmaier, New York, NY

Sheldon D. Wander, New York, NY

R. J. Warburton, Coral Gables, FL

G. T. Ward, Fairfax, VA

Robertson Ward Jr., Boston, MA

C. E. Ware, Rockford, IL

John Carl Warnecke, San Francisco, CA

Charles H. Warner Jr., Nyack, NY

Clyde K. Warner Jr., Louisville, KY

William D. Warner, Exeter, RI

Sharon F. Washburn, Bethesda, MD

Robert E. Washington, Richmond, VA

Barry L. Wasserman, Sacramento, CA

Joseph Wasserman, Southfield, MA

David H. Watkins, Bellaire, TX

Donald R. Watson, Trumbull, CT

Raymond L. Watson, Newport Beach, CA

William J. Watson, LaJolla, CA

John L. Webb, Ponchatoula, LA

P. R. Webber, Rutland, VT

Arthur M. Weber, Aiea, HI

Frederick S. Webster, Cazenovia, NY

C. R. Wedding, St. Petersburg, FL

Benjamin H. Weese, Chicago, IL

Cynthia Weese, Chicago, IL

Gary K. Weeter, Dallas, TX

Bryce Adair Weigand, Dallas, TX

Joe Neal Weilenman, Pago Pago, American Samoa

Nicholas H. Weingarten, Chicago, IL

Amy Weinstein, Washington, DC

Edward Weinstein, Seattle, WA

Jane Weinzapfel, Boston, MA

Gerald G. Weisbach, San Francisco, CA

Sarelle T. Weisberg, New York, NY

Steven F. Weiss, Chicago, IL

Martha L. Welborne, Los Angeles, CA

Frank D. Welch, Dallas, TX

John A. Welch, Tuskegee, AL

William P. Wenzler, Milwaukee, WI

Helge Westermann, Cambridge, MA

Merle T. Westlake, Lexington, MA

Paul E. Westlake Jr., Cleveland, OH

I. Donald Weston, Brooklyn, NY

Charles H. Wheatley, Charlotte, NC

C. Herbert Wheeler, State College, PA

Daniel H. Wheeler, Chicago, IL

James H. Wheeler Jr., Abilene, TX

Kenneth D. Wheeler, Lake Forest, IL

Richard H. Wheeler, Los Angeles, CA

Murray Whisnant, Charlotte, NC

Arthur B. White, Havertown, PA

George M. White, Bethesda, MD

Janet Rothberg White, Bethesda, MD

Norval C. White, Salisbury, CT

Samuel G. White, New York, NY

Stephen Q. Whitney, Detroit, MI

Leonard S. Wicklund, Long Grove, IL

Chester A. Widom, Santa Monica, CA

William Wiese, II, Shelburne, VT

E. D. Wilcox, Tyler, TX

Jerry Cooper Wilcox, Little Rock, AR

Gordon L. Wildermuth, Greeley, PA

James E. Wiley, Dallas, TX

Fellows of The American Institute of Architects (Con't)

Charles E. Wilkerson, Richmond, VA

Joseph A. Wilkes, Annapolis, MD

Michael B. Wilkes, San Diego, CA

Barbara E. Wilks, Baltimore, MD

Paul Willen, Yorktown Heights, NY

A. Richard Williams, Saint Ignace, MI

Allison G. Williams, San Francisco, CA

Daniel E. Williams, Coconut Grove, FL

E. Stewart Williams, Palm Springs, CA

F. Carter Williams, Raleigh, NC

Frank Williams, New York, NY

George Thomas Williams, Kitty Hawk, NC

Harold L. Williams, Los Angeles, CA

Homer L. Williams, Riverside, MO

John G. Williams, Fayetteville, AR

Lorenzo D. Williams, Minneapolis, MN

Mark F. Williams, Ambler, PA

Roger B. Williams, Seattle, WA

Terrance R. Williams, Washington, DC

Tod C. Williams, New York, NY

W. Gene Williams, The Woodlands, TX

Wayne R. Williams, Harmony, CA

Beverly A. Willis, New York, NY

Michael E. Willis, San Francisco, CA

John C. Wilmot, Damascus, MD

Jeffrey Wilson, Anchorage, AK

John E. Wilson, Richmond, VA

John L. Wilson, Boston, MA

William D. Wilson, Bridgehampton, NY

Steven R. Winkel, Berkeley, CA

Jon Peter Winkelstein, San Francisco, CA

John H. Winkler, Verbank, NY

Paul D. Winslow, Phoenix, AZ

Arch R. Winter, Mobile, AL

Steven Winter, Norwalk, CT

Marjorie M. Wintermute, Lake Oswego, OR

Norman E. Wirkler, Denver, CO

Joseph J. Wisnewski, Alexandria, VA

Gayland B. Witherspoon, Pendleton, SC

Charles Witsell Jr., Little Rock, AR

Gordon G. Wittenberg, Little Rock, AR

Fritz Woehle, Birmingham, AL

Robert L. Wold, Hilton Head, SC

Martin F. Wolf, Wilmette, IL

Harry C. Wolf, III, Malibu, CA

Richard Wolf, San Mateo, CA

Gin D. Wong, Los Angeles, CA

Kellogg H. Wong, New York, NY

William Wong Jr., Taikooshing, PRC

Carolina Y. Woo, San Francisco, CA

George C. Woo, Dallas, TX

Kyu S. Woo, Cambridge, MA

H. A. Wood III, Boston, MA

John M. Woodbridge, Sonoma, CA

David Geoffrey Woodcock, College Station, TX

David Woodhouse, Chicago, IL

Robert S. Woodhurst III, Augusta, GA

Stanford Woodhurst Jr., Augusta, GA

Enrique Woodroffe, Tampa, FL

Thomas E. Woodward, Buena Vista, CO

Evans Woollen, Indianapolis, IN

J. R. Wooten, Fort Worth, TX

John C. Worsley, Portland, OR

David H. Wright, Seattle, WA

George S. Wright, Fort Worth, TX

Henry L. Wright, Canby, OR

John L. Wright, Redmond, WA

Marcellus Wright Jr., Richmond, VA

Rodney H. Wright, Liberty, KY

Thomas W. D. Wright, Washington, DC

Cynthia Wuellner, Kansas City, MO

Scott W. Wyatt, Seattle, WA

Y

Jack R. Yardley, Dallas, TX

Fellows of The American Institute of Architects (Con't)

John L. Yaw, Aspen, CO

Zeno Lanier Yeates, Memphis, TN

Raymond W. Yeh, Honolulu, HI

Ronald W. Yeo, Corona Del Mar, CA

David N. Yerkes, Washington, DC

William R. Yost, Portland, OR

Clayton Young, Seattle, WA

Joseph L. Young, Clemson, SC

Norbert Young Jr., New York, NY

Theodore J. Young, Greenwich, CT

Hachiro Yuasa, Orleans, CA

Robert J. Yudell, Santa Monica, CA

Z

James Zahn, Chicago, IL

Saul Zaik, Portland, OR

H. Alan Zeigel, Denver, CO

J. Zemanek, Houston, TX

Golden J. Zenon Jr., Omaha, NE

Robert L. Ziegelman, Birmingham, MI

Raymond Ziegler, Altadena, CA

Frank Zilm, Kansas City, MO

John J. Zils, Chicago, IL

Bernard B. Zimmerman, Los Angeles, CA

Gary V. Zimmerman, Milwaukee, WI

Thomas A. Zimmerman, Rochester, NY

Hugh M. Zimmers, Philadelphia, PA

Peter Jay Zweig, Houston, TX

Source: The American Institute of Architects

Fellows of the American Society of Interior Designers

The American Society of Interior Designers (ASID) grants fellowship to those members who have made notable and substantial contributions to the profession and society. The following individuals are current, active fellows of the ASID.

Stanley Abercrombie
Dan Acito
Stephen W. Ackerman
Gail Adams
Joy E. Adcock
Estelle Alpert
Jerry R. Alsobrook
William F. Andrews
Ellen Angell
Robert H. Angle*
Robert A. Arehart
Warren G. Arnett
Anita Baltimore
David Barrett
Nancy Hoff Barsotti
Jeannine Bazer-Schwartz
Tamara A. Bazzle
Roy F. Beal
Marjorie A. Bedell
Frank Lee Berry
Hal F.B. Birchfield
Adriana Bitter
Edwin Bitter*
Joan Blutter
Daisy Houston Bond*
Penny Bonda
William D. Bowden
Blair S. Bowen
Susan Bradford
Bruce J. Brigham
C. Dudley Brown
Everett Brown
R. Michael Brown
Walton E. Brown*
Mary A. Bryan
Eleanor Brydone

Joyce A. Burke-Jones
David M. Butler
Rosalyn Cama
Orville V. Carr
Elizabeth M. Castleman
Juliana M. Catlin
Carl E. Clark
John P. Conron
Loverne C. Cordes
Herbert Cordier
Jini Costello
Virginia W. Courtenay
P.A. Dale
Hortense Davis
Robert John Dean
Hon C. Doxiadis*
Dede Draper
Hilda M. East
H. Gerard Ebert
Barbara Ebstein
Garrett Eckbo*
Arlis Ede
Martin Elinoff
John Elmo
Joel M. Ergas
Sammye J. Erickson
Adele Faulkner
Jon J. Fields
Lyn Fontenot
John G. Ford
Thomas Frank
Charles D. Gandy
Marion Gardiner
Francis J. Geck*
Alexander Girard*
Judy Girod

Fellows of the American Society of Interior Designers (Con't)

Milton Glaser
Thomas C. Grabowski
Theodora Kim Graham
Stephen Greenberger
Roberta S. Griffin
Olga Gueft*
Rita C. Guest
David W. Hall
Lawrence Halprin*
James M. Halverson
William D. Hamilton*
A. Niolon Hampton
Patricia Harvey
Dennis Haworth
Dorothy G. Helmer
Albert E. Herbert
Fred B. Hershey
Joseph P. Horan
Elizabeth B. Howard
Nina Hughes
Dorian Hunter
H. Cliff Ivester
Barbara L. Jacobs
Sarah B. Jenkins
Connie Johannes
Wallace R. Jonason
Richard W. Jones
Henry Jordan
Henri V. Jova
Franklin S. Judson*
Janet E. Kane
Mary V. Knackstedt
Binnie Kramer
Gayle Kreutzfeld
Karlyn Kuper
Anita M. Laird*
Hugh L. Latta
Dennis W. Leczinski
Robert S. Lindenthal
Boyd L. Loendorf
Michael Love
Joseph LoVecchio*
Odette Lueck

Ruth K. Lynford
William M. Manly
Helen Masoner
Terri Maurer
Sandra McGowen
James E. McIntosh
James Mezrano
John Richard Miller
Thomas H. Miller
Susan I. Mole
Kathy Ford Montgomery
Mark Nelson
Roi C. Nevaril
Linda Newton
W. E. Noffke
Douglas Parker*
Suzanne Patterson
Lawrence Peabody
Edward J. Perrault
BJ Peterson
H. Albert Phibbs
Dianne H. Pilgrim*
Norman Polsky*
Betty J. Purvis
Catharine G. Rawson
William Dunn Ray
Martha Garriott Rayle
John Robinson
Pedro Rodriguez
Agnes H. Rogers
Wayne Ruga*
Jack G. Ruthazer
Chester F. Sagenkahn
Barbara A. Sauerbrey
Hollie Schick
Janet S. Schirn
Barbara Schlattman
E. Williard Schurz
Irving D. Schwartz
Otho S. Shaw
James L. Simpson
Theodore A. Simpson
Edna A. Smith

Fellows of the American Society of Interior Designers (Con't)

James Merrick Smith

Sandra H. Sober

Jerrold Sonet*

Michael Sorrentino*

Beulah G. Spiers

Paul D. Spreiregen*

Edward H. Springs

Rita St.Clair

Russell M. Stanley

Ed Starr

Karl L. Steinhauser

Deborah Steinmetz

C. Eugene Stephenson

Blanche F. Strater

Ann Sullivan

Doris Nash Upshur

Bernard Vinick

G.F. Weber

Maurice Weir

Vicki Wenger

Gary E. Wheeler

Miriam Whelan

William L. Wilkoff

Frances E. Wilson

John B. Wisner

D. C. Witte

Edmund D. Wood

Julie M. Wyatt

* Honorary Fellow

Source: American Society of Interior Designers

Fellows of the American Society of Landscape Architects

Fellows of the American Society of Landscape Architects (ASLA) are landscape architects of at least ten years standing as Full Members of the ASLA, elected to Fellowship in honor of their outstanding contributions to the profession. Categories of election are: works of landscape architecture, administrative work, knowledge, and service to the profession. There have been a total of 754 Fellows elected since 1899. The list below indicates current, active Fellows of the ASLA.

Howard G. Abel
Wm. Dwayne Adams Jr.
Marvin I. Adleman
Russell A. Adsit
John F. Ahern
J. Robert Anderson
Domenico Annese
Ellis L. Antuñez
David E. Arbegast
David S. Armbruster
Henry F. Arnold
Sadik C. Artunc
Roy O. Ashley
D. Lyle Aten
Donald B. Austin
Kenneth J. Backman
Ted Baker
William H. Baker
Harry J. Baldwin
Edward B. Ballard
Alton A. Barnes Jr.
Milton Baron
Cheryl Barton
James H. Bassett
Kenneth E. Bassett
Anthony M. Bauer
Clarence W. Baughman
Howard R. Baumgarten
Eldon W. Beck
Yoshiro Befu
Arthur G. Beggs
William A. Behnke

James R. Bell
Richard C. Bell
Vincent Bellafiore
Armand Benedek
Claire R. Bennett
Shary Page Berg
Charles A. Birnbaum
Calvin T. Bishop
David H. Blau
Kerry Blind
Lloyd M. Bond
Norman K. Booth
W. Frank Brandt
Michael Wayne Breedlove
Theodore W. Brickman Jr.
Samuel W. Bridgers
Donald Carl Brinkerhoff
Mark K. Brinkley
Robert F. Bristol
Joseph E. Brown
Jeffrey L. Bruce
Jackie Karl Bubenik
Alexander Budrevics
Robert S. Budz
Dennis R. Buettner
Wayne L. Buggenhagen
Frank Burggraf Jr.
Arthur E. Bye Jr.
Willard C. Byrd
Raymond F. Cain
Robert A. Callans
William B. Callaway

Fellows of the American Society of Landscape Architects (Con't)

Craig S. Campbell

Paschall Campbell

Dean Cardasis

Robert R. Cardoza

Charles Cares

Bryan D. Carlson

Dennis B. Carmichael

Derr A. Carpenter

Jot D. Carpenter

David B. Carruth

Donald R. Carter

Eugene H. Carter

Anthony B. Casendino

Carlos J. Cashio

James E. Christman

Ann Christoph

Alan B. Clarke

Lewis J. Clarke

Roger D. Clemence

Franklin C. Clements

Jon Charles Coe

Beatriz de Winthuysen Coffin

Laurence E. Coffin Jr.

John F. Collins

Dennis C. Colliton

George Glenn Cook

Fred J. Correale

Kenneth R. Coulter

Van L. Cox

H. Kenneth Crasco

George E. Creed

Samuel G. Crozier

Joseph H. Crystal

George W. Curry

Jack Curtis

John E. Cutler

Jack R. Daft

Peter Dangermond Jr.

Edward L. Daugherty

Stuart O. Dawson

Dennis J. Day

Francis H. Dean

Neil J. Dean

Roy H. DeBoer

Richard K. Dee

Robert B. Deering

Bruce Dees

C. Christopher Degenhardt

Roger DeWeese

P. Woodward Dike

F. Christopher Dimond

Nicholas T. Dines

Carlton T. Dodge

Dan W. Donelin

Thomas R. Dunbar

Robert W. Dyas

Robert P. Ealy

Garrett Eckbo

Allen R. Edmonson

Jon Stidger Emerson

Donald H. Ensign

Steve Estrada

Morgan Evans

L. Susan Everett

Julius Gy. Fabos

Barbara Faga

Oliver M. Fanning

Damon Farber

David Fasser

Rudy J. Favretti

Barbara V. Fealy

Bruce K. Ferguson

Donald L. Ferlow

John J. Fernholz

Phillip E. Flores

William L. Flournoy Jr.

Everett L. Fly

George E. Fogg

Donald Mark Fox

Kathleen M. Fox

Mark Francis

Carol L. Franklin

Fellows of the American Society of Landscape Architects (Con't)

Daniel B. Franklin
Robert L. Frazer
Jere S. French
John W. Frey
M. Paul Friedberg
John F. Furlong
Emily J. Gabel-Luddy
Paul Gardescu
Harry L. Garnham
Benjamin W. Gary Jr.
George G. Gentile
Richard George Gibbons
James E. Glavin
D. Newton Glick
Donald H. Godi
James B. Godwin
Robert E. Goetz
Susan M. Goltsman
Philip H. Graham Jr.
Leonard Grassli
Bradford M. Greene
Isabelle Clara Greene
E. Robert Gregan
John N. Grissim
Clare A. Gunn
Anthony M. Guzzardo
Richard Haag
Frederick Edward Halback
Lawrence Halprin
Calvin S. Hamilton
Asa Hanamoto
Byron R. Hanke
Becca Hanson
Richard E. Hanson
Nancy M. Hardesty
George Hargreaves
Terence G. Harkness
Charles W. Harris
Robert R. Harvey
Richard G. Hautau
William H. Havens
Richard S. Hawks

Robert Graham Heilig
Kenneth I. Helphand
Edith H. Henderson
Glenn O. Hendrix
Donald F. Hilderbrandt
Arthur W. Hills
Allen W. Hixon Jr.
Leonard J. Hopper
Perry Howard
Donovan E. Hower
Joseph Hudak
Sam L. Huddleston
Mark B. Hunner
Alice R. Ireys
Wayne D. Iverson
Ronald M. Izumita
H. Rowland Jackson
Bernard Jacobs
Peter D. A. Jacobs
Susan L.B. Jacobson
Dale G.M. Jaeger
Frederick D. Jarvis
Leerie T. Jenkins Jr.
Linda Lee Jewell
Carl D. Johnson
Carol R. Johnson
Dean A. Johnson
Mark W. Johnson
William J. Johnson
Grant R. Jones
Ilze Jones
Robert Trent Jones
Warren D. Jones
Dirk Jongejan
Gary E. Karner
Joseph P. Karr
Jean Stephans Kavanagh
Frank H. Kawasaki
James E. Keeter
Walter H. Kehm
J. Timothy Keller
Leslie A. Kerr

Fellows of the American Society of Landscape Architects (Con't)

Gary B. Kesler

Masao Kinoshita

Charles L. Knight

Harold Kobayashi

Ken R. Krabbenhoft

Brian S. Kubota

William B. Kuhl

Bruce G. Kulik

Ray O. Kusche

Joseph J. Lalli

Joe W. Langran

Lucille Chenery Lanier

Mary Ann Lasch

Warren E. Lauesen

Michael M. Laurie

Dennis L. Law

Richard K. Law

Jack E. Leaman

Donald F. Lederer

Donald W. Leslie

Aaron Levine

Philip H. Lewis Jr.

J. Roland Lieber

Mark S. Lindhult

Karl Linn

J. Mack Little

Susan P. Little

R. Burton Litton Jr.

Thomas A. Lockett

Nimrod W. E. Long III

David O. Lose

Eldridge Lovelace

Paul C. K. Lu

J. Douglas Macy

Michael H. Malyn

Cameron R. J. Man

Lane L. Marshall

Richard K. Marshall

Edward C. Martin Jr.

Roger B. Martin

Steve Martino

Robert E. Marvin

Robert M. Mattson

Lewis T. May

Richard E. Mayer

Carol Mayer-Reed

Earl Byron McCulley

Vincent C. McDermott

Roger B. McErlane

Ian McHarg

Kathryn E. McKnight-Thalden

David A. McNeal

Gary W. Meisner

Robert Melnick

Vincent N. Merrill

Stuart M. Mertz

Richard J. Meyers

Luciano Miceli

E. Lynn Miller

Patrick A. Miller

Ann Milovsoroff

Debra L. Mitchell

Michael T. Miyabara

Lawrence R. Moline

Donald J. Molnar

Lynn A. Moore

Patrick C. Moore

Richard A. Moore

Paul F. Morris

Darrel G. Morrison

Mark K. Morrison

Robert H. Mortensen

Robert K. Murase

Thomas A. Musiak

Kenneth S. Nakaba

Kenichi Nakano

Joan I. Nassauer

Darwina L. Neal

John A. Nelson

William R. Nelson Jr.

Joseph N. Nevius

Thomas J. Nieman

Fellows of the American Society of Landscape Architects (Con't)

Satoru Nishita

Robert L. O'Boyle

Patricia M. O'Donnell

William A. O'Leary

Cornelia A. Oberlander

Warren J. Oblinger

Neil Odenwald

Wolfgang W. Oehme

Laurie D. Olin

Peter J. Olin

Edward J. Olinger

Don H. Olson

Brian Orland

Theodore Osmundson

Dennis Y. Otsuji

. Steve Ownby

Michael Painter

Meade Palmer

Thomas P. Papandrew

Cary M. Parker

John G. Parsons

Tito Patri

Gerald D. Patten

Courtland P. Paul

Merlyn J. Paulson

Robert Perron

Robert C. Perry Jr.

Owen H. Peters

Karen A. Phillips

Robert W. Pierson

. Edward Pinckney

Marjorie E. Pitz

Kenneth J. Polakowski

Peter M. Pollack

Harry W. Porter

Joe A. Porter

Neil H. Porterfield

Marion Pressley

William Pressley

Rae L. Price

Paul N. Procopio

Edward L. Pryce

Helen M. Quackenbush

Nicholas Quennell

F. Truitt Rabun Jr.

David C. Racker

John Rahenkamp

Robert S. Reich

Robert G. Reimann

John J. Reynolds

Artemas P. Richardson

Donald Richardson

Jane S. Ries

Robert B. Riley

William H. Roberts

Gary O. Robinette

Richard H. Rogers

Peter G. Rolland

Clarence Roy

Robert N. Royston

Harvey M. Rubenstein

Robert H. Rucker

Virginia Lockett Russell

Terry Warriner Ryan

Paul M. Saito

Margaret Sand

William D. Sanders

Hideo Sasaki

George J. Sass

Terry W. Savage

William Scatchard

Herbert R. Schaal

Horst Schach

Janice C. Schach

Sally Schauman

Mario G. Schjetnan

Arno S. Schmid

Helmut Schmitz

Gunter A. Schoch

Ollie Schrickel

Sunny Jung Scully

Bradford G. Sears

Jonathan G. Seymour

Bruce Sharky

Fellows of the American Society of Landscape Architects (Con't)

Juanita D. Shearer-Swink
Ruth P. Shellhorn
Dr. Hamid Shirvani
J. Kipp Shrack
Jeffrey L. Siegel
Kenneth B. Simmons Jr.
John Ormsbee Simonds
John B. Slater
Herrick H. Smith
Jerrold Soesbe
Stanley V. Specht
James C. Stansbury
Barry W. Starke
Richard G. Stauffer
Robert Steenhagen
John Goddfrey Stoddart
Edward D. Stone Jr.
Edward H. Stone II
Allen D. Stovall
William G. Swain
Rodney L. Swink
Austin Paul Tao
Leslee A. Temple
Barry R. Thalden
Robert Thayer Jr.
Michael Theilacker
J. William Thompson
William H. Tishler
Donald H. Tompkins
L. Azeo Torre
Shavaun Towers
Roger T. Trancik
Howard E. Troller
Peter J. Trowbridge
Stephen J. Trudnak
James R. Turner
Jerry Mitchell Turner
Ronald W. Tuttle
Anthony Tyznik
Raymond L. Uecker
James R. Urban

James Van Sweden
Michael R. Van Valkenburgh
Albert R. Veri
John Wacker
Lawrence L. Walker
Peter E. Walker
Theodore D. Walker
Victor J. Walker
Thomas H. Wallis
Ronald M. Walters
Thomas C. Wang
Barry J. Warner
Kent E. Watson
Dwight W. Weatherford
E. Neal Weatherly Jr.
Richard K. Webel
Scott S. Weinberg
V. Michael Weinmayr
Roger Wells
William E. Wenk
Robert A. Weygand
James K. Wheat
Morgan Dix Wheelock
Robert F. White
George W. Wickstead
Sara Katherine Williams
Richard A. Wilson
Theodore J. Wirth
Robert L. Woerner
J. Daniel Wojcik
David G. Wright
Patrick H. Wyss
Joseph Y. Yamada
Mark J. Zarillo
Floyd W. Zimmerman
Robert L. Zion
Robert W. Zolomij
Ervin H. Zube
Laurence W. Zuelke
K. Richard Zweifel

Source: American Society of Landscape Architects

Fellows of the Construction Specifications Institute

Fellowship in the Construction Specifications Institute (CSI) is the highest honor granted to its members. Fellows are chosen by their peers from those who have been members in good standing for at least five years and who have demonstrated extraordinary service to CSI and notably contributed to the advancement of construction technology, the improvement of construction specifications, and education in the construction profession. The following individuals are current, active Fellows of the CSI.

Jerome H. Alciatore
Joel R. Aftland
John C. Anderson
Stephen John Andros
John C. Arant
Robert E. Armitage
Robert L. Ashbrook
Livingston E. Atkins Jr.
R. Stanley Bair
Jane D. Baker
Frank L. Barsotti
Richard P. Bastyr
Gary A. Betts
Walter F. Bishop
S. Steve Blumenthal
H. Maynard Blumer
I. Steven Bonner
I. Gregg Borchelt
James C. Bort
William Calvin Bowne Jr.
Charles Chief Boyd
William M. Brenan
William R. Brightbill
Wayne C. Brock
Larry Brooks
A. Larry Brown
Robert G. Burkhardt
Scott Campbell
Charles R. Carroll Jr.
Michael D. Chambers
S. Elmer Chambers
James A. Chaney

Gary D. Church
Donald G. Clark
Thomas L. Clarke Jr.
Melvin G. Cole
Pamela J. Cole
Lynton B. Cooper Jr.
Eugene H. Cortrell
Frank L. Couch
John Milton Creamer
Wrenn M. Creel
Ray E. Cumrine
Walter E. Damuck
Douglas W. Day
Larry Craig Dean
Christopher G. Delgado
Charles M. Denisac Jr.
James N. De Serio
Wesley J. Dolginoff
Jo Drummond
William P. Dunne
Jerry W. Durham
R. Grant Easterling
Paul Edlund
Joseph H. Edwards
Richard C. Ehmann
Donald G. Engelhard
Rodney E. Erickson
Richard A. Eustis
Dell R. Ewing
Larry G. Fisher
John C. Fleck
Glenn G. Frazier

Fellows of the Construction Specifications Institute (Con't)

Elliot H. Gage
Woodward Garber
George S. George
Michael F. Gibbons
William Goudeket Jr.
Jorgen Graugaard
Alana S. Griffith
Benjamin M. Gruzen
Kenneth E. Guthrie
Dennis J. Hall
Diana M. Hamilton
Craig K. Haney
James B. Hardin
Robert W. Harrington
Robert V.M. Harrison
Douglas C. Hartman
Betty C. Hays
Paul Heineman
Raymond H. Helfer
Marshall A. Hildebrand Jr.
Robert C. Hockaday
Robert W. Holstein
Herman R. Hoyer
Gilman K.M. Hu
Thomas D. Hubbard
Clarence Huettenrauch
Mary A. Hutchins
Harry F. Iram
Sheldon B. Israel
James Jackson
R. Graham Jackson
Seth Jackson
W.L. Jacobsen
Martin J. Janka
Edwin J. Johnson
Harry L. Johnson Jr.
Robert W. Johnson
Wilbur L. Johnson
Joseph H. Kasimer
Walter R. Kaye
Lee F. Kilbourn
Clarence H. King Jr.
Michael J. King

Frederick J. Klemeyer Jr.
Norman Kruchkow
John William Kuremsky
Ralph G. Lane
John B. Lape
Grant Alvin Larsen
Curtis H. Lee
Thomas E. Lewis
William T. Lohmann
David E. Lorenzini
Lendall W. Mains
Donald W. Manley
Dr. Oscar E. Marsch
Mortimer M. Marshall Jr.
Marvin Martin
Robert Kipp Mayer
Charles E. McGuire
Joseph J. McGuire
Robert L. McManus
Hans W. Meier
Donald D. Meisel
Arthur J Miller
Mori Mitsui
Robert B. Moleseed
Thomas D. Montero
Peter J. Monterose
Kenneth J. Moore
Robert J. Morin
Lee C. Murray
Robert William Myers
Kenneth T. Nagie
Weldon W. Nash Jr.
Ronald R. Nattress
R. James Noone
Robert W. Nordstrom
Arthur A. Nording
Roger A. Nourse
Harold L. Olsen
Jerome I. Orland
Edwin T. Pairo
Dennis M. Pelletier
Herbert F. Pendleton
Daniel A. Perkins

Fellows of the Construction Specifications Institute (Con't)

Richard C. Perrell

Robert L. Petterson

Milton C. Potee

James Owen Power

Manuel Press

Jerry W. Preston

Katherine S. Proctor

Andrew D. Rae

John A. Raeber

Vincent G. Raney

Larry T. Raymond

Raymond R. Rieger

William F. Riesberg

James M. Robertson

Richard C. Robinson

Harold J. Rosen

Bernard B. Rothschild

Kelsey Y. Saint

Louis H. Sams

Maxwell L. Saul

Kenneth M. Schaefer

Carole E. Schafmeister

Richard C. Schroter

Lawrence E. Schwietz

Kenneth L. Searl

Alice Elizabeth Shelly

Paul W. Simonsen

Robert E. Simpson

Edward F. Smith

William A. Skoglund

Roscoe D. Smith

Tom F. Sneary

Edward L. Soenke

Richard B. Solomon

Michael L. Spence

Ross Spiegel

Everett G. Spurling Jr.

Norbert R. Steeber

Joel E. Stegall Jr.

J. Stewart Stein

Howard R. Steinmann

Terry J. Strong

Albert E. Taylor

David E. Thomas

Paul H. Tiffin

David F.M. Todd

Philip J. Todisco

Knox H. Tumlin

Albert R. Vallin

Donald P. Van Court

George A. Van Niel

William P. Vickers

Terry M. Wadsworth

Edith S. Washington

Wayne N. Watson

E. Ernest Waymon

Richard T. Weatherby

Roger T. Welcome

Raymond Whalley

George F. White Jr.

Thomas I. Young

Werner Edwin Zarnikow

Source: Construction Specifications Institute

Fellows of the Industrial Designers Society of America

Membership in the Industrial Designers Society of America's (IDSA) Academy of Fellows is conferred by a two-thirds majority vote of its Board of Directors. Fellows must be Society members in good standing who have earned the special respect and affection of the membership through distinguished service to the Society and to the profession as a whole. The following individuals are the current, active fellows of the IDSA.

James M. Alexander
Wallace H. Appel
Alfons Bach
Alexander Bally
George Beck
Nathaniel Becker
Arthur N. BecVar
Melvin H. Best
Robert I. Blaich
Alfred M. Blumenfeld
Eugene Bordinat
William Bullock
Peter Bresseler
Joseph Carriero
Arthur H. Crapsey
Donald E. Dailey
Thomas David
Niels Diffrient
Jay Doblin
H. Creston Doner
Henry Dreyfuss
Arden Farey
Vincent M. Foote
James F. Fulton
Roger Funk
Walter Furlani
Carroll M. Gantz
Franceco Gianninoto
Henry P. Glass
William Goldsmith
John S. Griswold
Robert Gruen

Olle E. Haggstrom
James G. Hansen
Jon W. Hauser
Stephen G. Hauser
Richard Hollerith
Robert H. Hose
James L. Hvale
Marnie Jones
Lorraine Justice
Belle Kogan
George Kosmak
Rowena Reed Kostellow
Rudolph W. Krolopp
David Kusuma
LeRoy LaCelle
Richard S. Latham
Raymond Loewy
Peter E. Lowe
Paul MacAlister
Tucker P. Madawick
Joseph R. Mango
Katherine J. McCoy
Donald McFarland
Leon Gordon Miller
Dana W. Mox
Peter Müller-Munk
C. Stowe Myers
George Nelson
Joseph M. Parriott
Lee Payne
Charles Pelly
Nancy Perkins

ellows of the Industrial Designers Society of America (Con't)

ames J. Pirkl
Villiam L. Plumb
rthur J. Pulos
obert E. Redmann
ean Otis Reinecke
Iarold Reynolds
eane W. Richardson
ames Ryan
lair A. Samhammer
enneth Schory
. Eugene Smith
obert G. Smith
aul B. Specht
aymond Spilman
arrell S. Staley
udd Steinhilber
rooks Stevens

Philip H. Stevens
Ernest L. Swarts
Sharyn Thompson
David D. Tompkins
Herbert H. Tyrnauer
John Vassos
Read Viemeister
Tucker Viemeister
Noland Vogt
Sandor Weisz
Arnold Wolf
Peter Wooding
Cooper C. Woodring
Edward J. Zagorski

Source: Industrial Designers Society of America

Did you know...

Eero Saarinen's 1948 womb chair, part of the Museum of Modern Art's collection, was the first fiberglass chair to be mass-produced.

Fellows of the International Interior Design Association

Professional members of the International Interior Design Association (IIDA) are inducted into the College of Fellows by a two thirds vote by their Board of Directors. This honor recognizes members who have demonstrated outstanding service to the IIDA, the community, and the interior design profession. The following individuals are current, active fellows of the IIDA.

Robin Klehr Avia
Laura Bailey
Jeanne Baldwin
Claude Berube
Charles Blumberg
Dan Bouligny
Michael Bourque
Rus Calder
Richard Carlson
Particia Gutierrez Castellanos
Amarjeet Chatrath
Susan Coleman
David Cooke
Eleanor Corkle
Christine Dandan
Eugene Daniels
Carol Disrud
Jacqueline Duncan
Cheryl Duvall
Hilda East
Marilyn Farrow
James Ferguson II
Dorothy Fowles
Neil Frankel
Angela Frey
Charles D. Gandy
Gerald Gelsomino
M. Arthur Gensler Jr.
Carol S. Graham
Karen Guenther
Beth Harmon-Vaughan
Judith Hastings
Jo Heinz

Edna Henner
John Herron
Frederick Hutchirs
David Immenschuh
Christina Johnson
Carol Jones
Margo Jones
Robert Kennedy
Tessa Kennedy
Sooz Klinkhamer
Mary Knackstedt
Lili Kray
Marjorie Kriebel
Michael Kroelinger
Robert Ledingham
Fola Lerner-Miller
Jack Levin
Neville Lewis
Charles Littleton
Ronald Lubben
Hiroko Machida
Candace MacKenzie
Richard Mazzucotelli
Jose Medrano
Ruth Mellergaard
Kenneth Muller
Donald Parker
Janie Petkus
Paul Petrie
Richard N. Pollack
Shirley Pritchard
Carole Price Shanis
Sandra Ragan

Fellows of the International Interior Design Association (Con't)

Charles Raymond
Patti Richards
Wayne Ruga
Joyce Saunders
Allan Shaivitz
Donald Sherman
Rayne Sherman
Gail Shiel
Bernard Soep
Henrietta Spencer-Churchill
Andre Staffelbach
Andrew Stafford
William Stankiewicz
Janice Stevenor-Dale
Donald Thomas
Joann Thompson

Betty Treanor
Marcia Troyan
Robert Valentine
Margaret Velardo
Roen Viscovich
Allison Carll White
Ron Whitney-Whyte
Glenda Wilcox
Frances Wilson
M. Judith Wilson
D. Geary Winstead
Michael Wirtz
Susan Wood
Minoru Yokoyama
Janice Young

Source: International Interior Design Association

Fellows of the Society of Architectural Historians

Fellowship in the Society of Architectural Historians is granted for "exceptional and distinguished service to the Society."

H. Allen Brooks
Marian C. Donnelly
Alan W. Gowans
Carol Herselle Krinsky
Elisabeth Blair MacDougall
Carter H. Manny
Henry A. Millon
Osmund Overby
Seymour H. Persky
Charles E. Peterson
William H. Pierson Jr.
Adolf K. Placzek
George B. Tatum

Source: Society of Architectural Historians

Honorary Fellows of The American Institute of Architects

The American Institute of Architects (AIA) grants Honorary Fellowship to non-members, both architects and non-architects, who have made substantial contributions to the field of architecture. The following individuals are current Honorary Fellows of the AIA.

Kurt H.C. Ackermann, Munich, Germany

Gunnel Adlercreutz, Helsinki, Finland

O. J. Aguilar, Lima, Peru

Hisham Albakri, Kuala Lumpur, Malaysia

William A. Allen, London, England

Alfred V. Alvares, Vancouver, Canada

Jose Alvarez, Lima, Peru

Mario R. Alvarez, Buenos Aires, Argentina

Tadao Ando, Osaka, Japan

John H. Andrews, Australia

Carlos D. Arguelles, Manila, Philippines

Gordon R. Arnott, Regina, Canada

Carl Aubock, Austria

Carlo Aymonino, Venice, Italy

George G. Baines, England

W. D. Baldwin, Sterling, Canada

W. K. Banadayga, Sterling, Canada

Essy Baniassad, Halifax, Canada

Nikolai B. Baranov, Moscow, Russia

Geoffrey M. Bawa, Columbo, Sri Lanka

Eugene Beaudouin, France

Gerard Benoit, Paris, France

Jai R. Bhalla, New Delhi, India

Jacob Blegvad, Aalborg, Denmark

Ricardo L. Bofill, Barcelona, Spain

Oriol Bohigas, Barcelona, Spain

Irving D. Boigon, Richmond Hill, Canada

Ferenc Callmeyer, Telki, Hungary

Santiago A. Calvo, Lima, Peru

Felix Candela, Raleigh, North Carolina

Rifat Chadirji, Surrey, England

Suk-Woong Chang, Seoul, Korea

Te L. Chang, Taipei, Taiwan

Bill Chomik, Calgary, Canada

Adolf Ciborowski, Warsaw, Poland

E. Gresley Cohen, Dalkeith, Australia

Charles M. Correa, Bombay, India

Philip S. Cox, Sydney, Australia

Charles H. Cullum, Newfoundland, Canada

Carlos E. Da Silva, Rizal, Philippines

John M. Davidson, Richmond, Australia

David Y. Davies, Surrey, England

Sara T. De Grinberg, Mexico

Rafael De La Hoz, Spain

S. D. De La Tour, Durville, France

Eduardo De Mello, Braga, Portugal

Costantin N. Decavalla, Greece

Ignacio M. Delmonte, Mexico City, Mexico

A. J. Diamond, Toronto, Canada

Ignacio Diaz-Morales, Jalisco, Mexico

Balkrishna V. Doshi, Ahmedabad, India

Philip Dowson, London, England

Kiril Doytchev, Sofia, Bulgaria

G. M. Dubois, Toronto, Canada

Allan F. Duffus, Halifax, Canada

Werner Duttman, Lindenalle, Germany

David W. Edwards, Regina, Canada

Yehya M. Eid, Cairo, Egypt

Abdel W. El Wakil, Kent, England

Arthur C. Erickson, Vancouver, Canada

Lord Esher, England

Inger Exner, Denmark

Honorary Fellows of The American Institute of Architects

Johannes Exner, Denmark

Tobias Faber, Copenhagen, Denmark

Francisco B. Fajardo, Philippines

Hassan Fathy, Egypt

Sverre Fehn, Oslo, Norway

Bernard M. Feilden, Norfolk, England

Ji Z. Feng, Shanghai, PRC

Angelina Munoz Fernandez de Madrid, Sonora, Mexico

A. I. Ferrier, Red Hill, Australia

Jozsef Finta, Budapest, Hungary

Antonio F. Flores, Mexico

Cesar X. Flores, Mexico D.F., Mexico

Norman Foster, London, England

Charles A. Fowler, Canada

Jorge Gamboa de Buen, Mexico DF, Mexico

Juan Gonzalez, Spain

Roderick P. Hackney, Cheshire, England

Zaha Hadid, London, England

H. H. Hallen, Australia

Shoji Hayashi, Tokyo, Japan

Tao Ho, North Point, Hong Kong

Barry J. Hobin, Ottawa, Canada

Hans Hollein, Vienna, Austria

Wilhelm Holzbauer, Vienna, Austria

Sir Michael Hopkins, London, England

Lady Patricia Hopkins, London, England

Thomas Howarth, Toronto, Canada

Nobuo Hozumi, Tokyo, Japan

Arata Isozaki, Tokyo, Japan

Toyo Ito, Tokyo, Japan

Daryl Jackson, Melbourne, Australia

R. D. Jackson, Sydney, Australia

Alvaro Joaquim de Meio Siza, Porto, Portugal

P. N. Johnson, Australia

Achyut P. Kanvinde, New Dehli, India

Vladimir Karfik, Brno, Czech Republic

Kiyonori Kikutake, Tokyo, Japan

Reiichiro Kitadai, Tokyo, Japan

Azusa Kito, Tokyo, Japan

Josef P. Kleihues, Berlin, Germany

Rob Krier, Berlin, Germany

Dogan Kuban, Istanbul, Turkey

Alexandr P. Kudryavtsev, Moscow, Russia

Kisho Kurokawa, Tokyo, Japan

Colin Laird, Port of Spain, Trinidad and Tobago

Jean L. Lalonde, Canada

Henning Larsen, Denmark

Denys L. Lasdun, London, England

Kwang-Ro Lee, Seoul, Korea

Kyung-Hoi Lee, Seoul, Korea

Juha Ilmari Leiviska, Helsinki, Finland

Jaime Lerner, Parana, Brazil

Wu Liang Yong, Beijing, PRC

Kington Loo, Kuala Lumpur, Malaysia

Aldana E. Lorenzo, San Jeronimo, Mexico

Serapio P. Loza, Jalisco, Mexico

Kjell Lund, Oslo, Norway

Olufemi Majekodunmi, Gaborone, Botswana

Fumihiko Maki, Tokyo, Japan

Matti K. Makinen, Finland

Rutilo Malacara, Mexico D. F., Mexico

Motlatsi Peter Malefane, Johannesburg, South Africa

Albert Mangones, Port Au Prince, Haiti

Yendo Masayoshi, New York, New York

Robert Peter McIntyre, Victoria, Australia

Rodrigo Mejia-Andrion, Panama

Hector Mestre, Mexico, D.F., Mexico

Jose Raphael Moneo, Madrid, Spain

Raymond Moriyama, Toronto, Canada

Padraig Murray, Dublin, Ireland

Toshio Nakamura, Tokyo, Japan

Nikola I. Nikolov, Sofia, Bulgaria

Juan Bassegoda Nonell, Barcelona, Spain

Honorary Fellows of The American Institute of Architects

Rafael Norma, Mexico City, Mexico

Jean Nouvel, Paris, France

Jorge Nu Ex Verdugo, Mexico

Carl J.A. Nyren, Stockholm, Sweden

ShinIchi Okada, Tokyo, Japan

Oluwole O. Olumyiwa, Lagos, Nigeria

Georgui M. Orlov, Moscow, Russia

Juhani Pallasmaa, Helsinki, Finland

Gustav Peichl, Wein, Austria

Raili Pictila, Helsinki, Finland

Methodi A. Pissarski, Sofia, Bulgaria

Ernst A. Plischke, Wien, Austria

Christian de Portzamparc, Paris, France

Ivor C. Prinsloo, Rondebosch, South Africa

Victor M. Prus, Montreal, Canada

Luis M. Quesada, Lima, Peru

Hector M. Restat, Santiago, Chile

Jose F. Reygadas, Mexico City, Mexico

Philippe Robert, Paris, France

Jerry Menzies Robertson, Picton, Canada

Ivan J. Rocco, Montevideo, Uruguay

Javier Cortes Rocha, Coyoacan, Mexico

Aldo A. Rossi, Milano, Italy

Witold Rybczynski, Philadelphia, PA

Thomas J. Sanabria, Miami, FL

Alberto Sartoris, Cossonay Ville, Switzerland

Helmut C. Schulitz, Braunschweig, Germany

Michael Scott, Ireland

Harry Seidler, Australia

Vassilis C. Sgoutas, Athens, Greece

Taigo T.H. Shen, Taipei, Taiwan

Peter F. Shepheard, Philadelphia, PA

Dr. Tsutomu Shigemura, Kobe, Japan

Kazuo Shinohara, Yokohama, Japan

Brian Sim, Vancouver, Canada

Antonio S. Sindiong, Rizal, Philippines

Heikki Siren, Helsinki, Finland

Kaija Siren, Helsinki, Finland

Nils Slaatto, Oslo, Norway

Vladimir Slapeta, Praha, Czech Republic

Inette L. Smith, Cornwall, England

J. M. Smith, Cornwall, England

Gin Su, Bethesda, Maryland

Timo Suomalainen, Espoo, Finland

Minoru Takeyama, Littleton, Colorado

Yoshio Taniguchi, Tokyo, Japan

German Tellez, Bogota, Colombia

Anders Tengbom, Sweden

Paul-Andre Tetreault, Montreal, Canada

Alexandros N. Tombazis, Athens, Greece

Luben N. Tonev, Bulgaria

Marion Tournon-Branly, Paris, France

Shozo Uchii, Tokyo, Japan

Lennart Uhlin, Stockholm, Sweden

Jorn Utzon, Denmark

Pierre Vago, Noisy, France

Gino Valle, Udine, Italy

Marcelo E. Vargas, Lima, Peru

Pedro R. Vasquez, Mexico City, Mexico

Eva Vecsei, Montreal, Canada

Jorge N. Verdugo, Mexico City, Mexico

Tomas R. Vicuna, Santiago, Chile

Ricardo L. Vilchis, Mexico City, Mexico

Eduardo O. Villacortaq, Lima, Peru

William Whitefield, London, England

Terence J. Williams, Victoria, Canada

Roy W. Willwerth, Halifax, Canada

C. A. Wnderlich, Guatemala City, Guatemala

Chung Soo Won, Seoul, Korea

Bernard Wood, Ottawa, Canada

Rutang Ye, Beijing, PRC

Richard Young, Sterling, Canada

Abraham Zabludovsky, Codesa, Mexico

Jose M. Zaragoza, Philippines

Eberhard Heinrich Zeidler, Toronto, Canada

Source: The American Institute of Architects

Honorary Members of The American Institute of Architects

The American Institute of Architects (AIA) grants honorary membership to individuals outside the architecture profession who are not otherwise eligible for membership in the Institute. They are chosen for their distinguished service to architecture or the allied arts and sciences. Nominations may be submitted by the national AIA Board of Directors or a component PIA. National and component staff with 10 years or more of service are also eligible for Honorary Membership. The following individuals are Honorary Members of the AIA.

Ava J. Abramowitz, Chevy Chase, MD
Joseph F. Addonizio, New Rochelle, NY
His Highness The Aga Khan
Joseph Ahearn, Littleton, CO
Michael L. Ainslie, New York, NY
R. Mayne Albright, Charlotte, NC
Barbara Allan, Seattle, WA
George A. Allen, CAE, Tallahassee, FL
Trudy Aron, Topeka, KS
Ludd Ashley, Washington, DC
Janice Axon, Laguna Niguel, CA
Mariana Barthold, Oklahoma City, OK
Augustus Baxter, Sr., Philadelphia, PA
Stephen M. Bennett, Columbus, OH
Elaine Bergman, Tulsa, OK
James Biddle, Andalusia, PA
J. Bidwill, Chicago, IL
Sherry Birk, Washington, DC
The Honorable Sherwood L. Boehlert
Oriol Bohigas, Barcelona, Spain
Sara H. Boutelle, Santa Cruz, CA
A. S. Boyd, Washington, DC
Ann Marie Boyden, Arlington, VA
Eleanor K. Brassel, Bethesda, MD
John W. Braymer, Richmond, VA
David Brinkley, Chevy Chase, MD
Jack Brooks, Washington, DC
A. B. Brown, Providence, RI

J. N. Brown, Providence, RI
William A. Brown Sr., Washington, DC
John M. Bryan, Columbia, SC
Muriel Campaglia, Washington, DC
Donald Canty, Seattle, WA
Joan Capelin, New York, NY
Edward Carlough, Washington, DC
Charles M. Cawley, Wilmington, DE
Henry C. Chambers, Beaufort, SC
Mary Chapman-Smith, Mancelona, MI
William W. Chase, Alexandria, VA
Henry Cisneros, San Antonio, TX
F. J. Clark, Washington, DC
Grady Clay Jr., Louisville, KY
Ernest A. Connally, Alexandria, VA
S. B. Conroy, Washington, DC
Rolaine V. Copeland, Seattle, WA
Weld Coxe, Block Island, RI
Lois Craig, Cambridge, MA
James P. Cramer, Norcross, GA
Alfonse M. D'Amato, Washington, DC
Kathleen L. Daileda, Washington, DC
Ann Davidson, North Canton, OH
Joan K. Davidson, New York, NY
Mabel S. Day, Alexandria, VA
Fred R. Deluca, Washington, DC
Deborah Dietsch, Washington, DC
Carlos Diniz

Honorary Members of The American Institute of Architects (Con't)

ae Dumke, Detroit, MI

. Durning, Seattle, WA

Sprigg Duvall, Washington, DC

inda J. Ebitz, Oakland, PA

idy A. Edwards, New Haven, CT

. D. Egan, Anderson, SC

imes R. Ellis, Seattle, WA

ohn D. Entenza, Santa Monica, CA

Iarie L. Farrell, Belvedere, CA

lan M. Fern, Chevy Chase, MD

ngelina Munoz Fernandez de Madrid,
    Sonora, Mexico

. A. Ferre, San Juan, Puerto Rico

avid W. Field, CAE, Columbus, OH

Iarold B. Finger, Washington, DC

imes M. Fitch, New York, NY

D. Forbes, Charlottesville, VA

Jilliam S. Fort, Eugene, OR

rthur J. Fox Jr., New York, NY

oris C. Freedman, New York, NY

Iildred Friedman, New York, NY

atsy L. Frost, Columbus, OH

uth Fuller, Houston, TX

aul Gapp, Chicago, IL

. E. Gardner, Delaware, OH

aul Genecki, Kensington, MD

. D. Gibson, Ogden, UT

rendan Gill, New York, NY

rge Glusberg, Buenos Aires, Argentina

lfred Goldberg, Belvedere Tiburo, CA

Ioward G. Goldberg, Esq.

aul Goldberger, New York, NY

ouglas E. Gordon, Washington, DC

. B. Gores, Alpharetta, GA

. R. Graham, Tallahassee, FL

inny W. Graves, Prairie Village, KS

arbara Gray, Takoma Park, MD

oberta Gratz

ecil H. Green, Dallas, TX

Thomas Griffith, New York, NY

Roberta J. Guffey, Charleston, WV

Robert Gutman, Princeton, NJ

Richard Hagg

Donald J. Hall, Kansas City, MO

William L. Hall, Eden Prairie, MN

Donalee Hallenbeck, Sacramento, CA

P. Hammer, Beverley Beach, MD

Marga Rose Hancock, Seattle, WA

Partrick K. Harrison, London, England

Dr. F. Otto Hass, Philadelphia, PA

Arthur A. Hart, Boise, ID

Dianne Hart, California

Beverly E. Hauschild-Baron, Minneapolis, MN

A. Hecksher, New York, NY

Andrew Heiskell, New York, NY

Amy Hershfang

Gerald D. Hines, Houston, TX

Charles L. Hite

William Houseman, Portland, ME

Thomas P. Hoving, New York, NY

Philip A. Hutchinson, Harwood, MD

Ada L. Huxtable, New York, NY

J. Michael Huey, Esq.

Donald G. Iselin, Santa Barbara, CA

Kathy C. Jackson, CAE, Jackson, MS

J. B. Johnson, Watertown, NY

Dr. Joseph E. Johnson

Lady B. Johnson, Austin, TX

Gerre Jones, Albuquerque, NM

V. Jordan, Jr., New York, NY

H. A. Judd, Beaverton, OR

Lloyd Kaiser, Oakmont, PA

Shelly Kappe

Robert J. Kapsch, Gaithersburg, MD

Suzanne Keller, Princeton, NJ

Dorothy Kender

Roger G. Kennedy, Alexandria, VA

Jonathan King, Houston, TX

Honorary Members of The American Institute of Architects (Con't)

R. Lawrence Kirkegaard, Downers Grove, IL

Lee E. Koppelman, Stonybrook, NY

Peter H. Kostmayer, Washington, DC

Mabel Krank, Oklahoma City, OK

Florence C. Ladd, Cambridge, MA

Anita M. Laird, Cape May, NJ

George Latimer, St. Paul, MN

William J. Le Messurier, Cambridge, MA

Aaron Levine, Menlo Park, CA

E. H. Levitas, Washington, DC

Lawrence Lewis Jr.

Weiming Lu, St. Paul, MN

Major General Eugene Lupia

Jane Maas, New York, NY

Diane Maddox, Washington, DC

Randell Lee Makinson

Stanley Marcus, Dallas, TX

Louis L. Marines, Corte Madera, CA

Judy Marks, Washington, DC

Albert R. Marschall, Alexandria, VA

Maureen Marx, Springfield, VA

Mary Tyler Cheek McClenaham

F M. McConihe, Potomac, MD

Terrence M. McDermott, Chicago, IL

Evelyn B. McGrath, Holiday, FL

Ian L. McHarg, Philadelphia, PA

Cheri C. Melillo, New York, NY

Paul Mellon, Upperville, VA

Betty H. Meyer

E. P. Mickel, Bethesda, MD

J. I. Miller, Columbus, IN

Martha P. Miller, Portland, OR

R. Miller, Sherman Oaks, CA

Richard B. Miller, Elmsford, NY

Roger Milliken, Spartanburg, SC

Hermine Mitchell, Philadelphia, PA

Martha Barber Montgomery, Ph.D.

William B. Moore Jr., Kilmarnock, VA

John W. Morris, Arlington, VA

Philip A. Morris, Birmingham, AL

Terry B. Morton, Chevy Chase, MD

Woolridge Brown Morton III

Jean G. Muntz, Omaha, NE

Martha Murphree, Houston, TX

Maria Murray, Kensington, MD

Betty J. Musselman, Accokeek, MD

Raymond D. Nasher

Doreen Nelson, Los Angeles, CA

Shirley J. Norvell, Springfield, IL

Laurie D. Olin, Philadelphia, PA

Mary E. Osman, Columbia, SC

Ronald J. Panciera, Bradenton, FL

R. B. Pease, Pittsburgh, PA

C. Ford Peatross, Washington, DC

Robert A. Peck, Esq, Washington, DC

Claiborne Pell, Washington, DC

David Perdue, Silver Spring, MD

Honorable Pete Wilson, Washington, DC

G. E. Pettengill, Arlington, VA

Janet D. Pike, Lexington, KY

Philip W. Pillsbury Jr., Washington, DC

Walter F. Pritchard II, Costa Mesa, CA

Jay A. Pritzker, Chicago, IL

Jody Proppe, Portland, OR

Sidney A. Rand, Minneapolis, MN

David P. Reynolds, Richmond, VA

William G. Reynolds Jr., Richmond, VA

Brenda Richards

Carolyn Richie

Raymond P. Rhinehart, Washington, DC

Joseph P. Riley, Charleston, SC

J. P. Robin, Pittsburgh, PA

Laurance Rockefeller, New York, NY

Barbara J. Rodriguez, Albany, NY

Gini Rountree, Sacramento, CA

Mario G. Salvadori, New York, NY

Carl M. Sapers, Boston, MA

William D. Schaefer, Baltimore, MD

Martin Schaum, Garden City, NY

Paul Schell, Seattle, WA

Ionorary Members of The American Institute of Architects
Con't)

incent C. Schoemehl Jr., Clayton, MO

hilip Schreiner, Washington, DC

osemary Schroeder, Dallas, TX

usan E. Schur

rederick D. Schwengel

uzanne K. Schwengels, Des Moines, IA

ex Scouten, Washington, DC

. Sebastian, San Francisco, CA

imes H. Semans, Durham, NC

ilian B. Serrill, Des Moines, IA

laine K. Sewell Jones, Los Angeles, CA

olly E. Shackleton, Washington, DC

ilius Shulman, Los Angeles, CA

etty W. Silver, Raleigh, NC

lice Sinkevitch, Chicago, IL

ohn B. Skilling, Seattle, WA

J. L. Slayton, Washington, DC

leanor McNamara Smith, Somerset, WI

ancy Somerville, Washington, DC

. Spencer, Washington, DC

nn Stacy, Baltimore, MD

. Steinborn, Seattle, WA

aundra Stevens, Portland, OR

. D. Stitt, Yreka, CA

eborah Sussman, Culver City, CA

nne J. Swager, Pittsburg, PA

Pipsan S. Swanson, Bloomfield, MI

G. B. Tatum, Chester, CT

Anne Taylor, Kansas City, MO

Richard Thevenot, Baton Rouge, LA

J. S. Thurmond, Washington, DC

Carolyn H. Toft, St. Louis, MO

Bernard Tomson, Voorheesville, NY

W. F. Traendly, Thetford Center, VT

R. E. Train, Washington, DC

Pierre Vago, Noisy, France

Mariana L. Verga, Edmond, OK

Wolf Von Eckardt, Washington, DC

Connie C. Wallace, CAE, Nashville, TN

Paul Weidlinger, New York, NY

Paul W. Welch, Jr. Sacramento, CA

Emmet L. Wemple, Los Angeles, CA

Katie Westby, Tulsa, OK

Frank J. Whalen Jr., Cheverly, MD

Richard Guy Wilson, Charlottesville, VA

Gloria Wise, Dallas, TX

Arol Wolford, Norcross, GA

Marilyn Wood, Santa Fe, NM

Tony P. Wrenn, Fredricksburg, VA

Honorable Sidney Yates, Washington, DC

Jill D. Yeomans, Santa Barbara, CA

John Zukowsky, Chicago, IL

Source: The American Institute of Architects

Architecture is the reaching out for the truth.

Louis Kahn

Honorary Members of the American Society of Landscape Architects

Honorary Membership is granted by the American Society of Landscape Architects' (ASLA) Board of Directors, to persons, other than landscape architects, who have performed notable service to the profession of landscape architecture. The following individuals are current, active Honorary Members of the ASLA.

Edward H. Able Jr.
Hon. Douglas Bereuter
Randall Biallas
Hon. Dale Bumpers
Pres. James Earl Carter Jr.
Grady Clay
Russell E. Dickenson
Walter L. Doty
Marvin Durning
Carolyn B. Etter
Don D. Etter
Albert Fein
Charles E. Fraser
Marshall M. Fredericks
Gwen Frostic
Donald M. Harris
George B. Hartzog Jr.
Vance R. Hood
Patrick Horsbrugh
Thomas Hylton
Lyndon B. Johnson
Dr. Harley Jolley
Genevieve Pace Keller
Hon. Edward M. Kennedy
Peter A. Kirsch

Balthazar Korab
Norbert Kraich
Prof. Walter H. Lewis
Dr. Binyi Liu
John A. Love
Lee MacDonald
Prof. E. Bruce MacDougall
Charles C. McLaughlin
Hugh C. Miller
Philip A. Morris
Frederick L. Noland
Gyo Obata
Ross D. Pallay
R. Max Peterson
William Phelps
Richard Pope, Sr.
Gen. Colin Powell
Peter H. Raven
Hon. Joseph P. Riley Jr.
L. S. Rockefeller
Martin J. Rosen
John Seiberling
Ron Taven
Dr. Ralph J. Warburton

Source: American Society of Landscape Architects

Honorary Members of the Industrial Designers Society of America

The Board of Directors of the Industrial Designers Society of America (IDSA) grants honorary membership to individuals whose relationship to, involvement with, or special efforts on behalf of the design profession merit the recognition and gratitude of the Society. Honorary membership is awarded by a three-quarters majority vote by the Board of Directors.

1965   R. Buckminster Fuller
1965   Edgar Kaufmann Jr.
1981   Ray Eames
1982   Florence Knoll Bassett
1983   Ralph Caplan
1988   Brian J. Wynne
1998   Bruce Nussbaum

Source: Industrial Designers Society of America

Did you know...

The 1949 Ericofon telephone, designed by L. M. Ericsson, was the first compact plastic telephone to include all components—earpiece, mouthpiece, dial, and switch—in one unit.

Honorary Members of the International Interior Design Association

The International Interior Design Association (IIDA) grants honorary membership to individuals who, although they are not interior designers, have made substantial contributions to the interior design profession. The following individuals are current Honorary Members of the IIDA.

Stanley Abercrombie
Clarellen Adams
George Baer
Shirley Black
Charles Blumberg
Chilton Brown
Margaret Buckingham
Len Corlin
Christine Cralle
James P. Cramer
Tom Cramer
Lori Graham
Dianne Jackman

Cynthia Leibrock
Paul Leonard
Viscount David Linley
Chris McKellar
Doug Parker
Norman Polsky
Lois Powers
John Sample
Thomas Sutton Jr.
Dean Thompson
Jan Toft
Jill Vanderfleet-Scott
John West

Source: International Interior Design Association

Interior Design Hall of Fame

In 1985 *Interior Design* magazine established the Interior Design Hall of Fame to recognize individuals who have made significant contributions to the growth and prominence of the Interior Design profession. New inductees are presented every December at an awards ceremony at New York's Waldorf-Astoria Hotel. This event also serves as a fundraising effort for the non-profit Foundation for Interior Design Education Research (FIDER) and other charitable organizations supporting interior design educational initiatives.

Hall of Fame Members:

Marvin. B Affrime
Kalef Alaton
Davis Allen
Pamela Babey
Benjamin Baldwin
Florence Knoll Bassett
Louis M.S. Beal
Ward Bennett
Maria Bergson
Laura Bohn
Joseph Braswell
Robert Bray
Don Brinkmann
Tom Britt
R. Scott Bromley
Denise Scott Brown
Mario Buatta
Richard Carlson
Francois Catroux
Steve Chase
Clodagh
Celeste Cooper
Robert Currie
Barbara D'Arcy
Joseph D'Urso
Thierry W. Despont
Orlando Diaz-Azcuy
Angelo Donghia
Jack Dunbar
Tony Duquette
Melvin Dwork
David Easton

Henry End
Mica Ertegun
Bernardo Fort-Brescia
Billy W. Francis
Neil Frankel
Frank Gehry
Arthur Gensler
Richard Gluckman
Mariette Himes Gomez
Jacques Grange
Margo Grant
Michael Graves
Bruce Gregga
Charles Gwathmey
Albert Hadley
Anthony Hall
Mel Hamilton
Mark Hampton
Antony Harbour
Hugh Hardy
David Hicks
Edith Mansfield Hills
Richard Himmel
Howard Hirsch
William Hodgins
Malcolm Holzman
Franklin D. Israel
Carolyn Iu
Eva Jiricna
Jed Johnson
Melanie Kahane
Robert Kleinschmidt
Ronald Krueck

Interior Design Hall of Fame (Con't)

Gary Lee
Sarah Tomerlin Lee
Naomi Leff
Debra Lehman-Smith
Joseph Lembo
Lawrence Lerner
Neville Lewis
Sally Sirkin Lewis
Eva Maddox
Stephen Mallory
Peter Marino
Patrick McConnell
Margaret McCurry
Kevin McNamara
Richard Meier
Robert Metzger
Lee Mindel
Juan Montoya
Frank Nicholson
James Northcurr
Mrs. Henry Parish II
Norman Pfeiffer
Charles Pfister
Warren Platner
Donald D. Powell
William Pulgram
Andrée Putman
Chessy Rayner
Lauren Rottet
Rita St. Clair
John F. Saladino
Michael Schaible
Peter Shelton
Berry Sherrill
Robert Siegel
Ethel Smith
Laurinda Spear
Jay Spectre
Andre Staffelbach
Philippe Starck
Robert A.M. Stern
Rysia Suchecka
Lou Switzer
Rose Tarlow
Michael Taylor

Stanley Tigerman
Adam Tihany
Billie Tsien
Carleton Varney
Robert Venturi
Lella Vignelli
Massimo Vignelli
Kenneth H. Walker
Sally Walsh
Kevin Walz
Bunny Williams
Tod Williams
Trisha Wilson
Vincente Wolf

Special Honorees:
Robert O. Anderson
Jaime Ardiles-Arce
Stanley Barrows
Howard Brandston
Adele Chatfield-Taylor
John L. Dowling
Lester Dundes
Sherman R. Emery
Karen Fisher
Arnold Friedmann
Alberto Paolo Gavasci
Jeremiah Goodman
Louis Oliver Gropp
Olga Gueft
Jack Hedrich
Benjamin D. Holloway
Philip E. Kelly
Kips Bay Decorator Show House
Jack Lenor Larsen
Santo Loquasto
Ruth K. Lynford
Gene Moore
Diantha Nype
Dianne Pilgrim
Paige Rense
Ian Schrager
Tony Walton
Winterthur Museum and Gardens

Source: Interior Design *magazine*

Leading Women Architects and Designers of the 20th Century

The following women are some of many female leaders in the design professions throughout the 20th Century, selected by the editors of the *Almanac of Architecture & Design* to broaden awareness of and generate interest in the contributions of women to design. There are, however, many outstanding female contributors to the profession, and, as such, this is list is only intended to serve as the beginnings of an understanding of the influential role of women architects and designers during the last century.

Aino Aalto

Finnish. Born Aino Marso (1894-1949). Aino Aalto graduated from the Helsinki University of Technology in 1919. In 1921 she married and formed a professional partnership with Alvar Aalto in Jyväskylä, Finland. Aino designed interiors, furniture, fixtures and glass objects. Her glass designs, which were awarded a prize at the Milan Triennial in 1936, are still being manufactured today. She was the principal in Artek, which manufactured furniture and artifacts, from its founding in 1936 until her death. Aino designed the majority of Artek's furniture, lamps, screens, household objects, mats and other textiles. Up until 1949, all of Alvar Aalto's exhibitions and works were signed 'Aino and Alvar Aalto.'

Suzana Antonakakis

Greek. Born Suzana-Maria Kolokytha in Athens, Greece on June 25, 1935. Suzana Antonakakis studied at the National Technical University, School of Architecture, in Athens, 1954-59, and established a partnership with her husband Dimitris in 1958. She has also worked as an architect/consultant for the Archaeological and Restoration Service of Athens and has lectured internationally. Her firm has been influenced by Modernism and the rich historical environ-

ment of Greece. Her architecture demonstrates a creative use of space. Geometry, materials, and socio-cultural values are combined in a rational yet complex structure.

Gae(tana) Aulenti

Italian. Born in Palazolo dello Stella (Udine), Italy on December 4, 1927. Gae Aulenti received her Dip. Arch. from the Milan Polytechnic's School of Architecture in 1954. She has been in private practice in Milan as an exhibition and industrial designer since 1954. She has also taught in Venice, Milan, Barcelona, and Stockholm. Her other professional involvements include serving as a member of the editorial staff of *Casabella-Continuità* from 1955-65 and on the Directional Board of *Lotus International* magazine since 1974. Aulenti's work, which includes exhibition design, interiors as well as architecture, evolved in the Milanese architecture scene of which she has become one of its major exponents. She has won many prestigious industrial design and architectural prizes. Her most famous work to date is her conversion of the Gare d'Orsay in Paris into the highly successful Museum d'Orsay.

Mary Jane Elizabeth Colter

American. Born in Pittsburgh, Pennsylvania (1869-1958). Mary Jane Colter attended the

Leading Women Architects and Designers of the 20th Century (Con't)

California School of Design in 1886 and then apprenticed at a local architect's office in 1887. In 1901 she began a forty-year career as a designer for the Fred Harvey Company, which operated hotels, restaurants, shops and dining cars for the Santa Fe Railway. She was one of the few female architects working in the United States at that time. Her buildings include Hopi House, Lookout Studio, Hermit's Rest, and the Watchtower (all at the Grand Canyon). Colter used local building traditions and materials to create buildings that appropriately fit into the spectacular natural wonder of the South Rim of the Grand Canyon.

Sylvia Crowe

British. Born in Barnbury, Oxfordshire, England (1901-97). Sylvia Crowe studied at Swanley Horticultural College in Kent, 1920-22, and worked in private practice as a landscape architect in London beginning in 1945. Crowe was President of the Institute of Landscape Architects in London from 1957-61. She also won the Woman of the Year Award from London's Architects' Journal in 1970. Sylvia Crowe held Honorary Doctorates from the University of Newcastle, Heriot–Watt University in Edinburgh, University of Sussex, and University of Brighton. She was also made an Honorary Fellow of the Royal Institute of British Architects in 1969. Although Crowe was first recognized for her domestic garden designs, her career was largely served with postwar architects and town planners. Through her professional work and books, Crowe dedicated her career to the interests of landscape as a whole.

Jane Beverly Drew

British. Born in Thornton Heath, Surrey, England (1911-96). Drew received her diploma from London's Architectural Association School of Architecture in 1934. She worked with her husband, E. Maxwell Fry, from 1945-77 in Fry Drew and Partners, London, and served as the joint editor of the *Architects Yearbook* from 1946-62. Drew also taught at the Massachusetts Institute of Technology and Harvard University. Among her awards are Honorary Doctorates from the University of Ibadan, Nigeria; Open University, Milton Keynes, Buckinghamshire; University of Newcastle; and Witwaterstrand University, Johannesburg. Much of Drew's work was in Africa and on the Indian continent. Her architecture is characterized by a functional adaptation of the modern idiom to tropical buildings. Some of her best earlier work was in conjunction with Le Corbusier, Pierre Jeanneret and Maxwell Fry in Chandigarh, India.

Joan Edelman Goody

American. Born Joan Edelman in New York City, December 1, 1935. Joan Goody studied at the University of Paris from 1954-55, received her B.A from Cornell University in 1956, and earned a M. Arch. degree from the Harvard Graduate School of Design in 1960. She has been a principal at Goody, Clancy and Associates in Boston since 1961. In 1983 she received *Progressive Architecture's* Urban Planing Award and has won numerous awards from The American Institute of Architects, the Boston Society of Architects, and the American Planning Association. Much of Good's work is contextual and demonstrates sensitivity to community, scale, and regional building traditions.

Leading Women Architects and Designers of the 20th Century (Con't)

Eileen Gray

Irish. Born in Brownswood, Enniscorthy, County Wexford, Ireland, (1879-1976). Eileen Gray studied at the Slate School of Art in London from 1898-1902 and worked as an architect in France from 1926 until her death in 1976. She was awarded the Honorary Royal Designer for Industry from the Royal Society of Arts, London, in 1972 and was made a Fellow of the Royal Institute of Irish Architects, Dublin, in 1973. Eileen Gray was a furniture designer who also designed a small number of buildings and interiors. Her architecture reflected the close affinity between furniture and building. She also brought humanity to modernism. Although small in number, her architectural work was quite original and skillful, such as her house, E. 1027, which was sometimes attributed to Le Corbusier or to the architect and critic Jean Badovici who assisted Gray on the house.

Zaha Hadid

Iraqi. Born in Baghdad in 1950. Zaha Hadid studied at the American University in Beirut and under Rem Koolhaas at London's Architectural Association, School of Architecture from which she graduated in 1977. She was a Unit Master at the Architectural Association from 1977-87 and a visiting professor at Harvard and Columbia University in 1986 and 1987. Hadid received the British Architectural Awards' Gold Medal in 1982. Although she won numerous first prizes in international building competitions during the 1980s, Hadid actually built little during that period. Generally known as a Deconstructivist, Hadid has been classified in this group since the 1988 MoMA exhibition entitled "Deconstructive Architecture." Her

recent work, such as the Vitra Fire Station and her garden pavilion, both in Weil am Rhein, Germany, displays a mastery of form and technology.

Itsuko Hasegawa

Japanese. Born in Yaizu City, Japan in 1941. Itsuko Hasegawa graduated from the College of Engineering, Kanto Gakuin University in 1964. In 1976 she established the Itsuko Hasegawa Atelier, which was renamed the Architectural Design Studio in 1979. Hasegawa has also served as lecturer at the Women's College of Art in Tokyo since 1972 and has lectured internationally. She won the Prize of Architectural Institute of Japan for Design in 1986 and the Grand Prize of Proposal Design Competition for the Niigata Municipal Cultural Hall in 1993. Hasegawa is one of the most famous female architects practicing in Japan today. Her architecture combines expressive forms inspired by nature with the innovative use of leading edge materials.

Florence Knoll

American. Born Florence Schust in Saginaw, Michigan in 1917. Florence Knoll graduated from the Cranbrook Academy of Art and studied under LeCorbusier at the Architectural Association in London. In 1942 she completed her architectural training under Ludwig Mies van der Rohe at the Armour Institute (now the Illinois Institute of Technology) in Chicago. In 1946 with her husband Hans Knoll, she formed Knoll Associates in which she organized and directed Knoll's Planning Unit to handle its interior-design operations. She was a pioneer for modern design and designed offices, furniture, and the Knoll show rooms which pro-

Leading Women Architects and Designers of the 20th Century (Con't)

jected the company's image. Hers was the mind, the controlling hand and the animating spirit behind Knoll's success.

Julia Morgan

American. Born in San Francisco (1872-1957). Julia Morgan studied at the University of California at Berkeley where she was one of the first women to graduate with a Degree in Civil Engineering in 1894. With the encouragement of Bernard Maybeck, she went to Paris to study architecture and became the first women architect granted a L'Ecole des Beaux Arts certificate in 1902. She established her own practice in San Francisco in 1904 and over her long career designed over 700 buildings – from the Hearst Castle at San Simeon, to private homes and pubic buildings. Morgan's approach to architecture reflected the classicism of her Beaux-Arts education and the influence of the California Arts and Crafts movement.

Käpy Paavilainen

Finish. Born in Vaasa, Finland in 1944. Käpy Paavilainen studied at the Helsinki University of Technology where she received a Dip. Arch. in 1975. In 1977 she established a partnership with her husband in Helsinki. She has been a visiting lecturer at the Helsinki University of Technology since 1982 and served as a visiting lecturer in Barcelona and Berlin. Paavilainen won the Architectural Prize, Tiili, in 1983 and the State Award for Architecture and Community Planning. Most of her work is in Finland. Her architecture is minimal yet has important classical influences and is characterized by close attention to place with materials that provide a contextual richness.

Patricia Patkau

Canadian. Born in Winnipeg, Manitoba in 1950. Patricia Patkau received a BA in 1973 from the University of Manitoba and a MA from Yale University in 1978. Since 1992 she has been an associate professor at the School of Architecture, University of British Columbia. In 1978 she established a partnership with her husband John in Edmonton, Alberta, which in 1984 moved to Vancouver, British Columbia. The firm has won numerous awards of excellence and many first prizes in competitions. Patricia Patkau describes her work as focusing on the particular in an effort to balance the tendency towards generalization which is increasingly dominant in Western culture.

Charlotte Perriand

French. Born in Paris, France (1903-99). Charlotte Perriand studied design at the Ecole de l'Union Centrale des Arts Décoratifs in Paris from 1920-25. She began working in private practice in Paris in 1927 when she established her own studio in the Place Saint Suplice, 1927-30, and in the Boulevard de Montparnasse, 1930-37. She also served as the associate in charge of furniture and fittings in the studio of Le Corbusier from 1927-37. From 1937-40 she worked with Jean Prouvé, Pierre Jeanneret, and Georges Blanchon in Paris. She also began an office for prefabricated building research in Paris in 1940. Throughout her career she worked frequently in Tokyo, Rio de Janeiro and other cities in Latin America. She served as a member of the editorial board for *Architecture d'aujourd'hui* in Paris, 1930-74. During her long and highly successful career, Perriand received international recognition for her interior designs as well as their furnishings.

Leading Women Architects and Designers of the 20th Century (Con't)

Elizabeth Plater-Zyberk

American. Born in Bryn Mawr, Pennsylvania in 1950. Elizabeth Plater-Zyberk received her B.A. in Architecture and Urban Planning from Princeton University in 1971 and a Master of Architecture from Yale in 1974. Plater-Zyberk is a co-founder and principal in Duany Plater-Zyberk & Company, which was begun in 1980, as well as an Associate Professor and Director of the Masters of Architecture program at the University of Miami. She and her partner, Andres Duany, have developed design principles of urban form based on traditional towns, which they implemented in the now famous town of Seaside, Florida. Since 1980 they have designed over eighty new towns and revitalization projects for existing communities and won many awards and much international recognition.

Madhu Sarin

Indian. Born in India in 1945. Madhu Sarin studied at the Punjab University, Chandigarh, India, where she received a Bachelor of Architecture in 1967. She also earned a post graduate diploma in Tropical Studies from the Architectural Association School of Architecture in London in 1980. She subsequently established her own practice and has worked as an advisor to the Indian Government and international organizations as well as directly with poor communities in the Punjab and Rajasthan. She has received several awards for professional excellence, including India's prestigious Vishwakarma Award in 1989. Madhu has always used her architectural training in creative ways to help those who most need her skills. In response to the fuel crisis in the Shiwalik foothills of the Himalayas, she designed a fuel efficient stove known as the Nadu Chula that has improved the lives of thousands of people living in many parts of the world where deforestation has occurred.

Denise Scott Brown

American. Born Denise Lakofskiin Nkana in Zambia, October 3, 1931. Denise Scott Brown emigrated to the United States in 1958 and was naturalized in 1967. Scott Brown studied at the University of the Witwaterstrand, Johannesburg, South Africa from 1948-51 and at the Architectural Association, School of Architecture in London, 1952-55, where she received an AA Diploma and Certificate in Tropical Architecture in 1956. She also studied at the University of Pennsylvania under Louis I. Kahn, 1958-60, and earned a Masters in City Planning in 1960. She has been the principal in charge of urban planning and design at Venturi, Scott Brown and Associates since 1989. Denise Scott Brown has taught at a number of Universities including Yale, University of Pennsylvania, Harvard, and MIT. Her work has received national and international recognition. Along with her husband, Robert Venturi, Scott Brown's built work and books such as *Learning from Las Vegas* ushered in Post-Modernism and influenced an entire generation of architects.

Alison Smithson

British. Born Alison Margaret Gill in Sheffield, England (1928-93). Alison Smithson studied architecture at the University of Durham, 1944-49. In 1950 she formed a partnership with her husband Peter. She was a founding member of Independent Group and was associated with Team 10 throughout her career. She also

Leading Women Architects and Designers of the 20th Century (Con't)

served as a lecturer at the Architectural Association, School of Architecture in London. Smithson practiced, taught, and also wrote a number of books. With her husband-partner, she formed a team whose architectural influence extended beyond England. Their work has been described as a "Gentle Cultural Accommodation." Through their teaching at the Architectural Association they influenced generations of students throughout the world, among these Denise Scott-Brown.

Laurinda Spear
American. Born 1951. Laurinda Spear studied Fine Arts at Brown University, receiving her BA in 1972. She also earned a MA from Columbia University in 1975. She won the Rome Prize in Architecture in 1978 and awards from *Progressive Architecture* in 1978 and 1980. Spear is the principal and co-founder of Arquitectonica, which she formed in 1977 with her husband Barnardo Fort-Brescia. Their work is characterized by sculpted intersecting geometric forms and bright colors and is recognized as being stylistically appropriate for Miami.

Helena Syrkus
Polish. Born Helena Niemirowska in Warsaw, Poland, (1900-82). Helena Syrkus studied architecture at Warsaw's Institute of Technology from 1918-23 and humanities and philosophy at the University of Warsaw from 1923-25. Syrkus combined practice with teaching for much of her career, lecturing at the Institute of Architecture and Town Planning in Warsaw. She established a partnership with her husband in 1962 until her death in 1982. She won many national awards for both her architectural work and her writings. The life and work of Helena and her husband Szymon Syrkus are linked to international avant-garde architectural thought. The fundamental principle of their long partnership is that social co-operation is more rewarding than competition and rivalry.

Susana Torre
American. Born in Puan, Buenos Aires, Argentina, November 2, 1944 and later emigrated to the United States. Torre studied at the Universidad de La Plata, 1961-63 and received her Dipl. Arch. from the Universidad de Buenos Aires in 1967. Susana Torre also did post-graduate studies at Columbia University. She has been a principal of Susana Torre and Associates in New York since 1988 and has lectured and been a visiting critic at Columbia University, Yale University, Cooper Union, Carnegie Mellon and Syracuse University. She also served as a member of the editorial board for the *Journal of Architectural Education* from 1983-85 and received awards from Architectural Record and the National Endowment for the Arts. Her work is interesting for its recognition of groups who have experienced displacement (i.e. new immigrants) and its critical feminist consciousness. Urban memory also plays an important role in her designs.

Eva Vecsei
Canadian. Born Eva Hollo in Vienna, Austria, August 21, 1930, and emigrated to Canada in 1957 where she was naturalized in 1962. Eva Vecsei studied at the University of Technical Sciences, School of Architecture in Budapest from 1948-52 where she earned a BA in 1952. She has been in partnership with Andrew Vescei at Vescei Architects since 1984. She has received 5 Massey Architecture

Leading Women Architects and Designers of the 20th Century (Con't)

Awards and an Award of Excellence from *Canadian Architect*. In her 30s, she became the head designer for one of the largest buildings in the world, the Place Bonaventure in Montreal. Her second mammoth project was La Cité, Montreal's first large-scale mixed-use downtown development. No woman architect has ever before had such broad responsibility for the design and construction of projects of this magnitude and excellence.

Source: Pauline Morin

Did you know...

A recent AIA Firm Survey found that only 10% of licensed architects in firms were women.

Presidents of The American Institute of Architects

1857-76	Richard Upjohn	1964	J. Roy Carroll Jr.
1877-87	Thomas U. Walter	1965	A. Gould Odell Jr.
1888-91	Richard M. Hunt	1966	Morris Ketchum Jr.
1892-93	Edward H. Kendall	1967	Charles M. Nes Jr.
1894-95	Daniel H. Burnham	1968	Robert L. Durham
1896-98	George B. Post	1969	George E. Kassabaum
1899	Henry Van Brunt	1970	Rex W. Allen
1900-1	Robert S. Peabody	1971	Robert F. Hastings
1902-3	Charles F. McKim	1972	Max O. Urbahn
1904-5	William S. Eames	1973	S. Scott Ferebee Jr.
1906-7	Frank M. Day	1974	Archibald C. Rogers
1908-9	Cass Gilbert	1975	William "Chick" Marshall Jr.
1910-11	Irving K. Pond	1976	Louis DeMoll
1912-3	Walter Cook	1977	John M. McGinty
1914-5	R. Clipston Sturgis	1978	Elmer E. Botsai
1916-8	John L. Mauran	1979	Ehrman B. Mitchell Jr.
1919-20	Thomas R. Kimball	1980	Charles E. Schwing
1921-2	Henry H. Kendall	1981	R. Randall Vosbeck
1923-4	William B. Faville	1982	Robert M. Lawrence
1925-6	Dan E. Waid	1983	Robert C. Broshar
1927-8	Milton B. Medary	1984	George M. Notter Jr.
1929-30	Charles H. Hammond	1985	R. Bruce Patty
1931-2	Robert D. Kohn	1986	John A Busby Jr.
1933-4	Earnest J. Russell	1987	Donald J. Hackl
1935-6	Stephen F. Voorhees	1988	Ted P. Pappas
1937-8	Charles D. Maginnis	1989	Benjamin E. Brewer Jr.
1939-40	Edwin Bergstrom	1990	Sylvester Damianos
1941-2	Richmond H. Shreve	1991	C. James Lawler
1943-4	Raymond J. Ashton	1992	W. Cecil Steward
1945-6	James R. Edmunds Jr.	1993	Susan A. Maxman
1947-8	Douglas W. Orr	1994	L. William Chapin Jr.
1949-50	Ralph T. Walker	1995	Chester A. Widom
1951-2	A. Glenn Stanton	1996	Raymond G. "Skipper" Post Jr.
1953-4	Clair W. Ditchy	1997	Raj Barr-Kumar
1955-6	George B. Cummings	1998	Ronald A. Altoon
1957-8	Leon Chatelain Jr.	1999	Michael J. Stanton
1959-60	John Noble Richards	2000	Ronald Skaggs
1961-2	Philip Will Jr.	2001	John D. Anderson
1963	Henry L. Wright		

Source: The American Institute of Architects

Presidents of the American Institute of Architecture Students

1956-57	James R. Barry, Rice Univ.	1977-78	Charles Guerin, Univ. of Houston
1957-58	Robert Harris, Princeton Univ.	1978-79	John Maudlin-Jeronimo, Univ. of Miami
1958-59	Paul Ricciutti, Case Western Reserve Univ.	1979-80	Richard Martini, Boston Architectural Center
1959-60	Charles Jones, Univ. of Arizona	1980-81	Alejandro Barbarena, Univ. of Houston
1960-61	Ray Gaio, Univ. of Notre Dame	1981-82	Bill Plimpton, Univ. of California at Berkeley
1961-62	Donald Williams, Univ. of Illinois at Urbana-Champaign	1982-83	Robert Klancher, Univ. of Cincinnati
1962-63	Carl Schubert, California State Polytechnic Univ.	1983-84	Robert Fox, Temple Univ.
1964-65	Joseph Morse, Howard Univ.	1984-85	Thomas Fowler IV, NYIT–Old Westbury
1965-66	Kenneth Alexander, Pratt Institute	1985-86	Scott Norberg, Univ. of Nebraska
1966-67	Jack Worth III, Georgia Institute of Technology	1986-87	Scott Norberg, Univ. of Nebraska
1967-68	Morten Awes, Univ. of Idaho	1987-88	Kent Davidson, Univ. of Nebraska
1968-69	Edward Mathes, Univ. of Southwestern Louisiana	1988-89	Matthew W. Gilbertson, Univ. of Minnesota
1969-70	Taylor Culver, Howard Univ.	1989-90	Douglas A. Bailey, Montana State Univ.
1970-71	Michael Interbartolo, Boston Architectural Center	1990-91	Alan D.S. Paradis, Roger Williams College
1971-72	Joseph Siff, Rice Univ.	1991-92	Lynn N. Simon, Univ. of Washington
1972-73	Fay D'Avignon, Boston Architectural Center	1992-93	Courtney E. Miller, Univ. of Maryland
1973-74	Fay D'Avignon, Boston Architectural Center	1993-94	Garen D. Miller, Drury College
1974-75	Patric Davis, Boston Architectural Center	1994-95	Dee Christy Briggs, City College of New York
1975-76	Ella Hall, North Carolina State Univ.	1995-96	Robert J. Rowan, Washington State Univ.
1976-77	Jerry Compton, Southern California Inst. of Arch.	1996-97	Raymond H. Dehn, Univ. of Minnesota

Presidents of the American Institute of Architecture Students (Con't)

1997-98   Robert L. Morgan,
           Clemson Univ.
1998-99   Jay M. Palu,
           Univ. of Nebraska
1999-00   Melissa Mileff,
           Univ. of Oklahoma
2000-01   Scott Baldermann,
           Univ. of Nebraska

Source: American Institute of Architects Students

Never look at an ugly thing twice. It is fatally easy to get accustomed to corrupting influences.

C.F.A. Voysey

Presidents of the American Society of Interior Designers

1974-75	Norman DeHann	1989-90	Elizabeth Howard
1974-76	Richard Jones	1990-91	Robert John Dean
1977-78	H. Albert Phibbs	1991-92	Raymond Kennedy
1978-79	Irving Schwartz	1992-93	Martha G. Rayle
1979-80	Rita St. Clair	1993-94	BJ Peterson
1980-81	Wallace Jonason	1994-95	Gary Wheeler
1981-82	Jack Lowery	1995-96	Penny Bonda
1982-83	Martin Ellinoff	1996-97	Kathy Ford Montgomery
1984-85	William Richard Waley	1997-98	Joyce Burke Jones
1985-86	Gail Adams	1998-99	Rosalyn Cama
1986-87	Janet Schirn	1999-2000	Juliana M. Catlin
1987-88	Joy Adcock	2000-01	Terri Maurer
1988-89	Charles Gandy		

Source: American Society of Interior Designers

Presidents of the American Society of Landscape Architects

1899-1901	John C. Olmsted*
1902	Samuel Parsons Jr.*
1903	Nathan F. Barrett*
1904-1905	John C. Olmsted*
1906-1907	Samuel Parsons Jr.*
1908-1909	Frederick Law Olmsted Jr.*
1910-1911	Charles N. Lowrie*
1912	Harold A. Caparn
1913	Ossian C. Simonds*
1914	Warren H. Manning*
1915-1918	James Sturgis Pray
1919-1922	Frederick Law Olmsted Jr.*
1923-1927	James L. Greenleaf
1927-1931	Arthur A. Shurcliff
1931-1935	Henry Vincent Hubbard
1935-1941	Albert D. Taylor
1941-1945	S. Herbert Hare
1945-1949	Markley Stevenson
1949-1951	Gilmore D. Clarke
1951-1953	Lawrence G. Linnard
1953-1957	Leon Zach
1957-1961	Norman T. Newton
1961-1963	John I. Rogers
1963-1965	John Ormsbee Simonds
1965-1967	Hubert B. Owens
1967-1969	Theodore Osmundson
1969-1971	Campbell E. Miller
1971-1973	Raymond L. Freeman
1973-1974	William G. Swain
1974-1975	Owen H. Peters
1975-1976	Edward H. Stone II
1976-1977	Benjamin W. Gary Jr.
1977-1978	Lane L. Marshall
1978-1979	Jot Carpenter
1979-1980	Robert L. Woerner
1980-1981	William A. Behnke
1981-1982	Calvin T. Bishop
1982-1983	Theodore J. Wirth
1983-1984	Darwina L. Neal
1984-1985	Robert H. Mortensen
1985-1986	John Wacker
1986-1987	Roger B. Martin
1987-1988	Cheryl L. Barton
1988-1989	Brain S. Kubota
1989-1990	Gerald D. Patten
1990-1991	Claire R. Bennett
1991-1992	Cameron R.J. Man
1992-1993	Debra L. Mitchell
1993-1994	Thomas Papandrew
1994-1995	Dennis Y. Otsuji
1995-1996	Vincent Bellafiore
1996-1997	Donald W. Leslie
1997-1998	Thomas R. Dunbar
1998-1999	Barry W. Starke
1999-2000	Janice Cervelli Schach
2000-2001	Leonard J. Hopper

*Charter Member

Source: American Society of Landscape Architects

What artist so noble as he who, with far reaching conception of beauty and designing power, sketches the outlines, arranges the colors, and directs the shadows of a picture upon which nature shall be employed for generations before the work he has prepared for her hand shall realize his intentions.

Frederick Law Olmsted

Presidents of the Association of Collegiate Schools of Architecture

1912-21	Warren Laird, Univ. of Pennsylvania
1921-23	Emil Lorch, Univ. of Michigan
1923-25	William Emerson, Massachusetts Institute of Technology
1925-27	Francke Bosworth, Jr., Cornell Univ.
1927-29	Goldwin Goldsmith, Univ. of Kansas
1929-31	Everett Meeks, Yale Univ.
1931-34	Ellis Lawrence, Univ. of Oregon
1934-36	Roy Childs Jones, Univ. of Minnesota
1936-38	Sherely Morgan, Princeton Univ.
1938-40	George Young, Jr., Cornell Univ.
1940-42	Leopold Arnaud, Columbia Univ.
1942-45	Wells Bennett, Univ. of Michigan
1945-47	Loring Provine, Univ. of Illinois
1947-49	Paul Weigel, Kansas State College
1949-51	B. Kenneth Johnstone, Carnegie Institute
1951-53	Thomas FitzPatrick, Iowa State College
1953-55	Lawrence Anderson, Massachusetts Institute of Technology
1955-57	Elliott Whitaker, Ohio State Univ.
1957-59	Buford Pickens, Washington Univ.
1959-61	Harlan McClure, Clemson College
1961-63	Olindo Grossi, Pratt Institute
1963-65	Henry Kamphoefner, North Carolina St. College
1965-67	Walter Sanders, Univ. of Michigan
1967-69	Robert Bliss, Univ. of Utah
1969-71	Charles Burchard, Virginia Polytechnic
1971-72	Alan Taniguchi, Rice Univ. & Univ. of Texas, Austin
1972-73	Robert Harris, Univ. of Oregon
1973-74	Sanford Greenfield, Boston Arch. Center
1974-75	Don Schlegal, Univ. of New Mexico
1975-76	Bertram Berenson, Univ. of Illinois at Chicago
1976-77	Donlyn Lyndon, Massachusetts Institute of Technology
1977-78	Dwayne Nuzum, Univ. of Colorado, Boulder
1978-79	William Turner, Tulane Univ.
1979-80	Robert Burns, North Carolina State Univ.
1980-81	Richard Peters, Univ. of California, Berkeley
1981-82	Eugene Kremer, Kansas State Univ.
1982-83	O. Jack Mitchell, Rice Univ.
1983-84	Charles Hight, Univ. of North Carolina, Charlotte
1984-85	Wilmot Gilland, Univ. of Oregon
1985-86	George Anselevicius, Univ. of New Mexico

Presidents of the Association of Collegiate Schools of Architecture (Con't)

1986-87   Blanche Lemco van Ginkel,
           Univ. of Toronto

1987-88   J. Thomas Regan,
           Univ. of Miami

1988-89   Robert Beckley,
           Univ. of Michigan

1989-90   Marvin Malecha,
           Cal. State Poly. Univ., Pomona

1990-91   John Meunier,
           Arizona State Univ.

1991-92   Patrick Quinn,
           Rensselaer Polytechnic Institute

1992-93   James Barker,
           Clemson Univ.

1993-94   Kent Hubbell,
           Cornell Univ.

1994-95   Diane Ghirardo,
           Univ. of Southern California

1995-96   Robert Greenstreet,
           Univ. of Wisconsin-Milwaukee

1996-97   Linda W. Sanders,
           Calif. State Polytechnic Univ.

1997-98   John M. McRae,
           Mississippi State Univ.

1998-99   R. Wayne Drummond,
           Univ. of Florida

1999-00   Jerry Finrow,
           Univ. of Washington

2000-01   Tony Schuman,
           New Jersey Institute of Technology

Source: Association of Collegiate Schools of Architecture

The stone and wood construction bears the same relation to architecture as the piano does to the music played upon it. Architecture and music are the conveyors of expression of human experience.

Bernard Maybeck

Presidents of the Construction Specifications Institute

1948-49	James B. Moore	1975-76	Larry C. Dean
1949-50	James B. Moore	1976-77	Philip J. Todisco
1950-51	Francis R. Wragg	1977-78	Louis H. Sams
1951-52	Carl J. Ebert	1978-79	R. Stanley Bair
1952-53	Carl J. Ebert	1979-80	Howard R. Steinmann
1953-54	Lester T. Burn	1980-81	George S. George
1954-55	Lester t. Burn	1981-82	Robert J. Schmidt
1955-56	Joseph A. McGinnis	1982-83	Terry J. Strong
1956-57	J. Norman Hunter	1983-84	Donald D. Meisel
1957-58	J. Norman Hunter	1984-85	Terry M. Wadsworth
1958-59	J. Stewart Stein	1985-86	Richard B. Solomon
1959-60	J. Stewart Stein	1986-87	Charles Chief Boyd
1960-61	Glen H. Abplanalp	1987-88	Robert L. McManus
1961-62	James C. Bort	1988-89	Weldon W. Nash, Jr.
1962-63	Edwin T. Pairo	1989-90	S. Steve Blumenthal
1963-64	Jack R. Lewis	1990-91	Robert W. Johnson
1964-65	Terrell R. Harper	1991-92	Sheldon B. Israel
1965-66	Henry B. Baume	1992-93	Thomas I. Young
1966-67	Henry B. Baume	1993-94	Jerome H. Alciatore
1967-68	John C. Anderson	1994-95	William F. Ricsberg
1968-69	Kelsey Y. Saint	1995-96	Jane D. Baker
1969-70	Arthur W. Brown	1996-97	Richard A. Eustis
1970-71	Ben F. Greenwood	1997-98	Robert R. Molseed
1971-72	Arthur J. Miller	1998-99	Kenneth E. Guthrie
1972-73	John C. Fleck	1999-00	Alana Griffith
1973-74	Robert E. Vansant	2000-01	James Chaney
1974-75	Larry C. Dean		

Source: Construction Specification Institute

Presidents of the Industrial Designers Society of America

1965	Henry Dreyfuss	1983-84	Katherine J. McCoy
1966	Joseph M. Parriott	1985-86	Cooper C. Woodring
1967-68	Robert Hose	1987-88	Peter H. Wooding
1969-70	Tucker Madawick	1989-90	Peter W. Bressler
1971-72	William Goldsmith	1991-92	Charles Pelly
1973-74	Arthur Pulos	1993-94	David Tompkins
1975-76	James Fulton	1995-96	James Ryan
1977-78	Richard Hollerith	1997-98	Craig Vogel
1979-80	Carroll M. Gantz	1999-00	Mark Dziersk
1981-82	Robert G. Smith	2000-01	Betty Baugh

Source: Industrial Designers Society of America

Did you know...

When Hans Knoll issued his first catalog in April 1942, fifteen of the twenty-five pieces offered were Jen Risom designs.

Presidents of the International Interior Design Association

1994-1995 Marilyn Farrow
1995-1996 Judith Hastings
1996-1997 Beth Harmon-Vaughan
1997-1998 Karen Guenther
1998-1999 Neil Frankel
1999-2000 Carol Jones
2000-2001 Richard Pollack

Source: International Interior Design Association

Presidents of the National Council for Architectural Registration Boards

1920-22	Emil Loch	1974	E.G. Hamilton
1923-24	Arthur Peabody	1975	John (Mel) O'Brien Jr.
1925	Miller I. Kast	1976	William C. Muchow
1926-27	W.H. Lord	1977	Charles A. Blondheim Jr.
1928	George D. Mason	1978	Paul H. Graven
1929-30	Clarence W. Brazer	1979	Lorenzo D. Williams
1931-32	James M. White	1980	John R. Ross
1933	A.L. Brockway	1981	Dwight M. Bonham
1933	A.M. Edelman	1982	Thomas H. Flesher Jr.
1934-35	Joseph W. Holman	1983	Sid Frier
1936	Charles Butler	1984	Ballard H.T. Kirk
1938-39	William Perkins	1985	Robert E. Oringdulph
1940-41	Mellen C. Greeley	1986	Theodore L. Mularz
1942-44	Louis J. Gill	1987	Robert L. Tessier
1945-46	Solis Seiferth	1988	Walter T. Carry
1947-49	Warren D. Miller	1989	George B. Terrien
1950	Clinton H. Cowgill	1990	Herbert P. McKim
1951	Roger C. Kirchoff	1991	Charles E. Garrison
1952-52	Charles E. Firestone	1992	Robert H. Burke Jr.
1954-55	Fred L. Markham	1993	Harry G. Robinson III
1956-58	Edgar H. Berners		William Wiese II (Honorary Past President)
1959-60	Walter F. Martens		
1961	A. Reinhold Melander	1994	Robert A. Fielden
1962	Chandler C. Cohagen	1995	Homer L. Williams
1963	Paul W. Drake	1996	Richard W. Quinn
1964	Ralph O. Mott	1997	Darrell L. Smith
1965	C.J. "Pat" Paderewski	1998	Ann R. Chaintreuil
1966	Earl L. Mathes	1999	Susan May Allen
1967	George F. Schatz	2000	Joseph P. Giattina Jr.
1968-69	Howard T. Blanchard	2001	Peter Steffian
1970	Dean L. Gustavson		
1971	William J. Geddis		
1972	Daniel Boone		
1973	Thomas J. Sedgewick		

Source: National Council for Architectural Registration Boards

---

Design should not be a fad but a philosophy.

Glen Walter

Presidents of the Royal Institute of British Architects

1835-59	Earl de Grey	1935-37	Sir Percy Thomas
1860	Charles Robert Cockerell	1937-39	H.S. Goodhart-Rendel
1861-63	Sir William Tite	1939-40	E. Stanley Hall
1863-65	Thomas L. Donaldson	1940-43	W.H. Ansell
1865-67	A.J.B. Beresford Hope	1943-46	Sir Percy Thomas
1867-70	Sir William Tite	1946-48	Sir Lancelot Keay
1870-73	Thomas Henry Wyatt	1948-50	Michael T. Waterhouse
1873-76	Sir Gilbert G. Scott	1950-52	A. Graham Henderson
1876-79	Charles Barry	1952-54	Sir Howard Robertson
1879 81	John Whichcord	1954-56	C.H. Aslin
1881	George Edmund Street	1956-58	Kenneth M.B. Cross
1882-84	Sir Horace Jones	1958-60	Sir Basil Spence
1884-86	Ewan Christian	1960-62	The Lord Holford
1886-87	Edward l'Anson	1962-64	Sir Robert Matthew
1888-91	Alfred Watershouse	1964-65	Sir Donald Gibson
1891-94	J. Macvicar Anderson	1965-67	The Viscount Esher
1884-96	Francis C. Penrose	1967-69	Sir Hugh Wilson
1896-99	George Aitchison	1969-71	Sir Peter Shepheard
1899-1902	Sir William Emerson	1971-73	Sir Alex Gordon
1902-04	Sir Aston Webb	1973-75	F.B. Pooley
1904-06	John Belcher	1975-77	Eric Lyons
1906-08	Thomas Edward Collcutt	1977-79	Gordon Graham
1908-10	Sir Ernest George	1979-81	Bryan Jefferson
1910-12	Leonard Stokes	1981-83	Owen Luder
1912-14	Sir Reginald Blomfield	1983-85	Michael Manser
1914-17	Ernest Newton	1985-87	Larry Rolland
1917-19	Henry Thomas Hare	1987-89	Rod Hackney
1919-21	Sir John William Simpson	1989-91	Max Hutchinson
1921-23	Paul Waterhouse	1991-93	Richard C. MacCormac
1923-25	J. Alfred Gotch	1993-95	Frank Duffy
1925-27	Sir Guy Dawber	1995-97	Owen Luder
1927-29	Sir Walter Tapper	1997-99	David Rock
1929-31	Sir Banister Fletcher	1999-	Marco Goldschmied
1931-33	Sir Raymond Unwin		
1933-35	Sir Giles Gilbert Scott		

Source: Royal Institute of British Architects

Presidents of the Society of Architectural Historians

1941-42	Turpin C. Bannister		1970-71	James F. O'Gorman
1943-44	Rexford Newcomb		1972-74	Alan W. Gowans
1945-47	Kenneth John Conant		1975-76	Spiro Kostof
1948-49	Carroll L.V. Meeks		1976-78	Marian C. Donnelly
1950	Buford L. Pickens		1978-80	Adolph K. Placzek
1951	Charles E. Peterson		1982-84	Damie Stillman
1952-53	Henry-Russell Hitchcock		1984-86	Carol Herselle Krinsky
1954	Agnes Addison Gilchrist		1986-88	Osmund Overby
1955-56	James G. Van Derpool		1988-90	Richard J. Betts
1957-58	Carroll L. V. Meeks		1990-93	Elisabeth Blair MacDougall
1959	Walter L. Creese		1993-94	Franklin Toker
1960-61	Barbara Wriston		1994-96	Keith N. Morgan
1962-63	John D. Forbes		1996-98	Patricia Waddy
1964-65	H. Allen Brooks		1998-00	Richard Longstreth
1966-67	George B. Tatum		2000-02	Christopher Mead
1968-69	Henry A. Millon			

Source: Society of Architectural Historians

Nothing is ever reborn, but it never completely disappears either, everything that has ever been emerges in a new form.

Alvar Aalto

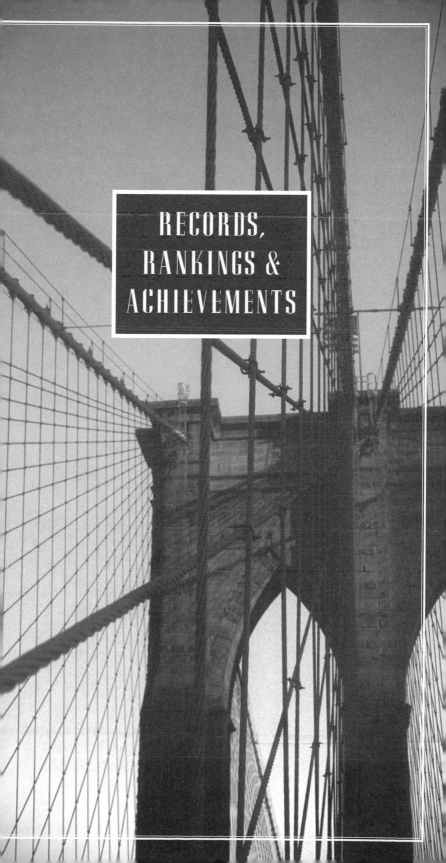

RECORDS,
RANKINGS &
ACHIEVEMENTS

Century's Top 10 Construction Achievements

The Top 10 Construction Achievements of the 20th Century were chosen from a list of over a 100 international nominations which included such diverse projects as bridges, dams, highways, roads, tunnels, buildings, stadiums, commercial centers, and transportation facilities. Besides requiring that the projects be entirely developed during the 20th century, the selection criteria also included integrity in construction and design, contribution to improving the quality of life, technological progressiveness, and positive economic impact. This program was established to promote the construction industry's increased contribution to the advancement of our society. The final judging occurred at the triennial CONEXPO-CON/AGG exposition in March 1999 in Las Vegas by a panel of editors and executives from the construction and construction materials industry

1. The Channel Tunnel between Dover, England and Calais, France
2. The Golden Gate Bridge, San Francisco
3. The U.S. Interstate Highway System
4. The Empire State Building, New York City
5. Hoover Dam, Nevada and Arizona
6. The Panama Canal
7. Sydney Opera House, Sydney, Australia
8. Aswan High Dam, Egypt
9. The World Trade Center, New York City
10. Chek Lap Kok Airport, Hong Kong

Source: Architecture *magazine and CONEXPO-CON/AGG*

Did you know...

The Øresund Fixed Link, the new ten-mile bridge connecting Denmark and Sweden, is composed of a two-and-half mile long artificial island, the longest immersed tube tunnel for both auto and rail traffic, and the longest cable-stayed main span in the world for both auto and rail traffic.

Construction Costs – 25 Least Expensive Cities

The following cities are currently the least expensive locales in the United States and Canada to construct a building according to R.S. Means, the country's leading construction costing company. This ranking is based on 2000 square foot costs for a 2-4 story office building of average construction type. Costs include labor, materials, and professional design fees.

1. Fayetteville, Arkansas
2. Alliance, Nebraska
3. Asheville, North Carolina
3. Charlotte, North Carolina
3. Columbia, South Carolina
6. Durham, North Carolina
6. Greensboro, North Carolina
6. Winston-Salem, North Carolina
6. Charleston, South Carolina
10. Raleigh, North Carolina
10. Abilene, Texas
10. McAllen, Texas
10. Martinsburg, West Virginia
14. Tallahassee, Florida

14. Jackson, Mississippi
14. Laredo, Texas
17. Columbus, Georgia
17. Aberdeen, South Dakota
17. Rapid City, South Dakota
17. El Paso, Texas
21. Knoxville, Tennessee
21. Corpus Christi, Texas
21. Lubbock, Texas
21. Waco, Texas
21. Wichita Falls, Texas

Source: R.S. Means

Construction Costs – 25 Most Expensive Cities

The following cities are currently the most expensive locales in the United States and Canada to construct a building according to R.S. Means, the country's leading construction costing company. This ranking is based on 2000 square foot costs for a 2-4 story office building of average construction type. Costs include labor, materials, and professional design fees.

1. New York, New York
2. Brooklyn, New York
3. Anchorage, Alaska
4. Fairbanks, Alaska
5. San Francisco, California
5. Honolulu, Hawaii
7. San Jose, California
7. Yonkers, New York
9. Berkeley, California
9. Oakland, California
11. Palo Alto, California
11. Santa Rosa, California
13. Boston, Massachusetts
13. Vallejo, California

15. Salinas, California
15. Minneapolis. Minnesota
15. Jersey City, New Jersey
15. Newark, New Jersey
15. Paterson, New Jersey
20. Chicago, Illinois
20. Trenton, New Jersey
20. Philadelphia, Pennsylvania
20. Toronto, Canada
24. Modesto, California
24. Sacramento, California
24 Saint Paul, Minnesota

Source: R.S. Means

Fastest Growing Firms

As part of *DesignIntelligence's* Leading Firms Survey, over 800 architecture firms were surveyed to determine which had experienced the greatest growth in the preceding year. In the case of firms with multiple offices, only information from their respective city offices was considered; no corporate-wide statistics were used. The following rankings are based on the percentage of growth experienced by the firms between 1999 and 2000 with the growth percentage indicated for each firm.

Atlanta
1. John Portman & Associates 33%
2. Godwin Associates 26%
3. Preston Phillips Partnership 21%
4. MSTSD, Inc. 19%
5. Warner Summers Ditzel Benefield Ward & Associates 13%
6. Cooper Carry, Inc. 13%

Boston
1. Einhorn Yaffee Prescott 98%
2. Cubellis Associates, Inc. 22%
3. Tsoi/Kobus & Associates 18%
4. Margulies & Associates 17%
5. Jung/Brannen Associates, Inc. 15%
6. Flansburgh Associates, Inc. 13%

Chicago
1. Holabird & Root 55%
2. Gensler 50%
3. RTKL Associates, Inc. 40%
4. Hellmuth, Obata + Kassabaum 21%
5. Ross Barney + Jankowski, Inc. 19%
6. HDR Architecture, Inc. 12%

Dallas
1. RTKL Associates, Inc. 68%
2. Beck Architecture 33%
3. SHW Group 24%
4. Harris Design Associates 17%
5. Wiginton Hooker Jeffry Architects 10%
6. Design International 10%

Detroit
1. Gunn Levine Associates 46%
2. Ghafari Associates, Inc. 22%
2. Harley Ellis 22%
4. FRENCH Associates Inc. 20%
4. Marco Design Group 20%
6. JGA, Inc. 10%

Florida
1. HNTB Corporation 90%
2. Euthenics 46%
3. Fugleberg Koch Architects & Interiors 28%
4. Yoshino Architects/Yoshino Design Group 25%
4. Charlan Brock & Associates, Inc. 25%
5. Dorsky Hodgson + Partners 23%

Houston
1. Wilson Architectural Group 33%
2. Kaufman Meeks & Partners 22%
3. EDI Architecture, Inc. 17%
4. FKP Architects, Inc. 12%
5. Barone Design Group 10%
6. Hermes Reed Architects 8%

Minneapolis
1. Walsh Bishop Associates, Inc. 60%
2. Meyer, Scherer & Rockcastle, Ltd. 32%
3. Tushie Montgomery Architects 25%
4. Hammel Green & Abrahamson, Inc. 18%
5. Leonard Parker Associates (Durrant) 17%
6. Cuningham Group 16%

Fastest Growing Firms (Con't)

New York

1. R.M. Kliment & Frances Halsband Architects 80%
2. Kapell and Kostow Architects, PC 43%
3. Larsen Shein Ginsberg + Magnusson, LLP 41%
4. MCG Architecture 38%
5. Fox & Fowle Architects 31%
6. Phillips Group 22%

San Francisco

1. Huntsman Architectural Group 73%
2. Studios Architecture 53%
3. Richard Pollack & Associates 26%
4. NBBJ 25%
5. SmithGroup 18%
6. Sandy & Babcock International 15%

Washington D.C.

1. Brennan Beer Gorman Monk 67%
2. Dorsky Hodgson + Partners 50%
3. OPX 40%
4. Studios Architecture 14%
5. Lehman - Smith + McLeish 12%
6. Spector, Knapp & Baughman 12%

Other Notable Increases:

Bower Lewis Thrower Architects, Philadelphia, Pennsylvania 33%

Flad Associates, Madison, Wisconsin 33%

The DeWolff Partnership, Rochester, New York 28%

Urban Design Group, Denver, Colorado 28%

Zimmer Gunsul Frasca Partnership, Portland, Oregon 28%

Dorsky Hodgson + Partners, Cleveland, Ohio 25%

RTKL, Baltimore, Maryland 22%

Kahler Slater Architects, Milwaukee, Wisconsin 20%

Space, Oakland, California 17%

Source: DesignIntelligence/*Counsel House Research*

Firm Anniversaries

The following currently practicing architecture firms were founded in 1901, 1926, 1951, and 1976 respectively.

Firms Celebrating their 100th Anniversary

Steed Hammond Paul Inc., Hamilton, OH
Wiley & Wilson, Lynchburg, VA

Firms Celebrating their 75th Anniversary

Arrasmith, Judd, Rapp, Inc., Louisville, KY
Robert Winston Carr Inc., Architects, Durham, NC
Kideney Architects/Laping Jaeger Associates, PC, Buffalo, NY
McCauley Associates, Inc., Birmingham, AL
Noyes-Vogt Architects, Guilford, CT
Spillis Candela & Partners, Inc., Coral Gables, FL
Spillman Farmer Shoemaker Pell Whildin, PC, Bethlehem, PA
The Spink Corporation, Sacramento, CA
Stuck Associates Architects, Little Rock, AR
Architects Wells Woodburn O'Neil, West Des Moines, IA

Firms Celebrating their 50th Anniversary

Barker, Cunningham, Barrington, PC, Buford, GA
Holland Brady, AIA, Architect, Tryon, NC
CH2M Hill, Corvallis, OR
Cone-Kalb-Wonderlick, Chicago, IL
Cordogan Clark & Associates, Chicago, IL
Crozier Gedney Architects, PC, Rye, NY
Duchscherer Oberst Design PC, Buffalo, NY
Farnsworth Group - Wischmeyer, Fayetteville, AR
GBKB Architects, Inc., Traverse City, MI
Gee & Jenson Engineers-Architects-Planners, Inc., West Palm Beach, FL
Arthur A. Gouvis, AIA, Chicago, IL
Kane and Johnson Architects, Inc., Rochester, MN
Kenyon and Associates, Architects, Peoria, IL
Klontz & Associates, Seattle, WA
Howard O. Krasnoff, AIA, Philadelphia, PA
Kring Architects, Johnstown, PA
Langdon Wilson Architecture Planning Interiors, Los Angeles, CA
Lanham Bros. General Contractors, Inc., Owensboro, KY
The Wendell Lovett Architects, Seattle, WA
MAI Architects Engineers Planners, Cleveland, OH
Eleanore Pettersen, FAIA, Saddle River, NJ
Sienna Architecture Company, Portland, OR
TC Architects Inc., Akron, OH
ThenDesign Architecture, Ltd., Willoughby, OH
Torno Nester Davison, Minot, ND
R. E. Warner Architects, Westlake, OH
The Wilson Design Group Inc., Fort Myers, FL

Firms Celebrating their 25th Anniversary

AAD, Scottsdale, AZ
Abo Copeland Architecture, Inc., Denver, CO
ACR Ltd., Englewood, CO
James E. Adkins Jr., AIA CSI, Specifications Consultant, Seattle, WA
AEPA Architects Engineers, Washington, DC
Akro Associates Architects, Hyannis, MA
James Alcorn AIA & Associates, La Jolla, CA
Cameron Alread Architects Inc., Fort Worth, TX
Ralph R. Alster Architect, Pittsburgh, PA
James R. Andersen Architect, St. Augustine, FL
John K. Anderson, AIA, Architect & Planner, High Point, NC
AR7 Hoover Desmond Architects, Denver, CO
ARC Architects, Seattle, WA
ARCHIspec, Carmel, NY

Firm Anniversaries (Con't)

Firms Celebrating their 25th Anniversary (Con't)

Architects BC, Inc., Lexington, SC

Architectural Horizons, Fort Collins, CO

Architectural Research Consultants, Inc., Albuquerque, NM

Architecture Incorporated, Sioux Falls, SD

Architecture/Design Alliance, Philadelphia, PA

Architecture Etc., Lake Jackson, TX

Architecture Solutions, Raleigh, NC

architrave PC Architects, Washington, DC

Chuck Bailey, AIA, Architect, Eugene, OR

Baker + Hogan + Houx Architecture & Planning PC, Breckenridge, CO

Barber Barrett Turner Architects Inc., Bend, OR

Barcelon & Jang, San Francisco, CA

Architects Barrentine.Bates.Lee, Lake Oswego, OR

James B. Bayley Consulting Architect, Wilmette, IL

Bearsch Compeau Knudson Architects & Engineers PC, Binghamton, NY

The Office of Rudolph Bedar, Westwood, MA

D. M. Bergerson Inc., Woodland Hills, CA

Charles Bettisworth & Company Inc., Fairbanks, AK

BG Consultants Inc., Manhattan, KS

Daniel Victor Bienko, AIA, Canfield, OH

Blumentals / Architecture, Inc., Brooklyn Center, MN

BMK, PC - Architects, Alexandria, VA

The Boudreaux Group (Boudreaux Hultstrand Quackenbush & Garvin), Columbia, SC

Broad Ripple Design Associates, Architects, Indianapolis, IN

The Brown Group, Tulsa, OK

Burns & Burns, Architects, Iowa City, IA

Campbell Thomas & Company Architects, Philadelphia, PA

Ronald G. Cannon, AIA, Gadsden, AL

Cathers & Associates Inc., Malvern, PA

Gordon H. Chong & Partners, San Francisco, CA

Lee N. Christensen & Associates Architecture & Planning, Sedona, AZ

CJS Group Architects Ltd., Honolulu, HI

Claflen Associates Architects & Planners, Philadelphia, PA

Clark & Associates Architects Inc., Clarksville, TN

Marshall Clarke Architects, Inc., Greenville, SC

Wesley M. Coble, Architect & Planner, Raleigh, NC

William Arthur Collier, Registered Architect, Cleveland, OH

Collignon & Nunley PSC, Owensboro, KY

Cooper/Roberts Architects, Salt Lake City, UT

CP&Associates/Architects & Planners, Kansas City, MO

Creative Designs Braxton Dennis / Architect, Carson, CA

Frank Dachille Architects, Johnstown, PA

Daniel Group Inc. Architects, Planners, Projects Managers, Philadelphia, PA

Dennis Davey Inc., Tolland, CT

Stanley W. Dawson Jr., AIA, Architect, Kilmarnock, VA

Design Associates of Lincoln, Inc., Lincoln, NE

DeWolf Architecture, PLLC, Highlands, NC

DiFazio Architects, Haddonfield, NJ

Anthony S. DiProperzio, AIA, Fresh Meadows, NY

Dorman & Breen Architects, Santa Fe, NM

EDI Architecture, Inc., Houston, TX

Elliott + Associates Architects, Oklahoma City, OK

Energy Management Consultants, Torrance, CA

EnvironMental Design, Breaux Bridge, LA

Eduardo Faxas/Architects & Planners, Holmes, NY

FFKR Architecture/Planning/Interior Design, Salt Lake City, UT

Filarski Architecture Planning Research, Providence, RI

Firm Anniversaries (Con't)

Firms Celebrating their 25th Anniversary (Con't)

Louis J. Fisher, AIA NOMA, Detroit, MI

Al Fitterer Architect PC, Mandan, ND

Frazier Group, Anaheim, CA

FWAI Architects Inc., Springfield, IL

John Garfield & Associates, St. Thomas,

Garfield Kindred Associates PC, Hancock, MI

Graham A. Geralds, Architect, Fort Lauderdale, FL

Glenn German, AIA, Midlothian, VA

Van H. Gilbert Architect, PC, Albuquerque, NM

Gary Glenn Architect, St. Louis, MO

GMR, Ltd., Cabin John, MD

Terence A. Golda, AIA, Ringoes, NJ

Goldman Firth Architects, Malibu, CA

Gorman Richardson Architects Inc., Hopkinton, MA

Grazado Velleco Architects, Marblehead, MA

Grooters Leapaldt Tideman Architects, St. Cloud, MN

Hammond Wilson Architects, PC, Annapolis, MD

Hance, Utz & Associates, LLC, Mattoon, IL

Thomas Harle / Architects, PS, Redmond, WA

Hasbrouck Peterson Zimoch Sirirattumrong, Chicago, IL

HDR Architecture, Inc., Chicago, IL

Richard Henry - Architect, Denver, CO

Herrman & Gordon Architects, PA, Hilton Head Island, SC

The Office of Allen Charles Hill, AIA, Woburn, MA

Hohenschau Associates Architects, Sherborn, MA

Holden & Johnson Architects, Palm Desert, CA

Holleyman Associates, Oklahoma City, OK

Alvin Holm, AIA, Architects, Philadelphia, PA

Houseal Architects, Brielle, NJ

Howell Associates Architects, Boone, NC

Hunter Grobe Architects/Planners, Fargo, ND

Inter Plan, Inc., Tequesta, FL

JCM Architectural Associates, Syracuse, NY

JDS Design Associates, Ardmore, PA

JMS Architect & Planner PC, Glen Cove, NY

Henry W. Johnston, AIA, Architects, Wilmington, NC

JPRA Architects, Farmington Hills, MI

JRA Architecture LLC, Indianapolis, IN

Glenn A. Kahley, AIA, Millville, NJ

John M. Kaiser, AIA, Architect Planner, Somerdale, NJ

Kanakanui Associates, Beckley, WV

Karlsberger Architecture PC, New York, NY

David Kehle, Architect, Seattle, WA

Reiner Keller, AIA, Architect, Sonoma, CA

Kelly/Maiello Inc. Architects & Planners, Philadelphia, PA

David L. Kinderfather, AIA, Friday Harbor, WA

Kirkegaard & Associates, Chicago, IL

Mark C. Klingerman Architect, Chartered, Sun Valley, ID

Christopher Knoop Architect, Cincinnati, OH

Kohn Pedersen Fox Associates, PC, New York, NY

Korte Design, St. Louis, MO

Kraly Consulting, Shaker Heights, OH

Kenneth R. Krause Architects, Sugar Land, TX

Robert Kubicek Architects, Phoenix, AZ

John R. Kulseth Associates Ltd., Tucson, AZ

Lagerquist & Morris, PS, Seattle, WA

Lark & Associates Architects & Planners, St. Louis, MO

LaRock Associates, PC, Denver, CO

Jeff Laur & Associates, Harrison, AR

Lavallee/Brensinger PA, Manchester, NH

Lerner | Ladds + Bartels, Inc., Providence, RI

Ray L. Logan, AIA, & Company, Gonzales, TX

LRS Architects, Portland, OR

Lucas Associates, Architects, Boalsburg, PA

Lundahl & Associates, Architects, Reno, NV

MacDonald Architecture & Technology, Fredericksburg, VA

T. Scott MacGillivray, AIA, Architect, Los Angeles, CA

Firm Anniversaries (Con't)

Firms Celebrating their 25th Anniversary (Con't)

Marshburn/Bunkley Associates, Portage, MI
McGraw/Baldwin Architects, San Diego, CA
Thomas McKenzie Architect, Denver, CO
MCM Architects PC, Portland, OR
George Merges Jr./Architect, Aliquippa, PA
H. L. Mohler & Associates PC, Lafayette, IN
Clifford Moles Associates, Redwood City, CA
Morley & Associates Inc., Evansville, IN
Prescott Muir Architects, Salt Lake City, UT
Muller & Caulfield Architects, Oakland, CA
John V. Mutlow Architects, Los Angeles, CA
Carl Myatt, Architect, Greensboro, NC
The Nelson Architectural Group, Inc., Pine Bluff, AR
Nudell Architects, Inc., Farmington Hills, MI
Odell Associates Inc., Greenville, SC
Omega Design Services Inc., Grandville, MI
Omni Architecture, Charlotte, NC
Orr/Houk & Associates Architects, Inc., Nashville, TN
Paoletti Associates Inc., San Francisco, CA
Pasanella + Klein Stolzman + Berg Architects, PC, New York, NY
L. A. Paul & Associates, Architecture/Planning, San Francisco, CA
PEG/Park LLC, White Plains, NY
John M. Pflueger Architect, Glen Ellen, CA
Frederick F. Phillips & Associates, Inc., Chicago, IL
O. Douglas Phillips, AIA, Architect, Los Angeles, CA
Mark L. Pierce, AIA, San Francisco, CA
Milton Powell & Partners, Dallas, TX
Power Engineers, Inc., Hailey, ID
Quincy Johnson Barretta, Boca Raton, FL
The Resort Design Collaborative International, San Francisco, CA
Reynolds Architects, PC, Gainesville, GA
RFL Architects, PC, Rochester, NY
Rierson/Duff & Associates, Tustin, CA
Walter B. Rise Jr., Architect, Bradenton, FL

Roark Kramer Kosowski Design, Minneapolis, MN
Thomas Rochon Associates, New York, NY
Rundquist Partnership, Inc., Spokane, WA
Robert B. Salsbury Associates, PA, Morganton, NC
Saltz Michelson Architects, Fort Lauderdale, FL
L. Lane Sarver Inc., Chapel Hill, NC
Saxon/Capers Architects, Philadelphia, PA
Philip V. Scalera, AIA Architect, Tampa, FL
Schmidt Associates, Inc., Indianapolis, IN
Andrew J. Schmitz & Associates, Huntington, NY
Ronald A. Sebring Associates, Manasquan, NJ
Shapiro Petrauskas Gelber, Philadelphia, PA
Sillman/Wyman, Inc., San Diego, CA
The Singleton Associates Architecture, Seattle, WA
R. Kenneth Skay, Architect, Traverse City, MI
The S/L/A/M Collaborative, Glastonbury, CT
S.L.I. Group, Inc., Houston, TX
SLR Architects, Palo Alto, CA
Smith & Thompson Architects, New York, NY
Marvin J. Sparn Architect, Boulder, CO
Stanius Johnson Architects, Duluth, MN
Stec & Company, PA, Greensboro, NC
Arthur Craig Steinman & Associates, Architects, Palo Alto, CA
Stephens Aylward & Associates/Clas Riggs Owens & Ramos, Beltsville, MD
William H. Stevens, AIA, Architect, Clifton Park, NY
Thomas P. Strahan Associates, Kansas City, MO
A. K. Strotz & Associates, Tiburon, CA
Susman Tisdale Gayle, Austin, TX
A. Y. Taniguchi Architects & Associates, Austin, TX
J. Knox Tate IV, Architect, Chapel Hill, NC
Taylor Associates Architects, PC, Atlanta, GA
Bruce S. Taylor, AIA, West Newbury, MA
Teitsch-Kent-Fay Architects, Cazenovia, NY
Thorp Associates PC Architects & Planners, Estes Park, CO

Firm Anniversaries (Con't)

Firms Celebrating their 25th Anniversary (Con't)

Danny J. Tosh, AIA, Architect & Planner, Dallas, TX

Triarch, New York, NY

Triebwasser Helenske & Associates, Fargo, ND

TSP Two, Inc., Sheridan, WY

James F. Tucker, AIA, Warrenton, VA

Underwood Associates Architects, Decatur, AL

Vaughn Architects Plus, Fort Worth, TX

VMDO Architects, PC, Charlottesville, VA

The Wallace Group, Inc., Waco, TX

David L. Warren, AIA, Architect, Rochester, MI

Architect Charles Weiler, Haddonfield, NJ

Don West AIA, Morro Bay, CA

James D. Wheat, Architect, Fenton, MI

Charles A. Wiechers Jr., AIA, Architect, Lexington, KY

Williams & Dean Associated Architects, Inc., Little Rock, AR

William Wilson Architects, PC, Portland, OR

Laurence Winters & Associates, Grants Pass, OR

Wisnewski Blair and Associates, Ltd., Alexandria, VA

WKA Architects, Inc, Dallas, TX

WLW & Associates, San Antonio, TX

Wolfberg Alvarez and Partners, Miami, FL

Warren C. Wuertz, AIA Emeritus, Consulting Architect, Bradenton, FL

WYK Associates, Inc., Clarksburg, WV

Paul Frederick Wynn, Dallas, TX

Yarger Associates Inc., St. Louis, MO

Yoder Architectural Exclusives, Virginia Beach, VA

Yoshino Shaw & Associates, Turlock, CA

George E. Yundt IV, Architect & Consultant, Macungie, PA

Zenon Beringer Mabrey/Partners, Inc., Architects, Omaha, NE

D. F. Zimmer, AIA, Fort Lauderdale, FL

Source: Counsel House Research

Largest Architecture Firms

As part of *DesignIntelligence's* annual Leading Firms study, data is collected from over 800 architecture firms to determine the largest firms in the United States. The following Top 25 ranking is derived from the total staff size for each firms' U.S. operations.

1. HDR Architecture, Inc., Omaha, Nebraska
2. HNTB, Kansas City, Missouri
3. Gensler, San Francisco, California
4. Hellmuth, Obata + Kassabaum, St. Louis, Missouri
5. SmithGroup, Detriot, Michigan
6. NBBJ, Seattle, Washington
7. Skidmore, Owings & Merrill, Chicago, Illinois
8. Heery International, Atlanta, Georgia
9. HKS, Dallas, Texas
10. RTKL Associates, Inc., Baltimore, Maryland
11. A. Epstein and Sons International, Chicago, Illinois
12. Ellerbe Becket, Minneapolis, Minnesota
13. Leo A. Daly, Omaha, Nebraska
14. DLR Group, Omaha, Nebraska
15. The Hillier Group, Princeton, New Jersey
16. SSOE, Inc., Toledo, Ohio
17. Callison, Seattle, Washington
18. Kohn Pedersen Fox Associates, New York, New York
19. Zimmer Gunsel Fraska, Portland, Oregon
20. Hammel, Green and Abrahamson, Minneapolis, Minnesota
21. Thompson, Ventulett and Stainbeck, Atlanta, Georgia
22. Einhorn Yaffee Prescott, Boston, Massachusetts
23. Kling-Lindquist Partnership, Philadelphia, Pennsylvania
24. HLM Design, Charlotte, North Carolina
25. Fanning/Howey Associates, Inc., Celina, Ohio

Source: DesignIntelligence/Counsel House Research

Longest Covered Bridges in the World

Covered bridges still survive throughout the world from many periods of history. Bridges are also being resorted and rebuilt by covered bridge enthusiasts. The following list contains the 30 longest covered bridges in the world.

For additional information about covered bridges, contact the National Society for the Preservation of Covered Bridges at *dickroych1 @juno.com*, or visit *www.atawalk.com* on the Web for covered bridge items of interest from around the world.

Rank	Bridge	Feet	Location	Truss Type	# spans	Year built
1	Hartland Bridge	1282	Carleton County, New Brunswick, Canada	Howe	7	1921
2	Reinbrücke	673	Between Stein, Switzerland and Sackingen, Germany	Multiple Queen (overlapping)	7	1803
3	Kapellbrücke	656	Luzern, Switzerland	1 multiple King span, 25 stringers	26	1333
4	St. Nicholas River Bridge	504	Kent County, New Brunswick, Canada	Howe	3+	1919
5	Marchand Bridge	499	Pontiac County, Quebec, Canada	Town lattice & Queen	6	1898
6	Perrault Bridge	495	Beauce County, Quebec, Canada	Town lattice variation	4	1928
7	Sevelen/Vaduz Bridge	480	Liechtenstein-Canton of St. Gallen, Switzerland	Howe (double X)	6	1901
8	Cornish-Windsor Bridge	460	Sullivan County, New Hampshire & Windsor County, Vermont	Timber Notch Lattice	2	1866
9	Rosenstein Park Footbridge	449	Baden-Wurrtemberg State, Germany	Ext. Queen & Ext. Steel Queen	2	1977
10	Medora Bridge	434	Jackson County, Indiana	Burr Arch	3	1875
11	unknown	410	Heilbronn-Kochendorf, Germany	Stringer	6	1976
12	Ashnola River Road Bridge	400	Similkameen Division, British-Columbia, Canada	Howe	3	1923

Longest Covered Bridges in the World (Con't)

Rank	Bridge	Feet	Location	Truss Type	# spans	Year built
13	Williams Bridge	376	Lawrence County, Indiana	Howe	2	1884
13	Bath Bridge	376	Grafton County, New Hampshire	Multiple King Post	4	1832
15	Degussa Footbridge	369	Baden-Wurtemberg State, Germany	Stringer	7	1979
16	Schwäbisch-Hall's Stadtwerke footbridge	362	Schwabisch-Hall, Germany	Inverted Multiple King	6	1981
17	Cesky-Krumov Footbridge	361	Southern Bohemia, Czech Republic	unknown		
17	Betlemska-Kaple Bridge	361	Central Bohemia, Czech Republic	unknown		
19	Medno Footbridge	348	Mendo, Slovenia	Suspension	1	1934
20	Moscow Bridge	334	Rush County, Indiana	Burr Arch	2	1886
21	Shieldstown Bridge	331	Jackson County, Indiana	Burr Arch	2	1876
22	Bell's Ford Bridge	330	Jackson County, Indiana	Post	2	1869
22	Kasernenbrücke	330	Bern Canton, Switzerland	Ext. King	5	1549
22	Knights Ferry Bridge	330	Stanislaus County, California	Pratt	4	1864
25	Swann or Joy Bridge	320	Blount County, Alabama	Town lattice	3	1933
26	West Union Bridge	315	Parke County, Indiana	Burr Arch	2	1876
27	Academia/ Pomeroy	305	Juniata County, Pennsylvania	Burr Arch	2	1901
27	Eschikofen-Bonau Bridge	305	Thurgau Canton, Switzerland	Multiple Queen	5	1837
29	Philippi Bridge	304	Barbour County, West Virginia	Burr Arch variation	2	1852
30	St-Edgar Bridge	293	Bonaventure County, Quebec, Canada	Town lattice variation	2	1938

Source: National Society for the Preservation of Covered Bridges, Inc.

Oldest Practicing Architecture Firms in the United States

The following firms were all founded prior to 1900 (their specific founding dates indicated below) and are still operational today.

1827	The Mason & Hanger Group, Inc., Lexington, KY
1832	Lockwood Greene, Spartanburg, SC
1853	Luckett & Farley Architects, Engineers and Construction Managers, Inc., Louisville, KY
1853	SmithGroup, Detroit, MI
1862	Freeman White, Inc., Raleigh, NC
1868	Jensen and Halstead Ltd., Chicago, IL
1868	King & King Architects, Manlius, NY
1870	Harriman Associates, Auburn, ME
1871	Scholtz-Gowey-Gere-Marolf Architects & Interior Designers, PC, Davenport, IA
1872	Brunner & Brunner Architects & Engineers, St. Joseph, MO
1873	Graham Anderson Probst & White, Chicago, IL
1874	Chandler, Palmer & King, Norwich, CT
1874	Shepley Bulfinch Richardson and Abbott Inc., Boston, MA
1878	The Austin Company, Kansas City, MO
1878	Ballinger, Philadelphia, PA
1880	Beatty Harvey & Associates, Architects, New York, NY
1880	Green Nelson Weaver, Inc., Minneapolis, MN
1880	Holabird & Root LLP, Chicago, IL
1880	Zeidler Roberts Partnership, Inc., Toronto, Canada
1881	Keffer/Overton Architects, Des Moines, IA
1883	Ritterbush-Ellig-Hulsing PC, Bismarck, ND
1883	SMRT Architecture Engineering Planning, Portland, ME
1885	Cromwell Architects Engineers, Little Rock, AR
1885	HLW International LLP, New York, NY
1887	Bradley & Bradley, Rockford, IL
1888	Reid & Stuhldreher, Inc., Pittsburgh, PA
1889	Architectural Design West Inc., Salt Lake City, UT
1889	CSHQA Architects/Engineers/Planners, Boise, ID
1889	MacLachlan, Cornelius & Filoni, Inc., Pittsburgh, PA
1889	Wank Adams Slavin Associates, New York, New York
1890	Kendall, Taylor & Company, Inc., Billerica, MA
1890	The Mathes Group PC, New Orleans, LA
1890	Plunkett Raysich Architects, Milwaukee, WI
1891	Shive/Spinelli/Perantoni & Associates, Somerville, NJ
1891	Wilkins Wood Goforth Mace Associates Ltd., Florence, SC
1892	Bauer Stark + Lashbrook, Inc., Toledo, OH
1893	Foor & Associates, Elmira, NY
1893	Wright, Porteous & Lowe/Bonar, Indianapolis, IN
1894	Colgan Perry Lawler Architects, Nyack, NY
1894	Freese and Nichols, Inc., Fort Worth, TX
1894	Parkinson Field Associates, Austin, TX
1895	Brooks Borg Skiles Architecture Engineering LLP, Des Moines, IA
1895	Albert Kahn Associates, Inc., Detroit, MI
1896	Hummel Architects, PA, Boise, ID
1896	Kessels DiBoll Kessels & Associates, New Orleans, LA

Oldest Practicing Architecture Firms in the United States (Con't)

1896 Lehman Architectural Partnership, Roseland, NJ

1897 Baskervill & Son, Richmond, VA

1897 L_H_R_S Architects, Inc., Huntington, IN

1898 Beardsley Design Associates, Auburn, NY

1898 Berners/Schober Associates, Inc., Green Bay, WI

1898 Bottelli Associates, Summit, NJ

1898 Burns & McDonnell, Kansas City, MO

1898 Eckles Architecture, New Castle, PA

1898 Emery Roth Associates, New York, NY

1898 Foss Associates, Fargo, ND & Moorhead, MN

1898 PageSoutherlandPage, Austin, TX

1899 William B. Ittner, Inc., St. Louis, MO

Source: Counsel House Research

Opposite: Bronson Medical Center, Kalamazoo, MI, Shepley Bullfinch Richardson and Abbott
Photographer: Peter Moss

State Capitols and their Architects

The architect(s) of each U.S. state capitol and the national Capitol is listed below. When available, the contractor(s) is also listed immediately below the architect in italics.

Alabama
Montgomery, 1851
George Nichols

Alaska
Juneau, 1931
Treasury Department architects with James
  A. Wetmore, supervising architect
N.P. Severin Company

Arizona
Phoenix, 1900
James Riley Gordon
Tom Lovell

Arkansas
Little Rock. 1911-1915
George R. Mann; Cass Gilbert
Caldwell and Drake; William Miller & Sons

California
Sacramento, 1874
Miner F. Butler; Ruben Clark and G. Parker
  Cummings

Colorado
Denver, 1894-1908
Elijah E. Myers, Frank E. Edbrooke

Connecticut
Hartford, 1779
Richard M. Upjohn
James G. Batterson

Delaware
Dover, 1933
William Martin

Florida
Tallahassee, 1977
Edward Durell Stone with Reynolds, Smith
  and Hills

Georgia
Atlanta, 1889
Edbrooke & Burnham
Miles and Horne

Hawaii
Honolulu, 1969
John Carl Warnecke with Belt, Lemman and
  Lo
Reed and Martin

Idaho
Boise, 1912-1920
John E. Tourtellotte
*Stewart and Company with Herbert Quigley,
  construction supervisor*

Illinois
Springfield, 1877-87
J. C. Cochrane with Alfred H. Piquenard; W.
  W. Boyington

Indiana
Indianapolis, 1888
Edwin May; Adolf Scherrer
*Kanmacher and Dengi; Elias F. Gobel and
  Columbus Cummings*

Iowa
Des Moines, 1884-86
J. C. Cochrane and Alfred H. Piquenard;
  M.E. Bell and W. F. Hackney

State Capitols and their Architects (Con't)

Kansas
Topeka, 1873-1906
John G. Haskell; E.T. Carr and George Ropes
D. J. Silver & Son; Bogart and Babcock;
William Tweeddale and Company

Kentucky
Frankfort, 1910
Frank Mills Andrews

Louisiana
Baton Rouge, 1931
Weiss, Dryfous and Seiferth
Kenneth McDonald

Maine
Augusta, 1832
Charles Bulfinch; John C. Spofford, 1891 rear
    wing addition; G. Henri Desmond, 1911
    expansion

Maryland
Annapolis, 1779
Joseph Horatio Anderson and Joseph Clark,
    interior architect; Baldwin and
    Pennington, 1905 rear annex
Charles Wallace; Thomas Wallace

Massachusetts
Boston, 1798
Charles Bulfinch; Charles Brigham, 1895 rear
    addition; R. Clipson, William Chapman,
    and Robert Agnew, 1917 side wing addi-
    tions

Michigan
Lansing, 1878-79
Elijah E. Myers
N. Osborne & Co.

Minnesota
St. Paul, 1905
Cass Gilbert

Mississippi
Jackson, 1903
Theodore C. Link; George R. Mann, dome
Wells Brothers Company

Missouri
Jefferson City, 1917
Tracy and Swartwout
T.H. Johnson; A. Anderson & Company; John
*   Gill & Sons*

Montana
Helena, 1902
Bell and Kent; Frank Mills Andrews and Link
    & Hare, 1912 east and west wing addition

Nebraska
Lincoln, 1932
Bertram Grosvenor Goodhue
W.J. Assenmacher Company; J.H. Wiese
*   Company; Peter Kewittand Sons; Metz*
*   Construction Company*

Nevada
Carson City, 1871
Joseph Gosling; Frederic J. Delongchamps
    and C.G. Sellman, 1913 addition
Peter Cavanough and Son

New Hampshire
Concord, 1819
Stuart James Park; Gridley J. F. Bryant and
    David Bryce, 1866 addition; Peabody and
    Stearns, 1909 addition

New Jersey
Trenton, 1792
Jonathan Doane; John Notman, 1845 expan-
    sion and renovation; Samuel Sloan, 1872
    expansion; Lewis Broome and James
    Moylan, c.1885 renovations; Karr Poole
    and Lum, 1900 expansion; Arnold Moses,
    1903 Senate wing renovations

State Capitols and their Architects (Con't)

New Mexico
Santa Fe, 1966
W. C. Kruger & Associates with John Gaw
    Meem, design consultant
Robert E. McKee General Contractor, Inc.

New York
Albany, 1879-99
Thomas Fuller; Leopold Eidlitz, Frederick
    Law Olmsted, Henry Hobson Richardson;
    Isaac G. Perry

North Carolina
Raleigh, 1840
Town and Davis, David Paton

North Dakota
Bismarck, 1934
Holabird & Root with Joseph B. DeRemer
    and William F. Kirke
Lundoff and Bicknell

Ohio
Columbus, 1857-1861
Henry Walter; William R. West; Nathan B.
    Kelly

Oklahoma
Oklahoma City, 1917
Layton and Smith

Oregon
Salem, 1938
Francis Keally of Trowbridge and Livingston

Pennsylvania
Harrisburg, 1906
Joseph M. Huston
George F. Payne Company

Rhode Island
Providence, 1904
McKim, Mead and White
Norcross Brothers Construction

South Carolina
Columbia, 1854-1907
John Rudolph Niernsee, 1854-85; J. Crawford
    Neilson, 1885-88; Frank Niernsee, 1888-
    91; Frank P. Milburn, 1900-04; Charles
    Coker Wilson, 1904-07

South Dakota
Pierre, 1911
C.E. Bell and M.S. Detwiler
*O.H. Olsen with Samuel H. Lea, state engineer
    and construction supervisor*

Tennessee
Nashville, 1859
William Strickland
A.G. Payne

Texas
Austin, 1888
Elijah E. Myers
*Mattheas Schnell; Taylor, Babcock & Co. with
    Abner Taylore*

Utah
Salt Lake City, 1915-16
Richard K. A. Kletting
James Stewart & Company

Vermont
Montpelier, 1859
Thomas W. Silloway; Joseph R. Richards

Virginia
Richmond, 1789
Thomas Jefferson with Charles-Louis
    Clérisseau; J. Kevin Peebles, Frye &
    Chesterman,1906 wings

State Capitols and their Architects (Con't)

Washington
Olympia, 1928
Walter R. Wilder and Harry K. White

West Virginia
Charleston, 1932
Cass Gilbert
George H. Fuller Company; James Baird
Company

Wisconsin
Madison, 1909-1915
George B. Post & Sons

Wyoming
Cheyenne, 1890
David W. Gibbs; William Dubois, 1915 extension
Adam Feick & Brother; Moses P. Keefe, 1890
wings; John W. Howard, 1915 extension

U.S. Capitol
Washington, DC, 1800-1829
William Thornton, 1793; Benjamin Henry
Latrobe, 1803-11, 1815-17; Charles Bulfinch,
1818-29; Thomas Ustick Walter, 1851-65;
Edward Clark, 1865-1902; Elliot Woods,
1902-23; David Lynn, 1923-54; J. George
Stewart, 1954-70; George Malcolm White,
FAIA, 1971-95; Alan M. Hantman, AIA,
1997-present

Source: Counsel House Research

Tallest Buildings in the World

The following list ranks the 100 tallest buildings in the world. Each building's architect, number of stories, height, location, and completion year are also provided. (Buildings which are under construction are deemed eligible and are indicated with a 'UC' in the year category.)

For additional resources about tall buildings, visit the Council on Tall Buildings and Urban Habitat on the Internet at *www.ctbuh.org* or *www.worldstallest.com*.

#	Building	Year	City/Country	Feet/ Meters	Stories	Architect
1	Petronas Tower 1	1998	Kuala Lumpur, Malaysia	1483/452	88	Cesar Pelli & Associates
2	Petronas Tower 2	1998	Kuala Lumpur, Malaysia	1483/452	88	Cesar Pelli & Associates
3	Sears Tower	1974	Chicago, USA	1450/442	110	Skidmore, Owings & Merrill
4	Jin Mao Building	1999	Shanghai, China	1381/421	88	Skidmore, Owings & Merrill
5	World Trade Center One	1972	New York, USA	1368/417	110	M. Yamasaki, Emery Roth & Sons
6	World Trade Center Two	1973	New York, USA	1362/415	110	M. Yamasaki, Emery Roth & Sons
7	CITIC Plaza	1996	"Guangzhou, China"	1283/391	80	Dennis Lau & Ng Chun Man
8	Shun Hing Square	1996	Shenzhen, China	1260/384	69	K.Y. Cheung Design Associates
9	Empire State Building	1931	New York, USA	1250/381	102	Shreve, Lamb & Harmon
10	Central Plaza	1992	Hong Kong, China	1227/374	78	Ng Chun Man & Associates
11	Bank of China	1989	Hong Kong, China	1209/369	70	I.M. Pei & Partners
12	Emirates Tower One	UC00	Dubai, U.A.E	1165/355	55	NORR Group Consultants
13	The Center	1998	Hong Kong, China	1148/350	79	Dennis Lau & Ng Chun Man

Tallest Buildings in the World (Con't)

#	Building	Year	City/Country	Feet/ Meters	Stories	Architect
14	T & C Tower	1997	Kaohsiung, Taiwan	1140/348	85	C.Y. Lee/Hellmuth, Obata & Kassabaum
15	Amoco Building	1973	Chicago, USA	1136/346	80	Edward D. Stone
16	Kingdom Centre	UC00	Riyadh, Saudi Arabia	1132/345	30	Altoon + Porter Architects
17	John Hancock Center	1969	Chicago, USA	1127/344	100	Skidmore, Owings & Merrill
18	Burj al Arab Hotel	UC00	Dubai, U.A.E.	1053/321	60	W. S. Atkins & Partners
19	Baiyoke Tower II	1997	Bangkok, Thailand	1050/320	90	Plan Architects Co.
20	Chrysler Building	1930	New York, USA	1046/319	77	William van Alen
21	Bank of America Plaza	1993	Atlanta, USA	1023/312	55	Kevin Roche, John Dinkeloo & Associates
22	Library Tower	1990	Los Angeles, USA	1018/310	75	Pei Cobb Freed & Partners
23	Telekom Malaysia Headquarters	1999	Kuala Lumpur, Malaysia	1017/310	55	Daewoo & Partners
24	Emirates Tower Two	UC00	Dubai, U.A.E	1014/309	54	NORR Group Consultants
25	AT&T Corporate Center	1989	Chicago, USA	1007/307	60	Skidmore, Owings & Merrill
26	Chase Tower	1982	Houston, USA	1000/305	75	I. M. Pei & Partners
27	Two Prudential Plaza	1990	Chicago, USA	995/303	64	Leobl Schlossman Dart & Hackl
28	Ryugyong Hotel	1995	Pyongyang, N. Korea	984/300	105	Baikdoosan Architects & Engineers
29	Commerzbank Tower	1997	Frankfurt, Germany	981/299	63	Sir Norman Foster & Partners
30	Wells Fargo Plaza	1983	Houston, USA	972/296	71	Skidmore, Owings & Merrill
31	Landmark Tower	1993	Yokohama, Japan	971/296	70	Stubbins Associates

Tallest Buildings in the World (Con't)

#	Building	Year	City/Country	Feet/ Meters	Stories	Architect
32	311 S. Wacker Drive	1990	Chicago, USA	961/293	65	Kohn Pederson Fox Associates
33	American International Building	1932	New York, USA	952/290	67	Clinton & Russell
34	Cheung Kong Centre	1999	Hong Kong, China	951/290	70	Cesar Pelli & Associates, Leo A. Daly
35	First Canadian Place	1975	Toronto, Canada	951/290	72	Bregman + Hamann Architects
36	Key Tower	1991	Cleveland, USA	950/290	57	Cesar Pelli & Associates
37	One Liberty Place	1987	Philadelphia, USA	945/288	61	Murphy/Jahn
38	Plaza66	UC00	Shanghai, China	945/288	66	Kohn Peterson Fox Associates
39	Columbia Seafirst Center	1984	Seattle, USA	943/287	76	Chester Lindsey Architects
40	Sunjoy Tomorrow Square	1999	Shanghai, China	934/285	59	John Portman and Associates
41	The Trump Building	1930	New York, USA	927/283	72	H. Craig Severance
42	NationsBank Plaza	1985	Dallas, USA	921/281	72	JPJ Architects
43	Overseas Union Bank Centre	1986	Singapore	919/280	66	Kenzo Tange Associates
44	United Overseas Bank Plaza	1992	Singapore	919/280	66	Kenzo Tange Associates
45	Republic Plaza	1995	Singapore	919/280	66	Kisho Kurakawa
46	Citicorp Center	1977	New York, USA	915/279	59	Stubbins Associates
47	Scotia Plaza	1989	Toronto, Canada	902/275	68	The Webb Zerafa Menkes Housden Partnership
48	Williams Tower	1983	Houston, USA	901/275	64	Johnson/Burgee Architects
49	Faisaliah Complex	UC00	Riyadh, Saudi Arabia	899/274	30	Sir Norman Foster & Partners

Tallest Buildings in the World (Con't)

#	Building	Year	City/Country	Feet/Meters	Stories	Architect
68	CitySpire	1989	New York, USA	814/248	75	Murphy/Jahn
69	Rialto Tower	1985	Melbourne, Australia	814/248	63	Gerard de Preu & Partners
70	One Chase Manhattan Plaza	1961	New York, USA	813/248	60	Skidmore, Owings & Merrill
71	MetLife	1963	New York, USA	808/246	59	Emery Roth & Sons, Pietro Belluschi
72	JR Central Towers	UC00	Nagoya, Japan	804/245	51	Kohn Peterson Fox Associates
73	Shin Kong Life Tower	1993	Taipei, Taiwan	801/244	51	K.M.G. Architects & Engineers
74	Malayan Bank	1988	Kuala Lumpur, Malaysia	799/244	50	Hijjas Kasturi Associates
75	Tokyo Metropolitan Government	1991	Tokyo, Japan	797/243	48	Kenzo Tange Associates
76	Woolworth Building	1913	New York, USA	792/241	57	Cass Gilbert
77	Mellon Bank Center	1991	Philadelphia, USA	792/241	54	Kohn Pedersen Fox Associates
78	John Hancock Tower	1976	Boston, USA	788/240	60	I. M. Pei & Partners
79	Bank One Center	1987	Dallas, USA	787/240	60	Johnson/Burgee Architects
80	Canadian Imperial Bank of Commerce	1973	Toronto, Canada	784/239	57	Page & Steele, I. M. Pei & Partners
81	Moscow State University	1953	Moscow, Russia	784/239	26	L. Roudnev, P. Abrossimov, A. Khariakov
82	Empire Tower	1994	Kuala Lumpur, Malaysia	781/238	62	ADC AKITEK
83	NationsBank Center	1984	Houston, USA	780/238	56	Johnson/Burgee Architects
84	Bank of America Center	1969	San Francisco, USA	779/237	52	Skidmore, Owings & Merrill
85	Office Towers	1985	Caracas, Venezuela	778/237	60	

Tallest Buildings in the World (Con't)

#	Building	Year	City/Country	Feet/ Meters	Stories	Architect
86	Worldwide Plaza	1989	New York, USA	778/237	47	Skidmore, Owings & Merrill
87	First Bank Place	1992	Minneapolis, USA	775/236	58	Pei Cobb Freed & Partners
88	IDS Center	1973	Minneapolis, USA	775/236	57	Johnson/Burgee Architects
89	One Canada Square	1991	London, UK	774/236	50	Cesar Pelli & Associates
90	Norwest Center	1988	Minneapolis, USA	773/235	57	Cesar Pelli & Associates
91	Treasury Building	1986	Singapore	771/235	52	Stubbins Associates
92	191 Peachtree Tower	1992	Atlanta, USA	770/235	50	Johnson/Burgee Architects
93	Opera City Tower	1997	Tokyo, Japan	768/234	54	NTT, Urban Planning & Design, TAK
94	Shinjuku Park Tower	1994	Tokyo, Japan	764/233	52	Kenzo Tange Associates
95	Heritage Plaza	1987	Houston, USA	762/232	52	M. Nasr & Partners
96	Kompleks Tun Abdul Razak Building	1985	Penang, Malaysia	760/232	65	International Sdn./Jurubena Bertiga Intnl. Sdn.
97	Palace of Culture and Science	1955	Warsaw, Poland	758/231	42	L. W. Rudinev
98	Carnegie Hall Tower	1991	New York, USA	757/231	60	Cesar Pelli & Associates
99	Three First National Plaza	1981	Chicago, USA	753/230	57	Skidmore, Owings & Merrill
100	Equitable Center	1986	New York, USA	752/229	51	Edward Larrabee Barnes Associates

Source: Council on Tall Buildings and Urban Habitat, Lehigh University

Opposite: Jin Mao Building, Shanghai, China, Skidmore, Owings and Merrill
Photographer: Hedrich Blessing

Tallest Free-Standing Towers

Because of their primarily utilitarian function as platforms for transmission equipment, the following structures are considered free-standing towers, not skyscrapers. According to internationally-recognized standards, a structure must be intended for human habitation with the great majority of its height divided into habitable floors in order to be deemed a skyscraper. The following free-standing towers are the tallest in the world. A (*) denotes buildings which are under construction.

#	Name	City	Country	Height(m)	Height(ft.)	Completion Year
1	CN Tower	Toronto	Canada	553	1815	1976
2	Ostankino Tower	Moscow	Russia	540	1772	1967
3	Oriental Pearl Television Tower	Shanghai	China	468	1535	1995
4	Teheran Telecommunications Tower*	Teheran	Iran	430	1411	2000
5	Manara Kuala Lumpur	Kuala Lumpur	Malaysia	420	1379	1996
6	Beijing Radio & T.V. Tower	Beijing	China	417	1369	1992
7	Tianjin Radio & T.V. Tower	Tianjin	China	415	1362	1991
8	Tashkent Tower	Tashkent	Uzbekistan	375	1230	1985
9	Alma-Ata Tower	Alma-Ata	Kazakhstan	370	1214	1982
9	Liberation Tower	Kuwait City	Kuwait	370	1214	1996
11	T.V. Tower	Riga	Latvia	368	1208	1987
12	Fernsehturm Tower	Berlin	Germany	365	1198	1969
13	Stratosphere Tower	Las Vegas	United States	350	1149	1996
14	Macau Tower*	Macau	China	338	1109	2001
15	Tokyo Tower	Tokyo	Japan	333	1092	1958

#	Name	City	Country	Height(m)	Height(ft.)	Completion Year
16	T.V. Tower	Frankfurt	Germany	331	1086	1979
17	National Telecommunications Transmitter	Emely Moor	United Kingdom	329	1080	
18	Sky Tower	Auckland	New Zealand	328	1075	1997
19	Vilnius T.V. Tower	Vilnius	Lithuania	327	1072	1980
20	KCTV Tower	Kansas City	United States	318	1042	1956
21	T.V. Tower	Tallinn	Estonia	314	1030	1975
22	Nanjing T.V. Tower	Nanjing	China	310	1017	
23	Nuremberger Fernmeldeturm	Nuremburg	Germany	308	1011	1977
24	T.V. Tower	Shenyang	China	307	1006	
25	Centrepoint Tower	Sydney	Australia	305	1000	1981
26	Eiffel Tower	Paris	France	300	986	1889
26	T.V. Tower	Bombay	India	300	984	1974
28	Sutro Tower	San Francisco	United States	298	977	1972
29	Olympic Tower	Munich	Germany	290	951	1968
30	Torre de Collserola	Barcelona	Spain	288	945	1992
31	Heinrich Hertz Tower	Hamburg	Germany	285	933	1967
32	Telemaxx Tower	Hannover	Germany	277	908	1992
33	J.G. Strijdom Tower	Johannesburg	South Africa	269	882	1970
34	Colonius Tower	Cologne	Germany	266	872	1981
35	Koblenz Tower	Koblenz	Germany	255	837	1976

Tallest Free-Standing Towers (Con't)

#	Name	City	Country	Height(m)	Height(ft.)	Completion Year
36	T.V. Tower	Brussels	Belgium	253	830	
37	Donauturm	Vienna	Austria	252	827	1964
38	Dresden Tower	Dresden	Germany	252	826	1966
39	Saint Chrischona Telecommunications Tower	Basel	Switzerland	249	817	1976
40	Seoul Tower	Seoul	South Korea	237	777	1980
41	TV Tower	New Dehli	India	235	771	1988
42	Rheinturm	Dusseldorf	Germany	234	768	1982
43	Fukuoka Tower	Fukuoka	Japan	234	768	1996
44	Johannesburg Tower	Johannes-burg	South Africa	232	761	1958
45	Fernmeldeturm Kiel	Kiel	Germany	230	753	1972
46	Torre de Espana	Madrid	Spain	220	721	1982
47	Dortmund Tower	Dortmund	Germany	219	720	
48	Fernmeldeturm	Stuttgart	Germany	217	711	1956
49	Zizkov T.V. Tower	Prague	Czech Republic	216	709	1992
50	West Berlin Tower	Berlin	Germany	212	695	

Source: Marshall Gerometta & Jeff Hertzer

10 Greenest Designs

The 10 Greenest Designs were selected by The American Institute of Architects' (AIA) Committee on the Environment (COTE) to highlight viable architectural design solutions that protect and enhance the environment. COTE represents architects who are committed to making environmental considerations and sustainable design integral to their practice. The following projects address one or more significant environmental challenges such as energy and water conservation, use of recycled construction materials, and designs which improve indoor air quality. Responsible use of building materials, use of daylight over artificial lighting, designs that produce efficiency in heating or cooling, and overall sensitivity to local environmental issues were some of the reasons COTE selected these projects.

To view photographs and descriptions, visit *www.e-architect.com/ia/cote/earthda00/earth00.asp* on the Internet.

Bainbridge Island City Hall
Bainbridge Island, Washington
The Miller|Hull Partnership

C. K. Choi Building for The Institute of Asian Research, University of British Columbia
Vancouver, British Columbia, Canada
Matsuzaki Wright Architects Inc.

The Emeryville Resourceful Building Project
Emeryville, California
Siegel & Strain Architects

The Green Institute's Phillips Eco-Enterprise Center (PEEC)
Minneapolis, Minnesota
Laney Architects, Master Planning
Workplace Designers, Architects
LHB Engineers & Architects, Engineers
Applied Ecology, Restoration Ecology
The Weidt Group, Energy Analysis

Hanover House
Hanover, New Hampshire
Energysmiths

Lady Bird Johnson Wildflower Center
Austin, Texas
Overland Partners, Inc.

New South Jamaica Branch Library
Queens, New York
Stein White Architects

Department of Environmental Living and Learning Center (ELLC)
Northland College, Ashland, Wisconsin
LHB Engineers & Architects, Architect of Record & Sustainable Building Design Consultant
HGA, Design Architect/Engineers
The Weidt Group, Energy Analysis

World Resources Institute Headquarters Office
Washington, D.C.
Sandra Mendler, AIA for HOK

Source: The American Institute of Architects

Top 15 Colleges and Universities of Interior Design

Each year *DesignIntelligence* and the Design Futures Council conduct a study in conjunction with the *Almanac of Architecture & Design* to determine the best colleges and universities for interior design in the United States. Principals of over 300 leading U.S. interior design and A/ID firms were asked the question "From which schools have you had the best experience hiring employees?" – relative to their experience during the past ten years. Respondents chose from FIDER (Foundation for Interior Design Education Research) accredited programs.

This research is the first 'customer-satisfaction' oriented study of leading firms, including industry giants, top sector leaders, and award winning firms. Firms in each market sector and throughout all regions of the country were contacted. The results of the study are presented below, with the schools ranked in the order of the most highly acclaimed (with last year's ranking given in parenthesis)

1. University of Cincinnati (1)
2. Pratt Institute (2)
3. Kansas State University* (6)
4. Cornell University (2)
5. Syracuse University* (7)
6. Auburn University (11)
6. University of Texas at Austin (4)
6. Arizona State University (9)
9. Drexel University (9)
9. University of Oregon
11. Texas Tech University
11. University of Florida

13. Virginia Polytechnic Institute and State University
13. Florida State University
13. Louisiana State University (11)

* This survey combined Kansas State University's Interior Architecture and Interior Design programs and Syracuse University's Environmental Design/Interior and Interior Design programs.

Source: DesignIntelligence and Counsel House Research

Top 15 Schools and Colleges of Architecture

Each year *DesignIntelligence* and the Design Futures Council conduct a study in conjunction with the *Almanac of Architecture & Design* to determine the best schools and colleges for architecture in the United States. Principals of over 800 leading U.S. architecture firms were asked the question "From which schools have you had the best experience hiring employees?" – relative to their experience during the past ten years. Respondents chose from NAAB (National Architectural Accrediting Board) accredited programs.

This research is the first 'customer-satisfaction' oriented study of leading firms, including industry giants, top sector leaders, and award winning firms. Firms in each market sector – including commercial, health care, education, hospitality, residential, institutional, laboratory, sports facilities, and office buildings – and throughout all regions of the country were contacted. The results of the study are presented below, with the schools ranked in the order of the most highly acclaimed (with last year's ranking given in parenthesis).

Cornell University (1)
Harvard University (2)
Yale University (6)
Rice University
University of Michigan (3)
University of Cincinnati (3)
Columbia University (10)
Massachusetts Institute of Technology
University of California, Berkeley
University of Texas, Austin
Princeton University (13)
University of Pennsylvania (5)
Rhode Island School of Design (7)
University of Virginia (7)
Texas A&M University

The following schools ranked in the Top 5 in their region.

East

1. Cornell University
2. Harvard University
3. Yale University
4. Columbia University
5. Massachusetts Institute of Technology

South

1. Rice University
2. University of Texas at Austin
3. Texas A&M University
4. Georgia Institute of Technology
5. Auburn University

Top 15 Schools and Colleges of Architecture (Con't)

Midwest

1. University of Michigan
2. University of Cincinnati
3. University of Illinois, Champaign-Urbana
4. Kansas State University
5. Ohio State University

West

1. University of California, Berkeley
2. Washington University
3. California Polytechnic State University, San Luis Obispo
4. University of California, Los Angeles
5. Arizona State University
5. Southern California Institute of Architecture
5. University of Oregon

Source: DesignIntelligence *and Counsel House Research*

29 Best Buildings of the 20th Century

The following 29 buildings were judged by a panel of industry experts to be the Best Buildings of the 20th Century. Buildings designed and constructed during the 20th century, regardless of location, were deemed eligible. Buildings were judged based on the following: their influence on the course of 20th century architecture, significant aesthetic contribution, promotion of design principles which have had a positive impact on the built environment, and/or a lasting impact on the history of the 20th century. The buildings below are listed alphabetically and are not ranked in any order.

Air Force Academy Chapel,
Colorado Springs, CO
SOM

Chrysler Building
New York, NY
William Van Allen

Dulles Airport
Chantilly, VA
Eero Saarinen

East Wing of the National Gallery
Washington, D.C.
I.M. Pei

Fallingwater
Bear Run, PA
Frank Lloyd Wright

Flatiron Building
New York, NY
Daniel Burnham

Gamble House
Pasadena, CA
Greene and Greene

Getty Center
Los Angeles, CA
Richard Meier

Glass House
New Canaan, CT
Philip Johnson

Guggenheim Museum
Bilbao, Spain
Frank Gehry

Hearst Castle
San Simeon, CA
Julia Morgan

Hong Kong and Shanghai Bank
Hong Kong SAR
Norman Foster

Il Palazzo Hotel
Fukuota, Japan
Aldo Rossi

John Deere Headquarters
Moline, IL
Eero Saarinen

John Hancock Building
Chicago, IL
SOM

S.C. Johnson & Son Administration Building
Racine, WI
Frank Lloyd Wright

369

29 Best Buildings of the 20th Century (Con't)

Kimbell Art Musuem
Fort Worth, TX
Louis Kahn

La Sagrada Familia
Barcelona, Spain
Antonio Gaudi

National Farmers' Bank
Owatonna, MN
Louis Sullivan

Nebraska State Capitol
Lincoln, NE
Bertram Goodhue

Notre Dame-du-Haut
Ronchamp, France
Le Corbusier

Salk Institute
La Jolla, CA
Louis Kahn

Seagram Building
New York, NY
Mies van der Rohe

Stockholm City Hall
Stockholm, Sweden
Ragnar Ostburg

Sydney Opera House
Sydney, Australia
Jorn Utzon

Thorncrown Chapel
Eureka Springs, AR
Fay Jones

Tokyo City Hall
Tokyo, Japan
Kenzo Tange

Villa Savoye
Poissy, France
Le Corbusier

Woolworth Building
New York, NY
Cass Gilbert

Source: Council House Research/Greenway Group

World's Best Skylines

This list ranks the world's 25 best skylines according to the density and height of the skyscrapers in each city's skyline. Each building over 90 meters (295 feet) tall contributes points to its home city's score equal to the number of meters by which it exceeds this benchmark height. This list also provides the name of the tallest buildings in each city along with its height and world ranking.

For more information about skyscrapers worldwide, visit Egbert Gramsbergen's Web site, the compiler of this list, at *www.library. tudelft.nl/~egram/skystats.htm* and *www.worldstallest.com*.

Ranking	Points	City	Country	# Buildings >90m	Tallest Bldg./World Ranking
1	28554	New York	USA	586	One World Trade Center (417m, #5)
2	19499	Hong Kong	China	493	Central Plaza (374m, #10)
3	12456	Chicago	USA	256	Sears Tower (442m, #3)
4	9986	Shanghai	China	226	Jin Mao Building (421m, #4)
5	5562	Tokyo	Japan	125	Tokyo Metropolitan Government Bldg. (243m, #75)
6	4370	Sydney	Australia	120	M. L. C. Center (228m)
7	4204	Houston	USA	82	Chase Tower (305m, #26)
8	4194	Singapore	Singapore	81	Overseas Union Bank Cetnre (280m, #43)
9	4110	Manila	Philippines	76	Sky City, Ortigas (300m, u/c)
10	3550	Kuala Lumpur	Malaysia	61	Petronas Tower 1 (452m, #1)
11	3477	San Francisco	USA	108	Transamerica Pyramid (260m, #57)
12	3400	Los Angeles	USA	72	Library Tower (310m, #23)
13	3209	Toronto	Canada	66	First Canadian Place (290m, #35)
14	2902	Bangkok	Thailand	58	Baiyoke Tower II (320m, #19)

World's Best Skylines (Con't)

Ranking	Points	City	Country	# Buildings >90m	Tallest Bldg./World Ranking
15	2634	Melbourne	Australia	53	Rialto Towers (248m, #69)
16	2600	Dallas	USA	53	NationsBank Plaza (281m, #42)
17	2440	Atlanta	USA	52	NationsBank Plaza (312m, #21)
18	2311	Paris	France	74	Tour Maine Montparnasse (209m)
19	2240	Boston	USA	50	John Hancock Tower (241m, #78)
20	2100	Philadelphia	USA	56	One Liberty Place (287m, #37)
21	2087	Jakarta	Indonesia	40	BNI Tower (250m, 66)
22	2052	Osaka	Japan	35	Rinku Gate Tower (256m, #63)
23	2034	Miami	USA	60	Four Seasons Hotel & Tower (240m, u/c)
24	1950	Calgary	Canada	51	Petro Canada Tower (210m)
25	1841	Seattle	USA	38	Columbia Seafirst Center (287m, #38)

Source: Egbert Gramsbergen

DESIGN &
HISTORIC
PRESERVATION

Abbott Lowell Cummings Award

The Abbott Lowell Cummings Award is presented annually by the Vernacular Architecture Forum (VAF), honoring outstanding books published about North American vernacular architecture and landscape. A review committee prioritizes submissions on new information, the role of fieldwork in research, critical approach and the model provided in writing and research methods. A founder of the VAF, Abbott Lowell Cummings was a prolific researcher and writer. He is best known for his magnum opus, *The Framed Houses of Massachusetts Bay, 1625-1725* (1979).

For additional information, visit the VAF's Web site at *www.vernacular architecture.org*.

1983
"'In a Manner and Fashion Suitable to Their Degree': An Investigation of the Material Culture of Early Rural Pennsylvania," in *Working Papers from the Regional Economic History Research Center vol. 5 no. 1*, by Jack Michel

1984
no award granted

1985
Big House, Little House, Back House, Barn: The Connected Farm Buildings of New England by Thomas Hubka (University Press of New England)

1986
Hollybush by Charles Martin (University of Tennessee Press)

1987
Holy Things and Profane: Anglican Parish Churches in Colonial Virginia by Dell Upton (Architectural History Foundation)

1988
Architecture and Rural Life in Central Delaware, 1700-1900 by Bernard L. Herman (University of Tennessee Press)

1989
Study Report for Slave Quarters Reconstruction at Carter's Grove by the Colonial Williamsburg Foundation

Study Report for the Bixby House Restoration by Old Sturbridge Village

1990
Manhattan for Rent, 1785-1850 by Elizabeth Blackmar (Cornell University Press)

Building the Octagon by Orlando Rideout (American Institute of Architects)

1991
Architects and Builders in North Carolina by Catherine Bishir, Charlotte Brown, Carl Lounsbury, and Ernest Wood, III (University of North Carolina Press)

1992
Alone Together: A History of New York's Early Apartments by Elizabeth Cromley (Cornell University Press)

A Place to Belong, Community, Order and Everyday Space in Calvert, Newfoundland by Gerald Pocius (University of Georgia Press)

Abbott Lowell Cummings Award (Con't)

1993

Homeplace: The Social Use and Meaning of the Folk Dwelling in Southwestern North Carolina by Michael Ann Williams (University of Georgia Press)

The Park and the People: A History of Central Park by Roy Rosenzweig and Elizabeth Blackmar (Cornell University Press)

1994

The Stolen House by Bernard L. Herman (University Press of Virginia)

1995

Living Downtown: The History of Residential Hotels in the United States by Paul Groth (University of California Press)

1996

An Illustrated Glossary of Early Southern Architecture and Landscape by Carl Lounsbury (Oxford University Press)

1997

Unplanned Suburbs: Toronto's American Tragedy, 1900-1950 by Richard Harris (Johns Hopkins University Press)

1998

City Center to Regional Mall: Architecture, the Automobile, and Retailing in Los Angeles, 1920-1950 by Richard Longstreth (MIT Press)

1999

The Myth of Santa Fe: Creating a Modern Regional Tradition by Chris Wilson (University of New Mexico Press)

Architecture of the United States by Dell Upton (Oxford University Press)

2000

Delta Sugar: Louisiana's Vanishing Plantation Landscape by John B. Rehder (Johns Hopkins University Press)

Honorable Mentions

Cheap, Quick & Easy: Imitative Architectural Materials, 1870-1930 by Pamela H. Simpson (University of Tennessee Press)

Building Community, Keeping the Faith: German Catholic Vernacular Architecture in a Rural Minnesota Parish by Fred W. Peterson (Minnesota Historical Society Press)

Source: Vernacular Architecture Forum

America's 11 Most Endangered Historic Places

Every June the National Trust for Historic Preservation, in conjunction with the History Channel, compiles a list of the 11 most threatened historic sites in the United States. Since 1988, the 11 Most Endangered list has highlighted more than 100 historic places threatened by neglect, deterioration, insufficient funds, inappropriate development, or insensitive public policy. While being listed does not guarantee protection or financial support, in the past the attention generated by the Endangered Historic Places has brought a broader awareness to the country's diminishing historic resources and generated local support for the threatened sites.

For photos and a history about each site, visit the National Trust's Web site at *www.nthp.org/11most/*.

2000 America's 11 Most Endangered Historic Places

Abraham Lincoln's Retreat - The Soldiers' Home, *Washington, D.C.*
The summer home where Lincoln drafted the Emancipation Proclamation awaits restoration.

Dwight D. Eisenhower VA Medical Center, *Leavenworth, Kansas*
39 historic buildings may be torn down.

Historic Neighborhood Schools, *Nationwide*
Abandonment, demolition, and suburban sprawl threaten these community icons.

Hudson River Valley, *New York*
Industrialization and sprawl threaten scenic area rich in historic landmarks.

Fifth and Forbes Historic Retail Area, *Pittsburgh, Pennsylvania*
Scores of historic buildings to be demolished for large-scale shopping and entertainment complex.

Nantucket, Massachusetts
"Teardowns" and "gut rehabs" of buildings imperil historic island character.

Okeechobee Battlefield, *Okeechobee, Florida*
Development threatens archaeological resources and important Second Seminole War battlefield.

Red Mountain Mining District, *Ouray and San Juan Counties, Colorado*
Sprawl and logging may overwhelm scenic historic mining sites.

Santa Anita Racetrack, *Arcadia, California*
Expansion will ruin historic Art Deco structure.

Valley Forge National Historical Park, *Valley Forge, Pennsylvania*
Revolutionary War buildings need immediate stabilization.

Wheelock Academy, *Millerton, Oklahoma*
Native American school buildings are seriously deteriorating.

Source: National Trust for Historic Preservation

Antoinette Forrester Downing Award

The Society for Architectural Historians annually grants the Antoinette Forrester Downing Award to an author for an outstanding publication in the field of historic preservation. Works published in the two years prior to the award are eligible.

For more information contact the SAH at 312-573-1365 or visit their web site at *www.sah.org*.

1987
: *Providence, A Citywide Survey of Historic Resources* by William McKenzie Woodward and Edward F. Sanderson (Rhode Island Historic Preservation Commission)

1990
: *East Cambridge: A Survey of Architectural History in Cambridge* by Susan E. Maycock (MIT Press)

1991
: *Somerset: An Architectural History* by Paul Baker Touart (Maryland Historical Trust and Somerset County Historical Trust)

1994
: *The Buried Past: An Archaeological History of Philadelphia* by John L. Cotter (University of Pennsylvania Press)

1995
: *Along the Seaboard Side: the Architectural History of Worcester County, Maryland* by Paul Baker Touart (Worcester County)

1996
: *The Historic Architecture of Wake County, North Carolina* by Kelly A. Lally (Wake County Government)

1997
: *A Guide to the National Road and The National Road* by Karl B. Raitz (Johns Hopkins University Press)

1998
: *A Guide to the Historic Architecture of Eastern North Carolina* by Catherine W. Bishir & Michael T. Southern (Chapel Hill University of N.C. Press)

1999
: no award granted

2000
: *Boston's Changeful Times* by Michael Holleran (Johns Hopkins University Press)

Source: Society for Architectural Historians

Crowninshield Award

The National Trust for Historic Preservation's highest honor, the Louise DuPont Crowninshield Award, each year recognizes an individual or organization who has demonstrated extraordinary lifetime achievement in the preservation of America's heritage. Winners are selected by the Preservation Committee of the National Trust's Board of Trustees.

For more information contact the National Trust at (800) 944-6847 or visit their Web site at *www.nthp.org*.

1960 The Mount Vernon Ladies Association	1984 Leopold Adler II
1961 Henry Francis DuPont	1985 James Marston Fitch
1962 Katherine Prentis Murphy	1986 Antoinette Downing
1963 Martha Gilmore Robinson	1987 Blair Reeves
1964 Mr. and Mrs. Bertram R. Little	1988 Robert Stipe
1965 Charles E. Peterson	1989 Fred Rath
1966 Ima Hogg	Association of Junior Leagues
Mary Gordon Latham Kellenberger	1990 Frederick Gutheim
1967 no award granted	1991 Robert Garvey
1968 St. Clair Wright	1992 Joan Bacchus Maynard
1969 Mr. and Mrs. Henry N. Flynt	1993 Carl B. Westmoreland
1970 Frank L. Horton	Arthur P. Ziegler Jr.
1971 Frances R. Edmunds	1994 Walter Beinecke Jr.
1972 Alice Winchester	1995 Dana Crawford
1973 Dr. Ricardo E. Alegria	1996 Richard H. Jenrette
1974 Mr. and Mrs. Jacob H. Morrison	1997 Marguerite Neel Williams
1975 no award granted	1998 Frederick Williamson
1976 Katherine U. Warren	Anice Barber Read
1977 San Antonio Conservation Society	1999 Senator Daniel Patrick Moynihan
1978 Helen Duprey Bullock	2000 National Park Service
1979 Old Post Office Landmark Committee	
1980 William J. Murtagh	
Ernest Allen Connally	*Source: National Trust for Historic Preservation*
1981 Gordon C. Gray	
1982 Helen Abell	
1983 Historic American Buildings Survey (HABS) of the National Park Service, U.S. Department of the Interior, in cooperation with The American Institute of Architects and the Library of Congress, Washington, D.C.	

DOCOMOMO International

DOCOMOMO (Documentation and Conservation of Buildings, Sites and Neighborhoods of the Modern Movement) International is headquartered in Eindhoven, Holland, with working parties in 33 countries. Membership consists of architects, engineers, historians, and others dedicated to preserving the architectural heritage of the Modern Movement through documentation and conservation. Founded in 1990, the group has six specialist committees concentrating on registers, technology, education, urbanism, landscapes and gardens, and publications. They also produce the *DOCOMOMO Journal*, published twice a year, with thematic articles and news from the individual chapters. Their technical publications focus on conservation issues related to modern structures.

Address:
Delft University of Technology
Faculty of Architecture
Berlageweg 1
2628 CR Delft
The Netherlands
Telephone: +31 15-2788755
Internet: www.docomomo.com

Great American Main Street Awards

Each year the National Trust for Historic Preservation's National Main Street Center selects five communities that have demonstrated considerable success with preservation based revitalization. These towns have all generated broad based support from its residents and business leaders, drawn financial assistance from both public and private sources, and created innovative solutions for their unique situations. Winners each receive $5000 to be used towards further revitalization efforts, a bronze plaque, road signs, and a certificate. Since its inception, the Main Street Center has helped over 1400 communities, which has resulted in an average of $35 in new downtown investments for every dollar spent on the revitalization effort.

For more information, visit the Main Street Center's Web site at *www.mainst.org* or contact them at (202) 588-6219.

1995
Clarksville, MO
Dubuque, IA
Franklin, TN
Sheboygan Falls, WI
Old Pasadena, CA

1996
Bonaparte, IA
Chippewa Falls, WI
East Carson Street Business District,
    Pittsburgh, PA
Saratoga Springs, NY
Wooster, OH

1997
Burlington, VT
DeLand, FL
Georgetown, TX
Holland, MI
Libertyville, IL

1998
Corning, IA
Lanesboro, MN
Morgantown, WV
Thomasville, GA
York, PA

1999
Bay City, MI
Cordell, OK
Denton, TX
Lafayette, IN
San Luis Obispo, CA

2000
Coronado, CA
Keokuk, IA
Newkirk, OK
Port Townsend, WA
St. Charles, IL

Source: The National Trust Main Street Center

Did you know...

Since 1980 total public and private reinvestment in Main Street programs has totaled $12.8 billion.

Guidelines for the Treatment of Cultural Landscapes

The Secretary of the Interior is responsible for establishing professional standards and providing advice on the preservation of cultural resources listed or eligible for listing on the National Register of Historic Places. As the definition and scope of preservation has continued to broaden, the Secretary of the Interior developed the Guidelines for the Treatment of Cultural Landscapes to provide expert guidance when planning and implementing work involving cultural landscapes. A cultural landscape is defined as "a geographic area, including both cultural and natural resources and the wildlife or domestic animals therein, associated with a historic event, activity, or person or exhibiting other cultural or aesthetic values."

For more information about cultural landscapes and their preservation, visit the National Park Service's Web site at *www2.cr.nps.gov/hli/introguid.htm.*

1. Before undertaking project work, research of a cultural landscape is essential. Research findings help to identify a landscape's historic period(s) of ownership, occupancy and development, and bring greater understanding of the associations that make them significant. Research findings also provide a foundation to make educated decisions for project treatment, and can guide management, maintenance, and interpretation. In addition, research findings may be useful in satisfying compliance reviews (e.g. Section 106 of the National Historic Preservation Act as amended).

2. Although there is no single way to inventory a landscape, the goal of documentation is to provide a record of the landscape as it exists at the present time, thus providing a baseline from which to operate. All component landscapes and features (see definitions below) that contribute to the landscape's historic character should be recorded. The level of documentation needed depends on the nature and the significance of the resource. For example, plant material documentation may ideally include botanical name or species, common name and size. To ensure full representation of existing herbaceous plants, care should be taken to document the landscape in different seasons. This level of research may most often be the ideal goal for smaller properties, but may prove impractical for large, vernacular landscapes.

3. Assessing a landscape as a continuum through history is critical in assessing cultural and historic value. By analyzing the landscape, change over time -the chronological and physical "layers" of the landscape –can be understood. Based on analysis, individual features may be attributed to a discrete period of introduction, their presence or absence substantiated to a given date and, therefore the landscape's

Guidelines for the Treatment of Cultural Landscapes (Con't)

significance and integrity evaluated. In addition, analysis allows the property to be viewed within the context of other cultural landscapes.

4. In order for the landscape to be considered significant, character-defining features that convey its significance in history must not only be present, but they also must possess historic integrity. Location, setting, design, materials, workmanship, feeling and association should be considered in determining whether a landscape and its character-defining features possess historic integrity.

5. Preservation planning for cultural landscapes involves a broad array of dynamic variables. Adopting comprehensive treatment and management plans, in concert with a preservation maintenance strategy, acknowledges a cultural landscape's ever-changing nature and the interrelationship of treatment, management and maintenance.

Source: Department of the Interior, National Park Service

> Places give roots to people, anchors which we need so much in rootless times when one after another codes of behaviour, established institutions, ways of looking at the world are called into question.
>
> *Christopher Day*

Historic American Buildings Survey (HABS)

The Historic American Buildings Survey (HABS) operates as part of the National Park Service and is dedicated to recording America's historic buildings through measured drawings, written histories, and large-format photographs. The program was started in 1933 as a Civil Works Administration project using unemployed architects to make permanent records of historic American architecture. Following a drop-off in activity after World War II, the program was restored in the early 1950's with student architects providing the research, a practice that continues to the present day. In 1969, the Historic American Engineering Record (HAER) was established as a companion program focusing on America's technological heritage. Records of the over 32,000 recorded historic structures and sites are available to the public through the Prints and Photographs Division of the Library of Congress.

Address:
National Park Service
HABS/HAER Division
849 "C" Street, NW, Room NC300
Washington, D.C. 20240
Telephone: (202) 343-9625
Internet: www.cr.nps.gov/habshaer/

For information on HABS and HAER archives, contact:

Prints and Photographs Reading Room
Library of Congress
James Madison Building, Room LM-337
Washington, DC 20540-4730
Telephone: (202) 707-6394
Internet: http://lcweb.gov/rr/print/

The ordinary and the familiar can become surprising and inspiring.

Robert Venturi

International Centre for the Study of the Preservation and Restoration of Cultural Property (ICCROM)

Founded by the United Nations' Educational, Scientific and Cultural Organization (UNESCO) in 1956, the International Centre for the Study of the Preservation and Restoration of Cultural Property (ICCROM) is an intergovernmental organization dedicated to the conservation of heritage of all types. It is funded by contributions from its 95 Member States, plus donors and sponsors. ICCROM provides members with information, publications and training; offers technical assistance and sponsors workshops; performs ongoing research and archives findings; and serves as an advocate for preservation. The group maintains one of the largest conservation libraries in the world.

Address:
13, Via di San Michele
I-00153 Rome, Italy
Telephone: +39 06 585 531
Internet: www.iccrom.org

Did you know...

Recent archaeological findings outside of Tokyo have uncovered the remains of what experts believe to be the world's oldest human-made structure – estimated at half a million years old.

International Council on Monuments and Sites (ICOMOS)

Dedicated to the conservation of the world's historic monuments and sites, the International Council on Monuments and Sites (ICOMOS) is an international, non-governmental organization with National Committees in over 90 countries. The group is the United Nations' Educational, Scientific and Cultural Organization's (UNESCO) principal advisor in matters concerning the conservation of monuments and sites. With the World Conservation Union (IUCN), ICOMOS advises the World Heritage Committee and UNESCO on the nomination of new sites to the World Heritage List. The group also works to establish international standards for the preservation, restoration and management of the cultural environment. ICOMOS members are professional architects, archaeologists, urban planners, engineers, heritage administrators, art historians, and archivists. All members join ICOMOS through the National Committee of their respective countries.

Address:
49-51 rue de la Fédération
75015 Paris, France
Telephone: +33 (0) 1 45 67 67 70
Internet: www.icomos.org

Did you know...
During his 72-year career, Frank Lloyd Wright completed approximately 500 buildings and also designed roughly that many unbuilt projects.

Most Visited Historic House Museums in the United States

Every year Counsel House Research, in conjunction with the *Almanac of Architecture & Design,* polls America's historic house museums to determine which are the most popular destinations. The following are this year's most visited historic house museums.

1. Mount Vernon, Mount Vernon, VA
    George Washington, 1785-86

2. Biltmore Estate, Asheville, NC
    Richard Morris Hunt, 1895

3. Hearst Castle, San Simeon, CA
    Julia Morgan, 1927-1947

4. Graceland, Memphis, TN
    Architect unknown, 1939

5. Monticello, Home of Thomas Jefferson,
    Charlottesville, VA
    Thomas Jefferson, 1768-79, 1793-1809

6. Martin Luther King Jr. Birth Home,
    Atlanta, GA
    Architect unknown, c. 1893

7. Arlington House, The Robert E. Lee
    Memorial, Arlington, VA
    George Hadfield, 1817

8. Maymont, Richmond, VA
    Edgeton Rogers, 1893

9. Lincoln Home, Springfield, IL
    Architect unknown, 1839

10. The Breakers, Newport, RI
    Richard Morris Hunt, 1895

11. Vanderbilt Mansion, Hyde Park, NY
    McKim, Mead, and White, 1898

12. Betsy Ross House, Philadelphia, PA
    Architect unknown, 1740

13. Paul Revere House, Boston, MA
    Architect unknown, c.1680

14. Carter's Grove, Williamsburg, VA
    John Wheatley, c. 1750-55

15. The Hermitage: Home of President
    Andrew Jackson, Hermitage, TN
    Architect unknown, 1819

16. Marble House, Newport, RI
    Richard Morris Hunt, 1892

17. Beehive House, Salt Lake City, Utah
    Truman Angel, 1854

18. George Eastman House, Rochester, NY
    J. Foster Warner, 1905

19. Viscaya, Miami, FL
    Burrall Hoffman, 1916

20. House of the Seven Gables, Salem, MA
    Architect unknown, 1668

21. Fallingwater, Mill Run, PA
    Frank Lloyd Wright, 1939

22. Franklin D. Roosevelt Home,
    Hyde Park, NY
    Architect unknown, 1826

23. Fair Lane, The Henry Ford Estate,
    Dearborn, MI
    William H. Van Tine, 1915

24. Taliesen West, Scottsdale, AZ
    Frank Lloyd Wright, 1937

25. Little White House, Warm Springs, GA
    Henry Toombs, 1932

Source: Counsel House Research

Opposite: Hearst Castle. ©Hearst Castle®/CA State Parks

National Center for Preservation Technology and Training (NCPTT)

The National Center for Preservation Technology and Training (NCPTT) promotes and enhances the preservation and conservation of prehistoric and historic resources in the United States through the advancement and dissemination of preservation technology and training. Created by Congress, the NCPTT is an interdisciplinary program of the National Park Service intended to advance the art, craft and science of historic preservation in the fields of archeology, historic architecture, historic landscapes, objects, materials conservation, and interpretation through research, education and information management. The Center also administers the Preservation Technology and Training Grants Program, one of the few preservation and conservation grants programs devoted to training, technology and basic research issues.

Address:
Northwestern State University
Box 5682
Natchitoches, LA 71497
Telephone: (318) 357-6464
Internet: www. ncptt.nps.gov

National Preservation Honor Awards

The National Preservation Honor Awards are the National Trust for Historic Preservation's annual program to recognize projects which demonstrate a high level of dedication and support of the ideals and benefits of historic preservation. A jury of preservation professionals and representatives selects winning projects based on their positive effect on the community, pioneering nature, quality, and degree of difficulty. Special interest is placed on those undertakings which utilize historic preservation as a method of revitalization.

For photos and descriptions of the winning projects, visit the National Trust on the Web at *www.nthp.org*.

2000 Award Winners:

Belton Chalet, West Glacier, Montana
The first of the Great Northern Railroad's Glacier Park hotels is restored to its original use

Chicago Military Academy, Chicago, Illinois
A community turns its landmark armory into a groundbreaking military academy

Denver Public Schools, Denver, Colorado
A continuing-use preservation education program saves historic schools

Egyptian Theatre, Los Angeles, California
After its near-destruction in an earthquake, the Egyptian rises from the ashes in all its glory

George Meyer, Milwaukee, Wisconsin
The "father of Wisconsin preservation" has blazed a trail with his pioneering vision

Kimpton Hotels, San Francisco, California
A hotel operator that practices preservation-minded rehabilitation

Kona Historical Society, Kona, Hawaii
A Japanese coffee farm is restored to become Hawaii's first living history museum

MASS MoCA, North Adams, Massachusetts
The opening of the world's largest modern art gallery helps save a depressed mill town

Pennsylvania Historic Schools Initiative, Pennsylvania
Preservationists help level the legislative playing field for historic schools

Radio City Music Hall, New York, New York
An intensive renovation returns the dazzling Art Deco masterpiece to its former glory

Did you know...

In 1931, Charleston, South Carolina, created the nation's first historic district when it passed a zoning ordinance to preserve and protect its historic neighborhood known as 'The Battery.'

National Preservation Honor Awards (Con't)

Roger Williams Park, Providence, Rhode Island
A premier Olmsted-inspired historic landscape is restored

Southwestern University School of Law, Los Angeles, California
A landmark department store becomes a beautiful law school

Stanford University, Stanford, California
Its 10-year seismic strengthening program restored 85 historic buildings

Union Station, Seattle, Washington
After a dazzling restoration, the Beaux-Arts landmark is now the regional transit agency's headquarters

USS Missouri, Honolulu, Hawaii
20,000 volunteers restore the battleship where Japan surrendered to the Allies in 1945

Walnut Cove Colored School, Inc., Walnut Cove, North Carolina
This former Rosenwald Fund school is now a senior citizens' center

Source: National Trust for Historic Preservation

Opposite: Grand Foyer, Radio City Music Hall after renovation, New York, NY, Hardy Holzman Pfeiffer Associates, renovation architect
Photographer: Whitney Cox ©2000

National Preservation Institute (NPI)

The National Preservation Institute (NPI) is a non-profit organization dedicated to the management, development, and preservation of historic, cultural, and environmental resources. Toward this end, NPI offers specialized information, continuing education, and, upon request, professional training tailored to the sponsor's needs. Many preservation-related services are available from NPI, including authentication of historic reproductions and historic real estate. NPI is also registered with The American Institute of Architects Continuing Education System.

Address:
P.O. Box 1702
Alexandria, VA 22313
Telephone: (703) 765-0100
Internet: www.npi.org

National Trust for Historic Preservation

Since its founding in 1949, the National Trust for Historic Preservation (NTHP) has worked to preserve historic buildings and neighborhoods. Through educational programs, publications, financial assistance and government advocacy, the National Trust has been successful in revitalizing communities across the country. This private, non-profit organization operates six regional offices, 20 historic sites, publishes the award winning *Preservation* magazine, hosts the nation's largest preservation conference every year, and works with thousands of local community groups nationwide, through such programs as Main Street, to preserve their history and buildings.

Address:
1785 Massachusetts Avenue, NW
Washington, DC 20036
Telephone: (202) 588-6000
www.nthp.org

Preservation engages the past in a conversation with the present over a mutual concern for the future.

William J. Murtagh

National Trust Historic Hotels of America

The properties listed on the National Trust for Historic Preservation's Historic Hotels of America are a compilation of some of the country's most noteworthy historic hotels, resorts, and inns. Each of the properties are fifty years or older. In addition, they are either eligible for or listed on the National Register of Historic Places or of locally recognized historic significance.

For more information, contact the National Trust for Historic Preservation at (800) 944-6847 or visit the Historic Hotels of America on the Web at *www.nthp.org/main/hotels/hotelsmain.htm*.

ALABAMA
Radisson Admiral Semmes, Mobile
St. James Hotel, Selma

ARIZONA
San Carlos, Phoenix
Royal Palms Hotel and Casitas, Phoenix
Arizona Inn, Tucson

ARKANSAS
Crescent Hotel & Spa, Eureka Springs

CALIFORNIA
La Playa, Carmel
Hotel Del Coronado, Coronado
Furnace Creek Inn, Death Valley
Eureka Inn, Eureka
Grande Colonial, La Jolla
La Valencia, La Jolla
Regal Biltmore, Los Angeles
Mendocino Hotel & Garden Suites, Mendocino
Ojai Valley Inn & Spa, Ojai
Paso Robles Inn, Paso Robles
Mission Inn, Riverside
Delta King Hotel, Sacramento
Fairmont Hotel San Francisco, San Francisco
Sir Francis Drake, San Francisco
Hyatt Sainte Claire, San Jose

El Encanto Hotel & Garden Villas, Santa Barbara
The Georgian Hotel, Santa Monica
Hotel La Rose, Santa Rosa

COLORADO
Hotel Jerome, Aspen
Hotel Boulderado, Boulder
The Brown Palace Hotel, Denver
The Oxford Hotel, Denver
Historic Strater Hotel, Durango
The Cliff House Inn, Manitou Springs
The Redstone Inn, Redstone

CONNECTICUT
The Lighthouse Inn, New London

DELAWARE
The Inn at Montchanin Village, Montchanin
Hotel du Pont, Wilmington

DISTRICT OF COLUMBIA
The Hay-Adams Hotel
Henley Park Hotel
The Jefferson Hotel
Morrison-Clark Inn
Renaissance Mayflower

National Trust Historic Hotels of America (Con't)

FLORIDA

The Biltmore, Coral Gables
The Colony Hotel & Cabaña Club, Delray
Beach
Greyfield Inn, Fernandina Beach
Gulf Stream Hotel, Lake Worth
The Hotel, Miami Beach
Lakeside Inn, Mt. Dora
Park Central Hotel, South Beach
Casa Monica Hotel, St. Augustine
Don CeSar Beach Resort and Spa, St. Pete
Beach
Renaissance Vinoy Resort, St. Petersburg

GEORGIA

The Windsor Hotel, Americus
The Georgian Terrace, Atlanta
The Partridge Inn, Augusta
Jekyll Island Club, Jekyll Island
Marshall House, Savannah
River Street Inn, Savannah
The King and Prince Beach & Golf Resort,
St. Simons Island
Melhana Plantation, Thomasville

ILLINOIS

Omni Ambassador East, Chicago
Regal Knickerbocker, Chicago
The Whitehall Hotel, Chicago
Deer Path Inn, Lake Forest
Hotel Baker, St. Charles

INDIANA

French Lick Springs Resort, French Lick

IOWA

Hotel Winneshiek, Decorah
Hotel Savery, Des Moines
Hotel Pattee, Perry

KENTUCKY

Boone Tavern Hotel, Berea
The Brown Hotel, Louisville

LOUISIANA

Delta Queen Steamboat, New Orleans

Fairmont New Orleans, New Orleans
Le Pavillon Hotel, New Orleans
Hotel Maison de Ville, New Orleans
Hotel Monteleone, New Orleans

MAINE

The Colony Hotel, Kennebunkport
Asticou Inn, Northeast Harbor
Portland Regency Inn, Portland

MARYLAND

Historic Inns of Annapolis, Annapolis
Admiral Fell Inn, Baltimore
Kent Manor Inn, Stevensville

MASSACHUSETTS

Boston Park Plaza Hotel, Boston
The Fairmont Copley Plaza, Boston
The Lenox, Boston
Chatham Bars Inn, Chatham
Harbor View Hotel, Edgartown
Cranwell Resort & Golf Club, Lenox
Hotel Northampton, Northampton
Hawthorne Hotel, Salem
The Red Lion Inn, Stockbridge

MICHIGAN

Grand Hotel, Mackinac Island
The Landmark Inn, Marquette

MINNESOTA

St. James Hotel, Red Wing
The Saint Paul Hotel, St. Paul

MISSISSIPPI

Monmouth Plantation, Natchez

MISSOURI

Raphael Hotel, Kansas City
Hyatt Regency St. Louis at Union Station,
St. Louis

MONTANA

The Pollard, Red Lodge

National Trust Historic Hotels of America (Con't)

NEW HAMPSHIRE
Mount Washington Hotel & Resort, Bretton Woods
The Balsams, Dixville Notch
Eagle Mountain House, Jackson

NEW JERSEY
Seaview Marriott Resort, Absecon

NEW MEXICO
Hotel St. Francis, Santa Fe
La Fonda, Santa Fe
Bishop's Lodge, Sante Fe

NEW YORK
The Sagamore, Bolton Landing, Lake George
Otesaga Hotel, Cooperstown
Mohonk Mountain House, New Paltz
The Algonquin, A Camberley Hotel, New York City
The Plaza, New York City
The Sherry Netherland, New York City
The Waldorf-Astoria, New York City
The Warwick, New York City
American Hotel, Sag Harbor
Hotel Saranac of Paul Smith's College, Saranac Lake

NORTH CAROLINA
Grove Park Inn, Ashville
The Carolina Inn, Chapel Hill
The Dunhill, Charlotte
Lords Proprietors' Inn, Edenton

OHIO
The Cincinnatian, Cincinnati
Omni Netherland Plaza, Cincinnati
Renaissance Cleveland Hotel, Cleveland
The Lafayette, Marietta

OKLAHOMA
Hotel Ambassador, Tulsa

OREGON
The Governor Hotel, Portland
The Heathman, Portland

PENNSYLVANIA
The Hotel Hershey, Hershey
Leola Village Inn & Suites, Leola
Park Hyatt Philadelphia at the Bellevue, Philadelphia
Skytop Lodge, Skytop
Nittany Lion Inn, State College
Yorktowne Hotel, York

PUERTO RICO
Hotel El Convento, Old San Juan

RHODE ISLAND
Inn at Newport Beach, Middletown
Hotel Viking, Newport

SOUTH CAROLINA
John Rutledge House Inn, Charleston
Kings Courtyard Inn, Charleston
Westin Francis Marion Hotel, Charleston

TENNESSEE
The Peabody, Memphis
The Hermitage Hotel, Nashville

TEXAS
The Driskill, Austin
Stoneleigh Hotel, Dallas
Camino Real Hotel, El Paso
Stockyards Hotel, Ft. Worth
Renaissance Casa de Palmas, McAllen
The Menger, San Antonio

UTAH
Ben Lomond Historic Suite Hotel, Ogden

VERMONT
The Old Tavern at Grafton, Grafton
The Equinox, Manchester Village
Middlebury Inn, Middlebury
Green Mountain Inn, Stowe
Basin Harbor Club, Vergennes

National Trust Historic Hotels of America (Con't)

VIRGINIA

Abingdon's Martha Washington Inn, Abingdon
Boar's Head Inn, Charlottesville
Bailiwick Inn, Fairfax
The Homestead, Hot Springs
Wayside Inn, Middletown
The Jefferson, Richmond
Linden Row Inn, Richmond
Williamsburg Inn, Williamsburg
Williamsburg Colonial Houses, Williamsburg

WASHINGTON

Rosario Resort, Eastsound, Orcas Island
The Paradise Inn, Mt. Rainier National Park
Mayflower Park Hotel, Seattle

WEST VIRGINIA

The Greenbrier, White Sulphur Springs

WISCONSIN

The American Club, Kohler
Hotel Metro, Milwaukee
The Pfister Hotel, Milwaukee

Hotel names in italics are new members in 2001.

Source: National Trust for Historic Preservation

Did you know...

Licensed architects receive a reduced rate at the newly converted Hotel Burnham located in the 1895 Reliance Building in Chicago.

Rural Heritage Program

The Rural Heritage Program (RHP), a part of the National Trust for Historic Preservation, is dedicated to the recognition and preservation of rural historic and cultural resources. Through their educational programs, publications, and technical assistance, the RHP supports the efforts of rural communities across the United States to both preserve and live with their heritage. The program works with communities on such topics as farmland preservation, scenic byways, heritage areas and parks, historic roads, and sprawl.

Address:
1785 Massachusetts Avenue, NW
Washington, DC 20036
Telephone: (202) 588-6279
Internet: www.ruralheritage.org

People want to be from a place, not just a place-name. What makes a place is the story you tell about it – its history, in other words – and the determination of people to build community based on that story.

Tom Isern

Save America's Treasures

Launched in May 1998, Save America's Treasures is a public-private initiative between the White House Millennium Council and the National Trust for Historic Preservation dedicated to identifying and rescuing the enduring symbols of America and to raising public awareness and support for their preservation. This national effort to protect America's threatened cultural treasures includes significant documents, works of art, maps, journals, and historic structures that document and illuminate the history and culture of the United States. Applications to be designated an Official Project are accepted on an ongoing basis from non-profit organizations and federal, state, and local agencies that are involved in the preservation, restoration, or conservation of historic buildings, sites, documents, artifacts, objects, or related educational activities. Becoming an Official Project is the first step towards eligibility for Save America's Treasures grants and, in and of itself, often generates local support. In the two years since its founding, Save America's Treasures has designated 523 Official Projects, a list of which is available on their Web site, and raised over $100 million in public-private funds to support preservation efforts.

Address:
785 Massachusetts Avenue, N.W.
Washington, D.C. 20036
Telephone: (202) 588-6202
Internet: www.saveamericastreasures.org

Secretary of the Interior's Standards for Rehabilitation

The Secretary of the Interior's Standards for Rehabilitation were developed to help protect our nation's irreplaceable cultural resources by promoting consistent preservation practices. The Standards recognize the need to alter or add to a historic property in order to meet continuing or changing uses. Following the Standards helps to preserve the distinctive character of a historic building and its site while accommodating new uses. The Standards (36 CFR Part 67) apply to historic buildings of all periods, styles, types, materials, and sizes, as well as to both the exterior and the interior of historic buildings. The Standards also encompass related landscape features and the building's site and environment as well as attached, adjacent, or related new construction. In addition, in order for a rehabilitation project to be eligible for the 20% rehabilitation tax credit, the Standards must be followed.

For more information about how to apply these Standards to restoration projects and tax credits, visit the National Park Service's Web site at *www2.cr.nps.gov/tps/tax/rehabstandards.htm.*

1. A property shall be used for its historic purpose or be placed in a new use that requires minimal change to the defining characteristics of the building and its site and environment.

2. The historic character of a property shall be retained and preserved. The removal of historic materials or alteration of features and spaces that characterize a property shall be avoided.

3. Each property shall be recognized as a physical record of its time, place, and use. Changes that create a false sense of historical development, such as adding conjectural features or architectural elements from other buildings, shall not be undertaken.

4. Most properties change over time; those changes that have acquired historic sig-

nificance in their own right shall be retained and preserved.

5. Distinctive features, finishes, and construction techniques or examples of craftsmanship that characterize a historic property shall be preserved.

6. Deteriorated historic features shall be repaired rather than replaced. Where the severity of deterioration requires replacement of a distinctive feature, the new feature shall match the old in design, color, texture, and other visual qualities and, where possible, materials. Replacement of missing features shall be substantiated by documentary, physical, or pictorial evidence.

7. Chemical or physical treatments, such as sandblasting, that cause damage to historic materials shall not be used. The

surface cleaning of structures, if appropriate, shall be undertaken using the gentlest means possible.

8. Significant archeological resources affected by a project shall be protected and preserved. If such resources must be disturbed, mitigation measures shall be undertaken.

9. New additions, exterior alterations, or related new construction shall not destroy historic materials that characterize the property. The new work shall be differentiated from the old and shall be compatible with the massing, size, scale, and architectural features to protect the historic integrity of the property and its environment.

10. New additions and adjacent or related new construction shall be undertaken in such a manner that if removed in the future, the essential form and integrity of the historic property and its environment would be unimpaired.

Source: Department of the Interior, National Park Service

Did you know...

Rehabilitation projects that used federal tax incentives in 1998 created 40,404 jobs and leveraged $2.08 billion in private investment.

Threatened National Historic Landmarks

National Historic Landmarks are buildings, sites, districts, structures, and objects determined by the Secretary of the Interior to possess national significance to American history and culture and are deemed worthy of preservation. Every two years, out of the over 2,300 National Historic Landmarks, the National Park Service compiles a list of those that are in eminent danger of destruction due to deterioration, incompatible new construction, demolition, erosion, vandalism, and looting. The purpose of this list is to alert the Federal government and the American people to this potential loss of their heritage.

For additional information about the National Historic Landmarks program or the Threatened List, visit the National Park's web site at *www2.cr.nps.gov/nhl/* or contact Heritage Preservation Services at (202) 343-9583.

2000 Threatened National Historic Landmarks – Buildings and Historic Districts

Alaska
Kake Cannery, Kake

Arizona
Fort Huachuca
Old Oraibi, Oraibi
Yuma Crossing & Associated Sites, Yuma

California
Aquatic Park Historic District, San Francisco
Locke Historic District, Locke
Presidio of San Francisco

Colorado
Central City/Black Hawk Historic District, Central City
Cripple Creek Historic District, Cripple Creek

District of Columbia
Terrell (Mary Church) House

Illinois
Adler Planetarium, Chicago
Grant Park Stadium. Chicago
Kennicott Grove, Glenview
Montgomery Ward Company Complex, Chicago
Orchestra Hall, Chicago
Room 405, George Herbert Jones Laboratory, University of Chicago, Chicago
Sears, Roebuck, and Company 1905-6 Complex, Chicago
Shedd Aquarium, Chicago

Indiana
Bailly (Joseph) Homestead, Porter County

Kansas
Fort Leavenworth, Leavenworth

Louisiana
Courthouse (The) and Lawyer's Row, Clinton
Fort St. Philip, Triumph

Threatened National Historic Landmarks (Con't)

Maryland
Chestertown Historic District,
Chestertown
Resurrection Manor, Hollywood

Massachusetts
Boston Naval Shipyard
Fenway Studio, Boston
Nantucket Historic District, Nantucket

Michigan
Fair Lane, Dearborn
Pewabic Pottery, Detroit

Minnesota
Fort Snelling, Minneapolis-St. Paul
Volstead (Andrew J.) House, Granite Falls

Mississippi
Montgomery (I.T.) House, Mount Bayou

Missouri
Tower Grove Park, St. Louis
Westminster College Gymnasium, Fulton

Montana
Butte Historic District, Butte
Fort Benton
Great Northern Railway Buildings, Glacier
National Park

Nevada
Virginia City Historic District, Virginia
City

New Jersey
Abbott Farm Historic District, Trenton
Cape May Historic District, Cape May
Fort Hancock and Sandy Hook Proving
Ground Historic District, Sandy Hook
Great Falls of the Passaic Society for
Universal Manufacturing Historic
District, Patterson

New Mexico
Lincoln Historic District, Lincoln
National Park Service Region III

Headquarters Building, Santa Fe
Seton Village, Santa Fe
San Estevan Del Ray Mission Church,
Acoma
Village of Columbus and Camp Furlong,
Columbus
Watrous (La Junta), Watrous

New York
Mount Lebanon Shaker Village, Mount
Lebanon
New York State Inebriate Asylum,
Binghamton

Ohio
Kettering (Charles F.) House, Kettering
Rocket Engine Test Facility, Cleveland
Young (Colonel Charles) House,
Wilberforce

Oklahoma
Cherokee National Capitol, Tahlequah
Fort Gibson
Wheelock Academy, Durant

Pennsylvania
Bedford Springs Hotel Historic District,
Bedford
Cambria Iron Company, Johnstown
Eastern State Penitentiary, Philadelphia
Gallatin (Albert) House, Point Marion
Harrisburg Station and Train Shed,
Harrisburg
Meason (Isaac) House, Dunbar Township
United States Naval Asylum, Philadelphia
Woodlands, Philadelphia

Rhode Island
Fort Adams, Newport

South Carolina
Chapelle Administration Building,
Columbia
Fort Hill (John C. Calhoun House),
Clemson

Threatened National Historic Landmarks (Con't)

South Dakota
Frawley Ranch Historic District, Spearfish

Tennessee
The Hermitage, Nashville

Vermont
Robbins and Lawrence Armory and
Machine Shop, Windsor

Virginia
Bacon's Castle, Surry County
Jackson Ward Historic District, Richmond

West Virginia
Elkins Coal and Coke, Bretz
Weston Hospital Main Building, Weston

Wyoming
Old Faithful Inn, West Thumb
Sun (Tom) Ranch, Casper vicinity
Swan Land and Cattle Company
Headquarters, Chugwater

Source: National Park Service

Did you know...

In Columbus, Indiana, the modern architecture mecca, six of its buildings, each completed between 1942 and 1965, recently received National Historic Landmark status.

Vernacular Architecture Forum (VAF)

Devoted to the "ordinary" architecture of North America, the Vernacular Architecture Forum (VAF) was formed in 1980 to encourage the study and preservation of traditional structures and landscapes. These include agricultural buildings, industrial and commercial structures, twentieth-century suburban houses, settlement patterns and cultural landscapes, and areas historically overlooked by scholars. The VAF embraces multidisciplinary interaction. Historians, designers, archaeologists, folklorists, architectural historians, geographers, museum curators and historic preservationists contribute to the organization. The VAF holds its conference every spring with part of the agenda focusing on the vernacular architecture of that region. Every few years papers are selected from past conferences and published in the series *Perspectives in Vernacular Architecture*. The VAF presents two annual awards: the Abbott Lowell Cummings Award for the best book published on North American vernacular architecture and cultural landscapes, and the Paul E. Buchanan Award for the best non-published work on North American vernacular architecture.

Address:
Internet: www.vernaculararchitecture.org

Did you know...

Now considered historic treasures, between 1908 and 1940 Sears Roebuck and Co. manufactured and sold an estimated 100,000 kit houses, in more than 450 different styles, through its mail-order catalog.

World Heritage List

Since 1972 the World Heritage Committee has inscribed 582 properties on the World Heritage List (445 cultural, 117 natural and 20 mixed properties in 114 States Parties). The World Heritage List was established under terms of The Convention Concerning the Protection of the World Cultural and Natural Heritage, adopted in November 1972 at the 17th General Conference of the United Nations Educational, Scientific, and Cultural Organization (UNESCO). The Convention states that a World Heritage Committee "will establish, keep up-to-date and publish" a World Heritage List of cultural and natural properties, submitted by the States Parties and considered to be of outstanding universal value. One of the main responsibilities of this Committee is to provide technical cooperation under the World Heritage Fund for the safeguarding of World Heritage properties to States Parties whose resources are insufficient. Assistance with the nomination process, training, grants, and loans is also available.

For a complete listing of all the World Heritage properties with detailed descriptions and photographs of each, visit their Web site at *www.unesco.org/whc.*

Algeria:
M'Zab Valley
Djémila
Tipasa
Timgad
Kasbah of Algiers

Argentina and Brazil:
Jesuit Missions of the Guaranis: San Ignacio Mini, Santa Ana, Nuestra Señora de Loreto and Santa Maria Mayor (Argentina), Ruins of Sao Miguel das Missoes (Brazil)

Armenia:
Monastery of Haghpat

Austria:
City of Graz - Historic Centre
Historic Centre of the City of Salzburg
Palace and Gardens of Schönbrunn
Hallstatt-Dachstein Salzkammergut Cultural Landscape
Semmering Railway

Bangladesh:
Historic Mosque City of Bagerhat
Ruins of the Buddhist Vihara at Paharpur

Belgium:
Belfries of Flanders and Wallonia
Flemish Béguinages
The Four Lifts on the Canal du Centre and their Environs, La Louvière and Le Roeulx (Hainault)
Grand-Place, Brussels

Benin:
Royal Palaces of Abomey*

World Heritage List (Con't)

Bolivia:
  City of Potosi
  Jesuit Missions of the Chiquitos
  Historic City of Sucre
  El Fuerte de Samaipata

Brazil:
  Historic Centre of the Town of
      Diamantina
  Historic Town of Ouro Preto
  Historic Centre of the Town of Olinda
  Historic Centre of Salvador de Bahia
  Sanctuary of Bom Jesus do Congonhas
  Brasilia
  Historic Centre of São Luis

Bulgaria:
  Boyana Church
  Rock-hewn Churches of Ivanovo
  Thracian Tomb of Kazanlak
  Ancient City of Nessebar
  Rila Monastery
  Thracian Tomb of Sveshtari

Cambodia:
  Angkor*

Canada:
  Quebec (Historic Area)
  Lunenburg Old Town

China:
  The Great Wall
  Mount Taishan
  Imperial Palace of the Ming and Qing
      Dynasties
  Mausoleum of the First Qin Emperor
  The Mountain Resort and its Outlying
      Temples, Chengde
  Temple and Cemetery of Confucius, and
      the Kong Family Mansion in Qufu
  Ancient Building Complex in the Wudang
      Mountains
  Potala Palace, Lhasa
  Lushan National Park
  Mount Emei and Leshan Giant Buddha

  Old Town of Lijiang
  Ancient City of Ping Yao
  Classical Gardens of Suzhou
  Summer Palace, an Imperial Garden in
      Beijing
  Temple of Heaven -- an Imperial
      Sacrificial Altar in Beijing

Colombia:
  Port, Fortresses and Group of
      Monuments, Cartagena
  Historic Centre of Santa Cruz de Mompox

Croatia:
  Old City of Dubrovnik
  Historic Complex of Split with the Palace
      of Diocletian
  Episcopal Complex of the Euphrasian
      Basilica in the Historic Centre of Porec
  Historic City of Trogir

Cuba:
  Old Havana and its Fortifications
  Trinidad and the Valley de los Ingenios
  San Pedro de la Roca Castle, Santiago de
      Cuba

Cyprus:
  Paphos
  Painted Churches in the Troodos Region
  Choirokoitia

Czech Republic:
  Historic Centre of Prague
  Historic Centre of Cesky Krumlov
  Historic Centre of Telc
  Pilgrimage Church of St. John of
      Nepomuk at Zelena Hora
  Kutná Hora: Historical Town Centre with
      the Church of Saint Barbara and the
      Cathedral of Our Lady at Sedlec
  Lednice-Valtice Cultural Landscape
  Holasovice Historical Village Reservation
  Gardens and Castle at Kromeríz
  Litomysl Castle

World Heritage List (Con't)

Denmark:
Roskilde Cathedral

Dominican Republic:
Colonial City of Santo Domingo

Ecuador:
City of Quito
Historic Center of Santa Ana de los Rios de Cuenca

Egypt:
Memphis and its Necropolis - the Pyramid Fields from Giza to Dahshur
Ancient Thebes with its Necropolis
Nubian Monuments from Abu Simbel to Philae
Islamic Cairo
Abu Mena

Estonia:
The Historic Centre (Old Town) of Tallinn

Ethiopia:
Rock-hewn Churches, Lalibela
Fasil Ghebbi, Gondar Region
Aksum

Finland:
Old Rauma
Fortress of Suomenlinna
Petäjävesi Old Church
Verla Groundwood and Board Mill

Former Yugoslav Rep. of Macedonia
Ohrid Region, including its cultural and historic aspects, and its natural environment

France:
Mont-Saint-Michel and its Bay
Chartres Cathedral
Palace and Park of Versailles
Vézelay, Church and Hill
Palace and Park of Fontainebleau
Chateau and Estate of Chambord
Amiens Cathedral

Roman Theatre and its Surroundings and the "Triumphal Arch" of Orange
Roman and Romanesque Monuments of Arles
Cistercian Abbey of Fontenay
Royal Saltworks of Arc-et-Senans
Place Stanislas, Place de la Carrière, and Place d'Alliance in Nancy
Church of Saint-Savin sur Gartempe
Pont du Gard (Roman Aqueduct)
Strasbourg-Grande île
Paris, Banks of the Seine
Cathedral of Notre-Dame, Former Abbey of Saint-Remi and Palace of Tau, Reims
Bourges Cathedral
Historic Centre of Avignon
Canal du Midi
Historic Fortified City of Carcassonne
Routes of Santiago de Compostela in France
Historic Site of Lyons
The Jurisdiction of Saint-Emilion

Georgia:
City-Museum Reserve of Mtskheta
Bagrati Cathedral and Gelati Monastery
Upper Svaneti

Germany:
Aachen Cathedral
Speyer Cathedral
Würzburg Residence, with the Court Gardens and Residence Square
Pilgrimage Church of Wies
The Castles of Augustusburg and Falkenlust at Brühl
St. Mary's Cathedral and St. Michael's Church at Hildesheim
Roman Monuments, Cathedral and Liebfrauen-Church in Trier
Hanseatic City of Lübeck
Palaces and Parks of Potsdam and Berlin
Abbey and Altenmünster of Lorsch
Mines of Rammelsberg and Historic Town of Goslar

World Heritage List (Con't)

Town of Bamberg

Maulbronn Monastery Complex

Collegiate Church, Castle, and old Town of Quedlinburg

Völklingen Ironworks

Cologne Cathedral

Bauhaus and its sites in Weimar and Dessau

Luther Memorials in Eisleben and Wittenberg

Classical Weimar

Museumsinsel (Museum Island)

Wartburg Castle

Ghana:

Forts and Castles, Volta Greater Accra, Central and Western Regions

Ashanti Traditional Buildings

Greece:

Temple of Apollo Epicurius at Bassae

Archaeological Site of Delphi

Acropolis, Athens

Mount Athos

Meteora

Paleochristian and Byzantine Monuments of Thessalonika

Archaeological Site of Epidaurus

Medieval City of Rhodes

Mystras

Archaeological Site of Olympia

Delos

Monasteries of Daphni, Hossios Luckas and Nea Moni of Chios

Pythagoreion and Heraion of Samos

The Historic Centre (Chorá) on the Island of Pátmos

Guatemala:

Antigua Guatemala

Haiti:

National History Park – Citadel, Sans-Souci, Ramiers

Holy See:

Vatican City

Honduras:

Mayan Site of Copan

Hungary:

Budapest, the Banks of the Danube and the Buda Castle Quarter

Hollokö

Millenary Benedictine Monastery of Pannonhalma and its Natural Environment

India:

Ajanta Caves

Ellora Caves

Agra Fort

Taj Mahal

Sun Temple, Konarak

Group of Monuments at Mahabalipuram

Churches and Convents of Goa

Khajuraho Group of Monuments

Group of Monuments at Hampi

Fatehpur Sikri

Group of Monuments at Pattadakal

Brihadisvara Temple, Thanjavur

Buddhist Monuments at Sanchi

Humayun's Tomb, Delhi

Qutb Minar and its Monuments, Delhi

Indonesia:

Borobudur Temple Compounds

Prambanan Temple Compounds

Iran:

Tchogha Zanbil

Persepolis

Meidan Emam, Esfahan

Iraq:

Hatra

Ireland:

Skellig Michael

World Heritage List (Con't)

Italy:

The Church and Dominican Convent of
Santa Maria delle Grazie with "The Last
Supper" by Leonardo da Vinci
Historic Centre of Florence
Venice and its Lagoon
Piazza del Duomo, Pisa
Historic Centre of San Gimignano
I Sassi di Matera
City of Vicenza and the Palladian Villas of
the Veneto
Historic Centre of Siena
Historic Centre of Naples
Crespi d'Adda
Ferrara: City of the Renaissance
Castel del Monte
The Trulli of Alberobello
Early Christian Monuments of Ravenna
Historic Centre of the City of Pienza
18th-Century Royal Palace at Caserta with
the Park, the Aqueduct of Vanvitelli
and the San Leucio Complex
Residences of the Royal House of Savoy
Botanical Garden (Orto Botanico), Padua
Portovenere, Cinque Terre, and the
Islands (Palmaria, Tino and Tinetto)
Cathedral, Torre Civica and Piazza
Grande, Modena
Archaeological Areas of Pompei,
Herulaneum, and Torre Annunziata
Costiera Amalfitana
Villa Romana del Casale
Archaeological Areas of Agrigento
Su Nuraxi di Barumini
Archaeological Area and the Patriarchal
Basilica of Aquileia
Cilento and Vallo di Diano National Park
with the Archeological Sites of Paestum
and Velia, and the Certosa di Padula
Historic Centre of Urbino
Villa Adriana

Italy/Holy See:

Historic Centre of Rome, the Properties of
the Holy See in that City Enjoying
Extraterritorial Rights, and San Paolo
Fuori le Mura

Japan:

Buddhist Monuments in the Horyu-ji
Area
Himeji-jo
Historic Monuments of Ancient Kyoto
(Kyoto, Uji and Otsu Cities)
Historic Villages of Shirakawa-go and
Gokayama
Itsukushima Shinto Shrine
Historic Monuments of Ancient Nara
Shrines and Temples of Nikko

Jerusalem:

Old City of Jerusalem and its Walls*

Jordan:

Petra
Quseir Amra

Lao People's Democratic Republic:

Town of Luang Prabang

Latvia:

Historic Centre of Riga

Lebanon:

Anjar
Baalbek
Byblos
Tyre
Ouadi Qadisha (the Holy Valley) and the
Forest of the Cedars of God (Horsh Arz
el-Rab)

Libyan Arab Jamahiriya:

Archaeological Site of Leptis Magna
Archaeological Site of Sabratha
Archaeological Site of Cyrene
Old Town of Ghadames

World Heritage List (Con't)

Lithuania:
Vilnius Historic Centre

Luxembourg:
City of Luxemburg: its Old Quarters and
Fortifications

Mali:
Old Towns of Djenné
Timbuktu*

Malta:
City of Valetta
Megalithic Temples of Malta

Mauritania:
Ancient Ksour of Ouadane, Chinguetti,
Tichitt and Oualata

Mexico:
Pre-Hispanic City and National Park of
Palenque
Historic Centre of Mexico City and
Xochimilco
Pre-Hispanic City of Teotihuacan
Historic Centre of Oaxaca and
Archaeological Site of Monte Alban
Historic Centre of Puebla
Historic Town of Guanajuato and
Adjacent Mines
Pre-Hispanic City of Chichen-Itza
Historic Centre of Morelia
El Tajin, Pre-Hispanic City
Historic Centre of Zacatecas
Earliest 16th-Century Monasteries on the
Slopes of Popocatepetl
Pre-Hispanic Town of Uxmal
Historic Monuments Zone of Querétaro
Hospicio Cabañas, Guadalajara
Archaeological Zone of Paquimé, Casas
Grandes
Historic Monuments Zone of Tlacotalpan
Historic Fortified Town of Campeche

Morocco:
Medina of Fez
Medina of Marrakesh
Ksar of Aït-Ben-Haddou
Historic City of Meknes
The Medina of Tétouan (formerly known
as Titawin)

Mozambique:
Island of Mozambique

Nepal:
Kathmandu Valley
Lumbini, the Birthplace of the Lord Buddha

Netherlands:
Schokland and Surroundings
Defense Line of Amsterdam
Mill Network at Kinderdijk-Elshout
Historic Area of Willemstad, Inner City,
and Harbour, the Netherlands Antilles
Ir.D.F. Woudagemaal (D.F. Wouda Steam
Pumping Station)
Droogmakerij de Beemster (The Beemster
Polder)

Nigeria:
Sukur Cultural Landscape

Norway:
Urnes Stave Church
Bryggen
Røros

Oman:
Bahla Fort*

Pakistan:
Archaeological Ruins at Moenjodaro
Taxila
Buddhist Ruins of Takht-i-Bahi and
Neighbouring City Remains at Sahi-i-
Bahlol
Historic Monuments of Thatta
Fort and Shalamar Gardens in Lahore
Rohtas Fort

World Heritage List (Con't)

Panama:

Fortifications on the Caribbean side of Panama: Portobelo-San Lorenzo

The Historic District of Panamá, with the Salón Bolivar

Paraguay:

Jesuit Missions of La Santisima Trinidad de Parana and Jesus de Tavarangue

Peru:

City of Cuzco

Historic Sanctuary of Machu Picchu

Chavin

Chan Chan Archaeological Zone*

Historic Centre of Lima

Philippines:

Baroque Churches of the Philippines

Historic Town of Vigan

Poland:

Cracow's Historic Centre

Wieliczka Salt Mine

Historic Centre of Warsaw

Old City of Zamosc

The Medieval Town of Torun

Castle of the Teutonic Order in Malbork

Kalwaria Zebrzydowska

Portugal:

Central Zone of the Town of Angra do Heroismo in the Azores

Monastery of the Hieronymites and Tower of Belem in Lisbon

Monastery of Batalha

Convent of Christ in Tomar

Historic Centre of Evora

Monastery of Alcobaça

Cultural Landscape of Sintra

Historic Centre of Oporto

Republic of Korea:

Sokkuram Buddhist Grotto

Haiensa Temple Changgyong P'ango, the Depositories for the Tripitaka Koreana Woodblocks

Chongmyo Shrine

Ch'angdokkung Palace Complex

Hwasong Fortress

Romania:

Biertan and its Fortified Church

Monastery of Horezu

Churches of Moldavia

Historic Centre of Sighisoara

The Wooden Churches of Maramures

The Dacian Fortresses of the Orastie Mountains

Saint Christopher & Nevis

Brimstone Hill Fortress National Park

Russian Federation:

Historic Centre of St. Petersburg and Related Groups of Monuments

Kizhi Pogost

Kremlin and Red Square, Moscow

Historic Monuments of Novgorod and Surroundings

Cultural and Historic Ensemble of the Solovetsky Islands

White Monuments of Vladimir and Suzdal

Architectural Ensemble of the Trinity Sergius Lavra in Sergiev Posad

Church of the Ascension, Kolomenskoye

Senegal:

Island of Gorée

Slovakia:

Vlkolinec

Banska Stiavnica

Spissky Hrad and its Associated Cultural Monuments

South Africa:

Robben Island

Spain:

Historic Centre of Cordoba

Alhambra, Generalife and Albayzin, Granada

World Heritage List (Con't)

Burgos Cathedral
Monastery and Site of the Escurial, Madrid
Parque Güell, Palacio Güell and Casa Mila in Barcelona
Old Town of Segovia and its Aqueduct
Monuments of Oviedo and the Kingdom of the Asturias
Santiago de Compostela (Old town)
Old Town of Avila, with its Extra-Muros Churches
Mudejar Architecture of Teruel
Historic City of Toledo
Old Town of Caceres
Cathedral, Alcazar and Archivo de Indias in Seville
Old City of Salamanca
Poblet Monastery
Archaeological Ensemble of Mérida
Royal Monastery of Santa Maria de Guadalupe
Route of Santiago de Compostela
Historic Walled Town of Cuenca
La Lonja de la Seda de Valencia
Las Médulas
The Palau de la Música Catalana and the Hospital de Sant Pau, Barcelona
San Millán Yuso and Suso Monasteries
University and Historic Precinct of Alcalá de Henares
San Critóbal de la Laguna

Sri Lanka:
Sacred City of Anuradhapura
Ancient City of Polonnaruva
Ancient City of Sigiriya
Sacred City of Kandy
Old Town of Galle and its Fortifications
Golden Temple of Dambulla

Sweden:
Royal Domain of Drottningholm
Birka and Hovgården
Engelsberg Ironworks
Skogskyrkogården

Hanseatic Town of Visby
Church Village of Gammelstad, Luleå
Naval Port of Karlskrona

Switzerland:
Convent of St. Gall
Benedictine Convent of St. John at Müstair
Old City of Berne

Syrian Arab Republic:
Ancient City of Damascus
Ancient City of Bosra
Site of Palmyra
Ancient City of Aleppo

Thailand:
Historic Town of Sukhothai and Associated Historic Towns
Historic City of Ayutthaya and Associated Historic Towns

Tunisia:
Medina of Tunis
Site of Carthage
Amphitheatre of El Jem
Punic Town of Kerkuane and its Necropolis
Medina of Sousse
Kairouan
Dougga/Thugga

Turkmenistan:
State Historical and Cultural Park 'Ancient Merv'

Turkey:
Historic Areas of Istanbul
Göreme National Park and the Rock Sites of Cappadocia
Great Mosque and Hospital of Divrigi
Hattusha
Nemrut Dag
Xanthos-Letoon
Hierapolis-Pamukkale
City of Safranbolu
Archaeological Site of Troy

World Heritage List (Con't)

Ukraine:
Kiev: Saint-Sophia Cathedral and Related
Monastic Buildings, Kiev-Pechersk
Lavra
L'viv - the Ensemble of the Historic Centre

United Kingdom:
Durham Castle and Cathedral
Ironbridge Gorge
Studley Royal Park, including the Ruins of
Fountains Abbey
Stonehenge, Avebury and Associated Sites
Castles and Town Walls of King Edward in
Gwynedd
St. Kilda
Blenheim Palace
City of Bath
Hadrian's Wall
Westminster Palace, Westminster Abbey,
and Saint Margaret's Church
Tower of London
Canterbury Cathedral, St. Augustine's
Abbey and St. Martin's Church
Old and New Towns of Edinburgh
Maritime Greenwich

United Republic of Tanzania:
Ruins of Kilwa Kisiwani and Ruins of
Songo Mnara

United States of America:
Independence Hall
La Fortaleza and San Juan Historic Site in
Puerto Rico
The Statue of Liberty
Monticello, and University of Virginia in
Charlottesville
Pueblos de Taos

Uruguay:
Historic Quarter of the City of Colonia del
Sacramento

Uzbekistan:
Itchan Kala
Historic Centre of Bukhara

Venezuela:
Coro and its Port

Viet Nam:
Complex of Hué Monuments
Hoi An Ancient Town
My Son Sanctuary

Yemen:
Old Walled City of Shibam
Old City of Sana'a
Historic Town of Zabid

Yugoslavia:
Stari Ras and Sopocani
Natural and Culturo-Historical Region of
Kotor*
Studenica Monastery

Zimbabwe:
Khami Ruins National Monument

* *Indicates the site is also on the List of World*
Heritage in Danger as determined by the
World Heritage Committee.

Source: World Heritage Committee, UNESCO

World's 100 Most Endangered Sites

The World Monuments Fund's biennial List of the 100 Most Endangered Sites designates those cultural sites most in danger of destruction, either by natural or man-made causes. Initial nominations for the list are solicited annually from governments, heritage conservation organizations, and concerned individuals. Each nominated site must have the support of a sponsoring institution, substantial cultural significance, an urgent need for intervention, and a viable recovery plan. The final selection committee is comprised of a panel of international experts. Limited financial support is also available from the World Monuments Watch Fund and is awarded on a competitive basis to selected sites on the list. The World Monuments Fund is a private, non-profit organization created in 1965 with the purpose of fostering a greater awareness of the world's cultural, artistic, and historic resources; facilitating preservation and conservation efforts; and generating private financial assistance.

For more information or to find out how to nominate a site, visit the World Monuments Fund's Web site at *www.worldmonuments.org* or contact them at 212-517-9367.

Albania
Butrint Archaeological Site, Sarande

Algeria
Tipasa Archaeological Park, Tipasa

Belgium
Tour and Taxis (transport hub), Brussels

Bosnia and Herzegovina
Mostar Historic Center, Mostar

Brazil
Santo Antonio do Paraguaçu, São Francisco do Paraguaça, Bahia
Vila de Paranapiacaba, Santo André, São Paulo

Bulgaria
Ivanovo Rock Chapels, Rousse Region

Cambodia
Banteay Chhmar Temple of Jayavarman VII, Thmar Puok

Chile
Orongo Ceremonial Site, Easter Island

China
Dulan County Tibetan Royal Tomb Group, Reshuixiang-Xuewei, Dulan
Palpung Monastery, Babang Village, Sichuan
Temple of Agriculture (Xiannongtan), Beijing
Xuanjian Tower, Yuci City, Shanxi

Croatia
Vukovar City, Center Vukovar

World's 100 Most Endangered Sites (Con't)

Cuba
National Art Schools, Cubanacán, Havana
San Isidro de los Destiladeros, Valle de los
Ingenios, Trinidad
Santa Teresa de Jesús Cloisters, Havana

Czech Republic
Kuks Forest Sculptures, Kuks

Dominican Republic
Puerto Plata Lighthouse, Puerto Plata

Egypt
Khasekhemwy at Hierakonpolis, Edfu,
Kom el Ahmar
Sultan Qa'itbay Complex, Cairo
Valley of the Kings, Thebes, Luxor

El Salvador
Suchitoto City, Cuscatlán

Ethiopia
Mentewab-Qwesqwam Palace, Gondar

France
Saint Pierre Cathedral, Beauvais

Georgia
Ikorta Church of the Archangel, Zemo
Artsevi Village
Tbilisi Historic District, Tbilisi

Germany
Gartenreich Dessau-Wörlitz, Dessau
Thomaskirche, Leipzig

Greece
Kahal Shalom Synagogue, Rhodes

India
Basgo Gompa (Maitreya Temples),
Ladakh, Leh
Champaner Archaeological Site,
Panchmahal, Gujarat
Jaisalmer Fort, Rajasthan
Metropolitan Building, Calcutta
Saint Anne Church, Talaulim, Goa

Indonesia
Omo Hada (Royal Palace Complex), Nias,
North Sumatra
Tanah Lot Temple, Tabanan, Bali

Iraq
Erbil Citadel, Kurdish Autonomous
Region

Ireland
Saint Brendan's Cathedral, Clonfert,
County Galway

Israel
Tel-Dan Canaanite Gate, near Kibbutz
Dan, Upper Galilee
Ramle White Mosque Archaeological Site,
Ramle

Italy
Ancient Pompeii, Naples
Bridge of Chains, Bagni di Lucca
Cinque Terre, Liguria
Santi Quattro Coronati Cloister, Rome

Jamaica
Falmouth Historic Town, Trelawny Parish

Jordan
Petra Archaeological Site, Wadi Mousa

Kenya
Thimlich Ohinga Cultural Landscape,
Migori

Lebanon
Enfeh Archaeological Site, Enfeh, near
Tripoli

Malaysia
George Town Historic Enclave, Penang
State
Kampung Cina River Frontage, Kuala
Terengganu

Opposite: The Petra Archaeological Site in Jordan
© The World Monuments Fund (J. Stubbs)

World's 100 Most Endangered Sites (Con't)

Malta
  Mnajdra Prehistoric Temples, Mnajdra

Mexico
  Madera Cave Dwellings, Madera,
    Chihuahua
  San Juan de Ulúa Fort, Veracruz
  Santa Prisca Parish Church, Taxco de
    Alarcón, Guerrero
  Teotihuacán Archaeological Site, San Juan
    Teotihuacán
  Yaxchilán Archaeological Zone, Cuenca
    del Usumacinta, Chiapas

Mongolia
  Bogd Khaan Palace Museum, Ulaanbaatar

Nepal
  Itum Monastery, Kathmandu
  Teku Thapatali Monument Zone,
    Kathmandu

Niger
  Giraffe Rock Art Site

Pakistan
  Uch Monument Complex, Bahawalpur,
    Punjab

Panama
  San Lorenzo Castle and San Gerónimo
    Fort, Colón and Portobelo

Peru
  Cusco Historic Center, Cusco
  Los Pinchudos Archaeological Site, Rio
    Abiseo National Park
  Machu Picchu, Urubamba, Cusco

Philippines
  Rice Terraces of the Cordilleros, Ifugao

Poland
  Vistulamouth Fortress, Gdansk

Romania
  Bánffy Castle, Bontida

Russia
  Arkhangelskoye State Museum, Moscow
  Irkoutsk Historic Center, Irkoutsk
  Oranienbaum State Museum, Lomonosov
  Paanajärvi Village, Kemi Province
  Rostov Veliky Historic Center, Rostov
    Veliky
  Russakov Club, Moscow
  Viipuri Library, Vyborg

Slovakia
  Basil the Great Church, Krajné Cierno

Sudan
  Gebel Barkal Archaeological Site, Karima

Suriname
  Jodensavanne Archaeological Site, Redi
    Doti

Turkey
  Ani Archaeological Site, Ocarli Köyü, Kars
  Çatalhöyük, Çumra, Konya
  Mount Nemrut Archaeological Site, Kâhta
  Zeyrek Mosque, Istanbul

Turkmenistan
  Merv Archaeological Site, Bairam Ali

Ukraine
  Kamyanets Podilsky Castle Bridge,
    Kamyanets Podilsky
  Zhovkva Synagogue, Zhovkva

United Kingdom
  Abbey Farmstead, Faversham, Kent,
    England
  Saint Francis Church and Monastery, East
    Manchester, England

United States of America
  Eastern State Penitentiary, Philadelphia,
    Pennsylvania
  Lancaster County, Pennsylvania
  Seventh Regiment Armory, New York,
    New York

World's 100 Most Endangered Sites (Con't)

Tree Studios and Medinah Temple,
   Chicago, Illinois

VDL Research House II, Los Angeles,
   California

Uzbekistan
   Abdulazizkhan Complex, Bukhara

Venezuela
   San Francisco Church, Coro, Falcón

Vietnam
   Minh Mang Tomb, Hue
   My Son Temple Complex, Duy Xuyen,
      Quang Nam

Yemen
   Tarim Historic City, Wadi Hadhramaut

Yugoslavia
   Subotica Synagogue, Subotica

Zimbabwe
   Khami National Monument, Bulawayo

Source: World Monuments Fund

Did you know...

**Of the sites listed on the 1998
World Monuments Watch list,
73 are no longer endangered
and have been removed from
the list.**

DESIGN
ECONOMETRICS

Annual Value of Construction Put in Place: 1995-1999

Type of construction	Constant (1996) dollars (in millions)				
	1995	1996	1997	1998	1999
Total construction	567,900	613,454	635,765	670,859	692,477
Private construction	434,450	474,307	486,273	520,613	535,625
Residential buildings	251,937	281,229	280,748	297,886	315,757
New housing units	174,585	191,212	192,386	212,068	225,896
1 unit	156,363	170,865	170,154	188,785	201,210
2 units or more	18,222	20,347	22,232	23,283	24,686
Improvements	77,352	90,018	88,362	85,818	89,860
Nonresidential buildings	139,711	153,866	166,754	177,639	175,048
Industrial	34,814	36,215	35,411	37,715	31,214
Office	26,218	27,875	33,058	39,333	41,643
Hotels, motels	7,274	10,909	12,438	13,794	14,262
Other commercial	43,636	48,170	49,948	49,915	51,067
Religious	4,426	4,531	5,565	6,139	6,701
Educational	5,621	6,737	8,375	9,039	8,743
Hospital and institutional	11,512	11,778	13,066	12,853	12,183
Miscellaneous [1]	6,209	7,650	8,892	8,850	9,235
Farm nonresidential	3,084	3,657	3,675	3,989	3,977
Public utilities	36,740	33,124	32,884	38,616	38,166
Telecommunications	11,556	11,791	12,159	13,036	15,142
Other public utilities	25,184	21,333	20,725	25,581	23,024
Railroads	3,609	4,391	4,745	5,463	4,540
Electric light and power	14,310	11,209	11,122	11,885	13,393
Gas	6,329	4,720	3,911	7,020	3,690
Petroleum pipelines	936	1,013	947	1,213	1,401
All other private [2]	2,979	2,431	2,212	2,482	2,678

Annual Value of Construction Put in Place: 1995-1999 (Con't)

Type of construction	Constant (1996) dollars (in millions)				
	1995	1996	1997	1998	1999
Public construction	133,450	139,147	149,493	150,246	156,852
Buildings	59,074	63,446	69,319	68,334	69,497
Housing and redevelopment	4,786	5,046	5,084	4,853	5,088
Industrial	1,544	1,390	965	941	828
Educational	26,374	28,577	33,136	33,743	35,497
Hospital	4,335	4,617	4,970	3,642	3,548
Other 3	22,034	23,815	25,164	25,155	24,537
Highways and streets	38,952	39,412	42,535	45,877	48,827
Military facilities	3,102	2,593	2,466	2,377	1,909
Conservation and develop.	6,443	6,000	5,541	5,219	5,602
Sewer systems	8,600	9,778	10,034	9,743	10,438
Water supply facilities	4,809	5,609	6,275	6,552	7,142
Miscellaneous public 4	12,468	12,310	13,323	12,145	13,436

Includes amusement and recreational buildings, bus and airline terminals, animal hospitals and shelters, etc.

Includes privately owned streets and bridges, parking areas, sewer and water facilities, parks and playgrounds, golf courses, airfields, etc.

Includes general administrative buildings, prisons, police and fire stations, courthouses, civic centers, passenger terminals, space facilities, postal facilities, etc.

Includes open amusement and recreational facilities, power generating facilities, transit systems, airfields, open parking facilities, etc.

Source: U.S. Census Bureau

Architecture Firm Profiles by State: 1997

	Number of Establishments	Receipts ($1,000)	Annual Payroll ($1,000)	Paid Employees [1]
U.S Total	20,602	16,988,338	6,468,524	146,702
Alabama	229	154,208	55,838	1,352
Alaska	47	45,369	16,417	337
Arizona	474	323,750	116,499	2,910
Arkansas	147	80,119	29,606	811
California	2,789	2,482,256	909,074	18,911
Colorado	596	382,471	143,569	3,389
Connecticut	324	238,061	85,065	1,727
Delaware	38	30,790	9,918	227
District of Columbia	122	243,985	91,375	1,901
Florida	1,472	937,583	307,179	7,826
Georgia	538	506,929	200,887	4,222
Hawaii	165	141,688	45,767	1,013
Idaho	119	66,761	25,544	678
Illinois	1,023	772,167	326,319	7,015
Indiana	287	206,895	86,331	2,114
Iowa	130	86,271	33,124	840
Kansas	160	122,655	48,643	1,282
Kentucky	161	115,140	42,390	1,098
Louisiana	262	143,042	52,856	1,428
Maine	83	49,569	21,270	529
Maryland	378	281,833	109,403	2,372
Massachusetts	699	1,147,248	393,708	8,005
Michigan	559	416,101	184,418	4,137
Minnesota	378	377,127	165,869	3,701
Mississippi	112	68,175	27,343	679
Missouri	400	427,846	177,863	3,767

	Number of Establishments	Receipts ($1,000)	Annual Payroll ($1,000)	Paid Employees [1]
Montana	82	43,134	16,486	519
Nebraska	116	108,018	45,516	1,115
Nevada	131	144,766	49,791	1,069
New Hampshire	66	32,192	12,718	313
New Jersey	610	387,938	143,028	3,381
New Mexico	161	85,771	30,154	962
New York	1,614	1,455,388	548,028	11,890
North Carolina	513	355,173	148,493	3,375
North Dakota	36	24,442	8,465	251
Ohio	665	520,814	216,760	5,212
Oklahoma	168	170,195	63,231	1,685
Oregon	308	247,565	91,205	2,215
Pennsylvania	693	655,071	263,098	6,284
Rhode Island	75	32,226	12,588	341
South Carolina	229	141,394	61,209	1,337
South Dakota	40	20,915	8,417	239
Tennessee	296	292,064	116,769	2,623
Texas	1,306	1,160,271	444,352	9,746
Utah	168	110,703	41,372	1,133
Vermont	84	28,757	10,291	328
Virginia	514	369,194	147,818	3,521
Washington	661	494,026	181,146	4,363
West Virginia	45	22,702	9,428	222
Wisconsin	286	217,008	86,594	2,125
Wyoming	43	20,572	5,292	182

Paid employees for the pay period including March 12

Source: U.S. Census Bureau, 1997 Economic Census

Architecture Student Demographics

Based on a study conducted by the National Architectural Accrediting Board (NAAB), the following information outlines demographic information about NAAB accredited architecture degree programs at U.S. colleges and universities.

	1993/94	1994/95	1995/96	1996/97	1997/98	1998/99
Pre-professional Undergrad. Programs						
Full-time students	10,420	10,790	9,655	12,130	11,789	12,062
Part-time students	1,504	1,577	1,494	1,602	1,524	1386
Women students	3,419	3,895	3,432	4,317	4,419	4499
African-American students	635	723	496	660	682	641
American Indian students	59	59	80	62	67	78
Asian/Pacific Isle students	929	1,010	807	1,112	1,065	1042
Hispanic students	1,144	967	750	991	955	929
Total Graduates	2,260	2,369	2,154	2,324	2,199	2397
Women graduates	662	708	603	746	807	774
African-American graduates	105	75	74	83	81	85
American Indian graduates	7	7	6	10	9	12
Asian/Pacific Isle graduates	238	219	198	225	233	226
Hispanic graduates	149	147	101	157	162	157
Accredited B. Arch Programs						
Full-time students	16,899	16,500	16,424	16,025	16,423	15312
Part-time students	1,924	1,500	1,364	1,178	1,377	1606
Women students	5,007	5,107	5,155	5,046	5,413	5201
African-American students	1,252	1,174	1,247	1,122	1,165	1243
American Indian students	101	143	195	163	138	151
Asian/Pacific Isle students	1,699	1,735	1,665	1,591	1,497	1425
Hispanic students	1,473	1,466	1,436	1,340	1,249	1184
Total Graduates	3,206	2,837	2,948	3,028	2,710	2617
Women graduates	832	775	742	849	762	754
African-American graduates	152	144	148	131	111	131
American Indian graduates	20	16	14	14	8	13
Asian/Pacific Isle graduates	282	277	276	307	294	239
Hispanic graduates	188	185	215	223	222	198

Architecture Student Demographics (Con't)

	1993/94	1994/95	1995/96	1996/97	1997/98	1998/99
Accredited M. Arch Programs						
Full-time students	4,812	4,664	5,196	5,252	5,461	5769
Part-time students	537	491	724	533	677	689
Women students	1,855	1,883	2,164	2,143	2,273	2210
African-American students	117	121	142	133	133	119
American Indian students	18	11	21	17	20	12
Asian/Pacific Isle students	521	508	540	522	550	607
Hispanic students	260	235	267	302	301	427
Total Graduates	1,654	1,629	1,676	1,645	1,799	2002
Women graduates	541	580	558	580	747	744
African-American graduates	28	28	26	45	32	40
American Indian graduates	1	3	5	3	9	10
Asian/Pacific Isle graduates	158	169	140	156	164	197
Hispanic graduates	75	87	83	82	92	104

Source: National Architectural Accrediting Board

Commercial Building Characteristics: 1995 (in thousands)

Building Characteristics	All Buildings	Buildings by Size			
		1,001 to 5,000 Square Feet	5,001 to 10,000 Square Feet	10,001 to 25,000 Square Feet	25,001 to 50,000 Square Feet
All Buildings	4,579	2,399	1,035	745	213
Principal Building Activity					
Education	309	100	60	62	49
Food Sales	137	108	Q	Q	Q
Food Service	285	210	52	Q	Q
Health Care	105	57	Q	16	
Lodging	158	46	40	43	14
Mercantile and Service	1,289	736	295	195	3
Office	705	405	131	94	3
Public Assembly	326	128	110	64	1
Public Order and Safety	87	Q	Q	23	
Religious Worship	269	92	84	78	1
Warehouse and Storage	580	2B6	135	95	3
Other	67	Q	Q	Q	
Vacant	261	149	68	34	
Year Constructed					
1919 or Before	353	175	92	65	
1920 to 1945	562	309	145	70	
1946 to 1959	867	461	222	123	
1960 to 1969	718	343	159	135	
1970 to 1979	813	428	174	137	
1980 to 1989	846	422	151	186	4
1990 to 1992	218	132	50	16	
1993 to 1995	202	129	43	13	
Floors					
One	3,018	1,894	618	358	
Two	1,002	378	283	236	
Three	399	123	97	115	
Four to Nine	148	Q	37	35	
Ten or More	12	Q	Q	Q	

Buildings by Size				
50,001 to 100,000 Square Feet	100,001 to 200,000 Square Feet	200,001 to 500,000 Square Feet	Over 500,000 Square Feet	Building Characteristics
115	48	19	6	**All Buildings**
				Principal Building Activity
26	9	3	Q	Education
Q	Q	Q	Q	Food Sales
Q	Q	0	Q	Food Service
2	Q	2	1	Health Care
9	4	2	Q	Lodging
18	8	2	2	Mercantile and Service
22	10	5	1	Office
7	2	1	Q	Public Assembly
Q	Q	Q	Q	Public Order and Safety
Q	Q	Q	Q	Religious Worship
17	9	3	1	Warehouse and Storage
Q	Q	Q	Q	Other
3	Q	Q	Q	Vacant
				Year Constructed
6	2	Q	Q	1919 or Before
11	6	2	1	1920 to 1945
19	5	3	*	1946 to 1959
21	12	3	1	1960 to 1969
20	9	4	1	1970 to 1979
26	9	4	1	1980 to 1989
6	3	1	*	1990 to 1992
6	Q	*	*	1993 to 1995
				Floors
37	16	4	1	One
32	8	2	1	Two
18	7	2	*	Three
26	14	7	1	Four to Nine
Q	3	4	2	Ten or More

Commercial Building Characteristics: 1995 (Con't)

Building Characteristics	All Buildings	Buildings by Size			
		1,001 to 5,000 Square Feet	5,001 to 10,000 Square Feet	10,001 to 25,000 Square Feet	25,001 to 50,000 Square Feet
Census Region					
Northeast	725	351	162	139	38
Midwest	1,139	638	224	181	48
South	1,750	953	380	276	74
West	964	457	269	149	53
Ownership and Occupancy					
Nongovernment Owned	4,025	2,176	909	646	158
Owner Occupied	3,158	1,746	704	503	109
Nonowner Occupied	698	325	163	126	47
Unoccupied	170	105	Q	Q	Q
Government Owned	553	223	125	98	55
Predominant Ext. Wall Material					
Masonry	3,061	1,454	749	545	170
Siding or Shingles	639	465	116	50	5
Metal Panels	662	390	146	97	18
Concrete Panels	106	Q	10	30	14
Window Glass	46	Q	Q	Q	4
Other	50	Q	Q	Q	Q
No One Major Type	15	Q	Q	Q	Q
Predominant Roof Material					
Built-up	1,369	591	331	258	97
Shingles (Not Wood)	1,486	915	331	191	29
Metal Surfacing	908	512	192	158	26
Synthetic or Rubber	351	133	62	71	49
Slate or Tile	202	105	60	21	10
Wooden Materials	152	72	50	Q	0
Concrete	58	Q	Q	Q	0
Other	36	Q	Q	Q	0
No One Major Type	Q	Q	Q	Q	0

Q: Data withheld because the Relative Standard Error (RSE) was greater than 50 percent, or fewer than 20 buildings were sampled.

* = Value rounds to zero in the units displayed.

Buildings by Size				Building Characteristics
50,001 to 100,000 Square Feet	100,001 to 200,000 Square Feet	200,001 to 500,000 Square Feet	Over 500,000 Square Feet	
				Census Region
20	10	5	2	Northeast
28	14	5	1	Midwest
42	17	6	1	South
24	8	3	1	West
				Ownership and Occupancy
83	35	13	4	Nongovernment Owned
58	24	10	4	Owner Occupied
24	10	3	*	Nonowner Occupied
Q	Q	Q	Q	Unoccupied
32	13	6	1	Government Owned
				Predominant Ext. Wall Material
91	35	14	4	Masonry
Q	Q	Q	Q	Siding or Shingles
7	2	Q	*	Metal Panels
12	6	2	*	Concrete Panels
3	2	1	1	Window Glass
Q	Q	*	Q	Other
Q	Q	Q	Q	No One Major Type
				Predominant Roof Material
54	25	10	3	Built-up
14	4	1	*	Shingles (Not Wood)
13	3	1	Q	Metal Surfacing
25	13	5	2	Synthetic or Rubber
4	Q	Q	Q	Slate or Tile
Q	Q	Q	Q	Wooden Materials
Q	Q	Q	*	Concrete
Q	0	Q	Q	Other
Q	Q	Q	Q	No One Major Type

Source: Energy Information Administration, Office of Energy Markets and End Use,1995 Commercial Buildings Energy Consumption Survey

Construction Costs by City (in dollars per square foot)

Location	CCI	Apartment 1-3 Story	Church	College Classroom 2-3 Story	College Dorm 2-3 Story	College Laboratory	Fire Station 1 Story	Hospital 4-8 Story	Hotel 8-24 Story
National Average		101.45	115.95	110.7	117.3	117.35	102.25	122.15	96.05
ALABAMA									
Birmingham	0.87	88.26	100.88	96.31	102.05	102.09	88.96	106.27	83.56
Huntsville	0.83	84.2	96.24	91.88	97.36	97.4	84.87	101.38	79.72
Mobile	0.83	84.2	96.24	91.88	97.36	97.4	84.87	101.38	79.72
Montgomery	0.81	82.17	93.92	89.67	95.01	95.05	82.82	98.94	77.8
ALASKA									
Anchorage	1.25	126.81	144.94	138.38	146.63	146.69	127.81	152.69	120.06
Fairbanks	1.24	125.8	143.78	137.27	145.45	145.51	126.79	151.47	119.1
ARIZONA									
Mesa/Tempe	0.85	86.23	98.56	94.1	99.71	99.75	86.91	103.83	81.64
Phoenix	0.89	90.29	103.2	98.52	104.4	104.44	91	108.71	85.48
Tucson	0.87	88.26	100.88	96.31	102.05	102.09	88.96	106.27	83.56
ARKANSAS									
Fayetteville	0.67	67.97	77.69	74.17	78.59	78.62	68.51	81.84	64.35
Little Rock	0.81	82.17	93.92	89.67	95.01	95.05	82.82	98.94	77.8
CALIFORNIA									
Anaheim	1.09	110.58	126.39	120.66	127.86	127.91	111.45	133.14	104.69
Bakersfield	1.06	107.54	122.91	117.34	124.34	124.39	108.39	129.48	101.81
Berkeley	1.18	119.71	136.82	130.63	138.41	138.47	120.66	144.14	113.34
Fresno	1.08	109.57	125.23	119.56	126.68	126.74	110.43	131.92	103.73
Inglewood	1.06	107.54	122.91	117.34	124.34	124.39	108.39	129.48	101.81
Long Beach	1.07	108.55	124.07	118.45	125.51	125.56	109.41	130.7	102.77
Los Angeles	1.08	109.57	125.23	119.56	126.68	126.74	110.43	131.92	103.73
Modesto	1.1	111.6	127.55	121.77	129.03	129.09	112.48	134.37	105.66
Oakland	1.18	119.71	136.82	130.63	138.41	138.47	120.66	144.14	113.34
Oxnard	1.09	110.58	126.39	120.66	127.86	127.91	111.45	133.14	104.69
Palo Alto	1.17	118.7	135.66	129.52	137.24	137.3	119.63	142.92	112.38
Pasadena	1.06	107.54	122.91	117.34	124.34	124.39	108.39	129.48	101.81
Riverside	1.08	109.57	125.23	119.56	126.68	126.74	110.43	131.92	103.73
Sacramento	1.1	111.6	127.55	121.77	129.03	129.09	112.48	134.37	105.66
Salinas	1.12	113.62	129.86	123.98	131.38	131.43	114.52	136.81	107.58
San Bernardino	1.05	106.52	121.75	116.24	123.17	123.22	107.36	128.26	100.85

Jail	Library	Nursing Home	Office 2-4 Story	Office 11-20 Story	Post Office	School Elementary	School High 2-3 Story	Store Department 3 Story	Location
177.8	103.1	101.1	105	89.15	84.55	86.7	92.1	87.15	**National Average**
									ALABAMA
154.69	89.7	87.96	91.35	77.56	73.56	75.43	80.13	75.82	Birmingham
147.57	85.57	83.91	87.15	73.99	70.18	71.96	76.44	72.33	Huntsville
147.57	85.57	83.91	87.15	73.99	70.18	71.96	76.44	72.33	Mobile
144.02	83.51	81.89	85.05	72.21	68.49	70.23	74.6	70.59	Montgomery
									ALASKA
222.25	128.88	126.38	131.25	111.44	105.69	108.38	115.13	108.94	Anchorage
220.47	127.84	125.36	130.2	110.55	104.84	107.51	114.2	108.07	Fairbanks
									ARIZONA
151.13	87.64	85.94	89.25	75.78	71.87	73.7	78.29	74.08	Mesa/Tempe
158.24	91.76	89.98	93.45	79.34	75.25	77.16	81.97	77.56	Phoenix
154.69	89.7	87.96	91.35	77.56	73.56	75.43	80.13	75.82	Tucson
									ARKANSAS
119.13	69.08	67.74	70.35	59.73	56.65	58.09	61.71	58.39	Fayetteville
144.02	83.51	81.89	85.05	72.21	68.49	70.23	74.6	70.59	Little Rock
									CALIFORNIA
193.8	112.38	110.2	114.45	97.17	92.16	94.5	100.39	94.99	Anaheim
188.47	109.29	107.17	111.3	94.5	89.62	91.9	97.63	92.38	Bakersfield
209.8	121.66	119.3	123.9	105.2	99.77	102.31	108.68	102.84	Berkeley
192.02	111.35	109.19	113.4	96.28	91.31	93.64	99.47	94.12	Fresno
188.47	109.29	107.17	111.3	94.5	89.62	91.9	97.63	92.38	Inglewood
190.25	110.32	108.18	112.35	95.39	90.47	92.77	98.55	93.25	Long Beach
192.02	111.35	109.19	113.4	96.28	91.31	93.64	99.47	94.12	Los Angeles
195.58	113.41	111.21	115.5	98.07	93.01	95.37	101.31	95.87	Modesto
209.8	121.66	119.3	123.9	105.2	99.77	102.31	108.68	102.84	Oakland
193.8	112.38	110.2	114.45	97.17	92.16	94.5	100.39	94.99	Oxnard
208.03	120.63	118.29	122.85	104.31	98.92	101.44	107.76	101.97	Palo Alto
188.47	109.29	107.17	111.3	94.5	89.62	91.9	97.63	92.38	Pasadena
192.02	111.35	109.19	113.4	96.28	91.31	93.64	99.47	94.12	Riverside
195.58	113.41	111.21	115.5	98.07	93.01	95.37	101.31	95.87	Sacramento
199.14	115.47	113.23	117.6	99.85	94.7	97.1	103.15	97.61	Salinas
186.69	108.26	106.16	110.25	93.61	88.78	91.04	96.71	91.51	San Bernardino

Construction Costs by City (Con't)

Location	CCI	Apartment 1-3 Story	Church	College Classroom 2-3 Story	College Dorm 2-3 Story	College Laboratory	Fire Station 1 Story	Hospital 4-8 Story	Hotel 8-24 Story
San Diego	1.06	107.54	122.91	117.34	124.34	124.39	108.39	129.48	101.81
San Francisco	1.23	124.78	142.62	136.16	144.28	144.34	125.77	150.24	118.14
San Jose	1.2	121.74	139.14	132.84	140.76	140.82	122.7	146.58	115.26
Santa Ana	1.06	107.54	122.91	117.34	124.34	124.39	108.39	129.48	101.81
Santa Rosa	1.17	118.7	135.66	129.52	137.24	137.3	119.63	142.92	112.38
Stockton	1.09	110.58	126.39	120.66	127.86	127.91	111.45	133.14	104.69
Vallejo	1.15	116.67	133.34	127.31	134.9	134.95	117.59	140.47	110.46
COLORADO									
Colorado Springs	0.92	93.33	106.67	101.84	107.92	107.96	94.07	112.38	88.37
Denver	0.95	96.38	110.15	105.17	111.44	111.48	97.14	116.04	91.25
Fort Collins	0.92	93.33	106.67	101.84	107.92	107.96	94.07	112.38	88.37
CONNECTICUT									
Bridgeport	1.05	106.52	121.75	116.24	123.17	123.22	107.36	128.26	100.85
Hartford	1.05	106.52	121.75	116.24	123.17	123.22	107.36	128.26	100.85
New Haven	1.05	106.52	121.75	116.24	123.17	123.22	107.36	128.26	100.85
Stamford	1.08	109.57	125.23	119.56	126.68	126.74	110.43	131.92	103.73
D.C.									
Washington	0.95	96.38	110.15	105.17	111.44	111.48	97.14	116.04	91.25
DELAWARE									
Wilmington	1.01	102.46	117.11	111.81	118.47	118.52	103.27	123.37	97.01
FLORIDA									
Jacksonville	0.83	84.2	96.24	91.88	97.36	97.4	84.87	101.38	79.72
Fort Lauderdale	0.86	87.25	99.72	95.2	100.88	100.92	87.94	105.05	82.6
Miami	0.86	87.25	99.72	95.2	100.88	100.92	87.94	105.05	82.6
Orlando	0.86	87.25	99.72	95.2	100.88	100.92	87.94	105.05	82.6
St. Petersburg	0.84	85.22	97.4	92.99	98.53	98.57	85.89	102.61	80.68
Tallahassee	0.78	79.13	90.44	86.35	91.49	91.53	79.76	95.28	74.92
Tampa	0.83	84.2	96.24	91.88	97.36	97.4	84.87	101.38	79.72
GEORGIA									
Atlanta	0.86	87.25	99.72	95.2	100.88	100.92	87.94	105.05	82.6
Columbus	0.79	80.15	91.6	87.45	92.67	92.71	80.78	96.5	75.88
Macon	0.81	82.17	93.92	89.67	95.01	95.05	82.82	98.94	77.8
Savannah	0.82	83.19	95.08	90.77	96.19	96.23	83.85	100.16	78.76

Jail	Library	Nursing Home	Office 2-4 Story	Office 11-20 Story	Post Office	School Elementary	School High 2-3 Story	Store Department 3 Story	Location
188.47	109.29	107.17	111.3	94.5	89.62	91.9	97.63	92.38	San Diego
218.69	126.81	124.35	129.15	109.65	104	106.64	113.28	107.19	San Francisco
213.36	123.72	121.32	126	106.98	101.46	104.04	110.52	104.58	San Jose
188.47	109.29	107.17	111.3	94.5	89.62	91.9	97.63	92.38	Santa Ana
208.03	120.63	118.29	122.85	104.31	98.92	101.44	107.76	101.97	Santa Rosa
193.8	112.38	110.2	114.45	97.17	92.16	94.5	100.39	94.99	Stockton
204.47	118.57	116.27	120.75	102.52	97.23	99.71	105.92	100.22	Vallejo
									COLORADO
163.58	94.85	93.01	96.6	82.02	77.79	79.76	84.73	80.18	Colorado Springs
168.91	97.95	96.05	99.75	84.69	80.32	82.37	87.5	82.79	Denver
163.58	94.85	93.01	96.6	82.02	77.79	79.76	84.73	80.18	Fort Collins
									CONNECTICUT
186.69	108.26	106.16	110.25	93.61	88.78	91.04	96.71	91.51	Bridgeport
186.69	108.26	106.16	110.25	93.61	88.78	91.04	96.71	91.51	Hartford
186.69	108.26	106.16	110.25	93.61	88.78	91.04	96.71	91.51	New Haven
192.02	111.35	109.19	113.4	96.28	91.31	93.64	99.47	94.12	Stamford
									D.C.
168.91	97.95	96.05	99.75	84.69	80.32	82.37	87.5	82.79	Washington
									DELAWARE
179.58	104.13	102.11	106.05	90.04	85.4	87.57	93.02	88.02	Wilmington
									FLORIDA
147.57	85.57	83.91	87.15	73.99	70.18	71.96	76.44	72.33	Jacksonville
152.91	88.67	86.95	90.3	76.67	72.71	74.56	79.21	74.95	Fort Lauderdale
152.91	88.67	86.95	90.3	76.67	72.71	74.56	79.21	74.95	Miami
152.91	88.67	86.95	90.3	76.67	72.71	74.56	79.21	74.95	Orlando
149.35	86.6	84.92	88.2	74.89	71.02	72.83	77.36	73.21	St. Petersburg
138.68	80.42	78.86	81.9	69.54	65.95	67.63	71.84	67.98	Tallahassee
147.57	85.57	83.91	87.15	73.99	70.18	71.96	76.44	72.33	Tampa
									GEORGIA
152.91	88.67	86.95	90.3	76.67	72.71	74.56	79.21	74.95	Atlanta
140.46	81.45	79.87	82.95	70.43	66.79	68.49	72.76	68.85	Columbus
144.02	83.51	81.89	85.05	72.21	68.49	70.23	74.6	70.59	Macon
145.8	84.54	82.9	86.1	73.1	69.33	71.09	75.52	71.46	Savannah

Construction Costs by City (Con't)

Location	CCI	Apartment 1-3 Story	Church	College Classroom 2-3 Story	College Dorm 2-3 Story	College Laboratory	Fire Station 1 Story	Hospital 4-8 Story	Hotel 8-24 Story
HAWAII									
Honolulu	1.23	124.78	142.62	136.16	144.28	144.34	125.77	150.24	118.14
IDAHO									
Boise	0.94	95.36	108.99	104.06	110.26	110.31	96.12	114.82	90.29
ILLINOIS									
Bloomington	0.99	100.44	114.79	109.59	116.13	116.18	101.23	120.93	95.09
Champaign	1	101.45	115.95	110.7	117.3	117.35	102.25	122.15	96.05
Chicago	1.11	112.61	128.7	122.88	130.2	130.26	113.5	135.59	106.62
North Suburban	1.09	110.58	126.39	120.66	127.86	127.91	111.45	133.14	104.69
Peoria	1.01	102.46	117.11	111.81	118.47	118.52	103.27	123.37	97.01
Rockford	1.04	105.51	120.59	115.13	121.99	122.04	106.34	127.04	99.89
South Suburban	1.08	109.57	125.23	119.56	126.68	126.74	110.43	131.92	103.73
Springfield	0.98	99.42	113.63	108.49	114.95	115	100.21	119.71	94.13
INDIANA									
Bloomington	0.93	94.35	107.83	102.95	109.09	109.14	95.09	113.6	89.33
Columbus	0.92	93.33	106.67	101.84	107.92	107.96	94.07	112.38	88.37
Evansville	0.95	96.38	110.15	105.17	111.44	111.48	97.14	116.04	91.25
Fort Wayne	0.91	92.32	105.51	100.74	106.74	106.79	93.05	111.16	87.41
Gary	1.01	102.46	117.11	111.81	118.47	118.52	103.27	123.37	97.01
Indianapolis	0.95	96.38	110.15	105.17	111.44	111.48	97.14	116.04	91.25
South Bend	0.91	92.32	105.51	100.74	106.74	106.79	93.05	111.16	87.41
IOWA									
Cedar Rapids	0.92	93.33	106.67	101.84	107.92	107.96	94.07	112.38	88.37
Des Moines	0.92	93.33	106.67	101.84	107.92	107.96	94.07	112.38	88.37
Dubuque	0.89	90.29	103.2	98.52	104.4	104.44	91	108.71	85.48
KANSAS									
Kansas City	0.94	95.36	108.99	104.06	110.26	110.31	96.12	114.82	90.29
Topeka	0.85	86.23	98.56	94.1	99.71	99.75	86.91	103.83	81.64
Wichita	0.86	87.25	99.72	95.2	100.88	100.92	87.94	105.05	82.6
KENTUCKY									
Frankfort	0.87	88.26	100.88	96.31	102.05	102.09	88.96	106.27	83.56
Lexington	0.85	86.23	98.56	94.1	99.71	99.75	86.91	103.83	81.64
Louisville	0.92	93.33	106.67	101.84	107.92	107.96	94.07	112.38	88.37

Jail	Library	Nursing Home	Office 2-4 Story	Office 11-20 Story	Post Office	School Elementary	School High 2-3 Story	Store Department 3 Story	Location
									HAWAII
218.69	126.81	124.35	129.15	109.65	104	106.64	113.28	107.19	Honolulu
									IDAHO
167.13	96.91	95.03	98.7	83.8	79.48	81.5	86.57	81.92	Boise
									ILLINOIS
176.02	102.07	100.09	103.95	88.26	83.7	85.83	91.18	86.28	Bloomington
177.8	103.1	101.1	105	89.15	84.55	86.7	92.1	87.15	Champaign
197.36	114.44	112.22	116.55	98.96	93.85	96.24	102.23	96.74	Chicago
193.8	112.38	110.2	114.45	97.17	92.16	94.5	100.39	94.99	North Suburban
179.58	104.13	102.11	106.05	90.04	85.4	87.57	93.02	88.02	Peoria
184.91	107.22	105.14	109.2	92.72	87.93	90.17	95.78	90.64	Rockford
192.02	111.35	109.19	113.4	96.28	91.31	93.64	99.47	94.12	South Suburban
174.24	101.04	99.08	102.9	87.37	82.86	84.97	90.26	85.41	Springfield
									INDIANA
165.35	95.88	94.02	97.65	82.91	78.63	80.63	85.65	81.05	Bloomington
163.58	94.85	93.01	96.6	82.02	77.79	79.76	84.73	80.18	Columbus
168.91	97.95	96.05	99.75	84.69	80.32	82.37	87.5	82.79	Evansville
161.8	93.82	92	95.55	81.13	76.94	78.9	83.81	79.31	Fort Wayne
179.58	104.13	102.11	106.05	90.04	85.4	87.57	93.02	88.02	Gary
168.91	97.95	96.05	99.75	84.69	80.32	82.37	87.5	82.79	Indianapolis
161.8	93.82	92	95.55	81.13	76.94	78.9	83.81	79.31	South Bend
									IOWA
163.58	94.85	93.01	96.6	82.02	77.79	79.76	84.73	80.18	Cedar Rapids
163.58	94.85	93.01	96.6	82.02	77.79	79.76	84.73	80.18	Des Moines
158.24	91.76	89.98	93.45	79.34	75.25	77.16	81.97	77.56	Dubuque
									KANSAS
167.13	96.91	95.03	98.7	83.8	79.48	81.5	86.57	81.92	Kansas City
151.13	87.64	85.94	89.25	75.78	71.87	73.7	78.29	74.08	Topeka
152.91	88.67	86.95	90.3	76.67	72.71	74.56	79.21	74.95	Wichita
									KENTUCKY
154.69	89.7	87.96	91.35	77.56	73.56	75.43	80.13	75.82	Frankfort
151.13	87.64	85.94	89.25	75.78	71.87	73.7	78.29	74.08	Lexington
163.58	94.85	93.01	96.6	82.02	77.79	79.76	84.73	80.18	Louisville

Construction Costs by City (Con't)

Location	CCI	Apartment 1-3 Story	Church	College Classroom 2-3 Story	College Dorm 2-3 Story	College Laboratory	Fire Station 1 Story	Hospital 4-8 Story	Hotel 8-24 Story
LOUISIANA									
Baton Rouge	0.82	83.19	95.08	90.77	96.19	96.23	83.85	100.16	78.76
Lafayette	0.82	83.19	95.08	90.77	96.19	96.23	83.85	100.16	78.76
New Orleans	0.86	87.25	99.72	95.2	100.88	100.92	87.94	105.05	82.6
Shreveport	0.81	82.17	93.92	89.67	95.01	95.05	82.82	98.94	77.8
MAINE									
Bangor	0.92	93.33	106.67	101.84	107.92	107.96	94.07	112.38	88.37
Portland	0.9	91.31	104.36	99.63	105.57	105.62	92.03	109.94	86.45
MARYLAND									
Annapolis	0.9	91.31	104.36	99.63	105.57	105.62	92.03	109.94	86.45
Baltimore	0.92	93.33	106.67	101.84	107.92	107.96	94.07	112.38	88.37
MASSACHUSETTS									
Boston	1.15	116.67	133.34	127.31	134.9	134.95	117.59	140.47	110.46
Lowell	1.08	109.57	125.23	119.56	126.68	126.74	110.43	131.92	103.73
Springfield	1.02	103.48	118.27	112.91	119.65	119.7	104.3	124.59	97.97
Worcester	1.06	107.54	122.91	117.34	124.34	124.39	108.39	129.48	101.81
MICHIGAN									
Ann Arbor	1.04	105.51	120.59	115.13	121.99	122.04	106.34	127.04	99.89
Detroit	1.06	107.54	122.91	117.34	124.34	124.39	108.39	129.48	101.81
Flint	1	101.45	115.95	110.7	117.3	117.35	102.25	122.15	96.05
Grand Rapids	0.86	87.25	99.72	95.2	100.88	100.92	87.94	105.05	82.6
Lansing	0.98	99.42	113.63	108.49	114.95	115	100.21	119.71	94.13
MINNESOTA									
Bemidji	1	101.45	115.95	110.7	117.3	117.35	102.25	122.15	96.05
Duluth	1.07	108.55	124.07	118.45	125.51	125.56	109.41	130.7	102.77
Minneapolis	1.12	113.62	129.86	123.98	131.38	131.43	114.52	136.81	107.58
Rochester	1.03	104.49	119.43	114.02	120.82	120.87	105.32	125.81	98.93
Saint Paul	1.1	111.6	127.55	121.77	129.03	129.09	112.48	134.37	105.66
MISSISSIPPI									
Biloxi	0.81	82.17	93.92	89.67	95.01	95.05	82.82	98.94	77.8
Jackson	0.78	79.13	90.44	86.35	91.49	91.53	79.76	95.28	74.92
MISSOURI									
Kansas City	1	101.45	115.95	110.7	117.3	117.35	102.25	122.15	96.05

Jail	Library	Nursing Home	Office 2-4 Story	Office 11-20 Story	Post Office	School Elementary	School High 2-3 Story	Store Department 3 Story	Location
									LOUISIANA
145.8	84.54	82.9	86.1	73.1	69.33	71.09	75.52	71.46	Baton Rouge
145.8	84.54	82.9	86.1	73.1	69.33	71.09	75.52	71.46	Lafayette
152.91	88.67	86.95	90.3	76.67	72.71	74.56	79.21	74.95	New Orleans
144.02	83.51	81.89	85.05	72.21	68.49	70.23	74.6	70.59	Shreveport
									MAINE
163.58	94.85	93.01	96.6	82.02	77.79	79.76	84.73	80.18	Bangor
160.02	92.79	90.99	94.5	80.24	76.1	78.03	82.89	78.44	Portland
									MARYLAND
160.02	92.79	90.99	94.5	80.24	76.1	78.03	82.89	78.44	Annapolis
163.58	94.85	93.01	96.6	82.02	77.79	79.76	84.73	80.18	Baltimore
									MASSACHUSETTS
204.47	118.57	116.27	120.75	102.52	97.23	99.71	105.92	100.22	Boston
192.02	111.35	109.19	113.4	96.28	91.31	93.64	99.47	94.12	Lowell
181.36	105.16	103.12	107.1	90.93	86.24	88.43	93.94	88.89	Springfield
188.47	109.29	107.17	111.3	94.5	89.62	91.9	97.63	92.38	Worcester
									MICHIGAN
184.91	107.22	105.14	109.2	92.72	87.93	90.17	95.78	90.64	Ann Arbor
188.47	109.29	107.17	111.3	94.5	89.62	91.9	97.63	92.38	Detroit
177.8	103.1	101.1	105	89.15	84.55	86.7	92.1	87.15	Flint
152.91	88.67	86.95	90.3	76.67	72.71	74.56	79.21	74.95	Grand Rapids
174.24	101.04	99.08	102.9	87.37	82.86	84.97	90.26	85.41	Lansing
									MINNESOTA
177.8	103.1	101.1	105	89.15	84.55	86.7	92.1	87.15	Bemidji
190.25	110.32	108.18	112.35	95.39	90.47	92.77	98.55	93.25	Duluth
199.14	115.47	113.23	117.6	99.85	94.7	97.1	103.15	97.61	Minneapolis
183.13	106.19	104.13	108.15	91.82	87.09	89.3	94.86	89.76	Rochester
195.58	113.41	111.21	115.5	98.07	93.01	95.37	101.31	95.87	Saint Paul
									MISSISSIPPI
144.02	83.51	81.89	85.05	72.21	68.49	70.23	74.6	70.59	Biloxi
138.68	80.42	78.86	81.9	69.54	65.95	67.63	71.84	67.98	Jackson
									MISSOURI
177.8	103.1	101.1	105	89.15	84.55	86.7	92.1	87.15	Kansas City

Construction Costs by City (Con't)

Location	CCI	Apartment 1-3 Story	Church	College Classroom 2-3 Story	College Dorm 2-3 Story	College Laboratory	Fire Station 1 Story	Hospital 4-8 Story	Hotel 8-24 Story
Springfield	0.87	88.26	100.88	96.31	102.05	102.09	88.96	106.27	83.56
St. Louis	1.03	104.49	119.43	114.02	120.82	120.87	105.32	125.81	98.93
MONTANA									
Billings	0.96	97.39	111.31	106.27	112.61	112.66	98.16	117.26	92.21
Great Falls	0.96	97.39	111.31	106.27	112.61	112.66	98.16	117.26	92.21
NEBRASKA									
Lincoln	0.83	84.2	96.24	91.88	97.36	97.4	84.87	101.38	79.72
Omaha	0.91	92.32	105.51	100.74	106.74	106.79	93.05	111.16	87.41
NEVADA									
Las Vegas	1.05	106.52	121.75	116.24	123.17	123.22	107.36	128.26	100.85
Reno	1	101.45	115.95	110.7	117.3	117.35	102.25	122.15	96.05
NEW HAMPSHIRE									
Manchester	0.94	95.36	108.99	104.06	110.26	110.31	96.12	114.82	90.29
Portsmouth	0.91	92.32	105.51	100.74	106.74	106.79	93.05	111.16	87.41
NEW JERSEY									
Elizabeth	1.09	110.58	126.39	120.66	127.86	127.91	111.45	133.14	104.69
Jersey City	1.12	113.62	129.86	123.98	131.38	131.43	114.52	136.81	107.58
Newark	1.12	113.62	129.86	123.98	131.38	131.43	114.52	136.81	107.58
Paterson	1.12	113.62	129.86	123.98	131.38	131.43	114.52	136.81	107.58
Trenton	1.11	112.61	128.7	122.88	130.2	130.26	113.5	135.59	106.62
NEW MEXICO									
Albuquerque	0.91	92.32	105.51	100.74	106.74	106.79	93.05	111.16	87.41
Santa Fe	0.91	92.32	105.51	100.74	106.74	106.79	93.05	111.16	87.41
NEW YORK									
Albany	0.97	98.41	112.47	107.38	113.78	113.83	99.18	118.49	93.17
Brooklyn	1.3	131.89	150.74	143.91	152.49	152.56	132.93	158.8	124.87
Buffalo	1.02	103.48	118.27	112.91	119.65	119.7	104.3	124.59	97.97
New York	1.34	135.94	155.37	148.34	157.18	157.25	137.02	163.68	128.71
Rochester	1	101.45	115.95	110.7	117.3	117.35	102.25	122.15	96.05
Syracuse	0.96	97.39	111.31	106.27	112.61	112.66	98.16	117.26	92.21
Yonkers	1.2	121.74	139.14	132.84	140.76	140.82	122.7	146.58	115.26
NORTH CAROLINA									
Asheville	0.75	76.09	86.96	83.03	87.98	88.01	76.69	91.61	72.04

Jail	Library	Nursing Home	Office 2-4 Story	Office 11-20 Story	Post Office	School Elementary	School High 2-3 Story	Store Department 3 Story	Location
154.69	89.7	87.96	91.35	77.56	73.56	75.43	80.13	75.82	Springfield
183.13	106.19	104.13	108.15	91.82	87.09	89.3	94.86	89.76	St. Louis
									MONTANA
170.69	98.98	97.06	100.8	85.58	81.17	83.23	88.42	83.66	Billings
170.69	98.98	97.06	100.8	85.58	81.17	83.23	88.42	83.66	Great Falls
									NEBRASKA
147.57	85.57	83.91	87.15	73.99	70.18	71.96	76.44	72.33	Lincoln
161.8	93.82	92	95.55	81.13	76.94	78.9	83.81	79.31	Omaha
									NEVADA
186.69	108.26	106.16	110.25	93.61	88.78	91.04	96.71	91.51	Las Vegas
177.8	103.1	101.1	105	89.15	84.55	86.7	92.1	87.15	Reno
									NEW HAMPSHIRE
167.13	96.91	95.03	98.7	83.8	79.48	81.5	86.57	81.92	Manchester
161.8	93.82	92	95.55	81.13	76.94	78.9	83.81	79.31	Portsmouth
									NEW JERSEY
193.8	112.38	110.2	114.45	97.17	92.16	94.5	100.39	94.99	Elizabeth
199.14	115.47	113.23	117.6	99.85	94.7	97.1	103.15	97.61	Jersey City
199.14	115.47	113.23	117.6	99.85	94.7	97.1	103.15	97.61	Newark
199.14	115.47	113.23	117.6	99.85	94.7	97.1	103.15	97.61	Paterson
197.36	114.44	112.22	116.55	98.96	93.85	96.24	102.23	96.74	Trenton
									NEW MEXICO
161.8	93.82	92	95.55	81.13	76.94	78.9	83.81	79.31	Albuquerque
161.8	93.82	92	95.55	81.13	76.94	78.9	83.81	79.31	Santa Fe
									NEW YORK
172.47	100.01	98.07	101.85	86.48	82.01	84.1	89.34	84.54	Albany
231.14	134.03	131.43	136.5	115.9	109.92	112.71	119.73	113.3	Brooklyn
181.36	105.16	103.12	107.1	90.93	86.24	88.43	93.94	88.89	Buffalo
238.25	138.15	135.47	140.7	119.46	113.3	116.18	123.41	116.78	New York
177.8	103.1	101.1	105	89.15	84.55	86.7	92.1	87.15	Rochester
170.69	98.98	97.06	100.8	85.58	81.17	83.23	88.42	83.66	Syracuse
213.36	123.72	121.32	126	106.98	101.46	104.04	110.52	104.58	Yonkers
									NORTH CAROLINA
133.35	77.33	75.83	78.75	66.86	63.41	65.03	69.08	65.36	Asheville

Construction Costs by City (Con't)

Location	CCI	Apartment 1-3 Story	Church	College Classroom 2-3 Story	College Dorm 2-3 Story	College Laboratory	Fire Station 1 Story	Hospital 4-8 Story	Hotel 8-24 Story
Charlotte	0.75	76.09	86.96	83.03	87.98	88.01	76.69	91.61	72.04
Durham	0.76	77.1	88.12	84.13	89.15	89.19	77.71	92.83	73
Greensboro	0.76	77.1	88.12	84.13	89.15	89.19	77.71	92.83	73
Raleigh	0.77	78.12	89.28	85.24	90.32	90.36	78.73	94.06	73.96
Winston-Salem	0.76	77.1	88.12	84.13	89.15	89.19	77.71	92.83	73
NORTH DAKOTA									
Bismarck	0.85	86.23	98.56	94.1	99.71	99.75	86.91	103.83	81.64
Fargo	0.84	85.22	97.4	92.99	98.53	98.57	85.89	102.61	80.68
Grand Forks	0.83	84.2	96.24	91.88	97.36	97.4	84.87	101.38	79.72
OHIO									
Akron	1	101.45	115.95	110.7	117.3	117.35	102.25	122.15	96.05
Cincinnati	0.95	96.38	110.15	105.17	111.44	111.48	97.14	116.04	91.25
Cleveland	1.03	104.49	119.43	114.02	120.82	120.87	105.32	125.81	98.93
Columbus	0.96	97.39	111.31	106.27	112.61	112.66	98.16	117.26	92.21
Dayton	0.93	94.35	107.83	102.95	109.09	109.14	95.09	113.6	89.33
Toledo	0.99	100.44	114.79	109.59	116.13	116.18	101.23	120.93	95.09
Zanesville	0.91	92.32	105.51	100.74	106.74	106.79	93.05	111.16	87.41
OKLAHOMA									
Oklahoma City	0.83	84.2	96.24	91.88	97.36	97.4	84.87	101.38	79.72
Tulsa	0.82	83.19	95.08	90.77	96.19	96.23	83.85	100.16	78.76
OREGON									
Eugene	1.06	107.54	122.91	117.34	124.34	124.39	108.39	129.48	101.81
Portland	1.07	108.55	124.07	118.45	125.51	125.56	109.41	130.7	102.77
Salem	1.06	107.54	122.91	117.34	124.34	124.39	108.39	129.48	101.81
PENNSYLVANIA									
Allentown	1.01	102.46	117.11	111.81	118.47	118.52	103.27	123.37	97.01
Erie	0.97	98.41	112.47	107.38	113.78	113.83	99.18	118.49	93.17
Philadelphia	1.11	112.61	128.7	122.88	130.2	130.26	113.5	135.59	106.62
Pittsburgh	1.01	102.46	117.11	111.81	118.47	118.52	103.27	123.37	97.01
RHODE ISLAND									
Providence	1.04	105.51	120.59	115.13	121.99	122.04	106.34	127.04	99.89
SOUTH CAROLINA									
Charleston	0.76	77.1	88.12	84.13	89.15	89.19	77.71	92.83	73

Jail	Library	Nursing Home	Office 2-4 Story	Office 11-20 Story	Post Office	School Elementary	School High 2-3 Story	Store Department 3 Story	
133.35	77.33	75.83	78.75	66.86	63.41	65.03	69.08	65.36	Charlotte
135.13	78.36	76.84	79.8	67.75	64.26	65.89	70	66.23	Durham
135.13	78.36	76.84	79.8	67.75	64.26	65.89	70	66.23	Greensboro
136.91	79.39	77.85	80.85	68.65	65.1	66.76	70.92	67.11	Raleigh
135.13	78.36	76.84	79.8	67.75	64.26	65.89	70	66.23	Winston-Salem
									NORTH DAKOTA
151.13	87.64	85.94	89.25	75.78	71.87	73.7	78.29	74.08	Bismarck
149.35	86.6	84.92	88.2	74.89	71.02	72.83	77.36	73.21	Fargo
147.57	85.57	83.91	87.15	73.99	70.18	71.96	76.44	72.33	Grand Forks
									OHIO
177.8	103.1	101.1	105	89.15	84.55	86.7	92.1	87.15	Akron
168.91	97.95	96.05	99.75	84.69	80.32	82.37	87.5	82.79	Cincinnati
183.13	106.19	104.13	108.15	91.82	87.09	89.3	94.86	89.76	Cleveland
170.69	98.98	97.06	100.8	85.58	81.17	83.23	88.42	83.66	Columbus
165.35	95.88	94.02	97.65	82.91	78.63	80.63	85.65	81.05	Dayton
176.02	102.07	100.09	103.95	88.26	83.7	85.83	91.18	86.28	Toledo
161.8	93.82	92	95.55	81.13	76.94	78.9	83.81	79.31	Zanesville
									OKLAHOMA
147.57	85.57	83.91	87.15	73.99	70.18	71.96	76.44	72.33	Oklahoma City
145.8	84.54	82.9	86.1	73.1	69.33	71.09	75.52	71.46	Tulsa
									OREGON
188.47	109.29	107.17	111.3	94.5	89.62	91.9	97.63	92.38	Eugene
190.25	110.32	108.18	112.35	95.39	90.47	92.77	98.55	93.25	Portland
188.47	109.29	107.17	111.3	94.5	89.62	91.9	97.63	92.38	Salem
									PENNSYLVANIA
179.58	104.13	102.11	106.05	90.04	85.4	87.57	93.02	88.02	Allentown
172.47	100.01	98.07	101.85	86.48	82.01	84.1	89.34	84.54	Erie
197.36	114.44	112.22	116.55	98.96	93.85	96.24	102.23	96.74	Philadelphia
179.58	104.13	102.11	106.05	90.04	85.4	87.57	93.02	88.02	Pittsburgh
									RHODE ISLAND
184.91	107.22	105.14	109.2	92.72	87.93	90.17	95.78	90.64	Providence
									SOUTH CAROLINA
135.13	78.36	76.84	79.8	67.75	64.26	65.89	70	66.23	Charleston

Construction Costs by City (Con't)

Location	CCI	Apartment 1-3 Story	Church	College Classroom 2-3 Story	College Dorm 2-3 Story	College Laboratory	Fire Station 1 Story	Hospital 4-8 Story	Hotel 8-24 Story
Columbia	0.75	76.09	86.96	83.03	87.98	88.01	76.69	91.61	72.04
SOUTH DAKOTA									
Aberdeen	0.79	80.15	91.6	87.45	92.67	92.71	80.78	96.5	75.88
Rapid City	0.79	80.15	91.6	87.45	92.67	92.71	80.78	96.5	75.88
Sioux Falls	0.82	83.19	95.08	90.77	96.19	96.23	83.85	100.16	78.76
TENNESSEE									
Chattanooga	0.81	82.17	93.92	89.67	95.01	95.05	82.82	98.94	77.8
Knoxville	0.8	81.16	92.76	88.56	93.84	93.88	81.8	97.72	76.84
Memphis	0.86	87.25	99.72	95.2	100.88	100.92	87.94	105.05	82.6
Nashville	0.86	87.25	99.72	95.2	100.88	100.92	87.94	105.05	82.6
TEXAS									
Abilene	0.77	78.12	89.28	85.24	90.32	90.36	78.73	94.06	73.96
Amarillo	0.81	82.17	93.92	89.67	95.01	95.05	82.82	98.94	77.8
Austin	0.82	83.19	95.08	90.77	96.19	96.23	83.85	100.16	78.76
Corpus Christi	0.8	81.16	92.76	88.56	93.84	93.88	81.8	97.72	76.84
Dallas	0.85	86.23	98.56	94.1	99.71	99.75	86.91	103.83	81.64
El Paso	0.79	80.15	91.6	87.45	92.67	92.71	80.78	96.5	75.88
Fort Worth	0.83	84.2	96.24	91.88	97.36	97.4	84.87	101.38	79.72
Houston	0.88	89.28	102.04	97.42	103.22	103.27	89.98	107.49	84.52
Laredo	0.78	79.13	90.44	86.35	91.49	91.53	79.76	95.28	74.92
Lubbock	0.8	81.16	92.76	88.56	93.84	93.88	81.8	97.72	76.84
McAllen	0.77	78.12	89.28	85.24	90.32	90.36	78.73	94.06	73.96
San Antonio	0.83	84.2	96.24	91.88	97.36	97.4	84.87	101.38	79.72
Waco	0.8	81.16	92.76	88.56	93.84	93.88	81.8	97.72	76.84
Wichita Falls	0.8	81.16	92.76	88.56	93.84	93.88	81.8	97.72	76.84
UTAH									
Provo	0.9	91.31	104.36	99.63	105.57	105.62	92.03	109.94	86.45
Salt Lake City	0.9	91.31	104.36	99.63	105.57	105.62	92.03	109.94	86.45
VERMONT									
Burlington	0.86	87.25	99.72	95.2	100.88	100.92	87.94	105.05	82.6
Montpelier	0.84	85.22	97.4	92.99	98.53	98.57	85.89	102.61	80.68
VIRGINIA									
Alexandria	0.91	92.32	105.51	100.74	106.74	106.79	93.05	111.16	87.4

Jail	Library	Nursing Home	Office 2-4 Story	Office 11-20 Story	Post Office	School Elementary	School High 2-3 Story	Store Department 3 Story	Location
133.35	77.33	75.83	78.75	66.86	63.41	65.03	69.08	65.36	Columbia
									SOUTH DAKOTA
140.46	81.45	79.87	82.95	70.43	66.79	68.49	72.76	68.85	Aberdeen
140.46	81.45	79.87	82.95	70.43	66.79	68.49	72.76	68.85	Rapid City
145.8	84.54	82.9	86.1	73.1	69.33	71.09	75.52	71.46	Sioux Falls
									TENNESSEE
144.02	83.51	81.89	85.05	72.21	68.49	70.23	74.6	70.59	Chattanooga
142.24	82.48	80.88	84	71.32	67.64	69.36	73.68	69.72	Knoxville
152.91	88.67	86.95	90.3	76.67	72.71	74.56	79.21	74.95	Memphis
152.91	88.67	86.95	90.3	76.67	72.71	74.56	79.21	74.95	Nashville
									TEXAS
136.91	79.39	77.85	80.85	68.65	65.1	66.76	70.92	67.11	Abilene
144.02	83.51	81.89	85.05	72.21	68.49	70.23	74.6	70.59	Amarillo
145.8	84.54	82.9	86.1	73.1	69.33	71.09	75.52	71.46	Austin
142.24	82.48	80.88	84	71.32	67.64	69.36	73.68	69.72	Corpus Christi
151.13	87.64	85.94	89.25	75.78	71.87	73.7	78.29	74.08	Dallas
140.46	81.45	79.87	82.95	70.43	66.79	68.49	72.76	68.85	El Paso
147.57	85.57	83.91	87.15	73.99	70.18	71.96	76.44	72.33	Fort Worth
156.46	90.73	88.97	92.4	78.45	74.4	76.3	81.05	76.69	Houston
138.68	80.42	78.86	81.9	69.54	65.95	67.63	71.84	67.98	Laredo
142.24	82.48	80.88	84	71.32	67.64	69.36	73.68	69.72	Lubbock
136.91	79.39	77.85	80.85	68.65	65.1	66.76	70.92	67.11	McAllen
147.57	85.57	83.91	87.15	73.99	70.18	71.96	76.44	72.33	San Antonio
142.24	82.48	80.88	84	71.32	67.64	69.36	73.68	69.72	Waco
142.24	82.48	80.88	84	71.32	67.64	69.36	73.68	69.72	Wichita Falls
									UTAH
160.02	92.79	90.99	94.5	80.24	76.1	78.03	82.89	78.44	Provo
160.02	92.79	90.99	94.5	80.24	76.1	78.03	82.89	78.44	Salt Lake City
									VERMONT
152.91	88.67	86.95	90.3	76.67	72.71	74.56	79.21	74.95	Burlington
149.35	86.6	84.92	88.2	74.89	71.02	72.83	77.36	73.21	Montpelier
									VIRGINIA
161.8	93.82	92	95.55	81.13	76.94	78.9	83.81	79.31	Alexandria

Construction Costs by City (Con't)

Location	CCI	Apartment 1-3 Story	Church	College Classroom 2-3 Story	College Dorm 2-3 Story	College Laboratory	Fire Station 1 Story	Hospital 4-8 Story	Hotel 8-24 Story
Arlington	0.9	91.31	104.36	99.63	105.57	105.62	92.03	109.94	86.45
Fairfax	0.9	91.31	104.36	99.63	105.57	105.62	92.03	109.94	86.45
Fredericksburg	0.85	86.23	98.56	94.1	99.71	99.75	86.91	103.83	81.64
Newport News	0.82	83.19	95.08	90.77	96.19	96.23	83.85	100.16	78.76
Portsmouth	0.82	83.19	95.08	90.77	96.19	96.23	83.85	100.16	78.76
Richmond	0.84	85.22	97.4	92.99	98.53	98.57	85.89	102.61	80.68
WASHINGTON									
Seattle	1.04	105.51	120.59	115.13	121.99	122.04	106.34	127.04	99.89
Spokane	0.98	99.42	113.63	108.49	114.95	115	100.21	119.71	94.1
Tacoma	1.03	104.49	119.43	114.02	120.82	120.87	105.32	125.81	98.9
WEST VIRGINIA									
Charleston	0.94	95.36	108.99	104.06	110.26	110.31	96.12	114.82	90.29
Martinsburg	0.77	78.12	89.28	85.24	90.32	90.36	78.73	94.06	73.90
Morgantown	0.94	95.36	108.99	104.06	110.26	110.31	96.12	114.82	90.29
WISCONSIN									
Milwaukee	1	101.45	115.95	110.7	117.3	117.35	102.25	122.15	96.0
Green Bay	0.97	98.41	112.47	107.38	113.78	113.83	99.18	118.49	93.1
Madison	0.98	99.42	113.63	108.49	114.95	115	100.21	119.71	94.1
WYOMING									
Casper	0.83	84.2	96.24	91.88	97.36	97.4	84.87	101.38	79.7
Cheyenne	0.82	83.19	95.08	90.77	96.19	96.23	83.85	100.16	78.7
CANADA									
Calgary	0.97	98.41	112.47	107.38	113.78	113.83	99.18	118.49	93.1
Charlottetown	0.91	92.32	105.51	100.74	106.74	106.79	93.05	111.16	87.4
Edmonton	0.97	98.41	112.47	107.38	113.78	113.83	99.18	118.49	93.1
Halifax	0.96	97.39	111.31	106.27	112.61	112.66	98.16	117.26	92.2
Moncton	0.91	92.32	105.51	100.74	106.74	106.79	93.05	111.16	87.4
Montreal	1.03	104.49	119.43	114.02	120.82	120.87	105.32	125.81	98.9
Ottawa	1.07	108.55	124.07	118.45	125.51	125.56	109.41	130.7	102.7
Quebec	1.04	105.51	120.59	115.13	121.99	122.04	106.34	127.04	99.8
Regina	0.92	93.33	106.67	101.84	107.92	107.96	94.07	112.38	88.3
Saint John	0.95	96.38	110.15	105.17	111.44	111.48	97.14	116.04	91.2
Saskatoon	0.92	93.33	106.67	101.84	107.92	107.96	94.07	112.38	88.3

Jail	Library	Nursing Home	Office 2-4 Story	Office 11-20 Story	Post Office	School Elementary	School High 2-3 Story	Store Department 3 Story	Location
160.02	92.79	90.99	94.5	80.24	76.1	78.03	82.89	78.44	Arlington
160.02	92.79	90.99	94.5	80.24	76.1	78.03	82.89	78.44	Fairfax
151.13	87.64	85.94	89.25	75.78	71.87	73.7	78.29	74.08	Fredericksburg
145.8	84.54	82.9	86.1	73.1	69.33	71.09	75.52	71.46	Newport News
145.8	84.54	82.9	86.1	73.1	69.33	71.09	75.52	71.46	Portsmouth
149.35	86.6	84.92	88.2	74.89	71.02	72.83	77.36	73.21	Richmond
									WASHINGTON
184.91	107.22	105.14	109.2	92.72	87.93	90.17	95.78	90.64	Seattle
174.24	101.04	99.08	102.9	87.37	82.86	84.97	90.26	85.41	Spokane
183.13	106.19	104.13	108.15	91.82	87.09	89.3	94.86	89.76	Tacoma
									WEST VIRGINIA
167.13	96.91	95.03	98.7	83.8	79.48	81.5	86.57	81.92	Charleston
136.91	79.39	77.85	80.85	68.65	65.1	66.76	70.92	67.11	Martinsburg
167.13	96.91	95.03	98.7	83.8	79.48	81.5	86.57	81.92	Morgantown
									WISCONSIN
177.8	103.1	101.1	105	89.15	84.55	86.7	92.1	87.15	Milwaukee
172.47	100.01	98.07	101.85	86.48	82.01	84.1	89.34	84.54	Green Bay
174.24	101.04	99.08	102.9	87.37	82.86	84.97	90.26	85.41	Madison
									WYOMING
147.57	85.57	83.91	87.15	73.99	70.18	71.96	76.44	72.33	Casper
145.8	84.54	82.9	86.1	73.1	69.33	71.09	75.52	71.46	Cheyenne
									CANADA
172.47	100.01	98.07	101.85	86.48	82.01	84.1	89.34	84.54	Calgary
161.8	93.82	92	95.55	81.13	76.94	78.9	83.81	79.31	Charlottetown
172.47	100.01	98.07	101.85	86.48	82.01	84.1	89.34	84.54	Edmonton
170.69	98.98	97.06	100.8	85.58	81.17	83.23	88.42	83.66	Halifax
161.8	93.82	92	95.55	81.13	76.94	78.9	83.81	79.31	Moncton
183.13	106.19	104.13	108.15	91.82	87.09	89.3	94.86	89.76	Montreal
190.25	110.32	108.18	112.35	95.39	90.47	92.77	98.55	93.25	Ottawa
184.91	107.22	105.14	109.2	92.72	87.93	90.17	95.78	90.64	Quebec
163.58	94.85	93.01	96.6	82.02	77.79	79.76	84.73	80.18	Regina
168.91	97.95	96.05	99.75	84.69	80.32	82.37	87.5	82.79	Saint John
163.58	94.85	93.01	96.6	82.02	77.79	79.76	84.73	80.18	Saskatoon

Construction Costs by City (Con't)

Location	CCI	Apartment 1-3 Story	Church	College Classroom 2-3 Story	College Dorm 2-3 Story	College Laboratory	Fire Station 1 Story	Hospital 4-8 Story	Hotel 8-24 Story
St. John's	0.94	95.36	108.99	104.06	110.26	110.31	96.12	114.82	90.2
Thunder Bay	1.03	104.49	119.43	114.02	120.82	120.87	105.32	125.81	98.9
Toronto	1.11	112.61	128.7	122.88	130.2	130.26	113.5	135.59	106.6
Vancouver	1.07	108.55	124.07	118.45	125.51	125.56	109.41	130.7	102.7
Victoria	1.06	107.54	122.91	117.34	124.34	124.39	108.39	129.48	101.8
Winnipeg	0.97	98.41	112.47	107.38	113.78	113.83	99.18	118.49	93.1

Jail	Library	Nursing Home	Office 2-4 Story	Office 11-20 Story	Post Office	School Elementary	School High 2-3 Story	Store Department 3 Story	Location
67.13	96.91	95.03	98.7	83.8	79.48	81.5	86.57	81.92	St. John's
183.13	106.19	104.13	108.15	91.82	87.09	89.3	94.86	89.76	Thunder Bay
97.36	114.44	112.22	116.55	98.96	93.85	96.24	102.23	96.74	Toronto
90.25	110.32	108.18	112.35	95.39	90.47	92.77	98.55	93.25	Vancouver
88.47	109.29	107.17	111.3	94.5	89.62	91.9	97.63	92.38	Victoria
72.47	100.01	98.07	101.85	86.48	82.01	84.1	89.34	84.54	Winnipeg

Source: R.S. Means

Did you know...

In 1999, New York and Chicago were the only metropolitan areas with the majority of office space located in their primary downtown.

Source: The Brookings Institution

Expenditures to Owner-Occupied Residential Properties: 1993 to 1998 (Millions of dollars)

Type of job [1]	1993	1994	1995	1996	1997	1998
Total	72,882	81,737	78,583	80,070	85,305	90,20
Additions	11,519	8,793	6,576	10,276	8,838	8,8
Decks and porches	1,856	1,618	2,419	2,356	2,792	1,6
Attached garages	2,290	1,618	1,688	1,312	460	1,6
Rooms	7,372	5,556	2,468	6,608	5,587	5,4
Alterations	18,514	22,996	19,176	21,667	23,817	24,8
Plumbing	877	658	1,050	771	1,547	64
HVAC	955	1,591	1,232	1,940	1,902	1,68
Electrical	528	796	485	720	542	47
Flooring	1,791	2,202	2,000	2,952	2,508	3,2
Kitchen remodeling	1,564	1,379	1,716	2,038	3,141	2,5
Bathroom remodeling	2,246	3,643	2,501	2,609	3,675	4,74
Kitchen and bathroom remodeling	630	1,470	608	845	167	9
Finishing space	967	709	1,146	1,196	1,185	1,0
Interior restructuring	1,275	2,855	2,249	3,318	3,187	2,9
Siding	977	1,245	550	685	1,134	6
Windows and doors	848	703	359	538	605	4
Other alterations	5,858	5,746	5,280	4,055	4,224	5,35
Outside Additions and Alterations	6,516	8,904	8,221	8,387	8,424	9,07
Detached buildings	577	1,895	1,271	1,868	2,038	2,3
Patios and terraces	520	775	484	983	1,323	66
Driveways and walkways	818	468	814	497	1,209	1,3
Fences	1,176	1,280	1,447	1,419	1,524	1,5
Other outside additions and alterations	3,427	4,486	4,204	3,621	2,329	3,1
Major Replacements	14,200	15,869	18,348	18,053	17,600	21,5
Plumbing	1,655	1,811	1,997	1,312	1,516	1,12
HVAC	3,331	2,815	5,014	3,719	4,487	4,02
Siding	1,169	978	1,056	1,849	1,077	1,5
Roofing	3,006	4,030	4,176	5,212	5,312	6,44
Driveways and walkways	760	875	438	457	537	1,1
Windows	1,838	2,487	2,435	3,030	2,739	3,90
Doors	958	1,157	1,020	986	982	1,06
Other major replacements	1,484	1,716	2,213	1,489	950	2,25

Expenditures to Owner-Occupied Residential Properties: 1993 to 1998 (Con't)

Type of job [1]	1993	1994	1995	1996	1997	1998
Maintenance and Repairs	22,133	25,175	26,262	21,687	26,626	25,998
Painting and papering	6,833	6,669	6,660	7,247	7,748	8,641
Plumbing	2,002	2,945	2,281	2,285	2,618	2,240
HVAC	1,680	1,687	1,692	2,044	1,375	1,845
Electrical	483	551	615	418	503	493
Siding	584	497	587	241	706	298
Roofing	2,707	2,439	2,902	1,670	2,666	2,297
Flooring	774	1,490	1,417	1,093	1,638	826
Windows and doors	351	855	726	515	853	797
Materials to have on hand	1,965	2,270	1,990	2,650	2,726	3,234
Other maintenance and repairs	4,752	5,771	7,392	3,523	5,793	5,326

Note: Components may not add to totals because of rounding.
NA: Not applicable
[1] The expenditures given for each specified type of job consist of those outlays which have been identified as being primarily of the specified type. Thus, expenditures for one type of job done incidental to another type are included under the latter classification. For example, the relatively minor cost of painting done in conjunction with a roofing job is included in the roofing category.

Source U.S. Census Bureau

Did you know...

One in ten homeowners spends over $5,000 a year on remodeling.

Homeownership Rates (percentage)

	1900	1910	1920	1930	1940
U.S. Total	46.50	45.90	45.60	47.80	43.60
Alabama	34.40	35.10	35.00	34.20	33.60
Alaska	(N/A)	(N/A)	(N/A)	(N/A)	(N/A)
Arizona	57.50	49.20	42.80	44.80	47.90
Arkansas	47.70	46.60	45.10	40.10	39.70
California	46.30	49.50	43.70	46.10	43.40
Colorado	46.60	51.50	51.60	50.70	46.30
Connecticut	39.00	37.30	37.60	44.50	40.50
Delaware	36.30	40.70	44.70	52.10	47.10
District of Columbia	24.00	25.20	30.30	38.60	29.90
Florida	46.80	44.20	42.50	42.00	43.60
Georgia	30.60	30.50	30.90	30.60	30.80
Hawaii	(N/A)	(N/A)	(N/A)	(N/A)	(N/A)
Idaho	71.60	68.10	60.90	57.00	57.90
Illinois	45.00	44.10	43.80	46.50	40.30
Indiana	56.10	54.80	54.80	57.30	53.10
Iowa	60.50	58.40	58.10	54.70	51.50
Kansas	58.10	59.10	56.90	56.00	51.00
Kentucky	51.50	51.60	51.60	51.30	48.00
Louisiana	31.40	32.20	33.70	35.00	36.90
Maine	64.80	62.50	59.60	61.70	57.30
Maryland	40.00	44.00	49.90	55.20	47.40
Massachusetts	35.00	33.10	34.80	43.50	38.10
Michigan	62.30	61.70	58.90	59.00	55.40
Minnesota	63.50	61.90	60.70	58.90	55.20
Mississippi	34.50	34.00	34.00	32.50	33.30
Missouri	50.90	51.10	49.50	49.90	44.30
Montana	56.60	60.00	60.50	54.50	52.00
Nebraska	56.80	59.10	57.40	54.30	47.10
Nevada	66.20	53.40	47.60	47.10	46.10
New Hampshire	59.30	51.20	49.80	55.00	51.70
New Jersey	34.30	35.00	38.30	48.40	39.40
New Mexico	68.50	70.60	59.40	57.40	57.30
New York	33.20	31.00	30.70	37.10	30.30
North Carolina	46.60	47.30	47.40	44.50	42.40
North Dakota	80.00	75.70	65.30	58.60	49.80

1950	1960	1970	1980	1990	
55.00	61.90	62.90	64.40	64.20	**U.S. Total**
49.40	59.70	66.70	70.10	70.50	Alabama
54.50	48.30	50.30	58.30	56.10	Alaska
56.40	63.90	65.30	68.30	64.20	Arizona
54.50	61.40	66.70	70.50	69.60	Arkansas
54.50	61.40	54.90	55.90	55.60	California
58.10	63.80	63.40	64.50	62.20	Colorado
51.10	61.90	62.50	63.90	65.60	Connecticut
58.90	66.90	68.00	69.10	70.20	Delaware
32.30	30.00	28.20	35.50	38.90	District of Columbia
57.60	67.50	68.60	68.30	67.20	Florida
46.50	56.20	61.10	65.00	64.90	Georgia
33.00	41.10	46.90	51.70	53.90	Hawaii
65.50	70.50	70.10	72.00	70.10	Idaho
50.10	57.80	59.40	62.60	64.20	Illinois
65.50	71.10	71.70	71.70	70.20	Indiana
63.40	69.10	71.70	71.80	70.00	Iowa
63.90	68.90	69.10	70.20	67.90	Kansas
58.70	64.30	66.90	70.00	69.60	Kentucky
50.30	59.00	63.10	65.50	65.90	Louisiana
62.80	66.50	70.10	70.90	70.50	Maine
56.30	64.50	58.80	62.00	65.00	Maryland
47.90	55.90	57.50	57.50	59.30	Massachusetts
67.50	74.40	74.40	72.70	71.00	Michigan
66.40	72.10	71.50	71.70	71.80	Minnesota
47.80	57.70	66.30	71.00	71.50	Mississippi
57.70	64.30	67.20	69.90	68.80	Missouri
60.30	64.00	65.70	68.60	67.30	Montana
60.60	64.80	66.40	68.40	66.50	Nebraska
48.70	56.30	58.50	59.60	54.80	Nevada
58.10	65.10	68.20	67.60	68.20	New Hampshire
53.10	61.30	60.90	62.00	64.90	New Jersey
58.80	65.30	66.40	68.10	67.40	New Mexico
37.90	44.80	47.30	48.60	52.20	New York
53.30	60.10	65.40	68.40	68.00	North Carolina
66.20	68.40	68.40	68.70	65.60	North Dakota

Homeownership Rates (Con't)

	1900	1910	1920	1930	1940
Ohio	52.50	51.30	51.60	54.40	50.00
Oklahoma	54.20	45.40	45.50	41.30	42.80
Oregon	58.70	60.10	54.80	59.10	55.40
Pennsylvania	41.20	41.60	45.20	54.40	45.90
Rhode Island	28.60	28.30	31.10	41.20	37.40
South Carolina	30.60	30.80	32.20	30.90	30.60
South Dakota	71.20	68.20	61.50	53.10	45.00
Tennessee	46.30	47.00	47.70	46.20	44.10
Texas	46.50	45.10	42.80	41.70	42.80
Utah	67.80	64.80	60.00	60.90	61.10
Vermont	60.40	58.50	57.50	59.80	55.90
Virginia	48.80	51.50	51.10	52.40	48.90
Washington	54.50	57.30	54.70	59.40	57.00
West Virginia	54.60	49.50	46.80	45.90	43.70
Wisconsin	66.40	64.60	63.60	63.20	54.40
Wyoming	55.20	54.50	51.90	48.30	48.60

1950	1960	1970	1980	1990	
61.10	67.40	67.70	68.40	67.50	Ohio
60.00	67.00	69.20	70.70	68.10	Oklahoma
65.30	69.30	66.10	65.10	63.10	Oregon
59.70	68.30	68.80	69.90	70.60	Pennsylvania
45.30	54.50	57.90	58.80	59.50	Rhode Island
45.10	57.30	66.10	70.20	69.80	South Carolina
62.20	67.20	69.60	69.30	66.10	South Dakota
56.50	63.70	66.70	68.60	68.00	Tennessee
56.70	64.80	64.70	64.30	60.90	Texas
65.30	71.70	69.30	70.70	68.10	Utah
61.30	66.00	69.10	68.70	69.00	Vermont
55.10	61.30	62.00	65.60	66.30	Virginia
65.00	68.50	66.80	65.60	62.60	Washington
55.00	64.30	68.90	73.90	74.10	West Virginia
63.50	68.60	69.10	68.20	66.70	Wisconsin
54.00	62.20	66.40	69.20	67.80	Wyoming

Note: Alaska and Hawaii are NOT included in the 1950 US total.

Source: U.S. Census Bureau

Did you know...

According to Harvard University's Joint Center for Housing Studies, 40% of Americans over the age of 60 will move at least once.

Housing Characteristics: 1997 (percentage)

Housing Unit Characteristics	Total	Census Region			
		Northeast	Midwest	South	West
Total	100.0	100.0	100.0	100.0	100.0
Census Region and Division					
Northeast	19.4	100.0	-	-	-
New England	5.2	26.9	-	-	-
Middle Atlantic	14.2	73.1	-	-	-
Midwest	23.7	-	100.0	-	-
East North Central	16.7	-	70.3	-	-
West North Central	7.0	-	29.7	-	-
South	35.4	-	-	100.0	-
South Atlantic	18.4	-	-	52.1	-
East South Central	6.3	-	-	17.7	-
West South Central	10.7	-	-	30.2	-
West	21.5	-	-	-	100.0
Mountain	6.1	-	-	-	28.3
Pacific	15.4	-	-	-	71.7
Urban Status					
Urban	77.5	82.5	73.9	70.6	88.4
Central City	36.2	30.3	36.2	34.0	45.5
Suburban	41.2	52.2	37.7	36.6	42.9
Rural	22.5	17.5	26.1	29.4	11.6
Estimated Floorspace [1] (in square feet)					
Fewer than 600	7.8	9.7	6.9	5.7	10.3
600 to 900	21.2	22.4	21.3	19.0	23.4
1000 to 1,599	29.9	25.8	28.8	32.8	30.0
1,600 to 1,999	15.1	12.2	17.5	15.8	13.7
2,000 to 2,399	7.8	6.9	7.6	8.3	7.9
2,400 to 2,999	5.3	4.9	5.8	5.0	5.3
3,000 or more	4.1	3.4	4.1	5.1	3.0
No estimate provided	9.0	14.8	7.9	8.2	6.3

Housing Characteristics: 1997 (Con't)

Housing Unit Characteristics	Total	Census Region			
		Northeast	Midwest	South	West
Ownership of Unit					
Owned	67.4	64.6	71.8	70.7	59.8
Rented	32.6	35.4	28.2	29.3	40.2
Type and Ownership of Housing Unit					
Single-Family Detached	62.8	54.0	69.1	66.6	57.7
Owned	54.8	49.9	61.7	57.6	46.9
Rented	8.0	4.1	7.4	9.0	10.7
Single-Family Attached	9.8	15.6	7.6	7.7	10.6
Owned	5.4	9.7	3.9	4.8	4.2
Rented	4.4	5.9	3.7	2.8	6.4
Multifamily (2 to 4 units)	5.5	8.6	7.1	3.9	3.7
Owned	0.9	1.7	1.7	Q	Q
Rented	4.6	6.9	5.4	3.6	3.5
Multifamily (5 or more units)	15.6	19.3	11.7	13.4	20.1
Owned	1.1	1.5	Q	1.0	1.7
Rented	14.4	17.8	11.1	12.4	18.3
Mobile Home	6.2	2.5	4.6	8.3	8.0
Owned	5.2	1.8	4.0	6.9	6.7
Rented	1.0	Q	0.5	1.5	1.3
Year of Construction					
1939 or before	18.4	32.2	30.0	8.6	9.5
1940 to 1949	9.1	9.8	8.7	7.9	10.7
1950 to 1959	12.4	13.7	11.3	11.7	13.4
1960 to 1969	14.3	13.2	13.2	14.2	16.5
1970 to 1979	19.3	13.4	16.7	21.8	23.4
1980 to 1989	17.1	11.9	12.0	22.8	17.8
1990 to 1997 [2]	9.6	5.9	8.2	12.9	8.8
Observed Location of Household					
City	47.5	34.8	47.3	45.8	62.1
Town	17.9	26.2	18.8	14.8	14.8

Housing Characteristics: 1997 (Con't)

Housing Unit Characteristics	Total	Census Region			
		Northeast	Midwest	South	West
Suburbs	18.3	21.8	18.7	19.3	13.1
Rural or Open Country	16.2	17.2	15.1	20.1	10.0
Total Number of Rooms (Excluding Bathrooms)					
1 or 2	3.0	3.2	2.3	1.7	5.8
3	9.0	11.3	6.2	7.9	12.0
4	18.0	18.1	17.8	16.2	21.2
5	20.9	17.3	20.1	24.2	19.9
6	19.7	19.8	20.1	20.7	17.8
7	14.0	14.1	15.0	15.0	11.3
8	8.2	8.7	10.7	7.6	6.2
9 or more	6.9	7.4	7.8	6.8	5.8
Bedrooms					
None or 1	13.0	16.6	11.4	9.7	16.9
2	28.4	28.2	27.7	27.4	30.9
3	40.3	36.1	40.6	46.1	34.5
4 or More	18.3	19.1	20.4	16.8	17.7
Other Rooms (Excluding Bathrooms)					
None or 1	5.0	5.0	3.1	3.6	9.3
2	38.1	35.4	34.8	38.1	43.9
3	30.5	31.8	30.5	31.3	28.2
4	17.3	18.5	20.1	18.2	11.7
5 or More	9.1	9.3	11.5	8.1	6.9
Full Bathrooms					
None or 1	58.5	71.9	64.5	50.6	52.8
2	35.4	25.4	30.2	42.4	38.9
3 or More	6.1	2.7	5.4	7.0	8.3
Half Bathrooms					
None	72.0	66.4	68.7	74.0	77.2
1	26.1	30.9	28.9	24.5	21.5
2 or More	Q	Q	Q	Q	Q

Housing Characteristics: 1997 (Con't)

Housing Unit Characteristics	Total	Census Region			
		Northeast	Midwest	South	West
Number of Stories					
Single-Family Homes	72.7	69.7	76.7	74.3	68.2
1 Story	40.5	19.3	33.7	53.0	46.5
2 Stories	26.5	42.8	34.6	17.4	18.1
3 Stories	3.2	5.7	3.6	2.3	1.9
Split-Level	2.4	1.6	4.7	1.6	1.7
Other	Q	Q	Q	Q	Q
Mobile Homes	6.2	2.5	4.6	8.3	8.0
Foundation/Basement of Single-Family Homes (More than one may apply)					
Basement	32.7	57.1	58.6	13.7	13.3
Crawlspace	22.2	7.2	16.1	30.1	29.3
Concrete Slab	22.6	9.8	9.5	34.2	29.7
Not Asked (Mobile Homes and Multi-Family Units)	27.3	30.3	23.3	25.7	31.8
Garage/Carport					
Yes	53.7	47.4	62.1	48.3	58.9
1-Car Garage	16.0	22.9	17.3	13.0	13.3
2-Car Garage	29.2	21.5	38.0	24.2	34.7
3-Car Garage	2.7	1.9	4.6	1.2	3.8
Covered Carport	6.3	1.4	2.3	10.9	7.8
No	25.2	24.7	19.1	34.3	17.3
Not Asked (Apartments)	21.1	27.9	18.8	17.4	23.8
Main Heating Fuel					
Natural Gas	52.4	46.7	73.4	38.4	57.5
Electricity	29.6	12.2	12.4	48.7	33.0
Fuel Oil	9.2	35.0	4.3	3.2	1.0
LPG	4.4	1.2	7.1	5.5	2.6
Wood	2.2	2.2	1.9	1.9	3.1
Kerosene	0.9	1.9	Q	1.2	Q
Solar	Q	Q	Q	Q	Q
Other/None	0.3	0.7	Q	Q	Q

Estimated based on heated floorspace area.

Does not include all new construction for 1997.

Q: Data withheld either because the Relative Standard Error (RSE) was greater than 50 percent or fewer than 10 households were sampled.

Source: Energy Information Administration, Office of Energy Markets and End Use, 1997 Residential Energy Consumption Survey

Housing Density: 1940 to 1990

	Total Housing Units	Total Land Area (in square miles)	Housing Density (per square mile)	Total Population	Population Density (per square mile)
1990	102,263,678	3,536,338	28.9	248,709,873	70.3
1980	88,410,627	3,539,289	25.0	226,542,199	64.0
1970	68,704,315	3,536,855	19.4	203,302,031	57.5
1960	58,326,357	3,540,911	16.5	179,323,175	50.6
1950	46,137,076	3,550,206	13.0	151,325,798	42.6
1940	37,438,714	3,554,608	10.5	132,164,569	37.2

Source: US Census Bureau

Interior Design Firm Profiles by State: 1997

	Number of Establishments	Receipts ($1,000)	Annual Payroll ($1,000)	Paid Employees [1]
U.S Total	9,612	4,945,340	1,021,531	33,915
Alabama	126	41,901	5,695	338
Alaska	9	5,249	1,131	40
Arizona	169	88,732	14,273	465
Arkansas	35	D	D	c
California	1,122	791,655	171,073	5,169
Colorado	228	112,807	20,557	729
Connecticut	132	78,739	18,181	479
Delaware	24	D	D	c
District of Columbia	51	62,038	20,540	377
Florida	1,096	566,916	88,792	3,363
Georgia	349	210,603	48,584	1,380
Hawaii	28	D	D	b
Idaho	31	18,860	2,023	118
Illinois	533	266,766	68,911	1,978
Indiana	170	55,904	10,743	520
Iowa	55	15,975	2,301	117
Kansas	66	D	D	c
Kentucky	90	28,226	4,951	259
Louisiana	93	33,153	6,127	325
Maine	24	D	D	b
Maryland	199	82,918	17,592	591
Massachusetts	213	122,184	29,392	812
Michigan	287	107,290	19,969	841
Minnesota	178	82,482	16,618	562
Mississippi	49	12,652	1,415	126
Missouri	183	64,571	14,242	573
Montana	18	D	D	b
Nebraska	43	18,844	3,720	225
Nevada	87	46,674	9,635	326
New Hampshire	27	9,214	1,687	58

Interior Design Firm Profiles by State: 1997 (Con't)

	Number of Establishments	Receipts ($1,000)	Annual Payroll ($1,000)	Paid Employees [1]
New Jersey	276	117,941	21,140	715
New Mexico	31	8,426	1,454	69
New York	878	638,212	144,230	3,328
North Carolina	307	118,018	19,037	807
North Dakota	14	3,736	580	49
Ohio	337	162,636	34,824	1,306
Oklahoma	94	28,930	5,286	240
Oregon	107	43,064	7,100	310
Pennsylvania	281	141,426	33,193	1,132
Rhode Island	36	15,388	4,755	173
South Carolina	105	42,192	6,150	317
South Dakota	12	2,219	281	22
Tennessee	136	68,323	12,391	458
Texas	649	323,655	70,325	2,464
Utah	65	30,098	4,435	222
Vermont	18	5,373	1,864	63
Virginia	250	79,247	20,224	812
Washington	151	60,898	12,075	465
West Virginia	21	6,568	1,358	84
Wisconsin	121	48,201	9,203	459
Wyoming	8	1,173	164	10

1 Paid employees for the pay period including March 12
D: Withheld to avoid disclosing data of individual companies
b: 20 to 99 employees
c: 100 to 249 employees

Source: U.S. Census Bureau, 1997 Economic Census

Metro Areas Adding More Than 25% to their Housing Stocks: 1990-1998 (in thousands)

	Total Permits 1990-98	1990 Housing Stock	Permits as share of 1990 stock (%)
Las Vegas, NV	233.6	376.1	62.1
Naples, FL	44.1	94.2	46.9
Provo, UT	28.4	72.8	38.9
Boise City, ID	44.2	114.0	38.8
Laredo, TX	12.9	37.2	34.7
Wilmington, NC	30.2	94.2	32.1
Raleigh-Durham, NC	113.8	359.3	31.7
Orlando, FL	163.2	524.2	31.1
Atlanta, GA	361.0	1224.4	29.5
Fort Collins, CO	22.8	77.8	29.3
Greenville, NC	12.5	43.1	28.9
Fayetteville, AR	25.5	88.8	28.7
Myrtle Beach, SC	25.2	90.0	28.0
Lawrence, KS	8.9	31.8	28.0
Phoenix, AZ	278.2	1004.8	27.7
Fort Walton Beach, FL	16.9	62.6	27.0
Clarksville, TN	16.4	60.7	27.0
Columbia, MO	12.0	44.7	26.7
Charlotte, NC	124.1	472.9	26.2
McAllen, TX	32.9	128.2	25.7
Reno, NV	28.6	112.2	25.5
Bellingham, WA	14.2	55.7	25.5
Fort Myers, FL	47.6	189.1	25.2

Note: The above metropolitan areas are defined by the Office of Management and Budget.

Sources: Joint Center for Housing Studies, Census Bureau, Construction Reports C-40, and 1990 Decennial Census

Metro Areas With More Than 200,000 Housing Permits Issued : 1990-1998 (in thousands)

	Total Permits 1990-98	Total 1990 Population	Total Permits per 1,000 Population
Las Vegas, NV	233.6	852.6	274.0
Phoenix, AZ	278.2	2,238.50	124.3
Atlanta, GA	361	2,959.50	122.0
Seattle, WA	226.6	2,970.30	76.3
Dallas, TX	296.4	4,037.30	73.4
Washington, DC	379.9	6,726.40	56.5
Houston, TX	210.4	3,731.00	56.4
Detroit, MI	201.1	5,187.20	38.8
Chicago, IL	314.2	8,239.80	38.1
Los Angeles, CA	351.8	14,531.50	24.2
New York, NY	321.3	19,565.40	16.4

Note: The above metropolitan areas are defined by the Office of Management and Budget.

Sources: Joint Center for Housing Studies, Census Bureau, Construction Reports C-40, and Metropolitan and County Population Estimates

If I were asked to name the chief benefits of the house I should say: the house shelters daydreaming, the house protects the dreamer, the house allows one to dream in peace.

Gaston Bachelard

Number of Licensed Landscape Architects by State

The number of licensed landscape architects in a state is determined by both the number of registered landscape architects who are residents and those who are registered as reciprocal or out-of-state registrants. Based on current population levels, the chart below also provides the number of resident landscape architects per 100,000 of population in each state.

State	Resident	Non-Resident	Total	Population [1]	# Resident Arch. Per 100,000
Alabama	104	97	201	4,351,999	2
Alaska	253	364	617	614,010	41
Arizona	253	364	617	4,668,361	5
Arkansas	484	778	1,262	2,538,303	19
California	16,415	4,476	20,891	32,666,550	50
Colorado	2,603	3,135	5,738	3,970,971	66
Connecticut	1,391	7,879	9,270	3,274,069	42
Delaware	120	1,009	1,129	743,603	16
D.C.	546	2,632	3,178	523,124	104
Florida	4,477	3,526	8,003	14,915,980	30
Georgia	2,232	2,665	4,897	7,642,207	29
Hawaii	977	814	1,791	1,193,001	82
Idaho	490	1,312	1,802	1,228,684	40
Illinois	5,475	3,686	9,161	12,045,326	45
Indiana	1,095	3,248	4,343	5,899,195	19
Iowa	419	1,018	1,437	2,862,447	15
Kansas	980	1,496	2,476	2,629,067	37
Kentucky	701	1,757	2,458	3,936,499	18
Louisiana	1,123	1,509	2,632	4,368,967	26
Maine	327	796	1,123	1,244,250	26
Maryland	1,658	2,826	4,484	5,134,808	32
Massachusetts	3,290	2,698	5,988	6,147,132	54
Michigan	2,472	2,378	4,850	9,817,242	25
Minnesota	1,762	1,445	3,207	4,725,419	37
Mississippi	271	973	1,244	2,752,092	10
Missouri	1,854	2,374	4,228	5,438,559	34

Number of Licensed Landscape Architects by State (Con't)

State	Resident	Non-Resident	Total	Population [1]	# Resident Arch. Per 100,000
Montana	349	655	1,004	880,453	40
Nebraska	546	944	1,490	1,662,719	33
Nevada	446	1,928	2,374	1,746,898	26
New Hampshire	252	764	1,016	1,185,048	21
New Jersey	2,400	4,600	7,000	8,115,011	30
New Mexico	725	1,291	2,016	1,736,931	42
New York	8,000	5,000	13,000	18,175,301	44
North Carolina	1,860	2,626	4,486	7,546,493	25
North Dakota	125	375	500	638,244	20
Ohio	3,521	2,881	6,402	11,209,493	31
Oklahoma	749	1,240	1,989	3,346,713	22
Oregon	1,399	1,150	2,549	3,281,974	43
Pennsylvania	3,595	3,536	7,131	12,001,451	30
Rhode Island	257	1,011	1,268	988,480	26
South Carolina	950	2,038	2,988	3,835,962	25
South Dakota	111	559	670	738,171	15
Tennessee	1,600	1,590	3,190	5,430,621	29
Texas	6,825	3,187	10,012	19,759,614	35
Utah	837	800	1,637	2,099,758	40
Vermont	294	524	818	590,883	50
Virginia	2,306	3,121	5,427	6,791,345	34
Washington	3,290	1,627	4,917	5,689,263	58
West Virginia	130	920	1,050	1,811,156	7
Wisconsin	1,502	2,815	4,317	5,223,500	29
Wyoming	112	724	836	480,907	23
Totals	**96,966**	**105,466**	**202,432**	**270,298,254**	

[1] 1998 Population Estimate from the U.S. Census Bureau

Source: Council of Landscape Architectural Registration Boards

Number of Months From Start to Completion of New One-Family Houses (Average)

Year	United States	Region				Construction Purpose		
		Northeast	Midwest	South	West	Built for Sale	Contractor	Owner
1989	6.4	9.3	5.8	5.6	6.5	5.9	5.3	10.2
1990	6.4	9.3	5.6	5.7	6.9	5.9	5.3	10.3
1991	6.3	8.9	5.6	5.5	6.9	5.6	5.1	10.2
1992	5.8	7.6	5.6	5.1	6.1	5.0	5.0	9.5
1993	5.6	7.2	5.5	5.2	6.0	4.9	5.4	9.0
1994	5.6	7.1	5.7	5.3	5.6	4.9	5.3	9.1
1995	5.9	7.4	6.0	5.4	6.0	5.2	5.8	9.5
1996	6.0	8.2	6.1	5.6	5.6	5.2	5.8	9.9
1997	6.0	7.3	6.2	5.6	5.8	5.2	5.9	9.8
1998	6.0	7.1	6.2	5.5	6.1	5.4	6.0	9.5
1999	6.2	7.1	7.0	5.7	6.3	5.6	6.4	9.6

Source: US Census Bureau

Did you know...

7.5 million or approximately 7% of American homes are equipped with some degree of computer networking that automates security, entertainment, lighting, mechanical systems, and/or climate control – an increase from 2 million in 1995.

Number of New Privately Owned Housing Units Completed
(in thousands of units)

Period	Total	In structures with-			
		I unit	2 units	3 and 4 units	5 units or more
1989	1,422.8	1,026.3	24.1	34.6	337.9
1990	1,308.0	966.0	16.5	28.2	297.3
1991	1,090.8	837.6	16.9	19.7	216.6
1992	1,157.5	963.6	15.1	20.8	158.0
1993	1,192.7	1,039.4	9.5	16.7	127.1
1994	1,346.9	1,160.3	12.1	19.5	154.9
1995	1,312.6	1,065.5	14.8	19.8	212.4
1996	1,412.9	1,128.5	13.6	19.5	251.3
1997	1,400.5	1,116.4	13.6	23.4	247.1
1998	1,474.2	1,159.7	16.2	24.4	273.9
1999	1,636.1	1,307.2	12.0	25.2	291.8

Did you know...

During the last three decades, the average residential floor area per person rose 77% from 427 to 756 square feet.

Period	Inside MSAS[1]	Outside MSAS[1]	Northeast	Midwest	South	West
1989	1,181.20	241.7	218.8	267.1	549.4	387.5
1990	1,060.20	247.7	157.7	263.3	510.7	376.3
1991	862.1	228.7	120.1	240.4	438.9	291.3
1992	909.5	248	136.4	268.4	462.4	290.3
1993	943	249.8	117.6	273.3	512	290
1994	1,086.30	260.6	123.4	307.1	580.9	335.5
1995	1,065.00	247.6	126.9	287.9	581.1	316.7
1996	1,163.40	249.4	125.1	304.5	637.1	346.2
1997	1,152.80	247.7	134	295.9	634.1	336.4
1998	1,228.50	245.7	137.3	305.1	671.6	360.2
1999	1,378.10	258	145.4	337.5	750.4	402.7

Note: Detail may not add to total because of rounding.
N/A: Not available.
[1] Metropolitan statistical areas.

Source: U.S. Census Bureau

Number of Registered Architects by State

Registered architects in each state can be divided into two categories - those who are residents and reciprocal or out-of-state registrants. Based on current population levels, the chart below also calculates the number of resident architects per 100,000 of population in each state.

State	Resident Architects	Reciprocal Registrations	Total	Population [1]	# Resident Architects per 100,000 Population
Alabama	718	979	1,697	4,351,999	16
Alaska	300	204	504	614,010	49
Arizona	1,975	3,300	5,275	4,668,361	42
Arkansas	484	778	1,262	2,538,303	19
California	16,415	4,476	20,891	32,666,550	50
Colorado	2,603	3,135	5,738	3,970,971	66
Connecticut	1,391	7,879	9,270	3,274,069	42
Delaware	120	1,009	1,129	743,603	16
D.C.	546	2,632	3,178	523,124	104
Florida	4,477	3,526	8,003	14,915,980	30
Georgia	2,232	2,665	4,897	7,642,207	29
Hawaii	977	814	1,791	1,193,001	82
Idaho	490	1,312	1,802	1,228,684	40
Illinois	5,475	3,686	9,161	12,045,326	45
Indiana	1,095	3,248	4,343	5,899,195	19
Iowa	419	1,018	1,437	2,862,447	15
Kansas	980	1,496	2,476	2,629,067	37
Kentucky	701	1,757	2,458	3,936,499	18
Louisiana	1,123	1,509	2,632	4,368,967	26
Maine	327	796	1,123	1,244,250	26
Maryland	1,658	2,826	4,484	5,134,808	32
Massachusetts	3,290	2,698	5,988	6,147,132	54
Michigan	2,472	2,378	4,850	9,817,242	25
Minnesota	1,762	1,445	3,207	4,725,419	37
Mississippi	271	973	1,244	2,752,092	10
Missouri	1,854	2,374	4,228	5,438,559	34
Montana	349	655	1,004	880,453	40
Nebraska	546	944	1,490	1,662,719	33
Nevada	446	1,928	2,374	1,746,898	26

Number of Registered Architects by State (Con't)

State	Resident Architects	Reciprocal Registrations	Total	Population [1]	# Resident Architects per 100,000 Population
New Hampshire	252	764	1,016	1,185,048	21
New Jersey	2,400	4,600	7,000	8,115,011	30
New Mexico	725	1,291	2,016	1,736,931	42
New York	8,000	5,000	13,000	18,175,301	44
North Carolina	1,860	2,626	4,486	7,546,493	25
North Dakota	125	375	500	638,244	20
Ohio	3,521	2,881	6,402	11,209,493	31
Oklahoma	749	1,240	1,989	3,346,713	22
Oregon	1,399	1,150	2,549	3,281,974	43
Pennsylvania	3,595	3,536	7,131	12,001,451	30
Rhode Island	257	1,011	1,268	988,480	26
South Carolina	950	2,038	2,988	3,835,962	25
South Dakota	111	559	670	738,171	15
Tennessee	1,600	1,590	3,190	5,430,621	29
Texas	6,825	3,187	10,012	19,759,614	35
Utah	837	800	1,637	2,099,758	40
Vermont	294	524	818	590,883	50
Virginia	2,306	3,121	5,427	6,791,345	34
Washington	3,290	1,627	4,917	5,689,263	58
West Virginia	130	920	1,050	1,811,156	7
Wisconsin	1,502	2,815	4,317	5,223,500	29
Wyoming	112	724	836	480,907	23
Totals	**96,336**	**104,819**	**201,155**	**270,298,254**	

[1] 1998 Population Estimate from the U.S. Census Bureau

Source: National Council of Architectural Registration Boards

Office Building Vacancy Rates: 1980 to 1998

	1980	1985	1990	1991	1992
Total [1]	4.6	16.9	20.0	20.2	20.5
Atlanta, GA	10.0	21.0	19.1	19.5	19.4
Baltimore, MD	7.2	11.5	20.0	21.0	20.6
Boston, MA	3.8	13.1	19.6	19.1	17.5
Charlotte, NC	(N/A)	16.7	16.5	19.4	(N/A)
Chicago, IL	7.0	16.5	18.6	20.0	22.1
Cincinnati, OH	(N/A)	(N/A)	(N/A)	(N/A)	19.4
Dallas, TX	8.6	23.0	25.8	26.0	31.3
Denver, CO	6.6	24.7	24.8	23.0	21.5
Detroit, MI	(N/A)	(N/A)	(N/A)	(N/A)	(N/A)
Fort Lauderdale, FL	(N/A)	(N/A)	23.0	24.9	22.9
Houston, TX	4.0	27.6	24.9	27.3	27.0
Indianapolis, IN	(N/A)	(N/A)	21.2	21.4	22.4
Los Angeles, CA	0.9	15.3	16.8	20.2	21.2
Memphis, TN	(N/A)	(N/A)	(N/A)	(N/A)	(N/A)
Miami, FL	2.4	20.9	23.4	22.6	18.5
Minneapolis, MN	(N/A)	(N/A)	(N/A)	18.9	19.9
Nashville, TN	(N/A)	(N/A)	25.1	18.4	(N/A)
New Jersey (Central)	(N/A)	(N/A)	(N/A)	(N/A)	(N/A)
New Jersey (North)	(N/A)	(N/A)	(N/A)	(N/A)	(N/A)
New York, NY [2]	3.1	7.9	16.0	18.8	18.3
Orlando, FL	(N/A)	(N/A)	(N/A)	(N/A)	(N/A)
Philadelphia, PA	6.3	14.5	18.2	17.3	19.0
Phoenix, AZ	(N/A)	(N/A)	27.6	24.8	24.4
Pittsburgh, PA	1.2	(N/A)	16.3	14.2	(N/A)
Portland, OR	(N/A)	(N/A)	(N/A)	(N/A)	14.5
Raleigh, NC	(N/A)	(N/A)	(N/A)	(N/A)	(N/A)
Richmond, VA	(N/A)	(N/A)	(N/A)	(N/A)	(N/A)
Sacramento, CA	(N/A)	(N/A)	(N/A)	(N/A)	(N/A)
San Diego, CA	(N/A)	24.7	19.5	23,7	23.8
San Francisco, CA	0.3	13.7	14.7	13.3	12.5
Seattle, WA	(N/A)	(N/A)	12.3	12.8	15.9
Silicon Valley, CA	(N/A)	(N/A)	(N/A)	(N/A)	(N/A)
St. Louis, MO	(N/A)	(N/A)	21.0	20.5	21.8
St Paul, MN	(N/A)	(N/A)	(N/A)	19.7	18.5
Tampa/St. Petersburg, FL	(N/A)	(N/A)	(N/A)	(N/A)	(N/A)
Washington, DC	2.5	9.0	19.0	17.6	15.4
West Palm Beach, CA	(N/A)	(N/A)	(N/A)	(N/A)	(N/A)
Wilmington, DE	(N/A)	(N/A)	20.3	21.0	19.8
Winston-Salem/Greensboro, NC	(N/A)	(N/A)	(N/A)	(N/A)	(N/A)

[1] Includes other North American markets not shown separately. In 1998, 45 markets were covered.
[2] Refers to Manhattan

1993	1994	1995	1996	1997	1998	
19.4	16.2	14.3	12.4	10.4	9.7	Total [1]
16.8	13.0	10.4	9.2	10.5	11.2	Atlanta, GA
17.3	15.5	17.0	14.3	11.6	10.0	Baltimore, MD
17.7	13.3	10.4	6.2	4.4	7.1	Boston, MA
(N/A)	10.0	8.9	8.2	7.1	7.2	Charlotte, NC
21.4	18.7	15.5	15.5	(NA)	14.4	Chicago, IL
(N/A)	15.3	(N/A)	13.1	11.5	9.9	Cincinnati, OH
29.5	21.7	18.7	16.2	14.7	15.0	Dallas, TX
15.9	12.8	12.1	10.8	9.3	7.6	Denver, CO
21.4	19.7	16.9	11.1	8.5	6.9	Detroit, MI
(N/A)	10.8	(N/A)	10.5	10.4	10.0	Fort Lauderdale, FL
25.1	24.7	21.9	17.5	12.1	10.7	Houston, TX
18.8	18.4	14.3	(N/A)	14.2	11.2	Indianapolis, IN
21.0	19.6	23.2	22.1	13.8	14.2	Los Angeles, CA
(N/A)	(N/A)	(N/A)	13.6	12.0	12.5	Memphis, TN
19.0	15.4	13.8	12.4	11.2	11.4	Miami, FL
(N/A)	8.2	(N/A)	6.5	6.2	7.0	Minneapolis, MN
(N/A)	7.5	(N/A)	6.9	6.0	7.5	Nashville, TN
(N/A)	20.7	(N/A)	16.0	11.2	9.9	New Jersey (Central)
(N/A)	16.5	(N/A)	14.5	11.9	10.0	New Jersey (North)
17.9	16.3	17.0	16.0	(N/A)	8.6	New York, NY [2]
(N/A)	12.1	(N/A)	6.5	6.4	7.1	Orlando, FL
17.8	16.3	16.2	13.7	10.9	12.4	Philadelphia, PA
(N/A)	11.8	(N/A)	11.5	9.3	8.9	Phoenix, AZ
17.0	15.8	14.5	(N/A)	15.4	14.0	Pittsburgh, PA
(N/A)	9.4	(N/A)	5.8	5.6	(NA)	Portland, OR
(N/A)	(N/A)	(N/A)	(N/A)	(N/A)	6.0	Raleigh, NC
(N/A)	11.9	(N/A)	9.7	9.7	10.7	Richmond, VA
(N/A)	14.1	(N/A)	12.4	12.3	11.8	Sacramento, CA
22.1	18.8	17.4	14.1	10.1	9.1	San Diego, CA
13.7	11.7	10.2	5.4	4.0	(NA)	San Francisco, CA
17.6	14.7	7.1	5.3	4.5	(NA)	Seattle, WA
(N/A)	12.7	(N/A)	8.7	5.8	8.3	Silicon Valley, CA
19.1	18.1	12.7	13.4	12.3	9.6	St. Louis, MO
(N/A)	15.2	(N/A)	12.5	9.9	7.2	St Paul, MN
(N/A)	(N/A)	(N/A)	13.0	9.1	8.8	Tampa/St. Petersburg, FL
14.1	13.4	10.8	9.3	8.0	5.8	Washington, DC
(N/A)	16.8	(N/A)	12.0	12.3	13.5	West Palm Beach, CA
(N/A)	16.7	(N/A)	9.5	9.7	8.7	Wilmington, DE
(N/A)	13.2	(N/A)	14.1	12.3	14.5	Winston-Salem/Greensboro, NC

Source: ONCOR International, Houston, TX, 1980 and 1985, National Office Market Report, semi-annual; 1989-1990, International Office Market Report, semi-annual; thereafter, Year-End (year) Market Data Book, annual (copyright).

Salary and Compensation Guide

Each year Greenway Consulting tracks the hiring of design professionals and reviews compensation packages for marketplace competitiveness. The following cash compensation figures reflect actual base salaries and incentive compensation for positions filled or adjusted in each category since January 2000 based on Greenway's research and experience. All figures include bonus and profit sharing unless otherwise indicated. Approximately 75% of Principals received a bonus in the last fiscal year. The national average information is derived from a composite of research information from association and industry surveys and updated based upon Greenway's specific national experience. Greenway Consulting estimates that 2001 cash compensation will increase 4.75% depending on regional economies, building segment strength factors, and micro economy fluctuations in the design disciplines.

For further information, contact Greenway Consulting at (770) 209-3770, The American Institute of Architects at (202) 626-7300, the International Interior Design Association at (312) 467-1950, and the Industrial Designers Society of America at (703) 759-0100.

Intern Architects

Minneapolis	$34,450
Memphis	$32,000
Los Angeles	$44,000
Washington DC	$42,500
Atlanta	$36,000
National Average	$35,500

Architects – 5 Years Experience

Seattle	$48,200
Phoenix	$44,000
New York City	$52,000
Boston	$47,450
Sioux Falls	$36,200
National Average	$45,000

Architects – 10 Years Experience

Detroit	$56,500
Miami	$51,000
Atlanta	$49,800
Minneapolis	$75,500
New Orleans	$52,000
National Average	$56,500

Architects – 15 Years Experience

Omaha	$67,000
Minneapolis	$69,000
Nashville	$57,500
Washington DC	$90,000
Denver	$73,500
National Average	$68,000

Architect/Principal/Owner – Small Sole Proprietorship

Des Moines	$120,000
Los Angeles	$168,000
Miami	$95,000
Chicago	$135,000
Boise	$104,000
National Average	$102,000

Salary and Compensation Guide (Con't)

Interior Designer — 10-15 Years Experience

Minneapolis	$49,000
Atlanta	$55,000
New York City	$57,500
Washington DC	$67,000
Seattle	$54,750
National Average	$55,500

Interior Designer – Principal

Sacramento	$88,000
Los Angeles	$134,000
Kansas City	$85,000
New York City	$158,000
Boston	$150,000
National Average	$98,000

Design Technology Supervisor

New York City	$67,000
Washington DC	$75,000
Charlotte	$55,000
San Francisco	$73,500
Portland	$62,500
National Average	$58,000

Industrial Designer/Product Designer in Private Practice

Chicago	$65,000
Palo Alto	$73,000
San Francisco	$68,000
New York City	$62,800
Cincinnati	$72,500
National Average	$73,000

Industrial Design – Principal/President

San Francisco	$235,000
Palo Alto	$350,000
New York City	$185,000
Minneapolis	$135,000
Chicago	$152,500
National Average	$135,000

Landscape Architect – Principal

Des Moines	$80,000
St. Louis	$90,500
Chicago	$103,500
Boston	$120,000
Seattle	$98,500
National Average	$104,000

Architect – Principal – Medium Size Firm

Dallas	$140,000
Phoenix	$102,000
Denver	$120,000
New York City	$130,000
Los Angeles	$146,250
National Average	$118,000

Architect – Principal, Non-CEO – Large Firm

Miami	$235,000
Los Angeles	$188,000
Atlanta	$240,000
New Haven	$275,000
Baltimore	$160,000
National Average	$130,000

CEO/President – Medium/Large Firm A/E/ID

Denver	$500,000
Salt Lake City	$375,000
San Francisco	$675,000
New York City	$750,000
Orlando	$250,000
National Average	$235,000

Architects (Vice President A/E/C, Chief Architect, Executive Vice President, etc) in Industry and Government

Washington DC	$167,000
Washington DC	$225,000
San Francisco Area	$350,000
New York City Area	$290,000
Austin, TX	$144,000
Atlanta Area	$130,000

University Architecture and Design Faculty

Dean – Architecture	$128,000
Physical Plant Chief	$94,000
Professor	$71,000
Associate Professor	$55,000
Assistant Professor	$44,000
Instructor	$34,000

Source: Counsel House Research, Greenway Consulting, The American Institute of Architects, International Interior Design Association, Industrial Designers Society of America, Chronicle of Higher Education

Value of Construction Work by Region: 1997 (in U.S. dollars)

Type of Construction	Value of Construction Work			
	Total	New Construction	Additions, Alterations, or Reconstruction	Maintenance and Repair
UNITED STATES				
Building Construction, Total	667,892,335	441,085,796	160,098,787	66,707,752
Single-family houses, detached and attached	23,830,160	179,325,838	38,743,071	20,232,700
Single-family houses, detached	20,863,659	157,912,589	33,607,561	17,116,443
Single-family houses, attached	29,665,014	21,413,248	5,135,510	3,116,256
Apartment buildings/condos/cooperatives	35,912,059	23,549,029	7,294,218	5,068,813
All other residential building	1,450,935	879,677	409,889	161,370
Manufacturing/light industrial buildings	64,026,464	33,796,938	18,857,654	11,371,872
Manufacturing/light industrial warehouses	20,252,089	13,494,830	4,676,949	2,080,311
Hotels and motels	17,209,304	12,623,672	3,254,698	1,330,934
Office buildings	80,588,781	44,449,862	27,694,812	8,444,108
All other commercial buildings	69,545,794	43,566,415	18,638,395	7,340,984
Commercial warehouses	16,628,141	11,912,121	3,298,378	1,417,642
Religious buildings	9,400,127	5,343,590	2,969,442	1,087,095
Educational buildings	46,826,417	28,102,206	15,751,455	2,972,756
Health care and institutional buildings	33,942,469	19,754,714	11,763,387	2,424,369
Public safety buildings	10,119,930	7,346,218	2,200,704	573,008
Farm buildings, non-residential	3,473,574	2,508,098	530,901	434,575
Amusement/recreational buildings	10,429,599	7,893,895	2,073,509	462,196
Other building construction	9,785,043	6,538,695	1,941,327	1,305,021
NORTHEAST				
Building Construction, Total	114,550,714	61,638,403	38,682,611	14,229,699
Single-family houses, detached and attached	33,390,774	21,353,228	8,110,557	3,926,988
Single-family houses, detached	29,304,397	18,772,133	7,165,276	3,366,988
Single-family houses, attached	4,086,377	2,581,095	945,281	560,000
Apartment buildings/condos/cooperatives	6,792,548	3,020,707	2,338,623	1,433,218
All other residential building	194,851	96,982	61,320	36,550
Manufacturing and light industrial buildings	10,582,581	4,601,673	3,964,725	2,016,184
Manufacturing/light industrial warehouses	3,034,256	1,725,600	918,682	389,974
Hotels and motels	2,905,562	2,118,378	552,064	235,121
Office buildings	18,254,802	7,394,081	8,494,958	2,365,764
All other commercial buildings	12,565,856	6,637,924	4,331,737	1,596,195
Commercial warehouses	2,400,908	1,499,852	648,143	252,913
Religious buildings	1,348,655	530,739	539,552	278,365

Type of Construction	Value of Construction Work			
	Total	New Construction	Additions, Alterations, or Reconstruction	Maintenance and Repair
Educational buildings	9,726,636	4,946,851	4,114,060	665,725
Health care and institutional buildings	7,175,532	3,598,754	3,033,203	543,575
Public safety buildings	2,134,622	1,386,588	593,033	155,002
Farm buildings, non-residential	297,071	180,313	S	63,762
Amusement/recreational buildings	1,941,746	1,365,768	474,866	101,112
Other building construction	1,804,313	1,180,965	454,095	169,253
MIDWEST				
Building Construction, Total	158,651,020	101,737,168	39,706,572	17,207,280
Single-family houses, detached and attached	53,833,933	38,958,807	9,656,226	5,218,899
Single-family houses, detached	45,147,441	32,478,358	8,219,880	4,449,202
Single-family houses, attached	8,686,491	6,480,448	1,436,346	769,697
Apartment buildings/condos/cooperatives	7,209,912	4,935,375	1,317,092	957,444
All other residential building	244,676	144,642	75,448	24,586
Manufacturing/light industrial buildings	20,345,765	9,903,563	6,734,854	3,707,348
Manufacturing/light industrial warehouses	6,825,379	4,550,954	1,615,813	658,612
Hotels and motels	3,084,878	2,277,278	505,195	302,405
Office buildings	15,997,117	9,507,477	4,824,179	1,665,460
All other commercial buildings	16,070,258	9,829,218	4,397,665	1,843,375
Commercial warehouses	4,078,833	2,878,960	804,428	395,445
Religious buildings	2,571,423	1,357,789	879,028	334,606
Educational buildings	11,876,924	6,844,123	4,204,103	828,697
Health care and institutional buildings	9,171,992	5,303,575	3,162,981	705,437
Public safety buildings	2,189,952	1,519,131	521,041	149,781
Farm buildings, non-residential	1,558,036	1,148,443	224,798	184,796
Amusement/recreational buildings	1,918,469	1,400,700	425,435	92,333
Other building construction	1,673,473	1,177,131	358,286	138,056
SOUTH				
Building Construction, Total	229,801,000	161,014,229	46,788,740	21,998,031
Single-family houses, detached and attached	83,894,701	66,017,870	11,198,818	6,678,013
Single-family houses, detached	74,615,340	59,110,291	9,817,716	5,687,334
Single-family houses, attached	9,279,361	6,907,580	1,381,101	990,679
Apartment buildings/condos/cooperatives	13,425,146	9,679,705	2,136,636	1,608,805
All other residential building	553,268	373,872	123,283	56,113
Manufacturing/light industrial buildings	19,050,234	10,219,135	4,779,694	4,051,405

Value of Construction Work by Region: 1997 (Con't)

Type of Construction	Value of Construction Work			
	Total	New Construction	Additions, Alterations, or Reconstruction	Maintenance and Repair
Manufacturing/light industrial warehouses	6,064,446	4,231,672	1,212,149	620,625
Hotels and motels	5,781,393	4,202,038	1,136,776	442,579
Office buildings	27,062,275	16,141,975	8,233,658	2,686,642
All other commercial buildings	24,678,078	16,771,875	5,509,675	2,396,528
Commercial warehouses	5,627,487	4,150,277	1,027,871	449,339
Religious buildings	4,156,019	2,722,947	1,106,427	326,645
Educational buildings	15,749,219	10,556,575	4,348,666	843,977
Health care and institutional buildings	12,010,633	7,409,749	3,852,706	748,178
Public safety buildings	3,484,524	2,665,738	660,353	158,433
Farm buildings, non-residential	1,084,727	798,042	164,109	122,575
Amusement/recreational buildings	3,567,082	2,777,176	625,841	164,064
Other building construction	3,611,768	2,295,582	672,077	644,109
WEST				
Building Construction, Total	164,889,602	116,695,996	34,920,864	13,272,741
Single-family houses, detached and attached	67,182,200	52,995,932	9,777,470	4,408,799
Single-family houses, detached	59,569,415	47,551,807	8,404,689	3,612,919
Single-family houses, attached	7,612,785	5,444,124	1,372,781	795,880
Apartment buildings/condos/cooperatives	8,484,453	5,913,242	1,501,866	1,069,345
All other residential building	458,140	264,182	149,837	44,121
Manufacturing/light industrial buildings	14,047,884	9,072,567	3,378,382	1,596,935
Manufacturing/light industrial warehouses	4,328,009	2,986,604	930,304	411,100
Hotels and motels	5,437,471	4,025,979	1,060,663	350,829
Office buildings	19,274,587	11,406,329	6,142,017	1,726,242
All other commercial buildings	16,231,602	10,327,398	4,399,318	1,504,887
Commercial warehouses	4,520,913	3,383,032	817,936	319,946
Religious buildings	1,324,029	732,114	444,436	147,479
Educational buildings	9,473,638	5,754,656	3,084,625	634,357
Health care and institutional buildings	5,584,312	3,442,635	1,714,497	427,179
Public safety buildings	2,310,831	1,774,761	426,278	109,792
Farm buildings, non-residential	533,740	381,300	88,999	63,441
Amusement/recreational buildings	3,002,303	2,350,250	547,366	104,687
Other building construction	2,695,489	1,885,017	456,870	353,602

S: Information withheld because estimates did not meet publication standards.

Source: U.S. Census Bureau, 1997 Economic Census

REGISTRATION
LAWS

Architecture Registration Laws

The following information provides a brief overview of the major components of initial licensure requirements for architects including work experience, degree requirements, and the Architectural Registration Exam (ARE). Complete information regarding registration requirements, renewal procedures, interstate registration, and corporate practice guidelines is available from the individual state boards at the phone numbers listed below. Due to the complex and changing nature of the requirements, it is recommended that the state licensing board(s) be contacted to receive the most up-to-date information. The National Council of Architectural Registration Boards (NCARB) also maintains information about registration on their Web site at *www.ncarb.org/stateboards/*.

States and State Boards	Type of Law		Initial Requirements			Ongoing Requir.
	Title Act	Practice Act	College Degree Required	Internship Required	ARE Exam Required	Continuing Education Required
Alabama (334) 242-4179	X	X	X	X	X	X
Alaska (907) 465-1676	X	X	X	X	X	
Arizona (602) 255-4053 x210	X	X			X	
Arkansas (501) 682-3171	X	X	X	X	X	X
California (916) 445-3394	X	X			X	
Colorado (303) 894-7801	X	X		X	X	
Connecticut (860) 713-6145	X	X	X	X	X	
Delaware (302) 739-4522	X	X	X	X	X	P
District of Columbia (202) 442-4461	X	X	X	X	X	P
Florida (850) 488-1470	X	X	X	X	X	X
Georgia (912) 207-1400	X	X		X	X	
Hawaii (808) 586-2702	X	X		P	X	
Idaho (208) 334-3233	X	X		X	X	
Illinois (217) 785-0877	X	X		X	X	

Architecture Registration Laws (Con't)

States and State Boards	Type of Law		Initial Requirements			Ongoing Requir.
	Title Act	Practice Act	College Degree Required	Internship Required	ARE Exam Required	Continuing Education Required
Indiana (317) 233-6223	X	X	X	X	X	
Iowa (515) 281-4126	X	X	X	X	X	X
Kansas (785) 296-3053	X	X	X	X	X	X
Kentucky (859) 246-2069	X	X		X	X	X
Louisiana (225) 925-4802	X	X	X	X	X	X
Maine (207) 624-8522	X	X		X	X	
Maryland (410) 333-6322	X	X		X	X	
Massachusetts (617) 727-3072	X	X	X	X	X	
Michigan (517) 241-9253	X	X	X	X	X	P
Minnesota (651) 296-2388	X	X	X	X	X	P
Mississippi (601) 359-6020	X	X	X	X	X	
Missouri (573) 751-0047	X	X			X	
Montana (406) 444-3745	X	X	X	X	X	P
Nebraska (402) 471-2021	X	X	X	X	X	P
Nevada (702) 486-7300	X	X	X	X	X	P
New Hampshire (603) 271-2219	X	X		X	X	
New Jersey (973) 504-6385	X	X	X	X	X	P
New Mexico (505) 827-6375	X	X	X	X	X	X
New York (518) 474-3930	X	X		X	X	
North Carolina (919) 733-9544	X	X	X	X	X	X
North Dakota (701) 223-3184	X	X	X	X	X	
Ohio (614) 466-2316	X	X	X	X	X	
Oklahoma (405) 751-6512	X	X	X	X	X	X

Architecture Registration Laws (Con't)

States and State Boards	Type of Law		Initial Requirements			Ongoing Requir.
	Title Act	Practice Act	College Degree Required	Internship Required	ARE Exam Required	Continuing Education Required
Oregon (503) 378-4270	X	X	X	X	X	X
Pennsylvania (717) 783-3397	X	X	X	X	X	
Rhode Island (401) 222-2565	X	X	X	X	X	
South Carolina (803) 896-4408	X	X	X	X	X	
South Dakota (605) 394-2510	X	X	X	X	X	X
Tennessee (615) 741-3221	X	X		X	X	X
Texas (512) 305-8535	X	X		X	X	P
Utah (801) 530-6551	X	X	X	X	X	P
Vermont (802) 828-2373	X	X		P	X	P
Virginia (804) 367-8506	X	X	X	X	X	
Washington (360) 664-1388	X	X		P	X	
West Virginia (304) 528-5825	X	X	X	X	X	X
Wisconsin (608) 266-5511 x42	X	X		X	X	
Wyoming (307) 777-7788	X	X	X	X	X	P

P = There is current legislation pending regarding this requirement.

Source: National Council of Architectural Registration Boards

Global Architecture Practice Standards

The following guidelines outline the major requirements for U.S. architects and architecture firms to practice in other countries. This information is meant to be an overview and should not be used as a substitute for or synthesis of the complex and changing stipulations. Architects should contact the appropriate agency in each country (indicated below) prior to beginning a project in order to obtain the most up-to-date requirements. U.S Embassies in each country may also be helpful in understanding and fulfilling requirements.

Country	License or Reg. Required for Indigenous Arch.	License or Reg. Required for Foreign Arch.	Local Representative Required	Local Participation Required	English Official Language	Metric System Standard	Official Licensing Body
Australia	X	X			X	X	Architects Registration Boards in each state
Austria	X	3	X	X		X	Federal Ministry of Economic Affairs +43 (1) 71-1000
Belgium	X	X			4	X	Orde Van Architecten, Nationale Raad
Bermuda	X	X	X	X	X	X	Architects Registration Council (809) 297-7705
Brazil	X	X		X	4	X	Regional Council of Engineering, Architecture, and Agronomy in each state
Canada	X	X	X	X	X	X	Professional bodies in each province
China	X	X	X		4	X	National Administrative Board of Architectural Registration +86 (1) 839-4250
Colombia	X	X	X	X		X	Consejo Profesional Nacional de Ingeniería y Arquitectura
Czech Republic	X		X	X		X	Czech Chamber of Architects +42 (2) 2451-0112

Global Architecture Practice Standards (Con't)

Country	License or Reg. Required for Indigenous Arch.	License or Reg. Required for Foreign Arch.	Local Representative Required	Local Participation Required	English Official Language	Metric System Standard	Official Licensing Body
Denmark	X					X	None
Egypt	X	X	X	X	4	X	Egyptian Engineering Syndicate +20 (2) 74-0092
El Salvador	X	X		X		X	Registro Nacional de Arquitectos e Ingenieros
Finland	1	2		X	4	X	None
France	1	X				X	Ministere de l'Equipment, des Transports et du Tourisme
Germany	X	X				X	Chamber of Architects in each state
Greece	X	X	X		4	X	Technical Chamber of Greece +30 (1) 325-4590
Guatemala	X		X	X		X	Colegio de Arquitectos +50 (2) 69-3672
Honduras	X	X	X	U		X	National Autonomous University of Honduras & Colegio de Arquitectos de Honduras +504 38-5385
Hungary	X	X			4	X	Registration Board of Ministry of Environmental Protection & Regional Development
Iceland	X	X			4	X	Ministry of Industry +354 (1) 60-9420
India	X	X			X	X	Council of Architecture +91 (11) 331-5757

Country	License or Reg. Required for Indigenous Arch.	License or Reg. Required for Foreign Arch.	Local Representative Required	Local Participation Required	English Official Language	Metric System Standard	Official Licensing Body
Indonesia	X	X	X	U	X	X	Ministry of Internal Affairs
Ireland					X	X	None
Israel	X	X	X	U	4	X	Architects and Engineers Registrar
Italy	X	X	X		4	X	Consiglio Nazionale Architetti
Jamaica	X	X	X		4	X	Architects Registration Board
Japan	X	X	X			X	Ministry of Construction +81 (3) 3580-4311
Jordon	X	X	X	X	X	X	Jordon Engineers Association +926 (6) 607-616
Kenya	X	X	X	X	X	X	Board of Registration of Architects and Quantity Surveyors +254 (2) 72-0438
Korea	X	X	X	U		X	Ministry of Construction +82 (2) 503-7357
Lebanon	X	X	X		4	X	Order of Engineers +961 (1) 83-0286
Luxembourg	X	X	U	U		X	Ordre des Architectes et des Ingenieurs Conseils +352 42-2406
Malaysia	X	X	X	X	4	X	Lembaga Arkitek Malaysia +60 (3) 298-8733

Global Architecture Practice Standards (Con't)

Country	License or Reg. Required for Indigenous Arch.	License or Reg. Required for Foreign Arch.	Local Representative Required	Local Participation Required	English Official Language	Metric System Standard	Official Licensing Body
Mexico	X	X	X	U		X	Direccion General de Professiones en Mexico +52 (5) 550-9000
Netherlands						X	Stichting Bureau Architectenregister +31 (70) 360-7020
New Zealand					X	X	Architects Education and Registration Board
Nicaragua	X	X	X				Asociacion Nicarguense de Arquitectos Camara de La Construcion + 505 (2) 43-796
Norway						X	None
Panama	X		X	U		X	Junta Tecnica de Ingenieria y Arquitectura +507 23-7851
Peru	1	2	X			X	Colegio de Arquitectos del Peru +51 (41) 71-3778
Philippines	X	3	X	X	X	X	Professional Regulation Commission +63 (2) 741-6076
Poland	X	X		X		X	Government Offices in each province
Portugal	1	2				X	Associaçao dos Arquitectos Portugueses +351 (1) 343-2454
Romania	X	X	X		4	X	Union of Romanian Architects +40 (1) 312-0956
Russia	X	3	X	X		X	Russian License Architectural Centre

Global Architecture Practice Standards (Con't)

Country	License or Reg. Required for Indigenous Arch.	License or Reg. Required for Foreign Arch.	Local Representative Required	Local Participation Required	English Official Language	Metric System Standard	Official Licensing Body
Saudi Arabia	X	X	X	X		X	Ministry of Commerce +966 (1) 401-2222
Singapore	X	X			X	X	Board of Architects +65 222-5295
South Africa	X	X			X	X	South African Council for Architects +27 (11) 486-1683
Spain	X	X	U	U	4	X	Colegios de Arquitectos in each region
Sweden						X	None
Switzerland	X	U			4	X	Schweizerisches Register der Ingenieure, Architekten und Techniker +41 (1) 252-3222
Taiwan	X	X	X	X		X	Construction & Planning Administration , MOI +886 (4) 328-1560
Turkey	X	X			4	X	Turkiye Mimarlar Odasi +90 (4) 417-3727
United Kingdom	U	X			X	X	Architects Registration Council of the United Kingdom +44 (71)580-5861
Venezuela	X	X				X	Colegio de Ingenieros, Arquitectos y Profesiones Afines de Venezuela +58 (2) 241-8007

Specific requirements are unclear. The local agency should be contacted.
A license or registration is not required for indigenous architects; however, there are other stipulations which must be met in order for indigenous persons to practice architecture.
A license or registration is not required for foreign architects; however, there are other stipulations which must be met in order for a foreign architect to practice architecture.
Generally US architects may not practice in the country independently.
Although not the official language, English is commonly used in the commercial arena.

Source: National Council of Architectural Registration Boards

Interior Design Registration Laws

The following information provides a brief overview of the major components of initial registration for interior designers including work experience, degree requirements and the National Council for Interior Design Qualification (NCIDQ) exam. More specific information about these requirements is available from the individual state board phone numbers listed below. Due to the complex and changing nature of the requirements, it is recommended that the state licensing board(s) be contacted to receive the most up to date information. The American Society of Interior Designers (ASID) also maintains information about registration on their Web site at *www.asid.org.*

States and State Board Phone Numbers	Type of Law		Initial Requirements			Ongoing Req.
	Title Act	Practice Act	Post-HS Education Required	Work Experience Required	NCIDQ Exam Required	Continuing Education Required
Alabama (256) 340-9003	X		X		X	
Arkansas (501) 664-3008	X		X	X	X	X
California (760) 761-4734	*			X	X	X
Connecticut (860) 713-6135	X		X	X	X	
Florida (850) 488-6685	X	X	X	X	X	X
Georgia (404) 656-3941	X		X		X	X
Illinois (217) 785-0813	X		X	X	X	
Louisiana (225) 925-3921	X	X	X	X	X	X
Maine (207) 624-8603	X		X	X	X	
Maryland (410) 333-6322	X		X	X	X	X
Minnesota (651) 296-2333	X		X	X	X	X
Missouri (573) 522-4683	X		X	X	X	X
Nevada (702) 486-7300	X	X	X	X	X	

Interior Design Registration Laws (Con't)

States and State Board Phone Numbers	Type of Law		Initial Requirements			Ongoing Req.
	Title Act	Practice Act	Post-HS Education Required	Work Experience Required	NCIDQ Exam Required	Continuing Education Required
New Mexico (505) 476-7077	X		X	X	X	X
New York (518) 474-3846	X		X	X	X	
Tennessee (615) 741-3221	X		X	X	X	X
Texas (512) 305-8539	X		X	X	X	X
Virginia (804) 367-8514	X		X	X	X	
Washington, D.C. (202) 442-4330	X	X	X	X	X	X
Wisconsin (608) 266-5439	X		X	X	X	X

Self-Certification Act

Source: American Society of Interior Designers

Landscape Architecture Licensure Laws

The following information provides a brief overview of the major components of initial licensure for landscape architects. Complete information regarding licensing requirements, renewal procedures, and reciprocity is available from the individual state boards, at the phone numbers listed below. It is recommended that the state licensing board(s) be contacted to receive the most up to date information. The Council of Landscape Architectural Registration Boards (CLARB) also maintains information about licensure on their Web site at *www.clarb.org*.

States & State Board Phone Numbers	Type of Law		Initial Requirements			Ongoing Req.
	Title Act	Practice Act	College Degree Required	Work Experience Required	LARE Exam Required	Continuing Education Required
Alabama (334) 262-1351	X	X		X	X	X
Alaska* (907) 465-2540						
Arizona (602) 255-4053	X	X		X	X	
Arkansas* (501) 682-3171						
California (916) 445-4954	X	X	**	X	X	
Connecticut (860) 566-5130		X	X	X	X	X
Delaware (302) 739-4522	X		X	X	X	X
Florida (850) 488-6685 x2		X		***	X	
Georgia (404) 656-3941	X	X	X	X	X	X
Hawaii (808) 586-2702	X	X		X	X	
Idaho (208) 334-3233	X			X	X	
Illinois* (217) 785-0800						
Indiana (317) 232-2980	X			***	X	
Iowa (515) 281-5596	X			X	X	X
Kansas (913) 296-3053	X	X	X	X	X	X

States & State Board Phone Numbers	Type of Law		Initial Requirements			Ongoing Req.
	Title Act	Practice Act	College Degree Required	Work Experience Required	LARE Exam Required	Continuing Education Required
Kentucky (606) 245-2434	X	X	X	X	X	X
Louisiana (504) 925-7772	X	X		X	X	
Maine (207) 624-8522	X		X	X	X	
Maryland (410) 333-6322	X	X		X	X	
Massachusetts (617) 727-3072	X		X	X	X	
Michigan (517) 241-9253	X			X	X	
Minnesota (651) 296-2388	X	X		X	X	
Mississippi (601) 359-6020	X			***	X	
Missouri (573) 751-0039	X		X	X	X	
Montana (406) 444-5924	X				X	
Nebraska (402) 344-8711	X	X		X	X	X
Nevada (775) 626-0604	X	X	X	X	X	
New Jersey (973) 504-6385			X	X	X	X
New Mexico (505) 476-7077	X	X	X	X	X	X
New York (518) 474-3930	X	X		X	X	
North Carolina (919) 850-9088		X		X	X	X
Ohio (614) 466-2316	X			X	X	
Oklahoma (405) 751-6512	X		X	X	X	X
Oregon (503) 589-0093	X		X	***	X	
Pennsylvania (717) 772-8528	X	X		X	X	X
Rhode Island (401) 222-2565	X	X	X	X	X	
South Carolina (803) 734-9129	X	X		X	X	

Landscape Architecture Licensure Laws (Con't)

States & State Board Phone Numbers	Type of Law		Initial Requirements			Ongoing Req.
	Title Act	Practice Act	College Degree Required	Work Experience Required	LARE Exam Required	Continuing Education Required
South Dakota (605) 394-2510	X	X	X	X	X	X
Tennessee (615) 741-3221	X	X	X	X	X	X
Texas (512) 305-8539	X			***	X	
Utah (801) 530-6632	X	X		***	X	
Virginia (804) 367-8514	X			***	X	
Washington (360) 753-6967	X			X	X	
West Virginia (304) 293-2141 x4490	X		X	X	X	
Wisconsin* (608) 266-3423						
Wyoming (307) 777-7788	X	X	X	X	X	

*   Information from these state licensing boards was not available.
**   Some post-high school course work is required.
*** No experience is required with a Landscape Architectural Accreditation Board (LAAB) accredited Landscape Architecture degree; however, other degree types may require experience.
+   Also referred to as Professional Development Hours (PDH).

Note: Colorado, Washington, D.C., North Dakota, and Vermont currently do not have a Landscape Architecture licensure program.

Source: Council of Landscape Architectural Registration Boards

LEADING FIRMS

100 Leading Architecture Firms — 2001

Each year *DesignIntelligence*, the strategy and trends newsletter of the Design Futures Council, researches architecture firms for size, growth rates, recent award activity, noteworthy design contributions, level of published activity, and a subjective analysis of peer respect. This year over 800 architecture firms were analyzed to determine which are the 100 Leading Architecture Firms. This list is not a ranking as much as it is a source list of noteworthy firms who are leading their markets and receiving attention for their professional work. Their design richness and reach qualifies them for benchmark status and models for best practices. To receive consideration for next year's study, firms are invited to complete the form at the back of the *Almanac*.

For additional information about U.S. architecture firms, refer to *ProFile: The Architects Sourcebook* published by CMD Group in cooperation with The American Institute of Architects. This annual directory includes approximately 19,000 U.S.-based architecture firms. It can be found on the Web at *www.cmdg.com/profile*.

Anshen + Allen
San Francisco, California
Tel: (415) 882-9500
www.anshen.com

Arquitectonica
Miami, Florida
Tel: (305) 372-1812
www.arqintl.com

Bentz Thompson Reitow
Minneapolis, Minnesota
Tel: (612) 332-1234
www.btr-architects.com

Bohlin Cywinski Jackson
Wilkes-Barre, Pennsylvania
Tel: (717) 825.8756
www.bcj.com

BOORA Architects, Inc.
Portland, Oregon
Tel: (503) 226-1575
www.boora.com

Brennan Beer Gorman/Architects
New York, New York
Tel: (212) 888-7663
www.bbg-bbgm.com

Burt Hill Kosar Rittelmann Associates
Butler, Pennsylvania
Tel: (724) 285-4761
www.burthill.com

Callison Architecture, Inc.
Seattle, Washington
Tel: (206) 623-4646
www.callison.com

2001 Leading Architecture Firms (Con't)

Cannon
Grand Island, New York
Tel: (716) 773-6800
www.cannondesign.com

Centerbrook Architects
Essex, Connecticut
Tel: (860) 767-0175
www.centerbrook.com

Cesar Pelli & Associates
New Haven, Connecticut
Tel: (203) 777-2515
www.cesar-pelli.com

Cooper Carry, Inc.
Atlanta, Georgia
Tel: (404) 237-2000
www.coopercarry.com

Cooper, Robertson & Partners
New York, New York
Tel: (212) 247-1717
www.cooperrobertson.com

Cuningham Group
Minneapolis, Minnesota
Tel: (612) 379-6854
www.cuningham.com

Leo A. Daly
Omaha, Nebraska
Tel: (402) 391-8111
www.leodaly.com

Davis Brody Bond Architects
New York, New York
Tel: (212) 633-4700
www.davisbrody.com

Duany Plater-Zyberk & Company
Miami, Florida
Tel: (305) 644-1023
www.dpz.com

Durrant Group, Inc., The
Dubuque, Iowa
Tel: (604) 535-9801
www.durrant.com

Einhorn Yaffee Prescott
Albany, New York
Tel: (518) 431-3300
www.eypae.com

Eisenman Architects
New York, New York
Tel: (212) 645-1400

Elkus/Manfredi Architects
Boston, Massachusetts
Tel: (617) 426-1300
www.elkus-manfredi.com

Ellerbe Becket
Minneapolis, Minnesota
Tel: (612) 376-2000
www.ellerbebecket.com

Ewing Cole Cherry Brott
Philadelphia, Pennsylvania
Tel: (215) 923-2020
www.ewingcole.com

Flad & Associates
Madison, Wisconsin
Tel: (608) 238-2661
www.flad.com

Fox & Fowle Architects
New York, New York
Tel: (212) 627-1700
www.foxfowle.com

FRCH Design Worldwide
Cincinnati, Ohio
Tel: (513) 241-3000
www.frch.com

2001 Leading Architecture Firms (Con't)

Gabellini Associates
New York, New York
(212) 388-1700
www.gabelliniassociates.com

Frank O. Gehry and Associates, Inc.
Santa Monica, CA 90404
Tel: (310) 828-6088
www.frankgehry.com

Gensler
San Francisco, California
Tel: (415) 433-3700
www.gensler.com

Goody, Clancy & Associates
Boston, Massachusetts
Tel: 617-262-2760
www.gcassoc.com

Graham Gund Architects, Inc.
Cambridge, Massachusetts
Tel: (617) 577-9600
www.grahamgund.com

Michael Graves & Associates, Inc.
Princeton, New Jersey
Tel: (609) 924-6409
www.michaelgraves.com

Group Mackenzie
Portland, Oregon
Tel: (503) 224-9560
www.groupmackenzie.com

Gwathmey Siegel & Associates Architects
New York, New York
Tel: (212) 947-1240
www.gwathmey-siegel.com

Hammel, Green and Abrahamson, Inc.
Minneapolis, Minnesota
Tel: (612) 337-4100
www.hga.com

Hammond Beeby Rupert Ainge
Chicago, Illinois
Tel: (312) 527-3200

Hardy Holzmann Pfeiffer Associates
New York, New York
Tel: (212) 677-6030
www.hhpa.com

Hartman-Cox Architects
Washington, DC
Tel: (202) 333-6446

HDR Architecture, Inc.
Omaha, Nebraska
Tel: (402) 399-1000
www.hdrinc.com

Hellmuth, Obata + Kassabaum, Inc.
St. Louis, Missouri
Tel: (314) 421-2000
www.hok.com

Herbert Lewis Kruse Blunck Architects
Des Moines, Iowa
Tel: (515) 288-9536
www.hlkb.com

Hillier Group, The
Princeton, New Jersey
Tel: (609) 452-8888
www.hillier.com

HKS Inc.
Dallas, Texas
Tel: (214) 969-5599
www.hksinc.com

HLM Design
Charlotte, North Carolina
Tel: (704) 358-0779
www.hlmdesign.com

2001 Leading Architecture Firms (Con't)

HLW International
New York, New York
Tel: (212) 353-4600
www.hlw.com

Holabird & Root
Chicago, Illinois
Tel: (312) 726-5960
www.holabird.com

Steven Holl Architects
New York, New York
Tel: (212) 989-0918
www.stevenholl.com

Hugh Newell Jacobsen
Washington, D.C.
Tel: (202) 337-5200
www.hughjacobsen.com

Jerde Partnership International, The
Venice, California
(310) 399-1987
www.jerde.com

Kahler Slater
Milwuakee, Wisconsin
Tel: (404) 272-2000
www.kahlerslater.com

Kallmann McKinnell & Wood Architects
Boston, Massachusetts
Tel: (617) 267-0808
www.kmwarch.com

Kaplan McLaughlin Diaz
San Francisco, California
Tel: (415) 398-5191
www.kmd-arch.com

R. M. Kliment & Frances Halsband Architects
New York, New York
Tel: (212) 243-7400
www.kliment-halsband.com

Koetter Kim & Associates
Boston, Massachusetts
Tel: (617) 536-8560
www.koetterkim.com

Kohn Pedersen Fox Associates
New York, New York
Tel: (212) 777-6500
www.kpf.com

Lee, Burkhart, Liu, Inc.
Santa Monica, California
Tel: (310) 829-2249
www.lblarch.com

LMN Architects
Seattle, Washington
Tel: (206) 682-3460
www.lmnarchitects.com

Machado and Silvetti Associates, Inc.
Boston, Massachusetts
Tel: (617) 426-7070
www.machado-silvetti.com

Meyer, Scherer and Rockcastle Architects
Minneapolis, Minnesota
Tel: (612) 375-0336
www.msrltd.com

Moore Ruble Yudell Architects & Planners
Santa Monica, California
Tel: (310) 450-1400
www.moorerubleyudell.com

Morphosis
Santa Monica, California
(310) 453-2247
www.morphosis.net

Morris Architects
Houston, Texas
Tel: (713) 622-1180
www.morrisarchitects.com

2001 Leading Architecture Firms (Con't)

Moshe Safdie Architects Limited
Sommerville, Massachusetts
Tel: (617) 629-2100
www.msafdie.com

Murphy/Jahn, Inc.
Chicago, Illinois
Tel: (312) 427-7300
www.murphyjahn.com

NBBJ
Seattle, Washington
Tel: (206) 223-5555
www.nbbj.com

Odell Associates Inc.
Charlotte, North Carolina
Tel: (704) 377-5941
www.odell.com

O'Donnell Wicklund Pigozzi & Peterson
Chicago, Illinois
Tel: (312) 332-9600
www.owpp.com

Page Southerland Page
Austin, Texas
Tel: (512) 472-6721
www.psp.com

Payette Associates, Inc.
Boston, Massachusetts
Tel: (617) 342-8200
www.payette.com

Pei Cobb Freed & Partners Architects
New York, New York
Tel: (212) 751-3122
www.pcfandp.com

Perkins & Will
Chicago, Illinois
Tel: (312) 755-0770
www.perkinswill.com

Perkins Eastman Architects
New York, New York
Tel: (212) 353-7291
www.peapc.com

Perry Dean Rogers & Partners Architects
Boston, Massachusetts
Tel: (617) 423-0100
www.perrydean.com

Polshek Partnership, The
New York, New York
Tel: (212) 807-7171
www.polshek.com

John Portman and Associates, Inc.
Atlanta, Georgia
Tel: (404) 614-5555
www.portmanholdings.com

Antoine Predock
Albuquerque, New Mexico
Tel: (505) 843-7390
www.predock.com

Richard Meier & Partners
New York, New York
Tel: (212) 967-6060
www.richardmeier.com

RMW Architecture & Design
San Francisco, California
Tel: (415) 781-9800
www.rmw.com

RNL Design
Denver, Colorado
Tel: (303) 295-1717
www.rnldesign.com

Kevin Roche John Dinkeloo & Associates
Hamden, Connecticut
Tel: (203) 777-7251
www.krjda.com

2001 Leading Architecture Firms (Con't)

RTKL International, Inc.
Baltimore, Maryland
Tel: (410) 528-8600
www.rtkl.com

Sasaki Associates, Inc.
Watertown, Massachusetts
Tel: (617) 926-3300
www.sasaki.com

Scogin Elam and Bray Architects
Atlanta, Georgia
Tel: (404) 525-6869
www.scoginelamandbray.com

Shepley Bulfinch Richardson & Abbott
Boston, Massachusetts
Tel: (617) 423-1700
www.sbra.com

Skidmore, Owings & Merrill
Chicago, Illinois
Tel: (312) 554-9090
www.som.com

Smallwood, Reynolds, Stewart, Stewart Associates, Inc.
Atlanta, Georgia
Tel: (404) 233-5453
www.srssa.com

SmithGroup Incorporated
Detroit, Michigan
Tel: (313) 983-3600
www.smithgroup.com

Smith - Miller + Hawkinson
New York, New York
Tel: (212) 966-3875
www.smharch.com

Robert A. M. Stern Architects
New York, New York
Tel: (212) 967-5100
www.ramsa.com

Stubbins Associates, Inc., The
Cambridge, Massachusetts
Tel: (617) 491-6450
www.tsa-arch.com

Studios Architecture
San Francisco, California
Tel: (415) 398-7575
www.studiosarch.com

Swanke Hayden Connell Architects
New York, New York
Tel: (212) 226-9696
www.shca.com

Thompson, Ventulett, Stainback & Associates, Inc.
Atlanta, Georgia
Tel: (404) 888-6600
www.tvsa.com

Tigerman McCurry Architects
Chicago, Illinois
Tel: (312) 644-5880
www.tigerman-mccurry.com

Tod Williams, Billie Tsien and Associates
New York, New York
Tel: (212) 582-2385
www.twbta.com

Tsoi/Kobus & Associates
Cambridge, Massachusetts
Tel: (617) 491-3067
www.tka-architects.com

Venturi, Scott Brown and Associates
Philadelphia, Pennsylvania
Tel: (215) 487-0400
www.vsba.com

Rafael Viñoly Architects
New York, New York
Tel: (212) 924-5060
www.rvapc.com

2001 Leading Architecture Firms (Con't)

Vitetta Group
Philadelphia, Pennsylvania
Tel: (215) 235-3500
www.vitetta.com

VOA Associates Incorporated
Chicago, Illinois
Tel: (312) 554-1400
www.voa.com

Wimberly Allison Tong & Goo
Honolulu, Hawaii
Tel: (808) 521-8888
www.watg.com

Zimmer Gunsul Frasca Partnership
Portland, Oregon
Tel: (503) 224-3860
www.zgf.com

Zimmerman Design Group, The
Milwaukee, Wisconsin
Tel: (414) 476-9500
www.zdg.com

Source: DesignIntelligence/*Counsel House Research*

BOOKSTORES

Architecture & Design Bookstores

The following list outlines the specialty bookstores of architecture and design throughout the United States including rare and out-of-print dealers that specialize in design titles.

ARIZONA
Builder's Book Depot
1033 E. Jefferson
Suite 500
Phoenix, AZ 85034
(800) 284-3434
www.buildersbookdepot.com

CALIFORNIA
Builders Booksource
1817 Fourth Street
Berkeley, CA 94710
(510) 845-6874
www.buildersbooksite.com

J.B. Muns Fine Arts Books
1162 Shattuck Avenue
Berkeley, CA 94707
(510) 525-2420

Moe's Art & Antiquarian Books
2476 Telegraph Avenue
Berkeley, CA 94704
(510) 849-2133

Builder's Book
8001 Canoga Avenue
Canoga Park, CA 91304
(818) 887-7828

Builders Booksource
Ghirardelli Square
900 North Point
San Francisco, CA 94109
(415) 440-5773
www.buildersbooksite.com

William Stout Architectural Books
804 Montgomery Street
San Francisco, CA 94133
(415) 391-6757
www.stoutbooks.com

Form Zero Architectural Books + Gallery
2433 Main Street
Santa Monica, CA 90405
(310) 450-0222
www.formzero.com

Hennessey & Ingalls Art and Architecture Books
1254 Third Street Promenade
Santa Monica, CA 90401
(310) 458-9074
www.hennesseyingalls.com

DISTRICT OF COLUMBIA
AIA Bookstore
The American Institute of Architects
1735 New York Avenue NW
Washington, DC 20006
(202) 626-7475
www.aiabooks.com

Franz Bader Bookstore
1911 I Street NW
Washington, DC 20006
(202) 337-5440

National Building Museum Shop
401 F Street NW
Washington, DC 20001
(202) 272-7706

Architecture & Design Bookstores (Con't)

FLORIDA
Construction Bookstore
1830 NE 2nd Street
Gainesville, FL 32602
(904) 378-9784
(800) 253-0541

GEORGIA
Architectural Book Center
231 Peachtree Street NE Suite B-4
Atlanta, GA 30303
(404) 222-9920

ILLINOIS
Chicago Architecture Foundation Bookstore
224 S. Michigan Avenue
Chicago, IL 60604
(312) 922-3432

Chicago Architecture Foundation Bookstore
John Hancock Center
875 N. Michigan Avenue
Chicago, IL 60611
(312) 751-1380

Contract Design Center Bookshop
1-111 Merchandise Mart
P.O. Box 3442
Chicago, IL 60654
(312) 527-3509

Prairie Avenue Bookshop
418 S. Wabash Avenue
Chicago, IL 60605-1209
(312) 922-8311
www.pabook.com

INDIANA
Architectural Center Bookstore
Indiana Society of Architects
47 S. Pennsylvania Street
Indianapolis, IN 46204
(317) 634-3871

MASSACHUSETTS
Ars Libri
560 Harrison Avenue
Boston, MA 02118
(617) 357-5212
www.arslibri.com

F.A. Bernett
144 Lincoln Street
Boston, MA 02111
(617) 350-7778

Cambridge Architectural Books
12 Bow Street
Cambridge, MA 02138
(617) 354-5300
www.archbook.com

Charles B. Wood III Antiquarian Booksellers
P.O. Box 2369
Cambridge, MA 02238
(617) 868-1711

MARYLAND
Baltimore AIA Bookstore
11 1/2 Chase Street
Baltimore, MD 21201
(410) 625 2585

NEW YORK
Royoung Bookseller
564 Ashford Avenue
Ardsley, NY 10502
(914) 693-6116
www.royoung.com

Academy Book Store
10 West 18th Street
New York, NY 10011
(212) 242-4848
www.academy-bookstore.com

Architecture & Design Bookstores (Con't)

Acanthus Books
48 W. 22nd Street, No. 4
New York, NY 10011
(212) 463-0750
www.acanthusbooks.com

Archivia: The Decorative Arts Bookshop
944 Madison Avenue
New York, NY 10021
(212) 439-9194

Argosy Bookstore
116 E. 59th Street
New York, NY 10022
(212) 753-4455
www.argosybooks.com

Cooper-Hewitt Musuem Bookstore
2 East 91st St
New York, NY 10128
(212) 849-8400

Hacker Art Books
45 W. 57th Street
New York, NY 10019
(212) 688-7600
www.hackerartbooks.com

Jaap Rietman
134 Spring Street
New York, NY 10012
(212) 966-8044

McGraw-Hill Bookstore
1221 Avenue of the Americas
New York, NY 10020
(212) 512-4100
www.bookstore.mcgraw-hill.com

Morton, The Interior Design Bookshop
989 Third Avenue
New York, NY 10022
(212) 421-9025

Perimeter Books
21 Cleveland Place
New York, NY 10012
(212) 334-6559
www.perimeterbooks.com

Rizzoli Bookstore
31 W. 57th Street
New York, NY 10019
(212) 759-2424

Strand Book Store
828 Broadway
New York, NY 10003
(212) 473-1452

Stubbs Books & Prints
153 E. 70th
New York, NY 10021
(212) 772-3120

Urban Center Books
Villard Houses
457 Madison Avenue
New York, NY 10022
(212) 935-3592
http://colophon.com/urbancenterbooks/

Ursus Books
981 Madison Avenue
New York, NY 10021
(212) 772-8787

375 West Broadway, 3rd Floor
New York, NY 10012
(212) 226-7858
www.ursusbooks.com

OHIO
Wexner Center Bookstore
1871 N. High Street
Columbus, OH 43210-1105
(614) 292-1807

Architecture & Design Bookstores (Con't)

PENNSYLVANIA
AIA Bookstore & Design Center
17th and Sansom Streets
Philadelphia, PA 19103
(215) 569-3188
www.aiaphila.org

Joseph Fox Bookshop
1724 Sansom Street
Philadelphia, PA 19103
(215) 772-8787
www.bookweb.org/bookstore/foxbook

TEXAS
Brazos Bookstore
2421 Bissonnet Street
Houston, TX 77005
(713) 523-0701
www.brazosbookstore.com

UTAH
Bibliotect
329 W. Pierpont Ave.
Salt Lake City, UT 84101-1712
(801) 236-1010

WASHINGTON
Peter Miller Architecture and Design Books
1930 First Avenue
Seattle, WA 98101
(206) 441-4114
www.petermiller.com

JOURNALS & MAGAZINES

Architecture & Design Journals & Magazines

The following is a list of major architecture and design journals and magazines from around the world, ranging from the most popular to the cutting edge. Whether looking for periodicals which take a less traditional approach or for exposure to the most recent projects and design news, it is hoped this list will provide an opportunity to explore new ideas and perspectives about design and expand knowledge about the profession.

U.S. PUBLICATIONS

Archi-Tech
P.O. Box 10915
Portland, ME 04104
(207) 761-2177
Published 5 times a year

Architectural Digest
6300 Wilshire Boulevard
Los Angeles, CA 90048
(800) 365-8032
www.archdigest.com
Published monthly by Conde Nast Publications, Inc.

Architectural Record
Two Penn Plaza
New York, NY 10121-2298
(212) 904-2594
www.architecturalrecord.com
The official magazine of the AIA, published monthly.

Architecture
770 Broadway
New York, NY 10003
(646) 654-5766
www.architecturemag.com
Published monthly by BPI Communications

ASID ICON
608 Massachusetts Ave. NW
Washington, D.C. 20002-6006
(202) 546-3480
www.asid.org
The magazine of the American Society of Interior Designers, published quarterly.

Communication Arts
410 Sherman Ave.
P.O. Box 10300
Palo Alto, CA 94303
(650) 326-6040
www.commarts.com
Published 8 times per year

Design Book Review
California College of Arts and Crafts
1111 Eighth Street
San Francisco, CA 94107
(415) 551-9232
Published quarterly by the California College of Arts and Crafts

Dwell
99 Osgood Place
San Francisco, CA 94133
(415) 743-9990
www.dwellmag.com
Published bi-monthly by Pixie Communications

Architecture & Design Journals & Magazines (Con't)

Engineering News Record
Penn Plaza
th Floor
New York, NY 10121
www.enr.com
Published by McGraw-Hill Construction
Information Group

Fine Homebuilding
Taunton Press
S. Main St.
P.O. Box 5506
Newtown, CT 06470-5506
(203) 426-8171
www.taunton.com/fh/
Published bi-monthly by Taunton Press.

Harvard Design Magazine
Quincy St.
Cambridge, MA 02138
(617) 495-7814
www.harvard.edu/hdm
Published 3 times a year by Harvard
University's Graduate School of Design

I.D.
6 East 27th St. Floor 6
New York, NY 10016
(212) 447-1400
www.idonline.com
Published 8 times per year

Innovation
42 Walker Rd.
Great Falls, VA 22066
(703) 759-0100
www.idsa.org
Quarterly Journal of the Industrial
Designers Society of America

Interior Design
345 Hudson St.
New York, NY 10014
(212) 519-7200
Published 15 times a year by Cahners
Publishing Co.

Interiors
770 Broadway
New York, NY 10003
(646) 654-5786
Published monthly by BPI
Communications

Interiors & Sources
666 Dundee Rd., Ste. 807
Northbrook, IL 60062-2769
(847) 498-6495
www.isdesignet.com
Published 8 times per year

Journal of Architectural Education (JAE)
Association of Collegiate Schools of
Architecture
1735 New York Avenue, NW
Washington, DC 20006
(202) 785-2324
www.acsa-arch.org
Published quarterly by MIT Press for the
ACSA

**Journal of the American Planning
Association**
122 S. Michigan Ave.
Suite 1600
Chicago, IL 60603-6107
(312) 431-9100
www.planning.org
Published quarterly

Architecture & Design Journals & Magazines (Con't)

Journal of the Society of Architectural Historians
1365 N. Astor St.
Chicago, IL 60610
(215) 735-0224
www.sah.org
Published quarterly by the Society of Architectural Historians

Landscape Architecture
636 Eye St. NW
Washington, DC 20001-3736
(800) 787-5257
www.asla.org
Published monthly by the American Society of Landscape Architects

Metropolis
61 W. 23rd St.
New York, NY 10010
(212) 627-9177
www.metropolismag.com
Published 10 times a year

Old House Journal
2 Main St.
Gloucester, MA 01930
(978) 283-3200
Published bimonthly

Perspective
341 Merchandise Mart
Chicago, IL 60654
(312) 467-1950
www.iida.org
The International Magazine of the International Interior Design Association, published quarterly

Places
Center for Environ. Design Research
University of California
390 Wurster Hall
Berkeley, CA 94720
(510) 642-1495
www.cedr.berkeley.edu
Published 3 times a year by the Design History Foundation

Preservation
1785 Massachucetts Ave. NW
Washington, DC 20036
(202) 588-6000
www.nthp.org
Published bimonthly by the National Trust for Historic Preservation

INTERNATIONAL PUBLICATIONS

Abitare
Editrice Abitare Segesta
15 Corso Monforte
Milano, 20122 - Italy
+39 027 60902202
www.abitare.it
Monthly magazine in Italian and English

AD (Architectural Design)
c/o John Wiley & Sons, Inc.
Journals Administration Department
605 Third Avenue
New York, NY 10158
(212) 850-6645
Bimonthly; Published by John Wiley & Sons

AJ (Architects' Journal)
151 Rosebery Avenue
33 39 Bowling Green Lane
London, EC1R 4GB - U.K.
+44 020 8956 3504
www.ajplus.co.uk
Published by EMAP Construct

Architecture & Design Journals & Magazines (Con't)

Arca
Via Valcava 6
Milano, 20155 - Italy
39 02 325246
www.arcadata.it
Published 11 times a year

Archis
Elsevier Bedrijfsinformatie bv
PO Box 4
7000 A Doetinchem, 7000
The Netherlands
31 314-349888
www.archis.org
Monthly bilingual magazine published by
the Netherlands Architecture Institute
(NAI) in collaboration with Elsevier
Business Information BV

**Architectural History: The Journal of the
Society of Architectural Historians of
Great Britain**
Pixham Mill, Pixham Lane
Dorking, Surrey, RH14 1PQ - U.K.
www.sahgb.org.uk
Published annually

Architectural Review
151 Rosebery Avenue
39 Bowling Green Lane
London, EC1R 4GB - U.K.
44 020 8956 3504
Published by EMAP Construct

Architecture Australia
4 Princes Street, Level 3
Port Melbourne, Victoria 3207
Australia
61 (03) 9646 4760
www.archmedia.com.au/aa/aa.htm
Official magazine of the RAIA

l'architecture d'aujourd'jui
6, rue Lhomond
Paris, F-75005 - France
+33 1 44321860
www.architecture-aujourdhui.presse.fr
Published 6 times a year in French and
English

Arkitektur
Norrlandsgatan 18, 2fr
P.O. Box 1742
Stockholm, S-111 87 - Sweden
+46 8 679 6105
www.arkitektur-forlag.se
Published eight times yearly; with English
summaries

a+u magazine
30-8, Yushima 2-chome, Bunkyo-ku
Tokyo, 113-0034 - Japan
+81 33816-2935
www.japan-architect.co.jp
Published monthly in Japanese and
English by A+U Publishing Co., Ltd.

Blueprint
Freepost, LON8209
London NW - U.K
+ 44 171 706 4596
Published monthly except August, by
Aspen Publishing

Canadian Architect
1450 Don Mills Road
Don Mills, Ontario, M3B 2X7 - Canada
(416) 510-6854
www.cdnarchitect.com
Published monthly by Southam Magazine
Group Limited

Architecture & Design Journals & Magazines (Con't)

Casabella
Via Manzoni 12
Rozzano
Milan, 20089 - Italy
+39 2 57512575
Published monthly in Italian with an English summary

El Croquis
Av. De los Reyes Catolicos 9
Madrid, E-28280 El Escorial - Spain
+34 918969414
www.elcroquis.es
Published bimonthly in Spanish and English

Daidalos
Redaktion Daidalos
Littenstra Be 106/107
Berlin, D-10179 - Germany
+49 30246575
www.gbhap.com/magazine
Published quarterly in English by The Gordon and Breach Publishing Group

Domus
Via Achille Grandi 5-7
Rozzano
Milan, 20089 - Italy
+39 0282472265
http://domus.edidomus.it
Published 11 times a year in Italian and English

Hinge
17/F, Queen's centre. Queen's Road east
Wanchai,
Hong Kong
+852 2520 2468
www.hingenet.com/hinge/hinge.htm
Published monthly

Japan Architect
31-2 Yshima 2-chome
Bunkyo-ku
Tokyo, 113-8501 - Japan
+81 33811-7101
www.japan-architect.co.jp
Published quarterly in Japanese and English

Journal of Architecture
11 New Fetter Lane
London, EC4P 4EE - U.K.
+44 171 583 9855
http://journals.routledge.com/
Published four times a year by Routledge for the RIBA

Journal of Urban Design
Institute of Urban Planning
University of Nottingham
University Park
Nottingham, NG7 2RD - U.K.
+44 115 951 4873
www.carfax.co.uk
Published 3 times a year by Carfax Publishing Limited for the Institute of Urban Planning

Ottagono
Via Stalingrado, 97/2
Bologna, 40128 - Italy
+39 051 4199711
www.ottagono.com
Published bimonthly in Italian and English

Rassegna
Via Stalingrado 97-2
Bologna, 40128 - Italy
+39 51 4199211
www.compositori.it
Published quarterly in Italian and English by Editrice Compositori

Architecture & Design Journals & Magazines (Con't)

World Architecture
Exchange Tower
5 Harbour Exchange Square
London, E14 9GE - U.K.
+44 171 560 4120
*Published 10 times a year by the Builder
Group*

Source: DesignIntelligence/*Counsel House Research*

What is far more important
than the structural economy
and its functional emphasis is
the intellectual achievement
which has made possible a
new spatial vision. For where-
as building is merely a matter
of methods and materials,
architecture implies the mastery of space.

Walter Gropius

COLLEGES & UNIVERSITIES

Degree Programs

The following chart provides a list of schools in the United States offering design and design related degrees. The degrees offered include associates (A), certificate (C), professional (P), bachelors (B), masters (M). All the architecture, interior design, landscape architecture, and planning programs indicated below are accredited by the disciplines' respective accrediting bodies: National Architectural Accrediting Board, Foundation for Interior Design Education Research, Landscape Architectural Accrediting Board, and Planning Accreditation Board. For degree programs not listed and accredited by other bodies and students seeking Ph.D. programs, the individual schools should be consulted. As the following is subject to change often, check with the schools for the most updated information.

School	City	Web Address	Architecture	Architecture History	Historic Preservation	Industrial Design	Interior Design	Landscape Architecture	Planning
ALABAMA									
Alabama A&M University	Normal	aamu.edu							B M
Auburn University	Auburn	auburn.edu	B			B M *	B	B	
Samford University	Birmingham	samford.edu					B		
Tuskegee University	Tuskegee	tusk.edu	B						
University of Alabama	Tuscaloosa	ua.edu					B		
ARIZONA									
Arizona State University	Tempe	asu.edu	M			B M	B	B	M
Frank Lloyd Wright School of Architecture	Scottsdale	taliesin.edu	M						
University of Arizona	Tucson	arizona.edu	B					M	M
ARKANSAS									
University of Arkansas	Fayetteville	uark.edu	B				B	B	

Degree Programs (Con't)

School	City	Web Address	Architecture	Architecture History	Historic Preservation	Industrial Design	Interior Design	Landscape Architecture	Planning
CALIFORNIA									
Academy of Art College	San Francisco	academyart.edu				B M *	B		
American Inter-Continental University	Los Angeles	aiuniv.edu					B		
Art Center College of Design	Pasadena	artcenter.edu				B M *			
Brooks College	Long Beach	brookscollege.edu					A		
California College of Arts and Crafts	San Francisco	ccac-art.edu	B			B *	B		
California Polytechnic State University	San Luis Obispo	calpoly.edu	B					B	B M
California State Polytechnic University	Pomona	csupomona.edu	B M					B	B M
California State University, Fresno	Fresno	csufresno.edu					B		
California State University, Long Beach	Long Beach	csulb.edu				B M *			
California State University, Northridge	Northridge	csun.edu				B	B		
California State University, Sacramento	Sacramento	csus.edu					B		
College of the Redwoods	Eureka	redwoods.cc.ca.us			C				
Design Institute of San Diego	San Diego	disd.edu					B		
Fashion Inst. of Design & Merchandising	Los Angeles	fidm.edu					A		
Interior Designers Institute	Newport Beach	idi.edu					B		
ITT Technical Institute	San Bernardino	itt-tech.edu				B			
Newschool of Architecture	San Diego	newschoolarch.edu	B M						
San Diego Mesa College	San Diego	Sdmesa.sdccd.cc.ca.us					A		
San Francisco State University	San Francisco	sfsu.edu				B M			
San Jose State University	San Jose	sjsu.edu				B *			M

Degree Programs (Con't)

School	City	Web Address	Architecture	Architecture History	Historic Preservation	Industrial Design	Interior Design	Landscape Architecture	Planning
Southern California Institute of Architecture	Los Angeles	sciarc.edu	B M						
Stanford University	Stanford	stanford.edu				B M			
University of California, Berkeley	Berkeley	berkeley.edu	M	M				M	M
University of California, Berkeley Extension	Berkeley	unex.berkeley.edu					C		
University of California at Davis	Davis	ucdavis.edu						B	
University of California at Irvine	Irvine	uci.edu							M
University of California at Los Angeles	Los Angeles	ucla.edu	M	M					M
University of California at Los Angeles Ext.	Los Angeles	unx.ucla.edu					P		
University of California at Santa Barbara	Santa Barbara	ucsb.edu		M					
University of Southern California	Los Angeles	usc.edu	B						M
West Valley College	Saratoga	westvalley.edu					C		
Woodbury University	Burbank	woodburyu.edu	B				B		
COLORADO									
Art Institute of Colorado	Denver	cia.aii.edu				B			
Colorado State University	Fort Collins	colostate.edu					B	B	
Metropolitan State College of Denver	Denver	mscd.edu				B			
University of Colorado at Denver/Boulder	Denver	cudenver.edu	M	M				M	M
CONNECTICUT									
University of Bridgeport	Bridgeport	bridgeport.edu				B *			
University of Connecticut	Storrs	uconn.edu						B	
Yale University	New Haven	yale.edu	M						

Degree Programs (Con't)

School	City	Web Address	Architecture	Architecture History	Historic Preservation	Industrial Design	Interior Design	Landscape Architecture	Planning
DISTRICT OF COLUMBIA									
Catholic University of America	Washington	cua.edu	B M						
George Washington University	Washington	www.gwu.edu		M					
George Wash. Univ. Mount Vernon College	Washington	www.mvc.gwu.edu					B		
Howard University	Washington	howard.edu	B						
FLORIDA									
Art Institute of Fort Lauderdale	Fort Lauderdale	aifl.edu				B			
Florida A&M University	Tallahassee	famu.edu	B M						
Florida Atlantic University	Fort Lauderdale	fau.edu	B						M
Florida International University	Miami	fiu.edu	M					M	
Florida State University	Tallahassee	fsu.edu		M			B		M
International Academy of Design, Tampa	Tampa	academy.edu					B		
International Fine Arts College	Miami	ifac.edu					A		
Ringling School of Art and Design	Sarasota	rsad.edu					B		
Seminole Community College	Sanford	seminole.cc.fl.us					A		
Florida Southern College	Lakeland	flsouthern.edu					A/4yr.		
University of Florida	Gainesville	ufl.edu	M				B	B M	M
University of Miami	Miami	miami.edu							
University of South Florida	Tampa	usf.edu	M						
GEORGIA									
American InterContinental Univ.	Atlanta	aiuniv.edu					B		

Degree Programs (Con't)

School	City	Web Address	Architecture	Architecture History	Historic Preservation	Industrial Design	Interior Design	Landscape Architecture	Planning
Art Institute of Atlanta	Dunwoody	aia.aii.edu					B		
Atlanta College of Art	Atlanta	aca.edu					B		
Bauder College	Atlanta	bauder.edu					A		
Brenau University	Gainesville	brenau.edu					B		
Georgia Institute of Technology	Atlanta	gatech.edu	M	M		B M			M
Georgia State University	Atlanta	gsu.edu			M				
Savannah College of Art and Design	Savannah	scad.edu	B	M	M B	B M			
Southern Polytechnic State University	Marietta	spsu.edu	B						
University of Georgia	Athens	uga.edu			C M		B	B M	
HAWAII									
University of Hawaii at Manoa	Honolulu	hawaii.edu	B M						M
IDAHO									
Ricks College	Rexburg	ricks.edu					P/3yr.		
University of Idaho	Moscow	uidaho.edu	B M					B	
ILLINOIS									
Harrington Institute of Interior Design	Chicago	interiordesign.edu					B		
Illinois Institute of Art at Schaumburg	Schaumburg	ilia.aii.edu					B		
Illinois Institute of Technology	Chicago	iit.edu	B M			M			
Int'l Academy of Merch. and Design, Chicago	Chicago	iamd.edu					B		
The Art Institute of Chicago	Chicago	artic.edu			M				
Southern Illinois University at Carbondale	Carbondale	siu.edu				B *	B		

Degree Programs (Con't)

School	City	Web Address	Architecture	Architecture History	Historic Preservation	Industrial Design	Interior Design	Landscape Architecture	Planning
University of Illinois at Chicago	Chicago	uic.edu	B M	M		B M			M
University of Illinois at Urbana-Champaign	Urbana-Champaign	uiuc.edu	M	M		B M *		B M	B M
INDIANA									
Ball State	Muncie	bsu.edu	B		M			B	B M
Indiana University	Bloomington	indiana.edu					B		
Purdue University	Lafayette	purdue.edu				B M	B	B	
ITT Technical Institute	Fort Wayne	itt-tech.edu				B			
University of Notre Dame	South Bend	nd.edu	B M			B M			
IOWA									
Iowa State University	Ames	iastate.edu	B M				B	B	B M
University of Iowa	Iowa City	uiowa.edu		M					M
KANSAS									
Kansas State University	Manhattan	ksu.edu	B				B	B M	M
University of Kansas	Lawrence	ukans.edu	B M			B M *			M
KENTUCKY									
University of Kentucky	Lexington	uky.edu	B		M		B	B	
University of Louisville	Louisville	louisville.edu		M			B		
LOUISIANA									
Louisiana State University	Baton Rouge	lsu.edu	B				B	B M	
Louisiana Tech University	Ruston	latech.edu	B				B		
Southern University A&M College	Baton Rouge	subr.edu	B						

Degree Programs (Con't)

School	City	Web Address	Architecture	Architecture History	Historic Preservation	Industrial Design	Interior Design	Landscape Architecture	Planning
Tulane University	New Orleans	tulane.edu	B M		M				
University of Louisiana at Lafayette	Lafayette	louisiana.edu	B			B	B		
University of New Orleans	New Orleans	uno.edu							M
MARYLAND									
Goucher College	Baltimore	goucher.edu			B M				
Morgan State University	Baltimore	morgan.edu	M					M	M
University of Maryland	College Park	umd.edu	B	M				M	M
MASSACHUSETTS									
Boston Architectural Center	Boston	the-bac.edu	B						
Boston University	Boston	bu.edu		M	M				
Endicott College	Beverly	endicott.edu					B		
Harvard University	Cambridge	harvard.edu	M					M	M
Massachusetts College of Art	Boston	massart.edu				B M *			
Massachusetts Institute of Technology	Cambridge	mit.edu	M	M					M
Mount Ida College	Newton	mountida.edu					B		
Newbury College	Brookline	newbury.edu					A		
New England School of Art & Des. at Suffolk U.	Boston	suffolk.edu					B		
University of Massachusetts/Amherst	Amherst	umass.edu					B	B M	M
Wentworth Institute of Technology	Boston	wit.edu	B			B	B		
MICHIGAN									
Andrews University	Berrien Springs	andrews.edu	B						
Center for Creative Studies	Detriot	ccscad.edu				B *			

Degree Programs (Con't)

School	City	Web Address	Architecture	Architecture History	Historic Preservation	Industrial Design	Interior Design	Landscape Architecture	Planning
Cranbrook Academy of Art	Bloomfield Hills	cranbrookart.edu				M *			
Eastern Michigan University	Ypsilanti	emich.edu			M		B		B
Kendall College of Art and Design	Grand Rapids	kcad.edu				B *	B		
Lawrence Technological University	Southfield	ltu.edu	B M				B		
Michigan State University	East Lansing	msu.edu					B	B	B M
University of Detroit Mercy	Detroit	udmercy.edu	B						
University of Michigan	Ann Arbor	umich.edu	M			B M *		M	M
Wayne State University	Detriot	wayne.edu							M
Western Michigan University	Kalamazoo	wmich.edu				B *	B		
MINNESOTA									
Alexandria Technical College	Alexandria	alextech.org					A		
Dakota County Technical College	Rosemount	dctc.mnscu.edu					Pre-P		
University of Minnesota	St. Paul/ Mpls.	umn.edu	B M				B	M	M
MISSISSIPPI									
Mississippi State University	Mississippi State	msstate.edu	B				B	B	
University of Southern Mississippi	Hattiesburg	usm.edu					B		
MISSOURI									
Drury University	Springfield	drury.edu	B						
Kansas City Art Institute	Kansas City	kcai.edu				B*			
Maryville University of St. Louis	St. Louis	maryvillestl.edu					B		
Southeast Missouri State University	Cape Girardeau	semo.edu			B M				

Degree Programs (Con't)

School	City	Web Address	Architecture	Architecture History	Historic Preservation	Industrial Design	Interior Design	Landscape Architecture	Planning
University of Missouri, Columbia	Columbia	missouri.edu		M			B		
Washington University	St. Louis	wsu.edu	M						
MONTANA									
Montana State University	Bozeman	montana.edu	B M						
NEBRASKA									
University of Nebraska	Lincoln	unl.edu	M				B		M
NEVADA							B		
University of Nevada, Las Vegas	Las Vegas	unlv.edu	M					B	
NEW JERSEY							A		
Berkeley College/ Bergen Campus	Waldwick	berkeleycollege. edu					B		
Kean University	Union	kean.edu					B		
New Jersey Institute of Technology	Newark	njit.edu	B M						
Princeton University	Princeton	princeton.edu	M						
Rutgers, The State Univ. of New Jersey	New Brunswick	rutgers.edu		M				B	M
NEW MEXICO									
University of New Mexico	Albuquerque	unm.edu	M	M					M
NEW YORK									
City College of the City University of New York	New York	ccny.cuny.edu	B						
Columbia University	New York	columbia.edu		M	M				M
Cooper Union	New York	cooper.edu	B						
Cornell University	Ithaca	cornell.edu	B	M	M		B	B M	M

Degree Programs (Con't)

School	City	Web Address	Architecture	Architecture History	Historic Preservation	Industrial Design	Interior Design	Landscape Architecture	Planning
Fashion Inst. of Tech. State Univ. of New York	New York	Fitnyc.suny.edu					A		
Hunter College, City University of New York	New York	hunter.cuny.edu							M
New York Inst. of Tech. - Old Westbury	Old Westbury	nyit.edu	B?				B		
New York School of Interior Design	New York	nysid.edu					B		
New York University	New York	nyu.edu		M					M
Parsons School of Design	New York	parsons.edu	M			B *			
Pratt Institute	Brooklyn	pratt.edu	B			B M *	B		M
Rensselaer Polytechnic Institute	Troy	rpi.edu	B M						
Rochester Institute of Technology	Rochester	rit.edu				B M *			
School of Visual Arts	New York	schoolofvisualarts.edu					B		
State University of New York at Binghamton	Binghamton	binghamton.edu		M					
State University of New York at Buffalo	Buffalo	buffalo.edu	M						M[I]
State University of New York at Syracuse	Syracuse	esf.edu						B M	
Suffolk County Community College	Riverhead	sunysuffolk.edu					A		
Syracuse University	Syracuse	syr.edu	B M	M		B M *	B		
University at Albany, Suny	Albany	albany.edu							M
Villa Maria College of Buffalo	Buffalo	villa.edu					A		
NORTH CAROLINA									
East Carolina University	Greenville	ecu.edu					B		
Meredith College	Raleigh	meredith.edu					B		
North Carolina A & T State University	Greensboro	ncat.edu					B		

Degree Programs (Con't)

School	City	Web Address	Architecture	Architecture History	Historic Preservation	Industrial Design	Interior Design	Landscape Architecture	Planning
North Carolina State University	Raleigh	ncsu.edu	B M			B M		B M	
University of North Carolina at Chapel Hill	Chapel Hill	unc.edu							M
University of North Carolina at Charlotte	Charlotte	uncc.edu	B						
University of North Carolina at Greensboro	Greensboro	uncg.edu					B		
Western Carolina University	Cullowhee	wcu.edu					B		
NORTH DAKOTA									
North Dakota State University	Fargo	ndsu.nodak.edu	B				B	B	
OHIO									
Belmont Technical College	St. Clairsville	belmont.cc.oh.us			A				
Cleveland Institute of Art	Cleveland	cia.edu				B *			
Cleveland State University	Cleveland	csuohio.edu							M
Columbus College of Art & Design	Columbus	ccad.edu				B *	B		
Kent State University	Kent	kent.edu	B				B		
Miami University	Oxford	muohio.edu	M						
Ohio State University	Columbus	ohio-state.edu	M	M		B M *	B	B M	M
Ohio University	Athens	ohiou.edu					B		
University of Akron	Akron	uakron.edu					B		
University of Cincinnati	Cincinnati	uc.edu	B			B M *	B		B M
OKLAHOMA									
Oklahoma State University	Stillwater	okstate.edu	B				B	B	
University of Oklahoma	Norman	ou.edu	B M				B	M	M

Degree Programs (Con't)

School	City	Web Address	Architecture	Architecture History	Historic Preservation	Industrial Design	Interior Design	Landscape Architecture	Planning
OREGON									
Portland State University	Portland	pdx.edu							M
University of Oregon	Eugene	uoregon.edu	B M	M	M		B M	B	M
PENNSYLVANIA									
Bucks County Community College	Newtown	bucks.edu			C				
Carnegie Mellon University	Pittsburgh	cmu.edu	B			B M *			
Drexel University	Philadelphia	drexel.edu	B				B		
La Roche College	Pittsburgh	laroche.edu					B		
Moore College of Art and Design	Philadelphia	moore.edu					B		
Pennsylvania State University	State College	psu.edu	B	M				B	
Philadelphia University	Philadelphia	philau.edu	B			B	B		
Temple University	Philadelphia	temple.edu	B					B	
University of Pennsylvania	Philadelphia	upenn.edu	M	M	M			M	M
University of Pittsburgh	Pittsburgh	pitt.edu		M					
University of the Arts	Philadelphia	uarts.edu				B M *			
RHODE ISLAND									
Brown University	Providence	brown.edu		M					
Rhode Island School of Design	Providence	risd.edu	B M			B M *		B M	
Roger Williams University	Bristol	rwu.edu	B		B				
University of Rhode Island	Kingston	uri.edu						B	M
SOUTH CAROLINA									
Clemson University	Clemson	clemson.edu	M					B	M

Degree Programs (Con't)

School	City	Web Address	Architecture	Architecture History	Historic Preservation	Industrial Design	Interior Design	Landscape Architecture	Planning
College of Charleston	Charleston	cofc.edu			B				
Winthrop University	Rock Hill	winthrop.edu					B		
TENNESSEE									
Middle Tennessee State University	Murfreesboro	mtsu.edu			M		B		
O'More College of Design	Franklin	omorecollege.edu					B		
University of Memphis	Memphis	memphis.edu							M
University of Tennessee, Knoxville	Knoxville	utk.edu	B M				B		M
Watkins College of Art & Design	Nashville	watkins.edu					A		
TEXAS									
El Centro College	Dallas	ecc.dcccd.edu					C		
Houston Comm. College System/Central College	Houston	hccs.cc.tx.us/					A		
Prairie View A&M University	Prairie View	pvamu.edu	B						
Rice University	Houston	rice.edu	B M						
Southwest Texas State University	San Marcos	swt.edu					B		
Stephen F. Austin State University	Nacogdoches	sfasu.edu					B		
Texas A&M University	College Station	tamu.edu	M					B M	M
Texas Christian University	Fort Worth	tcu.edu					B		
Texas Tech University	Lubbock	ttu.edu	B M				B	B	
University of Houston	Houston	uh.edu	B M						
University of North Texas	Denton	unt.edu					B		
University of Texas at Arlington	Arlington	uta.edu	M				B	M	M

Degree Programs (Con't)

School	City	Web Address	Architecture	Architecture History	Historic Preservation	Industrial Design	Interior Design	Landscape Architecture	Planning
University of Texas at Austin	Austin	utexas.edu	B M	M	C M		B		M
University of Texas at San Antonio	San Antonio	utsa.edu	M^2				B		
UTAH									
ITT Technical Institute	Murray	itt-tech.edu				B			
Utah State University	Logan	usu.edu					B	B M	
University of Utah	Salt Lake City	utah.edu	M		M				
VERMONT									
Norwich University	Northfield	norwich.edu	B M						
University of Vermont	Burlington	uvm.edu			M				
VIRGINIA									
Hampton University	Hampton	hamptonu.edu	B						
James Madison University	Harrisonburg	jmu.edu					B		
Marymount University	Arlington	marymount.edu					B		
Mary Washington College	Fredericks-burg	mwc.edu			B				
University of Virginia	Charlottesville	virginia.edu	M	M				M	B M
Virginia Commonwealth Univ.	Richmond	vcu.edu		M			B		M
Virginia Polytechnic Inst. and State Univ.	Blacksburg	vt.edu	B M			B M	B	B M	M
WASHINGTON									
Eastern Washington University	Spokane	ewu.edu							B M
Washington State University	Pullman	wsu.edu	B				B	B	
Western Washington University	Bellingham	wwu.edu				B			

Degree Programs (Con't)

School	City	Web Address	Architecture	Architecture History	Historic Preservation	Industrial Design	Interior Design	Landscape Architecture	Planning
University of Washington	Seattle	washington.edu	M	M		B M		B M	M
WEST VIRGINIA									
West Virginia University	Morgantown	wvu.edu					B	B	
WISCONSIN									
Milwaukee Institute of Art & Design	Milwaukee	miad.edu				B *			
Mount Mary College	Milwaukee	mtmary.edu					B		
University of Wisconsin, Madison	Madison	wisc.edu		M			B	B	M
University of Wisconsin, Milwaukee	Milwaukee	uwm.edu	M						M
Univ. of Wisconsin, Stevens Point	Stevens Point	uwsp.edu					B		
University of Wisconsin, Stout	Menomonie	uwstout.edu				B *	B		

1 This program is currently in probationary status with the Planning Accreditation Board (PAB).
2 This program is currently in candidate status for National Architectural Accreditation Board (NAAB) accreditation.
* This Program is accredited by the National Association of Schools of Art & Design.

Source: Foundation for Interior Design Education Research (FIDER), Industrial Designers Society of America (IDSA), Landscape Architectural Accreditation Board (LAAB), National Architectural Accrediting Board (NAAB), National Council for Preservation Education (NCPE), Planning Accreditation Board (PAB), Society of Architectural Historians (SAH)

Educational Resources

In addition to the individual schools, the following organizations can provide information about design education.

ARCHITECTURE

Association of Collegiate Schools of Architecture (ACSA)
1735 New York Avenue, NW
Washington, DC 20006
Tel: (202) 785-2324
Internet: www.acsa-arch.org

National Architectural Accrediting Board (NAAB)
1735 New York Avenue, NW,
Washington, DC 20006
Telephone: (202) 783-2007
Internet: www.naab.org

ARCHITECTURE HISTORY

Society of Architectural Historians (SAH)
1365 North Astor Street
Chicago, Illinois 60610
Telephone: (312) 573-1365
Internet: www.sah.org

HISTORIC PRESERVATION

National Council for Preservation Education (NCPE)
Internet: www.uvm.edu/histpres/ncpe/

INDUSTRIAL DESIGN

Industrial Designers Society of America (IDSA)
1142 Walker Road
Great Falls, VA 22066
Telephone: 703-759-0100
Internet: www.idsa.org

INTERIOR DESIGN

Foundation for Interior Design Education Research (FIDER)
60 Monroe Center NW, Suite 300
Grand Rapids, MI 49503-2920
Telephone: (616) 458-0400
Internet: www.fider.org

LANDSCAPE ARCHITECTURE

Council of Educators in Landscape Architecture (CELA)
Internet: www.uidaho.edu/cela/

Landscape Architectural Accreditation Board (LAAB)
Internet: www.asla.org/nonmembers/
accreditedprograms.cfm

PLANNING

Association of Collegiate Schools of Planning (ACSP)
Internet: www.uwm.edu/Org/acsp/

Planning Accreditation Board (PAB)
Internet: http://showcase.netins.net/
web/pabfi66/

Did you know...

In 1865, architect William Robert Ware began the United States' first school of architecture at the Massachucetts Institute of Technology.

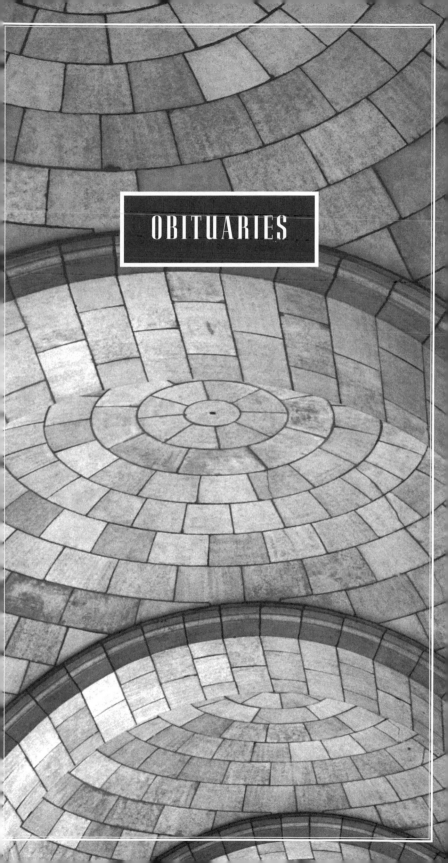

OBITUARIES

Leon Allain, 75

Leon Allain, one of the first black architects in Georgia, died June 20, 2000. Allain studied architecture at the University of Michigan, where he received his bachelor's degree in 1949. He worked for a few architecture firms in New York before moving to Atlanta, where he opened his own practice with Edward Miller in 1958. After nine years, he formed his own firm, Allain & Associates. Some of his notable Atlanta projects include the Martin Luther King Jr. International Chapel at Morehouse College, the Catholic Center at the Atlanta University Center, renovation of the Friendship Baptist Church, the Morehouse School of Medicine campus, and, in a joint venture, the Hartsfield International Airport and the Georgia Dome.

Tony Arefin, 38

Tony Arefin, former creative director of *I.D.* magazine, died May 19, 2000. Arefin was a self-taught designer and brilliant visual thinker. He was born in Pakistan and raised in Bangladesh and London, where he became a well-known designer of art catalogues and exhibition posters. His work is included in the collections of the Victoria & Albert Museum and the Design Museum. He was also a curator and design director for the Photographer's Gallery and the Institute of Contemporary Art. He came to the United States to take over creative direction for *I.D.* magazine in 1993, where he infused the publication with warmth and humanism, producing many notable issues. After leaving *I.D.* in 1997, he worked for the advertising firm Widen & Kennedy, then Ogilvy & Mather. In 2000 he won a Clio Award for his contribution to the IBM Magic Box campaign.

Walter Blackburn, 62

Walter Blackburn, FAIA, an Indianapolis architect and national leader on diversity issues, died August 9, 2000. Most recently, his Indianapolis firm, Blackburn Architects, completed the National Underground Railroad Freedom Center in Cincinnati, Ohio. During the 1990s, Blackburn was instrumental in raising awareness of diversity issues at The American Institute of Architects in Washington, D.C. spearheading the formation of the AIA Diversity Committee. He was also elected AIA national vice president in 1994. Blackburn received his architecture degree from Howard University in 1963.

Bruce Ethan Borland, 40

The prodigious golf course architect, Bruce Ethan Borland, died October 25, 1999. Borland received his landscape architecture degree from the University of Illinois at Urbana-Champaign in 1981. He worked for several firms in Chicago, including David Gill & Associates and Killiam and Nugent, before beginning his own design firm in 1989. Borland earned a reputation as a top designer of golf courses and, in 1990, joined Jack Nicklaus' golf course design firm as a design associate. Borland was also one of the first golf course architects to use computers in designing a course.

Theodore R. Butler, 70

Theodore R. (Ted) Butler, FAIA, retired vice president at Hammel, Green and Abrahamson (HGA), died September 23, 2000. During his 35-year career at HGA, Butler designed a number of buildings that won national awards. He received his architecture degree from the University of Minnesota and began working at HGA in 1960 where he specialized in church architecture. Some of his notable projects include the Colonial Church of Edina, MN, and St. Bede's Priory in Eau Claire, WI. Butler retired from HGA in 1996.

Martin Caroe, 66

English preservation architect Martin Caroe died November 19, 1999. Caroe came from a distinguished family of architects. His grandfather, W. D. Caroe, was an active member of the Arts and Crafts movement and founder of the family firm, now Caroe & Partners. Martin's father, Alban Caroe, was a successful cathedral and church architect, and Martin's son, Oliver, is now the fourth generation to run the practice. Martin's focus and finest successes were in church conservation, especially stone conservation techniques. His greatest achievement was the conservation of the sculpture on the west front of Wells Cathedral in England. He also served as consultant to the Tower of London between 1991 and 1998 regarding maintenance and conservation of the complex.

Jot D. Carpenter, 61

Jot D. Carpenter, FASLA, an Ohio State University professor of landscape architecture, died February 17, 2000. During his 28-year career at Ohio State University, Carpenter served as the chair of the Department of Landscape Architecture from 1972 to 1986. His teaching focus included site planning, history of the profession, and AUTOCAD/GIS applications. As an active member of the American Society of Landscape Architects (ASLA), Carpenter served as its president in 1978-79 and on numerous committees and task forces. His book *Handbook of Landscape Architectural Construction* was named one of the ten most influential books on landscape architecture of the past century by *Landscape Architecture* magazine. Carpenter received his bachelor's degree in landscape architecture from the University of Georgia in 1960 and a master's degree from Harvard University in 1962.

Carroll Cline, 72

Carroll B. Cline, a noted lighting designer, died February 24, 2000. Cline designed creative lighting schemes for the Santa Fe Opera Theater in Santa Fe, NM, the Norman Rockwell Museum in Stockbridge, MA, and the lobby of 1251 Avenue of the Americas in New York City. After studying architecture at the Illinois Institute of Technology, he joined Skidmore, Owings, and Merrill. In 1962 while collaborating with Edison Price, a lighting fixture manufacturer, Cline switched his career focus to lighting design and joined Price's company as a vice president. In 1985 he founded Cline Bettridge Bernstein Lighting Design.

Ernest Allen Connally, 78

Preservation leader Ernest Allen Connally died December 23, 1999. Throughout his long and varied career, Connally served as educator, author, government administrator, and national and international advocate for preservation. Connally graduated from the University of Texas at Austin with a degree in architecture in 1950. After receiving a master's and doctoral degree from Harvard University in the history and principles of fine arts, he taught at Miami University in Ohio, Washington University, and the University of Illinois at Champaign-Urbana. He joined the National Park Service in 1967, retiring in 1992 as its Associate Director and Chief Appeals Officer for the rehabilitation tax credit program. During his career, he also served as chairman and secretary-general of the U.S. Committee of the International Council of

Monuments and Sites (ICOMOS) and as a U.S. delegate to the United Nations Educational, Scientific and Cultural Organization (UNESCO). Among the many honors and awards bestowed upon him were the Louise duPont Crowninshield Award from the National Trust for Historic Preservation, the Department of the Interior's Distinguished Service Award, and honorary membership in The American Institute of Architects.

Jane Davies, 86

Jane Davies, an architectural historian and Alexander J. Davis scholar, died February 9, 2000. Davies first developed an interest in A. J. Davis in the 1950s and spent the rest of her life studying his work and collecting his prints, drawings, and furniture. She earned a B.A. from Wellesley College in 1935 and degrees in German history and library science from Columbia University in 1942 and 1944, where she subsequently became a reference librarian and rare books cataloguer. Although she never received a degree in art or architecture history, Davies was considered the pre-eminent authority on the nineteenth century American architect Alexander J. Davis. She wrote an introduction to the 1980 reprint of Davis's *Rural Residents*, the first American architectural patternbook for house plans; served as the consulting curator for the Metropolitan Museum of Arts' 1992-93 exhibition entitled "Alexander Jackson Davis, American Architect;" and spent more than 30 years researching and compiling a comprehensive biography of A. J. Davis.

Eladio Dieste, 83

The Uruguayan modernist Eladio Dieste died in 2000. This celebrated architect and engineer is virtually unknown outside of South America. Dieste studied engineering at the University of the Republic of Montevideo in Uruguay. During his early career, he worked in Uruguay's public works department specializing in bridges before becoming head of the technical section of the department's Architecture Office. He then established an architecture and engineering practice, Dieste y Montáñez, in Montevideo, Uruguay, in 1954. Dieste's designs combine the country's mid-century drive for large-scale urban modernization, the limited resources–both in material and skills, and expressive forms. Although Dieste never studied architecture, his work earned him honorary architecture degrees from the University of the Republic of Montevideo and the University of Buenos Aires in Argentina.

Garrett Eckbo, 89

Professor and modernist landscape architect Garrett Eckbo died May 14, 2000. Throughout his practice, Eckbo designed such diverse projects as the grounds for the Central Valley housing project for migrant farm workers to gardens for such Hollywood legends as Gary Cooper and Louis B. Mayer. Eckbo studied landscape architecture at the University of California Berkeley and Harvard University, where he studied under Walter Gropius and was exposed to the modern movement. These modernist ideals drove his approach to landscape design, and he soon became a leader in the modern landscape movement. After practicing in Los Angeles and San Francisco, he joined the landscape architecture faculty at the University of California, Berkeley in 1965. He served as department chairman until 1969 and retired in 1978. Throughout his career, Eckbo received numerous awards, including the American Society of Landscape Architects' Medal of Honor and wrote many influential books such as *Landscapes for Living* and *Urban Landscape Design*.

Milton Fischer, 89

Milton Fischer, a Washington, D.C. architect and former U.S Housing Authority official, died October 2, 1999. Following World War II, Fischer settled in Washington, D.C. and supervised the post-war housing boom as a regional director of the National Housing Agency. In the 1950s, he joined Corning and Moore, which later became Corning Moore, Elmore and Fischer, and then Fischer and Elmore. During his years with the firm, Fischer was an associate architect on the Watergate project and principal architect on the Foxhall housing complex, both in D.C. His other work included B'nai B'rith International, the national headquarters for the American Association of University Women, the Federal Bar Building, the Georgetown Inn, and St. Francis Episcopal Church in Potomac, Maryland.

James Marston Fitch, 90

Preservation leader, educator, historian, and architect James Marston Fitch died April 10, 2000. While teaching at Columbia University, Fitch began the country's first graduate program in historic preservation in 1964, which has graduated over 1,000 students in the last 35 years. He also served as the director of historic preservation for New York's Beyer Blinder Belle Architects for 21 years where he was involved in such notable restorations as Ellis Island and Grand Central

Station. Fitch's 1947 American Building: The Environmental Forces That Shape It (reprinted 1970, 1972, 1999) has influenced generations of architects and was an early proponent of green architecture. He served as an editor of Architectural Record from 1936 to 1939. Always concerned for the human element in design, Fitch believed that "the ultimate task of architecture is to act in favor of human beings."

Louis E. Fry Sr., 97

Louis E. Fry Sr., FAIA, an influential practitioner, teacher and mentor to many African-American architects, died June 10, 2000. Fry was also a founding member of the National Organization of Minority Architects (NOMA) and served as the chair of the architecture department at Tuskegee and Lincoln Universities. Fry established the first architecture program at Tuskegee University in 1935 and later designed the Tuskegee Chapel in conjunction with Paul Rudolph. From 1947 to 1954, he was a professor at Howard University, where he also designed Douglass Hall and the Founder's Library. Until his retirement in 1972, Fry practiced architecture at Fry and Welch, a firm he founded in 1954. He received a M.Arch degree from Harvard University in 1945.

Elizabeth Gordon, 94

Elizabeth Gordon, influential editor of *House Beautiful*, died September 3, 2000. During her 20 year career as editor of *House Beautiful*, a role she assumed in 1939, she used the magazine as a means to educate the American public about appropriate design and new American architecture. She spent whole issues discussing climate control, California ranch houses, and other emerging design trends to arm her readers against the overpowering influence of the International style, preferring instead to promote a softer approach to contemporary design. As a result of her views, Frank Lloyd Wright became a mentor and close friend. Gordon even arranged for the magazine to furnish one of his Usonian houses. She is also credited with introducing Shibui, a traditional Japanese design philosophy, to the United States in a 1960 essay. After her retirement in 1964, Gordon continued to lecture and consult on design matters. She became a knight, first class, in the Finnish Order of the Lion for her 1972 special issue on Scandinavian design and was appointed a honorary member of The American Institute of Architects in 1987.

Ted Graber, 80

Influential interior designer Ted Graber died June 3, 2000. Graber attended the Chouinard Art Institute of Los Angeles and received his first interior design commission at age 17. He began his career working with such notable clients as Alfred and Betsy Bloomingdale, Jack Benny, Joan Crawford, and Jack Warner. However, he received national attention for his work with Nancy Reagan to redesign and update the family living quarters at the White House. During this project, Graber lived at the White House for nine months to supervise the restoration of furniture and antiques; the replacement of wallpaper, paint, and fixtures; and the upgrading of the plumbing and electrical systems. The Reagans later hired Graber to refurbish their Bel-Air home. He retired in 1989.

Karl Greimel, 69

Karl Greimel, dean of architecture at Lawrence Technological University in Southfield, Michigan, died April 24, 2000. When Greimel became Dean at Lawrence Technological University in 1974, he turned the school into a nationally recognized university for architecture. He attracted top faculty members, raised money, toughened coursework, and eventually earned accreditation for the program. Through his ArchiLecture program, he brought a number of internationally renowned architects, such as Cesar Pelli and John Burgee, to the school to lecture and work with the students. The students themselves best remember him for the unwavering support and encouragement he gave them, especially at jury time when criticism typically runs high. In addition to his role as an educator, Greimel also practiced as an urban planning consultant.

Dale W. Gruyé, 70

Industrial designer, Dale W. Gruyé, died July 12, 2000. Gruyé attended the University of Minnesota and the Art Center College of Design in Los Angeles, California, where he received a bachelor's degree in industrial design in 1958. He began his career with General Electric, then became an industrial designer for Hewlett-Packard in Palo Alto, California, in 1960. Subsequently, he co-founded and was principal of Gruyé-Vogt Organization (GVO), an internationally known industrial design firm. In 1978 he formed his own firm, Gruyé Associates, which specialized in corporate identity development, graphics, and trade show exhibit design.

John Hejduk, I

Architect and educator John Hejduk, died July 3, 2000. Hejduk was the Dean of Architecture at the Cooper Union in New York City where he influenced some of today's most noteworthy architects such as Daniel Libeskind, Toshiko Mori, and Elizabeth Diller. He studied at Cooper Union and the University of Cincinnati and received a master's degree in architecture from the Harvard Graduate School of Design in 1953. Hejduk taught at the University of Texas at Austin with Colin Rowe and Robert Slutsky and later worked with I.M. Pei. In 1964 he began teaching at Cooper Union where he served as dean from 1975 until his retirement in June 2000.

George Hellmuth, 2

Co-founder of Hellmuth, Obata + Kassabaum (HOK), George Hellmuth, FAIA, died in November 1999. In 1955, with co-founders Gyo Obata and George E. Kassabaum, Hellmuth founded HOK in St. Louis. He spearheaded the firm's philosophy of market specialization in building type and location, which has helped the firm to grow from 26 employees to today more than 1,600 in 24 offices worldwide. Hellmuth served as HOK's board chair until 1979 when he became chair of HOK International, Inc. Some of the significant commissions he was instrumental in procuring include the terminal at Lambert-St. Louis International Airport; Southern Illinois University at Edwardsville; the Priory Chapel in St. Louis; and the E. R. Squibb & Sons, Inc. Headquarters and Research Center in Lawrenceville, New Jersey. He also served as the chair of St. Louis' Landmarks and Urban Design Commission for 20 years and was a member of the Board of Directors of Downtown St. Louis, Inc.

Richard Himmel, 79

Richard Himmel, FASID, an internationally acclaimed interior designer, died April 5, 2000. In addition to residential commissions from such prominent individuals as Irv Kupcinet and Mohammad Ali, Himmel produced designs for corporate jets, country clubs, banks, restaurants, and night clubs. He studied journalism and English at the University of Chicago and began an interior design business with his sister after serving in World War II. In 1985 Himmel was inducted into the Interior Designers Hall of Fame. He was also a founder of the Chicago Designers Club and a fellow of the American Society of Interior Designers. Besides a successful design career, Himmel was a novelist, writing more than a dozen books which have sold over 11 million copies.

Friedensreich Hundertwasser, 71

The colorfully expressive Austrian architect and painter Friedensreich Hundertwasser died February 19, 2000. Hundertwasser originally earned acclaim for his paintings but is currently better known for his unique architectural design with bright colors, wavy lines, and bold ornament as its hallmarks. He studied briefly at the Vienna Academy of Art, leaving to pursue painting. One of his most famous buildings is the Hundertwasserhaus, a residential block in Vienna which opened in 1985. Its bands of alternating color, unusual windows, and onion-dome cupolas have made it an attractive tourist destination. Hundertwasser's strong environmentalism was also evident in his buildings where he liked to incorporate gardens and plants on the rooftops.

Floyd Elmer Johnson, 90

Retired Charlottesville, Virginia, architect Floyd Elmer Johnson, FAIA, died October 9, 1999. He was a past chairman of the Virginia State Fine Arts Commission and a partner in the firm of Johnson, Craven and Gibson. During his years with the firm from 1940 to 1994, Johnson's many projects included the Albemarle County Courthouse, the Charlottesville airport terminal, and many buildings at the University of Virginia. Johnson also worked with the Thomas Jefferson Memorial Foundation at Monticello for over 50 years and was an instructor at the University of Virginia. Throughout his career, he received numerous honors from many organizations including the Association for the Preservation of Virginia Antiquities, the Civic League of Charlottesville & Albemarle County, and the Virginia chapter of The American Institute of Architects.

Robert Trent Jones Sr., 93

One of the world's most preeminent golf course designers who is credited with the design of over 500 courses in 40 states and 35 countries, Robert Trent Jones, died June 14, 2000. Jones helped to transform golf course architecture into the highly specialized profession it is today and is known as the creator of the "signature golf course." Over the years, his courses have hosted 79 national championships, including 20 U.S. Opens and 12 PGA Championships, and six of his foreign courses have hosted the World Cup of Golf. Jones attended Cornell University where he studied landscape architecture, agronomy, horticulture, hydraulics, and surveying, all subjects intended to help him become a golf course designer.

After working for Canadian golf course designer Stanley Thompson, Jones struck out on his own in the late 1930s. He designed public courses through the Depression until his career began to soar after World War II. Jones was a charter member of the American Society of Golf Course Architects in 1948.

im Kirby, 6

Specifications specialist Tim Kirby died in April 2000. He began his career with Atlanta's Thompson, Ventulett & Stainback International as the chief of specifications. He later established an Atlanta-based specifications consulting firm with William Dyer and was a partner in Construction Insights, a Chicago-based marketing consulting firm for manufacturers of construction building products. Kirby was also active in The American Institute of Architects. Most recently he served as chair of the Uniform Construction Index Task Force of the AIA Documents Committee and was past chair of the MASTERSPEC Review Committee.

Jwe F. Koehler

Ball State University architecture professor Uwe F. Koehler died October 22, 1999. Born in Germany, Koehler first came to the United States in 1968 on a Fulbright Scholarship. He received a master's degree in architecture and planning from the Technical University in Berlin and a master's degree in architecture from Virginia Polytechnic Institute and State University. He began teaching at Ball State University in 1971. Throughout his career, Koehler became involved in a number of projects throughout the U.S. and abroad. During his leave from Ball State in 1981-83, he served as an advisor to the Minister of Housing Affairs in Riyadh, Saudi Arabia. With his efforts in tornado research and seismic design, he also consulted with the National Safety Council. His most recent work involved research on elderly housing issues.

'rancisco Kripacz, 57

Francisco Kripacz, the 1985 *Interiors'* Designer of the Year and partner of the Vancouver-based interior design firm, Arthur Erickson, died April 3, 2000. After studying design at the Vancouver School of Art and the Pratt Institute in New York, Kripacz began his career in Arthur Erickson's Toronto office. He received his earliest recognition for his 1971 designs for the Ottawa residence and offices of Canadian Prime Minister Pierre Trudeau. Between 1981 and 1991, he headed Erickson' Los Angeles office. According to Erickson, Kripacz contributed "a true understanding of how much further an interior designer, when in sympathy with the work, can extend it beyond the limited vision of the architect."

Carl Lewis, 52

Carl Lewis, AIA, a partner of Fox & Fowle Architects in New York City, died May 29, 2000. Throughout his career, Lewis held high-level positions in corporate interiors at Hellmuth, Obata + Kassabaum (HOK), Beyer Blinder Belle, and Perkins & Will. He joined Fox & Fowle in 1993. Some of his notable projects include the Bausch & Lomb headquarters in Rochester, New York (1995); the Tenneco headquarters in Greenwich, Connecticut (1996); the Tommy Hilfiger administrative offices in South Brunswick, New Jersey (1996); the Herman Miller showroom in Manhattan (1996); and the American Bible Society in Manhattan (1998). He also served as chair of the national AIA Interiors Committee during the late 1980s.

Ross Littell, 75

Ross Littell, a furniture and textile designer, died April 17, 2000. According to Terence Riley, chief curator for architecture and design at the Museum of Modern Art, Littell was "one of the key designers during what was a golden moment for American design." Littell won many awards from the American Institute of Decorators for his furniture designs, which were known for their lightweight materials and minimalist style. In 1950, Littell and his partners, fellow Pratt Institute classmates William Katavolos and Douglas Kelly, created the T-chair, an elegant three-legged piece of chrome and leather, which is part of the Museum of Modern Art's permanent collection. After working for Knoll and Herman Miller in the 1950s and 1960s, Littell moved to Denmark, then Italy, where he worked on textile and furniture designs for European manufacturers.

Dominique Bonnamour Lloyd, 43

Architect and teacher Dominique Bonnamour Lloyd died in December 1999. Born and raised in Paris, Lloyd attended college in Zurich, Switzerland, and graduated from the Beaux Arts National Graduate School of Architecture in France. She came to the United States in 1981 and worked for various architecture firms in Arizona. In 1991 she opened her own firm, Accent Architecture, and the following year began teaching at the University of Arizona in Tucson. She subsequently was heavily recruited by the Georgia Institute of Technology in Atlanta. As a member of their faculty, she received numerous awards, including an early career achievement award and was awarded tenure in 1998. In addition to architecture, Lloyd was an avid painter.

Edward Louge, 78

Former director of the Boston Redevelopment Authority, Edward Louge, died January 27, 2000. Louge spent his career revitalizing communities on the east coast, first in New Haven, Connecticut, as the development administrator overseeing the rebuilding of that community's decaying downtown. His most notable project, the Faneuil Hall-Quincy Market restoration in Boston, became a much copied model around the United States. His other contributions in Boston included the new Government Center, completion of the Prudential Center, and various neighborhood revitalizations. He later worked in New York City in the South Bronx and other areas.

Maynard Lyndon, 92

Maynard Lyndon, a Los Angeles architect who was best known for his school designs, died November 30, 1999. During his career, Lyndon designed over 40 schools. His 1936 Northville Elementary School in Michigan, with its concrete, brick and glass construction, is considered the first modern public school in North America. Natural light and courtyards were central themes in his designs. He was also a pioneer in the use of large areas of glass. Lyndon's controversial 1964 design for UCLA's Bunche Hall, which utilized a three-dimensional waffle-like pattern of glass solar shields, is now considered one of the most distinctive buildings on the campus. Lyndon also taught at the University of Southern California during the 1940s, 1950s, and early 1960s.

John MacFadyen, 76

John Hayter MacFadyen, who designed some of the nation's premier performing art venues, died February 18, 2000. Some of his better known projects include the Mann Music Center in Philadelphia and the Wolf Trap Center for the Arts outside of Washington, D.C. MacFadyen studied architecture at Princeton University, earning his master's degree in 1949. After service in World War II, he joined the New York architecture firm of Harrison and Abramovitz, during which time he was a fellow in residence at the American Academy in Rome from 1952 to 1953. MacFadyen left the firm in 1960 to become the founding executive director of the New York State Council on the Arts where he played an important role in shaping the movement toward public support of the arts. Between 1964 and his retirement in 1986, MacFadyen maintained a private architecture practice, specializing in performing arts facilities and residences.

Sir Leslie Martin, 91

Architect Sir Leslie Martin, best known for his work on the Royal Festival Hall in London, died July 28, 2000. After studying architecture in Manchester, England, Martin became the head of the new architecture school at Hull University in 1938. With his wife and fellow architect, Sadie Speight, he collaborated on many projects including The Flat Book, a 1938 reference work on contemporary furniture, fabrics, and household products. After World War II, Martin became the deputy to the chief architect at the London County Council, where he became involved in plans for the Festival of Britain and the Royal Festival Hall. He was promoted to chief architect at the London County Council in 1953 and, three years later, was appointed chair of architecture at Cambridge University. Martin was knighted in 1957.

Wayne McAllister, 92

The architect known for his car culture designs, Wayne McAllister, died March 22, 2000. Some of his most notable projects include the Sands and El Rancho Hotel, both in Las Vegas, Nevada. McAllister began his training as an architect early, designing the Agua Caliente resort in Tijuana, Mexico, a popular locale of the period for Hollywood actors, when he was twenty-years old. He is credited with elevating the design of drive-in restaurants and theme resorts to an art form with his flamboyant use of neon and a streamlined aesthetic that reflected the period's car culture. He himself declared his designs to be "influenced by the automobile, not the architect." McAllister left the architecture profession in 1956 to become a vice president at the Marriott Corporation. Due to the rapid growth of Los Angeles and Las Vegas in recent years, the sites of many of his designs, only a few of his buildings survive. Interest in his work has increased during the past decade with the successful preservation effort to save his 1949 Bob's Big Boy restaurant on Riverside Drive in Los Angeles, the highlight of his work in recent books on Los Angeles and Las Vegas architecture, and a 1998 exhibit at the Pacific Design Center in Los Angeles.

Vinson McKenzie, 50

Vinson McKenzie, a lifelong champion of African-American architects, died May 5, 2000. McKenzie studied history at Albany State College and earned a master's degree in library science from Atlanta University. He worked as an architectural librarian at Auburn University until 1994 when he left to focus on his art. His 1994 exhibit "African-American Architects and Builders," a culmination of his lifelong passion, elaborated the numerous contributions made by African-American architects, and was featured during the 1996 Olympics in Atlanta. McKenzie also ran the African-American Institute of Architectural History and served as the historian of the National Organization of Minority Architects (NOMA).

Enric Miralles, 45

Spanish architect Enric Miralles died July 3, 2000. Miralles recently began to receive his first major international commissions, including the new Scottish Parliament in Edinburgh which is currently under construction. He graduated from the Escuela Tecnica Superior de Arquitectura in Barcelona in 1978 and subsequently attended Columbia University as a Fulbright scholar. He later returned to Columbia as a visiting professor and also taught at Harvard University, London's Architectural Association, and the Escuela Tecnica Superior de Arquitectura in Spain. Miralles' unique architectural expression combined a modern vocabulary with a Catalan expression. His career blossomed after the 1992 Barcelona Olympics for which he designed the Archery Range. Miralles was buried in one of his most celebrated works, the Igualada Cemetery (1995) outside of Barcelona.

Robert Johnson Nash, 70

Robert Nash, FAIA, a prominent Washington, D.C. architect, died December 5, 1999. Throughout his career, he designed over 100 churches and religious facilities in the D.C. metropolitan area, as well as public transit projects, healthcare facilities, educational buildings, and commercial structures. After graduating from Howard University in 1952, Nash spent a number of years in Nigeria as a partner in a design and construction firm. He opened his own architecture office in Washington, D.C. in 1960 and worked there until shortly before his death. In addition to his practice, Nash was a founder and former president of the National Organization of Minority Architects (NOMA). He was also the first African-American president of the Washington chapter of The American Institute of Architects (AIA), the first African-American national vice president of the AIA, and the first recipient of the AIA's Whitney M. Young Award.

Christian Norberg-Schulz, 73

Norwegian architectural theorist Christian Norberg-Schulz died March 28, 2000. Norberg-Schulz is recognized for his contributions to defining the phenomenon of place. During his career, he published more than 30 books; served as editor of *Byggekunst*, a Norwegian architecture journal, from 1963 to 1978; and was the co-director of Lotus International. He was also a professor of architecture and dean at the Oslo School of Architecture. Among his many honors, Norberg-Schulz received the Gold Medal of the Académie d'Architecture and was named a honorary fellow of the Royal Institute of British Architects.

Frederick Noyes, 87

Frederick "Fred" Noyes, a New York architect who helped design the Lever House, died June 10, 2000. Noyes received a bachelor's degree in architecture from the Massachusetts Institute of Technology in 1936. While at the firm of Skidmore, Owings & Merrill in the late 1940s and early 1950s, he worked under Gordon Bunshaft on the Lever House and other notable projects. He opened his own architecture office in Manhattan in 1954, retiring in 1982. In 1980 he won praise for his design for the T. Anthony Luggage store at 480 Park Avenue in New York City.

Gil Oberfield, 49

Vice president of Gensler's New York office, Gil Oberfield, died in March 2000. During his career, Oberfield specialized in project management. The studio he headed at Gensler focused on global professional service firms and included such clients as Kidder Peabody, McKinsey, and PriceWaterhouse Coopers. He also consulted for the State of Israel Government Centers in Jerusalem about strategic planning and was a past chair of the AIA New York Chapter's Interiors Committee. Oberfield received his bachelor's degree in architecture and urban studies from Yale University and a master's degree in architecture from the Harvard Graduate School of Design.

Edwin T. Pairo, 93

Washington architect Edwin T. Pairo died November 18, 1999. Pairo began his 50-year career in 1928 at the Washington architectural firm of Philip M. Julien. The following year he won the first prize in the Paris Beaux Arts Institute competition. As a civilian, he worked for the Allied Architects and between 1936 and 1953 as an architect for the federal government's public housing agency. In 1953 he became a partner and the chief of specifications with Chatelain, Gauger, and Chatelain until his retirement in 1974. Pairo was also instrumental in the formation of the Construction Specifications Institute. He served as the chair of its first national convention in 1957, president of the D.C. Metropolitan chapter in 1959-60, and its national president in 1963.

Joseph Parriott, 79

Industrial designer and teacher Joseph Marshall Parriott died March 13, 2000. Parriott was the chief designer for a number of well-known objects including the Steam-O-Matic steam iron and the WaterPik. He attended Colorado University and the Pratt Institute prior to serving the U.S. Army Corps of Engineers during World War II. In 1966, he became the chairman of the industrial design department at the Pratt Institute in Brooklyn, New York, a position he held for 24 years.

Kermit Carlyle Parsons, 72

Kermit Carlyle, "K.C.," Parsons, an influential planning professional and educator, died December 9, 1999. Parsons graduated from Miami University of Ohio in 1951 with a bachelor's degree in architecture and received a master's degree in regional planning from Cornell University in 1953. Subsequently, he spent four years at the Cleveland City Planning Commission, eventually becoming Head of the Community Planning Section. In 1957 he began teaching at Cornell and in 1967 was appointed Chairman of the City and Regional Planning Department. He became the Dean of the College of Architecture, Art, and Planning, in 1971, a position he held for nine years. Between 1980 and his retirement in 1999, he resumed teaching at Cornell. Throughout his career, Parsons published over 50 articles, research reports, and books on campus and downtown planning, urban renewal and policy, and the history of urban planning. He also worked as a planning consultant for many cities, countries, colleges, and architecture firms,

Charlotte Perriand, 96

Charlotte Perriand, the French designer who worked with Le Corbusier in the 1920s and 1930s designing furniture, died October 27, 1999 in Paris. Perriand had a very productive career as a furniture designer and collaborated with many architects, believing that furniture and architecture should be developed as a single entity. In the 1920s, Perriand attended the École de l'Union Central des Arts Décoratifs in Paris. A showing of her "bar under the roof' piece at the Exposition Internationale des Arts Décortatifs in Paris in 1926 brought her early acclaim. She worked with Le Corbusier and Pierre Jenneret designing furniture from 1927 to 1937. Later in her career, she collaborated with Le Corbusier again on his Unité d'Habitation housing project in Marseilles. Some of her most collectable pieces are a lighting table she designed with Jean Prouve in 1953 and a primary colored bookcase with cupboards she designed for Tunisian dormitory students at the Cité Universitaire in Paris. Although Perriand was a Modernist, she had a humanist agenda in her work that was manifested in her ideas about flexible space, free-form shapes, natural materials, and furniture. Perriand has been cited as "a major innovator in French design."

Adolf Placzek, 87

The distinguished architectural librarian and editor, Adolf Placzek, died March 19, 2000. Placzek was born in Vienna, Austria and immigrated to the United States in 1940. He studied library science and became a junior librarian at Columbia University's Avery Architectural Library. When he became its Director, Placzek expanded the library's holdings, transforming Avery into one of the world's finest repositories of architectural books and drawings. When he retired from Avery in 1980, he pursued many other noteworthy projects, such as the editor-in-chief of the four-volume *Macmillan Encyclopedia of Architects*, the founding editor of *The Buildings of the United States* series, and editor of numerous other architectural publications. Placzek also served as a commissioner on New York's Landmarks Preservation Commission.

Robert Probst, 78

Robert Probst, director of research for Herman Miller, died March 4, 2000. Probst is often considered "the father of the modern office" for his creation of the Action Office system in the 1960s, which is responsible for popularizing modular, reconfigurable office furniture. Probst held over 120 patents for such diverse products as office furniture, healthcare, waste management, timber harvesting, and concrete quality control – all products developed out of his interest in understanding in how people function and in making their lives simpler. Probst began his career teaching art at Stevens College and the University of Colorado, after serving in World War II. In 1953, he formed the Probst Company to focus on speculative product development. He became president of the Herman Miller Research Corp. in 1960 were he developed many innovative products, including the Action Office system and the Co/Struc system for hospitals. His 1968 book, The Office: A Facility Based on Change, predicted current trends in office design.

George T. Rockrise, 83

George T. Rockrise, renowned California architect, landscape architect, and urban planner, died July 7, 2000. His aesthetic adapted modern principles to a sensitivity to materials and the environment. Rockrise studied architecture at Syracuse University and received a master's degree from Columbia University in 1941. Following service in World War II, he became a staff designer for the United Nations headquarters in New York City. He gained landscape architecture training when he moved to San Francisco in 1947 to work for the renowned landscape architect Frederick Church. He also taught design at Stanford University and the University of California, Berkeley. In the early 1950s he founded the ROMA Design Group with three other architects. Their many notable designs include the U.S. Embassy in Manama, Bahrain, and urban design plans for over 25 cities. During his career, Rockrise received over 20 national and regional awards and a Fulbright Fellowship in urban design at the University of Rome.

Lloyd Rodwin, 80

Lloyd Rodwin, an international authority on urban planning, died December 7, 1999. Rodwin taught at the Massachusetts Institute of Technology for forty years, retiring in 1988 as the Ford International Professor of urban studies. He received a bachelor's degree from the City College in Manhattan and a doctorate in regional planning from Harvard University. Rodwin was the co-founder, along with Daniel Patrick Moynihan, of the M.I.T.-Harvard Joint Center for Urban Studies. Moynihan described Rodwin's impact on the field of urban studies as redefining "the study of cities, defin[ing] them in terms of the people who lived there rather than the building in which they lived." In addition to teaching, Rodwin advised on planning issues throughout the developing world, served as an advisor to the United Nations, and authored and edited a number of books on urban planning.

Robert Ross, 46

Founding member of the John Hardy Group in Atlanta, Georgia, Robert Ross, died May 23, 2000. Ross received both his bachelor's and master's degrees in architecture from the University of Pennsylvania. He began his career working for Bower Lewis Thrower/Architects in Philadelphia before moving to Atlanta where he worked for John Portman & Associates and several other firms. In 1992, he was a founding member of the John Hardy Group where he served as group leader of development.

Colin Rowe, 79

Colin Rowe, an architectural historian and teacher, died November 5, 1999. Rowe was the Andrew Dickson White Professor of Architecture at Cornell University from 1962 until his retirement in 1990. Although he produced a few books during his career, his real influence was through his teaching. Many of his students went on to become distinguished teachers themselves at Yale, Princeton, Harvard, the University of Pennsylvania, and many other architecture schools. Rowe was born in England and attended the Liverpool School of Architecture. Following service in the British Infantry, he taught at Liverpool where one of his students was James Stirling. Rowe came to the United States to teach at the University of Texas and, in 1962, began a 28-year career at Cornell. In the 1950s and 1960s Rowe heavily promoted a formalist approach to architecture. By the late 1960s, Rowe and his followers, which included Richard Meier, Peter Eisenman, Charles Gwathmey, and John Hejduk, were known as the "Whites" for the formal purity and absence of color in their designs. His philosophies further evolved in the 1970s into a more contextural approach in his efforts to reconcile the traditional urban center to the sprawling suburban landscape. In 1995 the Royal Institute of British Architecture awarded Rowe its prestigious Royal Gold Medal.

Francisco Javier Saenz de Oiza, 81

Spanish architect Francisco Javier Saenz de Oiza died July 18, 2000. Saenz is best known for his prominent design for the Banco Bilbao Vizcaya and the innovative, curvy Torres Blancas apartments, both in Madrid. As director of the School of Architecture of Madrid, he served as a mentor to many aspiring architects, including Rafael Moneo. Among the many awards and honors he received were the Prince of Asturias Prize for Arts in 1993 and the European Prize for Excellence in 1974.

Renny B. Saltzman, 69

Renny B. Saltzman, an interior designer and patron of modern architecture, died in January 2000. Saltzman attended the New York School of Interior Design after earning an undergraduate degree from New York University. Soon after opening his own design firm in 1956, he established a reputation for eclecticism. His many notable patrons included Charles Revson, the founder of Revlon, Herbert Siegel of Chris-Craft

Industries, and the publisher Richard Snyder of Simon & Schuster. In 1968 Saltzman provided architect Richard Meier with one of his first residential commissions, the Saltzman home in East Hampton, which has long been regarded a modernist landmark.

Hideo Sasaki, 80

Hideo Sasaki, a world renowned landscape architect and founder of Sasaki Associates Inc., died August 30, 2000. Sasaki is known for his multi-disciplinary approach to landscape and urban design and an influential teaching career. Sasaki attended the University of Illinois and received a master's degree in landscape architecture from the Harvard Graduate School of Design. While teaching at Harvard in 1953, he formed Sasaki Associates whose notable projects include Greenacre Park in New York City, the University of Colorado at Boulder campus expansion, Foothill College in Los Altos, California, and the Upjohn Headquarters in Kalamazoo, Michigan. He also served as the chair of the landscape architecture department at Harvard from 1958 to 1968 and on numerous commissions, panels, and juries, including the U.S. Fine Arts Commission and the Vietnam War Memorial Competition jury. Among his many honors and awards, Sasaki was the first recipient of the American Society of Landscape Architects' Medal in 1971 and was granted Harvard's Centennial Medal in honor of his extraordinary achievement in landscape architecture.

Kenneth L. Schnitzer, 70

Innovative Houston developer Kenneth. L. Schnitzer died November 1, 1999. Schnitzer's life-long career as a real estate developer produced many of the buildings that now comprise the Houston skyline, including the Wells Fargo Bank Plaza, Enron building, Mcorp Plaza, Greenway Plaza, and Citicorp Center. His 127-acre Greenway Plaza, which includes a 400-room hotel, underground shopping mall, sports arena, and 10 office towers, was one of the first large-scale, planned urban developments to utilize greenbelts and extensive landscaping. The Summit arena, now called the Compaq Center, served as a widely copied model throughout the United States of a public-private joint venture. Among other endeavors, he was a founding director of Houston Proud, founding Chairman of the Houston Economic Development Council, and director of the Greater Houston Partnership and the Greater Houston Convention and Visitors Bureau.

Margarete Schütte-Lihotzky, 102

Margarete Schütte-Lihotzky, one of Austria's first female architects and a prominent member of the anti-Nazi resistance movement, died January 18, 2000. Schütte-Lihotzky was the first woman to study architecture at the Vienna School of Arts and Crafts (now the Academy of Applied Arts), beginning in 1915. Always a social activist, she went on to design public housing for working people. In 1926 she moved to Germany where she worked with Ernst May and designed the first standardized built-in kitchen, commonly known as the "Frankfurt kitchen." She lived and practiced architecture in the Soviet Union during the 1930s, returning to Austria to take part in the anti-fascist resistance movement for which she was imprisoned. A 1986 Austrian television film, "One Minute of Darkness Does Not Make Us Blind," explored her experiences during this period. In 1980 she received the Architecture Award of the City of Vienna and, later, the Austrian Medal for Science and Art.

Michael T. Sheehan, 57

Michael T. Sheehan, executive director of the National Trust for Historic Preservation's Woodrow Wilson House in Washington, D.C., died March 4, 2000. Sheehan attended the University of Pennsylvania where he received a doctorate in American civilization. Prior to the Woodrow Wilson house, Sheehan served as the executive director for Oatlands Plantation in Leesburg, Virginia, and the Snug Harbor Cultural Center on Staten Island, New York. At the Wilson House, he was instrumental in establishing an international affairs program and the Woodrow Wilson Statesmanship Award. He was also a founding member of Historic House Museums of Metropolitan Washington and the D.C. Heritage Tourism Coalition.

Francis Cutler Turner, 90

Francis "Frank" Cutler Turner, the driving force and designer of the U.S. interstate highway system, died October 2, 1999. As a member of President Dwight D. Eisenhower's highway advisory committee, Turner spearheaded the interstate highway effort, often cited as the largest public works project in U.S. history. Not only did he help draft legislation for the project, Turner polled Americans about where the highways should be located by asking them to draw their preferences on a grided map of the country. He began his career in 1929 as a highway engineer with the Federal Bureau of Roads, culminating in his tenure as the head of the Federal Highway Administration from 1969 until his retirement in 1972. The Federal Highway Research Center in McLean, Virginia, is named for Turner.

F. Carter Williams, 87

Raleigh architect F. Carter Williams, FAIA, died in April 2000. After earning degrees in architectural engineering and design and serving in the U.S. Army during World War II, Williams opened his own architecture firm in Raleigh, North Carolina, in 1946. He also served as president of the North Carolina chapter of The American Institute of Architects (AIA) and was the recipient of the national chapter's Edward C. Kemper Award for outstanding service to the organization. He was also the former chair of the Raleigh Planning Commission.

Bruno Zevi, 80

Italian architect, proponent of organic design, and editor of *L'Architettura*, Bruno Zevi, died January 9, 2000. Zevi designed a few buildings, including the Italian pavilion for the 1967 World's Fair in Montreal, Canada, but was best known for his writings. After receiving an architecture degree from the Harvard Graduate School of Design in 1942, Zevi wrote his first of many books, *Toward an Organic Architecture*, which exposed his theory that architecture should have an integrated relationship with nature. He was a vociferous opponent of modernism and later postmodernism. In 1955 he founded the magazine *L'Architettura* and began writing a weekly column for *L'Expresso*. He also taught architecture history and criticism in Venice and Rome.

Robert L. Zion, 79

Prominent New York landscape architect, Robert L. Zion, died April 25, 2000. Zion and his firm, Zion and Breen, designed some of New York's most notable parks and public spaces, including Paley Park, the IBM building atrium, and the Abby Aldrich Rockefeller Sculpture Garden of the Museum of Modern Art. Zion studied landscape architecture at Harvard University where he received a master's degree in 1951 and opened his firm in 1957. Throughout his career, he collaborated with many distinguished architects, such as Philip Johnson, Edward Larrabee Barnes, and I.M. Pei. He also was a faculty member at the Pratt Institute, served on New York City's Arts Commission, and was a vice president of the Architectural League. His design for Paley Park is as popular and admired today as it was when it opened in 1967.

INDEX

Anchorage (Alaska), 338
Ancient Merv' State Historical and Cultural Park
   (Turkmenistan), 415
Andalous Residence (Tunisia), 54
Andersen, James R., 341
Anderson, Amy, 245
Anderson, Dorman D., 251
Anderson, Harry F., 251
Anderson, J. Macvicar, 331
Anderson, J. Robert, 287
Anderson, J. Timothy, 251
Anderson, John C., 293, 327
Anderson, John D., 251, 320
Anderson, John K , 341
Anderson, Joseph Horatio, 353
Anderson, Lawrence, 161, 325
Anderson, Richard, 251
Anderson, Robert O., 312
Anderson, Ross S., 245
Anderson, Samuel A., 251
Anderson, Sir Robert Rowand, 148
Anderson, William L., 251
Anderson Engineering & Surveying, Inc., 102
Ando, Dr. Yoichi, 70
Ando, Tadao
   awards and honors, 80, 88, 117, 139, 142, 148, 165
   organizational memberships, 301
Andreu, Paul, 57
Andrew J. Schmitz & Associates, 344
Andrews, Frank Mills, 353
Andrews, J. Philip, 251
Andrews, John H., 80, 301
Andrews, John Hamilton, 145
Andrews, Lavone D., 251
Andrews, Martha P., 251
Andrews, William F., 284
Andrews University (Michigan), 530
Andropogon Associates, LTD., 84
Andros, Stephen John, 293
Angel, Truman, 388
Angell, Ellen, 284
Angell, Robert H., 284
Angkor (Cambodia), 409
Angle, Robert H., 284
Angotti, Thomas, 248
Anhar (Lebanon), 412
Annapolis Historic Landmarks (Maryland), 131
Annese, Domenico, 287
Anselevicius, George, 98, 251, 325
Ansell, W. H., 331
Anshen + Allen, 500
Anstis, James H., 251
Antigua Guatemala (Guatemala), 411
Antoine, Jacques-Denis, 17
Antoinette Forrester Downing Award, 18, 379
Antonakakis, Dimitris, 313
Antonakakis, Suzana, 13, 312
Antuñez, Ellis L., 287
Anuradhapura (Sri Lanka), 415
APCO Graphics, 113
Apgar, Anne N., 77
Apgar, Mahlon, IV, 77
Apgar Award for Excellence, 77

Apollo Epicurius Temple (Greece), 411
Appel, Natalye, 251
Appel, Wallace H., 296
Applachian Trail (West Virginia), 133
Apple Computer, Inc. (California), 94, 111, 115, 152
Appleyard, Donald, 248
Applied Ecology, 365
Al-Aqsa Mosque (Jerusalem), 55
Aquatic Park Historic District (California), 404
Aqueduct of Vanvitelli (Italy), 412
Aquileia Archaeological Area and Patriarchal Basilica (Italy),
   412
AR7 Hoover Desmond Architects, 341
Arad, Ron, 240
Arant, John C., 293
Aranya Low-Cost Housing (India), 56
Arbegast, David E., 287
ARC Architects, 341
Archer, Richard M., 251
Archi-Tech, 516
Archis, 519
ARCHIspec, 341
Architects Barrentine.Bates.Lee, 342
Architects BC, Inc., 342
Architects Collaborative, 78
Architects' Council of Europe, 183
Architects/Designers/Planners for Social Responsibility, 70
Architects' Journal, 518
Architects Regional Council of Asia, 120
Architects Wells Woodburn O'Neill, 341
Architects Workshop of Pennsylvania, 170
Architectural Alliance, 129
Architectural Book Center, 511
Architectural Center Bookstore, 511
Architectural Design, 518
Architectural Design Studio, 315
Architectural Design West Inc., 349
Architectural Digest, 516
Architectural Digest Home Design Show, 22
*Architectural History: The Journal of the Society of Architectural
   Historians of Great Britain*, 519
Architectural Horizons, 342
Architectural Institute of Japan, 184
Architectural Record, 516
Architectural Record/Business Week Awards, 6, 8, 86
Architectural Research Consultants, 342
Architectural Review, 519
Architecture, 137, 516
Architecture and Design Charter High School, 368
Architecture Australia, 519
Architecture Design Alliance, 342
Architecture Etc., 342
Architecture Firm Award, 35–37, 78
Architecture Incorporated, 342
Architecture Resource Center, 71
Architecture Solutions, 342
Architecture Studio, 56
Architektur im Ringturm, 224
Architektur Zentrum Wien, 213
architrave PC Architects, 342
Archivia: The Decorative Arts Bookshop, 512
Archivo de Indias (Spain), 415
ARCOP Design Group, 54
Ardiles-Arce, Jaime, 312

Area, 115
Arefin, Tony, 542
Arehart, Robert A., 284
Arfaa, Peter F., 251
Argosy Bookstore, 512
Arguelles, Carlos D., 301
Arizona Inn (Arizona), 396
Arizona State Capitol, 352
Arizona State University, 366, 368, 524
Arkansas State Capitol, 352
Arkhangelskoye State Museum (Russia), 420
Arkitek Bersikutu, 54
Arkitektur, 519
Arles Roman and Romanesque Monuments (France), 410
Arlington House, Robert E. Lee Memorial (Virginia), 388
Arlington Village Creek (Texas), 101
Armajani, Siah, 70
Armand Hammer Museum of Art, 225
Armbruster, David S., 287
Armitage, Robert E., 293
Armstrong, Edward, 83
Armstrong, Eric, 247
Arnaud, Leopold, 325
Arneill, Bruce P., 251
Arnett, Warren G., 284
Arnold, Chris, 251
Arnold, Christopher C., 252
Arnold, Henry F., 287
Arnold Associates, 82
Arnold W. Brunner Memorial Prize, 80
Arnott, Gordon R., 301
Aron, Trudy, 304
Aronson, Joseph H., 248
Arquitectonica, 78, 167, 318, 500
Arraihana, Amin, 54
Arrasmith, Judd, Rapp, Inc., 341
Arrigoni, Robert V., 252
Ars Libri, 511
Art Center College of Design (California), 525
Art Institute of Atlanta (Georgia), 528
Art Institute of Chicago (Illinois), 70, 214–215, 528
Art Institute of Colorado, 526
Art Institute of Fort Lauderdale (Florida), 527
Artek, 313
Arthur, Dr. Eric R., 146
Arthur and Yvonne Boyde Education Center (Australia), 120, 121
Arthur Craig Steinman & Associates, Architects, 344
Arthur Ericson, 551
Artigas, Joao Baptista Vilanova, 85, 119
ARTScorpsLA, Inc. (California), 150
Artunc, Sadik C., 287
Arup, Ove, 9, 148
Ashanti Traditional Buildings (Ghana), 411
Ashbrook, Robert L., 293
Ashcraft Design, 111
Asher-Stubbins, Hugh, 250
Asheville (North Carolina), 337
Ashley, Ludd, 304
Ashley, Roy O., 287
Ashnola River Road Bridge (Canada), 347
ASHRAE, 14
Ashton, Raymond J., 320
ASID ICON, 516

Asilah (Morocco), 55
Asken, Yvonne W., 252
Askew, Laurin B., 252
Askew, Lee Hewlett, III, 252
ASLA Medal, 81
ASLA Professional Award, 82–84
Aslin, C. H., 331
Association de Sauvegarde de la Médina, 54, 56
Association for Computer Aided Design in Architecture, 20
Association for the Preservation of Virginia Antiquities, 70
Association of Collegiate Schools of Architecture, 539
      awards given by, 97
      meetings, 6, 12, 22
      Presidents, 325–326
Association of Collegiate Schools of Planning, 52, 539
Association of Junior Leagues, 380
Association pour le Développement naturel d'une
      Architecture et d'un Urbanisme Africains, 57
Asticou Inn (Maine), 397
Astle, Neil L., 252
Astorino, Louis D., 252
Astro Products Inc., 94
Asturias Kingdom (Spain), 415
Aswan High Dam (Egypt), 336
Atelier Enam Architects and Planners, 55
Aten, D. Lyle, 287
Athenaeum of Philadelphia (Pennsylvania), 216
Atherton, Charles H., 252
Atkin, Tony, 252
Atkins, John L., 252
Atkins, Livingston E., Jr., 293
Atkins, Tom, 84
Atlanta College of Art (Georgia), 528
Atlanta University Center Catholic Center (Georgia), 542
ATREA Co., 58
AT&T Corporate Center (Illinois), 357
Atwood, Charles, 11
a+u magazine, 519
Aubock, Carl, 301
Aubry, Eugene E., 252
Auburn University (Alabama), 366, 367, 524
Auerbach, Seymour, 252
Auguste Perret Prize, 85
Augustusburg Castle (Germany), 410
Aulenti, Gae, 25, 139, 313
Austin, Donald B., 287
Austin, Douglas H., 252
Austin-Bergstrom International Airport (Texas), 79
Austin Company, 129, 349
Austin Engineering, 130
Avchen, Daniel, 252
Avebury (United Kingdom), 416
Aveda Retail (Minnesota), 153
Avenue of Americas, 1251 (New York), 544
Avery Architectural Library, 559
Avia, Robin Klehr, 298
Avignon Historic Centre (France), 410
Avila Old Town and Extra-Muros Churches (Spain), 415
Awes, Morten, 321
Awqaf Department, 54
Awwad, Isam, 55
Axon, Donald C., 252
Axon, Janice, 304
Aydelott, Alfred L., 252

Barrick, Nolan E., 252
Barron, Errol, 252
Barrow, Richard E., 252
Barrows, Stanley, 312
Barry, Charles, 147, 331
Barry, James R., 321
Barsotti, Frank L., 293
Barsotti, Nancy Hoff, 284
Bart, Sir Thomas Graham Jackson, 147
Barthold, Mariana, 304
Bartholomew, Harland, 134
Bartholomew, Richard W., 245, 252
Bartlett, Jennifer, 69
Barton, Cheryl L., 287, 324
Bartos, Armand, 252
Barucki, Tadeusz, 119
Basgo Gompa (India), 418
Basil the Great Church (Slovakia), 420
Basin Harbor Club (Vermont), 398
Baskervill & Son, 350
Bassett, Edward Charles, 80, 252
Bassett, Edward M., 134
Bassett, Florence Knoll, 158, 309, 311
Bassett, James H., 287
Bassett, Kenneth E., 287
Bassetti, Fred, 252
Bastyr, Richard P., 293
Bat Dome Culvert (Texas), 91
Batalha Monastery (Portugal), 414
Batchelor, Peter, 252
Bath (United Kingdom), 416
Bath Bridge (New Hampshire), 348
Battaglia, Ronald J., 252
Batterson, James G., 352
Battery Park City Authority, 70
Bauder College (Georgia), 528
Bauer, Anthony M., 287
Bauer, Jay S., 252
BAUER AND WILEY Architects, 115
Bauer Stark + Lashbrook, Inc., 349
Baugh, Betty, 328
Baughman, Clarence W., 287
Bauhaus sites (Germany), 411
Baum, Edward, 252
Baum, Joseph H., 70
Baume, Henry B., 327
Baumgarten, Howard R., 287
Bausch & Lomb headquarters (New York), 552
Bausman, Karen, 248
Bavaro, Joseph D., 252
Bavinger House (Oklahoma), 164
Bawa, Geoffrey M., 301
Baxter, Augustus, Sr., 304
Bay City (Michigan), 382
Bay Engineering, 129
Bayley, James B., 342
Bayou Place (Texas), 166
Bazer-Schwartz, Jeannine, 284
Bazzle, Tamara A., 284
BD Medical Systems, 113
Beal, Louis M. S., 311
Beal, Roy F., 284
Beale, John Craig, 252
Beall, Burtch W., Jr., 252

Bean, Leroy E., 252
Beard, Alan J., 252
Beardsley Design Associates, 350
Bearsch, Lee P., 252
Bearsch Compeau Knudson Architects & Engineers, 342
Beasley, Ellen, 248
Beatty Harvey & Associates, 349
Beaty, William H., 252
Beaudouin, Eugene, 301
Bechhoefer, William B., 252
Bechtel, Riley P., 127
Bechtel, Stephen D., Jr., 127
Bechtel Group, 127
Beck, Eldon W., 287
Beck, George, 296
Beck Architecture, 339
Becker, Lee, 252
Becker, Nathaniel, 296
Becker, Rex L., 252
Beckhard, Herbert, 252
Beckley, Robert M., 252, 326
Becom, Jeff, 232
BecVar, Arthur N., 296
Bedar, Rudolph, 342
Bedell, Marjorie A., 284
Bedford Springs Hotel (Pennsylvania), 405
Bedford-Stuyvesant Restoration, 68
Bednar, Michael, 252
Bedons Alley (South Carolina), 82
Bee, Carmi, 252
Beeah Group Consultants, 55
Beehive Housze (Utah), 388
Beer, David W., 252
Beers, 130
Beery, Edgar C., 253
Befu, Yoshiro, 287
Beggs, Arthur G., 287
Beha, Ann M., 253
Behnisch, Stefan, 90
Behnke, William A., 287, 324
Behrens, Peter, 9
Beijing Radio & T.V. Tower (China), 362
Beinecke, Walter, Jr., 380
Belcher, John, 147, 331
Belem Tower (Portugal), 414
Belfries of Flanders and Wallonia (Belgium), 408
Bell, Byron, 253
Bell, C. E., 354
Bell, Frederic, 253
Bell, James R., 287
Bell, M. E., 352
Bell, M. Wayne, 253
Bell, Richard C., 247, 287
Bell and Kent, 353
Bellafiore, Vincent, 287, 292, 324
Bellavia, Regina, 84
Belle, John, 253
Bell's Ford Bridge (Indiana), 348
Belluschi, Pietro, 17, 60, 136, 164, 359
Belmont Technical College (Ohio), 534
Belt, Lemman and Lo, 352
Belt Collins Hawaii, 167
Belton Chalet (Montana), 391
Ben Lomond Historic Suite Hotel (Utah), 398

Bender, Ralph C., 253
Benedek, Armand, 287
Benepe, Barry, 253
Benisch, G., 85
Benjamin, Asher, 13
Benjamin Thompson & Associates, 78
Benktzon, Maria, 117
Bennet, H., 155
Bennett, Claire R., 287, 324
Bennett, Daniel D., 253
Bennett, David J., 253
Bennett, Edward H., 134
Bennett, Ralph, 98
Bennett, Stephen M., 304
Bennett, Ward, 69, 311
Bennett, Wells, 325
Benoit, Gerard, 301
Benson, John, 69
Bentel, Frederick R., 253
Bentel, Maria A., 253
Bentel & Bentel Architects/Planners, 115
Bentsen, Kenneth E., 253
Bentz, Frederick J., 253
Bentz Thompson Reitow, 500
BEQ-MCPON Plackett Manor and Naval Hospital (Illinois), 129
Berenson, Bertram, 325
Bercuter, Hon. Douglas, 308
Berg, Karl A., 253
Berg, Raymond, 145
Berg, Shary Page, 287
Berger, Lehman Associates, 102
Bergman, Elaine, 304
Bergmann, Richard R., 253
Bergquist, Lloyd F., 253
Bergson, Maria, 311
Bergstedt, Milton V., 170
Bergstrom, Edwin, 320
Berkebile, Robert J., 253
Berkeley (California), 338
Berkeley College/Bergen Campus (New Jersey), 532
Berkoff, Marlene J., 253
Berlage, Dr. Hendrik Petrus, 5, 148
Berlin Palaces and Parks (Germany), 410
Bernard Tschumi Architects, 62
Berne (Switzerland), 415
Berners, Edgar H., 330
Berners/Schober Associates, Inc., 350
Bernheim, Anthony N., 253
Bernstein, Phillip, 253
Berry, Frank Lee, 284
Berry, K. Norman, 253
Bertman, Richard J., 253
Bertone, Ronald P., 253
Bertram, Frederic A., 253
Berube, Claude, 298
Best, Melvin H., 296
Betac, 113
Beth Israel Memorial Garden (Texas), 82
Betlemska-Kaple Bridge (Czech Republic), 348
Betsy Ross House (Pennsylvania), 388
Bettman, Alfred, 134
Betts, Gary A., 293
Betts, Hobart, 253

Betts, Richard J., 332
Beyer, John H., 253
Beyer, William, 253
Beyer Blinder Belle, 62, 78, 106, 547
BG Consultants Inc., 342
Bhalla, Jai R., 301
Bhong Mosque (Pakistan), 55
Biallas, Randall, 308
Bibliotect, 513
Bibliotèque Nationale de France, 125
Bibliotheca Alexandrina, 231
Bickel, John H., 253
Biddle, James, 304
Bidwill, J., 304
Biebesheimer, Frederick C., III, 253
Bienko, Daniel Victor, 342
Biertan and Fortified Church (Romania), 414
Big Belt House (Montana), 137
Biggs, T. J., 253
Bilbao Subway (Spain), 168
The Biltmore (Florida), 397
Biltmore Estate (North Carolina), 388
Binder, Rebecca L., 253
Binkley, James, 253
Biokinetics, 111
Birchfield, Hal F. B., 284
Bird, Lance L., 253
Birge, John R., 253
Birk, Sherry, 304
Birka (Sweden), 415
Birkerts, Gunnar, 80, 97, 253
Birmingham Flight Sequence (Alabama), 153
Birnbaum, Charles A., 287
Bishir, Catherine W., 376, 379
Bishop, Calvin T., 287, 324
Bishop, James A., 253
Bishop, Walter F., 293
Bishop's Lodge (New Mexico), 398
Bissell, George, 253
Bitter, Adriana, 284
Bitter, Edwin, 284
Björn and Björn Design, 54
Black, J. Sinclair, 253
Black, Shirley, 310
Black & Decker, 111
Black & Veatch Construction, 129
Black Hawk Historic District (Colorado), 404
Blackburn, Walter, 542
Blackburn Architects, 542
Blackford, Leonard D., 253
Blackmar, Elizabeth, 376, 377
Blackmon, Jan Gaede, 253
Blackner, Boyd A., 253
Blackwood, Michael, 70
Blaich, Robert I., 296
Blake, Peter, 253
Blanc, Luis, 107
Blanchard, Howard T., 330
Bland, Frederick A., 253
Bland, John, 146
Blanski, William A., 172
Blau, David H., 287
Blau, Eve, 138, 157
Blegvad, Jacob, 301

Bourges Cathedral (France), 410
Bourque, Michael, 298
Boutelle, Sara H., 304
Bovis Management Group, 166
Bowden, Gary A., 254
Bowden, William D., 284
Bowen, Blair S., 284
Bowen, David M., 254
Bowen, Gary, 254
Bowen, Ronald Gene, 254
Bower, John A., Jr., 254
Bower Lewis Thrower Architects, 340
Bowers, Paul D., Jr., 254
Bowersox, William A., 254
Bowles, Chester, Jr., 254
Bowman, J. Donald, 254
Box, Hal, 98
Box, John Harold, 254
Boyana Church (Bulgaria), 409
Boyd, A. S., 304
Boyd, Charles Chief, 293, 327
Boyd, Robin, 145
Boyden, Ann Marie, 304
Boyer, M. Christine, 123
Boyington, W. W., 352
Boyle Engineering Corporation, 102
Boym Partners, 108
Boynton, Robert A., 254
Bozalis, John, 254
Bradburn, James H., 254
Braden, David R., 254
Bradfield, Richard H., 254
Bradford, Susan, 284
Bradley, Carl L., 100
Bradley, Thomas G., 254
Bradley & Bradley, 349
Brady, Clyde A., III, 254
Brady, Holland, 341
Braley, Scott W., 254
Brame, Ronald M., 254
Branch, Melville, 52
Brand, Joel, 254
Brandston, Howard, 71, 312
Brandt, W. Frank, 287
Brannen, Robert, 254
Branner, Robert, 72
Brasilia (Bolovia), 409
Brassel, Eleanor K., 304
Braswell, Joseph, 311
Braun, Charles S., 254
BraunPrize, 2
Braunschweiger, Robert W., 248
Bray, Paul M., 248
Bray, Robert, 311
Braymer, John W., 304
Brayton, Paul, 158
Brayton, Richard M., 254
Brazer, Clarence W., 330
Brazil Public Security, Human Rights and Citizenship, 99
Brazley, William E., Jr., 254
Brazos Bookstore, 513
Breakers (Rhode Island), 388
Brecher, Melvin, 254
Bredendieck, Hin, 110

Breedlove, Michael Wayne, 287
Bregenz Art Museum (Austria), 125
Breger, William N., 254
Bregman + Hamann Architects, 358
Breines, Simon, 254
Brenan, William M., 293
Brenau University (Georgia), 528
Brendle, John Michael, 254
Brennan Beer Gorman/Architects, 340, 500
Brents, Daniel R., 254
Bresnan, Adrienne G., 254
Bresnan, Joseph, 254
Bressler, Peter W., 296, 328
Breuer, Marcel, 11, 60, 161
Brewer, Benjamin E., Jr., 254, 320
Brewster, Elise, 247
Brickbauer, Charles G., 245
Brickman, Theodore W., Jr., 287
Bridge of Chains (Italy), 418
Bridgefarmer & Associates, Inc., 101
Bridgers, Samuel W., 287
Bridges, Leon, 170, 254
Briggs, Cecil C., 245
Briggs, Dee Christy, 321
Brigham, Bruce J., 284
Brigham, Charles, 353
Brightbill, William R., 293
Brihadisvara Temple (India), 411
Brill, Michael, 158
Brimstone Hill Fortress National Park (Romania), 414
Brinkerhoff, Donald Carl, 287
Brinkley, David, 304
Brinkley, Mark K., 287
Brinkman, Gail, 83
Brinkmann, Don, 311
Bristol, Robert F., 287
British Ministry for Education, 85
Britt, Stanford R., 254
Britt, Tom, 311
Broad Ripple Design Associates, Architects, 342
Brocato, Joseph M., Sr., 254
Brocchini, Myra M., 254
Broches, Paul, 254
Brochstein, Raymond D., 254
Brock, Wayne C., 293
Brockway, A. L., 330
Brockway, William R., 254
Brodie, M. J. "Jay," 160, 254
Brody, Samuel, 80
Bromley, R. Scott, 311
Bronson Medical Center (Michigan), 351
Bronx River Parkway (New York), 132
Brooke, Steven, 69, 248
Brooklyn (New York), 338
Brooks, H. Allen, 73, 300, 332
Brooks, H. Gordon, II, 254
Brooks, Honorable Jack, 160, 304
Brooks, James, 147
Brooks, Larry, 293
Brooks, Turner, 245
Brooks Borg Skiles Architecture Engineering, 349
Brooks College (California), 525
Broome, John W., 254
Broome, Lewis, 353

Broshar, Robert C., 254, 320
Brotman, David J., 254
Broudy, Charles E., 254
Brown, A. B., 304
Brown, A. Larry, 293
Brown, Andrea Clark, 245
Brown, Arthur W., 327
Brown, C. Dudley, 284
Brown, Charlotte, 376
Brown, Chilton, 310
Brown, Everett, 93, 284
Brown, George D., Jr., 254
Brown, J. Carter, 127
Brown, J. N., 304
Brown, Jennie Sue, 254
Brown, Joseph E., 287
Brown, Kenneth F., 120, 254
Brown, Paul B., 254
Brown, R. Michael, 284
Brown, Robert F., Jr., 254
Brown, Robert L., Jr., 254
Brown, Terrance, 254
Brown, Theodore L., 245
Brown, Walton E., 284
Brown, William A., Sr., 304
Brown, Woodlief, 254
Brown & Root Services, 101
Brown & Storey Architects, 137
Brown and Caldwell, 104
Brown Engineers, Inc., 130
Brown Group, 342
Brown Hotel (Kentucky), 397
Brown Palace Hotel (Colorado), 396
Brown Residence (Massachusetts), 115
Brown University (Rhode Island), 535
Browne, William Calvin, Jr., 293
Brownell, Charles, 138
Brownlee, David, 73, 138
Brubaker, C. William, 244, 254
Bruce, Barry B., 254
Bruce, Jeffrey L., 287
Bruder, Will, 75
Bruder, William, 245
Bruegmann, Robert, 157
Brugger, Benno, 156
Brukoff Design Associates, Inc., 115
Brunel, Isambard Kingdom, 221
Bruner, Van B., Jr., 170, 254
Bruner/Cott & Associates, 62
Bruner Foundation, 150
Brunner & Brunner Architects & Engineers, 349
Bruno, Harry A., 254
Brussels T.V. Tower (Belgium), 364
Bruton, Larry S., 254
Bryan, Harvey, 254
Bryan, John M., 304
Bryan, Mary A., 284
Bryant, Gridley J. F., 353
Bryant, John H., 254
Bryce, David, 353
Brydone, Eleanor, 284
Bryggen (Norway), 413
Brynildsen, Per Christian, 57
Buatta, Mario, 311

Bubenik, Jackie Karl, 287
Bublys, Algimantas V., 255
Buchanan, C., 155
Buchanan, Marvin H., 245, 255
Buchanan, Robert T., 247
Buchholz Sports Center (Switzerland), 58
Buckingham, Margaret, 310
Buckley, James W., 255
Buckley, Michael P., 255
Bucks County Community College (Pennsylvania), 535
Buda Castle Quarter (Hungary), 411
Budapest (Hungary), 411
Budrevics, Alexander, 287
Budz, Robert S., 287
Buehrer, Huber H., 255
Buenz, John B., 255
Buettner, Dennis R., 287
Buff, Glenn A., 255
Buggenhagen, Wayne L., 287
Build Boston, 22
Builder's Book, 510
Builder's Book Depot, 510
Builders Booksource, 510
Building Owners & Managers Association, 12
Bukhara Old City (Uzbekistan), 56, 416
Bukhara Restoration Office, 56
Bulfinch, Charles, 353, 355
Bull, Henrik H., 255
Bullock, Ellis W., Jr., 244, 255
Bullock, Helen Duprey, 380
Bullock, William, 296
Bumpers, Hon. Dale, 308
Bunch, Franklin S., 255
Bundy, Richard S., 255
Bunshaft, Gordon, 76, 80, 142, 556
Burchard, Charles, 161, 325
Burck, Richard, 247
Burdick Group, 113
Bureau of Labor, 181
Burgee, John H., 255
Burgess, Charles E., 255
Burggraf, Frank Jr., 287
Burgos Cathedral (Spain), 415
Burgun, J. Armand, 255
Burj al Arab Hotel (United Arab Emirates), 357
Burke, Edward M., 255
Burke, Robert H., Jr., 330
Burke-Jones, Joyce A., 284, 323
Burkhardt, Robert G., 293
Burlage, James E., 255
Burley, Robert, 255
Burlington (Vermont), 382
Burlington County (New Jersey), 132
Burn, Lester T., 327
Burnet, Sir John James, 148
Burnett, James, 82
Burnham, Daniel Hudson, 134, 139, 320, 369
Burns, Arthur L., 255
Burns, John A., 255
Burns, Norma DeCamp, 255
Burns, Robert P., 98, 255, 325
Burns & Burns, Architects, 342
Burns & McDonnell, 350
Burson, Rodger E., 255

urt Hill Kosar Rittelmann Associates, 500
usby, John A., Jr., 244, 255, 320
usiness Week, 94, 111
usiness Week/Architectural Record Awards, 6, 8, 86
uskuhl, C. Joe, 255
ussard, H. Kennard, 255
utler, Charles, 330
utler, David M., 284
utler, Jerome R., 255
utler, Miner F., 352
utler, Theodore R., 543
utner, Fred W., 255
utrint Archaeological Site (Albania), 417
utt, Thomas K., 255
utte Historic District (Montana), 405
utterfield, William, 147
utterworth, Richard, 145
uttrick, Harold, 255
yard, Paul Spencer, 167, 255
yblos (Lebanon), 412
ye, Arthur E. "Ed," Jr., 81, 287
yers, Brent, 255
yker (United Kingdom), 168
yrd, Willard C., 287
yrne, Jeanne, 255
yron White United States Courthouse (Colorado), 140
ystrom, Arne, 255

C

C. A. Pretzer Associates, 129
C. K. Choi Building for the Institute of Asian Research
   (Canada), 365
Cabinet GERAU, 54
Caceres (Spain), 415
Caddell Construction Company, Inc., 130
Cadwalader, Burns, 255
Cadwell, Michael B., 248
Cafritz, Morris, 127
Cain, Raymond F., 287
Cain, Walker O., 245
Cairo, Islamic (Egypt), 410
Cakirhan, Nail, 54
Cakirlar, Ertan, 53
Calatrava, Santiago, 15, 85
Calcutta Metropolitan Building (India), 418
Calder, Rus, 298
Caldwell, Alfred, 97
Caldwell and Drake, 352
Caldwell Architects, 86
Calhoun, Harold, 255
California College of Arts and Crafts, 516, 525
California Polytechnic State University, 368, 525
California State Capitol, 352
California State Polytechnic University, 525
California State University, Fresno, 525
California State University, Long Beach, 525
California State University, Northridge, 525
California State University, Sacramento, 525
California State University Monterey Bay Master Plan, 83
Callans, Robert A., 287
Callaway, William B., 287
Callison, 346
Callison Architecture, Inc., 500

Callmeyer, Ferenc, 301
Calvo, Santiago A., 301
Cama, Rosalyn, 284, 323
Cambria State Penitentiary (Pennsylvania), 405
Cambridge Architectural Books, 511
Cambridge Seven Associates Inc., 78
Camenzind Gafensteiner Architects, 58
Cameron Alread Architects Inc., 341
Camino Real Hotel (Texas), 398
Camp Dresser & McKee, Inc., 101, 130
Camp Furlong (New Mexico), 405
Campaglia, Muriel, 304
Campbell, Barbara J., 90
Campbell, Craig S., 288
Campbell, Leroy M., 170
Campbell, Paschall, 288
Campbell, Robert, 68, 144, 249, 255
Campbell, Scott, 293
Campbell, Wendell J., 68, 170, 255
Campbell Thomas & Company Architects, 342
Campeche (Mexico), 413
Canada Square (United Kingdom), 360
Canadian Architect, 519
Canadian Centre for Architecture, 70, 217
Canadian Council on Rehabilitation and Work, 12
Canadian Imperial Bank of Commerce, 359
Canal du Centre Lifts and Environs (Belgium), 408
Canal du Midi (France), 410
Candela, Felix, 3, 301
Candela, F., 85
Candela, H. F., 255
Canine, Luigi, 147
Canizaro, Robert H., 255
Cannady, William T., 255
Cannon, 501
Cannon, Jamie, 255
Cannon, Ronald G., 342
Cansever, Feyza, 56
Cansever, Turgut, 53, 56
Canterbury Cathedral (United Kingdom), 416
Cantor, Marvin J., 255
Cantrell, Horace S., Jr., 255
Canty, Donald, 69, 304
Canyon Forest Villiage II Corp. (Arizona), 83
Caparn, Harold A., 324
Cape Hatteras Light Station (North Carolina), 102
Cape May Historic District (New Jersey), 405
Capelin, Joan, 304
Caplan, Ralph, 309
Cappadocia Rock Sites (Turkey), 415
Caracas Office Towers (Venezuela), 359
Carcassonne Historic Fortified City (France), 410
Cardasis, Dean, 288
Cardinal, Douglas, 146
Cardoso, J., 85
Cardoza, Robert R., 288
Cardwell, Kenneth Harvey, 255
Cares, Charles, 288
Carey, Hillary, 113
Caribiner International, 153
Carl, Peter, 245
Carlhian, Jean P., 100, 255
Carlisle, William A., 255
Carlough, Edward, 304

Carlsberg Architectural Prize, 88
Carlson, Bryan D., 288
Carlson, DeVon M., 255
Carlson, Donald Edwin, 255
Carlson, Richard, 298, 311
Carlson Technology, 113
Carmichael, Dennis B., 288
Carnegie Hall Tower (New York), 360
Carnegie Mellon University (Pennsylvania), 535
Carnegie Museum of Art, 222
Caroe, Alban, 543
Caroe, Martin, 543
Caroe, W. D., 543
Caroe & Partners, 543
Carol R. Johnson Associates, Inc., 82
Carolina Inn (North Carolina), 398
Carpenter, Clyde R., 255
Carpenter, Derr A., 288
Carpenter, Jack A., 255
Carpenter, James Fraser, 70, 106
Carpenter, Jot D., 288, 324, 544
Carpenter, William J., 172
Carr, E. T., 353
Carr, Oliver T., Jr., 127
Carr, Orville V., 284
Carré d'Art Plaza (France), 168
Carrére, John Mervin, 23
Carriero, Joseph, 296
Carroll, Charles R., Jr., 293
Carroll, Edwin Winford, 255
Carroll, Jefferson Roy, Jr., 244, 320
Carroll, M. E., 255
Carroll, Marley, 255
Carruth, David B., 288
Carry, Walter T., 255, 330
Carson, Chris, 255
Carson, Heather, 248
Cartagena Port, Fortresses and Monuments (Colombia), 409
Carter, Donald K., 255
Carter, Donald R., 288
Carter, Eugene H., 288
Carter, James Earl, Jr., 308
Carter, Virgil R., 255
Carter & Burgess, Inc., 101, 102
Carter's Grove (Virginia), 388
Carthage Site (Tunisia), 415
Cartnal, David R., 255
Caruso Affiliated Holdings, 166
Casa Mila (Spain), 415
Casa Monica Hotel (Florida), 397
Casabella, 520
Casai, Timothy A., 255
Casale Villa Romana (Italy), 412
Casbarian, John J., 248, 255
Cascieri, A., 255
Cascio, Joe, 83
Casendino, Anthony B., 288
Caserta Royal Palace (Italy), 412
Cashio, Carlos J., 288
Caskey, Donald W., 255
Cass, Heather W., 255
Casserly, Joseph W., 255
Castel de Monte (Italy), 412
Castellana, John J., 255

Castellanos, Particia Gutierrez, 298
Castellanos, Stephan, 255
Castleman, Elizabeth M., 284
Castor, Daniel, 245
Castro-Blanco, David, 170
Çatalhöyük (Turkey), 420
Cathedral Church of St. John the Divine (New York), 69
Cathedral of Our Lady (Czech Republic), 409
Cathers & Associates Inc., 342
Catholic University of America (Washington, D.C.), 527
Catlin, Juliana M., 284, 323
Catroux, Francois, 311
Caudill, Samuel J., 255
Caudill, William Wayne, 60
Caudill Rowlett Scott, 78
Cavaglieri, Giorgio, 255
Cavin, W. Brooks, Jr., 256
Cawley, Charles M., 304
CDM Engineers and Constructors, Inc., 130
The Center (China), 356
Center for Creative Studies (Michigan), 530
Center for Health Design, 90
Center Street Park and Ride (Iowa), 62
Centerbrook Architects, 78, 501
Central City (Colorado), 404
Central Park (New York), 69, 132
Central Plaza (China), 356, 371
Central Valley housing project (California), 546
Centre for Experimentation, Research and Training, 155
Centrepoint Tower (Australia), 363
Cerasi, Vincent C., 247
Certosa di Padula (Italy), 412
Cesar Pelli & Associates, 62, 356, 358, 360, 501
Cesky Krumlov Footbridge (Czech Republic), 348
Cesky Krumlov Historic Centre (Czech Republic), 409
CH2M Hill, 341
Chabanne, Henri E., 247
Chadirji, Rifat, 57, 301
Chadwick & Associates, 94
Chafee, Judith, 245
Chaffin, Lawrence, Jr., 256
Chaintreuil, Ann R., 256, 330
Chaix, Alfred V., 256
Chambers, Henry C., 304
Chambers, Michael D., 293
Chambers, S. Elmer, 293
Chambliss, Dean B., 256
Chambord Chateau and Estate (France), 410
Champaner Archaeological Site (India), 418
Champeaux, Junius J., II, 256
Champneys, Basil, 147
Chan, Lo-Yi, 256
Chan Chan Archaeological Zone (Peru), 414
Chandler, Palmer & King, 349
Chaney, James A., 293, 327
Chang, Suk-Woong, 301
Chang, Te L., 301
Ch'angdokkung Palace Complex (Republic of Korea), 414
Channel Tunnel (England and France), 336
Chao, Wing T., 256
Chapelle Administration Building (South Carolina), 405
Chapin, F. Stuart, Jr., 52, 134
Chapin, L. William, Jr., 256, 320
Chapman, Donald D., 256

Clarke, Marshall F., 256
Clarke, Thomas L., Jr., 293
Clarksville (Missouri), 382
Clary, Charles, 256
Clause, Thomas R., 256
Clay, Grady, Jr., 304, 308
Clemence, Roger D., 288
Clement, Jerry L., 256
Clements, Franklin C., 288
Clemson University (South Carolina), 535
Clérisseau, Charles-Louis, 354
Cleveland Historic Landmarks (Ohio), 132
Cleveland Institute of Art (Ohio), 534
Cliff House Inn (Colorado), 396
Clifford Moles Associates, 344
Cline, Carroll, 544
Cline, Glen E., 256
Cline Bettridge Bernstein Lighting Design, 544
Clinton & Russell, 358
Clinton Courthouse and Lawyer's Row (Louisiana), 404
Clipson, R., 353
Clive Wilkinson Architects, 116
Clodagh, 311
Close, Elizabeth, 256
Clough, Robert K., 256
Clutts, James A., 256
CMR, Ltd., 343
CN Tower (Canada), 362
Cobb, Henry Nichols, 80, 161, 249, 256
Coble, Wesley M., 342
Cochrane, J. C., 352
Cockerell, Charles Robert, 9, 147, 331
Coe, Christopher W., 172
Coe, Jon Charles, 288
Coe, Theodore Irving, 100
Coenen, Jo, 228, 229
Coffee, R. F., 256
Coffin, Beatriz de Winthuysen, 288
Coffin, David, 72
Coffin, Laurence E., Jr., 288
Coffin, Margaret, 84
Coffman, Jim, 83
Cohagen, Chandler C., 330
Cohen, Andrew S., 256
Cohen, E. Gresley, 301
Cohen, Jack C., 256
Cohen, Martin H., 256
Cohen, Stuart, 256
Coia, Jack Antonio, 148
Coit, Elizabeth, 280
Coker, Coleman, 245
Cole, Doris, 256
Cole, Melvin G., 293
Cole, Pamela J., 293
Coleman, Susan, 298
Coleman Product Design, 113
Coles, Robert Traynham, 170, 244, 256
Colgan Perry Lawler Architects, 349
Collcutt, Thomas Edward, 147, 331
Colleen B. Rosenblat Jewelry Showroom and Office (Germany), 64
College Hill (Rhode Island), 132
College of Charleston (South Carolina), 536
College of the Redwoods (California), 525

Collier, William Arthur, 342
Collignon & Nunley, 342
Collins, David S., 256
Collins, John F., 288
Colliton, Dennis C., 288
Cologne Cathedral (Germany), 411
Colonia del Sacramento Historic Quarter (Uruguay), 416
Colonial Church (Minnesota), 543
Colonial Williamsburg Foundation, 376
Colonius Tower (Germany), 363
Colorado State Capitol, 352
Colorado State University, 526
Colter, Mary Jane Elizabeth, 313–314
Columbia (South Carolina), 337
Columbia Historic Landmarks (Maryland), 131
Columbia River Highway State Trail (Oregon), 91
Columbia Seafirst Center (Washington), 358, 372
Columbia University (New York), 367, 532, 559
Columbus (Georgia), 337
Columbus (Indiana), 406
Columbus (New Mexico), 405
Columbus College of Art & Design (Ohio), 534
CommArts, 152
Commerzbank Tower (Germany), 357
Commoner, Barry, 68
Commons at Calabasas (California), 166
Communication Arts, 516
Compaq Center (Texas), 562
Compton, Jerry, 321
CompUSA (California), 114, 152
Comstock, Donald, 256
Conant, Kenneth John, 72, 332
Concord Mills (North Carolina), 153
Cone-Kalb-Wonderlick, 341
Confucius Temple and Cemetary (China), 409
Conklin, William T., 256
Connally, Ernest Allen, 304, 380, 544–545
Connecticut State Capitol, 352
Conrad, Richard T., 256
Conrad, W. M., 256
Conron, John P., 256, 284
Conroy, J. J., 256
Conroy, S. B., 304
Conservation Trust of Puerto Rico, 70
Constant, Caroline B., 245
Construction Bookstore, 511
Construction Insights, 551
Construction Specifications Institute, 14, 185, 293–295, 327
Contract Design Center Bookshop, 511
Cook, Eugene E., 256
Cook, George Glenn, 288
Cook, Lawrence D., 256
Cook, Linda J., 247
Cook, Peter, 119
Cook, Richard B., 256
Cook, Walter, 320
Cook, William H., 256
Cook Hiltscher Associates, 167
Cooke, David, 298
Cooledge, Harold, Jr., 97
Coolidge, Frederic S., 245
Cooper, Alexander, 256

ooper, Celeste, 311
ooper, Douglas, 71
ooper, Jerome M., 256
ooper, Lynton B., Jr., 293
ooper, Robertson & Partners, 501
ooper, Sir Edwin, 148
ooper, W. Kent, 256
ooper Carry, Inc., 339, 501
ooper-Hewitt Museum (National Design Museum), 69, 141, 218
ooper-Hewitt Museum Bookstore, 512
ooper/Roberts Architects, 342
ooper Union (New York), 532, 549
oors Field (Colorado), 166
oover, Christopher, 256
ope, Gerald M., 256
opeland, Lee G., 256
opeland, Rolaine V., 304
oram Design Award, 6
orberó, Xavier, 125, 126
orbett, Harrison & MacMurray, 162
orbin Design, 153
orddry, Carpenter, Dietz & Zack, 102
ordell (Oklahoma), 382
ordes, Loverne C., 284
ordier, Herbert, 284
ordish Company, 166
ordoba Historic Centre (Spain), 414
ordogan Clark & Associates, 341
organ, C. Jack, 256
organ, Jack M., 256
orkle, Eleanor, 298
orlett, William, 256
orlin, Len, 310
ornell University (New York), 43, 366, 367, 532, 558, 561
orniche Mosque (Saudi Arabia), 55
orning (Iowa), 382
orning Incorporated, 70
orning Museum of Glass, 153
ornish-Windsor Bridge (New Hampshire and Vermont), 347
oro and its Port (Venezuela), 416
oronado (California), 382
orpus Christi (Texas), 337
orrea, Charles M., 57, 139, 148, 156, 165, 250, 301
orreale, Fred J., 288
ortrell, Eugene H., 293
ossutta, Araldo A., 256
osta, Lucio, 155
osta, Walter H., 257
ostello, Jini, 284
ostiera Amalfitana (Italy), 412
otacachi Canton (Ecuador), 99
ott, Leland, 257
otter, John L., 379
otton, John O., 257
ouch, Frank L., 293
oulter, Kenneth R., 288
ouncil of Educators in Landscape Architecture, 539
ouncil on Tall Buildings and Urban Habit, 186, 356
ounsel House Research, 388
ountry Club Plaza (Missouri), 132, 133
ourtenay, Virginia W., 284
ourtyard Houses (Morocco), 53

Cousins, Morison S., 248
Cowell, C. H., 257
Cowgill, Clinton H., 330
Cowling, Dan C., 257
Cox, David C., 257
Cox, Frederic H., 257
Cox, Philip Sutton, 145, 301
Cox, Van L., 288
Cox, Warren J., 257
Cox, Whitson W., 257
Coxe, Weld, 304
Coyle, Stephen, 70
CP&Associates/Architects & Planners, 342
Crabtree, Bruce I., Jr., 257
Cracow Historic Centre (Poland), 414
Craig, Kirk R., 257
Craig, Lois, 304
Craigo, Steade, 257
Cralle, Christine, 310
Cram, Ralph Adams, 25
Cram, Stephen, 170
Cramer, James P., 304, 310
Cranbrook Academy of Art, 69
Cranbrook Academy of Art (Michigan), 531
Crandall, George M., 257
Crane, David A., 257
Cranston Aqueduct (Rhode Island), 130
Cranwell Resort & Gold Club, 397
Crapsey, Arthur H., 296
Crasco, H. Kenneth, 288
Crawford, Dana, 380
Crawford, Ronald O., 257
Crawley, Stanley W., 98
Crayola Cafe & Store, 113
Creamer, John Milton, 293
Creative Designs Braxton Dennis/Architect, 342
Creed, George E., 288
Creel, Wrenn M., 293
Creer, Philip D., 100
Creese, Walter L., 332
Crennen, Martin W., 257
Crepsi d'Adda (Italy), 412
Crescent Hotel & Spa (Arkansas), 396
Cret, Paul Philippe, 60
Crimp, Frank W., 257
Cripple Creek Historic District (Colorado), 404
Crissman, James H., 257
Critchfield Mechanical, 129
Crittenden, Edwin B., 257
Crocco, K. C., 257
Croft, Charles B., 257
Cromley, Elizabeth, 376
Cromwell, Edwin B., 257
Cromwell Architects Engineers, 349
Cross, Eason, Jr., 257
Cross, Kenneth M. B., 331
Crothers, Samuel III, 257
Crouch, Dora P., 136
Crow Island School (Illinois), 162
Crowe, Dame Sylvia, 81
Crowe, Sylvia, 314
Crowley, Roger, 245
Crown Equipment, 111
Crowninshield Award, 380

Crowther, R. L., 257
Croxton, Randolph R., 257
Crozier, Samuel G., 288
Crozier Gedney Architects, 341
Crump, Metcalf, 257
Cruthers, Evan D., 257
Cruz, Teddy Edwin, 245
Crystal, Joseph H., 288
CSHQA Architects/Engineers/Planners, 349
Cubanacán National Art Schools (Cuba), 418
Cubellis Associates Inc., 339
Cuenca Walled Town (Spain), 415
Cullen, Gordon, 68
Cullum, Charles H., 301
Culp, Russell Rowe, 248
Culp & Tanner, 128
Culpin Planning, 55
Cultural Landscape Foundation, 84
Cultural Landscape Guidelines, 383–384
Culver, Taylor, 321
Cummings, Abbott Lowell, 73, 376
Cummings, Columbus, 352
Cummings, G. Parker, 352
Cummings, George B., 320
Cumrine, Ray E., 293
Cuningham, John W., 257
Cuningham Group, 339, 501
Cunningham, Gary M., 257
Cunningham, Warren W., 257
Currie, Robert, 311
Curry, Father Terrence, 172
Curry, George W., 288
Curtis, Jack, 288
Cusco Historic Centre (Peru), 420
Custer, Betty Lou, 100
Cutler, James L., 257
Cutler, John E., 288
Cutler, Phoebe, 248
Cuypers, Dr. P. J. H., 147
Cuzco (Peru), 414
Cyrene Archaeological Site (Libyan Arab Jamahiriya), 412
Cywinski, Bernard J., 257
Czarnowski, Thomas V., 245

D

D. J. Silver & Son, 353
D. M. Bergerson Inc., 342
Da Silva, Carlos E., 301
Dacian Fortresses (Romania), 414
Dada, Nayyar Ali, 57
Daewoo & Partners, 357
Daft, Jack R., 288
Dagit, Charles E., Jr., 257
Dahan, Fernand W., 257
Dahl, Taffy, 71
Dahshur Pyramids (Egypt), 410
Daileda, David A., 257
Daileda, Kathleen L., 304
Dailey, Donald E., 296
Dakota County Technical College (Minnesota), 531
Dale, Curt, 257
Dale, P. A., 284
Daley, Honorable Richard M., 122

Daley, Royston T., 245
Dalland, Todd, 257
Dallas Area Rapid Transit Mall (Texas), 82, 91
Daltas, Spero, 245
Dalton, J. E., 257
Daly, Cesar, 147
Daly, Leo A., III, 257
Daly, Leo A., 100, 346, 358, 501
Damascus (Syrian Arab Republic), 415
D'Amato, Alfonse M., 304
Damaz, Paul, 257
Dambulla Golden Temple (Sri Lanka), 415
Damianos, Sylvester, 100, 257, 320
Damora, Robert, 257
Damuck, Walter E., 293
Dandan, Christine, 298
Danforth, George E., 257
Dangermond, Peter, Jr., 288
Daniel Group Inc. Architects, Planners, Project Managers, 342
Danielian, Arthur C., 257
Daniels, Eugene, 298
Daniels, George N., 257
Daniels, Stanley L., 257
Danish Center for Architecture, 219
Danish Design Center, 70, 220
Dankovsky, Vladimir, 58
Danna, Doris Andrews, 257
Danube Banks (Hungary), 411
Daphni Monastery (Greece), 411
Dar Lamane Housing Community (Morocco), 54
Darb Qirmiz Quarter (Egypt), 54
Darby, Robert F., 257
D'Arcy, Barbara, 93, 311
Darden, Douglas, 245
Darden, Edwin S., 257
Darling, Frank, 148
Darmer, Ben R., 257
Daroff Design, 152
Dattner, Richard, 160, 257
Daugherty, Edward L., 288
Daumet, Honore, 147
David, Theoharis L., 257
David, Thomas, 296
David Wisdom and Associates, 56
Davidoff, Paul, 134
Davidson, Ann, 304
Davidson, Colin H., 98
Davidson, D. G., 257
Davidson, David S., 258
Davidson, Joan K., 304
Davidson, John M., 301
Davidson, Kent, 321
Davidson, Robert I., 258
Davidson and Jones Group, 130
Davidson County (Tennessee), 132
Davies, David Y., 301
Davies, Jane, 545
D'Avignon, Fay, 321
Davis, Albert J., 258
Davis, Alexander J., 545
Davis, Arthur Q., 258
Davis, Charles M., 258
Davis, Clark, 258

DeWolff Partnership, 340
Di Geronimo, Suzanne, 258
Di Maio, Judith, 245
Di Mambro, Antonio, 258
Diadalos, 520
Diamant, Robert, 258
Diamond, A. J., 301
Diamond, J. J. J., 258
Diamond, Katherine, 258
Diaz, Horacio, 258
Diaz, James R., 258
Diaz-Azcuy, Orlando, 158, 311
Diaz-Morales, Ignacio, 301
DiBenedetto, A. P., 258
Dibner, David R., 258
Dickenson, Russell E., 308
Dicker, Bruce, 258
Diedrich, 166
Diehl, Gerald G., 258
Dieste, Eladio, 545
Dieste y Montáñez, 545
Dietrich, Paul E., 258
Dietsch, Deborah, 304
Dietz, Robert H., 258
DiFazio Architects, 342
Diffrient, Niels, 70, 296
Dijkstra, Harry, 83
Dike, P. Woodward, 288
Dikis, William M., 258
DiLaura, Eugene L., 258
Diller, Elizabeth, 549
Diller + Scofidio, 137
Dimond, F. Christopher, 288
Dimster, Frank, 258
Dindorf, Carolyn J., 84
Dines, Nicholas T., 288
Diniz, Carlos, 304
Dinsmore, Philip, 258
Dioxiadis, G., 155
DiProperzio, Anthony S., 342
Dirsmith, Ronald L., 245
Disrud, Carol, 298
Distinguished Professor Award, 97–98
District Design, 90
Ditchy, Clair W., 320
Divrigi Great Mosque and Hospital (Turkey), 415
Dixon, David D., 258
Dixon, F. Dail, Jr., 258
Dixon, John M., 258
Dixon, Michael A., 258
Djémila (Algeria), 408
Djenné Old Towns (Mali), 413
DLR Group, 129, 346
Doane, Jonathan, 353
Doane, Lawrence S., 258
Doblin, Jay, 296
Doche, Jim C., 258
DOCOMOMO (Documentation and Conservation of
   Buildings, Sites and Neighborhoods of the Modern
   Movement), 381
DOCOMOMO Journal, 381
Dodge, Carlton T., 288
Dodge, Peter H., 258
Dohr, Joy, 124

Dolginoff, Wesley J., 293
Dolim, George S., 258
Dominick, Peter Hoyt, Jr., 258
Domus, 520
Don CeSar Beach Resort and Spa (Florida), 397
Donaldson, Milford W., 258
Donaldson, Thomas L., 147, 331
Donauturm (Austria), 364
Donelin, Dan W., 288
Donelson, Janet, 258
Doner, H. Creston, 296
Donghia, Angelo, 311
Donkervoet, Richard C., 258
Donnell, William S., 71
Donnelly, Marian C., 300, 332
Dorius, Kermit P., 258
Dorman, Albert A., 258
Dorman, Richard L., 258
Dorman & Breen Architects, 342
Dorpfeld, Wilhelm, 147
Dorsey, Robert W., 258
Dorsky Hodgson + Partners, 339, 340
Dortmund Tower (Germany), 364
Doshi, Balkrishna V., 56, 301
Doss, Darwin V., 258
Doty, Walter L., 308
Dougga/Thugga (Tunisia), 415
Dougherty, Betsey O., 259
Dougherty, Brian P., 259
Dougherty, Joanna, 247
Douglas, Frank F., 259
Douglass, H. Robert, 259
Dove, C. R. George, 259
Dow, Alden B., 75
Dowling, John L., 312
Downing, Antoinette Forrester, 69, 72, 380
Dowson, Sir Philip, 148, 301
Doxiadis, Dr. Constantinos, 146, 284
Doyle, Gerald A., 259
Doyle, Peter G., 259
Doytchev, Kiril, 301
Dragon Rock, 151
Drake, Paul W., 330
Dramov, Boris, 259
Drapeau, Mayor Jean, 146
Draper, Dede, 284
Draper, Earle S., 134
Dreiling, Helene, 259
Dresden Tower (Germany), 364
Drew, Jane Beverly, 7, 314
Drew, Roy M., 259
Drexel University (Pennsylvania), 366, 535
Drexler, Arthur, 68
Dreyer, Carl Theodor, 250
Dreyfuss, Albert M., 259
Dreyfuss, Henry, 296, 328
Dripps, Robert D., 98
The Driskill (Texas), 398
Droogmakerij de Beemster (Netherlands), 413
Drottningholm Royal Domain (Sweden), 415
Drummond, Jo, 293
Drummond, Robert Wayne, 259, 326
Drury University (Missouri), 531
Duany, Andres M., 19, 259, 317

Egan, M. David, 98, 305
Eggers, David L., 259
Egnell, Stig, 54
Egyptian Antiquities Organization, 54
Egyptian Theater (California), 116, 391
Ehmann, Richard C., 293
Ehrenkrantz, Ezra D., 259
Ehrig, John P., 259
Ehrlich, Joseph, 259
Ehrlich, Steven D., 259
Eichbaum, Thomas N., 259
Eid, Yehya M., 301
Eidlitz, Leopold, 7, 354
Eiffel Tower (France), 363
Eifler, John A., 259
Eight Inc., 115
Einhorn, Steven L., 259
Einhorn Yaffee Prescott, 339, 346, 501
Eisenman, Peter D., 17, 19, 249, 259, 561
Eisenman, Peter K., 80
Eisenman Architects, 501
Eisenshtat, Sidney H., 259
Eisleben Luther Memorials (Germany), 411
Eisner, Richard Karl, 259
Eisner, Simon, 134
Ekuan, Kenji, 117
El Arco Iris, 84
El Camino Real Hotel (Mexico), 61
El Centro College (Texas), 536
El Croquis, 520
El Encanto Hotel & Garden Villas (California), 396
El Fuerte de Samaipata (Bolivia), 409
El Jem Amphitheatre (Tunisia), 415
El Paso (Texas), 337
El Rancho Hotel (Nevada), 554
El Tajin (Mexico), 413
El Wakil, Abdel W., 301
Elam, Merrill, 75
Elbasani, Barry P., 259
Eldem, Sedad Hakki, 54
Eldredge, Joseph L., 259
Electrolux, 109
Eleven Inc. (California), 115
Eleven Madison Park (New York), 115
Eley, Charles N., 259
Elinoff, Martin, 284
Eliot, Charles W., II, 81
Elizondo, Juan Gil, 155
Elkins Coal and Coke (West Virginia), 406
Elkus, Howard F., 259
Elkus/Manfredi Architects, 501
Ellenzweig, Harry, 259
Ellerbe Becket, 104, 346, 501
Ellerthorpe, Robin M., 259
Ellickson, Dale R., 259
Ellinoff, Martin, 323
Elliot Contracting Corporation, 129
Elliott, Benjamin P., 259
Elliott + Associates Architects, 64, 113, 342
Ellis, James R., 305
Ellis, John M., 259
Ellis, Prof. Margaret Holben, 247
Ellis Island (New York), 546
Ellison, James E., 259

Ellora Caves (India), 411
Elmo, John, 284
Elmore, James W., 259
Emerald Necklace Parks (Massachusetts), 131
Emerson, Jon Stidger, 247, 288
Emerson, Sir William, 325, 331
Emery, Sherman R., 312
Emery Roth & Sons, 350, 356, 359
Emeryville Resourceful Building Project (California), 365
Emilio Ambasz & Associates, 86, 113
Emirates Tower One (United Arab Emirates), 356
Emirates Tower Two (United Arab Emirates), 357
Emmons, Frederick E., 259
Emmons, Terrel M., 259
Empire State Building (New York), 336, 356
Empire Tower (Malaysia), 359
End, Henry, 311
Endicott College (Massachusetts), 530
Energy Management Consultants, 342
Energysmiths, 365
Enfeh Archaeological Site (Lebanon), 418
Eng, William, 259
Engebretson, Douglas K., 259
Engelbrecht, Mark C., 259
Engelhard, Donald G., 293
Engelsberg Ironworks (Sweden), 415
Engineering Excellence Awards, 2, 101–104
Engineering News Record, 517
Enron building (Texas), 562
Ensign, Donald H., 288
Ensign, William L., 259
Entenza, John D., 68, 305
Entrepreneurship Development Institute of India (India), 56
EnvironMental Design, 342
Environmental Design Research Association, 12
Environmental Services, Inc., 102
Enyart, Lawrence, 259
Epidaurus Archaeological Site (Greece), 411
Eppstein-Uhen Architects Inc., 166
Epstein, Herbert, 100, 259
The Equinox (Vermont), 398
Equitable Center (New York), 360
Equitable Savings and Loan Building (Oregon), 164
Erbil Citadel (Iraq), 418
Ergas, Joel M., 284
Ergonomic System Design, 111
Eric Owen Moss Architects, 137
Ericksen Roed & Associates, 129
Erickson, Arthur C., 60, 85, 146, 301, 552
Erickson, Rodney E., 293
Erickson, Sammye J., 284
Ericson, Elizabeth S., 259
Ericsson, L. M., 309
Ernest J. Kump Associates, 78
Ernst, Jerome R., 259
Erskine, Ralph, 146, 148, 168, 171
Ertegun, Mica, 311
Ertegün House (Turkey), 53
ESA Consultants Inc., 102
Eschikofen-Bonau Bridge (Switzerland), 348
Escurial Monastery and Site (Spain), 415
Eshbach, William W., 100
Esher, Lord, 301, 331
Esherick, Joseph, 60, 161

Ferrara, Jackie, 70
Ferrara (Italy), 412
Ferrari, Olivio C., 97
Ferre, L. A., 305
Ferrell, Stephanie E., 260
Ferrer, Miguel, 260
Ferrey, Benjamin, 147
Ferrier, A. I., 302
Ferrier, Richard B., 260
Ferris, James D., 260
Ferris, Robert D., 260
Ferro, M. L., 260
Ferry, Donald E., 260
Festival of Britain, 554
Fez Medina (Morocco), 413
FFKR Architecture/Planning/Interior Design, 342
Fickel, Michael T., 260
Field, David W., 305
Field, H. H., 260
Field, John L., 260
Fielden, Robert A., 260, 330
Fieldman, Michael M., 260
Fields, Jon J., 284
Fifth and Forbes Historic Retail Area (Pennsylvania), 378
Fifth Avenue Duplex (New York), 64
Figg Engineering Group, 140
Filarski, Kenneth J., 260
Filarski Architecture Planning Research, 342
Filer, R. Jerome, 260
Filippini, Ignacio, 113
Fillpot, Bob G., 260
Filson, Ronald C., 245, 260
Finch, Curtis, 260
Finch, James H., 260
Findlay, Robert A., 260
Fine, Steven, 138
Fine Homebuilding, 517
Finegold, Maurice N., 260
Finger, Harold B., 305
Finger & Moy Architects, 64
Fink, Ira S., 260
Finney, Garrett S., 245
Finnish Pavilion (New York), 125
Finrow, Jerry V., 260, 326
Finta, Jozsef, 302
Firestone, Charles E., 330
First Bank Place (Minnesota), 360
First Canadian Place, 358, 371
First Houses (New York), 132
First National Plaza (Illinois), 360
Fischer, Michael A., 172
Fischer, Milton, 546
Fischer and Elmore, 546
Fisher, A. Robert, 260
Fisher, Karen, 312
Fisher, Larry G., 293
Fisher, Louis J., 343
Fisher-Price, 111
Fisk, Hollye C., 260
Fitch, Inc., 94, 111, 114
Fitch, James Marston, 68, 97, 305, 380, 546–547
Fitterer, Al, 343
Fitts, Michael A., 260
Fitzgerald, Darrell A., 260

Fitzgerald, James T., 260
Fitzgerald, Joseph F., 260
Fitzgerald, Richard A., 260
FitzPatrick, Thomas, 325
FKP Architects, Inc., 339
Flad, Joseph H., 260
Flad & Associates, 340, 501
Flagg, Ernest, 5
Flansburg Associates, Inc., 339
Flansburgh, Earl Robert, 260
Flatiron Building (New York), 369
Flato, Ted, 260
Fleck, John C., 293, 327
Fleischer, Joseph L., 260
Fleischman, Richard J., 260
Flemish Béguinages (Belgium), 408
Flesher, Thomas H., Jr., 330
Fletcher, Norman C., 260
Fletcher, Shelley, 247
Fletcher, Sir Banister, 331
Flood, David J., 260
Florance, Colden R., 260
Florence Historic Centre (Italy), 412
Flores, Antonio F., 302
Flores, Cesar X., 302
Flores, Phillip E., 288
Flores-Dumont, Luis, 260
Florida A&M University, 527
Florida Atlantic University, 527
Florida International University, 527
Florida Keys Owners Demo Project, 102
Florida Southern College, 527
Florida State Capitol, 352
Florida State University, 366, 527
Flournoy, William L., Jr., 288
Floyd, J. Chadwick P., 260
Floyd, Richard F., 260
Floyd, W. Jeff, Jr., 260
Fly, Everett L., 141, 288
Flynn, Ligon B., 260
Flynn, Michael, 260
Flynt, Henry N., 380
Flynt, Mrs. Henry N., 380
Focke, John W., 260
Focus: HOPE Center for Advanced Technologies (Michigan)
  140
Foerster, Bernd, 97, 260
Fogg, George E., 288
Follett, James, 260
Fontenay Cistercian Abbey (France), 410
Fontenot, Lyn, 284
Foor & Associates, 349
Foote, Fred L., 261
Foote, Stephen M., 261
Foote, Vincent M., 110, 296
Foothill College (California), 562
Forbes, John D., 305, 332
Forbes, Peter, 261
Force, Kris, 108
Ford, George Burdett, 134
Ford, John G., 284
Ford, Robert M., 261
Ford Foundation Headquarters (New York), 164

Gerard de Preu & Partners, 359
Geren, Preston M., 261
German, Glenn, 343
German Archaeological Institute, 54
Gerou, Phillip H., 261
Getty Center (California), 62, 369
Ghadames Old Town (Libyan Arab Jamahiriya), 412
Ghafari Associate, Inc., 339
Ghirardo, Diane, 98, 326
Gianninoto, Franceco, 296
Giattina, Joe P., Jr., 261, 330
Gibbons, Michael F., 294
Gibbons, Richard George, 289
Gibbs, Dale L., 261
Gibbs, David W., 355
Gibbs, Donald H., 261
Gibson, C. D., 305
Gibson, John, 147
Gibson, Robin Findlay, 145
Gibson, Sir Donald, 331
Gideon, Randall C., 261
Gilbert, Cass
    awards, 76
    organizational memberships, 320
    quote by, 237
    works of, 352, 353, 355, 359, 370
Gilbert, Sidney P., 261
Gilbert, Van H., 343
Gilbertson, Matthew W., 321
Gilbertson, Victor C., 262
Gilchrist, Agnes Addison, 332
Gill, Brendan, 305
Gill, Louis J., 330
Gilland, Wilmot G., 262, 325
Giller, Norman M., 262
Gillette, 94
Gilling, Ronald Andrew, 145
Gilpin, W. Douglas, 262
Gimpel, James S., 262
Gindroz, Raymond L., 262
Ginsberg, David L., 262
Giordano, Jeanne, 248
Giraffe Rock Art Site (Niger), 420
Girard, Alexander, 218, 284
Girault, Charles Louis, 148
Girod, Judy, 284
Girvigian, Raymond, 262
Giuliani, Joseph Carl, 262
Giurgola, Renaldo, 19
Giurgola, Romaldo, 60, 80, 97, 145, 262
Giza Pyramids (Egypt), 410
Gladding, McBean & Company, 69
Glaser, Milton, 70, 285
Glaser, Richard E., 262
Glass, Henry P., 296
Glass, Lisa, 113
Glass, William R., 262
Glass House (Connecticut), 369
Glasser, David Evan, 262
Glavin, James E., 289
Glendening, E. A., 262
Glenn, Gary, 343
Glick, D. Newton, 289
Glitsch, Val, 262

GlobalShop, 6
GLS Landscape Architecture, 82
Gluckman, Richard J., 262, 311
Gluckman Mayner Architects, 64
Glucksman, Harold D., 262
Glusberg, Jorge, 119, 305
Glymph, James M., 262
Goa Churches and Convents (India), 411
Gobbell, Ronald V., 262
Gobel, Elias F., 352
Gobster, Paul, 83
Godfrey, William Purves Race, 145
Godi, Donald H., 289
Godwin, George, 147
Godwin, James B., 289
Godwin Associates, 339
Goettsch, James, 262
Goetz, Robert E., 289
Goff, Bruce, 13, 164
Gokayama Historic Village (Japan), 412
Golda, Terence A., 343
Goldberg, Alan E., 262
Goldberg, Alfred, 305
Goldberg, Howard G., 305
Goldberg, Jeff, 71
Goldberg, Steven M., 262
Goldberger, Paul, 69, 144, 305
Golden Bear International, 167
Golden Gate Bridge (California), 336
Golder, Robert M., 245
Goldfinger, M. H., 262
Goldman, Ron, 262
Goldman Firth Architects, 343
Goldman Properties, 167
Goldschmied, Marco, 331
Goldsmith, Goldwin, 325
Goldsmith, Nicholas, 262
Goldsmith, William, 296, 328
Goldstein, Roger Neal, 262
Goldstein, Stanley J., 262
Goldstone, Harmon H., 262
Golemon, Albert S., 244
Golemon, Harry A., 262
Goltsman, Susan M., 289
Gomez, Mariette Himes, 311
Gonzales, Bennie M., 262
Gonzalez, Juan, 302
Goo, Donald W. Y., 262
Good, Karen, 84
Good, R. L., 262
Goodhart-Rendel, H. S., 331
Goodhue, Bertram Grosvenor, 60, 353, 370
Goodhue, D. B., 262
Goodkind & O'Dea Inc., 130
Goodman, Cary C., 262
Goodman, Jeremiah, 312
Goodman, John P., 262
Goodman, Paul, 114
Goodwin, Michael K., 262
Goody, Clancy & Associates, 314, 502
Goody, Joan Edelman, 25, 262, 314
Gordon, Cynthia Nicole, 109
Gordon, Douglas E., 305
Gordon, Elizabeth, 547

Gordon, Eric, 247
Gordon, Ezra, 262
Gordon, Harry T., 262
Gordon, James Riley, 352
Gordon, Sir Alex, 331
Gordon H. Chong & Partners, 342
Gorée Island (Senegal), 414
Göreme National Park (Turkey), 415
Gores, H. B., 305
Gorlin, Alexander C., 245
Gorman Richardson Architects Inc., 343
Gorski, Gilbert, 107
Goslar Historic Town (Germany), 410
Gosling, Joseph, 353
Gotch, J. Alfred, 331
Goucher College (Maryland), 530
Goudeket, William, Jr., 294
Gould, Robert E., 262
Gourley, Ronald, 262
Gouvis, Arthur A., 341
Governor Hotel (Oregon), 398
Governors Island (New York), 106
Gowans, Alan W., 72, 300, 332
Graber, Ted, 548
Grabowski, Thomas C., 285
Graceland (Tennessee), 388
Gracey, Brian, 262
Grad, Bernard J., 262
Graham, Bruce J., 262
Graham, Carol S., 298
Graham, D. R., 305
Graham, Gary L., 262
Graham, Gordon, 331
Graham, Lori, 310
Graham, Philip H., Jr., 289
Graham, Roy E., 262
Graham, Theodora Kim, 285
Graham Anderson Probst & White, 349
Graham Gund Architects, Inc., 502
Gramann, Robert E., 262
Grameen Bank, 55
Grameen Bank Housing (Bangladesh), 55
Gramsbergen, Egbert, 371
Gran, Warren Wolf, 262
Grand Central Station (New York), 62, 91, 132, 153, 546–547
Grand Forks (North Dakota), 102
Grand Hotel (Michigan), 397
Grand-Place (Austria), 408
Grande Colonial (California), 396
Grange, Jacques, 311
Grant, Margo, 311
Grant Park Stadium (Illinois), 404
Grassimuseum, 239
Grassli, Leonard, 289
Gratz, Roberta, 305
Graugaard, Jorgen, 294
Graven, Paul H., 330
Graves, Charles P., 262
Graves, Dean W., 262
Graves, Ginny W., 305
Graves, Michael
    awards and honors, 60, 80, 136, 151, 245, 311
    birthday, 15
    organizational memberships, 262

Gray, Aelred Joseph Gray, 134
Gray, Ann E., 71
Gray, Barbara, 305
Gray, David Lawrence, 262
Gray, Eileen, 17, 315
Gray, Gordon C., 380
Gray, Thomas A., 262
Graz Historic Centre (Austria), 408
Grazado Velleco Architects, 343
Graziani, Lyn E., 262
Greager, Robert E., 262
Great American Main Street Awards, 22, 382
Great Falls of Passaic Society for Universal Manufacturing (New Jersey), 405
Great Northern Railway Buildings (Montana), 405
Great Stuff, 113
Great Wall (China), 409
Grebner, Dennis W., 262
Greeley, Mellen C., 330
Green, Aaron G., 262
Green, Cecil H., 305
Green, Curtis H., 262
Green, Pat, 83
Green, Richard J., 262
Green, Thomas G., 262
Green, William Curtis, 148
Green Institute's Phillips Eco-Enterprise Center (Minnesota), 365
Green Mountain Inn (Vermont), 398
Green Nelson Weaver, Inc., 349
Greenacre Park (New York), 562
Greenbelt (Maryland), 131
Greenberg, Aubrey J., 262
Greenberger, Stephen, 285
The Greenbrier (West Virginia), 399
Greendale (Wisconsin), 133
Greene, Bradford M., 289
Greene, Isabelle Clara, 289
Greene, James A., 262
Greene and Greene, 369
Greenfield, Sanford, 262, 325
Greenfield/Belser Ltd., 141
Greenhills (Ohio), 132
Greenleaf, James L., 324
Greensboro (North Carolina), 337
Greenstreet, Robert, 98, 326
Greenwald, Susan, 262
Greenway Consulting, 476
Greenway Plaza (Texas), 562
Greenwell Goetz Architects Design Studio, 64
Greenwell Goetz Architects Design Studio Offices (Washington, D.C.), 64
Greenwood, Ben F., 327
Greer, John O., 262
Gregan, E. Robert, 289
Gregg, Glenn H., 262
Gregga, Bruce, 311
Gregory, Jules, 100
Greimel, Karl, 548
Grenader, Nonya, 262
Grenald, Raymond, 262
Gresham, James A., 245, 262
Grey, Earl de, 331
Greyfield Inn (Florida), 397

Hass, Dr. F. Otto, 305
Hasselman, Peter M., 264
Hassid, Sami, 264
Hassinger, Herman A., 264
Hasslein, George J., 264
Hastings, Hubert de Cronin, 148
Hastings, Judith, 298, 329
Hastings, L. Jane, 244, 264
Hastings, Robert F., 320
Hastings, Thomas, 148
Hastings & Chivetta Architects, Inc., 129
Hatami, Marvin, 264
Hatch Mott MacDonald, 101
Hatra (Iraq), 411
Hattusha (Turkey), 415
Hauf, Harold D., 264
Haus, Stephen C., 247
Hauschild-Baron, Beverly E., 305
Hauser, III, 114
Hauser, Jon W., 296
Hauser, Stephen G., 296
Hausner, Robert O., 264
Hautau, Richard G., 289
Havana, and Fortifications, Old (Cuba), 409
Havana, Old (Cuba), 409
Havekost, Daniel J., 264
Havens, William H., 289
Haviland, David S., 70
Haviland, Perry A., 264
Hawaii State Capitol, 352
Hawes, Velpeau E., Jr., 264
Hawkins, Dale H., 247
Hawkins, H. Ralph, 264
Hawkins, Jasper Stillwell, 264
Hawkins, William J., III, 264
Hawkins Partners, Inc., 84
Hawks, Richard S., 289
Hawley, William R., 264
Haworth, Dennis, 285
Hawthorne Hotel (Massachusetts), 397
Hawtin, Bruce A., 264
Hay-Adams Hotel (Washington, D.C.), 396
Hayashi, Shoji, 302
Hayden, Richard S., 264
Hayes, J. F., 264
Hayes, John Freeman, 264
Haynes, Irving B., 264
Hays, Betty C., 294
Haystack Mountain School of Crafts (Maine), 164
Hayy Assafarat (Saudi Arabia), 55
Hazelhurst, Franklin Hamilton, 73
HDR Architecture, Inc., 339, 343, 346, 502
HDR Engineering, Inc., 101
Healey, Edward H., 264
Heapy Engineering, 128
Hearn, Michael M., 264
Hearst Castle (California), 316, 369, 388, 389
The Heathman (Oregon), 398
Heatly, Bob E., 98
Hebron Old Town (Palestine), 57
Hebron Rehabilitation Committee, 57
Heck, Robert, 98
Hecksher, A., 305
Hedrich, Jack, 312

Heery, George T., 264
Heery International, Inc., 129, 130, 346
Heilig, Robert Graham, 289
Heimbaugh, John D., Jr., 245
Heimsath, Clovis, 264
Heineman, Paul, 294
Heinfeld, Dan, 264
Heinrich Hertz Tower (Germany), 363
Heinz, Jo, 298
Heinz Architectural Center, 222
Heiskell, Andrew, 305
Hejduk, John, 80, 161, 264, 549, 561
Helfand, Margaret, 264
Helfer, Raymond H., 294
Heller, Jeffrey, 264
Heller o Manus Architects, 64
Hellmann, Maxwell Boone, 264
Hellmuth, George F., 264, 549
Hellmuth, Obata & Kassabaum, Inc. (HOK), 502
        awards, 153, 154, 365
        founding of, 549
        growth rate, 339
        HOK Sports Facilities Group Inc., 166
        size ranking, 346
        works of, 357, 365
Helman, A. C., 264
Helmer, Dorothy G., 285
Helmut Lang Flagship Retail Boutique (New York), 64
Helpern, David P., 264
Helphand, Kenneth I., 289
Hemphill, James C., Jr., 264
Henderson, A. Graham, 331
Henderson, Arn, 264
Henderson, Edith H., 289
Henderson, John D., 264
Henderson, Philip C., 264
Henderson, Richard, 80
Hendricks, James L., 264
Hendrix, Glenn O., 289
Henley Park Hotel (Washington, D.C.), 396
Hennepin Counservation District, 84
Henner, Edna, 298
Hennessey & Ingalls Art and Architecture Books, 510
Henry, Richard, 343
Henry, William R., 264
Hensel Phelps Construction Company, 129
Hensman, Donald C., 264
Herbert, Albert E., 285
Herbert, Charles, 264
Herbert Lewis Kruse Blunck Architects, 62, 66, 78, 86, 502
Herbst LaZar Bell, 111, 113, 114
Heritage Plaza (Texas), 360
Heritage Preservation Services, 404
Herlihy, Elisabeth, 134
Herman, Bernard L., 376, 377
Herman, Robert G., 264
Herman & Gordon Architects, 343
Herman Miller Inc., 69, 95, 559
Herman Miller showroom (New York), 552
Hermann, Elizabeth Dean, 247
Hermes Reed Architects, 339
The Hermitage (Tennessee), 388, 406
Hermitage Hotel (Tennessee), 398
Herrin, William W., 264

Hood, Raymond, 7
Hood, Vance R., 308
Hood, Walter, 247
Hook, Alfred Samuel, 145
Hooker, Van D., 265
Hooper, Vicki L., 172
Hoover, G. N., 265
Hoover, George, 265
Hoover, Ray C., III, 265
Hoover Dam (Nevada and Arizona), 336
Hope, A. J. B. Beresford, 331
Hope, Frank L., Jr., 265
Hopkins, Alden, 247
Hopkins, Gene C., 265
Hopkins, Lady Patricia, 302
Hopkins, Patty, 148
Hopkins, Sir Michael, 148, 302
Hopper, Leonard J., 289, 324
Hopprier, Peter, 245
Horan, Joseph P., 285
Hord, Edward M., 265
Horezu Monastery (Romania), 414
Horii, Howard N., 265
Horn, Gerald, 265
Horns, Miller, 248
Horsbrugh, Patrick, 265, 308
Horsh Arz el-Rab (Lebanon), 412
Horsky, Charles A., 127
Horton, Frank L., 380
Horty, T., 265
Horyu-ji Area Buddhist Monuments (Japan), 412
Hose, Robert H., 296, 328
Hospicio Cabañas (Mexico), 413
Hossios Luckas Monastery (Greece), 411
The Hotel (Florida), 397
Hotel Ambassador (Oklahoma), 398
Hotel Baker (Illinois), 397
Hotel Boulderado (Colorado), 396
Hotel Burnham (Illinois), 399
Hotel Del Coronado (California), 396
Hotel du Pont (Delaware), 396
Hotel El Convento (Puerto Rico), 398
Hotel Hershey (Pennsylvania), 398
Hotel Jerome (Colorado), 396
Hotel La Rose (California), 396
Hotel Maison de Ville (Louisiana), 397
Hotel Metro (Wisconsin), 399
Hotel Monteleone (Louisiana), 397
Hotel Northampton (Massachusetts), 397
Hotel Pattee (Iowa), 397
Hotel Saranac of Paul Smith's College (New York), 398
Hotel Savery (Iowa), 397
Hotel St. Francis (New Mexico), 398
Hotel Viking (Rhode Island), 398
Hotel Winneshiek (Iowa), 397
Houben, Francine, 229
Hough, Reginald D., 265
House Beautiful, 547
House of the Seven Gables (Massachusetts), 388
Houseal Architects, 343
Houseman, William, 305
Houston Community College System/Centrl College (Texas), 536
Housworth, Marvin C., 265

Hovey, David C., 265
Hovgarden (Sweden), 415
Hoving, Thomas P., 305
Howard, Elizabeth B., 285, 323
Howard, J. Murray, 265
Howard, John Tasker, 134
Howard, John W., 355
Howard, Perry, 289
Howard University (Washington, D.C.), 527, 547
Howarth, Thomas, 72, 302
Howe, George, 13
Howell Associates Architects, 343
Hower, Donovan E., 289
Howey, John, 265
Howorth, Thomas Sommerville, 172, 265
Hoyer, Herman R., 294
Hoyt, Charles K., 265
Hozumi, Nobuo, 302
Hricak, Michael M., Jr., 265
HSH Design/Build Inc., 129
Hsiung, Robert Y., 265
Hu, Gilman K. M., 294
Hualalai at Historic Ka'upulehu (Hawaii), 167
Hubacek, Karl, 85
Hubbard, Charles A., 265
Hubbard, Henry Vincent, 134, 324
Hubbard, Theodora Kimball, 134
Hubbard, Thomas D., 294
Hubbard Educational Trust, 84
Hubbell, Kent, 326
Huberman, Jeffrey A., 265
Huberty, Daniel, 265
Hubka, Thomas, 376
H.U.D. Plaza (Washington, D.C.), 83
Hudak, Joseph, 289
Huddleston, Sam L., 289
Hudson River Valley (New York), 378
Hué Monuments (Viet Nam), 416
Huettenrauch, Clarence, 294
Huey, J. Michael, Esq., 305
Huffman, Richard W., 265
Hugh Ferris Memorial Prize, 24, 107
Hugh Stubbins & Associates, 78
Hughes, Nina, 285
Hughes, Robert S. F., 249
Huh, Stephan S., 265
Hull, Robert E., 265
Humayun's Tomb (India), 411
Hummel, Charles F., 265
Hummel, Fred E., 265
Hummel Architects, 349
Humstone, Elizabeth, 245
Hunderman, Harry J., 265
Hundertwasser, Friedensreich, 550
Hundertwasserhaus (Austria), 550
Hungary Office for Study of Industrial and Agricultural Buildings, 85
Hunner, Mark B., 289
Hunt, Gregory, 265
Hunt, Richard Morris, 147, 320, 388
Hunt Design Associates, 153
Hunter, Dorian, 285
Hunter, J. Norman, 327
Hunter College, City University of New York, 532

Hunter Grobe Architects/Planners, 343
Huntsman Architectural Group, 340
Huppert, Frances P., 265
Hursley, Timothy, 70
Hurst, Sam T., 265
Husain, Syed V., 265
Huston, Joseph M., 354
Hutchins, Mary Alice, 265, 294
Hutchins, Robert S., 244
Hutchinson, Max, 331
Hutchinson, Philip A., 305
Hutchirs, Frederick, 298
Huxtable, Ada Louise, 119, 144, 249, 305
Huygens, Remmert W., 265
Hvale, James L., 296
Hwasong Fortress (Republic of Korea), 414
Hyatt Foundation, 142
Hyatt Regency St. Louis at Union Station (Missouri), 397
Hyatt Saint Claire (California), 396
Hyde, Bryden B., 265
Hyderabad Development Authority, 56
Hylton, Thomas, 308
Hynek, Fred J., 265

I

I. M. Pei & Partners, 78, 356, 357, 359
    See also Pei, I. M.
I Sassi di Matera (Italy), 412
IBM building atrium (New York), 565
IBM Corp., 127
Ibrahim Engineering, 130
ICCROM (International Centre for the Study of Preservation
    and Restoration of Cultural Property), 55, 386
I.D., 517, 542
I.D. Annual Design Review, 108–109
Idaho State Capitol, 352
IDEO, 108, 113, 114
Ideya Restaurant (New York), 116
IDI/Innovations & Development Inc., 94
IDS Center (Minnesota), 360
IDSA Education Award, 110
Igualada Cemetery (Spain), 555
Ikorta Church of the Archangel (Georgia), 418
Il Palazzo Hotel (Japan), 369
Iliescu, Sanda D., 245
Illingworth, Dean, 265
Illinois Institute of Art at Schaumburg, 528
Illinois Institute of Technology, 528
Illinois State Capitol, 352
Illuminating Engineers Society of North America, 16
al-Imam, Shafiq, 54
Immenschuh, David, 298
Imperial Palace of Ming and Qing Dynasties (China), 409
In-Cheurl, Kim, 120
Independence Hall (Pennsylvania), 416
Independent Group, 317
India Sanitation Systems, 99
Indiana Automotive Fasters Manufacturing Plant/Office
    Headquarters, 128
Indiana State Capitol, 352
Indiana University, 529
Indianapolis Downtown Signage (Indiana), 153
Indore City Slum Networking (India), 57

Industrial Design Excellence Awards, 111–116
Industrial Designers Society of America (IDSA), 539
    awards given by, 94–96, 110, 111–116
    Fellows, 296
    Honorary Members, 309
    meetings, 16
    organizational profile, 190
    Presidents, 328
    publications, 517
Ingraham, Elizabeth W., 265
Initiative for Architectural Research, 191
Inner Harbor Development of the City of Baltimore, 69
Innovation, 517
Insas Insaat Taahut Ve Ticaret, 66
Inserra, Louis, 98
InSideOutSide house (Texas), 137
Institut du Monde Arabe (France), 56
Institute for Architecture and Urban Studies, 68
Institute of Urban Planning, 520
Inter-Continental Hotel and Conference Centre (Saudi
    Arabia), 53
Inter Plan, Inc., 343
Interbartolo, Michael, 321
Interior Design, 115, 517
Interior Design Competition, 6, 115
Interior Design Hall of Fame, 311–312
Interior Designers Institute (California), 525
Interiors, 116, 517
Interiors & Sources, 517
Interiors Annual Design Awards, 18, 116
International Academy of Design, Tampa (Florida), 527
International Academy of Merchandising and Design,
    Chicago (Illinois), 528
International Centre for the Study of Preservation and
    Restoration of Cultural Property (ICCROM), 55, 386
International Council for Innovation and Research in
    Building and Construction, 8
International Council of Societies of Industrial Design, 20,
    192
International Council on Monuments and Sites, 387
International Design Award, Osaka, 117
International Design Competition, Osaka, 2
International Design Resource Awards, 4
International Federation of Interior Architects/Designers,
    193
International Federation of Landscape Architects, 194
International Interior Design Association, 518
    awards given by, 115, 124, 158
    Fellows, 298–299
    Honorary Members, 310
    meetings, 12
    organizational profile, 195
    Presidents, 329
International Union of Architects, 85, 119, 155, 156, 165, 196
Interstate 90 (Washington), 141
Iowa State Capitol, 352
Iowa State University, 529
Iram, Harry F., 294
Ireys, Alice R., 289
Irkoutsk Historic Center (Russia), 420
Ironbridge Gorge (United Kingdom), 416
Irving, Robert Grant, 73
Iselin, Donald G., 305
Isern, Tom, 400

Kaedi Regional Hospital (Mauritania), 57
Kaelber, Carl F., Jr., 266
Kaeyer, Richard E., 266
Kagan, Gerald, 266
Kahal Shalom Synagogue (Greece), 418
Kahan, Richard A., 160
Kahane, Melanie, 311
Kahler, David T., 266
Kahler Slater, 340, 503
Kahley, Glenn A., 343
Kahn, Charles H., 266
Kahn, Louis I.
    awards, 56, 60, 76, 80, 148, 162, 164
    quotes by, 118, 307
    works of, 370
Kahn, Robert, 246
Kainlauri, Eino O., 266
Kairouan (Tunisia), 56, 415
Kaiser, John M., 343
Kaiser, Lloyd, 305
Kajima Construction Services, Inc., 128
Kalamazoo Mall (Michigan), 132
Kale, Harry, 266
Kalin, Mark, 266
Kallman, McKinnell & Wood, Architects, 66, 78, 503
Kallmann, Gerhard Michael, 249, 266
Kalwaria Zebrzydowska (Poland), 414
Kamekura, Yusaku, 117
Kamin, Blair, xi–xv, 71, 144
Kamphoefner, Henry, 161, 325
Kampung (Indonesia), 54
Kampung Cina River Frontage (Malaysia), 418
Kampung Kali Cho-de (Indonesia), 56
Kampung Kebalen (Indonesia), 55
Kampung Kebalen Community (Indonesia), 55
Kamyanets Podilsky Castle Bridge (Ukraine), 420
Kanakanui Associates, 343
Kandy (Sri Lanka), 415
Kane, Janet E., 285
Kane and Johnson Architects, 341
Kanmacher and Dengi, 352
Kanner, Stephen H., 266
Kansas City Art Institute (Missouri), 531
Kansas City Parks (Missouri), 132
Kansas State Capitol, 353
Kansas State University, 366, 368
Kanvinde, Achyut P., 302
Kapell and Kostow Architects, 340
Kapellbrücke (Switzerland), 347
Kaplan, Gary Y., 266
Kaplan, Richard H., 266
Kaplan, Wendy, 248
Kaplan McLaughlin Diaz, 129, 503
Kappe, Raymond L., 161, 266
Kappe, Shelly, 305
Kapsch, Robert J., 305
Karfik, Vladimir, 302
Karlova 21 Corporate Offices (Czech Republic), 58
Karlsberger Architecture, 343
Karlskrona Naval Port (Sweden), 415
Karner, Gary E., 289
Karr, Joseph P., 289
Karr Poole and Lum, 353
Kasbah of Algiers (Algeria), 408

Kasernenbrücke (Switzerland), 348
Kasimer, Joseph H., 294
Kaskey, Raymond J., 106, 266
Kass, Spence, 246
Kass, Thomas, 98
Kassabaum, George Edward, 244, 320, 549
Kast, Miller I., 330
Katavolos, William, 552
Kate Cannery (Alaska), 404
Katherine Spitz & Associates, 167
Kathmandu Valley (Nepal), 413
Kaufman, Donald, 71
Kaufman, Edgar, Jr., 309
Kaufman, Edward, 138
Kaufman Meeks & Partners, 339
Kaufmann House (California), 62
Ka'upulehu Makai Venture, 167
Kavanagh, Jean Stephans, 289
Kawasaki, Frank II., 289
Kaye, Walter R., 294
KCTV Tower (Missouri), 363
Keahey, Kirby M., 266
Keally, Francis, 354
Kean University (New Jersey), 532
Keane, Gustave R., 266
Keane, Jan, 266
Keating, Richard C., 266
Keay, Sir Lancelot, 331
Keefe, Moses P., 355
Keeter, James E., 289
Keffer/Overton Architects, 349
Kehle, David, 343
Kehm, Walter H., 289
Kelbaugh, Douglas S., 67, 266
Kell, Duane A., 266
Kell, John H., 266
Kellenberger, Mary Gordon Latham, 380
Kellenyi, Bernard, 266
Keller, Genevieve Pace, 308
Keller, J. Timothy, 289
Keller, Larry J., 266
Keller, Reiner, 343
Keller, Suzanne, 305
Kelly, Douglas, 552
Kelly, Frank S., 266
Kelly, Nathan B., 354
Kelly, Philip E., 312
Kelly/Maiello Inc. Architects & Planners, 66, 343
Kelsey, F. L., 266
Kemp, Diane Legge, 266
Kendall, Edward H., 320
Kendall, Henry H., 320
Kendall, Taylor & Company, Inc., 349
Kendall, William D., 266
Kendall College of Art and Design (Michigan), 531
Kender, Dorothy, 305
Kennard, Robert, 170
Kennedy, Hon. Edward M., 308
Kennedy, Raymond, 323
Kennedy, Robert N., 266, 298
Kennedy, Roger G., 305
Kennedy, Tessa, 311
Kenneth F. Brown Asia Pacific Culture & Architecture
    Design Award, 120

Kenneth R. Krause Architects, 343
Kennicott Grove (Illinois), 404
Kent, T. J., Jr., 134
Kent Manor Inn (Maryland), 397
Kent State University (Ohio), 534
Kentucky DOQQ Conversion/Web-Based GIS, 102
Kentucky State Capitol, 353
Kenyon and Associates, 341
Kenzo Tange Associates, 358, 359, 360
    See also Tange, Kenzo
Keokuk (Iowa), 382
Kerbis, Gertrude L., 266
Kerkaune and its Necropolis (Tunisia), 415
Kerns, Thomas L., 266
Kerr, Leslie A., 289
Kesler, Gary B., 290
Kessels DiBoll Kessels & Associates, 349
Kessler, George Edward, 134
Kessler, William H., 266
Ketcham, Herbert A., 266
Ketchum, Morris, Jr., 244, 320
Kettering House (Ohio), 405
Keune, Russell V., 266
Kevin Roche John Dinkeloo & Associates, 78, 164, 504
Key Tower (Ohio), 358
Keyes, A. H., Jr., 267
Keystone Award, 122
Khajuraho Monuments (India), 411
Khami Ruins National Monument (Zimbabwe), 416, 421
Khan, Fazlur, 69
Khan, His Highness the Aga, 69
Khariakov, A., 359
Khasekhemwy at Hierakonpolis (Egypt), 418
KHR AS Arkitekten, 85
Khuda-ki-Basti (Pakistan), 56
Kidder, Bradley P., 100
Kideney Architects/Laping Jaeger Associates, 341
Kieran, Stephen J., 246, 267
Kiev-Pechersk Lavra (Ukraine), 416
Kiks Forest Sculptures (Czech Republic), 418
Kiku Obata & Company, 153
Kikutake, Kiyonori, 302
Kilbourn, Lee F., 267
Kiley, Daniel Urban, 80, 136
Killebrew, James R., 267
Killingsworth, Edward A., 267
Kilwa Kisiwani Ruins (United Republic of Tanzania), 416
Kim, Tai Soo, 267
Kim Ok-gill Memorial Hall (Korea), 120
Kimball, Thomas R., 320
Kimbell Art Museum (Texas), 164, 370
Kimm, Jong S., 267
Kimpton Hotels (California), 391
Kimsey, J. Windom, 172
Kinderdijk-Elshout Mill Network (Netherlands), 413
Kinderfather, David L., 343
al-Kindi Plaza (Saudi Arabia), 55
King, Clarence H., Jr., 294
King, David R. H., 267
King, Dennis M., 267
King, Donald, 267
King, Gordon L., 267
King, J. Bertram, 267
King, Jonathan, 305

King, Leland, 267
King, Michael J., 294
King, Sol, 267
King & King Architects, 349
King and Prince Beach & Gold Resort (Florida), 397
Kingdom Centre (Saudi Arabia), 357
Kings Courtyard Inn (South Carolina), 398
Kingston, M. Ray, 267
Kinnison, Paul, Jr., 267
Kinoshita, Masao, 290
Kinsler, Walt, 83
KIP Technical Unit, 54
Kips Bay Decorator Show House, 312
Kirby, Tim, 551
Kirchoff, Roger C., 330
Kirk, Ballard H. T., 267, 330
Kirk, D. W., Jr., 267
Kirk, Stephen J., 267
Kirke, William F., 354
Kirkegaard, R. Lawrence, 306
Kirkegaard & Associates, 343
Kirkland, J. Michael, 248
Kirkpatrick, John F., 247
Kirksey, John M., 267
Kirsch, Peter A., 308
Kirven, Peyton E., 267
Kitadai, Reiichiro, 302
Kitchell, 130
Kitchen, Robert S., 247, 267
Kito, Azusa, 302
Kitutake, Kiyonori, 85
Kizhi Pogost (Russian Federation), 414
KJWW Engineering Consultants, 128
Klancher, Robert, 321
Klasky Csupo, Inc. (California), 115
Kleihues, Josef P., 302
Klein, Henry, 267
Klein, J. Arvid, 267
Kleinschmidt, Robert, 311
Klemeyer, Frederick J., Jr., 294
Kletting, Richard K. A., 354
Kliment, Robert M., 64, 267
Kliment, Stephen A., 267
Klindtworth, Kenneth F., 267
Kline, Lee B., 267
Kling, Vincent G., 267
Kling-Lindquist Partnership, 346
Klingerman, Mark C., 343
Klinkhamer, Sooz, 298
Klontz & Associates, 341
Knackstedt, Mary V., 285, 298
Knapheide Mfg. Facility (Illinois), 130
Knight, Charles L., 290
Knight, James F., 267
Knight, Roy F., 267
Knight, William H., 267
Knights Ferry Bridge (California), 348
Knoll, Florence, 315–316
Knoll, Hans, 192, 315, 328
Knoll Associates, 315–316
Knoll International, 69
Knoop, Christopher, 343
Knoop, Stuart, 267
Knoops, Johannes M.P., 246

The Lighthouse, 223
Lighthouse Inn (Connecticut), 396
Lijiang (China), 409
Lim, Jimmy C. S., 57
Lima Historic Centre (Peru), 414
Lin, Maya, 75
Lin, T. Y., 69
Lin, Tiffany, 43–46
Lincoln Historic District (New Mexico), 405
Lincoln Home (Illinois), 388
Lincolne Scott & Kohloss, 130
Lind, John H., 268
Linden Row Inn (Virginia), 399
Lindenthal, Robert S., 285
Lindhult, Mark S., 290
Lindsey, David, 268
Lindström, Joe, 54
Lindström, Sune, 54
Link, Theodore C., 353
Link & Hare, 353
Linley, Viscount David, 310
Linn, Karl, 290
Linnard, Lawrence G., 324
Linwood and Howard Avenue Ozonation Facilities
    (Wisconsin), 129
Lippincott, H. Mather, Jr., 268
Lipton, Stuart, 244
Liskamm, William H., 268
Lister, James M., 247
Litomysl Castle (Czech Republic), 409
Littell, Ross, 552
Little, Bertram R., 380
Little, J. Mack, 290
Little, Mrs. Bertram R., 380
Little, Robert A., 268
Little, Susan P., 290
Little White House (Georgia), 388
Littleton, Charles, 298
Litton, R. Burton, Jr., 290
Liu, Dr. Binyi, 308
Livesey, Robert S., 246
Livingston, Stanley C., 268
Livingston, Thomas W., 268
Livingston, Walter R., Jr., 268
Lizon, Peter, 268
Lloyd, Dominique Bonnamour, 553
LMN Architects, 503
LMW Corporate Office, 120
Loch, Emil, 330
Lockard, W. Kirby, 268
Locke Historic District (California), 404
Lockett, Thomas A., 290
Lockwood Andrews & Newman, 101
Lockwood Greene, 349
Loeb Fellowship in Advanced Environmental Studies, 69
Loendorf, Boyd L., 285
Loewy, Raymond, 296
Loftis, James L., 268
Logan, Donn, 269
Lohan, Dirk, 269
Lohan Associates Inc., 64
Lohmann, William T., 294
Lollini, Thomas E., 269
Lomax, Jerrold E., 269

London County Council, 554
London Tower (United Kingdom), 416
Long, Margot, 83
Long, Nimrod W. E., III, 290
Long Island Parkways and Parks (New York), 132
Long Meadow Ranch Winery (California), 64
Longstreth, Richard, 123, 157, 332, 377
Loo, Kington, 302
Looney, J. Carson, 269
Loope, R. Nicholas, 269
Loquasto, Santo, 312
Lorant, Gabor, 269
Lorch, Emil, 325
Lord, Larry, 269
Lord, W. H., 330
Lords Proprietors' Inn, 398
Lorenc/Yoo Design, 153
Lorenzini, David E., 294
Lorenzo, Aldana E., 302
Lorsch Abbey and Altenmünster (Germany), 410
Los Angeles Co. Highways and Freeways (California), 131
Los Angeles Inner City Arts (California), 137
Los Pinchudos Archaeological Site (Peru), 420
Loschky, George H., 269
Lose, David O., 290
Loss, John C., 269
Lotery, Rex, 269
Lotus International, 556
Louge, Edward, 553
Louie, William C., 269
Louisiana State Capitol, 353
Louisiana State University, 366, 529
Louisiana Tech University, 529
Lounsbury, Carl, 376, 377
Louvain la Neuve (Belgium), 155
Love, John A., 308
Love, Michael, 285
Love, William, 269
LoVecchio, Joseph, 285
Lovelace, Eldridge, 290
Lovelace, Richard, 107
Lovell, Tom, 352
Lovett, Wendell H., 269
Lowe, Peter E., 296
Lowe, Rick, 122
Lowery, Jack, 323
Lowrie, Charles N., 324
Loxia, Karel Dudych, 167
Loza, Serapio P., 302
LRS Architects, 342
Lu, Paul C. K., 290
Lu, Weiming, 306
Luanda Sul (Angola), 99
Luang Prabang (Lao People's Democratic Republic), 412
Lubben, Ronald, 298
Lubbock (Texas), 337
Lübeck, Hanseatic City (Germany), 410
Lubetkin, Berthold, 148
Lucas, Frank E., 269
Lucas, Frederick Bruce, 145
Lucas, Thomas J., 269
Lucas Associates, Architects, 342
Lucey, Lenore M., 269
Luckenbach, Carl F., 269

Mangunwijaya, Yousef B., 56
Mangurian, Robert, 246
Manitoga (New York), 151
Manley, Donald W., 294
Manly, William M., 285
Mann, Arthur E., 269
Mann, George R., 352, 353
Mann, Lian Hurst, 71
Mann Music Center (Pennsylvania), 554
Manning, Warren H., 324
Manny, Carter H., Jr., 269, 300
Manser, Michael, 331
Manus, Clark D., 269
Maragall, Pasqual, 117
Maramures Wooden Churches (Romania), 414
Marble House (Rhode Island), 388
March, Virginia S., 269
Marchand Bridge (Canada), 347
marchFIRST, 152
Marco Design Group, 339
Marcus, Stanley, 306
Margerum, Roger W., 269
Margulies & Assoicates, 339
Mariani, Theodore F., 100
Marines, Louis L., 306
Maritime Greenwich (United Kingdom), 416
Mark O. Hatfield U.S. Courthouse (Oregon), 105
Markeluis, Sven Gottfrid, 148, 155
Market House Gallery (Rhode Island), 153
Markham, Fred L., 330
Marks, Judy, 306
Markwood, Phillip T., 269
Marmol and Radziner Architects, 62
Marmon, Harvey V., Jr., 269
Marquardt, Jud R., 269
Marquis, Robert B., 244
Marr, Clinton, Jr., 269
Marrakesh Medina (Morocco), 413
Marriott Corporation, 555
Marsch, Dr. Oscar E., 294
Marschall, Albert R., 306
Marschall, Denton Corker, 145
Marshall, Lane L., 290, 324
Marshall, Mortimer M., Jr., 269, 294
Marshall, Richard C., 269
Marshall, Richard K., 290
Marshall, William "Chick," Jr., 320
Marshall Clarke Architects, Inc., 342
Marshall House (Florida), 397
Marshburn/Bunkley Associates, 344
Martens, Walter F., 330
Martha Schwartz, Inc., 83, 106
Martin, Albert C., 269
Martin, Charles, 376
Martin, Christopher C., 269
Martin, David C., 269
Martin, Edward C., Jr., 290
Martin, Marvin, 294
Martin, Robert E., 269
Martin, Roger B., 247, 290, 324
Martin, Sir Leslie, 148, 554
Martin, W. Mike, 269
Martin, William, 352

Martin Luther King, Jr. Birth Home (Georgia), 388
Martin Luther King, Jr. International Chapel (Georgia), 542
Martin-Vegue, Phyllis, 93
Martinez, Walter B., 269
Martini, Richard, 321
Martino, Steve, 290
Martinsburg (West Virginia), 337
Marvel, Thomas S., 269
Marvin, Robert E., 290
Marx, Maureen, 306
Marx, Roberto Burle, 81
Mary Washington College (Virginia), 537
Maryland State Capitol, 353
Marymount University (Virginia), 537
Maryville University of St. Louis (Missouri), 531
Marzella, Joseph V., 269
Masayoshi, Yendo, 302
Mashantucket Pequot Museum and Research Center
   (Connecticut), 62
Mason, George D., 330
Mason, Ronald L., 269
Mason & Hangar Group, Inc., 349
Masoner, Helen, 285
Mass, Jane, 306
Mass, Marvin, 70
MASS MoCA (Massachusetts), 391
Massachusetts College of Art, 530
Massachusetts Historic Cemetary Preservation Initiative, 83
Massachusetts Institute of Technology. See M.I.T.
Massachusetts Museum of Contemporary Art, 62
Massachusetts State Capitol, 353
Massey, Honorable Vincent, 146
Massie, William E., 137
Mathes, Earl L., 330
Mathes, Edward, 321
Mathes Group, 349
Mathew, Sir Robert, 148
Mathews, Thomas F., 73
Matsumoto, George, 269
Matsuzaki Wright Architects Inc., 365
Matthei, Edward H., 269
Matthew, Sir Robert, 331
Mattox, Robert F., 269
Mattson, Robert M., 290
Matzke, Frank J., 270
Maudlin-Jeronimo, John M., 270, 321
Maufe, Sir Edward, 148
Mauk Design, 113, 152
Maulbronn Monastery Complex (Germany), 411
Maule, Tallie B., 246
Mauran, John L., 320
Maurer, Laurie M., 270
Maurer, Terri, 285, 323
Mausoleum of First Qin Emperor (China), 409
Maxman, Susan A., 270, 320
Maxwell, Murvan M., 270
May, Arthur, 80, 246, 270
May, Edwin, 352
May, Ernst, 563
May, Lewis T., 290
Mayan Site of Copan (Honduras), 411
Maybeck, Bernard Ralph, 60, 326
Maycock, Susan E., 379
Mayekawa, K., 85

Meidan Emam (Iran), 411
Meier, Hans W., 294
Meier, Henry G., 270
Meier, Richard
    awards and honors, 60, 80, 139, 142, 148, 249, 270, 312
    birthday, 21
    exhibitions, 229
    influences on, 561
    works of, 369, 562
    See also Richard Meier & Partners
Meigs, Montgomery C., 226
Meinhardt, Carl R., 270
Meisel, Donald D., 294, 327
Meisner, Gary W., 290
Mejia-Andrion, Rodrigo, 302
Meknes (Morocco), 413
Melander, A. Reinhold, 330
Melhana Plantation (Florida), 397
Melillo, Cheri C., 306
Melillo, Lawrence P., 270
Mellem, Roger C., 270
Mellergaard, Ruth, 298
Mellon, Paul, 306
Mellon Bank Center (Pennsylvania), 359
Melnick, Robert, 290
Melting, R. Alan, 248, 270
Memorial Tunnel (West Virginia), 91
Memphis and its Necropolis (Egypt), 410
Menara Mesiniaga (Malaysia), 57
Mendler, Sandra, 365
Mendocino Hotel & Garden Suites (California), 396
The Menger (Texas), 398
Mentewab-Qwesqwam Palace (Ethiopia), 418
Mercury cruise ship, 65
Meredith College (North Carolina), 533
Merges, George, Jr., 344
Mérida Archaeological Ensemble (Spain), 415
Merriam Center (Illinois), 131
Merricksmith, James, 93
Merrill, John O., 270
Merrill, Scott, 67
Merrill, Vincent N., 290
Merrill, William Dickey, 270
Mertz, Stuart M., 247, 290
Merv Archaeological Site (Turkmenistan), 420
Mesa Verde National Park (Colorado), 69
Messersmith, David R., 270
Mestre, Hector, 302
Metcalf, Robert C., 270
Metcalf, William H., 270
Meteora (Greece), 411
Methow Valley Cabin (Washington), 62, *63*
MetLife (New York), 359
Metropolis, 4, 518
Metropolitan Mechanical Contractors, Inc., 129
Metropolitan State College of Denver (Colorado), 526
Metter, Andrew, 270
Metz Construction Company, 353
Metzger, Robert, 312
Meunier, John, 326
Mexico City Historic Center, 168, 413
Mexico City Housing Reconstruction, 156
Meyer, Betty H., 306
Meyer, C. Richard, 270

Meyer, James H., 270
Meyer, Kurt W., 270
Meyer, Richard C., 270
Meyer, Scherer and Rockcastle Architects, 339, 503
Meyers, Marshall D., 270
Meyers, Richard J., 290
Meyerson, Martin, 52
Mezrano, James, 285
Miami-Dade Art in Public Places, 71
Miami University (Ohio), 534
Miao, Nancy A., 270
Miceli, Luciano, 290
Michael, Linda H., 271
Michael Barber Architecture, 140
Michael Graves & Associates, Inc., 43, 502
Michael Jordon's Steakhouse (New York), 153
Michael Maltzan Architecture, 137
Michael Rice and Co., 53
Michael Tatum Excellence in Education Award, 124
Michaelangelo, 7
Michaelides, Constantine E., 271
Michel, Jack, 376
Michelson, Valerius Leo, 271
Michigan State Capitol, 353
Michigan State University, 531
Michilin Manufacturing, 111
Mickel, E. P., 306
Mid-Embarcadero Open Space/Ferry Terminal (California), 66
Middle East Technical University (Turkey), 57
Middle Tennessee State University, 536
Middlebury Inn (Vermont), 398
Middleton, D. Blake, 246
Mies van der Rohe, Ludwig
    awards, 60, 76, 148, 162, 164
    museum collections and exhibitions, 214, 217, 224, 225, 238, 240
    works of, 370
Mies van der Rohe Award for European Architecture, 125
Mies van der Rohe Award for Latin American Architecture, 126
Mies van der Rohe Foundation, 125
Miklos, Robert, 271
Mikon, Arnold, 271
Milburn, Frank P., 354
Mildenberg, Juanita M., 271
Mileff, Melissa, 322
Miles, Don C., 271
Miles and Horne, 352
Millen, Daniel R., Jr., 271
Miller, Arthur J., 294, 327
Miller, Campbell E., 81, 324
Miller, Courtney E., 321
Miller, David E., 271
Miller, E. Lynn, 290
Miller, Ewing H., 271
Miller, Garen D., 321
Miller, George H., 271
Miller, Harold V., 134
Miller, Henry F., 271
Miller, Hugh C., 271, 308
Miller, J. Irwin, 127, 306
Miller, James W., 271
Miller, John F., 271

Morgantown (West Virginia), 382
Morgridge, Howard H., 271
Mori, Toshiko, 549
Moriarty, Stacy T., 247
Morin, Robert J., 294
Moris, Lamberto G., 271
Moriyama, Raymond, 146, 302
Morla Design, 153
Morley & Assoicates Inc., 344
Morphett, John, 145
Morphosis, 64, 75, 137, 165, 503
Morris, John W., 306
Morris, Paul F., 290
Morris, Philip A., 306, 308
Morris, Robert Schofield, 148
Morris, Seth I., 271
Morris Architects, 503
Morrison, Darrel G., 290
Morrison, Hunter, 160
Morrison, Jacob H., 380
Morrison, Lionel, 271
Morrison, Mark K., 290
Morrison, Mrs. Jacob H., 380
Morrison-Clark Inn (Washington, D.C.), 396
Mors, John, 232
Morse, John, 271
Morse, Joseph, 321
Mortensen, Robert H., 290, 324
Morter, James R., 271
Mortlock, Harold Bryce, 145
Morton, Terry B., 306
Morton, The Interior Design Bookshop, 512
Morton, Woolridge Brown, III, 306
Moscow Bridge (Indiana), 348
Moscow State University (Russia), 359
Moses, Allen D., 271
Moses, Arnold, 353
Moses, Robert, 134
Moshe Safdie Architects Limited, 504
Mosher, Robert, 271
Moskow, Keith, 172
Moskowitz, Samuel Z., 271
Moss, Eric Owen, 75, 271
Moss Engineering, 130
Mostar, Stari-Grad, 55
Mostar Historic Center (Bosnia-Herzegovina), 55, 417
Mostoller, G. Michael, 271
Motley, Kenneth L., 271
Motorola Inc., 94
Mott, John K., 271
Mott, Ralph O., 330
al-Mouhit Cultural Association, 55
Moule, Elizabeth, 92
Moulthrop, Edward A., 271
Moulton, Jennifer T., 271
Mount Athos (Greece), 411
Mount Emei (China), 409
Mount Ida College (Massachusetts), 530
Mount Laurel Township (New Jersey), 132
Mount Lebanon Shaker Village (New York), 405
Mount Mary College (Wisconsin), 538
Mount Nemrut Archaeological Site (Turkey), 420
Mount Taishan (China), 409
Mount Vernon (Virginia), 388

Mount Vernon Ladies Association, 380
Mount Washington Hotel & Resort (New Hampshire), 398
Mountain View Cemetary (Canada), 83
Mouton, Grover E., III, 246
Mox, Dana W., 296
Moyer, Frederic D., 271
Moylan, James, 353
Moynihan, Honorable Daniel Patrick, 127, 160, 380, 560
Mozambique, 413
MSTSD, Inc., 339
Mt. Hood National Forest Landscape (Oregon), 83
MTA 101 Pedestrian Bridge (California), 137
Mtskheta City-Museum Reserve (Georgia), 410
Muchow, William C., 244, 330
Mudano, Frank R., 271
Mughal Sheraton Hotel (India), 54
Muhanna, Rafi, 56
Muhanna, Raif, 56
Muhanna, Ziad, 56
Mularz, Theodore L., 271, 330
Mulcahy, Vincent, 246
Muldawer, Paul, 271
Mullen, John W., III, 271
Müller, Hans Heinrich, 240
Muller, Kenneth, 298
Müller, Lars, 108
Muller, Rosemary F., 271
Muller & Caufield Architects, 344
Muller/Hull Partnership, 105
Müller-Munk, Peter, 296
Mumford, Lewis, 134, 148
Munari, Bruno, 117
Munger, Harold C., 271
Municipal Art Society of New York, 70
Munly, Anne, 246
Muntz, Jean G., 306
Munzer, Frank W., 271
Murase, Robert K., 290
Murcutt, Glenn Marcus, 120, 145
Murdock, Richard C., 247
Murphree, Martha, 306
Murphy, Charles F., 271
Murphy, Frank N., 271
Murphy, Katherine Prentis, 380
Murphy Company, 129
Murphy/Jahn, Inc., 358, 359, 504
Murray, David G., 271
Murray, Lee C., 294
Murray, Maria, 306
Murray, Padraig, 302
Murtagh, William J., 380, 395
Muschamp, Herbert, 144
Muse, Stephen A., 271
Museum d'Orsay, 313
Museum of Contemporary Art, 225
Museum of Finnish Architecture, 224
Museum of Modern Art (New York), 117, 225, 565
Museumsinsel (Germany), 411
Musho, Theodore J., 246
Musiak, Thomas A., 290
Musselman, Betty J., 306
Mutchler, Robert C., 271
Mutlow, John V., 271
Muvico Paradise 24 Theater, 154

Oregon State Capitol, 354
Oregon State Library, 102
Oremen, Edward L., 272
Øresund Fixed Link (Denmark and Sweden), 336
Oriental Pearl Television Tower (China), 362
Oringdulph, Robert E., 272, 330
Orland, Brian, 291
Orland, Jerome I., 294
Orlov, Georgui M., 303
Orlov, Iosif Bronislavovitch, 155
Orongo Ceremonial Site (Chili), 417
Orr, Douglas W., 320
Orr, Gordon D., Jr., 272
Orr/Houk & Associates Architects, Inc., 344
Orto Botanico (Italy), 412
O'Shea, Peter, 247
Osler, David William, 272
Oslund, Thomas R., 247
Osman, Mary E., 306
Osmundson, Theodore O., 81, 291, 324
Ossipoff, Vladimir, 244
Ostankino Tower (Russia), 362
Östberg, Ragnar, 60, 148, 370
Otesaga Hotel (New York), 398
Otis Elevator Company, 107
Otsu Historic Monuments (Japan), 412
Otsuji, Dennis Y., 291, 324
Ottagono, 520
Otto, Atelier Frei, 53, 57, 85, 117, 171
Ouadane Ancient Ksour (Mauritania), 413
Oualata Ancient Ksour (Mauritania), 413
Oud, J. J. P., 5, 229
Oudens, G. F., 272
Ouro Preto (Bolovia), 409
"Outdoor Circle," 134
Outrigger Waikoloa Beach Resort (Hawaii), 130
Ove Arup & Partners, 70, 106
Overall, Sir John Wallace, 145
Overby, Osmund, 300, 332
Overland Partners, Inc., 365
Overseas Union Bank Centre (Singapore), 358, 371
Oviedo Monuments (Spain), 415
Ovresat, Raymond C., 272
Owens, Hubert B., 81, 324
Owens, Kenneth, Jr., 272
Owings, Nathaniel A., 60, 80
Ownby, J. Steve, 291
Oxford Automotriz de Mexico Stamping/Assembling
    Facility, 130
Oxford Hotel (Colorado), 396

P

P/A Awards, 24, 137
Paanajärvi Village (Russia), 420
Paavilainen, Käpy, 316
Paderewski, C. J. "Pat," III, 273, 330
Padjen, Elizabeth Seward, 273
Paepcke, Elizabeth, 90
Paestum Archaeological Site (Italy), 412
Page & Steele, 359
Page Southerland Page, 350, 504
Pahl, Pahl, Pahl Architects, 128
Pahlman, William, 93

Painted Churches in Troodos Region (Cyprus), 409
Painter, Michael, 291
Pairo, Edwin T., 294, 327, 557
Palace of Culture and Science (Poland), 360
Palace of Diocletian (Croatia), 409
Palace Parks (Turkey), 56
Palacio Güell (Spain), 415
Palacious, Jose Luis, 172
Palau de la Música Catalana (Spain), 415
Palenque City and National Park (Mexico), 413
Palermo, Gregory, 273
Paley, Albert, 70
Paley Park (New York), 565
Palladio, Andrea, 23
Pallasmaa, Juhani, 119, 303
Pallay, Ross D., 308
Palm Computing, 94
Palmaria (Italy), 412
Palmer, James F., 83
Palmer, Meade, 81, 291
Palmyra Site (Syrian Arab Republic), 415
Palo Alto (California), 338
Palo Alto Products International, 94
Palpung Monastery (China), 417
Palu, Jay M., 322
Pan, Joshua J., 273
Pan, Solomon, 273
Panafrican Institute for Development (Burkina Faso), 56
Panama Canal, 336
Panamá Historic District, 414
Panciera, Ronald J., 306
Pancoast, Lester C., 273
Pangrazio, John R., 273
Pannonhalma Millenary Benedictine Monastery and Natural
    Environment (Hungary), 411
Pansky, Stanley H., 246
Panton, Verner, 239
Panushka, Donald H., 273
Paoletti, Dennis A., 273
Paoletti Associates Inc., 344
Papachristou, Tician, 273
Papandrew, Thomas, 291, 324
Paphos (Cyprus), 409
Papp, Laszlo, 273
Pappageorge, George C., 273
Pappas, Nicholas A., 273
Pappas, Ted P., 273, 320
Paquimé Archaeological Zone (Mexico), 413
Paradis, Alan D. S., 321
Paradise Inn (Washington), 399
Paradise Valley Mall Children's Playcourt (Arizona), 153
Parc de la Solidaritat (Spain), 58
Parent, Claude, 119
Parikh, Himanshu, 57
Paris, Banks of Seine (France), 410
Paris Las Vegas Casino Resort (Nevada), 152
Parise, Charles J., 273
Parish, Mrs. Henry, II, 312
Park, Ki Suh, 170, 273
Park, Nell H., 247
Park, Sharon C., 273
Park, Stuart James, 353
Park Central Hotel (Florida), 397
Park DuValle (Kentucky), 67

Perkins, David L., 273
Perkins, George Holmes, 68, 161, 244, 273
Perkins, L. Bradford, 273
Perkins, Nancy, 296
Perkins, Wheeler & Will, 162
Perkins, William, 100, 330
Perkins & Will, 78, 504
Perkins Eastman Architects, 504
Perloff, Harvey S., 52, 134
Perrault, Dominique, 125
Perrault, Edward J., 93, 285
Perrault Bridge (Canada), 347
Perrell, Richard C., 295
Perret, Auguste, 60, 148
Perriand, Charlotte, 21, 316, 558
Perron, Robert, 291
Perry, Charles O., 246
Perry, Clarence Arthur, 134
Perry, Isaac G., 354
Perry, Robert C., Jr., 291
Perry Dean Rogers & Partners Architects, 504
Persepolis (Iran), 411
Persky, Seymour H., 300
Perspective, 518
Perspectives in Vernacular Architecture, 407
Perttula, Norman K., 273
Pertz, Stuart K., 273
Petäjävesi Old Church (Finland), 410
Petaluma (California), 131
Peter Cavanough and Son, 353
Peter Kewittand Sons, 353
Peter Miller Architecture and Design Books, 513
Peters, Charles E., 68
Peters, Owen H., 291, 324
Peters, Richard C., 98, 325
Peters, Robert W., 273
Peterson, BJ, 285, 323
Peterson, Carolyn S., 273
Peterson, Charles Emil, 160, 273, 300, 332, 380
Peterson, Fred W., 377
Peterson, Leonard A., 273
Peterson, R. Max, 308
Peterson, Warren A., 246
Peting, Donald, 248
Petkus, Janie, 298
Petr Franta Architects & Associates, 58
Petra (Jordan), 412, 418, 419
Petrazio, Edward G., 273
Petro Canada Tower, 372
Petronas Towers (Malaysia), 356, 371
Pettengill, G. E., 306
Pettersen, Eleanore, 273, 341
Petterson, Robert L., 295
Pettitt, Jay S., Jr., 273
Pevsner, Sir Nikolaus, 69, 148
Pewabic Pottery (Michigan), 405
Pfaller, Mark A., 273
Pfeiffer, Norman, 80, 273, 312
Pfister, Charles, 312
Pfister Hotel (Wisconsin), 399
Pflueger, John M., 344
Pfluger, J. D., 273
Phelps, Barton, 273
Phelps, William, 308

Phibbs, H. Albert, 285, 323
Phifer, Thomas M., 246
Philadelphia (Pennsylvania), 338
Philadelphia Historic Landmarks (Pennsylvania), 132
Philadelphia University (Pennsylvania), 535
Philadelphia Zoological Society, 70
Philae Nubian Monuments (Egypt), 410
Philip Johnson Award, 18, 138
Philip Johnson's Residence (Connecticut), 162
Philippi Bridge (West Virginia), 348
Philippines Baroque Churches, 414
Philips Design, 111, 113
Philips Wuori Long Inc., 83
Phillips, Frederick F., 273
Phillips, Karen A., 291
Phillips, O. Douglas, 344
Phillips, W. Irving, Jr., 273
Phillips Exeter Academy Library (New Hampshire), 164
Phoenix City Landscape Architects, 83
Phoenix Federal Building and U.S. Courthouse (Arizona), 106
Phoenix Zoo (Arizona), 82
Piano, Renzo, 19, 80, 139, 142, 148, 250
Piano & Rogers, 85
Piazza del Duomo (Italy), 412
Pickens, Buford L., 325, 332
Pienza Historic Centre (Italy), 412
Pierce, J. Almont, 273
Pierce, John Allen, 273
Pierce, Mark L., 344
Pierce, Walter S., 273
Pierson, Robert W., 291
Pierson, William H., Jr., 300
Pietila, Reima, 165
Pigozzi, Raymond A., 273
Pike, Janet D., 306
Pikes Peak (Colorado), 83
Pilgrim, Dianne H., 285, 312
Pilgrimage Church (Germany), 410
Pilgrimage Church of St. John of Nepomuk (Czech Republic), 409
Pillorge, George J., 273
Pillsbury, Philip W., Jr., 306
Pinckney, J. Edward, 291
Pinero, E. Pinez, 85
Ping Yao (China), 409
Pinto, John, 74
Piper, Robert J., 273
Piquenard, Alfred H., 352
Pirkl, James J., 297
Pirscher, Carl W., 273
Pissarski, Methodi A., 303
Pitman, John W., 273
Pitman, Karin M., 172
Pittsburgh History & Landmarks Foundation, 68
Pitz, Marjorie E., 291
Piven, Peter A., 273
Place Bonaventure (Montreal), 319
Place d'Alliance (France), 410
Place de la Carriére (France), 410
Place Stanislas (France), 410
Places, 518
Placzek, Adolph Kurt, 69, 300, 332, 559
Plan Architects Co., 357

Sacramento (California), 338
Sadler, Harold G., 276
Saenz de Oiza, Francisco Javier, 561
Safdie, Moshe, 15, 146, 250, 276
SAFECO Field (Washington), 101, *103*
Safranbolu (Turkey), 415
The Sagamore (New York), 398
Sagenkahn, Chester F., 285
Sahi-i-Bahlol City Remains (Pakistan), 413
Saïd Naum Mosque (Indonesia), 55
Saint, Kelsey Y., 295, 327
Saint Anne Church (India), 418
St. Augustine's Abbey (United Kingdom), 416
Saint Barbara Church (Czech Republic), 409
St. Bede's Priory (Wisconsin), 543
Saint Brendan's Cathedral (Ireland), 418
St. Charles (Illinois), 382
St. Charles County Family Arena (Missouri), 129
Saint Chrischona Telecommunications Tower (Switzerland), 364
Saint Christopher & Nevis (Romania), 414
St. Clair, Rita, 93, 286, 312, 323
Saint-Emilion Jurisdiction (France), 410
St. Florian, Friedrich, 246
Saint Francis Church and Monastery (United Kingdom), 420
St. Gall Convent (Switzerland), 415
St. Gall Plan, 69
Saint-Hyacinthe School of Trades and Technologies (Canada), 86, *87*
St. James Hotel (Alabama), 396
St. James Hotel (Minnesota), 397
St. Jean Vianney Catholic Church Sanctuary (Louisiana), 66
St. John Benedictine Convent (Switzerland), 415
St. Kilda (United Kingdom), 416
St. Louis Downtown (Missouri), 83
Saint Margaret's Church (United Kingdom), 416
St. Martin's Church (United Kingdom), 416
St. Mary's Cathedral (Germany), 410
St. Michael's Church (Germany), 410
St. Nicholas River Bridge (Canada), 347
Saint Paul (Minnesota), 338
Saint Paul Hotel (Minnesota), 397
St. Petersburg Historic Centre and Monuments (Russian Federation), 414
Saint Pierre Cathedral (France), 418
Saint-Remi Abbey, Former (France), 410
Saint-Savin sur Gartempe Church (France), 410
Saint-Sophia Cathedral and Related Monastic Buildings (Ukraine), 416
Saito, Paul M., 291
Sakata, Carol S., 276
Saksena, Raj, 276
Saladino, John F., 312
Salamanca (Spain), 415
Salem State College (Massachusetts), 153
Salinas (California), 338
Salinger Residence (Malaysia), 57
Salk Institute (California), 164, 370
Salmon, F. Cuthbert, 276
Salón Bolivar (Panama), 414
Salt River (Arizona), 131
Saltworks of Arc-et-Senans (France), 410
Saltz Michelson Architects, 344
Saltzman, Renny B., 561–562

Saltzman home (New York), 562
Salvadori, Mario G., 161, 306
Salvadori Educational Center of the Build Environment, 70
Salvin, Anthony, 147
Salzburh Historic Centre (Austria), 408
Salzman, Stanley, 97
Samford University (Alabama), 524
Samhammer, Clair A., 297
Samos Pythagoreion and Heraion (Greece), 411
Sample, John, 310
Sample, Nathaniel W., 276
Sams, Louis H., 295, 327
Samsung Electronics, 113
Samton, Peter, 276
Samuels, Danny M., 248, 276
Samuels, Thomas, 276
San Antonio Conservation Society, 71, 380
San Antonio River Walk (Texas), 69
San Carlos (Arizona), 396
San Critóbal de la Laguna (Spain), 415
San Diego Mesa College (California), 525
San Estevan Del Ray Mission Church (New Mexico), 405
San Francisco (California), 338
San Francisco Bay Historic Landmarks (California), 131
San Francisco Church (Venezuela), 421
San Francisco City Hall Improvement Project (California), 64
San Francisco Civic Center Complex (California), 129
San Francisco Historic Landmarks (California), 131
San Francisco Museum of Modern Art (California), 234–235
San Francisco State University (California), 525
San Gerónimo Fort (Panama), 420
San Gimignano Historic Centre (Italy), 412
San Ignacio Mini (Argentina), 408
San Isidro de los Destiladeros (Cuba), 418
San Jose (California), 338
San Jose State University (California), 525
San Juan de Ulúa Fort (Mexico), 420
San Juan Historic Site (Puerto Rico), 416
San Leucio Complex (Italy), 412
San Lorenzo Castle (Panama), 420
San Luis Obispo (California), 382
San Millián Yuso Monastery (Spain), 415
San Paolo Fuori le Mura (Italy), 412
San Pedro de la Roca Castle (Cuba), 409
Sana'a (Yemen), 416
Sanabria, Thomas J., 303
Sanchez, Gil A., 276
Sanchi Buddhist Monuments (India), 411
Sand, Margaret, 291
Sanders, James J., 276
Sanders, Linda W., 276, 326
Sanders, Walter, 325
Sanders, William D., 291
Sands Hotel (Nevada), 554
Sandy, Donald, Jr., 276
Sandy & Babcock International, 340
Sanford University (California), 393
Sanoff, Henry, 98
Sant Pau Hospital (Spain), 415
Santa Ana (Argentina), 408
Santa Ana de los Rios de Cuenca Historic Center (Ecuador), 410
Santa Anita Racetrack (California), 378

Schrickel, Ollie, 291
Schroeder, Douglas F., 276
Schroeder, Kenneth A., 276
Schroeder, Rosemary, 307
Schroter, Richard C., 295
Schruben, John H., 276
Schubert, Carl, 321
Schuett, George A. D., 276
Schulitz, Helmut C., 303
Schumacher, Thomas L., 98, 246
Schuman, Tony, 326
Schur, Susan E., 307
Schurz, E. Williard, 285
Schütte-Lihotzky, Margarete, 563
Schwäbisch-Hall's Stadtwerke Footbridge, 348
Schwarting, J. Michael, 246
Schwartz, Frederic D., 246
Schwartz, Irving D., 285, 323
Schwartz, Joel, 123
Schwartz, Kenneth E., 276
Schwartz, Robert, 276
Schwartzman, Alan, 276
Schwartzman, Daniel, 100
Schwartzman, Paul D., 248
Schwengel, Frederick D., 307
Schwengels, Suzanne K., 307
Schwietz, Lawrence E., 295
Schwing, Charles E., 276, 320
Sclater, Alan D., 276
Scogin, Mack, 75
Scogin Elam and Bray Architects, 505
Scotia Plaza (Canada), 358
Scott, David M., 276
Scott, Douglas, 117
Scott, Mel, 134
Scott, Michael, 148, 303
Scott, Sir George G. Gilbert, 147
Scott, Sir Gilbert G., 331
Scott, Sir Giles Gilbert, 148, 331
Scott, William W., 276
Scott Brown, Denise
    awards and honors, 97, 136, 161
    biographical profile, 317
    birthday, 21
    influences on, 318
    organizational memberships, 249
Scottish Parliament, 555
Scouten, Rex, 307
Scully, Daniel V., 246
Scully, Sunny Jung, 291
Scully, Vincent, J., Jr., 68, 72, 161, 168, 250
Scutt, Der, 276
Sea Ranch Condominium I (California), 164
Seablom, Seth H., 247
Seagram Building (New York), 164, 370
Sealy, Jim W., 276
Searl, Kenneth L., 295
Searl, Linda, 276
Sears, Bradford G., 291
Sears, Roebuck and Company (Illinois), 407
Sears, Roebuck and Company 1905-6 Complex (Illinois), 404
Sears, Stephen, 247
Sears Tower (Illinois), 177, 356, 371

Sease, Catherine, 248
Seaside (Florida), 70, 317
Seattle First Avenue Bridge (Washington), 102
Seaview Marriott Resort (New Jersey), 398
Seavitt, Catherine, 246
Sebastian, B., 307
Secretary of the Interior, 383, 402
SEDG Design Awards, 152–154
Sedgewick, Thomas J., 277, 330
Segal, Paul, 277
Segoe, Ladislas, 134
Segovia Old Town and Aqueduct (Spain), 415
Segrue, Lawrence P., 277
Seiberling, Hon. John F., 69, 308
Seibert, E. J., 277
Seidel, Alexander, 277
Seidler, Harry, 145, 148, 303
Seiferth, Solis, 330
Seiji Ozawa Hall at Tanglewood (Massachusetts), 64
Sejima, Kazuyo, 228
Sekler, Eduard Franz, 70, 119
Self, Larry D., 277
Seligmann, Werner, 161, 246
Seligson, Theodore, 277
Sellery, Bruce M., 277
Sellman, C. G., 353
Selzer, Dale E., 277
Semans, James H., 307
Seminole Community College (Florida), 527
Semmering Railway (Austria), 408
Semper, Gottfried, 23
Senegal Agricultural Training Center, 53
Senhauser, John C., 277
Senseman, Ronald S., 277
Seoul Tower (South Korea), 364
Seracuse, Jerome M., 277
Serber, Diane, 277
Serrill, Julian B., 307
Sert, Jackson and Associates, 78
Sert, Joseph Luis, 60
Seton Village (New Mexico), 405
Settecase, Phillip K., 277
Sevelen/Vaduz Bridge (Canada), 347
1747 Normandie Partners, 167
7th & Collins Public Parking/Retail Facility (Florida), 167
Seventh Regiment Armory (New York), 420
Severance, H. Craig, 358
Seville Cathedral (Spain), 415
Sewell Jones, Elaine K., 307
Seydler-Hepworth, Betty Lee, 277
Seymour, Jonathan G., 291
Sgoutas, Vassilis C., 303
Shackleton, Polly E., 307
Shadbolt, Doug, 97, 146
Shaffer, Marshall, 100
Shah Rukn-i-'Alam Tomb (Pakistan), 54
Shaivitz, Allan, 299
Shambob Brick Producers Co-operative (Sudan), 99
Shanghai Urban Planning and Design Research Institute, 67
Shanghai Waterfront (China), 67
Shanis, Carole Price, 298
Shannon & Wilson, 129
Shanti Weekend House (India), 120

Sir Robert Matthew Prize, 156
Siren, Heikki, 303
Siren, Kaija, 303
Sirney Architects, 365
Siza Vieira, Alvaro, 80, 125, 139, 142, 168, 250
Sizemore, Michael M., 277
Skaggs, Ronald L., 277, 320
Skay, R. Kenneth, 344
Skellig Michael (Ireland), 411
Skidmore, Louis, 60
Skidmore, Owings & Merrill (SOM), 505
    awards and honors, 54, 66, 67, 78, 105, 129, 137, 162,
        164, 165
    size ranking, 346
    works of, 356, 357, 359, 360, 369
Skilling, John B., 307
Skilling Ward Magnusson Barkshire Inc., 101, 102
Sklarek, Norma M., 277
Skog, Gary, 277
Skoglund, William A., 295
Skogskyrkogarden (Sweden), 415
Sky, Alison, 248
Sky City, Ortigas (Philippines), 371
Sky Tower (New Zealand), 363
Skyscraper Museum, 237
Skytop Lodge (Pennsylvania), 398
Slaatto, Nils, 303
Slama, Murray A., 277
Slapeta, Vladimir, 303
Slater, John B., 292
Slattery Skanska, 130
Slayton, W. L, 307
Sloan, Samuel, 7, 353
SLR Architects, 344
Slutsky, Rael D., 107
Slutsky, Robert, 549
Smallwood, Reynolds, Stewart, Stewart Associates, Inc., 505
Smart, Clifton M., Jr., 277
Smart Design, 94, 111, 113, 114
Smiley, Saul C., 277
Smirke, Sir Robert, 147
Smirke, Sydney, 147
Smith, Adrian D., 277
Smith, Andrew Travis, 172
Smith, Arthur, 277
Smith, Bill D., 277
Smith, Bruce H., 277
Smith, Charles E., 127
Smith, Christopher J., 277
Smith, Coin Stansfield, 148
Smith, Cole, 277
Smith, Colin L. M., 277
Smith, Darrell L., 277, 330
Smith, Edna A., 285
Smith, Edward F., 277, 295
Smith, Eleanor McNamara, 307
Smith, Elizabeth A. T., 138
Smith, Ethel, 312
Smith, Eugene W., 222
Smith, F. Eugene, 297
Smith, Fleming W., Jr., 277
Smith, Frank Folsom, 277
Smith, Gordon H., 70
Smith, Hamilton P., 277

Smith, Harwood K., 277
Smith, Herrick H., 292
Smith, Hinchman and Grylls, 164
Smith, Inette L., 303
Smith, Ivan H., 277
Smith, James Merrick, 286, 303
Smith, John R., 277
Smith, Joseph N., III, 277
Smith, Kenneth, 277
Smith, Macon S., 277
Smith, Robert G., 297, 328
Smith, Roscoe D., 295
Smith, Stephen B., 278
Smith, T. Clayton, 278
Smith, Thomas G., 246
Smith, Tyler, 278
Smith, Whitney R., 278
Smith - Miller + Hawkinson, 505
Smith & Thompson Architects, 344
Smith Hinchman & Grylls Associates, Inc., 140
Smith House (Connecticut), 162, 164
SmithGroup Incorporated, 128, 129, 130, 340, 346, 349, 505
Smithson, Alison, 317-318
Smithson, Peter, 19, 317-318
Smithson, Robert, 69
Smithsonian Associates, 69
Smithsonian Institution. See Cooper-Hewitt Museum
Smotrich, David I., 278
SMRT Architecture Engineering Planning, 349
Smull, Neil H., 278
Sneary, Tom F., 295
Snelson, Kenneth, 69
Snibbe, Richard, 278
Snider, Sheila, 278
Snow, Julie V., 278
Snozzi, Luigi, 168
Soane, Sir John, 217, 236
Sobel, Walter H., 278
Sober, Sandra H., 286
Society for American City and Regional Planning History,
    22, 123
Society for Architectural Historians, 138, 379
Society for Environmental Graphic Design, 2, 10, 152, 205
Society for Industrial Archeology, 10
Society for the Preservation of New England Antiquities, 70
Society of Architectural Historians, 539
    awards given by, 72-74, 157
    Fellows, 300
    meetings, 8, 18
    organizational profile, 204
    Presidents, 332
    publications, 518
Soekarno-Hatta Airport (Indonesia), 57
Soenke, Edward L., 295
Soep, Bernard, 299
Soesbe, Jerrold, 292
Sokkuram Buddhist Grotto (Republic of Korea), 414
Solbert Perkins Design Collaborative, 153
Soleri, Paolo, 13
Solomon, Barbara Stauffacher, 246
Solomon, Daniel, 278
Solomon, Richard B., 295, 327
Solomon, Richard J., 278
Solomon, Stuart B., 278

Stegall, Joel E., Jr., 295
Steger, Charles W., Jr., 278
Steidl, Douglas, 278
Stein, Carl, 278
Stein, Clarence S., 60, 135, 162
Stein, J. Stewart, 295, 327
Stein White Architects, 365
Steinberg, Goodwin B., 278
Steinberg, Paul L., 248
Steinberg, Robert T., 278
Steinberg, Saul, 68
Steinborn, S., 307
Steinbrueck, Peter, 172
Steiner, Prof. Frederick, 248
Steinglass, Ralph, 278
Steinhardt, Henry, 278
Steinhauser, Karl L., 286
Steinhilber, Budd, 297
Steinman, Douglas E., Jr., 278
Steinmann, Howard R., 295, 327
Steinmetz, Deborah, 286
Stenhouse, James A., 278
Stephen F. Austin State University (Texas), 536
Stephens, Donald J., 278
Stephens Aylward & Associates/Clas Riggs Owens & Ramos, 344
Stephenson, C. Eugene, 286
Stephenson, Sir Arthur, 145
Stepner, Michael J., 278
Stern, David, 115
Stern, Robert A. M., 11, 106, 278, 312
Stern, William F., 278
Sternfeld, Joel, 248
Steven Holl Architects, 137, 503
Stevenor-Dale, Janice, 299
Stevens, Brooks, 297
Stevens, Philip H., 297
Stevens, Preston, Jr., 278
Stevens, Saundra, 307
Stevens, William H., 344
Stevenson, James M., 278
Stevenson, Markley, 324
Steward, Prof. W. Cecil, 99, 161, 278, 320
Stewart, J. George, 355
Stewart, William W., 278
Stewart and Company, 352
Sticks Inc. (Iowa), 86
Stieber, Nancy, 157
Stifter, Charles, 246
Stillman, Damie, 332
Stirling, James, 80, 139, 142, 148, 561
Stitt, P. D., 307
Stockholm City Hall (Sweden), 370
Stockholm Town Planning Service, 155
Stockwell, Sherwood, 278
Stockyards Hotel (Texas), 398
Stoddart, John Goddfrey, 292
Stokes, Leonard, 148, 331
Stokoe, James S., 246
Stoller, Claude, 278
Stone, Edward D., Jr., 81, 292
Stone, Edward Durell, 352, 357
Stone, Edward H., II, 292, 324
Stone, Michelle, 248

Stone Building System (Syria), 56
Stonehenge (United Kingdom), 416
Stonehill, John J., 246
Stoneleigh Hotel (Texas), 398
Story Design Ltd., 128
Stovall, Allen D., 292
Stowe, Neal P., 278
Stowell, H. T., 278
Straka, Ronald A., 100, 278
Strand Book Store, 512
Stransky, Michael J., 278
Strasbourg-Grande Isle (France), 410
Strategiz I.D., 111, 114
Strater, Blanche F., 286
Strater Hotel (Colorado), 396
Stratosphere Tower (Nevada), 362
Straub, Calvin C., 97
Straub, Frank, 278
Strauss, Carl A., 278
Street, George Edmund, 147, 331
Street, John R., Jr., 278
Strickland, William, 354
Stroback, Jacey, 113
Strock, Arthur V., 278
Strong, Ann, 52
Strong, Terry J., 295, 327
Structural Preservations Systems, Inc., 130
Stuart Collection, 70
Stubbins, Hugh Asher, Jr., 278
Stubbins Associates, Inc., 357, 358, 360, 505
Stubbs, Sidney W., Jr., 279
Stubbs Books & Prints, 512
Stuck Associates Architects, 341
Studenica Monastery (Yugoslavia), 416
Studio Arts & Letters, 152
Studio E. Architects, 62
Studio Works, 137
Studios Architecture, 340, 505
Studley Royal Park and Fountains Abbey Ruins (United Kingdom), 416
Stuler, August, 147
Stull, Donald L., 279
Stull & Lee, 67
Stumpf, Karl W., 172
Stumpf, Weber + Associates, 94
Sturbridge Village (Massachusetts), 376
Sturgis, R. Clipston, 320
Sturgis, Robert S., 279
STV Construction Services, 130
Su, Gin, 303
Su Nuraxi di Barumini (Italy), 412
Subotica Synagogue (Yugoslavia), 421
Suchecka, Rysia, 312
Suchitoto City (El Salvador), 418
Sucre (Bolivia), 409
Sueberkrop, Erik, 279
Suer, Marvin D., 279
Suffolk County Community College (New York), 532
Sugden, John W., 279
Sugimoto, Hiroshi, 234
Suisman, Douglas R., 279
Sukhothai and Associated Historic Towns (Thailand), 415
Sukur Cultural Landscape (Nigeria), 413
Sullam, Edward, 279

Tobey + Davis, 105
Tobin, Calvin J., 279
Tobola, Logic, II, 279
Tod Williams, Billie Tsien and Associates, 505
Todd, Anderson, 279
Todd, David F. M., 279, 295
Todd, Thomas A., 279
Todisco, Philip J., 295, 327
Toft, Carolyn H., 307
Toft, Jan, 310
Toker, Franklin, 73, 332
Tokyo (Japan), 386
Tokyo City Hall (Japan), 370
Tokyo Metropolitan Government Building (Japan), 359, 371
Tokyo Tower (Japan), 362
Toledano, Roulhac, 73
Toledo (Spain), 415
Tolleson 91st Avenue WWTP Pipeline (Arizona), 104
Tolson Youth Activities Ctr. (North Carolina), 130
Tomar Convent of Christ (Portugal), 414
Tomassi, John, 279
Tomb, Bruce, 108
Tombazis, Alexandros N., 303
Tomblinson, James E., 279
Tompkins, David D., 297, 328
Tompkins, Donald H., 292
Tomsick, Frank, 279
Tomson, Bernard, 307
Tonev, Luben N., 303
Tongue River (Montana), 102
Toombs, Henry, 388
TOPAZ Medallion, 20, 161
Torno Nester Davison, 341
Toronto (Canada), 338
Torre, L. Azeo, 247, 292
Torre, Susana, 23, 318
Torre Annuziata Archaeological Area (Italy), 412
Torre de Collserola (Spain), 363
Torre de Espana (Spain), 364
Torres Blancas apartments (Spain), 561
Torti Gallas & Partners·CHK Inc., 66
Torus House and Studio for Eric Wolf (New York), 137
Tosh, Danny J., 345
Touart, Paul Baker, 379
Tough, Coulson, 279
Tour and Taxis (Belgium), 417
Tour Maine Montparnasse (France), 372
Tournon-Branly, Marion, 303
Tourtellotte, John E., 352
Tower Grove Park (Missouri), 405
Tower of London (United Kingdom), 416
Towers, Shavaun, 292
Town and Davis, 354
Toyomura, Dennis T., 280
Trachtenberg, Marvin, 73, 74
Tracy and Swartwout, 353
Traendly, W. F., 307
Trahan Architects, 66
Train, Jack D., 100, 280
Train, R. E., 307
Trampoline and Willow Garden (France), 82
Trancik, Roger T., 292

Transamerica Pyramid (California), 371
Travisano, Fred, 246
TRAX Light Rail (Utah), 102
Trcanor, Betty, 299
Treasury Building (Singapore), 360
Treberspurg, Martin, 156
Tree Studios and Medinah Temple (Illinois), 421
Treffinger, Karl E., Sr., 280
Tregre, Louis, 93
Treib, Edward Marc, 248
Treib, Marc, 138
Treister, Kenneth, 280
Trenton (New Jersey), 338
Triaco, 55
Triarch, 345
Tribble, Michael, 280
Tribble & Stephens, 166
Tribune Tower international design competition, 215
Triebwasser Helenske & Associates, 345
Trier Roman Monuments, Cathedral and Liebfrauen-Church
   (Germany), 410
Trigiani, David M., 280
Trinidad (Cuba), 409
Trinity Sergius Lavra (Russian Federation), 414
Trogdon, William H., 280
Trogir (Croatia), 409
Troller, Howard E., 292
Troodos Painted Churches (Cyprus), 409
Trotter, Morris E., 247
Trowbridge, Peter J., 292
Trowbridge and Livingston, 354
Troy Archaeological Site (Turkey), 415
Troyan, Marcia, 299
Troyer, Leroy, 280
Trudeau residence and offices (Canada), 552
Trudnak, Stephen J., 292
Truelove, James, 83
Trump Building (New York), 358
Tryba, Anne, 154
Tseckares, Charles N., 280
Tsien, Billie, 80, 512
Tsoi, Edward T. M., 280
Tsoi/Kobus & Associates, 339, 505
TSP Two, Inc., 345
Tsukasa, Tadashi, 117
Tuck, Seab A., III, 280
Tucker, Jack R., Jr., 280
Tucker, James F., 345
Tucker, Thomas B., 280
Tucker & Booker Inc., 67
Tueruel Mudejar Architecture (Spain), 415
Tugwell, Rexford Guy, 135
Tulane University (Louisiana), 530
Tulane University Center (Louisiana), 137
Tullier Marketing Communications, 106
Tully, Richard L., 280
Tumlin, Knox H., 295
Tunis Medina (Tunisia), 415
Tunis Technical Bureau of the Municipality (Tunisia), 53
Turano, Emanuel N., 280
Turkey Grand National Assembly Mosque, 57
Turkey National Palaces Trust, 56
Turkey Re-forestation Program, 57

Vick, William R., 280
Vickers, William P., 295
Vickery, Robert L., 280
Vickrey, Wilmont, 280
Vicuna, Tomas R., 303
Vidhan Bhavan (India), 57
Vidler, Anthony, 74
Viemeister, Read, 297
Viemeister, Tucker, 297
Vieux Carre (Louisiana), 131
Vigan (Philippines), 414
Vignelli, Lella, 312
Vignelli, Massimo, 312
Vihara Buddhist Ruins (Bangladesh), 408
Viipuri Library (Russia), 420
Vila de Paranapiacaba (Brazil), 417
Vilchis, Ricardo L., 303
Villa Maria College of Buffalo (New York), 532
Villa Savoye (France), 370
Villacortaq, Eduardo O., 303
Villanueva, Gregory D., 280
Vilnius Historic Centre (Lithuania), 413
Vilnius T.V. Tower (Lithuania), 363
Vincent J. Scully Prize, 169
Vincent James Associates, 137
Vinci, John, 280
Vinick, Bernard, 286
Vinohradsky Pavilion (Czech Republic), 167
Vinoly, Rafael, 280
Violett-le-Duc, E., 147
Violich, Francis, 135
Virginia City Historic District (Nevada), 405
Virginia Commenwealth University, 537
Virginia Polytechnic Institute and State University, 366, 537
Virginia State Capitol, 354
Virtual Ink, 111
Visby Hanseatic Town (Sweden), 415
Viscaya (Florida), 388
Viscovich, Roen, 299
Vistulamouth Fortress (Poland), 420
Vitetta Group, 66, 506
Vitols, Austris J., 246
Vitra Design Museum (Germany), 239, 240, 241
Vladimir White Monuments (Russian Federation), 414
Vlkolinec (Slovakia), 414
VMDO Architects, 345
VOA Associates Incorporated, 506
Vogel, Craig, 328
Vogel, Stephen, 280
Vogt, Noland, 297
Vogue, Marquis de, 147
Volk, Leonard W., II, 280
Völklingen Ironworks (Germany), 407, 411
Volkswagen, 96
Volstead House (Minnesota), 405
Volta Greater Accra (Ghana), 411
Von Brock, A. R., 280
Von Dohlen, Robert J., 280
Von Eckardt, Wolf, 307
von Ferstel, Baron, 147
von Hansen, Baron, 147
von Klenze, Leo, 147
Von Luhrte, Richard L., 280
von Schmidt, Baron, 147

Voorhees, Stephen F., 320
Voorsanger, Bartholome, 280
Vosbeck, R. Randall, 280, 320
Vosbeck, William F., 280
Vouga, J. P., 119
Voysey, Charles Francis Annesley, 11, 148, 322
Vreeland, Thomas R., 280
Vrooman, R. E., 280
V'Soske, 70
Vukovar City (Croatia), 417

W

W. C. Kruger & Associates, 354
W. J. Assenmacher Company, 353
W. S. Atkins & Partners, 357
W New York, 116
Wacker, Charles Henry, 135
Wacker, John, 292, 324
Wacker Drive, 311 S. (Illinois), 358
Waco (Texas), 337
Waddy, Patricia, 74, 332
Wadsworth, Terry M., 295, 327
Wagener, Hobart D., 280
Wagner, William J., 280
Waibel, Janet, 83
Waid, Dan E., 320
Waite, John G., 281
El-Wakil, Abdelwahed, 53, 55
Walbridge Aldinger Company, 128
Wald, Lillian, 135
Waldman, Peter D., 98, 246
Waldorf-Astoria (New York), 398
Waldron, Lawrence G., 281
Waley, William Richard, 323
Walker, Bruce M., 281
Walker, Kenneth H., 281, 312
Walker, Lawrence L., 292
Walker, Peter E., 70, 83, 292
Walker, Ralph Thomas, 60, 244, 320
Walker, Theodore D., 292
Walker, Victor J., 292
Walker Art Center, 68
Walker-Kluesing Design Group, 83
WalkerGroup/CNI, 64, 116
Wallace, Charles, 353
Wallace, Connie C., 307
Wallace, David A., 281
Wallace, David D., 281
Wallace, Donald Q., 281
Wallace, Thomas, 353
Wallace Group, Inc., 345
Wallace Roberts and Todd, 82
Wallach, Les, 281
Wallis, Thomas H., 292
Walnut Grove Colored School, Inc. (North Carolina), 393
Walsh, Charles G., 281
Walsh, Sally, 312
Walsh Bishop Associates, Inc., 339
Walter, Glen, 330
Walter, Henry, 354
Walter, Lloyd G., Jr., 281
Walter, Thomas Ustick, 320, 355
Walters, Ronald M., 292

Walton, Craig H., 246
Walton, Tony, 312
Walz, Kevin, 248, 312
Wampler, Jan, 98
Wandelmaier, W. G., 281
Wander, Sheldon D., 281
Wang, Thomas C., 292
Wank Adams Slavin Associates, 349
Warber, Curt, 84
Ward, Barbara, 68
Ward, G. T., 281
Ward, Robertson, Jr., 281
Ware, C. E., 281
Ware, William Robert, 11, 539
Warnecke, John Carl, 80, 281, 352
Warner, Barry J., 292
Warner, Charles H., Jr., 281
Warner, Clyde K., Jr., 281
Warner, J. Foster, 388
Warner, William D., 281
Warner Summers Ditzel Benefield Ward & Associates, 339
Warren, David L., 345
Warren, Katherine U., 380
Warren B. Rudman U.S. Courthouse (New Hampshire), 106
Warsaw Historic Centre (Poland), 414
Wartburg Castle (Germany), 411
The Warwick (New York), 398
Washburn, Sharon F., 281
Washington, D.C. Historic Landmarks, 131
Washington, D.C. Park Road Tunnels, 102
Washington, Edith S., 295
Washington, George, 388
Washington, Robert E., 281
Washington Metropolitan Area Transit Authority, 69
Washington State Capitol, 355
Washington State Department of Transportation, 141
Washington State University, 537
Washington TimePlaces Heritage Signs, 84
Washington University (Missouri), 368, 532
Wassef, Ramses Wissa, 54
Wasserman, Barry L., 281
Wasserman, Joseph, 281
Water Towers (Kuwait), 54
Watergate (Washington, D.C.), 546
Waterhouse, Alfred, 147
Waterhouse, Michael T., 331
Waterhouse, Paul, 331
Waterloo International Station (England), 125
Watershouse, Alfred, 331
Watkins, David H., 281
Watkins College of Art & Design (Tennessee), 536
Watrous (New Mexico), 405
Watson, Donald R., 281
Watson, J. Stroud, 98
Watson, Kent E., 292
Watson, Raymond L., 281
Watson, Wayne N., 295
Watson, William J., 281
Watterson, Joseph, 100
Waymon, E. Ernest, 295
Wayne State University (Michigan), 531
Wayside Inn (Virginia), 399
Weatherby, Richard T., 295

Weatherford, Dwight W., 292
Weatherly, E. Neal, Jr., 292
Webb, John L., 281
Webb, Sir Aston, 60, 147, 331
Webb Zerafa Menkes Housden Partnership, 358
Webber, Melvin M., 52
Webber, P. R., 281
Webcor Builders, 128
Webel, Richard K., 247, 292
Weber, Arthur M., 281
Weber, G. F., 286
Webster, Frederick S., 281
Wedding, C. R., 281
Weese, Benjamin H., 281
Weese, Cynthia, 281
Weese, Harry, 80
Weeter, Gary K., 281
Wegner, Hans J., 117
Weidlinger, Paul, 307
Weidlinger Associates Inc., 69, 101
Weidt Group, 365
Weigand, Bryce Adair, 281
Weigel, Paul, 325
Weilenman, Joe Neal, 281
Weiler, Charles, 345
Weimar, Classical (Germany), 411
Weimar Bauhaus sites (Germany), 411
Weinberg, Scott S., 292
Weingarten, Nicholas H., 281
Weinmayr, V. Michael, 292
Weinstein, Amy, 281
Weinstein, Edward, 281
Weinzapfel, Jane, 281
Weir, Maurice, 286
Weisbach, Gerald G., 281
Weisberg, Sarelle T., 281
Weiss, Dryfous and Seiferth, 353
Weiss, Steven F., 281
Weiss/Manfredi Architects, 64
Weisz, Sandor, 297
Welborne, Martha L., 281
Welch, Frank D., 281
Welch, John A., 281
Welch, Paul W., Jr., 307
Welcome, Roger T., 295
Weller, Louis L., 170
Wells, Roger, 292
Wells Brothers Company, 353
Wells Cathedral (England), 543
Wells Fargo Bank Plaza (Texas), 357, 562
Wemple, Emmet L., 70, 307
Wendell Lovett Architects, 341
Wenger, Vicki, 286
Wenk, William E., 292
Wentworth Institute of Technology (Massachusetts), 530
Wenzler, William P., 281
Weppner, Robert A., Jr., 246
Werner Design Werks, 108
Wescoat, Prof. James L., 247
West, Don, 345
West, John, 310
West, William R., 354
West Berlin Tower (Germany), 364
West Union Bridge (Indiana), 348

West Valley College (California), 526
West Virginia State Capitol, 355
West Virginia University, 538
Westby, Katie, 307
Westchester County Parkway System (New York), 132
Westermann, Helge, 281
Western Carolina University (North Carolina), 534
Western Michigan University, 531
Western Washington University, 537
Westin Francis Marion Hotel (South Carolina), 398
Westlake, Merle T., 281
Westlake, Paul E., Jr., 281
Westminister College Gymnasium (Missouri), 405
Westminster Abbey (United Kingdom), 416
Westminster Palace (United Kingdom), 416
Westmoreland, Carl B., 380
Weston, I. Donald, 281
Weston Hospital Main Building (West Virginia), 406
Westside Light Trail (Oregon), 91
Wethey, Harold, 72
Wetmore, James A., 352
Wexler, Allan, 234
Wexner Center Bookstore, 512
Weygand, Robert A., 292
Whalen, Frank J., Jr., 307
Whalley, Raymond, 295
Wheat, James D., 345
Wheat, James K., 292
Wheatley, Charles H., 281
Wheatley, John, 388
Wheeler, C. Herbert, 281
Wheeler, Daniel H., 281
Wheeler, Dr. George, 248
Wheeler, Gary E., 93, 286, 323
Wheeler, James H., Jr., 281
Wheeler, Kenneth D., 281
Wheeler, Nick, 69
Wheeler, Richard H., 281
Wheelock, Morgan Dix, 292
Wheelock Academy (Oklahoma), 378, 405
Whelan, Miriam, 286
Whichcord, John, 331
Whiffen, Marcus, 72
Whisnant, Murray, 281
Whitaker, Elliott, 325
White, Allison Carll, 299
White, Arthur B., 281
White, George F., Jr., 295
White, George Malcolm, 160, 281, 355
White, Harry K., 355
White, James M., 330
White, Janet Rothberg, 281
White, Norval C., 281
White, Robert F., 292
White, Samuel G., 281
White House (Washington, D.C.), 548
Whitefield, William, 303
Whitehall Hotel (Illinois), 397
Whiteside, Emily M., 248
Whitnall, Gordon, 135
Whitney, Stephen Q., 281
Whitney M. Young, Jr. Award, 20, 170
Whitney Museum of American Art, 153
Whitney-Whyte, Ron, 299

Whyte, William H., 69
Wichita Falls (Texas), 337
Wicklund, Leonard S., 281
Wickstead, George W., 292
Widom, Chester A., 281, 320
Wiechers, Charles A., Jr., 345
Wiedemann, Nichole, 246
Wiegmann & Associates, 129
Wieliczka Salt Mine (Poland), 414
Wiese, William, II, 281, 330
Wigginton, Brooks E., 247
Wight & Co., 129
Wiginton Hooker Jeffry Architects, 339
Wilcox, E. D., 281
Wilcox, Glenda, 299
Wilcox, Jerry Cooper, 281
Wilday, 82
Wilder, Walter R., 355
Wildermuth, Gordon L., 281
Wildhorse Saloon (Florida), 152
Wiley, Charles D., 247
Wiley, James E., 281
Wiley & Wilson, 341
Wilkerson, Charles E., 282
Wilkes, Joseph A., 282
Wilkes, Michael B., 282
Wilkins Wood Goforth Mace Associates Ltd., 349
Wilkinson, Emeritus Prof. Leslie, 145
Wilkoff, William L., 90, 286
Wilks, Barbara E., 282
Will, Philip, Jr., 320
Willemstad Historic Area (Netherlands Antilles), 413
Willen, Paul, 282
William B. Ittner, Inc., 350
William D. Warner, 141
William J. Nealon Federal Building and U.S. Courthouse (Pennsylvania), 105
William Miller & Sons, 352
William Rawn Associates Architects Inc., 64, 67
William Stout Architectural Books, 510
William Tweeddale and Company, 353
William Wilson Architects, 345
Williams, A. Richard, 282
Williams, Allison G., 282
Williams, Bunny, 312
Williams, Daniel E., 66, 282
Williams, David W., 166
Williams, Donald, 321
Williams, E. Stewart, 282
Williams, Edgar I., 244
Williams, F. Carter, 100, 282, 564
Williams, Frank, 282
Williams, George Thomas, 282
Williams, Harold L., 282
Williams, Homer L., 282, 330
Williams, John G., 97, 282
Williams, Lorenzo D., 282, 330
Williams, Marguerite Neel, 380
Williams, Mark F., 282
Williams, Michael Ann, 377
Williams, Paul, 263
Williams, Richard, 97
Williams, Roger B., 282
Williams, Sara Katherine, 292

Williams, Terence J., 303
Williams, Terrance R., 282
Williams, Tod C., 80, 247, 282, 312
Williams, W. Gene, 282
Williams, Wayne R., 282
Williams & Dean Associated Architects, Inc., 345
Williams Bridge (Indiana), 348
Williams-Russell & Johnson Inc., 130
Williams Tower (Texas), 358
Williamsburg Colonial Houses (Virginia), 399
Williamsburg Inn (Virginia), 399
Willis, Beverly A., 282
Willis, Daniel, 107
Willis, Michael E., 282
Willis, Rev. Robert, 147
Willwerth, Roy W., 303
Wilmot, John C., 282
Wilson, Charles Coker, 354
Wilson, Chris, 377
Wilson, David, 106
Wilson, Forrest, 98
Wilson, Frances E., 286, 299
Wilson, Honorable Pete, 306
Wilson, Jeffrey, 282
Wilson, John E., 282
Wilson, John L., 170, 282
Wilson, John Louis, 170
Wilson, M. Judith, 299
Wilson, Merrill & Alexander, 162
Wilson, Richard A., 292
Wilson, Richard Guy, 307
Wilson, Robert, 70
Wilson, Sir Hugh, 331
Wilson, Trisha, 312
Wilson, William D., 282
Wilson Architectural Group, 339
Wilson Design Group Inc., 341
Wimberly, Wisenand, Allison, Tong and Goo, 54
Wimberly Allison Tong & Goo, 506
Winchester, Alice, 380
Windsor Hotel (Georgia), 397
Windsor Town Center (Florida), 67
Winkel, Steven R., 282
Winkelstein, Jon Peter, 282
Winkler, John H., 282
Winslow, Paul D., 282
Winstead, D. Geary, 299
Winston-Salem (North Carolina), 337
Winter, Arch R., 282
Winter, Steven, 282
Wintermute, Marjorie M., 282
Winterthur Museum and Gardens, 312
Winthrop University (South Carolina), 536
Wirkler, Norman E., 282
Wirth, Conrad L., 81
Wirth, Theodore J., 292, 324
Wirtz, Michael, 158, 299
Wisconsin State Capitol, 355
Wise, Gloria, 307
Wiseman, Carter, 69
Wiseman, Paul Vincent, 93
Wisner, John B., 286
Wisnewski, Joseph J., 282
Wisnewski Blair and Associates, Ltd., 345

Wissel, Robyn, 47–49
Witherspoon, Gayland B., 282
Witsell, Charles, Jr., 282
Witte, D. C., 286
Wittenberg, Gordon G., 282
Wittenberg Luther Memorials (Germany), 411
Wittkower, Rudolf, 69, 73
Wittwer, Gall, 247
WKA Architects, Inc., 345
WLW & Associates, 345
Wnderlich, C. A., 303
Woehle, Fritz, 282
Woerner, Robert L., 292, 324
Wojcik, J. Daniel, 292
Wolbrink, Donald, 135
Wold, Robert L., 282
Wolf, Arnold, 297
Wolf, Dr. Ricardo, 171
Wolf, Harry C., III, 282
Wolf, Martin F., 282
Wolf, Richard, 282
Wolf, Vincente, 312
Wolf Foundation, 171
Wolf Prize for Architecture, 171
Wolf Trap Center for the Arts (Washington, D.C.), 554
Wolfberg Alvarez and Partners, 345
Wolff, Lynn, 84
Wolford, Arol, 307
Women's Memorial and Education Center (Virginia), 64
Won, Chung Soo, 303
Wong, F. Michael, 71
Wong, Gin D., 282
Wong, John L., 247
Wong, Kellogg H., 282
Wong, William, Jr., 282
Woo, Carolina Y., 282
Woo, George C., 282
Woo, Kyu S., 282
Wood, Bernard, 303
Wood, Edith Elmer, 135
Wood, Edmund D., 286
Wood, Ernest, III, 376
Wood, H. A., III, 282
Wood, Marilyn, 307
Wood, Susan, 299
Woodard & Curran, 102
Woodbridge, John M., 282
Woodbridge, Sally B., 70
Woodbury University (California), 526
Woodcock, David Geoffrey, 98, 282
Woodhouse, David, 282
Woodhurst, Robert S., III, 282
Woodhurst, Stanford, Jr., 282
Wooding, Peter H., 297, 328
Woodlands (Pennsylvania), 405
Woodlock, Honorable Douglas P., 160
Woodring, Cooper C., 297, 328
Woodrotte, Enrique, 282
Woodrow Wilson House (Washington, D.C.), 563
Woods, Elliot, 355
Woods, Lebbeus, 70
Woodward, Thomas E., 282
Woodward, William McKenzie, 379
Woodworth Building (New York), 370

2002 ORDER FORM

We welcome you to order the upcoming 2002 edition of the *Almanac of Architecture & Design*. Please return this form to us at the address listed below. You may pay by credit card or check. Volume discounts are available, call 1.800.726.8603 for information.

Almanac of Architecture and Design $34.95

Price	Quantity	Total
$34.95		
	Shipping	$4.95
	Order Total	

☐ **Check**   ☐ **Credit card**

Card #   Expiration Date

Signature

Contact Information

Name

Address

City   State   Zip

Telephone

Fax

Email

Please return this form to:
Greenway Consulting
ATTN: Almanac
30 Technology Parkway South, Suite 200
Norcross, GA 30092
Tel 770.209.3770
Fax 770.209.3778

Or email us at almanac@greenwayconsulting.com

COMMENT FORM

Invitation For Comments and Suggestions
Please include any ideas, comments, or suggestions for the *Almanac of Architecture & Design.*

Suggestions and Comments

_____

_____

_____

_____

_____

_____

_____

_____

_____

_____

Contact Information

Name _____

Address _____

City _____ State _____ Zip _____

Telephone _____

Fax _____

Email _____

Please return this form to:
Greenway Consulting
ATTN: Almanac
30 Technology Parkway South, Suite 200
Norcross, GA 30092
Tel 770.209.3770
Fax 770.209.3778

Or email us at almanac@greenwayconsulting.com

CMD Group

CMD Group, a leading worldwide provider of total construction information solutions, consists of three synergistic product groups crafted to be the complete resource for reliable, timely and actionable construction market data. The product groups — Product, Project and Cost & Estimating — are driven by some of the most powerful brands in the construction industry. CMD Group develops innovative products targeted to owners, developers, architects, engineers, design/build professionals, building product manufacturers, general contractors, sub contractors, distributors, suppliers, government agencies, bankers, lawyers, as well as homeowners. With a scope no other company matches, CMD Group takes as its mission to study all the information dynamics that affect construction – products, projects, cost and estimating – and report on them for the entire North American region and select international markets. CMD Group is a division of Cahners Business Information.

Greenway Consulting

Greenway Consulting is a research and management-consulting firm that specializes in organizational design and strategic advisory services. Greenway has clients worldwide in nine foreign countries and 39 states who are served by offices in Washington D.C., Atlanta, and Chicago. The firm publishes *DesignIntelligence*, a strategic change bulletin and letter published 12 times a year, *DesignTechnology*, a monthly e-publication, as well as dozens of custom and limited circulation research reports for the design professions, product manufacturers, and construction industry clients. Greenway is committed to helping organizations grow faster and healthier through knowledge sharing and strategic decision support. They conduct futures invention workshops and manage the Design Futures Council, the Washington, D.C.-based think-tank.

James Cramer

James Cramer is the founder and chairman of Greenway Consulting and Adjunct Professor of Architecture at the University of Hawaii. He researches, consults, and gives seminars for leading professional firms around the world. He is the author of 135 articles and several books, including the critically acclaimed *Design + Enterprise, Seeking a New Reality in Architecture*. He is co-author of the upcoming *How Firms Succeed, A Field Guide to Management Solutions*. Cramer is the former Chief Executive of The American Institute of Architects in Washington D.C. and is the former President of the American Architectural Foundation. The recipient of over eighty awards and honors, he was presented the University of Minnesota's Distinguished Service Medal for his work advocating the value of good design into the mainstream of corporate America. He is currently the co-chair of the Washington D.C.-based think-tank, the Design Futures Council. An educator, futurist, and business advisor, he is currently leading workshops on technology advancements and pending value migration changes in the design professions.

Blair Kamin

Blair Kamin is the architecture critic of the *Chicago Tribune* and a contributing editor of *Architectural Record*. He joined the *Tribune* as a reporter in 1987 and was appointed the newspaper's architecture critic in 1992. In 1999, Kamin was awarded the Pulitzer Prize for criticism for a body of work including a series of articles on Chicago's lakefront. He lectures widely and has appeared on television programs such as ABC's Nightline. His writing has received numerous honors in addition to the Pulitzer, including the Institute Honor for Collaborative

Achievement from The American Institute of Architects and the Chicago Headline Club's Peter Lisagor Award for Exemplary Journalism, which he has won eight times. Kamin wrote the commentary for *Tribune Tower: American Landmark*, a guidebook to the Chicago skyscraper published in 2000 by Tribune Company. He is the author of *Why Architecture Matters: Lessons from Chicago*, a collection of his columns to be published in the fall 2001 by the University of Chicago Press.

Jennifer Evans

Jennifer Evans is an Architectural Historian and Project Director at Greenway. Besides serving as the Managing Editor of the *Almanac of Architecture & Design*, she is also the Editor of the Archidek series of collectable, educational architecture trading cards. She has a Master's degree in Architecture History from the Georgia Institute of Technology. She also studied at Drake University, where she received her B.S. in Business Administration, and earned a Master's Degree in Heritage Preservation at Georgia State University. As a researcher, architectural historian, and project director, she leads Greenway's initiatives that bring historical perspective and fresh insight to futures invention assignments.